# BECOMING CHILDREN OF GOD

# The Bible & Liberation

## An Orbis Series in Biblical Studies

### Norman K. Gottwald and Richard A. Horsley,
### General Editors

The Bible & Liberation Series focuses on the emerging range of political, social, and contextual hermeneutics that are changing the face of biblical interpretation today. It brings to light the social struggles behind the biblical texts. At the same time it explores the ways that a "liberated Bible" may offer resources in the contemporary struggle for a more human world.

Already published:

*The Bible and Liberation: Political and Social Hermeneutics* (Revised edition), Norman K. Gottwald and Richard A. Horsley, Editors

*Josiah's Passover: Sociology and the Liberating Bible,* Shigeyuki Nakanose

*The Psalms: Songs of Tragedy, Hope, and Justice,* J. David Pleins

*Women and Jesus in Mark: A Japanese Feminist Perspective,* Hisako Kinukawa

*Liberating Paul: The Justice of God and the Politics of the Apostle,* Neil Elliott

The Bible & Liberation Series

# BECOMING CHILDREN OF GOD

## John's Gospel and Radical Discipleship

**Wes Howard-Brook**

ORBIS BOOKS

Maryknoll, New York 10545

The Catholic Foreign Mission Society of America (Maryknoll) recruits and trains people for overseas missionary service. Through Orbis Books, Maryknoll aims to foster the international dialogue that is essential to mission. The books published, however, reflect the opinions of their authors and are not meant to represent the official position of the society.

---

Copyright © 1994 by Orbis Books
Published in the United States by Orbis Books, Maryknoll, NY 10545
Manufactured in the United States of America

Queries regarding rights and permissions should be addressed to: Orbis Books, P.O. Box 308, Maryknoll, NY 10545–0308

---

**Library of Congress Cataloging-in-Publication Data**

Howard-Brook, Wes.
    Becoming children of God : John's Gospel and radical discipleship
/ Wes Howard-Brook
       p.   cm. — (Bible & liberation series)
    Includes bibliographical references and index.
    ISBN 0-88344-983-8 (pbk.)
    1. Bible. N.T. John — Commentaries.    2. Liberation theology.
I. Title.    II. Series.
BS2615.3.H68    1994
226.5'07—dc20                          94-21927
                                              CIP

# Contents

FOREWORD      xiii

PREFACE      xvii

INTRODUCTION      1

A. READING THE FOURTH GOSPEL: DARING TO ENCOUNTER
THE LOGOS      1

1. The Intimidating Task of Bible Study      1

2. "Where Are You From?": Naming One's Commitments before
Encountering the Word      4

3. Learning How to Read: The Invitation to Consider the Bible
on Its Own Terms      9

4. The Continuity of Biblical Discourse: The Fourth Gospel's
Simultaneously Unique and "Classic" Narrative Style      15

B. AND THE FLESH BECAME WORD: THE TRANSFORMATION
OF JESUS OF NAZARETH INTO THE FOURTH GOSPEL      19

1. The Challenge of Tearing the Seamless Garment into Pieces      19

2. The Historical Thread: Placing the Gospel in Its Social Context      20

3. The Ideological Thread: Placing the Gospel in Its Political/
Theological Context      24

4. The Literary Thread: The Word Becomes Text      37

5. "They Were Yours, and You Gave Them to Me":
The Johannine Community and the Provenance of the Gospel      49

**1. THE BEGINNING**
   *John 1:1–18*                                                51

   1. The Prologue as Poetic Overture                          51

   2. Becoming God's Children                                  55

   3. The Word Made Flesh                                      58

**2. THE FIRST DAYS OF CREATION**
   **"See! The Lamb of God Who Takes Away the Sin of the World!"**
   *John 1:19–51*                                              62

   1. The Witness of John:  The First Day                      63

   2. The Witness of John:  The Second and Third Days          67

   3. The Discipleship Call:  The Third Day                    69

   4. The Discipleship Call:  The Fourth Day                   72

**3. THE WEDDING AT CANA**
   **The Celebration of the Messiah's Advent**
   *John 2:1–12*                                               76

**4. "ZEAL FOR YOUR HOUSE WILL CONSUME ME"**
   **The First Visit to Jerusalem**
   *John 2:13–25*                                              82

**5. TO BE BORN OF WATER AND SPIRIT**
   **Nicodemus's Struggle to Commit**
   *John 3:1–21*                                               86

   1. The Difficult Dialogue of Rebirth                        86

   2. God So Loved the World                                   89

**6. JOHN MUST DECREASE**
   *John 3:22–4:3*                                             94

**7. THE SAVIOR OF THE WORLD**
   **Jesus Becomes a Samaritan**
   *John 4:4–45*                                               100

   1. Competing Baptisms                                       101

   2. Living Water                                             101

   3. Worship in Spirit and Truth                              105

   4. Food of Which You Do Not Know                            110

   5. The Savior of the World                                  112

8. "HIS WHOLE HOUSEHOLD BELIEVED"
**Royal Servanthood Comes to Faith**
*John 4:46–54* **116**

9. "MY FATHER IS WORKING NOW, AND I AM WORKING"
*John 5:1–47* **120**

   1. Healing on the Sabbath     120

   2. "The Hour Is Coming . . . and Is Here Now"     127

   3. The Witnesses to Jesus     134

10. THE NEW EXODUS
**Munching the Bread of Life**
*John 6:1–71* **140**

   1. Feeding with God's Bread: John 6:1–15     140

   2. "I AM, Have No Fear!": John 6:16–21     147

   3. Eucharist as Public Commitment to Jesus: John 6:22–71     150

11. TABERNACLES
**Crying Out to Quench Thirst**
*John 7:1–52* **171**

   1. Structure of 7:1–10:42: The Third "Ministry Tour"     171

   2. Seeking but Not Finding     172

   3. The Great Day of the Feast: 7:37–52     184

12. THE TRIAL CONTINUES
**Determining One's Paternity**
*John 8:12–59* **191**

   1. Introduction: The Woman Caught in Adultery     191

   2. The Light Shines at Tabernacles     192

   3. "Why Am I Speaking to You at All?"     197

   4. "We Are Abraham's Seed . . ."     202

   5. ". . . Then Do the Works of Abraham!"     203

   6. A Liar and Murderer from the Beginning     205

   7. "Who Do You Claim to Be?"     208

13. **HEALING HUMANITY'S BLINDNESS AND WITNESSING
TO ONE'S RE-CREATION**
    *John 9:1–41*                                                           **211**

    1. Setting the Stage for Humanity's Healing                              212

    2. Structuring Drama into Discipleship                                   212

    3. Asking Why versus Doing God's Work                                    214

    4. The Invitation to Be Born Again Accepted                             216

    5. Witnessing to the Truth:  Round 1                                     218

    6. The Sin of the Parents Visited on the Child                          222

    7. Witnessing to the Truth:  Round 2                                     224

    8. Finding Jesus on the Outside                                          228

    9. Are We Blind?                                                         229

14. **"THE SHEPHERD LAYS DOWN HIS LIFE FOR HIS SHEEP"**
    *John 10:1–39*                                                          **231**

    1. The Question of Setting and Continuity                               231

    2. Calling the Sheep by Name                                            233

    3. The Door of the Sheep                                                235

    4. "The Good Shepherd Lays Down His Life for the Sheep"                 237

    5. "You Are Gods"                                                       245

15. **"COME OUT!"**
    **Confronting the Final Fear**
    *John 10:40–12:11*                                                      **248**

    1. A Respite on "the Other Side"                                        248

    2. Conquering the Fear of Death                                         249

    3. "You Have Not Known Anything!"                                       264

    4. "Leave Her Alone!"                                                   268

16. **"THE HOUR HAS COME"**
    **"Father, Glorify Your Name!"**
    *John 12:12–50*                                                         **273**

    1. The Entry upon a Young Ass:  The Battle of Messianic Myths           273

    2. The Grain of Wheat Must Fall:  Subversive Agriculture                277

    3. Calling Isaiah as the Final Witness                                  284

    4. The Closing Argument                                                 287

17. **"I HAVE SET THE EXAMPLE"**
**The Final Initiation into the Johannine Community**
        *John 13:1–30*                                                    **289**

   1. Introduction to the Last Supper Discourse:  The Narrative Mosaic
      of Inheritance                                                        289

   2. Setting the Example:  John 13:1–30                                    292

18. **"WE DON'T KNOW WHERE YOU ARE GOING"**
**Teaching the Disciples the Way**
        *John 13:31–14:31*                                                **307**

   1. The Intricate Interweaving of Themes                                  307

   2. Asking Questions:  Daring to State Community Needs                    308

   3. Not Leaving Them Orphans:  The Promise of the Paraclete              318

19. **THE VINE AND THE BRANCHES**
**The Johannine Community's Model of Church**
        *John 15:1–25*                                                    **329**

   1. Bearing Fruit and Being Cleaned                                       329

   2. "You Are My Friends If . . . "                                        334

   3. "For This the World Hates You"                                        337

20. **"COURAGE! I HAVE CONQUERED THE WORLD!"**
        *John 15:26–16:33*                                                **341**

   1. The Painful Truth                                                     341

   2. "On That Day, You Will Ask No More Questions"                        348

21. **"KEEP THEM FROM THE EVIL ONE"**
**Jesus' Prayer for the Community**
        *John 17:1–26*                                                    **358**

   1. "This Is Eternal Life:  To Know You and the One
      Whom You Sent"                                                        359

   2. They Received, They Knew, and They Believed                          361

   3. "I Am No Longer in the World, but They Are in the World"             364

   4. "They Are Not of the World, Just as I Am Not of the World"          365

   5. "I in Them and You in Me":  Perfected in Unity                       367

**22. "WHOM ARE YOU LOOKING FOR?"**
**The Arrest of Jesus**
    *John 18:1–12*    **370**

1. "Having Said These Things, Jesus Came Out . . .": Introduction to
the Johannine Passion Narrative    370

2. "I Told You, 'I AM!' "    372

**23. THE FIRST TRIALS**
**Jesus and Peter Put to the Test**
    *John 18:13–27*    **381**

**24. "MY KINGDOM IS NOT OF THIS WORLD"**
**The Roman Trial of Jesus**
    *John 18:28–19:16a*    **391**

1. The "Nonscene" before Caiaphas and the Results of the Judean
"Trial"    391

2. "I Am Not a Judean, Am I?": The Savior of the World Confronts
the Power of the Empire    393

**25. CARRYING THE CROSS BY HIMSELF**
**The Moment of Glory Arrives**
    *John 19:17–30*    **413**

1. The Johannine Crucifixion Narrative: All Is Glory    413

2. The Moment of Truth: Jesus Is Lifted Up in Glory    415

**26. BOUND IN SPICES**
**The Removal of Jesus' Body**
    *John 19:31–42*    **426**

1. Blood and Water: The Final Fulfillment of Scripture    426

2. In Secret, for Fear of the Judeans: The Final Challenge to Commit    431

**27. "FOR THEY DID NOT YET KNOW THE SCRIPTURE . . ."**
**Encountering the Empty Tomb for the First Time**
    *John 20:1–18*    **437**

1. The Multilayered Structure of the First Resurrection Narrative    438

2. The First Reactions to the Empty Tomb    439

3. "Woman, Why Are You Weeping?"    447

**28. PENETRATING THE LOCKED DOORS**
**Finding Jesus in the Midst of the Community**
    *John 20:19–31*     **454**

    1. The Unity of the Remaining Resurrection Accounts     454

    2. "As the Father Has Sent Me, So I Am Sending You"     455

    3. "Blessed Are Those Not Having Seen but Having Believed!"     459

    4. The Chiastic Center of the Community's Stories of Resurrection:
    The Reason for the Fourth Gospel     462

**29. FISHING AT NIGHT IN GALILEE**
**Empowering the Christian Communities into the Common Mission**
    *John 21:1–25*     **464**

    1. The Continuity of the Galilean Resurrection Stories     464

    2. Drawing in the Multitude of Fish     466

    3. The Shepherd and the Witness Continue Together     475

**ABBREVIATIONS**     **483**

**BIBLIOGRAPHY**     **485**

**SCRIPTURE INDEX**     **495**

**GENERAL INDEX**     **503**

# Foreword

For too long, serious and critical Bible study in the First World has been equated almost exclusively with academic study of the Bible. This is *not* because ordinary people — particularly those identified with churches or synagogues — are incapable of reading the Bible seriously. Rather it is due to the ascendency of the quintessentially modern notion — championed by most professional scholars — that critical study of the Bible is best done in the academy, *apart* from communities of conviction and practice.

Christians who apprehend the biblical texts as obscure cultural artifacts, whose decoding necessitates scholarly mediation, have been quite willing to concede to academia a privileged franchise for biblical interpretation. Those, on the other hand, who see the Bible as a story to be lived out have refused to grant such a franchise. For most of these latter, unfortunately, this rejection has extended to the critical enterprise itself, so that genuine hermeneutic problems are dismissed altogether. In either case, it has become increasingly difficult to persuade laypeople to take the responsibility and embrace the discipline necessary for critical study of their own scriptures.

Meanwhile, the field of *professional* biblical studies is awash with interpretations that have little to do with the life of the church. Stephen Fowl and Gregory Jones, in their book *Reading in Communion: Scripture and Ethics in Christian Life,* have challenged the legitimacy of such "purely" academic approaches:

> For Christians, interpreting Scripture is a difficult task. But it is difficult *not* because one has to be a specialist in the archaeology of the ancient Near East, an expert in linguistics, or a scholar of the literature of the Greco-Roman world. Though . . . Christians can learn important things about the Bible from the investigations pursued by people who do have such expertise, they are not necessary for wise readings of Scripture. Rather, the interpretation of Scripture . . . is a difficult task because it is, and involves, a life long process of learning to become a wise reader of Scripture capable of embodying that reading in life.

Interpretations of the Bible that neither arise from nor are addressed to communities of practice may be "smart," but they are rarely "wise."

Fortunately, over the last quarter century we have seen a widespread revolt against such alienated and alienating approaches to Bible study in the First World. Theologies of liberation arising from women and people of color at home and abroad have begun reappropriating the Bible through the lens of distinct communities struggling against oppression. We might call this phenomenon "movement-based" Bible study: reading scripture while engaged in the work of social transformation. It proposes a more "embodied" reading strategy, insisting that interpretation must be held in relationship to actual liberative practice.

Joining this movement, perhaps surprisingly, have been a small number of first-world, middle-class, white, educated men — defectors from the very franchise they stood to inherit by gender, race, and class privilege. To use the Exodus metaphor, a few of Pharaoh's courtiers decided to skip out of town along with the Hebrews. One of the first of these unlikely dissidents was William Stringfellow, who proposed to reverse the hermeneutic equation: what might happen if we allowed the biblical narrative to interpret *us*? "My concern is to understand America biblically," he wrote in 1973 in the Preface to *An Ethic for Christians and other Aliens in a Strange Land,* "*not* to construe the Bible Americanly." Over the last two decades, others similarly situated have struggled to carry on Stringfellow's project: Daniel Berrigan, Jim Corbett, Jim Douglass, Bill Wylie Kellermann, and Walter Wink, to name only a few. Such work, though still unacknowledged within the guild of professional biblical studies, represents a significant body of critical and engaged biblical interpretation alongside the other voices of liberation.

Wes Howard-Brook belongs to this circle of movement-based Bible study, as his own preface attests — and whether he knows it or not, he is one of Stringfellow's progeny as well. He certainly is a defector from the imperial franchise, leaving a favored career in law and politics in Washington, D.C., and Washington state government to devote himself to full-time peace and justice work in Seattle. But like those mentioned above, if unlike most activists, Wes has insisted on making regular space and time for critical reflection, particularly in the context of Bible study. This is because he rightly feels a need to stay close to the stories which have called him to radical discipleship. Yet his devotion to Bible study also arises from his deep and abiding love for the Word, which I suspect is traceable to his Jewish roots.

Wes is a kind of "organic rabbi" (to paraphrase Antonio Gramsci), a practitioner of critical Bible study unlicensed by the guild, with a movement base, a keen eye and an open heart. His exposition of the Fourth gospel bobs in prayer and gestures passionately, as if he were standing before the Wailing Wall. Indeed, that is just what John's story has seemed like to many of us: an impenetrable, even lamentable wall of strange signs and obscure significations. I am certainly one of those to whom Wes alludes (p. 25): mystified by the complex symbolics of this gospel. I have always *believed* that a "political reading" would bear fruit as surely here as with any other biblical text. But this was such a formidable reclamation project, demanding devotion, fortitude, even a certain

relentlessness! Wes brought all this to the task, and the result is a great gift —
from, and to, the tradition of movement-based Bible study.

Wes finds his way through the thick weave of Johannine discourse by using
a thoroughgoing literary method. He grasps the academic literature and narratological labyrinths, but remains focused on the task of presenting a reading that
will be widely accessible and sharply relevant. His trust that the narrative itself will signal us along and over its shrouded terrain is, in my opinion, clearly
vindicated.

Still, this is a dense commentary, unfolding slowly, like the gospel it follows.
It demands and deserves careful study. Go deliberately, be patient, attend to
each chiasm, follow the correlation of parts to the whole. If you tarry with Wes
long enough to tune into that strange Johannine rhythm, you will surely share
the gratitude I experienced at being able to embrace again images that I had
reluctantly conceded to the religious privatists: Jesus the Light of the World, the
Bread of Life, the Way and the Truth.

Most importantly, however, this commentary restores John's gospel as a story
for our time and place — personally *and politically.* John reflects, Wes contends,
the perspective of a hard-pressed but uncompromising community of faith, as
wary of the established church as of the world itself. Today we first-world Christians confront daily the high theological claims of an imperious New World
Order, while our churches are in danger of becoming just another commodity
in the triumphant global market. We would do well to recapture a sense of an
undomesticated radicalism that dares to claim Jesus as the one true "exegete" —
which is to say interpreter — of the unseen God (Jn 1:18).

I am grateful to Wes Howard-Brook for his "wise" exegesis of John's exegesis of Jesus, the exegete of God. This book never loses sight of the fact that in
John's gospel, the Word *reads us.* As the Nigerian writer Chinau Achebe puts
it, "The story is our escort; without it we are blind. Does the blind man own
his escort? No, neither do we the story; rather it is the story that owns us and
directs us."

May the reading that follows direct us toward embodiment of the Way of
radical discipleship in our lives.

# Preface

Sometime in 1988, a couple of friends came back from a retreat in Philadelphia with stars in their eyes. They had heard Mark's gospel explained in a brand new way by a man named Ched Myers. The approach was filled with political drama, risky consequences, and incredible meaning for discipleship in our world.

Kim and Karen couldn't wait to share the good news with those of us who claimed the Christian tradition and were involved with resistance to the nuclear arms race. Ched's work and Kim and Karen's invitation led to a process of weekly Bible study that changed my life forever. The Galilee Circle community, which lived for five years in Seattle, was born out of this new understanding of scripture.

I had studied the Bible during my three years at Seattle University, but nothing prepared me for the excitement of Mark's story of Jesus according to Ched, which became the book *Binding the Strong Man* (Orbis, 1988). I began to wonder: Was there something particularly radical about Mark's gospel, or would the lenses and method that Ched used and taught produce similar results when applied to another gospel? I decided to experiment with the gospel of John, the story of Jesus most obviously different from Mark's story. This book is the result of that experiment.

As with *Binding the Strong Man,* this book is a product of community. Ched's Bartimaeus community in Berkeley tried to live the Markan Way for nine years, combining prayer, liturgy, study, and nonviolent direct action as illustrated by Jesus' acts of preaching, healing, and exorcising demons. Galilee Circle spent two years reading Mark's gospel, then followed with two years reading John. During that time, many of us faced the hostility of friends, family, and neighbors as we tried to take seriously the call to witness publicly to God's love for the world and denunciation of injustice and violence. Throughout the years, our scripture work invigorated us, challenged us, frightened us, and gave us hope.

It is my desire in this book to stir up in readers the possibility of living out the radicality of the fourth gospel in community. John's gospel stands as a powerful invitation to resist the seductiveness of all death-dealing cultures, including our own. In its place, it offers the intimacy of community life grounded in the love of God. It beckons us to start fresh, to be reborn, to live as children of God. If even one community of radical discipleship is formed and nurtured by these pages, I will be grateful.

Galilee Circle was made up of wonderful people whose lives remain a challenge and comfort: Kim and Bill, who gave up the safety of the suburbs for the inner city and made their home a center for community life; Susan and Daniel, whose lives as healers witnessed to the pain of people in El Salvador, until Daniel's tragic fall from a stormy mountain cut short his own life; Karl, who was never afraid to risk public embarrassment for the sake of the gospel; Janet and Don, whose persistence in prayerful struggle to discern our community call kept us grounded; Gina, whose love for the children and simplicity of life were constant signs of challenge and hope; Karen, whose blood and ashes exposed the death at the heart of our cultural symbols of battleship and courtroom; Greg and Joan, whose love for the garden kept us in touch with the earth's cycles of death and rebirth; Mark, whose Jesuit charism tested us and was itself tested to the limit during his time with us; and the children, Ana, Sarah, Kevin, Peter, and Michelle, whose presence gave us the strongest incentive to keep going when times were hard.

This book could not have been born without these people, as well as the teachers and mentors whose own work taught me so much. Jim Eblen and Karen Barta, my first Bible teachers, encouraged my questions and opened up the wonders of the Greek and Hebrew texts. Steve Rowan's enthusiastic literary introduction to John's gospel and joyous support of my work gave me the confidence to continue. Jack Morris's enthusiasm for my enthusiasm sent me out into the church with my ideas. Ched Myers's inspiration is present on every page. The people of *Sojourners* trusted in my writing and allowed it to blossom into full flower. Many resistance communities beyond Galilee Circle, both living and dead, kept me grounded in radical discipleship: Ground Zero, Bartimaeus (especially Clancy and Marcia, John and Carol), Jonah House, and L.A. Catholic Worker. The helpful reading of the manuscript by Jim Douglass, Obery Hendricks, Jr., and Alan Culpepper sharpened the text in many places. The confidence of Robert Ellsberg at Orbis allowed an unknown writer to share his ideas with others.

Most of all, this book would never have come to be without the constant support of my beloved life partner, Maggie. Her belief in my crazy idea of writing a book and willingness to listen to my latest insights as they arose cannot be measured. She led many beautiful rituals, created countless prayer environments, and challenged us all to be honest. Her joyous spirit radiates throughout this text.

"scientific" methods that obviated the need to claim the personal positions and limits of the interpreter, more and more we find scholars admitting what has been true all along. That is, each reader or community of readers comes to the Bible with a panoply of prejudices and commitments that necessarily play a powerful part in shaping how one hears the word of God speaking.[3] Poor peasants in Latin American can connect with Jesus' parables drawn with images of farming far more readily than clean-fingered university professors in the United States or Europe. Women can hear both the pain caused by the patriarchal mind-set that permeates the Bible and Jesus' shocking invitations to reshape that mind-set in ways that men such as myself can never do. People anywhere committed to the transformation of unjust social structures into God's realm of *shalom* will pick up the pervasive political context of the gospels when readers satisfied with the status quo find only "spiritual" messages.

This is not to suggest that one particular cultural perspective or sociopolitical ideology is "better" for reading the Bible. Rather, it is to call all prospective readers to the enlightening and humbling task of paying attention to how *who we are affects who we believe the God of the Bible to be*. At the same time, it is not to succumb to a trackless pluralism in which anyone and everyone can read the Bible and find their "opinion" equally valid. Criteria do exist for distinguishing among readings, just as distinctions between faith in Yahweh and faith in Baal, Marduk, or Caesar are not mere tricks of the text. Our image of God and sense of God's will for us and for creation powerfully influence our sense of what makes for a "right" world. Are we simply part of a dog-eat-dog, survival-of-the-fittest struggle to survive, or ought we to aim together for a harmonious interconnectedness that respects the dignity of all life? Our biblical interpretations are crucial to answering this eminently practical inquiry.

This getting to know ourselves in order to get to know the Bible can, of course, produce the same avoidance of the question as does the attempt to get to know the Bible "directly." We will never completely know ourselves any more than we will completely know the Bible. But just as we should not allow our ignorance of Greek or Pharisaic practice to prevent our encounter with the sacred texts, we should not stop reading the Bible simply because some unrevealed prejudice may be affecting our reading. Instead, we can, like the Hebrews in Egypt, courageously accept the invitation to leave our captivity behind and begin the journey toward liberation.

If we choose to accept this life-changing invitation, how do we start? How do we know that the path we take is not simply a trail that loops back to Egypt or ends in a cul de sac in the desert? If we journey alone, we indeed run a high risk of picking a futile road to nowhere or, worse, to a place of great danger. The Bible's narrative of God's mighty acts and words is heady stuff that can, to the misguided, justify the worst sort of violence and brutality. The antidote is the one given by the Bible itself in nearly every story: to journey not alone but in the community of fellow travelers. Whether that means starting a Bible

---

3. Culpepper 1993a.

study group, going to church, or delving into the scholarly conversation, the joyous task of encountering the Bible makes sense only as part of an interpretative community. From Eden to Revelation, the Bible's various forms of discourse present one of the most intensely social collections of writings known to humanity. Its people are constantly in dialogue, either with other people or with God directly. And its questions are persistently in the first-person plural: Who are *we* and where are *we* going? The Bible contains virtually no notion of the isolated individual, no flinty-faced Marlboro man gazing outward with a private vision. The first challenge of reading, then, is to share in whatever ways we can in acknowledging this most basic premise of the text.

This book is an attempt to share some of my own reading of a particular text from the Bible. By putting my reading into writing, I am aware that I risk the same freezing of live conversation that the gospel writers themselves risked. Each day, new insights unfold for me about the fourth gospel, as I continue to grow in my self-awareness and my awareness of the gospel's own intertextual and intercultural contexts. But, as with the gospel, I hope that readers of this writing will continue the conversation, albeit at a distance, by continuing to think, pray, and act in response to what they read here.

This work, as with the Bible, is the product not of an isolated individual but of the collection of energies that make up the matrix in which I journey. In the following section, I will state openly (see Jn 7:26; 18:20) some of my life commitments and reading strategies. I do this not so much to persuade readers that these are the best or the correct perspectives, but in the interest of encouraging all Bible readers to continue the process of demythologizing the notion of the "objective" or "scientific" reading.

## 2. "WHERE ARE YOU FROM?": NAMING ONE'S COMMITMENTS BEFORE ENCOUNTERING THE WORD

One of the curiously powerful aspects of the gospels in general that stands out for readers familiar at all with other ancient literature is the social context in which their stories are told. Whereas almost all other national epics and myths speak of the important events and struggles in the lives of gods, kings, or other nobles, the gospels' concern is almost exclusively with the lives of the poor and marginalized. Even literature after the New Testament, up until the Romantics' discovery of the tragic narrative power of stories of street urchins and other outcasts, primarily focused on the trials and tribulations of people of wealth and authority. Lives existing amidst material splendor and social power have always intrigued those who look longingly on what they imagine to be the "good life." In contrast, the lives of the poor have generally seemed banal and trivial, devoid of interest because of the supposed monochromatic pattern of hard work and routine demands.

If we have relatively lately learned to "enjoy" the stories of the poor and have come to accept the harsh beauty of emotions and minds living on the tense edge of daily despair, such a perspective would have been virtually unthinkable to those of biblical times. The biblical patriarchs were wealthy herdsmen who, with their families, became landowners of distinction in their local communities. If the exodus portrays the desperate struggle of an enslaved people, it is only to show that their imprisonment first in Egypt and then in the desert is but a temporary obstruction on their way to the Promised Land where they will eat their fill and gather abundant land and cattle. The longest continuous biblical narrative is the saga of Israel's poignantly ironic marriage to monarchy, in which the main characters literally stand head and shoulders above their peers (e.g., 1 Sam 10:23). Even the prophetic promise/threat of exile was of concern primarily to Israel's elite, as the majority of poor people remained in Palestine even after the Babylonian conquest. And the postexilic narratives of rebuilding are the stories of priests and scribes, the intellectual and cultural leaders of the Persian colonial territory that had once been a great nation.

In this context of national journey from the perspective of the leaders and other powerful figures, the gospels sound a harshly discordant note. Their tales of lepers, blind people, bleeding women, and landless peasants searching desperately for hope are a shocking contrast to their biblical predecessors. For as we know, the New Testament was originally a collection of writings aimed at providing a message of divine love and healing for people who could not hear such a word in the established religious institutions. Although the Christian "Way" amazingly quickly swept across social classes and national boundaries in its first centuries of proclamation, the stories themselves are most easily understood by people who have experienced for themselves the failure of governments and clergy to relieve either physical or spiritual hunger.

John's gospel, in contrast with Mark and Luke in particular, has little to say about poverty and God's promise to provide good things for those who have gone without because of injustice. The fourth gospel proclaims not that the poor are "blessed" but that they are "always with you" (Jn 12:8) — although the Johannine perspective is not the cynical acceptance of the permanent presence of an underclass that it might seem to be when heard out of context. In the fourth gospel, characterization and plot focus not so much on economic exclusion as on the social barriers of ethnicity, ritual impurity, and lack of "proper" belief. Those who have been denied privilege in the dominant culture because of their "wrong" birth (e.g., the Samaritan woman and the one born blind) are the ones upon whom Jesus' compassion centers. At the same time, those who are willing to be reborn, regardless of original birthplace (e.g., Nicodemus and the "Judeans"), are invited into the community to which the gospel calls its readers.

And this reality leads directly to the negative and positive poles of my own reading stance. As a "white" male citizen of the United States at the end of the twentieth century, I must engage in strenuous acts of imaginative projection and concrete insertion in order to begin to hear the power of this gospel's word to those on the margins. It is a twofold task that cannot be done exclusively from the comforts of my warm home. Each experience I have had in which

I have, albeit hesitatingly and feebly, touched the actual lives of the poor in our culture has been a hermeneutical gift of immeasurable proportions. An hour with street people in downtown Seattle metamorphoses the abstraction of "the homeless" into the broken yet still human lives of Junior, Charles, and Althea. A few days in jail transforms one's vague notion of "criminals" into a perception of ordinary people whose lives have either gone sour along the way or existed on a road of shattered glass from the moment of their births. Each walk through the Central Area in inner-city Seattle at night converts the frightening image of "urban gangs" into the reality of angry, scared, and often hopeless eyes glinting from street corners and alleys.

But despite these occasional experiences of contact, most of my life is spent amidst people of relative privilege and comfort. As I am often reminded, even if I were to become unemployed and homeless, I would remain among the elite because of my education, skills, and stubborn confidence bred of easy success in the face of only minor obstacles. I suspect that the large majority of those reading this book share this basic perspective. We are, regardless of our good will, faith, or love, at a huge distance from those in our inner cities or in the Third World to whom the gospels speak clear and almost obvious truths. Only by pushing out from our easy chairs and into the cold darkness of the streets, prisons, public hospitals, and other havens for outcasts can we begin to catch the radicality of the gospel's word.

If this is true at the level of our personal zone of daily life, it is all the more the case with regard to our political and social privilege. I come to recognize more and more each day how the wealth of our nation has been systematically taken from the mouths of others. Indigenous peoples of North America, Africa, Latin America, and Asia all cry out as just prophets condemning our theft, indifference, and brutality as a nation. We are slowly coming to grips with our responsibility for the genocide of the peoples of our own continent, symbolized in part by the whimper with which the Columbus quincentennial was celebrated. It is an easy *mea culpa,* for we do not for the most part really think that it was our responsibility at all. Our "ancestors" savaged the Indians, not us. But we are much slower to acknowledge the ongoing responsibility for our nation's decimation of tribal ways of life in more distant lands, largely in the name of "economic growth." The increasing clamor for immigration limits and border patrols bears powerful testimony against our claim of being a just and free land, open to accepting the world's poor. And, more to the point of the fourth gospel, we have again increased the sickening acceptance of racial and ethnic scapegoating, whether against poor African-Americans or wealthy Japanese and other Asians.

All of this puts us as a people squarely on the opposite side from the Johannine Jesus and the community of the fourth gospel. But this brings us to the positive pole in my own prerelationship with the text. Despite my personal and national privilege and responsibility for massive injustice, I believe in a God who invites people such as myself to work and pray with others for the liberation of all peoples. While acknowledging my participation in unjust structures and in enjoying the fruits of rotting trees, I trust in the God of all life, who constantly calls me to focus on God alone and the way of *shalom*. Without attempting to express a complete personal philosophy in this space, it is important to proclaim my commitment to helping to shape a future in which all creation will sing joyously of the God of nonviolent and interdependent love.

Thus, I come to my own reading of John with a dual awareness. My birthplace veils the gospel from me in certain ways, leading me to find new experiences that help penetrate into the place from which the text seems to speak. At the same time, my commitment to a God who breaks down injustice and generates true love and freedom for all people opens me in other ways to hear the text speak its challenges to the status quo.

Still another aspect of my own reading perspective is important to note at the outset. I am not a member of the academic guild of Bible scholars. My reading of the Bible generally and the fourth gospel in particular comes not out of the context of university conversation — whether secular or theological — but rather from the perspective of radical discipleship. That is, I am interested in the biblical texts not simply as objects of study and intellectual interest but as paradigmatic tales of God's relationship to our ancestors and to us. If I did not believe that the Bible offered insights that are essential to our negotiation of our way out of the desert of the decaying American empire and toward a more hopeful future, I would quickly move on to some other pursuit and urge all listeners and readers to do likewise.

Of course, many academic scholars share a commitment to the power of the Bible to liberate people and social structures. I do not intend by this description of my own reading location to characterize academia broadly as an ivory tower or as otherwise irrelevant. Many of my own ideas have been the fruit of seeds planted by scholars, and many people in universities actively promote the Bible's liberating message.[4] What is central here is not a critique of academia but *awareness of the different but equally credible reading perspectives* that flow from university and "grassroots" standpoints. The university environment is capable of nurturing conversation among other scholars, both within biblical studies and across disciplines. The radical discipleship environment is capable of nurturing conversation among people of various experiences and traditions about the value of the Bible for social transformation. Each standpoint has strengths and weaknesses too numerous to list here. But it is important for those who read the Bible without a doctorate to recognize that their own readings are not necessarily diminished as a result. It is, of course, almost trite to note that Jesus was not an academic; nor were his first fol-

---

4. University-based liberation theologians such as the Jesuits martyred in El Salvador as well as the numerous biblical scholars who have suffered varying degrees of persecution for their controversial positions taken from a feminist, Marxist, or other "marginal" viewpoint testify eloquently to the possibility of speaking powerfully prophetic words from within the academic guild. See, e.g., the programmatic presidential address of Elisabeth Schüssler Fiorenza to the Society of Biblical Literature (1988). For a reply from a South African perspective, see Botha (1992), noting correctly that "white males must, of necessity, assume responsibility for their role as oppressors" (p. 176).

lowers; nor were the first Christian preachers, teachers, and other leaders. The development of the perception of a privileged reading position by academics is a relatively recent phenomenon, based not on biblical criteria but on principles stemming from the Enlightenment's notion of the primacy of "scientific" reason.

This is not, to be sure, to revert to the celebration of naive or accidental interpretations that come from the fabled random opening of the Bible, with the expectation that God speaks through whatever passage one happens to land upon. Bible study, whether from within academia or from some other social location, requires hard work for our generation, so removed from the Bible's own worlds and ways of speaking and thinking. My own interpretation flows from the attempt to pay a respectful and sincere visit to the house of academia and then to share the insights gleaned within with those whose daily lives do not allow the luxury of such a visit.

Finally, a personal element of my experience that cannot be separated from my reading of the fourth gospel: I grew up Jewish as a member of the first post-Holocaust generation. Although this upbringing was largely a matter of ethnicity rather than religion (perhaps, in the end, a false distinction, no matter what one's beliefs about God), it seared into my consciousness a deep understanding of the capacity of human beings for evil as well as the ability of Christians to kill others in the name of Christ. It is a difficult social dislocation for someone of this background to learn to see the wisdom of Jesus and come to claim the Christian tradition as one's own. It is particularly difficult to embrace the fourth gospel, given centuries of powerful misreadings that have found the text's characterization of "the Jews" as a basis for two millennia of mistreatment, mayhem, and murder. My own experience of being a Jew who has come to accept the power of the church's memory of Jesus has given me a perspective on the experience of the first Johannine community that is certainly different from those whose Christianity came with their "first" birth. I engage John's story of Jesus with the knowledge that this aspect of who I am both reveals and conceals.

I invite readers of this book and of the fourth gospel itself to consider how their own stance affects their reading process. This is not a matter of "confessing" one's "sins" or "prejudices" as much as engaging in a reflective process that has been made necessary by insights gleaned by the deepest sort of philosophical and literary thinking.[5] The powerful tool known as *deconstruction* challenges us to dig beneath any viewpoints that claim to be "objective" or "foundational" for the preconceived notions and commitments that underlie them. If we believe that God calls us to break down the altars of idolatry that pose as divine centers in our society, we should also be willing to examine both our own false gods and the images of the true God that animate us.

---

5. E.g., Caputo (1987) (philosophy), Eagleton (1983), S. Moore (1989) (literary criticism).

## 3. LEARNING HOW TO READ: THE INVITATION TO CONSIDER THE BIBLE ON ITS OWN TERMS

Once we have begun the process of reflection on what we bring to our encounter with the text — a process that continues throughout our reading — we are almost ready to take up the text itself. But before we do, we must come to grips with the dizzying array of reading options that can be gathered under the general name "method." At this point, many readers may be tempted to skip ahead to the commentary, wishing to avoid getting caught up in esoteric and perhaps even irrelevant theoretical conversation. But the fact of the matter is that questions of method are avoidable only by remaining unconscious. Just as our reading benefits from increased awareness of our own prejudices and commitments, so it is enhanced by a degree of conscious choice in *how* we read.

The consideration of biblical reading methods has occupied readers since before the Bible was even completed.[6] And from the earliest New Testament times, readers have pondered how to interpret the Hebrew scriptures in light of the Christ event. To take a familiar example, consider the following famous passage from Isaiah:

> For a child has been born for us, a son given to us; authority rests upon his shoulders; and he is named Wonderful Counselor, Mighty God, Everlasting Father, Prince of Peace. (Isa 9:6)

The passage has been so consistently interpreted as referring to Jesus that it is almost impossible for Christians to consider any other possibilities.[7] However, the passage was written eight centuries before the Common Era in the midst of monarchical turmoil in Israel, and the prophet almost certainly was writing to deal with concerns of his own time. But because we almost always read or hear the verse removed from both textual and historical context, our Christian filter leads us to celebrate the supposed ancient proclamation of the birth of Jesus. How different Handel's *Messiah* would sound if we associated the lyrics with the birth of King Hezekiah!

This simple example might begin to awaken in us the need to consider the *how* of our reading experience. But to bring the point home to the context of reading the fourth gospel, consider also this passage:

> Instead, one of the soldiers pierced his side with a spear, and at once blood and water came out. (Jn 19:34)

What are we to make of this apparently straightforward piece of "eyewitness" testimony? Is it a report of an explainable biological event? Or is it describing

---

6. Fishbane (1985).

7. Cf. the *Shepherd of Hermas*, in which the anonymous second-century Christian author interprets a wide array of biblical images and stories as "types" of the Christ event.

a "miracle"? Perhaps it is a symbolic reference to the birth of the Johannine community. These and other interpretative options may leap to our minds as we read. How are we to distinguish among the possibilities? What are the criteria (*Are* there criteria?) for preferring one interpretation over another?

As we have seen, the first attempt at answering some of these questions lies in the consideration of our personal standpoint and its effect on our reading practice. Our preexisting notions of God, Jesus, and their relationship to "ordinary" reality will have an enormous influence on how we read. But we are also challenged to consider the other side of the relationship as well. How do we think of the *text itself* and its modes of communication?

At the most basic level of distinction, biblical scholars have come to practice one of two major modes of understanding texts. These can be grouped as *source-oriented* and *discourse-oriented* methods.[8] The main difference between the two approaches is between what each set of methods views as the object of attention. In source-oriented readings, the reader tries to look "behind" the text to determine the hypothetical "original" pieces that eventually made up the final text that we now have. The most famous result of this procedure is the designation of the supposed Pentateuchal sources: J, E, P, and D (or DtrH). In the New Testament environment, source-oriented readings have come to agreement on the supposed "Q" source, which comprises the material common to Matthew and Luke but not Mark.

In fourth gospel scholarship, the primary conclusions are that analysis of the text reveals an original, much-abbreviated version by the "Evangelist" and a later, severely edited and added to edition by an "Ecclesiastical Redactor."[9] The original version, in this theory, is derived from three sources: a "signs source," a "revelatory discourse source," and a "Passion narrative source." Once one accepts the premise of this type of exercise, many directions can be taken. For example, Rudolf Bultmann, whose work popularized this theory among scholars, saw the present form of the gospel as hopelessly disorganized. His response was to posit a "better" order for its narratives! Another angle has been provided by Raymond Brown, who has further subdivided the supposed genesis of the text into five stages, each representing a step in the growth and eventual dissolution of the Johannine community.[10] Much of what more recent scholars presume to be the historical setting and situation of the Johannine community is derived from source-oriented analysis of the fourth gospel.[11]

The general category of source-oriented methods includes a panoply of specific "tools" with which to dig beneath the surface of the text to get to the archaeological treasures awaiting the inquirer. Some of the most important of these are form criticism (seeking to determine the type or genre of text making up a segment of a larger text), redaction criticism (seeking to discern layers of editing and their contexts), and, more generally, historical criticism (seeking to

---

8. Sternberg (1985) introduces these terms and uses them throughout his book.
9. Bultmann was the pioneer of this perspective on John (1971).
10. R. Brown (1979).
11. Neyrey (1988).

dig deep enough to find out "what really happened" or what Jesus "really said"). All of these methods share the starting presumption that the goal of reading is to move beneath or behind the text.

The other major approach is what we call discourse-oriented reading methods. The starting point with these methods is precisely the opposite of that of source-oriented methods. These reading strategies aim to encounter the world "in front of" or "in" the text itself. Rather than trying to take the text apart, their goal is to read the text as a whole, much as one reads other kinds of books such as novels, history, or biography. If source-oriented methods can be grouped as "historical" approaches, then discourse-oriented strategies can be gathered as "literary" approaches. They have in common the desire to listen to *how the text speaks to its readers.* For example, in reading the stories of Israel's past, we can ignore or bracket the issue of J, E, D, and P to pay attention to how the complete collection of stories *and* each individual story attempt to engage our attention and, ultimately, our loyalty.[12] In the New Testament context, there has been a recent explosion of works that try to read entire gospels and other narratives as discrete and complete narratives of Christian discipleship.[13]

Johannine scholarship first began to consider the challenge of discourse-oriented reading with R. Alan Culpepper's *Anatomy of the Fourth Gospel.* The specific method used was derived from the discipline known as *narratology,* or the study of how narrative is constructed and achieves its effects.[14] Through this approach, readers are called to pay attention to the various aspects found in modern novels or plays: narrative point of view, plot, characterization, setting, and the role of irony and other rhetorical features. Culpepper's work has spawned a variety of narrative commentaries on the fourth gospel in the past decade.[15]

Narrative criticism leapt into New Testament studies generally and fourth gospel work in particular with a joyous sense not unlike the emergence of ecological awareness in the 1970s and 1980s. If source-oriented approaches could be likened to examining the text with a microscope, extracting lifeless units of material and subjecting them to "scientific" observation, discourse-oriented methods enthusiastically recover the sense of context and life in which a particular gospel came to be. However, the uncritical acceptance of these approaches by some led to a barrage of attacks, which can be loosely conceived of as coming from both the "right" and the "left."[16]

---

12. Alter (1981) and Sternberg (1985) have made the most persuasive cases for holistic reading of the Hebrew scriptures. An interesting hybrid approach is Bloom (1990), in which the author attempts a discourse-oriented reading of the product of source-oriented study.

13. E.g., Myers (1988); Schüssler Fiorenza (1991).

14. Chatman (1978) is Culpepper's main tool. However, numerous other works in narratology have influenced New Testament study in recent years, e.g., Gennette (1980) and Rimmon-Kenan (1983).

15. E.g., Stibbe (1992), Maloney (1993), Reinhartz (1992), O'Day (1988), Staley (1988), and Duke (1985).

16. A criticism from what might be termed the "center" is found in de Boer (1992), rejecting the presupposition of much narrative criticism (including the method used in this book) of the-

The challenge from the "right" consists of the questions insisted upon by source-oriented scholars. Hasn't the editing and transmission process hopelessly corrupted the possibility of finding a coherent interpretation of a complete gospel? Doesn't the subjectivity of reading the Bible as "literature" destroy the notion of finding the "correct" meaning of the text? If so, are the interpretations of discourse-oriented critics any more than opinions not unlike those of many film and book reviewers? Furthermore, doesn't the tendency of some discourse-oriented readers to "bracket" historical questions falsely isolate the gospel from what form critics call its *Sitz im Leiben* (life situation)? Is it fair to leap two thousand years or more to read a biblical text as if it were a modern novel or film?

This last question comes around the circle to where criticism is aimed from the left. Much of the method used by biblical discourse-oriented readers comes from literary criticism that developed under the rubric New Criticism. This consists of letting the text and only the text speak. That is, any question about the "author's intention" derived from extrinsic evidence such as personal letters, notes, or other "external" sources is excluded from consideration. For some scholars, this resulted in reading the text as a hermetically sealed artifact, a self-contained entity that contains "meaning" that is discoverable by alert readers. Marxist, feminist, and other analysts interested in the inseparably social aspect of writing have seriously undermined this starting point.[17] Another criticism from the left is that of *deconstruction,* which, as mentioned, practices the sublimely subversive act of knocking props out from under any supposedly certain foundation. Deconstruction has demolished this type of literary approach to the Bible by forcing the embarrassing questions of commitment, self-interest, and the inexorably social and disturbingly arbitrary nature of language itself upon scholars.[18] If language is not a starting point but instead an intrusion into an always and already ongoing historical conversation the origin of which is unrecoverable, how do we know that our own articulations of biblical discourse are not themselves hopelessly arbitrary, just as the conservative, source-oriented critics feared?

The result of this type of questioning can be either a reinspired if sometimes grim determination to find "true" methods in the face of the threat of chaotic pluralism or a joyous celebration of the "play" of texts that acknowledges their largely persuasive rather than scientific power to affect their readers.[19] That is, one can either deny the insights of deconstruction and continue the intellectually

---

matic coherence and narrative cohesion in the final biblical text. De Boer's critique, however, is itself grounded in a questionable assumption, namely, that "the Gospel is the literary product of a single community" and that "the original readers would have been familiar with any putative sources or previous editions of the Gospel" (pp. 45–46). My own premise is that, by the late first century C.E., the fourth gospel was presented *as is* to an existing community and to prospective new members. While these people were probably familiar with many stories about Jesus, there is no reason to assume that they were familiar with previous "editions" of the fourth gospel.

17. Jameson (1981), Eagleton (1983), Robinson (1985).
18. S. Moore (1989).
19. Caputo (1987, 257–264).

discredited but still popular illusion of scientific study of the Bible or admit "defeat" and acknowledge that one's act of interpretation is necessarily an act of political speech-making. A given interpretation can tend to enforce the (unjust) status quo either by consciously interpreting in order to justify current social structures and practices as divinely inspired[20] or by its attempt to bracket social questions and thereby distract readers from the inherently political message of biblical discourse. The alternative, then, is to acknowledge one's commitments and read the Bible (as any text) as either supporting or arguing with one's own perspective on social questions. This is not to engage in eisegesis, or "reading into" the text whatever one's own ideology suggests is "God's will," but rather to engage in the more humble and necessary act of acknowledging, as I have tried to do from the start, how one's own perspective shapes one's attempt to read fairly.

Given the inevitably political consequences of reading, then, the task remains to discern how best to understand the text. My own choice is in favor of a discourse-oriented approach. There are two principal reasons for this decision. First, people who are trying to read the Bible for the sake of gaining insight into how to live so as to be constructive instruments of transformation of self and world encounter the texts as printed in ordinary Bibles, not as imaginatively reconstructed by source-oriented scholarship. The texts that have, for better or worse, shaped the Western world are not J, Q, or the signs source but Genesis, Mark, and John. We are more likely to find common ground for community-based reading if we start with the texts that are common to the community.

Second, discourse-oriented approaches come to grips more directly with the implications of our quantum-mechanical, artistic-metaphorical world. Source-oriented methods are a reflection of an Enlightenment mentality in which reason was deemed the divinely given means to reach knowledge.[21] Despite the undeniable gains that we have made through scientific inquiry, the dominance of science has also revealed its terrible shadow in the form of nuclear weapons, environmental destruction, and the crushing capitalism that has enslaved the many with the dollars and marks of the few. Science itself has begun to question its own premises in the face of these realities.[22] The insights of Einstein and his successors into the inherent uncertainty involved in attempting to observe reality have spilled over from "hard" science into other fields such as the so-called human sciences.[23] This has led to the question of a general "paradigm shift" in all thinking away from "machine" and toward "creation" as the primary metaphor of human reality.[24] The implications of this shift for biblical studies is the movement away from source-oriented strategies and their attempt to reach

---

20. Berger and Luckmann (1967).

21. McKnight (1988) reviews the history of biblical method, indicating how each period's prevailing method reflects its dominant worldview.

22. The landmark study is Kuhn (1970), which has had an immeasurable influence on literary studies in general and theology and biblical studies in particular.

23. Ricoeur (1981).

24. Winter (1981).

scientific conclusions and toward discourse-oriented methods that seek to find artistic and creative responses to texts. While source-oriented methods are political about *other people's* behavior (i.e., ancient Israel or the early churches), they have a harder time being political about *their own* behavior. The Bible was written and collected in order to serve not as an object of disinterested study but as a vehicle for inculcating faith and loyalty to the one God. Our approach to interpreting its narrative ought to be as consonant as possible both with modern insights and with the Bible's own apparent strategy.

This leads directly to the work of Meir Sternberg in his *Poetics of Biblical Narrative.* Sternberg attempts not to apply modern novelistic literary methods to the Bible but rather to discern how the Bible itself teaches us to read its narrative. The primary reason for seeking this internally implicit reading method is to get past modern literary methodology's frequent false dichotomy between "history" and "fiction." That is, as creatures of a scientist ethos in which empirical fact-finding and documentation dominate our notion of showing "truth," we tend sharply to distinguish "history" as a writing genre concerned with truth from "fiction" as a genre involved in fantasy or other modes of nontruth. But in reality, "the linkage of history-writing to documentation is a rather late arrival, born of an empirical spirit."[25] Indeed, as Paul Ricoeur and others have shown, history-writing is simply another form of narrative, with no more privileged a claim to truth content than any other form of writing.[26]

For Sternberg, this confusion results in the inappropriate presumption that biblical narratives are a category of "prose fiction"[27] or other fiction-like genres simply because of their mode of characterization, narrative point of view, and other "literary" features. The clarification of this problem comes in redistinguishing the two realms not by their truth *value* but by their truth *claims:* "history-writing is not a record of fact — of what 'really happened' — but a discourse that *claims* to be a record of fact. Nor is fiction-writing a tissue of free inventions, but a discourse that *claims* freedom of invention."[28]

Thus, Sternberg's work offers us a way to pass between the Scylla of applying literary methods derived from the study of modern (and postmodern) fiction to the Bible and the Charybdis of treating the biblical texts with the tools of modern historical analysis. His work invites us to consider the Bible on its own terms. For example, he shows how our deductions of genre based on our implicit assumptions about an omniscient narrator throw us astray. That is, in writing of our era, a "fictional" narrator can be in two places at once, can read the minds of characters, and can otherwise offer a "God's-eye" perspective on plot, characterization, and other narrative features. Of course, we say, "real" people cannot do such things; therefore, a text with such a narrative perspective must be "fiction." Similarly, a narrative perspective that maintains a cautious distance from the interiority of characters, that makes statements only by offering quotations,

---

25. Sternberg (1985, 32).
26. Ricoeur (1981, 274–296) and sources cited therein.
27. The term of Alter (1981), criticized in Sternberg (1985, 27–28).
28. Sternberg (1985, 27–28).

supposedly verifiable statistics, and other "facts," and that offers only carefully circumscribed commentary on this "data," sounds to us like a "scientific" narrative that fits our notion of "history." But in the ancient world, Sternberg points out, omniscience "not only accommodates but also guarantees authenticity."[29] To apply our notions of fiction and history to the Bible is to risk missing the essential claims of the texts: "Were the narrative written or read as fiction, then God would turn from the lord of history into a creature of the imagination, with the most disastrous results."[30]

Sternberg's invitation, then, is not to reject literary analysis but rather to find the type of literary analysis suitable to the biblical text under consideration. From this perspective, previous attempts to apply modern narrative-critical criteria to the Bible in general and to the fourth gospel in particular must be seen as seriously flawed. They fail to take seriously the text's own claim, which Sternberg puts squarely before us, to be reporting and interpreting the history of God's relationship with humanity. No less than the Hebrew scriptures with which Sternberg is concerned, the fourth gospel's own conclusion forces us to deal with its truth claims. Its narrator, referring if not to the actual author then at least to the human source of its narrative, tells us of that one:

This is the disciple who is testifying to these things and has written them, and we know that his testimony is true. But there are also many other things that Jesus did; if every one of them were written down, I suppose that the world itself could not contain the books that would be written. (Jn 21:25)

Although this claim is saved until the very end of the gospel, allowing us to read the narrative once without knowledge of the statement, we are better off acknowledging this claim from the start of our reading so as to try our best to hear the entire narrative on its own terms.

## 4. THE CONTINUITY OF BIBLICAL DISCOURSE: THE FOURTH GOSPEL'S SIMULTANEOUSLY UNIQUE AND "CLASSIC" NARRATIVE STYLE

In responding to the Bible's narrative claims, we must resist, therefore, the twin temptations to deny its historiographic mode or its literary/aesthetic mode of storytelling. The challenge is circular: to read the text as a narrative while interpreting that narrative with principles derived from within the text itself. This distinguishes what we are about here from other literary biblical readings that posit an "implied reader" who knows *only* what the text unfolds as it un-

---

29. Ibid., 34.
30. Ibid., 32.

folds and also knows *everything* the text unfolds.[31] While my commentary will pay attention to how the text builds up suspense, surprise, and other readerly responses from within its linearity, I find no advantage in adopting this fiction-based category. Similarly, there is no value in pretending that any actual readers are encountering the fourth gospel without some preexisting awareness of its stories and characters. The fourth gospel, as far as we know, has never simply landed unannounced on someone's reading desk, but has always been part and parcel of a community's effort to both gather and support people on the path of discipleship. Thus, there is no methodological barrier to reading through the text numerous times in order to discern its narrative logic, then rereading with an awareness of that logic. This is not unlike our usual method of listening to music. With each hearing of an already familiar piece, we learn better how to anticipate the piece's melody, key changes, and other features. But each time, we listen in the order in which the piece was composed, and usually to the entire work at one time.

What, then, are the features of the fourth gospel's narrative that teach us how to read? One of the principal features of the text is its explicit claim to express God's word through the words and deeds of Jesus.[32] In this regard, its power derives in the first instance from its claim to be in continuity with the scriptures preceding it. It accomplishes this result in three primary ways: (1) by referring to scripture through direct or indirect quotation; (2) by constructing scenes that reenact moments from Israel's biblical history; and (3) by imitating scripture's own narrative mode. This last aspect returns us to Sternberg, who has brilliantly discerned the Hebrew scripture's unique way of telling its stories.

Sternberg summarizes the Bible's overall narrative method as the creative conjunction of three principles: ideology, history, and aesthetics. He says the following about these principles, taken simply as abstractions:

> Ideology ... presses for transparent representation. ... History ... would like nothing better than to tack fact onto fact. ... For aesthetics, the play's the thing. ... The choice lies between easy specialization and demanding coordination.[33]

But the Bible never deals in pure abstractions, striving instead to weave and blend these different modes into a single, continuous pattern of storytelling. This goal of mixing and matching modes, incidentally, is another implicit difficulty with source-oriented criticism's striving to unravel the various threads of "original" narrative. Perhaps J and E as well as the Johannine "signs source" and "revelatory discourse source" did once circulate as separate traditions. But

---

31. The notion of "implied reader," derived originally from the schema of Booth (1961), has been widely adopted by narrative critics of the Bible and of the fourth gospel. See, generally, S. Moore (1989), McKnight (1988), Culpepper (1983), Staley (1988), Reinhartz (1992), Maloney (1993).

32. E.g., Jn 14:24; 18:9.

33. Sternberg (1985, 44).

as such, they were apparently *never scripture,* probably because as specific modes, they lacked the interplay that comprises authentic biblical discourse. The scriptural texts imitated by the fourth gospel were not the relatively narrowly ideological narratives posited as David's court history (J) or the postexilic priestly justification for the second Temple (P), but the single, multicolored fabric of the Pentateuch, Prophets, and Wisdom books as complete works.[34]

The ultimate purpose of blending these otherwise divergent narrative modes is what Sternberg calls "the Bible's overarching principle of composition, its strategy of strategies, namely, maneuvering between the truth and the whole truth."[35] John's gospel could hardly be more aligned with this purpose, as indicated by its concluding statement quoted above. The text is a conscious *selection* of *historical* stories, told with the particular *ideological* goal of leading readers to faith in Jesus, through a complex and absorbing *aesthetic* structure and style. If the gospel is open about its decision not to tell the *whole* truth, it is equally adamant about its goal of relating *God's* truth as incarnate in Jesus. Twenty-six of the thirty-two uses of the word "truth" (Gk, *alētheia*) in all the gospels are found in John.

If its overall strategic truth-telling parallels that of the Hebrew scriptures, so does its way of telling stories as seen up close. As we will see throughout the commentary, the text repeatedly, even maddeningly at times, sets up scenes that suggest crucial questions that go unanswered, reveals characters whose response or other behavior is left hanging as the scene shifts to some other place never to return, and offers discourse from Jesus himself that seems almost impossible to understand without further elucidation. As with Hebrew scripture, these "gaps" in the text serve several crucial functions, not the least of which is preventing readers from claiming to know too much. As Sternberg puts it:

> The reader's drama is literally dramatized in and through an analogous ordeal of interpretation undergone by some character.... The resulting brotherhood in darkness and guesswork and error thus cuts across the barrier separating participant from observer to highlight the barrier separating both from divine omniscience.[36]

In the case of John's gospel, this invitation to share in the ordeal of the characters also bears a more literal aspect: the invitation to join the Johannine community in its pain and love. Dealing with the gaps forms a sort of initiation rite that marks off those for whom the gospel resonates as God's truth and those who cast it aside as misguided or worse. As Wayne A. Meeks puts it:

---

34. See Polzin's (1980; 1989; 1993) first three parts of a projected four-part series on the Deuteronomic History (Deuteronomy–2 Kings) for a brilliant example of biblical interpretation based on this distinction.

35. Sternberg (1985, 51).

36. Ibid., 48.

The reader cannot understand any part of the Fourth Gospel until he understands the whole. Thus the reader has an experience rather like that of the dialogue partners of Jesus: either he will find the whole business so convoluted, obscure, and maddeningly arrogant that he will reject it in anger, or he will find it so fascinating that he will stick with it until the progressive reiteration of themes brings, on some level of consciousness at least, a degree of clarity.... 

While the function of the book is undoubtedly the hallmark of some one author's genius, it is unthinkable apart from a particular kind of religious community.... Coming to faith in Jesus is for the Johannine group a change in social location. Mere belief without joining the Johannine community, without making the decisive break with "the world,"...is a diabolic lie.[37]

It is in the very process of developing its own unique aesthetic and ideological structure, then, that the fourth gospel both continues the scriptural genre and moves into its own special realm. Awareness of this process also sheds light on the inseparable nature of discourse mode and theological substance. Just as the gospel's way of storytelling starts from what has gone before and transforms it into a new word of God, so it portrays Jesus and the Johannine community both as in continuity with Moses, the prophets, and the "people of God" of ancient Israel *and* as issuing a call to a new kind of community not experienced before.

In addition to revealing the Bible's interweaving of ideology, history, and aesthetics as a unique genre of which the fourth gospel is an example, Sternberg's work points out further elements of biblical discourse that teach us how to read. Any reader of modern fiction or history will immediately be startled by the Bible's apparent paucity of detail. Whereas a nineteenth-century novel might spend several paragraphs describing a character's physiognomy or the setting's landscape, the Bible almost never provides this sort of information. Similarly, biblical narrative gives us only the most cursory sense of motivation for its characters' behavior, and the behavior itself is referred to in extremely brief bits of speech. This is part of the biblical strategy of maneuvering between the truth and the whole truth. It is also a style by which huge "gaps" are created in the text that allow, even require, interpretation by readers in order to make some sense of the narrative. How many beginning Bible readers find these gaps so frequent and wide as to make the reading process seem more work than it is worth!

It is important to note that these stylistic gaps are not the same as the gaps that result from our cultural separation from the worlds of the narrative. Even for readers familiar with the settings and context, the gaps leave enormous room for imagination, discussion, meditation, and prayer. Sternberg explicates the function of these narrative gaps in terms of three aspects of knowledge:

---

37. Meeks (1972, 68–69).

Insofar as knowledge is *information,* the ubiquity of gaps about character and plot exposes us to our own ignorance: history unrolls as a continuum of discontinuities, a sequence of *non sequiturs,* which challenge us to repair the omissions by our native wit.... Insofar as knowledge is *true judgment,* ... the scarcity of commentary forces us to evaluate agent and action by appeal to norms that remain implicit, to clues that may have more than one face, to structures that turn on reconstruction, to voices partial in both senses, to models of character that resist polarization.... Insofar as knowledge consists in the *relations between part and whole,* the piecemeal, secretive storytelling makes at best for difficult unity.[38]

Indeed, it is the presence of such gaps that allows for the continual publication of biblical commentaries! John's gospel clearly continues this tradition of biblical gap-making. The presence of these gaps is a major reason for the need to interpret the gospel as a whole in order to reach understanding of any of its parts. As we will see in the commentary, many of the gaps early in the gospel allow and invite broad speculation but are best left open until additional aspects of the narrative are revealed. Many of the worst examples of faulty exegesis of John, especially that done by fundamentalists and other exponents of individualistic religion, occur as a result of a too-quick assumption about how to fill the gaps or even the failure to read close enough to notice that the gaps are there.

# B. AND THE FLESH BECAME WORD: THE TRANSFORMATION OF JESUS OF NAZARETH INTO THE FOURTH GOSPEL

## 1. THE CHALLENGE OF TEARING THE SEAMLESS GARMENT INTO PIECES

As we have seen, the gospel of John fits well into Sternberg's biblical narrative paradigm of the interweaving of ideology, history, and aesthetics into a single textual fabric. The genre of Johannine commentary, however, has traditionally started by separating out these and other strands in order to learn about the "Johannine community," the "author," and the historical setting of the text. Given our attempt to read from within the text's own narrative poetics, is continuing such a tradition helpful or a temptation that is best left alone?

The answer is probably a qualified yes to both parts of the question. Given what we know about the cultural gap between our reading standpoint and the original cultural situation of the gospel, to proceed without discerning what we

---

38. Sternberg (1985, 47).

can about the world out of which the fourth gospel arose would be to retreat into the false naiveté against which I cautioned at the outset. The strands that form the narrative fabric will probably appear as loose threads unless we gain some understanding of the realities of first-century Palestine and its socioreligious matrix. What we need to remain careful of, however, is unraveling the text in a way that sees *only* the threads and not the fabric. Whether under the rubric of "gospel values" or "Christian ethics," it is very popular today to read the Bible so as to extract the "lesson" from the text, missing the point that the story as story *is* the lesson. Given this caution, examining the individual threads can give us sharper reading eyes and ears for perceiving the coherence of the gospel as a whole.

## 2. THE HISTORICAL THREAD: PLACING THE GOSPEL IN ITS SOCIAL CONTEXT

Almost all understanding of the social setting of the fourth gospel begins with the narrator's identifying remark in the midst of the formerly blind man's "trial":

His parents said this because they were afraid of the Judeans; for the Judeans had already agreed that anyone who confessed Jesus to be the Messiah would be put out of the synagogue. (Jn 9:22)

A whole range of time-blurred concepts are presented within this single verse: the "Judeans," the "Messiah," the "synagogue." The only external datum placing this idea in a historical context is the Eighteen Benedictions, a collection of Jewish prayers from the late first century that includes a prayer expressing the exclusionary principle in Jn 9:22.

At the other end of the time spectrum, manuscript evidence indicates that the fourth gospel is unlikely to be later in origin than early in the second century. What social factors were at work in this period from the 90s to 120s of the Common Era?[39]

The most determining event for the gospel and, indeed, for both Judaism and Christianity as broad religious systems was the Roman destruction of the Temple and of Jerusalem in 70. With that cataclysmic event, the era of Israel as a nation came to an end for the next nineteen hundred years. Perhaps

---

39. There is currently renewed debate about whether the so-called *birkat ha-minim* (expulsion of heretics) expressed negatively in the Eighteen Benedictions was meant to exclude all Jewish-Christians or just some subset, and therefore, whether the apparent reference in Jn 9:22 alone is enough on which to conclude that the fourth gospel is a late first-century document. See Stibbe (1992, 57–61). Regardless of the specific social function of the *birkat ha-minim*, other factors relevant to my reading tip the balance toward a late first-century date: the polemical contrasting characterizations of Peter and the Beloved Disciple as symbols of apostolic and Johannine ecclesiologies, the political use of "my Lord and my God" in reference to the Roman emperor Domitian (Jn 20:28), the explicit "prediction" of persecution and death at the hands of opponents (Jn 15:20; 16:2), the implicit polemic against gnosticism throughout the gospel (esp. Jn 1:14; cf. 1 Tim 6:20).

we can imagine what that must have been like for those whose traditions had named them as God's Chosen People. It would be as if the former Soviet Union had come and taken over the United States and made it into a colonial outpost for the Eastern empire. Then, further, it would be as if, after a span of around one hundred years of such a colonial existence, the empire's army had come in and wiped out Washington, D.C., and all the national monuments with it. How would the collective psyche of "Americans" survive such a shock?

For the people of Israel, response came in the narrowing of the tradition's symbols down to that of a collection of books. With the outward manifestation of God's election destroyed, all that remained was a life of quiet faithfulness, grounded in the written presence of God and the wisdom of those who studied those words. In many ways, the shuddering fall of Jerusalem was the birth of the religion that we call Judaism.

For followers of Jesus, the shock was equally strong, but its waves radiated in a different direction. As we can discern from the early letters of Paul[40] and perhaps also from Luke's book of Acts, the first decades of the Jesus movement did not clearly suggest that a new religion would be the outcome.[41] Jesus at first must have seemed to the believers in the Yahwistic covenant to be a prophetic light (a light similar in some ways to that shed by Martin Luther King, Jr., Oscar Romero, and Dorothy Day in our own time). He announced no new God, no new revelation that might have naturally led to a different religious structure and system. Rather, his message apparently bore the "conservative" sense of seeking to lead people back to the covenantal relationship that ancient Israel had established with its God. But with the destruction of Jerusalem and the religious institutions of Israel, Jesus' disciples were for the first time put to the test *because* of the developments in what became Judaism.

To understand how the crisis within the mainstream Jewish practice forced a crisis upon the discipleship movement, we must take a look at the social dynamics of first-century Palestine across the breach of 70 C.E. As Richard A. Horsley and John S. Hanson have shown, the combination of Roman and internal Temple-state oppression had pushed the submerged disgruntlement of the masses into the open in the middle part of the first century.[42] Despite the powerful cultural pressures not to make waves,[43] the intensity of combined foreign and domestic taxation upon a peasant population that, under the best of circumstances, lived in a precarious balance with nature, became too much for many people. Just as in previous crises when Israel's religious imagination had conjured a wide variety of scenarios by which God would relieve them of their pain,[44] so, in the current struggle, various kinds of messiahs and prophets

---

40. Meeks (1983).

41. Both Schillebeeckx (1987) and Schüssler Fiorenza (1983) offer a succinct and convincing narrative of the first generation of discipleship before the birth of "Christianity."

42. Horsley and Hanson (1985).

43. Malina (1981) shows how the complex system of honor and shame enforced an implicit acceptance of the status quo among the overwhelming majority of people.

44. Second Isaiah and the late portions of Jeremiah provided support during the Babylonian Exile of the sixth century B.C.E., while Daniel and other apocalyptic literature promised God's

emerged to proclaim God's favor and to attract a following that would topple the Temple, Rome, or both.

At the same time, less immediate but perhaps equally attractive options appeared on the social horizon. In the desert by the Dead Sea town of Qumran, a thriving community lived for some two hundred years awaiting the definitive act of God that would liberate the Temple-state from the corruption of the priests and aristocracy who controlled Jerusalem. The Qumran community — whose existence we know from the twentieth-century finding of the so-called Dead Sea Scrolls — offered its own version of the Yahwistic covenant to disaffected Jews. By living its life outside of the Judean authorities' jurisdiction, the Qumranians avoided the political turmoil between the oppressive institutions of colony and colonizer and the various rebel groups that sprang up like spring grasses. Similarly, various versions of gnosticism provided a different kind of escape from social struggle, inviting people to share insiders' "knowledge" of God that would give spiritual solace in a world increasingly battered by factional disputes. We will have more to learn about both Qumran and gnostic appeals later when we consider Johannine ideology. But for now, it is important simply to be aware that the previously tranquil Palestinian countryside was rife with religious and social turmoil by the middle first century C.E., a situation which continued and even intensified in certain ways after the destruction of Jerusalem.

For communities gathered around the memory of Jesus and the presence of the Spirit in this period, then, there was increasing pressure to solidify self-understanding in the face of forces that threatened to splinter or destroy altogether the sense of unity to which these disciples felt called. What became the mainstream church responded by shoring up its belief system inside the strong walls of hierarchical authority. Those of us who struggle with the often maddeningly obstinate and narrow perspective of persons occupying hierarchical offices within the churches must remember that the original impulse toward control was not simply a matter of the inherent dynamics of power. Rather, it was a rational and perhaps necessary choice for a tiny band of believers threatened with annihilation both by dissent and by persecution.

For as the communities of Christians continued to mushroom into being, the Roman empire found it more and more necessary to respond. While the obedience and cooperation of institutional Yahwism before 70 had been assured by the accommodations made by Israel's aristocracy, emerging Christianity had no such social class with which to achieve such a doubtful harmony. Also, whereas Israel was allowed its religious practice out of Rome's liberal attitude toward local traditions, Christians after 70 found themselves exposed to a new political charge: *atheism.* For once followers of Jesus were disowned by the synagogues, they were perceived as worshipers of a god with no official sanction, which, in the mind of the empire, was no god at all. Thus began the Roman persecution of

---

powerful intervention during the worst period of Hellenistic oppression. See, generally, Collins (1984).

Christians. The prevailing imperial attitude is best expressed through the words of the Roman historian Tacitus, writing of the period of Nero in the 50s and 60s:

> Nero looked around for a scapegoat [for a fire that had been set], and inflicted the most fiendish tortures on a group of persons already hated by the people for their crimes. This was the sect known as Christians. Their founder, one Christus, had been put to death by the procurator Pontius Pilate in the reign of Tiberius. This checked the abominable superstition for a while, but it broke out again and spread, not merely through Judea, where it originated, but even to Rome itself, the great reservoir and collecting ground for every kind of depravity and filth. Those who confessed to being Christians were at once arrested, but on their testimony a great crowd of people were convicted...of hatred of the entire human race. They were put to death amid every kind of mockery. Dressed in the skins of wild beasts, they were torn to pieces by dogs, or were crucified, or burned to death· when night came, they served as human torches to provide lights. Nero threw open his gardens for this entertainment....These Christians were guilty, and well deserved their fate.[45]

Simply to be known as a Christian in Rome was enough reason for the empire's terrible persecution. While Nero's behavior was a sign more of his personal depravity than of political opposition between Christians and the empire, it established a precedent that was soon to be imitated by other emperors. In particular, the emperor Domitian (81–96) created controversy by taking upon himself the titles "Master" and "God." Domitian's usurpation of these religious titles created a crisis both for Jews and Christians in the wider empire, probably resulting in widespread persecution.[46] Although Domitian's successors temporarily subsided in their pursuit of "atheists," the possibility of torture and death hung over the minds and hearts of Christian communities throughout the next two hundred years.

How did the fourth gospel, which tells a story not of late first-century Christianity but of the lifetime of Jesus and immediately thereafter, come to reflect these events? As we will see, the text devises an intricate literary pattern of blending "story time" (the period in which the narrative's plot takes place) and "telling time" (the period in which the gospel was written and first proclaimed). It is a clear example of how the Bible's historical narrative differs from modern historiography. On the one hand, it is clear that all historical narrative is written not so much to explain events of the past but to give meaning to the present and future of the historian's world.[47] Thus, modern works on World

---

45. Tacitus *Ann.* 353–354 (Dudley, trans.).

46. Chadwick (1967, 26–27).

47. White (1986) shows how historiography is the emplotment of events with the purpose of fitting them into a pattern that makes sense given readers' preexisting cultural presuppositions, which may or may not have been shared by those for whom the now-historical events were "present."

War II — or on early Christianity, for that matter — are written to help *us* find meaning in *our* world, rather than to "inform" us about a long-gone situation for its own sake. But the genre of modern historical writing generally includes the convention that the writer openly acknowledges the temporal, and perhaps cultural, distance between author and subject matter. There is no pretense that the historian witnessed or otherwise experienced direct knowledge of the events in question. With biblical historiography, on the other hand, there is usually no explicit narrative distance between the events being described and the time of the author. Scholars have labored long and hard to try to place the various segments of the Bible in their "telling" context as well as in their "story" context, with little direct help from the Bible itself. John's gospel is no exception to this pattern. While the narrator in the end acknowledges some passage of time between Jesus and the recording of the gospel (21:23–25), there is nothing in the text itself that positions the narrator two full generations away from the life of Jesus. Thus, we have a text that purports to speak of a world that had changed in unfathomable ways during the interlude between its events and their telling.

### 3. THE IDEOLOGICAL THREAD: PLACING THE GOSPEL IN ITS POLITICAL/THEOLOGICAL CONTEXT

Although proof-texters and others of a moralistic bent are often heard quoting scripture as if it contained detailed descriptions of God's will for humanity, the Bible actually is extremely indirect in conveying its ideological perspective. What appear at first to be clear statements of principle or teaching often are revealed, when considered in both social and literary context, to be highly ambiguous and imprecise. As Sternberg points out:

> If biblical narrative is didactic, then it has chosen the strangest way to go about its business. . . . Instead of polarizing the reader's emotional and ethical response in line with some preconceived scheme of values, the Bible habitually generates ambivalence. . . . Characterization is complex, the motives mixed, the plot riddled with gaps and enigmas, behavior unpredictable, surprises omnipresent, the language packed and playful.[48]

Again, what is true about the Hebrew scriptures in general is also true about the fourth gospel. The Johannine Jesus is not a law-giver but a riddle-spinner. Even his unusually long speeches in John are more like poetry than pedagogy. How, then, are we to discern the ideology of the text? Should we conclude, with many Johannine interpreters, that the gospel is not ideological at all but rather "mystical," "individualistic," or "personal"?

---

48. Sternberg (1985, 37–38).

This question, of course, presents a false choice, one perpetuated by many who opt for a separation of "spirituality" from "politics." If John is taken out of its social context, readers of a privatistic perspective certainly can read the gospel as an extended meditation on God's call to mystical union. The many passages expressing Jesus' desire for "oneness" with his disciples clearly beckon Christian readers to a closer relationship with each other and with God. But if one is to take seriously the challenge to interpret the entire text as a coherent whole, many other passages intrude on this "spiritual" reading. For example, how does one deal with Jesus' heated argument with his opponents at the feast of Tabernacles, at which mutual accusations of illegitimate parenthood fly? Or the continuous disparagement of the group of people called in Greek *Ioudaioi,* usually translated as "Jews" (see sec. B.4.c.1, below)? If the Johannine Jesus is "only" a mystic, he certainly does not act with the equanimity and peacefulness of some idealized versions of sanctity.

As we will see by examining the text in detail, the fourth gospel, like the entire Bible, is a social document through and through, virtually incomprehensible if read completely from an individualistic perspective. From the prologue onward, the text speaks relentlessly with plural references: "he came to his own *people*" (1:11); "to *all* who received him" (1:12); "*we* have seen his glory" (1:14); "from his fullness *we* have all received" (1:16); "*we* know that his testimony is true" (21:24). Even the apparently one-on-one dialogues between Jesus and another person often contain plural pronouns, indicating the representative nature of the characters with whom Jesus converses. For example, Nicodemus and Jesus each speak on behalf of others (3:2, 11), as do the Samaritan woman and Jesus (4:12, 20, 22). Thus, the first aspect of the gospel's ideological perspective that we in our individualistic culture must recognize is that *life is inherently social.* Biblical theologians have shown clearly that the entire tradition is grounded in the question of what it means to be God's people; existential inquiry about personal purpose and fate — a modern obsession — is not at issue.[49]

This does not imply, however, that the gospel is *not* concerned with one's relationship with God, often considered under the rubric of mysticism. What the gospel *does* reject is the pursuit of a personal relationship with God that remains content simply within that relationship as an enclosed spiritual space. Although the notion of a "personal relationship with Jesus Christ" is a modern phenomenon that threatens to trivialize the political power and authority of the fourth gospel, there were in fact many ideological options available in the first-century Mediterranean world that would reduce the challenge to keep religious questions in the public sphere. To understand how the fourth gospel fits itself among these many possibilities, we should take at least a brief look at each option and the fourth gospel's response to it.

---

49. Hanson (1986) traces the origin of the covenant relationship between Israel and God and its memory through the centuries, including the New Testament period.

### a. "We Have Abraham for Our Father": The Option of Post-Temple Mainstream Judaism

With the collapse of the Temple-state in 70 C.E., many of the social pillars of Israelite religion also collapsed. Gone was the priestly and Sadducean establishment. In its place, the emerging system of rabbinical Judaism under the intellectual authority of the Pharisees became dominant. Contrary to the caricature we find in the synoptics, the Pharisees are not fairly understood as a party of hypocritical legalists. On the contrary, they had been in pre-70 Israel the "liberals" among established groups, primarily because of their advocacy of the authority of "oral law" to supplement the written Torah.[50] The most significant theological doctrine that flowed from this oral law was the acceptance of the belief in resurrection of the dead, a notion that had been introduced to biblical tradition with the prophet Daniel two centuries previously (Dan 12:2). While we frequently may consider this belief as an aspect of concern with personal judgment and the prospect of an afterlife in the face of existential angst, for Daniel and the Pharisees, resurrection had powerful political implications. During the period of Hellenistic oppression during which Daniel wrote, belief in resurrection signaled trust that God would act to relieve the people's suffering, in contrast with the prevailing Maccabean ideology that counseled (successfully) in favor of violent revolt. As John J. Collins puts it:

> This imaginative construction enables the persecuted Jews to cope with the crisis of the persecution ... by providing assurance that the forces of evil will inevitably be overcome by a higher power, and ultimately by providing a framework for action since it furnishes an explanation of the world that supports those who have to lay down their lives if they remain faithful to their religion. It provides a basis for nonviolent resistance to Hellenistic rule, even in the throes of the Maccabean rebellion.[51]

The Pharisees' belief in resurrection allowed them to justify avoiding the attempt to rid Israel of Roman rule, trusting that God would act apart from the militaristic machinations of the rebel groups who led the disastrous revolt in 66. In a post-Temple world, the Pharisees incorporated this belief into the wider notion of practicing the ongoing Torah-based religion in the context of *home* rather than the Temple. So long as the Romans did not disturb the tranquility of the Pharisaic household, oral Torah could be obeyed regardless of political oppression in regard to taxation and other matters.

The ideological implications of this shift from Temple to home were dramatic. First of all, the primary ritual with which the Pharisees achieved their identity was the *community meal.* One's holiness was measured by one's obedience to the regulations for purity at a meal. This meant not only that one need

---

50. Neusner (1984, 50–51).
51. Collins (1984, 92).

not hold special office in order to seek holiness but also that *women* were for the first time invited into full participation in the life of Judaism.[52] In the highly patriarchal environment of the ancient world in general and of the Palestinian world in particular, this move was an incredibly liberating one by the Pharisees.

Another implication of the Pharisaic perspective was the generally tolerant attitude toward Hellenistic culture. This is indeed ironic given the grounding of the Pharisees' ideological predecessors, the *hasidim* of Daniel's period, in resistance to Hellenism as a threat to Israel's identity.[53] But not unlike the way in which nineteenth- and twentieth-century Judaism assimilated first to the cultures of eastern Europe and then to that of the United States,[54] the first-century C.E. Pharisees did not find Hellenistic culture inherently objectionable. This meant that mainstream Judaism under Pharisaic influence found itself comfortable within the urban settings both of Palestine and eventually of the entire Mediterranean region. The ability to practice Torah at home unhinged religion from its centuries-long link with Jerusalem and allowed Jews throughout the Diaspora to feel a sense of Jewish identity even within the Hellenistic world.

Thus, the Pharisees offered a religion that was both derived from the long tradition of Israel and open to new practices that fit well within the mainstream of the dominant culture. To be sure, when pressed, the Pharisees exhibited a zealous willingness to lay down their lives for the Torah, as the Jewish historian Josephus attests.[55] But for the most part, adherence to the Pharisaic way of life meant a relatively peaceful existence occupied with Torah study, table fellowship, and the tasks of ordinary life as signs of God's presence amidst the everyday details.

Given this picture, what led the gospels in general and the fourth gospel in particular to vent such wrath against the Pharisees? At one level, the harsh criticism expressed by the Matthean Jesus (e.g., Mt 5:20; 16:6–12) is in opposition to the religious hypocrisy that could certainly be found among some of the Pharisees just as it can among people of all religious viewpoints. The temptation to enjoy the public perception of one's holiness visits most sincere believers from time to time, especially those who feel called to express their faith through public witness. But at a deeper level, the gospels' challenge to the Pharisees is an expression of disagreement with the focus on ritual purity as the measure of holiness. While the synoptic picture of greater concern over tithing of spices than for compassion is surely an exaggeration arising from polemical debate,[56] the repeated emphasis on the apparent triviality of many aspects of the oral tradition reveals the gospels' rejection of *law as a basis for holiness*.

In the fourth gospel, this opposition reaches its zenith. The Johannine Jesus repeatedly chastises his opponents for their inability or unwillingness to follow what he calls "your Law" (7:19; 8:17; 10:34). It is not that Jesus rejects the

---

52. Neusner (1984, 59).
53. Hanson (1986, 342).
54. Auerbach (1990).
55. Josephus *Ant.* 17.2.4.
56. E.g., Myers (1988, 107).

Torah altogether. As we will see shortly, the gospel is completely incoherent unless we understand that it portrays Jesus as viewing himself as fulfilling the promises of God found in the Torah. What is rejected is the attitude that *limits God's authority to speak* to the words found either in scripture or in the Pharisees' own oral tradition. Just as the gospel of Mark begins with the implicit announcement that the age of prophecy, contrary to the prevailing Jewish attitude, was not dead, so the gospel of John begins with the announcement that God's word is eternal, free, and incarnate in Jesus the Christ.

This question of authority to speak God's word is the predominant ideological battleground between the Pharisees and the Johannine community. Over and over, the gospel portrays the challenges to Jesus' authority and, implicitly, the authority of his disciples, particularly in the arguments gathered in chapters 7–8. While the Pharisees and those whom the fourth gospel groups under the rubric "Judeans" see the authority issue as a matter of *inheritance* — "we are children of Abraham" (8:33) — the Johannine community came to see the issue as a matter of "rebirth" (1:11–13; 3:3–8; 9:2–7) and the presence of the one called the "paraclete" (14:16, 26; 15:26; 16:7). For this group, the spirit of God is like the wind, which blows where it wills (3:8) and cannot be controlled by rules of purity or by ethnic claims.

Disagreement over this authority question manifested itself in part in the issue of calling Jesus "messiah" (9:22). The question of Jewish beliefs generally at the time of Jesus about "the messiah" is enormously complex.[57] Research has shown that there was no clear and widespread expectation of a single messiah in the first century. The Pharisees' own postbiblical writings hardly deal with the issue at all until much later. There is evidence that numerous apocalyptic and other marginalized groups expressed diverse and inconsistent beliefs in messianic figures of one type or another. But examination of the Pharisees or other expressions of mainstream Judaism yields little help toward understanding the Johannine emphasis on Jesus' messiahship — an emphasis not found in the synoptics outside of the infancy narratives. What appears to be the case is that based on Jesus' own reflections on scripture, his followers reinterpreted the ancient texts in such a way that they came to characterize him as messianic. The quintessential example of this is the road to Emmaus story in Luke, in which the risen Jesus explains to his hearers how the ancient stories were "about" Jesus as the messiah (Lk 24:26–27). But many of the passages that the first Christians heard as messianic had not been considered to be so by other Jews (e.g., the Suffering Servant songs in Isaiah and the "child" passages in Isa 9:6–7 and Mic 5:2–6). Thus, the primary Pharisaic objection to the Christian proclamation of Jesus as the messiah was that it was *incomprehensible.* A category that became central to Christianity was simply not of major significance to Judaism until many centuries later.

Thus, to proclaim Jesus the messiah — and therefore, to proclaim his status as God's envoy — seemed to the Pharisees at best like nonsense and at worst

---

57. See, generally, Neusner (1984).

as subversive of the authority of the Torah in general and of the *Pharisees' own status as authorized interpreters.* The Pharisees' ideology forced a question upon the Johannine community that clarified its christology and notion of discipleship: What are the criteria for speaking in God's name? The more the Johannine community was ostracized from the mainstream Jewish reality because of its claims about Jesus, the stronger its claims got. Furthermore, as the members of the community found themselves increasingly the objects of ridicule and persecution within the public realm of the post-Temple synagogue (the place of ordinary worship for Jews throughout the world), they were cornered into claiming Jesus' (and hence their own) direct authority from God (and the paraclete) to speak and act. To be a member of the Chosen People for them was no longer a matter of ethnicity or inheritance but of commitment to belief in Jesus the messiah and the public and personal consequences of that belief.

Ultimately, this self-understanding led to the reversal of the Pharisees' challenge. If the Johannine community would be expelled from the synagogue if it proclaimed Jesus' messiahship, then those Pharisees who did believe in Jesus must *renounce their status as Pharisees* (3:1–11; 9:40–41; 12:42–43; 19:38–42). What came to be the most bitter battle between the Johannine community and mainstream Judaism was against those among the Pharisees who, while recognizing Jesus' authority from God, attempted to be believers from within the Jewish establishment. For the Johannine community, "crypto-Christians"[58] were the hardest to accept. The more Jesus' disciples over the first generations experienced the pain of rejection by their fellow Jews, the more difficult it was to deal with "secret" believers who would not put their lives where their hearts were.

This feeling should be familiar to those whose radical discipleship in our day has led to anger and sorrow at the willingness of "liberal" Christians to accept the excesses and oppressions of the dominant U.S. culture without public comment. Just as the Johannine community must have mourned the weakness of Nicodemus's attempt to gain "due process" for Jesus rather than openly proclaiming his allegiance (7:48–52), so radical Christians today frequently mourn the weak tolerance by their fellow believers of the type of public prophetic witness demanded by the gospel and the times. It is less painful to accept the behavior of nonbelievers than that of those who purport to share the following of Jesus but are unwilling to renounce the privileges that come with the "virtues" of U.S. citizenship. To be a member of the Johannine community required a *new birth*, a complete severing of one's association with the system of privilege and relative security that the Pharisees came to represent.

It was precisely because the Pharisees' invitation was so appealing in many ways that the gospels spend so much energy in portraying them as unworthy of association. For the Johannine community, belief in Jesus the messiah demanded participation in a society comprised not on the basis of precedent but on the basis of the living presence of God's word in their midst.

---

58. The term is from R. Brown (1979).

## b. "I Am Not Asking That You Take Them out of the World": Rejecting the Temptation of the Desert

If mainstream post-Temple Judaism presented an unacceptable option to the Johannine community, what other ideological possibilities were there to choose from? First-century Judaism, like its Christian counterpart, was far from a univocal religious system. Apart from the dominance of the Pharisees, several more marginal — and more radical — interpretations of the tradition were being lived out. Perhaps the most powerful of these was the vision of the covenant community at Qumran.

The discovery of the Dead Sea Scrolls revealed a rich portrait of the radical Jewish sect that withdrew from Jerusalem and the surrounding region to practice an alternative Judaism in the desert. Disgusted with the corruption of the Temple-state and the priestly establishment's accommodation to Rome, a band of Judeans left their homeland sometime in the first century B.C.E. to live a life of holiness while awaiting God's definitive acts of liberation and renewal.[59] As the expectation of immediate divine action receded with the passing years, the covenanters at Qumran began to live out their own relatively rigid and dualistic scheme of Torah purity. As S. Talmon suggests, they "began to perceive their own sinfulness . . . as a factor that had contributed to or had altogether caused the retardation of the redeeming event."[60]

In support of their system of priestly holiness, they developed a powerful myth built around the theme of the war between the "Spirit of Truth" and the "Spirit of Darkness." The imagery with which they expressed this myth bears powerful similarities to that in the fourth gospel: light versus dark generally, as well as the more specific image of children of light versus children of darkness; "walking in the light"; and the presence of the "Spirit of Truth" as a helper of the faithful. The Qumran community's analysis of the world's perversity would have found a receptive audience within the Johannine community. They saw themselves as guided by one they called the "Teacher of Righteousness," who is described in terms somewhat parallel to the Johannine description of Jesus as teacher and example.[61]

Despite the many links between the theological and political perspectives of the Qumran and Johannine communities, an essential difference divided them. Whereas the Qumran covenanters and their Teacher of Righteousness lived in total and absolute rejection of the world, the Johannine Jesus expressly refuses to ask God to remove his community from the world (17:15). Throughout the fourth gospel there is an emphasis on the call to be *in* the world but not *of* the world, to *love* the world that rejects and persecutes those who point out the world's evil (3:16–21; 17:16–18; 20:21–23). Despite the expectation of pain and suffering in "thanks" for the effort to convince the world of its evil ways

---

59. See, generally, Charlesworth (1990).
60. Cited in Neusner (1984, 121).
61. Charlesworth (1990, 28–37).

(16:1–12), the Johannine community heard God's call as insisting that the world not be given up on or withdrawn from. Those seen by Matthew's gospel as "enemies" are characterized in the fourth gospel as "the world." In either case, the disciple's response is to love regardless of cost.

Whether the fourth gospel's imagery of light/darkness and truth/lies is *from* Qumran or in *response* to it, we cannot know. But it seems unlikely that the parallel language is purely coincidental. Whichever way the relationship originated, it seems clear that the gospel of John rejects the option of trying to live a life of holiness apart from the context of violence and falsity in which we are all born.

### c. "You Will See Heaven Opened and the Angels of God...": The Question of Apocalyptic Judaism

Another Jewish mind-set that competed for attention in the late first century was that of *apocalypticism*. Numerous documents, gathered later under the rubric "Pseudepigrapha," were written during the intertestamental period to provide radical hope amidst the terrible suffering of the people.[62] Much of this literature was composed during the two centuries preceding Jesus and forms part of the literary background for the fourth gospel as well as other New Testament texts. Several apocalyptic writings, however, were apparently created in response to the cataclysm of 70 C.E.: 4 Ezra, 2 Baruch, and the Apocalypse of Abraham.[63] The thrust of 4 Ezra is that "the humiliation of Israel will not last forever and that the balance over against the other nations will be set right."[64] Likewise, 2 Baruch provides hope for survivors by suggesting that the criterion for membership in the Chosen People "is not ethnicity but observance of the Law [Torah]."[65] Both of these documents, as well as the Apocalypse of Abraham, attempt to buoy up a distraught people by "explaining" both the reason for the destruction of Jerusalem as well as the key to restoring a good relationship with God. But in contrast with the fourth gospel, the primary image of hope is a restored *nation* of Israel.

For whom were these documents written? Unlike the Qumran scrolls, the post-Temple apocalypses do not appear to have supported a Jewish community apart from the mainstream of Pharisaic dominance. Although they perpetuate a genre that had otherwise been used to give hope to marginal groups not given to participation in the mainstream of sociopolitical discourse and actions,[66] these particular apocalypses seem to have been aimed at supporting the rabbinic community, those who most hoped for a day when Israel would take its place at the head of the nations.[67] Thus, there does not appear to have been a radical Jewish

---

62. See, generally, Charlesworth (1983) and Collins (1984).
63. Collins (1984, 155–186).
64. Ibid., 167.
65. Ibid., 175.
66. E.g., Daniel 7 as support for a nonviolent resistance community apart from the dominance of the Maccabean rebellion two centuries earlier; cf. Mark 13.
67. Collins (1984, 169, 178).

community other than at Qumran that offered ideological competition with the fourth gospel. However, the apocalyptic attitude, expressed in both the pre-70 and post-70 texts, did permeate the mind-set of the fourth gospel, as will be seen below in the discussion of the literary thread comprising the Johannine fabric.

### d. "Simon, Son of John: Do You Love Me More Than These?": The Johannine Struggle with Apostolic Christianity

One of the first things one notes when trying to read the fourth gospel as a coherent unit is its *strangeness* in relation to the synoptic gospels. In all three threads of biblical narrative, John differs in substantial ways from Mark, Matthew, and Luke. Historically, John links the rabbinical condemnation of Christ-confessors with the mission and ministry of the earthly Jesus. From a literary perspective, as we will see, it substitutes its own style of "I AM" statements for synoptic parables, uses the farewell discourse genre rather than the synoptic teaching speech, and otherwise constructs its own unique narrative. And from an ideological perspective, the fourth gospel paints a picture of discipleship that is almost irreconcilable with the emerging institutional apostolic Christianity of the late first and second centuries.

The most striking aspect of this divergence is the gospel's refusal to use the word "apostle" (Gk, *apostolos*) to describe those who gather around Jesus.[68] Each of the synoptics refers specifically to the appointment by Jesus of "twelve" who are called "apostles" (Mt 10:2; Mk 3:14; Lk 6:13). Luke, in his combined two-volume work, uses the term some thirty-six times! Why does the fourth gospel refuse to share in this traditional apostolic establishment?

The key reason is in the difference in Johannine ecclesiology from that of all of the synoptics. While Mark has Jesus strongly criticize and perhaps even satirize the ambition of the lead apostles (Mk 10:35–45),[69] he does provide a basis for the development of an apostolic leadership that exercises official authority over the church. However one might read Mark now from a perspective that affirms the church leadership of women and rejects Christian patriarchy,[70] the historical result of the synoptics' combined affirmation of the authority of the "twelve" was the institution of a system of doctrinal and moral control under the leadership of those deemed to be successors to the "apostles." This development is clear in the specific vesting of ecclesial authority in Peter by Matthew (Mt 16:18–19; but cf. 18:18–19, where authority is given to "disciples") and in Peter and the "other" apostles by Luke throughout the book of Acts (e.g., Acts

---

68. The one possible exception is in the proverbial statement in 13:16, where Jesus tells those gathered after the footwashing at supper: "A slave is not greater than his lord, nor the one sent [*apostolos*] greater than the one having sent [*pempsantos*] him." But even there, it is clear that the statement is not referring to a privilege of a particular group of individuals, but to all whom Jesus sends as the Father has sent him (17:18; 20:21).

69. Myers (1988, 279).

70. Ibid., 280–281.

2:37). Paul, for his part, attempts to share in this authority despite his absence from the formal group of the "twelve" (e.g., 1 Cor 9:1–2).

Despite their other differences in style and emphasis, then, the non-Johannine Christian communities described within the New Testament texts share the crucial element of creating an elite class of persons on whom the responsibility for leadership rests. The fourth gospel's refusal to use "apostle" as a noun (the verb form meaning "to be sent" is used twenty-nine times) is a powerful symbol of the unwillingness to go along with this dominant ideology. As we will see below and throughout the commentary, the narrative uses the character of Peter as a representative of the apostolic churches and allows Johannine Christians a good laugh and a good cry at the foibles of the one whom other communities designate as the lead apostle.

In place of the development of an apostolic institution, the fourth gospel offers an ecclesiology grounded in egalitarian community led by the elusive presence of the *paraclete*, also referred to as "the spirit of truth" (Jn 14:16–17; 15:26). The text's central image is not the metaphor of the body used by the synoptics (e.g., Mk 9:44–47) or Paul (1 Cor 12:12–27) but that of the vine and branches (Jn 15:1–6). The differentiation of functions and offices that developed in the apostolic churches is nowhere to be found in the Johannine community. Instead, there is a tightly united gathering of persons discerning together the presence of Jesus in their midst (Jn 20:19, 26). The spirit that animates this community cannot be controlled by human structures — whether those of Pharisaic Judaism or of apostolic Christianity — but blows where it wills (Jn 3:8). The discipleship mission can be equally lived out by women (4:39; 12:2–7; 20:18) as by men, by outsiders (9:17–34) as by the "twelve," by named figures like Peter as by anonymous ones like the "Beloved Disciple" (21:20–24).

Of course, such a structureless gathering is a very precarious foundation for community, as many of us who have attempted to live out similar patterns of discipleship have experienced. If we may join those who see 1 John as written by the same person or at least out of the same community as the fourth gospel,[71] then the sad but unsurprising outcome of this charismatic community can be seen. What was encouraged to be a circle of self-sacrificing love and mutual commitment deteriorated into harsh mutual accusations and hatred. A brief passage or two provides the tone of what happened when the community came to disagreement over an aspect of its discipleship:

> Children, it is the last hour! As you have heard that Antichrist is coming, so now many Antichrists have come. From this we know that it is the last hour. They went out from us, but they did not belong to us; for if they had belonged to us, they would have remained with us. But by going out they made it plain that none of them belongs to us. (1 Jn 2:18–19)

> All who hate a brother or sister are murderers, and you know that murderers do not have eternal life abiding in them. (1 Jn 3:15)

---

71. E.g., R. Brown (1979).

As a matter of structure and process, the presence of an irreconcilable difference within the community apparently led first to a schism and then to condemnation. Without either a means of being clear about which group was speaking with the presence of the spirit or a structure that would resolve the conflict more forcefully, the community seems to have dissolved altogether as a distinct living model of discipleship.

The outcome seems to have been the attempt of some to live apart from the mother community (those condemned in 1 John) and the reconciliation of the others with the apostolic churches (Jn 21:15–19). But the basis for acceptance of the apostolic leadership of Peter and his successors is expressly *not* their holding of the office of "shepherd" but the willingness of the shepherds to lay down their lives for the sheep. By the time of the Johannine community, Peter's martyrdom was both fact and legend. So long as the institutional leaders were willing to live Jesus' example of love, the Johannine community that remained appears to have been willing to live within the sheltering wing of the apostolic churches.

### e. "If You Know These Things, Happy Are You if You Do Them": The Mixed Appeal of Gnosticism

The Johannine community's ideology lay on a spectrum about midway between that of the apostolic churches and that of the other major direction taken by Christian communities in the first centuries: gnosticism. Although not reducible to a unified concept, the various strains of gnostic Christianity apparently had a common perspective on several issues important to the Johannine community.

First, they generally shared with the fourth gospel a preference for spirit-based leadership, rejecting the apostolic authority — which was based on witnessing the resurrection — of the dominant church.[72] According to the highly biased responses of the apostolic fathers, many of the gnostic communities held the system of bishop, priest, and deacon in great contempt, seeing it as a sign of the ignorance and human-based nature of the emerging Catholic Church. Although the fourth gospel is clearly capable of expressing strong opposition to the perspectives of those with whom it disagrees, it never casts the apostolic churches in as dark a light as do some of the gnostic texts, saving its venom for the Temple-state and its Pharisaic successors. But the gnostic willingness to trust that the spirit could be present in anyone regardless of social status would certainly have found a friendly reception in the Johannine community.

Second, the notion that knowledge led not simply to imitation of Christ but to *equal status* with Christ was common to both gnosticism and Johannine Christianity. A comparison of two sets of texts reveals the point of christological connection:

---

72. Pagels (1979, 3–47).

It is certainly necessary to be born again through the image. Which one? Resurrection.... For this person is no longer a Christian but a Christ. (*Gos. Phil.* 67:14–15, 26)

No one can see the reign of God unless that one is born again [from above].... The one who believes in me will do the works I do and greater than these that one will do.... I call you no longer slaves but friends. (Jn 3:3; 14:12; 15:15)

Although this aspect of Johannine ideology was quickly submerged into the dominant apostolic doctrine of the royal Son of God who was essentially different from humanity, the fourth gospel itself clearly calls disciples to participate with Jesus in being "children of God" (Jn 1:13).

Third, the emphasis on "knowledge" implied in the very title "gnosticism" (from Gk, *gnōsis*, "knowledge") is also found within the fourth gospel to a much greater extent than in the synoptics (the verb form *ginōskō* appears sixty-one times total in the synoptics, and fifty-six times in John alone, plus twenty-five times in 1 John). It is not surprising that the second-century gnostic writers found John a valuable reference to support their own perspective.

However, upon closer examination, the Johannine and gnostic meanings of "knowledge" were considerably different, with crucial consequences for discipleship. For the gnostics, knowledge was basically a matter of intellectual and spiritual insight, an awareness of one's own true nature that allowed one to be free of the illusions of the world. Knowledge was something for an elite cadre of individuals who were let in on the secret. It was an essentially *Hellenistic* notion, something derived from the thought world of Plato and Aristotle. But for the fourth gospel, knowledge was essentially a *Hebraic, biblical* notion. The Hebrew word *yada*, used over nine hundred times in the Hebrew scripture, has many shades of meaning but is predominantly a term of *relationship and intimacy*.[73] As it describes relationships among humans, it also links human intimacy with God (e.g., 1 Sam 2:12; Jer 4:22). The fourth gospel continues this biblical understanding of knowing. When the Johannine Jesus and narrator speak of knowledge of people or of the things of God, it is always a matter of intimacy and personal connectedness, not of purely intellectual understanding. Thus, the gnostic use of the fourth gospel to support its ideology is just the beginning of the centuries-long tradition of refusing to listen to the text speaking out of its own social and literary context.

Another point of divergence between the Johannine community and the dominant gnostic tradition flows from this difference in Hellenistic and Hebraic origins. For the gnostics, creation is the act of at best a demigod; at worst, it is the act of a demon. It is a place of suffering, pain, and toil, unworthy of a "true" God. Similarly, the Creator revered in the Hebrew scriptures is frequently described with adjectives such as "arrogant" and "ignorant." The scriptures'

---

73. *TWOT* 366.

own quotations of the Creator as a "jealous" God seemed to prove for many gnostics that creation was originally and remained the act not of the divine spark living within each person but of a mischievous interloper whose behavior was the source of human misery. Thus, the gnostic goal was not to celebrate fleshly existence but to seek to overcome it, to escape it into a realm of spiritual understanding "above" the illusion and pain of earthly life.

The fourth gospel, in contrast, puts its affirmation of creation right at the beginning, with its joyous acclamation that "the Word became flesh" (Jn 1:14). As we shall see, the gospel's later distinction between the power of spirit and the "uselessness" of flesh arises from concerns that are totally different from those of the gnostic perspective. For throughout John, the God of the Hebrew scriptures and of Israel's memory is stated to be the "Father" of Jesus, the source of all that is, the one who *is* love (1 Jn 4:8).

This contrast had, of course, enormous implications for discipleship. The gnostics' rejection of creation led them to perceive Jesus' death as a trick: either Jesus was not really human, or the one who was crucified was not really Jesus.[74] Bizarre as such a notion might seem to us, it arose from a very real question about how to respond to the circumstances of the time. As Elaine Pagels puts it, the "controversy over the interpretation of Christ's suffering and death involved, for Christians of the first and second centuries, an urgent practical question: How are believers to respond to persecution, which raises the imminent threat of their *own* suffering and death?"[75]

Perhaps ironically, this is where the Johannine community found greater communion with the apostolic churches than with the gnostics. For the fourth gospel, to accept Jesus as the one sent from God was to see his crucifixion as his being "raised up" in "glory," rather than a humiliating and stupid failure (Jn 12:27–33). This meant that his followers were to imitate this example, starting with the already accomplished martyrdom of Peter (Jn 13:15; 21:19). The apostolic churches, for their part, also embraced this call to imitate their Lord, as the powerful statements of people like Ignatius of Antioch and Polycarp attest. For example, shortly before his death, Ignatius wrote:

> Just pray that I will have the strength both outwardly and inwardly so that I may not just talk about it but want to do it, that I might not merely be called a Christian, but actually prove to be one. . . . Let me be food for wild beasts, through whom I can reach God. I am God's wheat, and I am being ground by the teeth of the wild beasts, that I might prove to be pure bread.[76]

Similarly, the elderly bishop Polycarp responded to the Roman order to "swear by the genius of Caesar":

---

74. Pagels (1979, 70–101).
75. Ibid., 75.
76. Ignatius, *Rom.* 3–4, in Holmes (1989, 103).

If you vainly suppose that I will swear by the genius of Caesar, as you request, and pretend not to know who I am, listen carefully: I am a Christian. . . . We have been taught to pay proper respect to rulers and authorities appointed by God, as long as it does us no harm; but as for these, I do not think they are worthy, that I should have to defend myself before them.[77]

Polycarp's proclamation shows how clearly the apostolic churches linked the reality of Jesus' physical existence and crucifixion with the political consequences for discipleship. As with the differences between the Johannine community and the Qumran covenanters, the fourth gospel fits better with the apostolic resistance to the world than with the gnostic withdrawal from it.

Given these various similarities and differences between gnosticism and Johannine Christianity, what actual role might gnostic communities have played vis-à-vis the Johannine community? The difficulty with answering this question is that the evidence we have about gnosticism almost all comes from the second and third centuries, after the completion of the fourth gospel. Thus, rather than gnosticism offering a competing social ideology to the fourth gospel's notion of community, it was more likely one of the first viewpoints to *interpret* the fourth gospel in its own favor. Probably the earliest example of this process is found in the esoteric-sounding text *The Trimorphic Protennoia* (Three-formed divine first thought) from the first part of the second century. Its use of images from the prologue of John as well as numerous other similar phrases suggests that the fourth gospel was an early weapon in the battle of myths between the apostolic and gnostic communities. Indeed, it is quite possible that the defectors from the Johannine community condemned in 1 John found a new home among the gnostics, while the mother community reconciled with the apostolic church.

With this movement from ideological competition *between* the fourth gospel and other texts toward competition *over* the fourth gospel, we reach the third strand in our fabric of Johannine narrative. How did the way the story is told invite such a wide variety of interpretations, both in the early church and throughout the centuries? In other words, how do the literary aspects of the text shape its historical and ideological claims?

## 4. THE LITERARY THREAD: THE WORD BECOMES TEXT

As suggested earlier, the process by which we have tried to separate out the historical and ideological threads of the fourth gospel is somewhat violent. The gospel of John is not a collection of "facts" nor a didactic treatise, but primarily a dramatic narrative. As such, it consists of various elements usually associated with "fiction" but actually found in all narrative genres: a narrator, plot,

---

77. *Mart. Pol.* 9, 11, in Holmes (1989, 139).

characters, settings, and so on.[78] Furthermore, the text, like all of the biblical narratives, uses various aspects of language to create ambiguity, surprise, suspense, and wordplay.[79] Rather than attempt to summarize how each of these elements is manifested in John, I will allow the commentary to take readers along the unfolding path verse by verse.

But there are several aspects of the literary makeup of the fourth gospel that readers are best made familiar with before the start of the actual reading of the text. Without some sense of how these features work, it would be all too easy to find oneself dazed and confused before finishing the prologue.

### a. Centering the Word: The Role of Chiasm

Perhaps the most unfamiliar yet vitally important aspect of the structure of the fourth gospel is its intricate use of the device known as "chiasm" or "chiastic structure." A chiasm is a portion of the text in which the words are arranged to form a concentric pattern, usually in the form a-b-c-b¹-a¹. The purpose is to draw attention in a passage to the center as the focal point for the surrounding verses. The best way to understand this is to look at an example of how it works.

**Chiasm: John 3:1–10**

a: 1–2: we know you are a teacher

   b: 3–4: unless born *anōthen*; Nicodemus asks, "how can this happen?"

      c: 5–6: unless born of water/spirit

   b¹: 7–9: don't marvel at born *anōthen*; Nicodemus asks, "how can this happen?"

a¹: 10: you are a teacher and don't know

In Jn 3:1–10, Jesus has a conversation with the person from the Pharisees, Nicodemus. At one level, the narrative proceeds in the normally conceived, linear progression of discussion, with one person speaking, then another, and so on, reaching its conclusion at the end. However, one can also see the verses as revealing parallels that center around the powerful "amen, amen" statement by Jesus in verses 5–6. That is, at beginning and end are statements about *knowledge* and being a *teacher.* In the first case, Nicodemus, speaking for an unspecified "we," proclaims their awareness of Jesus' status as a teacher. In the second case, Jesus mocks Nicodemus's own status as a teacher because he does not know what Jesus is talking about! Similarly, in the "b" parallels that fit inside the broader frame of the "a" parallels, the verses express Nicodemus's twice-asked question, "how can this happen?" in response to Jesus' twice-made statement about being born *anōthen*, that is, again/from above.

The effect of this structuring is not only to draw our attention to the verses in the center but also to help us see the surrounding parallels as corollaries or other

---

78. See, e.g., Chatman (1978); Culpepper (1983).
79. Sternberg (1985).

related statements grounded in the centrality of the "c" portion of the chiasm. Another effect of chiasm — perhaps even more for today's readers than for those of the gospel's own day — is to lead readers into paying close attention to the text as they search out the chiasms that fit the entire text together.

Chiasm was not invented by the author of the fourth gospel. It is found both in biblical narrative as well as in other ancient texts.[80] Its presence in the fourth gospel is not a new discovery but one that commentators have long seen in certain passages, notably the trial before Pilate in 18:28–19:16.[81] However, what scholars have not broadly acknowledged is the dominance of chiasm as the structural key to the fourth gospel. Peter Ellis, in his otherwise unremarkable commentary, *The Genius of John*, building on an obscure doctoral dissertation, was the first to claim that the entire text is structured around chiastic parallelism. Other literary critics have resisted this larger claim. Jeff Staley, for example, argues that "Ellis' failure to consider the possibility of a plot structure related to the chiastic symmetry of the book is a rejection of a narrative critical approach, and turns the gospel into an incredible mosaic that makes reading virtually impossible."[82] Staley's reproach, though, is not so much of the chiastic structure posited by Ellis, but of Ellis's unwillingness to see the *twofold* structure of the gospel as *both* chiastic *and* plot-centered.

In my own reading, I attempt to follow Staley's implicit suggestion of reading the fourth gospel through the double device of chiasm and narrative structuring. Once one begins to become familiar with the pattern of chiastic parallelism, one will perhaps find it not an impediment to reading but an aid to the gospel's *own method* of organizing itself. If reading in this way seems to violate norms grounded either in our unconscious reading methods or in the highly reflected upon notions of narrative critics such as Staley and Culpepper, we might try to recall Sternberg's guiding principle of trying to let the text teach us its own way of reading.

Another scholarly objection to chiasm is that it often seems to be in the eye of the interpreter rather than "in the text."[83] Two points may be helpful in response. First, any discourse-based reading method must recognize that any structure or meaning is not "in the text" but *in the relationship between the text and readers*.[84] The verbal or thematic parallels that make up a chiasm are "facts" of the sequence of words and ideas, but the decision to call such an arrangement a "chiasm" and to draw interpretative inferences from that decision is part of the act of reading, not the text itself.

Second, my attention to chiasm regularly notes that multiple patterns may be found within the gospel. I am not arguing for the "correct" chiasms. How-

---

80. E.g., Rosenberg (1986, 62, 84), using the term "palistrophe" to describe the same phenomenon as chiasm, shows how it structures both the garden of Eden story in Genesis 2–3 and the Abraham story in Genesis 11–25, which is usually seen as a loose collection of narratives from several sources, into a coherent whole.

81. E.g., R. Brown (1966, cxxxv).

82. Staley (1988, 58 n. 26).

83. Culpepper (1988); Stibbe (1992, 20).

84. McKnight (1988, 258–259).

ever, my experience with real readers of the fourth gospel — especially those unfamiliar with the whole concept of chiasm — is that the *process of looking for parallels is an effective reading strategy for inculcating skills of close and disciplined reading.* In many places, I go further and use the parallel structure as a factor in reaching interpretive conclusions. Rarely, though, is a chiasm itself the sole basis for reading a particular scene. As noted above, my reading of the fourth gospel pays simultaneous attention to chiasm and numerous other narrative aspects of the text.

### b. Johannine Irony:  The Choice of Whether to Laugh or Cry

If chiasm is a somewhat controversial aspect of Johannine literary design, irony is not. Scholars are virtually unanimous in noting the powerful role of irony in leading readers into the narrative.[85] Its ubiquitous presence will become apparent as we follow the text itself. For now, it is important simply to consider the overall purpose in using such a device. Why develop a narrative in which characters are constantly saying and doing things that seem to support precisely the opposite point apparently intended by their words and actions?

The answer shows how tightly wound are the literary and ideological threads of the gospel. The primary purpose of all irony is to get readers to identify with the point of view of the author or, in this case, the reliable narrator. As Paul Duke puts it: "Having already danced with the author, the reader is much more prone to consider marriage."[86] Irony presents readers with a sly choice: either to reject or ignore its presence — and risk being identified with the dullards and blind ones who populate the story — or to accept it and rise "above" the characters' ignorance and foolishness. A prime example from the gospel of John is the brutal irony with which the author has the Judeans respond to Pilate's "threat" to "crucify your king": "The chief priests answered, 'We have no king but Caesar!'" (Jn 19:15). Having walked with Jesus throughout his ministry, dare readers side with the blasphemous priests of Israel who proclaim their total allegiance to the imperial despot? The irony almost compels us to accept the author's perspective on the priests, who have completely abandoned their loyalty to Yahweh at the very moment when they are insisting that Jesus should be executed in order to preserve the integrity of the Torah!

Although we might think of irony as a form of humor, as the example just given shows, it often contains elements of the tragic as well. Whether in lampooning the Temple officials or Jesus' own disciples, the fourth gospel's use of irony constantly reminds us of the presence of a creative force that has shaped the narrative for a particular ideological purpose.

---

85. Culpepper (1983), Duke (1985), O'Day (1988), and Staley (1988) join the previous generation of historical commentators such as Brown (1966) and Schnackenburg (1990) in pointing out the role of irony in the fourth gospel, adding the particular value of it from various literary-critical perspectives.

86. Duke (1985, 37).

### c. Characterization: The Shifting Sands of Naming

The ideological and literary are perhaps most tightly entwined when it comes to the fourth gospel's way of presenting characters. Whether the majestic figure of Jesus going calmly to the cross to "complete" God's work for him or the combative discipleship of the once blind man in chapter 9, the text presents an incredible parade of persons who stand out from the landscape of Palestine in ways vastly different from the synoptics.

Some of the portraits are similar to the characterizations found in the synoptics, while others are hardly identifiable as the same people. For example, Peter as the too brash leader of the group is common to all the gospels, and the Johannine picture of the sisters Mary and Martha is consistent with the Lukan images (cf. Jn 12:2–3 and Lk 10:38–42). On the other hand, Jesus' mother in the Matthean and Lukan infancy narratives is so strongly identified by name that other Marys need additional description to be distinguished from the one who is simply "Mary," while in John, she is given no name at all. Most of these characterizations are best revealed by observing the text as it unfolds. However, some particular Johannine usages are best noted before reading begins.

### i. The "Judeans": Ideological, Not Religious, Opponents of the Johannine Community

One of the least understood yet most important aspects of the fourth gospel is its criticism of the people often referred to as "the Jews." No Christian text has been a stronger basis for two thousand years of unjustified anti-Semitism than the gospel of John. But reading the text from within its own poetics shows how, not surprisingly, modern anti-Jewish attitudes should find no support in the fourth gospel.

The issue arises from the question of how to translate the Greek word *Ioudaioi,* which is used seventy times in John and only sixteen times in the synoptics combined. Virtually all scholars recognize that the word has the root meaning not of "Jews" but of "Judeans," yet not a single major Bible translation renders it "Judeans." Why not?

One reason is that if one considers "Judeans" to refer simply to people living in Judea, then *Ioudaioi* must mean something else, for chapter 6 shows Jesus arguing with people called *Ioudaioi* while in the geographic location of *Galilee* (6:41). Unless one entertains the far-fetched but not impossible scenario of people coming from Judea to Galilee to speak with Jesus (officials come in the first scene from Jerusalem to talk with John the Baptist [1:19]), it seems that *Ioudaioi,* at least in this place in the text, must refer to the logical alternative, Jews. Once one reaches this point in the argument, the issue is reduced to whether the term is criticizing all Jews or some subgroup, such as the synagogue leaders or Sanhedrin.

However, two important matters argue against following this line of reasoning. First, the term *Ioudaioi* in its original context did not refer exclusively to "Jews" until after the failed Bar-Kochba revolt in 135 C.E. when the religious center for the first time shifted to Galilee, at least forty to fifty years *after* the composition of the fourth gospel.[87] Before that, it had had a variety of meanings, depending on the stage of history one is examining. Originally, the term applied more precisely to people of the tribe of Judah, but, during the period of the Hasmonean priestly dynasty roughly two centuries before Jesus, religious converts from other ethnic groups began to be referred to as *Ioudaioi*. John Ashton suggests that Josephus used the term to refer first to the returning exiles from Babylon, "the people responsible for the reconstruction of the Temple."[88] This would identify the term with the elite of Judah, those most identified with the Torah/Temple symbolic universe. Thus, at the time of the gospels generally, *Ioudaioi* conveyed both the geographic/ethnic-political sense as well as the more broad religious sense.

Of course, commentators who choose to translate the term as "Jews" must deal with the fact that Jesus and his first followers were obviously Jewish themselves. It cannot be, therefore, that the gospel is criticizing *all* Jews. This leads to the second fork in the road: either the term means some subgroup as already mentioned, or it means different things in different places in the text. For clearly, the same passage mentioned as evidence against the purely geographic connotation (6:41) also seems to exclude the idea that official leaders are the sole referent, for those who come to Jesus in the wilderness are unlikely to be the officials from Jerusalem!

Scholars caught in this dilemma frequently find themselves turning to the social setting of the gospel, the painful experience of a community of Jewish-Christians who have been excommunicated from the synagogue. Thus, if the gospel sounds anti-Jewish to our ears, perhaps we can reduce its sting by trying to limit its polemic to the particular situation in which it arose, one very much unlike the situation faced by most modern readers.[89] However, this whole "problem" — which admittedly results in reducing the value of the gospel for today's readers — can be avoided by recognizing the deeper reality of the social situation and the gospel's literary method of expressing it.

Judea in the time of Jesus was not only the place in which some Jewish people lived but also the *symbolic and economic center* of Palestine. Before 70 C.E., everything in Jerusalem and its environs turned on the presence of the Temple as a religious pilgrimage site. Located on top of a three-thousand-foot mountain and off the usual trade routes (unlike Galilee, which lay directly on common roads for many cultures), Jerusalem would have had no meaning and no economic base apart from the religious justification that led thousands to come three times a year with much money to spend and turn over as tithes to the Temple authorities.

---

87. Lowe (1976, 109).

88. Ashton (1991, 153).

89. E.g., Kysar (1992, 3–4): "Although the historical origin of the Gospel of John makes its anti-Semitic tone understandable, it does not alter the basic reality of that tone as the Gospel is read and heard.... Herein lies a dreadful danger! It is now read and interpreted outside of its original situation and beyond its original purpose."

For the ordinary people living in Judea, then, the Temple was the lifeblood of the region. Not unlike major defense contractors or military bases in the United States today, the presence of such a powerful entity would necessarily shape the attitudes of the population beyond their personal political or religious views. We are not surprised when people whose jobs depend on the viability of a Navy base or bomb factory become strong supporters of defense spending. The situation in Judea was much like this. Whatever one might have thought about the corruption of the Temple priests and the hypocrisy of the Sadducees' collaboration with Rome, the Temple and its supporting aristocracy were all that provided for economic success for every inhabitant of Judea. Anything that was a threat to the Temple was a threat to them, just as peace activists are often perceived as a threat by the "ordinary" people in militarized areas.

And into this situation, Jesus comes overturning the tables of the Temple money changers and dove sellers! Not only would the officials be aroused by such a direct action, but so would all the ordinary folks whose security depended on the Temple system of tithing and sacrifice. But in the northern reaches of Palestine, such economic dependence and the resulting ideological loyalty would not only be diluted but could easily be seen as a provincial problem of those in the south. For as far back as the initial break in the United Monarchy of Israel, the first king of the north recognized the economic and political difficulty of a populace traveling regularly to the south not only siphoning money out of his treasury but also subjecting themselves to the ideological influence of Jerusalem (1 Kgs 12:26–29). In Jesus' time, the Galileans would certainly have perceived the southern province as an at best ambiguous place of religious tradition and economic burden. It is thus not surprising that all of the gospels show Jesus having his best success in the north rather than in the south. Indeed, in the synoptics, Jesus does not go to Jerusalem at all until the final week of his life, where he is immediately arrested and executed!

Throughout the fourth gospel, therefore, the text works to establish opposition not between "Christians" and "Jews" but between *Galileans* and *Judeans.* It is not the strict sense of geography that is at issue[90] but the ideological *site* with which a person is identified. As we will see, the *Ioudaioi* in 6:41 may be from Galilee, but their behavior reveals their loyalty to the ways of Judea. To be a member of the *Ioudaioi* is thus not a matter purely of religion or geography but of ideological *choice.* This produces some interesting ironic twists in the text, the most striking of which is Pilate's question to Jesus, "I am not a Judean [*Ioudaios*], am I?" (18:35).

From this perspective, then, all of the problems related to supposed multiple meanings of "Jews" are seen to be false issues, eliminated by translating the term as "Judeans" throughout the text. The gospel is not anti-Semitic or anti-Jewish but anti-Judean, where "Judean" is a symbol for those whose allegiance is to the "world."

---

90. Cf. Meeks (1966) with Bassler (1981).

### ii. God as "Father": Where Patriarchy and Intimacy Clash

Another characterization that creates numerous social difficulties in our time is the repeated use of the term "Father" by Jesus to refer to the "one who sent" him. This time, no translation alternative can take away the clearly male characterization of God by the Johannine Jesus. Given appropriate feminist criticism in our day of the church's nearly exclusive use of male imagery for God and the consequent damage that has been done to the dignity and authority of women in the church and beyond, it is not surprising to find many readers repelled by this aspect of the fourth gospel.

A common but unfortunately unsatisfying option is to boldly change the term to a gender-neutral image such as Creator or Parent. While such images for the divine have their place among the burgeoning variety of God-names thankfully available to believers today, neither conveys the essence of what John's gospel is trying to tell us about Jesus' relationship with the one with whom he invites us to share a similar relationship.

The central purpose of Jesus' constant use of "Father" is not to impose the idea that God is male but to restore the then-repressed idea that God is *close*. To understand how this takes place, we need to consider briefly the history of Israel's sense of God's presence. In the chronological picture presented by the Bible, God started the relationship with humanity as one who walked in the garden in the cool of the evening (Gen 3:8). Throughout the narratives of the patriarchs and exodus, God was portrayed as the all-powerful but still accessible one who spoke regularly to human beings. As time passed, God spoke less and less directly, using the prophets as an instrument for expressing the divine word. Eventually, the period of prophecy was declared to be over. Apparently, God's willingness to speak to humans was a thing of the past. What remained was a powerful symbolic system for mediating the presence of an otherwise distant God, that is, the Temple-state and the Torah's official interpreters.

Thus, at the time of Jesus and the Johannine community, God was conceived largely as a transcendent deity who was completely unapproachable by ordinary people. Into this scene, Jesus comes speaking of God as his own Father and calling his disciples to the same intimacy with the divine that he experiences each moment of his own life (e.g., Jn 17:20–23). From this perspective, we can see that Jesus' claim to such a shocking intimacy with the God of Israel would be a subversive threat to the legitimation of the Temple and the Torah as exclusive avenues of encountering God. "Father" was not a new title for God but rather an ancient one, a title that had been suppressed by a religious establishment invested in keeping God at a distance, traversable across bridges that they controlled.

One cannot deny that this title is a male image, one that has roots in a patriarchal culture and that has perpetuated an unjust patriarchy over the centuries. But there is nothing in the fourth gospel that commands others to use this particular title for God. Unlike Matthew (6:9) and Luke (11:2), which seem to tell followers that the way to pray includes calling God "Father," the Johannine Jesus offers no formula for prayer. With one exception (Jn 20:17), the fourth gospel never extends the image of God as Father beyond Jesus' own experience. Thus, while not altering the gospel's claim to Jesus' choice of the image of "Father" to describe his relationship with the Holy One, we should feel free to claim whatever other images describe our own experience, whether Creator, Parent, or some other metaphor altogether.

### iii. Peter and the Beloved Disciple: The Struggle between Apostolic and Johannine Models of Christian Community

As pointed out above, one of the primary ideological options with which the fourth gospel competed for the hearts and minds of its readers was the emerging mainstream of apostolic Christianity. One of the main ways in which the text expresses this struggle is by the unique description of the relationship between Simon Peter and an anonymous character whom the text simply calls "the disciple whom he loved" (19:26) or "the one whom Jesus loved" (13:23).

In the synoptics, Peter is often associated with James and John, the "sons of thunder," who are referred to by Paul as the "pillars" (Gal 2:9). Together, these three are the "inner circle" of apostles who are given the privilege of experiencing the Transfiguration and the healing of Jairus's daughter (e.g., Mk 5:37; 9:2). But in the fourth gospel, Peter's primary companion is the anonymous Beloved Disciple, to whom the narrator attributes the authorship of the gospel itself (Jn 21:24). As we will see in the commentary, each of the occasions in which Peter and the Beloved Disciple are found together — or are not together — is a crucial step on the path of discipleship and formation of the community. These occasions include the scene regarding the question of knowledge of the betrayer at the Last Supper (13:21–26), the incidents at the foot of the cross (19:26–27), the race to Jesus' empty tomb (20:2–10), and the postresurrection recognition on the Sea of Galilee and subsequent call to follow (21:7, 20–23). Thus, the fourth gospel places the Rock on whom Matthew builds his church in at least an equal and perhaps even a subservient position to the Beloved Disciple himself. By linking Peter's presence and absence to the one on whose witness the gospel expressly claims its authority, the text allows Peter to be a symbol for the apostolic churches themselves, with whom the Johannine community had such an ambivalent relationship.

This characterization is just one pairing in the fourth gospel's pattern of "representative figures."[91] Throughout the text, individuals often stand for entire mind-sets or communities of interest, for example, Nicodemus for the Pharisees who are "secret disciples" and the once blind man for the ideal Johannine disciple. Rather than engage in the direct polemic that took place in the following decades between the apostolic churches and the gnostic communities, the fourth gospel chose to express the tension between its own perspective and the apostolic mind-set through the device of characterization. The result is a narrative in which readers are challenged to reflect on their own model of community and church through the interplay of Peter and the Beloved Disciple.

---

91. Collins (1976).

### d. "I Have Many More Things to Say to You": The Role of Jesus' Extended Speeches

One of the most difficult aspects of the fourth gospel for modern readers is the repetitive and seemingly abstract nature of Jesus' long monologues. Readers who have enjoyed the exciting drama of the Cana narrative and Temple exorcism sometimes drag by the end of chapter 3's discourse on the ways of light and dark; the Lazarus episode, the anointing at Bethany, and the Judean conspiracy — each a powerful scene — are followed by Jesus' long talk (five chapters, to be exact) referred to as the farewell or Last Supper discourse. Not a few reading groups have become so exhausted by this point that they miss out on the classic drama of the Johannine Passion narrative that follows. Why does the gospel include these repetitive speeches? What role do they play in weaving the ideological and historical threads together?

One answer is provided by Wayne Meeks, who uses anthropological insights about the task of communication in the presence of multiple background messages emanating from the culture:

> If a message is to be conveyed in the face of pervasive distractions — "noise," or, in the case of myth, the overwhelming complexity of the total social matrix — then the communicator must resort to "redundance." He must repeat the signal as many times as possible, in different ways.[92]

In our own world, we can see how this process works by observing political or marketing campaigns that mention their candidate or product repeatedly on television, radio, and other media. We may find this boring, but it is unquestionably effective.

But this explains only the *repetitive* element of Jesus' speeches. Even if there is method in the apparent madness of stating the same core of images and ideas over and over, why are Jesus' monologues so *long?* Part of the answer comes from our cultural difference from the world of the text itself. We are used to skimming material for the "point" and then getting on to the next matter on our reading list. Also, we are so inundated with "action" in our films and television shows that we have lost the art of listening to an eloquent speech that occupies even ten minutes of time. Indeed, the entire Last Supper discourse could be read aloud in less time than it takes to watch the evening news on television. It is no surprise that in our culture Shakespeare is not popular entertainment. So, to appreciate the gospel's own way of telling its story of Jesus, we simply must get past cultural craving for unceasing movement and learn to read and to listen to the text on its own terms.

---

92. Meeks (1972, 48).

## e. "This Was to Fulfill the Scripture...": The Intertextuality of the Gospel

In earlier, source-oriented commentary on the fourth gospel, an area of dispute arose from what appears at first glance to be the text's "dependence" on certain kinds of gnostic literature.[93] As we have seen, though, references to "knowledge" and other terminology that some gnostic literature also uses are only superficially connected to the main ideological struggle of the Johannine community. The primary battle of the fourth gospel — as is the case for the synoptics as well — is over the meaning of "scripture," the various texts now collected as the Hebrew Bible.

The gospel six times states that Jesus' words or actions "fulfill" the scriptures, offering specific texts (12:38; 13:18; 15:25; 19:24, 28, 36). On another eight occasions, the narrator or Jesus refer to "scripture(s)" as an explanation for what is taking place or being said. The synoptics together have only twelve such references. Thus, even at the surface level, it is clear that the fourth gospel makes an important point of portraying Jesus' mission as in continuity with and as a completion of the previous sacred texts.

But these express quotations or references to scripture are just the tip of the intertextual iceberg. Virtually every scene is grounded in a narrative from the Hebrew scriptures. Jesus constantly speaks as one in intimate relationship with the word of God, which should not be surprising for one who is the Logos incarnate.

The ideological tension arises with the Johannine Jesus' unique references to "your Law" (8:17; 10:34; cf. 15:25) in his speeches to the Pharisees or Judeans. It would miss the primary battleground in the war of myths to interpret these verses as suggesting that the "Law" — that is, the Torah — was "theirs" and therefore *not* the word of God for Jesus or the Johannine community. Jesus uses the term to point out that even if his opponents do not accept *his* word (e.g., 5:24; 8:31–7), they at least ought to accept and practice the word that they do believe comes from God. But as it is, none of them observes the Torah (7:19).

Thus, the questions of what constitutes God's word, what it means to observe it, and who in fact practices it are the foremost ideological issues in the gospel, fought on the battleground of the Hebrew scriptures.

In the face of the pervasive presence of the Hebrew scriptures, other intertextual sources pale in comparison. As we have seen, the Johannine community confronted the ideological appeal of other competing groups, such as the Qumran covenanters and the emerging apostolic and gnostic communities. Although there are certainly images in the fourth gospel that suggest familiarity with the *mythos* of those social groups, they are not nearly as central to the gospel's literary thread as are the scriptural texts.

In particular, it is the Septuagint version of scripture that is most often cited. This Greek translation of the original Hebrew narratives changed the texts in

---

93. E.g., Bultmann; criticized by R. Brown and others.

many places. Its influence indicates that the author, if not the Johannine community itself, was most familiar with the scriptures in this form, used throughout the Diaspora by Jews for centuries, starting around the first century B.C.E. Thus, it is a cosmopolitan version of scripture, one readable by both Jews and Gentiles in the Hellenistic world, that forms the primary literary background.

### f. "We Know That His Witness Is True": The Role of the Johannine Narrator

Throughout the commentary, we will see the powerful way in which the storyteller — referred to as the "narrator" — shapes the plot, characterizations, and other aspects of the narrative. As mentioned above (sec. A.3), certain narrative qualities — omniscience, omnipresence, interpretation of psychological states of characters — that suggest "fictionality" in modern literature instead assure truth-telling in scriptural texts. The Johannine narrator, like all biblical narrators, exploits these abilities to maximum ideological benefit.

However, the role of the Johannine narrator goes farther. At the gospel's conclusion, we are told that the narrator (in the first-person *plural*) *has based the text not on the words of Jesus but on the witness of the Beloved Disciple* (21:24). This bombshell is reserved for the end so that a more subtle process can take place throughout the act of reading: the replacement of "Jesus" first with the Beloved Disciple and subsequently with the narrator of the gospel. That is, the gospel calls readers to faith in Jesus only through the commitment to faith in the gospel's narrator.

Robert Polzin has shown how this is precisely the process that took place in the movement from faith in Moses as divine agent and prophet to the "prophet like Moses" (Deut 18:18) who is the narrator of the Deuteronomic History itself.[94] Postexilic Israel interpreted its history and faith through the *character* of Moses as reported by the *narrator* of Deuteronomy. Similarly, the fourth gospel interprets the schism with synagogue Judaism and emerging Christian faith through the character of Jesus as God's agent and prophet as reported by the narrator of John through the witness of the Beloved Disciple.

The clearest instance of this relationship is the parallel between "the only begotten god who is at the bosom [*kolpon*] of the Father who has explained him" and "the disciple Jesus loved, reclining at Jesus' bosom [*kolpō*]" (1:17; 13:23). Throughout the narrative, the narrator acts with knowledge of God and of Jesus that is matched only by Jesus' own knowledge. For the Johannine community and all subsequent believers, Jesus has "gone away." But the word remains, through the power of the paraclete and the agency of the fourth gospel's narrator.

---

94. Polzin (1980).

## 5. "THEY WERE YOURS, AND YOU GAVE THEM TO ME": THE JOHANNINE COMMUNITY AND THE PROVENANCE OF THE GOSPEL

Although it is customary to attempt to make an educated guess about the authorship and place in which a biblical text was composed, to do so in the case of the fourth gospel is largely an exercise in pious speculation. The text seems to go out of its way to keep its authorship secret (e.g., 21:24). Ancient legend linked the gospel with the John who is named in the synoptics as one of the inner circle of apostles and with his supposed location of Ephesus.[95] However, this seems to have been an unconsciously ironic attempt by the mainstream church in the second century to shroud the text in the mantle of apostolic authority. Rather than take sides in the debates that attempt to argue the merits of this connection, I prefer to take a more cautious abstention, for the evidence as a whole seems terribly weak all around.

At the same time, it is crucially important to underscore the community context out of which the text clearly arose. The narrator at the end speaks in the plural of those who believe in the testimony of the Beloved Disciple. And the disciples themselves — with the notable exception of Peter — generally also speak in the plural when conversing to or about Jesus. Conversely, Jesus' words to them, especially in the Last Supper discourse, are constantly directed to the behavior of a collective audience, not simply to individuals. Recent scholarship, of both the source- and discourse-oriented methods, has begun to form a consensus around this theme, breaking down the earlier idea of the text as "individualistic."[96]

Who comprised this community? We certainly cannot claim precision, but some elements seem discernible. It was a community of both men and women, of Jew and Gentile and Samaritan. Some of the members certainly must have been deeply familiar with the biblical tradition. Given the absence of stories focusing on economic conditions, it was probably a relatively prosperous group, in contrast with the Markan or Lukan communities, which seem to have included many of the Palestinian poor. At the same time, Jesus expressly notes the long-term presence of the poor "with you" (12:8), a technical term indicating that the poor were not simply present in the society but were a part of the Johannine community (cf. 9:40; 18:5, 18). Thus, in every way possible within the universe of its time, the gospel's primary social group was multicultural.

Perhaps more than any other gospel community of the first century, the Johannine community seems to have been conscious of its participation in the formation of a new religion based on discipleship of Jesus. Although that community saw Jesus as the fulfillment of scripture, its terrible experience of

---

95. E.g., Schnackenburg (1990, 75–104).

96. Beginning with Martyn's and Brown's notion of the "Johannine community," commentaries have generally supported the community-based nature of the text. E.g., Minear (1984), Rensberger, Miranda, Culpepper (1983).

rejection, excommunication, and persecution led it to abandon the practices that formed the socioreligious world of the Judeans (sabbath, Passover, Tabernacles, Dedication observances, as well as the other aspects of the Torah) and build its unity around a new set of rituals (baptism, eucharist, footwashing). It came to see Jesus' word as sharing in the traditional scriptural feature of being capable of fulfillment (18:9, 32). It almost certainly conceived of the fourth gospel itself as scriptural, a new word of God spoken for a new age. And although the apostolic churches shared the practice of baptism and eucharist and would eventually adopt footwashing and the gospel itself as sacred elements of the Christian tradition, it was for a particular community — and those who continue to hear the fourth gospel as God's word — that this text was truly a new beginning.

# *1*

# The Beginning

## John 1:1–18

**A. Chiasm:**

    a: 1–5: relationship of Logos to God, creation, humanity

      b: 6–8: witness of John (the Baptist) (negative)

        c: 9–11: journey of light/Logos (negative)

          d: 12–13: gift of empowerment

        $c^1$: 14: journey of Logos (positive)

      $b^1$: 15: witness of John (the Baptist) (positive)

    $a^1$: 16–18: relationship of Logos to humanity, re-creation (Law), God

**B. Location:** none given

**C. Time:** none given

**D. Hebrew scripture context:** Genesis 1; the exodus (event); Prov 8:22–31

**E. Social factors:** synagogue vs. Johannine community; gnostic communities vs. Johannine community; John (the Baptist's) communities vs. Johannine community

**F. Themes:** light/darkness; Law/grace; becoming/being; children of God

**G. Key words:** Logos, being, came to be, light, life, witness, the world, will, grace and truth

## 1. THE PROLOGUE AS POETIC OVERTURE

The beginning of John's gospel sings poetic music that will echo throughout the twenty-one chapters of the text. It is also a road map to what will unfold along the way through the gospel. When one is in doubt as to the meaning of a given passage, a return to the first eighteen verses will often shed clarifying light.

The prologue is a wistful summary of the unsure dance between *being* and *becoming,* between What Is and What Has Come To Be. It offers a commentary on the poignant, ironic relationship between Creator and created, the Word and the world. Its verses form one of the three seven-part chiasms (see introduction, sec. B.4.a, above) in the gospel (the others being the story of the blind one in chapter 9 and the trial between Jesus, Pilate, and the crowd in chapters 18 and 19). The rarity of the extended chiasm signals special importance in a passage. The prologue calls us to study, meditate over, and, finally, surrender to its promise and challenge.

"In the beginning..." Consciously molding itself in dialogue with the opening words of the Hebrew scriptures, the prologue starts in verse 1 with an ancient belief that becomes sparkling new for the Johannine community and its successors. The synoptic gospels settle for calling the reader back in time to specific persons at their start: the prophets (Mark), Abraham (Matthew), or Adam (Luke). John, though, returns the audience to the timeless moment, before Israel, before the patriarchs, before humanity. "In the beginning" is a cosmic opening, putting John's text at once within and beyond the tradition of the Hebrew scriptures. It challenges readers to consider primal origins, sources of power and creativity, one's relationship with what is.

"What Is" in the beginning is "the Word," *logos* in Greek. The Greek word *logos* represents complex and multivalent concepts. It translates the Hebrew *dabar,* which is often used in the Bible to relate the unseeable God to the concrete world.[1] Francis J. Moloney notes that "rabbinic and targumic literature often avoided the use of the name and the presence of God by replacing it with 'the Word' (Aramaic *mêmrâ*)."[2] In the Greek world, the word *logos* underwent its own "becoming" over time, evolving from its root meaning, "to gather" (*legō*), into a term for the rational element in human behavior (Socrates), to the source of human virtue (Aristotle), and finally to the ordered and goal-oriented aspect of the universe (the Stoics).[3] Philo of Alexandria, the Jewish-Hellenistic philosopher of the first century C.E., gave this account of the two powers contained in the Logos:

> One is the creative power through which the Artificer placed and ordered all things: this is named "God." And the other is the royal power, since through it the Creator rules over created things; this is called "Lord."[4]

Thus, Logos/Lord/God form an inseparable unit at the start of the gospel, which cannot be overcome by whatever derivative power might be contained in What Has Come To Be. As verse 3 insists both positively and negatively: "All things came to be through him, and apart from him nothing came to be."

---

1. O. Procksch, *TDNT* 4:91–100.
2. Moloney (1993, 30).
3. H. Kleinknecht, *TDNT* 4:77–91.
4. Cited in Neyrey (1988, 26).

The Logos tradition provides imagery grounded in male archetypes and language to paint the prologue's poetry of Creator and creation. "Logos" itself is a male-gender word, and its association with royalty, rationality, and the ordering of chaos conveys masculine images. At the same time, though, these verses also reflect the feminine imagery of the Wisdom tradition in Hebrew scripture. In various places in the Wisdom literature, the texts describe Wisdom incarnate walking with people, just as the prologue will feature the presence of the Logos in the world (e.g., Bar 3:9–4:4; Sirach 1; 4:11–19; Wisdom 6–10). Both Greek (*sophia*) and Hebrew (*hokma*) express "Wisdom" in feminine language. Proverbs 8:22–31 in particular shows how the imagery of Sophia (*hokma*) underlies the first verses of the prologue equally with the Logos imagery. A few excerpts illustrate the links:

> The Lord made me the beginning [LXX, *archōn*] of his ways for his works. He made me before time, in the beginning, before he made the earth. . . . When he made the heaven, I was with him. (Prov 8:22, 27)

The fourth gospel, however, does not "use" the Sophia tradition; it *subverts* it. As Norman Petersen has shown, much of the Sophia imagery that we will find in John was itself a revision of Deuteronomic language by and about Moses.[5] Thus, where Proverbs describes Sophia as a "firstborn" of God, in John, the Word *is* God. Here, the contrast is: Sophia was created *by* God, but the Word co-creates *with* God.

The next sentence in verses 3b–4 adds three elements of "becoming" to the equation: "What has come to be in him was life, and the life was the light of humanity [*anthrōpōn*]." Life, light, and humanity — all make their appearance at once. We might never fully unravel the complexity wound into the interdependence of these three realities, either in the sentence of the text or in the world. What is clear is that all have come to be through the Logos.

And immediately upon consideration of this lofty unity at the core of creation, we are disrupted by the introduction of an opposing force in verse 5: "And the light in the darkness [*skotia*] is shining, and the darkness has not overpowered it." What is this "darkness," over which the spirit of God broods in Gen 1:2? A vague threat? The great unknown? Evil itself? We are told nothing about the nature of darkness but rather are given the powerful assurance that whatever it is, it has not "overpowered" the light. However, if we read closely, we notice that the prologue does not establish the overpowering of the darkness by the light, either. Darkness will not win, the prologue claims; as to the victory of the light, we must wait to find out. In the meantime, the light does not withdraw into its own realm as in some kinds of gnosticism, but offers itself into the darkness, illuminating what is otherwise hidden from view. For the Jewish members of the audience, it provides the opening salvo in the battle of myths

---

5. Petersen (1993, 111–132).

over messiahship. Whoever or whatever the light is, it acts as the one described in Isaiah 9 acts:

> O people walking in darkness, behold a great light! You who dwell in the land of shadow and death, a light shall shine on you!...Because the yoke that was laid upon them has been taken away, and the rod that was on their neck: for he has broken the rod of the captors. (Isa 9:2, 4)

This veiled citation of the prophet continues the ambiguous relationship between the gospel and Hebrew scripture. Jesus will refer contemptuously to what he describes as "your Law" when pointing out the burdens that the religious authorities establish but do not practice (e.g., 7:19; 10:34). At the same time, the narrator will constantly remind us of how Jesus' actions are in accordance with scripture (e.g., 2:22; 19:36). Behind nearly every sentence or deed of Jesus is the living word that explains and justifies both Jesus and the Johannine community.

The prologue moves on to continue its description of the penetration of being into becoming with greater specificity in verses 6–8. From the broad concept of "humanity" we move quickly to the concrete historical existence of a person named John. With John's appearance comes the introduction of two themes central to the Johannine notion of discipleship. John is first described in verse 6 as "having been sent forth" (*apestalmenos*) from God. Throughout the gospel, we will see that "apostle" is a verb, not a noun. On the heels of this characteristic of God's messenger, the purpose of his apostleship is given in verse 7: "that he might witness [*martyrēsē*] about the light so that all might believe through him." Almost nothing more needs be said about the task and purpose of Johannine discipleship. The gospel will offer little concrete specificity to fill in the archetypal model of John. There is no rabbinical Sermon on the Mount or the Plain as in Matthew and Luke, no "discipleship catechism"[6] of action-examples as in Mark. Instead, the fourth gospel gives an image of the first disciple in the simple terms of witness that leads others to faith.

Verse 8 provides our first window into the specific social situation of the Johannine community. By insisting that John was "not the light" but simply "a witness to the light," the text sets up its first opposition between religious communities. The historical John the Baptist is credited with building up his own alternative community, one founded in the repentance and baptism attributed to him in the synoptics. It is possible that this community or communities continued to flourish throughout the first century and that some members saw the growing Jesus movement as a threat. This would explain the fourth gospel's immediate emphasis on John as witness to Jesus rather than as charismatic cult figure in his own right.

Coming behind John is the true light, who offers the gift of enlightenment to everyone in "the world." The *kosmos,* named four times in verses 9–10, is the paradoxical object of God's creation and place of God's rejection. The world's

---

6. Myers (1988, 236).

failure is stated in terms of two more Johannine themes introduced in verses 10–11: its lack of *knowledge* (*gnosis*) and its failure to *receive* the light. With the appearance of *gnosis,* we have the first occasion for the battle with other competing religious groups, the various gnostic communities. As discussed in the introduction (sec. B.3.e), John's gospel has throughout the centuries been perceived by many as supportive of a gnostic viewpoint because of its emphasis on the distinction between those who "know" and those who do not. But, as we will see repeatedly in the fourth gospel, Johannine *gnosis* is a matter not of secret information shared by insiders but of relational intimacy between Creator and creature, and among humans sharing community. If the *kosmos* does not know the light, it is not because of an information gap but because of a closure of mind and heart that seals it off in darkness.

The second basis for the world's failure is its unwillingness to receive the light. A powerful Hebrew scriptural theme that recurs in the fourth gospel is *hospitality* ("to receive," *lambanō*) as a sign of openness to God. Jesus will be received by foreigners, but the world rejects what is its own.

In particular, the Word is described as coming to and being rejected by "his own" (*oi idioi*) in "his own homeland" (*ta idia*). We will have to await the narrative to find out the specific contours of who and where the Word's "own" are, whether "Jews," "Judeans," or "humans" in general (cf. 4:44). But the use of *ta idia* is another aspect of the polemic against the gnostics, who thought of their "homeland" as in heaven, not on earth.[7]

With the statement of this tragic rejection, the prologue reaches the end of its first chiastic curve, setting up readers for the central element of the prologue and of the entire gospel.

## 2. BECOMING GOD'S CHILDREN

The prologue does not describe the fate of those who reject the light, offering only a positive promise to those who accept it. Verses 12–13 summarize the entire Johannine discipleship call in poetic speech that must be considered very carefully to absorb its full power and meaning.

The promise: "authority to become children of God." In John's gospel, status is not given by birth or heritage but by a combination of merit and grace. Modern theology may allow us to describe all people as "children of God" simply by the fact of our creation, but for the fourth gospel, this relationship is something given *and* something achieved. The term "children of God" in Hebrew scripture first denotes tribal status, then relationship with Yahweh, which, of course, occurred by *adoption* in the desert at Sinai.[8] What is remarkable about its usage in John is the way it points to an equivalence between Jesus' relationship with God and that of his disciples. If Jesus is declared "God's Son" and hence el-

---

7. Moloney (1993, 38).
8. Culpepper (1981, 18).

evated to high status, then so are all those who are given authority to become God's children! Conversely, if Jesus suffers persecution because he claims God as his Father — allegedly "making himself equal to God" (5:18) — then what is to be the fate of those others who are God's children? For now, the prologue simply states the claim of child/parent relationship, leaving the narration of consequences until much later. Further, the emphasis, from the beginning, is on the communal aspect of discipleship: "He gave *them* authority to become God's *children.*" Throughout the gospel, we will hear echoes of the first and third-person plural, although often spoken through representative individuals. For the fourth gospel, individual "childhood" is incomprehensible; it is the call to join a Johannine community that is this text's primary message.

The prologue now focuses on the antithetical means of receiving this breath-taking authority. Positively, people can become children of God by "believing in his name" and by being born of the will of God. Negatively, it is by *not* being born of "blood," the "will of the flesh," or "a man's will." These poetic images do not provide propositional theology. The best we can do now is to interpret their deliberately rich yet ambiguous terms in a general direction, leaving the body of the text to illustrate their meaning more fully.

The trio of negatives provides a broad overview of the causes of evil, according to the Johannine ideology. First is being "born of blood." Raymond Brown points out that the Greek word translated "blood," *aimatōn,* is plural and represents a Hebrew idiom for *bloodshed,* a usage also found in contemporaneous Roman literature.[9] The nonchild of God is the one born out of bloodshed, violence, and, ultimately, in the Genesis thematic, fratricide. That this interpretation was likely one understood by the Johannine community is reinforced by what may well be an extended commentary on this verse, found in 1 Jn 2:28–3:12. The passage from 1 John is also chiastic as follows:

a: 2:28–29: practicing justice
   b: 3:1–3: children of God
      c: 3:4–8: practicing sin; practicing justice
   b¹: 3:9–10: children of God
a¹: 3:11–12: practicing justice

Throughout the passage, the theme of the distinction between the children of God and the children of the devil is reiterated in typical Johannine manner. The clearest statement is in 1 Jn 3:12:

The children of God and the children of the devil are evident by this: everyone who does not practice justice is not out of God, nor is the one who does not love their brother. For this is the message which we heard

---

9. Brown (1966, 12); Ovid *Metamorphoses* 33: "Men thus born, no less than the giants, were contemptuous of the gods, violent and cruel, with a lust to kill: it was obvious that they were the children of blood."

from the beginning: that we should love one another, not as Cain, who is out of the evil one and killed his brother.

José Miranda adds that this is the primary distinguishing factor between the children of the devil and the children of God: those who, like Cain, practice fratricide versus those who love the fellow children of God.[10]

In this context, the other negative factors can be seen as further examples of sinfulness that prevents one's claim of God's parenthood. "Born of the will of the flesh" may seem superficially to relate to lust or other sexual behavior, but in the context of the entire gospel's distinction between "flesh" and "spirit," "earth" and "heaven," "below" and "above," we must see this exclusionary factor in broader terms. It is the entire "way of the flesh" that is the problem. It is the manner of behavior that is focused on superficial satisfaction, the culturally acceptable, the easy and comfortable. As we will hear, the Johannine Jesus is not antiflesh in the sense of asceticism or in the gnostic sense of rejecting creation. Rather, it is the way of thinking and acting that originates from "below" that prevents one's bond with one's heavenly Parent.

Finally, we have the term "will of man." To understand this term, we must pause to consider the Greek word being used in 1:13 for "man," *andros.* Throughout the gospel, the text uses a form of the more inclusive term, *anthrōpos,* to refer to human beings (despite the tradition of exclusive translations like "man"). In this rare circumstance,[11] the text chooses the specifically male term. Why? What social evil is the gospel concerned about in addition to bloodshed and cultural comfort? As we shall see, one of the primary communal values for the Johannine community is *egalitarian leadership,* regardless of gender or office. The Samaritan woman, Mary and Martha, and Mary Magdalene all have important leadership roles to play. The disciples are never called "apostles," and Peter's leadership authority will come only after much effort and is based on his willingness to die and the quality of his love, not his official precedence. With these themes in mind, one can read "will of man" as patriarchal leadership that passes on authority in the manner of royal succession. For John's gospel, whoever receives the gift of the spirit is qualified to lead, regardless of social location or prior experience. To be "born of the will of man" is to receive one's power through heredity, like the Judeans who claim Abraham as father but do not know God (e.g., 8:31–47).

There is another specific aspect of patriarchal leadership with which the fourth gospel takes issue. A central theme throughout the Hebrew scriptures, especially from the Deuteronomic History forward through the Prophets, is Israel's struggle to avoid becoming "like the nations" in worshiping the power of monarchy and militarism rather than God. In 1 Samuel 8 we find the oft-repeated view that acceptance of a king is equivalent to rejection of God and will bring about the consequences of slavery, conscription, economic exploita-

---

10. Miranda (1977, 94).
11. The only other use of *andros* is in John the Baptist's reference to Jesus in 1:30.

tion, and the sacrifice of Israel's finest youth to the idols of war. In the fourth gospel, this basic theological premise is carried forward in the tension between Israel as "nation" (*ethnos*) or as "people" (*laos*). This is most clearly and ironically expressed in Caiaphas's only line in the gospel at 11:50: "You do not understand that it is better for one person to die for the people than for the whole nation to be destroyed." The ultimate condemnation of Israel's leaders' choice of nationalism over religious community comes from their own mouths in response to Pilate's taunting question in 19:15: " 'Shall I crucify your king?' The chief priests answered, 'We have no king but Caesar.' " Throughout the gospel, Jesus challenges Judeans to share with him in being born from God rather than from the "fatherland" (cf. 4:44, *patridi*). Thus, in addition to a cry against patriarchy in general, the condemnation of birth "from the will of man" echoes the ancient prophetic cry against loyalty to the king instead of loyalty to God.

Given these negative elements, what can we infer from the positive factors stated in 1:12–13? First, to "believe in his name" is to believe in the person bearing the name, that is, Jesus. As 1 John expresses it, this means, in practice, to do the works of justice and to love one another. Throughout the Last Supper discourse, Jesus will emphasize this theme as the key to discipleship. It is the single great commandment in the gospel: love one another as I have loved you (e.g., 13:34; 15:12, 17). Thus, the ending factor, to be "born from God," is really just the concluding summary of the meaning of the previous negative and positive factors. The theme of birth and parenthood will follow us throughout the entire gospel, filling in the poetic image provided in the prologue.

### 3. THE WORD MADE FLESH

With this glorious centerpiece, the prologue continues its chiastic progress down the other side of the curve. What Jeff Staley calls the positive travels of the Logos, in contrast to the negative travels in verses 9–11,[12] begin in verse 14 with the classic incarnational line: "The Word became flesh and dwelt in us." The one who is *being* enters the realm of *becoming,* for all to behold. In Frank Kermode's wonderful phrase, we experience "the violent conceit of incarnation, wasness surrendering to becoming."[13]

The particular verb used for "dwelt," *eskēnōsen,* literally means "tented," calling forth images of God's presence with the Israelites on their exodus pilgrimage. It is another subversion of the Wisdom tradition found in Sir 24:8, where Wisdom metaphorically "tented" in Israel, while the prologue claims that the Word became a real person.[14] Besides recalling the glory days of Israel, the gospel implicitly brings up a theme prominent in Deuteronomy: the children of God exist on pilgrimage, in the between-places separating captivity to exter-

---

12. Staley (1988, 54–57).
13. Kermode (1986, 10).
14. Petersen (1993, 122).

nal masters from captivity to ego and self. Behind is Egypt/Jerusalem; ahead is Israel/church (as imperial monarchy). The center for the fourth gospel is on the move, not bound up in a human-made system of law, cult, and authority. The true children of God follow this free spirit, themselves remaining free to the extent that the journey continues in openness. The sentence also has connotations of intense intimacy: "dwelt *in us.*" This free God is found in the believing community, within the shared life that is born out of God.

Verse 14 introduces yet another important Johannine theme: glory. This exhilarating yet perhaps frightening word is given no specific meaning at this point, allowing its shades to be revealed in the gospel's own time. All we are told is that "we saw" it, for the first time expressing the communal aspect of the gospel's narrative voice. This glory is visible to the community of faith, a glory fitting for one begotten of a father.

This visible one was "full of grace and truth." Miranda explains this phrase as an attempt to translate the Hebrew *chesed v'emet,* that central, unitary characteristic of God often translated in the Hebrew scriptures as "loving-kindness" or "covenant love." Miranda sees this term as emphasizing God's (and the Word's) compassion and goodness, revealing here and in 1:16–17 the success of the Word where the Law failed in its identical purpose.[15] But between these two occurrences, we find the return of John, as the chiasm continues to sound its opening measures.

As we were told in 1:6–8 that John came as a witness, in verse 15 we have his actual witness, in a single sentence worded as cryptically as a Zen koan. In terms of the structure of the prologue, this witness statement marks the in-breaking of narrative into poetry, the movement of space and time in the world of becoming amidst the eternity of being. John's witness expresses in three parallel lines this paradoxical in-breaking of being into the world that it both created and sustains. I have translated them overliterally so that we can see the temporal and spatial effect in the Greek text:

1. The one *behind* me *is coming*

2. in *front* of me *has come to be*

3. because *prior* to me he *was*

As John is "surrounded" by the light to which he witnesses, his statement is textually surrounded by the fullness of grace, repeated in verses 14 and 16. As "we" saw his glory in verse 14, "we all received" out of the same fullness in verse 16. Whether this "we all" refers to the entire Johannine community or the entire human race is left ambiguous. Throughout the gospel, the text will leave open the question of whether the receiving of grace is meant to be something only a select few experience or a universal phenomenon. For now, the emphasis is not on the scope of the "we" but on the bounty of grace upon whomever it

---

15. Miranda (1977, 149–153).

is poured and whomever receives it. The word *charis* is repeated three times in ten words in verses 16–17, seeming to overflow and overcome the rejection of the light experienced on the opposite side of the chiasm in verses 10–11.

Verse 17 brings in still another frequent Johannine theme: the replacement of "the Law *given* by Moses" with "grace and truth which *came to be* through Jesus Christ." Like a whodunit waiting to spring the announcement of the killer, the prologue waits until the last moment to mention the name of the one whose life-creating story is being told. No longer coded as Logos or light, the one through whom the ancient offering of *chesed v'emet* comes to be is Jesus, the messiah. For a Jewish audience of the time, the opposition of Moses/Law and Jesus/grace-truth would have been a shocking climax to the poem. The Law — *nomos,* translating the Hebrew *torah* — was meant to embody the very *chesed v'emet* that it is now claimed had not come to be until Jesus. The Law was God's word — the Ten Commandments and all the related legislation Moses brought back directly from God's mouth on Mt. Sinai. The prologue now appears to proclaim this *torah* empty of value, a mere piece of human legislation given by *Moses,* but not by *God.* What a contrast with the Matthean "not one jot or tittle of the Law will pass away" (Mt 5:18)! For the fourth gospel, the *torah* was at best a valiant attempt to legislate morality and holiness, but one doomed to failure, for reasons to be revealed in the course of the story.

Petersen shows how this theme of countering Moses with Jesus, both personally and theologically, is part of the "anti-structural" undermining of the dominant culture with which the gospel argues throughout.[16] He says:

> The disciples of Moses control both the political situation and the terms in which the politics are played out.... From the perspective of the disciples of Moses, their language has a positive value and the language of the disciples of Jesus has a negative value.... John accepts the polarization, in all probability because, as the rejected, he and his people had no choice in the matter, but he *inverts* the terms of the conflict.[17]

Thus, the prologue reverses the hermeneutics of Jesus' opponents. It is Moses who is interpreted through the "grace and truth" of Jesus, not Jesus who is interpreted through the principles of the Law and the Pharisees' oral tradition. This is one of the major fields in the battle of myths between the Johannine community and its opponents.

To pound the distinction between Moses and Jesus home, the prologue concludes in verse 18 by emphasizing that "no one has ever seen God" — not Moses on Mt. Sinai, not the patriarchs or prophets, not even the Johannine community, except through the "only-begotten God, the one who is in the bosom of the Father." There can be no more intimate image linking this "only-begotten God" with the Father. It is not simply a matter of oneness of mind, but of total and

---

16. Petersen (1993, 80–110).
17. Ibid., 87.

complete union. Verse 18 uses "a technical [Greek] word for the exposition of poetry [or] 'law'" (*exēgēsato*, from which "exegesis")[18] to describe what this one has done in relation to God. It suggests we continue reading the gospel as if God were a poem and Jesus — not Moses! — the interpreter.

The prologue offers image after image to begin to open up space in the darkened world in which the light might shine. As we continue on our journey, we will find ourselves referring over and over to this treasure chest of Johannine reflection, as its themes reverberate throughout the entire gospel.

---

18. F. Bushsel, *TDNT* 2:907–909.

# 2

# The First Days of Creation

## *"See! The Lamb of God Who Takes Away the Sin of the World!"*

## John 1:19–51

A. **Chiasms:**

**Chiasm: 1:19–51**

a: 19–39: John (the Baptist) witnesses to Jesus

  b: 40–41: Andrew finds Simon

    c: 42: Simon=Cephas

  b¹: 43–45: Philip finds Nathanael

a¹: 46–51: Nathanael witnesses to Jesus[1]

**Chiasm: 1:19–36**

a: 19–24: John (the Baptist) witnesses

  b: 25–28: baptism in water: one you don't know

    c: 29–30: Lamb of God

  b¹: 31–33: baptism in water: I don't know

a¹: 34–36: John (the Baptist) witnesses

B. **Location:** Bethany across the Jordan

C. **Time:** the first days

D. **Hebrew scripture context:** Genesis 1

E. **Social factors:** Jerusalem establishment vs. John; Judea vs. Galilee

F. **Themes:** witness, baptism, discipleship

G. **Key words:** water/spirit, following, knowing, Lamb of God

---

1. Ellis (1984, 30).

## 1. THE WITNESS OF JOHN: THE FIRST DAY

**Chiasm: 1:19–28**

a: 19: from Jerusalem (Judea): who are you?

   b: 20–22: Christ, Elijah, prophet: those who sent us

      c: 23: voice in wilderness

   b$^1$: 24–25: sent from Pharisees: Christ, Elijah, prophet

a$^1$: 26–28: one coming after: in Bethany (non-Judea)

**Chiasm: 1:19–22**

a: 19: sent from Jerusalem: who are you?

   b: 20: not the Christ

      c: 21a: not Elijah

   b$^1$: 21b: not the prophet

a$^1$: 22: who are you? those who sent us

Without a moment of delay, the overture ends and the curtain rises in verse 19: "And this is the witness of John...." The portrait of John (the Baptist) in the fourth gospel is in dramatic contrast with the prophet of repentance found in the synoptics. Here, John's sole function is to proclaim the coming of the Lamb of God. The dramatic urgency of his witness is underscored by the introduction of his inquisitors in the first sentence of the narrative: "The Judeans sent forth to him priests and Levites from Jerusalem." There is no time to remind readers that John, in contrast, is sent from God (1:6). It is the first of innumerable instances wherein readers are expected to look back to the prologue to interpret the scene.

Verse 19 announces several dramatis personae: "Judeans," "priests," "Levites," and the home of the Law, Jerusalem. An array of religious officialdom has descended upon this obscure witness in the desert, asking one question: "Who are you?" Immediately, the primary opposition that will take us through the entire gospel is established: on the one hand, the one sent from God, and, on the other, the religious officials sent from Jerusalem. To modern Christians, this might seem a familiar confrontation. But to the original audience, it expressed a most shocking and radical claim: those who are descended from the tribe of Levi, those who claim the inheritance of the priestly office among the Chosen People, are in opposition to the one who is a representative of the very God they supposedly serve!

To understand the import of this initial inquiry, we must look closely at other factors revealed in the scene set out in 1:19–28. When the question-and-answer session is over, we are told in verse 28 that the discussion took place in "Bethany across the Jordan, where John was baptizing." The geographic opposition between Jerusalem and Bethany forms the opposing links in the chiasm that structures this scene. The place where John, the voice of Isaiah, is speaking and baptizing is outside Judea and even outside the ancient Promised Land. It is "across the Jordan," on the other side, away from the sacred covenantal territory, and, hence, outside the jurisdiction of the Law and the Jerusalem Temple. One might liken the presence of these inquiring officials to a team of FBI agents poking around in Juárez. Whatever John is doing, it is suspicious enough — and threatening enough — to lead these important Judeans many miles from their base of authority and into foreign territory.

However, this information is withheld until the story has been told. It is part of a common Johannine pattern in which the narrator invites us to go back and reread from a new perspective. On our first reading, we know only of the place from which the inquisitors have been sent. The second time through, we know just how far they have traveled to satisfy their senders. In addition, on a first reading, the sending of these officials to this witness is incomprehensible. Who, indeed, is this John who has attracted attention in high places? We do not find out until verse 28 that the reason for the inquiry in the first place must be the *baptizing ministry* of John.

In the fourth gospel, we are given no reason whatsoever for John's baptism. We are simply told twice that John baptized "in water" (1:26, 31), in contrast with Jesus' baptism in "holy spirit" (1:33). In the Jewish custom, sprinkling with water symbolized a purification that marked entry of a convert into the Jewish community as well as general purification of the people from idolatry (e.g., Ezek 36:25–26). Whatever its specific meaning when performed by John, it was well understood to be a sacred act authorized by God, an authority John had certainly not received from Jerusalem and its Law.

John's denial of being the messiah, the most obvious candidate for such extralegal authority, could hardly be stated more emphatically in verse 20. The literal Greek gives a three-part narrative preface to John's own words: "He confessed and did not deny, and confessed. . . ." Further, John's actual words are carefully chosen in specific contrast with Jesus': "I am not the Christ" (*egō ouk eimi ho cristos*). Starting in 4:26 in speaking to the Samaritan woman at the well and throughout the gospel, Jesus will claim for himself the holy phrase *egō eimi*. The words are those found in the Septuagint translation of the Hebrew scriptures for the response of God to Moses' request at the burning bush for a divine identification to give the people (Ex 3:14). *Egō eimi* represents the translation of what in Hebrew was the four-letter word YHWH, the virtually untranslatable nonname that maintained God's power in the face of Moses' attempt to pin God down to a specific title. In Greek, the term becomes at once the simple and everyday declaration, "I am," and the reference to this ancient encounter between humanity and divinity. Thus, John's *egō ouk eimi* — literally, "I not am" — prepares the way for Jesus' powerful claim.

John specifically ties his confessionary denial to the title *christos*, that is, messiah. We have already been told in the prologue that Jesus is the messiah, and we will be reminded of it near the end of the story (20:31). For now, John, the key first witness, goes out of his way to answer the officials' question with this eschatological title, making clear that his baptismal authority is different than Jesus'.

This leads the inquirers to a second possibility: Elijah. According to one strand of tradition, Elijah was not only the forerunner of the messiah but also the one who anointed one to be messiah who otherwise was unaware of his role.[2] If this tradition was in the background of the scene, it would suggest the reason for both the question and the answer. If John is Elijah, the next challenge for John would be to tell the authorities who would become the Anointed One. John's denial makes clear that John does not have this role in the fourth gospel, because Jesus the messiah is aware of who he is from "the beginning."

In one of the gospel's first ironies, there is even a more important implication of the official question: John's being Elijah would proclaim the reality of resurrection! Although a relatively obscure scriptural reference led to the tradition/legend that Elijah had never died (2 Chron 21:12),[3] the more common expectation was that Elijah would rise again in order to prepare the way for the messiah. John is indeed pictured this way in the synoptics in his camel's hair cloak and with his diet of locusts and honey.[4] But these details are omitted in the fourth gospel, to back up John's express denial of his identity with the ancient messenger. Thus, the question of resurrection is saved for another confrontation.

The final option in the authorities' mind to justify John's behavior is that he was "the prophet." Raymond Brown, like many commentators, identifies this expectation with the prophet-like-Moses suggested in Deut 18:15–18, one who would be a great arbiter of the Law and provider of justice.[5] Once more, John denies this guess, leaving the exasperated officials to repeat their initial question in verse 22, filling in the chiastic parallel. They back up the narrator's expression in verse 19 of their purpose with the classic statement of those serving human authority: "We must give an answer to the ones who sent us!"

John's response in verse 23, citing Isa 40:3, affirms his role as messianic precursor, but without the Elijah implications: "I am the voice of one crying in the wilderness, 'Make straight the way of the Lord!'" It fills in the center of the interlocking chiasm extending from 1:19 to 1:28 and leads to the introduction of another factor identifying John's inquisitors. They are not only priests and Levites; they are from the *Pharisees* (verse 24). In considering this new piece of information, we must remember the multilayered temporal setting of the gospel. In the *story* world — that narrated within the text — it is the time of John, Jesus, and the Jerusalem Temple with its priestly establishment. In the *discourse* world — that of the storyteller and the original audience — all these characters are gone from the scene, except for Jesus as risen king. However, the Pharisees were alive and well in late first-century Palestine, in fact, more powerful than

---

2. De Jonge (1972–73, 255).
3. R. Brown (1966, 47) discusses this tradition.
4. Myers (1988, 126–127).
5. R. Brown (1966, 49).

before. From being one party among several at the time of Jesus, the Pharisees became the only Jewish establishment group to survive the destruction of the Temple in 70 C.E. The power of the Pharisees upon a Jewish community of Jesus-followers at that time would have been tremendous. Thus, although priests and Levites populate the story world as an accurate reflection of *Jesus'* actual opponents, the Pharisees are brought to prominence to highlight the primary opponents of the *Johannine community*.

These Pharisaic representatives, given John's answers, get to the heart of the matter in verse 25: "If you are not the messiah, Elijah, or the prophet, why do you baptize?" Put in modern terms: If John cannot claim any traditional (legal) basis for his cultic activity, why is he engaging in this "civil disobedience"? Like many successors over the centuries, John refuses to answer the question as framed by the prosecution. Instead, he performs in verses 26–27 the role he has been sent by God to do, witnessing to the one to come. After the simple declaration, "I baptize in water," John's response looks back to the prologue and forward to the resurrection. The statement, "In your midst is standing one whom you do not know," will be poignantly echoed by the narrator in 20:19 and 20:26 when the frightened disciples encounter Jesus standing in their midst behind locked doors. "Coming behind me" backs up the narrator's quote of John in 1:15, adding to the reader's faith in the newborn narrative. The final element of John's response, "I am not worthy to loosen the lace of his sandal," provides the classic statement of John's humble status in relation to the one to come, heard in every gospel (Mk 1:8; Mt 3:11; Lk 3:16). The particular image expresses John's willingness to do even that which was not expected of a student for a teacher, taking off his shoes.[6]

The chiasm comes to a close with the revelation of the place in which these events have taken place, Bethany across the Jordan. By withholding this information until now, the text allows the illusion of a conversation outside of time and space between official authority and its challenger. Once we have the specific location, the story becomes grounded in Palestine, where it will remain until the heavenly discourse extending from chapter 13 through chapter 17.

Although the exact location of this Bethany is not known, the likely region on the plains outside Jericho situated John's ministry in the place in which Elijah was swept up into heaven and his successor Elisha received a share of his spirit (2 Kgs 2:9–15).[7] This detail is the fourth gospel's version of the synoptic description of John as dressing and eating like Elijah (Mk 1:6; Mt 3:4), suggesting without stating that John is linked with the memory and power of the prophet. However, the narrator is focused not on John's resemblance to his predecessors but on his role in witnessing to "the Lamb of God."

---

6. Carson (1991, 146).
7. C. Koester (1994, chap. 5).

## 2. THE WITNESS OF JOHN:
## THE SECOND AND THIRD DAYS

### Chiasm 1:29–36

a: 29–30: saw Jesus; Lamb; he was before me

  b: 31: did not know him/baptism with water

    c: 32: witness/spirit

  b[1]: 33: did not know him/baptism with water

a[1]: 34–36: saw Jesus; Lamb; Son of God

Seemingly out of nowhere, Jesus enters the stage in verse 29, "coming to-ward" John. The scene is described as "the next day," presumably in the same place; we are told nothing further about the questioning officials' whereabouts. Whether they have remained to hear the messianic announcement or have taken John's response back to the ones who sent them in Jerusalem, we do not know. We will not hear about Pharisees again until one of them goes to speak with Jesus in chapter 3, perhaps paralleling this opening inquiry.

With the spotlight now on the featured actor, everyone else falls into shadow. John performs his designated function, identifying Jesus with the loaded title, "the Lamb of God who takes away the sin of the world." The reader might have expected something more like, "Look, there is the messiah!" John's alternative immediately calls up both apocalyptic and paschal associations. The image of God's conquering hero as "Lamb" was prevalent at the time, as illustrated by its centrality in the book of Revelation[8] and elsewhere in apocalyptic literature.[9] This avenging lamb is also associated with the removal of sins, an association that is obvious to Christians of our day but that was perhaps surprising to the gospel's first hearers. This image goes back to the Passover lamb and the Isaian pictures of the Suffering Servant (e.g., Isaiah 42 and 53). It also foreshadows the fate of the Lamb by recalling the Levitical tradition of the scapegoat, who bore Israel's sins in an annual ritual (Lev. 16, esp. 16:22). Looking more closely, we notice that John's proclamation speaks in the singular of "sin," not "sins," indi-cating a condition rather than a particular act or acts. This Lamb will, according to John, change the situation in which "the world" finds itself. This proclamation is the centerpiece of the chiasm that extends from 1:19 to 1:36.

John then echoes in verse 30 the prologue's quote from him verbatim, indi-cating that it is something he has been saying to his own audience and further giving credibility to our narrator. His next words, in verse 31, though, are surprising: "Even I did not know him." What sounded like an accusation of ignorance when directed at the Pharisees in verse 26 now turns out to be John's

---

8. The term is used twenty-nine times in Revelation; e.g. Rev 7:17. See, generally, Schüssler Fiorenza (1991).

9. E.g., *TJos.* 19:8, in Charlesworth (1983, 824).

own shared condition. The statement is repeated for emphasis in verse 33 (filling in the chiastic parallel). In case we doubted, John is certainly not the Elijah who will help the messiah to discover his own identity. John may be on the level of the Pharisees in terms of his before-the-fact ignorance, but there is a crucial distinction: when John sees the Lamb, he knows him immediately and proclaims his presence. This challenge will stand before the Pharisees — and any other prospective followers of the messiah — throughout the gospel.

After disclaiming his preexisting knowledge, John answers in verse 31 the question left hanging in verse 25: "This is why I came baptizing in water — that he might be revealed to Israel." Standing outside the Promised Land, John expresses his God-given purpose as providing a revelation of the awaited messiah to the Chosen People. Upon first glance, his statement appears to be a non sequitur. What does baptizing in water have to do with revealing the messiah? In the synoptics, the connection is made clear by the coming of Jesus to be baptized by John in the Jordan and the descent of the dove-spirit that identifies Jesus as God's Chosen One. In the fourth gospel, though, the scene is carefully crafted with a different emphasis. We are not told that Jesus was ever baptized by John or that the dove appeared during baptism at all. Rather, the enigmatic "reason" is followed in verse 32 by John's additional "witness" that he "saw the spirit like a dove come down from heaven and remain on him." As Jeff Staley has pointed out, rather than allow readers to "see" the dove-spirit, the narrator instead gives us John's "witness."[10] For the fourth gospel, believing on the witness of another *without* seeing is "blessed" (20:29). For a Johannine community struggling to establish its credibility with an emerging apostolic Christian authority founded on the direct sight of the risen Jesus (whether immediately, like Peter, or remotely, like Saul/Paul; see introduction, B.3.d, above), this distinction is foundational. John provides the first disciple-witness to Jesus, upon which all subsequent witness is measured. John's witness concludes with the specific divine mandate that he is carrying out, establishing for the first time the contrast between John's thrice-repeated "baptize in water" and the Chosen One's baptism in "holy spirit."

Two more details of John's witness deserve note. The reference to "Israel" as the recipient of John's revelatory witness leaves ambiguous (for the moment) whether John is naming "God's people" or simply a nation. Given the emphasis throughout the gospel on "the Judeans" as the primary title for those who (falsely) claim the heritage of Abraham, Moses, and the Law (see introduction, B.4.c.1), this reference to Israel should be considered carefully as we proceed. For now, its ambiguity is left open as the text emphasizes John's witness and the one being witnessed to.

Finally, in verses 32–33, John introduces still another Johannine metaphor that will recur repeatedly: to "remain" (*menein*). It is the primary symbol for the incarnation of the steadfast nature of the love — the *chesed v'emet*, grace and truth — that links God and those who receive and respond to God's invitation

---

10. Staley (1985, 79).

to loving intimacy. By establishing it at the outset as the relationship between the spirit and Jesus, the text provides a measure by which any relationship in the gospel can be tested.

Verse 35 starts the third day, which in a purely sequential reading appears to begin a new scene. But from a chiastic perspective, the scene(s) begun in 1:19 and 1:28 do not end until 1:36, with the transition from John's (partially) repeated proclamation to the movement of his own disciples from John to Jesus. It is the third day, the messianic moment.

We are given in verse 35 the first evidence that there is any audience at all to John's witness: "John stood with two of his disciples." For the moment, they are unnamed individuals who hear the magic words, "See! The Lamb of God!" What they are not told is the all-important relationship between this Lamb and the sin of the world. Whether they have heard this detail from John in his first proclamation or overnight, we do not know. Given the artistry and care of the text down to the most minute detail, we should not be too quick to presume. If anything, given the subsequent ignorance of Jesus' disciples throughout the story, there is a stronger basis for limiting their awareness to what we hear them hear in verse 36 than the opposite. In any event, the chiasm and John's witness close with this powerful but ambiguous proclamation.

## 3. THE DISCIPLESHIP CALL: THE THIRD DAY

**Chiasm: 1:37–51**

a: 37–38: seeing/Rabbi

   b: 39–41: come and see/Andrew finds Simon/followed

      c: 42: you are Cephas

   $b^1$: 43–46: come and see/Philip finds Nathanael/Philip follows

$a^1$: 47–51: seeing/Rabbi

**Chiasm: 1:37–44**

a: 37: follow

   b: 38–40: Rabbi (which means teacher); where are you remaining?

      c: 41: we have found the messiah

   $b^1$: 42–43a: Cephas (which means Peter); Jesus goes to Galilee

$a^1$: 43b–44: follow

With nothing to go on except John's identification of the one they beheld as the Lamb of God, two of his disciples leave him and follow Jesus. Whether this was a response John expected or hoped for, we are not told at this point, although his approval might well be implied by the exaltation formula expressed by John in verse 27. Jesus' own response in verse 38 is to "turn" (*strapheis*). Although this term on its face simply refers to the physical movement, it generates overtones through repetition in the gospel that suggest a deepening of relationship, a movement toward intimacy (e.g., 20:14, 15). It is one of the many subtle yet powerful images from everyday activity that the fourth gospel uses to generate theological and dramatic significance, just as the character of Jesus uses everyday objects and ideas to generate a sense of his own relationship with God and prospective disciples. Jesus, apparently minding his own business walking along, turns toward these two disciples and looks at them for the first time, asking the penetrating question: "What are you seeking [*zēteite*]?" The verb *zeteo* is used twenty-three times in the fourth gospel and carries the ambiguous meaning of seeking either God's will/glory or that of oneself or humanity (e.g., 7:18). Deep within Jesus' simple inquiry of these would-be followers is this challenge: Whose ways are you seeking? Are you looking for a hero, a sage, a teacher? Someone to cling to, someone to make you famous? Or are you seeking your deepest self, the most profound truths of life, the reality that few can face directly?

Their response in verse 38b is itself ambiguous and indirect: "Rabbi (which means, when translated, 'Teacher'), where are you remaining?" Raymond Brown points out that there is no Jewish evidence for the title Rabbi before the destruction of the Temple.[11] They are willing to see Jesus as a holy teacher but want to know to what or whom Jesus is bonded. In this initial repartee, Jesus comes back in verse 39 with still another indirect statement: "Come and you will see." Although the narrator proceeds to use the special word *menein* twice in the next sentence to affirm their positive response to Jesus' invitation, we are in fact not told a word about *where* Jesus was remaining. When we might be expecting a *spatial* signal, we are given a *temporal* signal instead at the end of verse 39: "It was the tenth hour." Not a word of elaboration is offered for the significance of this particular information.

The dance-like conversation between Jesus and these first disciples is interrupted in verse 38 by the narrator's translation note explaining the meaning of the Hebrew word *rabbi*. The threefold use of this technique in this small chiasm insists that readers pay attention. In addition to setting up the chiastic parallel between verses 38 and 42, it provides the social implication that at least some of the audience was not Jewish, or at least not Hebrew-speaking. The gospel oscillates between the assumption of audience familiarity with things Jewish (e.g., the meaning of sabbath/Tabernacles, etc.; the implicit use of Hebrew scripture) and the provision, as here, of detailed explanation (e.g., the relationship between Judeans and Samaritans in 4:9; the implication of proclaiming Jesus "messiah" in 9:22). The overall effect of this inconsistency is to suggest that the translation notes are given not so much to provide "information" as for the literary purpose of drawing readers' attention to the Jewish/Hebrew context of this first discipleship call. As the prologue has told us, the light "came into his own" (1:11) to an at-best mixed reception. Perhaps we are meant to recall this scene when, in discussion with the Samaritan woman, Jesus tells her, "Salvation is from the

---

11. R. Brown (1966, 74).

Judeans" (4:22). The notes not only emphasize the original Jewish context but also ironically point out the eventual mixed community that received Jesus (and the fourth gospel), including those who need the notes to understand the Hebrew terms.

In verse 40, we are given the name of one of these first disciples: Andrew, the brother of Simon Peter. Poor Andrew, the disciple who in every gospel exists in the long shadow of his more (in)famous brother! Andrew can hardly spend an hour with Jesus without inviting Simon in. Andrew has only one other line to speak in the gospel (6:8), when he is again named as the brother of Simon Peter. But what a line he speaks in verse 41: "We have found the messiah!" The transliterated Hebrew word *messiah* occurs in the New Testament only in the fourth gospel, and only here and in 4:25.[12] Whatever Andrew and his nameless companion in discipleship have experienced in their brief time with Jesus, it has led him to this most remarkable of conclusions. The one whom Israel has been awaiting, the one to set Israel free for all time, God's Anointed One, is present in Jesus! Andrew's proffered title has profoundly different implications in tradition than John's "Lamb of God" (see introduction, B.3.a). Throughout this first discipleship passage, a heap of titles is poured upon Jesus, suggesting in their entirety that in Jesus is everything a child of the covenant could hope for. Yet it is important to see that none of these titles — including John's — comes from the mouth of Jesus. As we will see, Jesus has a very different form of self-reference, with tremendous implications for discipleship and community. For the moment, we can only accept Andrew's naming of his own and his partner's experience of Jesus as just that, their own experience, which will exist alongside many variations throughout the story.

After naming Jesus as messiah, Andrew "leads" Simon to Jesus. The narrator's introduction of Andrew's brother contains an odd sequence of naming. In verse 40, he is identified as "Simon Peter"; then in verse 41, he is referred to as simply "Simon"; finally, in verse 42, Jesus identifies him as "Simon son of John, you will be called Cephas (which is translated 'Peter')." We are told nothing at all about this brother other than his name: no details about the nets and boats of a fisherman as in the synoptics, no words or action of response. Jesus takes command of this relationship from the beginning. Whether in fact Simon goes with Jesus and his emerging band of followers we are not told until 6:68, when he is named as "one of the twelve."

With this ambiguous transaction, the third day ends. In verse 43, we are given the first geographic reference to this discipleship calling, and it is in terms of movement rather than present location. Jesus "willed to go into Galilee." We can only assume that this is movement across the Jordan and away from the place of John, although the absence of a specific reference to the location of the conversation in 1:35–42 gives the scene a certain spaceless quality that universalizes the invitation of Jesus to those who would be his followers. As with the previous unit of text, the scene carries over into the next day, concluding with

---

12. Ibid., 76.

the chiasm-completing call to Philip in verse 43 to "follow me." Once again, we are given no word of response from this new addition to the group. Instead, the narrator adds in verse 44 that Philip is from the same obscure city in Galilee as Andrew and "Peter" (without the "Simon" at all, a usage that will alternate with "Simon Peter" through the rest of the story).

A strong symbolic opposition between the northern province of Palestine, Galilee, and the southern home of the Temple and the Law, Judea, begins to develop with this story. Jerusalem has already been the source of sharp inquiry to John, while Galilee is identified as the home of Jesus' first followers. Although scholars disagree over how precise an identification can be made between Galilee as hospitable to Jesus and Judea as hostile,[13] it seems clear that the text invites readers to consider geography as more than simply information about Jesus' historical comings and goings. The implications of Galilee versus Judea will continue to unfold with each new scene.

Specifically, none of the synoptics give Bethsaida as the home of the first disciples. What little we know about the historical town of Bethsaida provides a powerful undertone for the reference in the fourth gospel. Sometime before 2 B.C.E., the tetrarch Philip renamed the fishing village "Bethsaida-Julias, in honor of the daughter of Caesar Augustus."[14] To name this city as the home of Jesus' disciple Philip — as well as Andrew and Simon Peter — was an ironic slap at Rome's power alliance with the Jerusalem elite in this outpost of the empire. A Jewish client-ruler might offer tribute to the emperor by naming a village after his daughter, but the town would go on to obtain a much greater claim to fame!

## 4. THE DISCIPLESHIP CALL: THE FOURTH DAY

**Chiasm: 1:45–51**

a: 45–46: the "earthly" identity of Jesus: Moses/the Law/prophets/son of Joseph/Nazareth; come see

  b: 47–8: know/fig tree/I saw you

    c: 49: Son of God/king of Israel

  b¹: 50: believe/fig tree/I saw you

a¹: 51: the "heavenly" identity of Jesus: heaven/angels/ascend-descend/Son of *anthrōpos*: you shall see

The final chiasm of the first days of Jesus' ministry begins in verse 45 with Philip "finding" Nathanael, a character encountered only in the fourth gospel and only in this scene (and by narrative reference in 21:2). He is greeted by Philip's breathless proclamation containing three distinct aspects of his perception of Jesus' identity: (1) the one of whom Moses and the prophets wrote, (2) the son of Joseph, and (3) the one from Nazareth. The first designation

---

13. Meeks (1966); Bassler (1981).
14. *HBD* 108.

seems broader than the one referred to by John's inquisitors in verse 21, but if the messiah is meant, Moses did *not* write about that one. Brown suggests the statement summarizes the general expectation of the Hebrew scriptures for one-to-come without the specific sense of a particular figure.[15] But in light of future expression (and lack thereof) of the disciples' limited awareness of their own scriptural tradition, it might also suggest Philip's *ignorance* of the Law and the Prophets. This would fit both the Pharisees' eventual derision of the "accursed" crowd following Jesus who do not know the Law (7:49) and Jesus' (and the narrator's) struggle to get the disciples (and readers) to understand how the Johannine Jesus' words and actions fulfill the scripture (e.g., 2:22; 20:9).

The second designation, son of Joseph, is the first of two references in the fourth gospel to Jesus' earthly father (6:42). On the lips of a disciple, it sounds innocent enough but will run wholly contrary to Jesus' repetitive naming of God as his Father. Of course, Philip cannot be faulted for not yet knowing what Jesus has not stated. It simply shows the limited basis upon which Philip makes his claim.

Finally, Philip adds another "earthly" element to Jesus' origin: "from Nazareth." The slight regard for which this country village was held is expressed in Nathanael's ironic reply in verse 46, literally, "Out of Nazareth can anything good come to be?" For alert readers, the prologue has expressed clearly that what has "come to be" is out of God, not Nazareth, but Nathanael's awareness does not include this insider's perspective. Philip, the quick learner, gives Nathanael the same response that Jesus gave the first two disciples: "Come and see."

In verse 47, Nathanael meets Jesus by overhearing Jesus' surprisingly insightful statement about him, "See! A true Israelite in whom there is no deceit." The statement contrasts Nathanael with Jacob, the first "Israel" (Gen 27:35–36), and evokes the blessing in Ps 32:2. One can only imagine Nathanael's feelings in being described in such a strongly positive way by a person he has never met!

Nathanael's questioning response in verse 48 is both natural and deeply symbolic. At the earthly level, he asks the obvious: How do you know me? But at the "heavenly" or spirit-level, his question reads: "From where [*pothen*] are you knowing [*ginōskeis*] me?" The source or *pothen* of Jesus and his authority is one of the prime elements of mystery and contention in the gospel (e.g., 2:9; 4:11; 19:9). Furthermore, the question of knowledge or *gnosis* has a double aspect. It implicitly puts the gospel in conversation with the gnostic versions of Christianity in circulation in the late first century. At the same time, it introduces a Johannine metaphor for the intimacy into which the discipleship community is called throughout the Last Supper discourse. Nathanael's unwitting inquiry gets right to the heart of the matter.

Jesus answers the question with the Zen-like, "Before Philip called you, I

---

15. R. Brown (1966, 86).

saw you under the fig tree." The fig tree is a powerful image throughout the Hebrew scriptures, symbolizing from 1 Kgs 4:25 through Zech 3:10 a place of peace and tranquility. In particular, it is associated with the fulfillment of Israel's dreams, whether through the military conquests of Solomon or the messianic achievements of Zechariah's "Branch." The Zecharian context sheds even more light on the usage here:

> Then he showed me the high priest Joshua [LXX, *Iēsoun*=Jesus] standing before the angel of the Lord, and the Devil standing at his right hand to accuse him. And the Lord said to the Devil, "The Lord rebuke you, O Devil! The Lord who has chosen Jerusalem rebuke you!" . . . Then the angel of the Lord witnessed to Joshua, saying, "Thus says the Lord of All, 'If you will walk in my ways, and keep my rules, then you shall judge my house, and if you keep my courts, I will give you these standing here. . . . I will remove the guilt of this land in a single day. On that day, says the Lord of All, you shall call each other to come under your vine and fig tree.' " (Zech 3:1–2, 6–7, 9–10)

In light of the sequence of days being counted out in the first chapter of the gospel and the Genesis context of the prologue, we might also consider as background the Eden story with its only named tree, the fig (Gen 3:7). Whether any of this leads to Nathanael's total reversal of his earlier doubts about one from Nazareth, we cannot know for sure. In any event, his response in verse 49 repeats the title Rabbi (matching the chiastic parallel in 1:38) and adds two more titles to Jesus' collection: "Son of God" and "king of Israel." Whatever Nathanael might mean by them, Jesus interprets them in verse 50 as an expression of belief, but perhaps with a comic undertone in light of the largeness of Nathanael's response in comparison with the relative smallness of Jesus' insight about him. Nathanael the Galilean whom Jesus named a true Israelite, sees and proclaims Jesus in a way those who reside in the home of Israel's Law and Temple cannot do. By responding with a question, though, Jesus puts at issue whether Nathanael's *expression* of faith really indicates the *presence* of faith (cf. 13:38, 16:31).

In verse 51, addressing those gathered with him, Jesus speaks the first of twenty-five double-amen sayings found only in the fourth gospel: "Amen, amen I am saying to you: you will see the heaven opened and the angels of God ascending and descending upon *ton huion tou anthrōpou*." He associates an image from Gen 28:12, Jacob's ladder, with a self-designation from apocalyptic sources (including Daniel) common to all the gospels, *ton huion tou anthrōpou*, the Son of Humanity, the Human One.[16] The transition from the earthly titles given to Jesus by Philip and Nathanael to the heavenly yet human

---

16. Douglass (1992, 39–40) discusses the Aramaic root of this term at length. The title "Human One" is used by Myers (1988).

title chosen by the Johannine Jesus is sudden and stark. Its apocalyptic background suggests that Jesus, "the Human One," is the successor to the "beasts" who have ruled over the people for so long. No response by the hearers is given at this point to this solemn statement by Jesus. The fourth day and the discipleship-selecting stories come to an open conclusion, leaving both characters and readers to ponder the mysterious meaning of the words and presence of this one from God.

# 3

# The Wedding at Cana

## *The Celebration of the Messiah's Advent*

### John 2:1–12

A. **Chiasm:**

  a: 1–2: Jesus, mother and disciples at Cana

    b: 3–5: wine/servants

      c: 6–8: water changed to wine

    b$^1$: 9–10: wine/servants

  a$^1$: 11–12: Jesus, mother and disciples at Cana[1]

B. **Location:** Cana in Galilee

C. **Time:** "the third day" (the last day of the first week of re-creation)

D. **Hebrew scripture context:** Wisdom, messianic/eschatological prophecy

E. **Social factors:** Judean purification rituals; women/servants

F. **Themes:** Jesus' "hour"; replacement of Judean ritual with Jesus; the first "sign"

G. **Key words:** "hour"; "purification" (*katharismon*); "draw"; "source" (*pothen*)

The first four days of the first week of the gospel are occupied with John's witness and Jesus' gathering of his first disciples. What takes place on the fifth and sixth days, we are not told. But on the seventh day of the week, the "third day" since the last scene, we find Jesus for the first time in a public setting. The wedding at Cana overflows with images from Hebrew scripture and breaks open the ministry of Jesus with a superabundance previously thought reserved for the "last days."

---

1. Ellis (1984, 40).

The scene in 2:1–12 establishes a narrative pattern that will recur many times in the fourth gospel. A setting in space or time is given, someone other than Jesus speaks, Jesus responds with an unexpected word and/or deed, and reactions are sorted out. Frequently, the formula will involve the transformation of an "earthly" reality (e.g., wine, water, birth) into a "heavenly" one (e.g., God's bounty, commitment to the faith community). Often, it will suggest the replacement of a Jewish/Judean religious practice with Jesus himself or an apparent practice of the Johannine community. Inevitably, it will lead some to faith and drive some away.

The first of these formulaic scenes opens with the loaded temporal reference in verse 1 to "the third day." Despite some commentators' willingness to attribute details such as this to accident, my working premise is that nothing in the gospel is "accidental." Many numbers are given to describe quantities; each is fraught with symbolic value, as would be expected for a people who found number itself to be a revelatory phenomenon. This first number in the gospel carries a rich background both in Hebrew scripture and Christian tradition. For example, the number three

> came to represent the smallest complete cycle. It cannot be accidental that periods of three days, weeks, months or years are so frequently encountered in the Scripture.... A period of three units of time seems to have been appropriate for justice to have run its course when tempered by grace.[2]

In Hebrew scripture, "the third day" is a common term in the Pentateuch and the Deuteronomic History, but it is rarely used in the Prophets. In the specific context that unfolds in John 2, a particular use of the phrase may have significance:

> The Lord said to Moses: "Go to the people and consecrate them today and tomorrow. Have them wash their garments and prepare for the third day, because on the third day the Lord will come down upon Mount Sinai in the sight of all the people." (Ex 19:10–11)

Of course, for Christians, "the third day" is an expression of the period between Jesus' crucifixion and resurrection. Thus, the scene at Cana opens in the double context of consecration for receiving God's revelation and expectation of resurrection.

Literally, the text continues: "Marriage came to be in Cana of Galilee." The geographic site of Cana is unique to the fourth gospel, being mentioned here, in 4:46–54, and in 21:2 as the home of Nathanael, a detail not given in chapter 1. Little else is known about this village, although there is some evidence that it was located near the legendary birthplace of Dionysus, the Greek god of fertility,

---

2. *TWOT* 933.

whose feasts were celebrated with huge outpourings of wine.[3] Whatever Cana may be, it is a long way from Jerusalem, where one might otherwise expect the sorts of events described in this passage to take place. Jesus begins his activity not in the headquarters of the Law, not in the center of the religious world of Israel, but on the obscure margins, hidden, quiet, yet invited.

At the end of verse 1 we are introduced to a new character: "Jesus' mother." Jesus' mother remains unnamed throughout the fourth gospel, in contrast with the synoptics. Her appearance here and at the foot of the cross is grounded not in her being the mother of Jesus but in her faith, as we will see shortly. Along with his mother, Jesus and his disciples — the first time we are told that Jesus in fact *has* disciples — are also "called [*eklēthē*] into the marriage" in verse 2.

We are given no information whatever about the identity of the bride or groom but rather are directed in verse 3 immediately to an apparent problem, the absence of wine. Jesus' mother announces this fact simply and straightforwardly, with not a hint that Jesus or anyone else can or should do anything about it. Jesus' response in verse 4 seems surprisingly gruff: "What is this to me and to you, woman? Not yet has my hour come." Raymond Brown notes that the first phrase is a common one in Hebrew scripture as an expression of either unjust bothering of one party by another or the more everyday equivalent, "none of your business."[4] José Miranda goes further to say that the phrase "is invariably addressed to someone who represents a threat or a danger to the speaker."[5] The title "woman" intensifies the surprising tone of irritation and distress with which Jesus addresses his mother for the first time in the story. Although it was a title that men commonly used to address women and although it had no derogatory connotation, it was not a title a son would have used to address his mother. Jesus treats this "woman" as just that, without any privilege due to her blood relationship with him. In light of the tightly knit family dynamics of the biblical world,[6] Jesus' apparent disregard for his mother's honor/shame is shocking.

He follows this brusque comment with a mysterious one: "Not yet has my hour come." This "hour" will approach throughout the first part of the gospel. It is the time of judgment, of darkness, of death, and of ultimate fidelity. For the moment, none of this is revealed either to his mother or to readers.

How does this response follow from his mother's simple statement? We are given no clue as to why Jesus interprets her statement as a request for action on his part. What might she have been expecting? Again, we are not told. His mother again speaks simply in verse 5, this time to the "servants": "Whatever he says to you, you do." As Francis Moloney observes, she "is the first person, in the experience of the reader, to manifest trust in the word of Jesus."[7] Whether

---

3. C. Koester (1994, chap. 3).
4. R. Brown (1966, 99).
5. Miranda (1977, 104).
6. Malina (1981, 102).
7. Moloney (1993, 84).

these servants overheard the dialogue between Jesus and his mother or whether she had gone to find them, we do not know.

The narrator intervenes at this point in verse 6 to inform readers of the presence of "six stone water jars, according to the Judean purification." Suddenly, the problem of the paucity of wedding wine is transformed into an issue of ritual-run-dry. For the first time, the gospel presents Jesus in confrontation with the Law. The six jars are juxtaposed with the six days of the gospel's first week: the old order is being replaced by the new.

In verse 7, Jesus, as his mother had predicted, gives a command to the servants to fill the jars, and they obey. Without gesture or other physical action on his part, Jesus gives a second command to the servants in verse 8: "Draw and bring" the jars to the feastmaster, which the servants again obey. The narrator describes the feastmaster's reaction as if readers already knew the effect of Jesus' command and the servants' obedience. In Greek, the "miracle" is described in verse 9 by the simple juxtaposition of words: "Water wine had become [*hydōr oinon gegenēmenon*]." The emphasis of the narrator's comment is not on the fact of the transformation but on the questions of knowledge and source. What the feastmaster does not know *is* known to the servants, who say nothing at all about their knowledge. The feastmaster naturally assumes that the newly found wine is the result of crafty planning by "the bridegroom," whom he contrasts with "every person."

As the narrative reaches its climax in the superabundance of quality wine and in the feastmaster's proclamation, the entire scene takes on a new scale of mammoth proportions. The purification jars, which were at best only partly filled with water, have become vessels of the best wine. Two different images from Hebrew scripture are pulled together in this scene to provide an initial assessment of the meaning of Jesus' presence in the world. The wedding itself was a common prophetic image for the final healing of God's relationship with the Chosen People. For example, Isa 62:4–5 expresses it:

> You shall no more be called Forsaken,
> and your land shall no more be called Desolate;
> but you shall be called My Delight Is in Her,
> and your land Married;
> for the Lord delights in you
> and your land shall be married.
> For as a young man marries a young woman,
> so shall your builder marry you,
> and as the bridegroom rejoices over the bride,
> so shall your God rejoice over you.

The bountiful wine was similarly a symbol of the eschatological banquet's overflowing, reconciling joy, as found in Amos 9:13–14 at the conclusion of the prophet's oracles:

> The time is surely coming, says the Lord,
> when the one who plows shall overtake the one who
>     reaps,
> and the treader of grapes the one who sows the seed;
> the mountains shall drip sweet wine,
> and all the hills shall flow with it.
> I will restore the fortunes of my people Israel,
> and they shall rebuild the ruined cities and inhabit them;
> they shall plant vineyards and drink their wine,
> and they shall make gardens and eat their fruit.

These prophetic poems expressing the deepest hopes of Israel's future joyful relationship with their God and one another find their fulfillment at the wedding at Cana. The Judean ritual purification, intended as a means of reconciling the broken with the community, had lost its power to bring celebration. The wedding was out of wine, the jars sitting uselessly on the sidelines. Jesus steps forward into this situation and, by the sheer power of his creative word, transforms the Law-laden jars into vessels of grace and truth. The feastmaster does not know the "source" (*pothen*) of this renewed celebration, so he cannot ask Jesus directly the question Nathanael had asked in 1:48. But the servants — those who minister to the bridegroom — *do* know. Given the prophetic poetry, it is not unrealistic to suggest that the bridegroom is the God of Israel, who is unknown to the leaders but known to the servants.

In this context, the feastmaster's speech to the bridegroom is triply ironic. He knows not the source of the wine, but he knows it is superior to what preceded it. At one level, the statement expresses the Johannine community's sense of being included at God's banquet even if disapproved of by the Judean cult leaders, those who came from Jerusalem to question John on "the other side." At another level, it is an unconscious affirmation that the story we are reading *is itself scripture*, in fact, scripture superior to the "Law" brought by Moses! Finally, in suggesting that "every person" puts the inferior wine out once people are drunk, the statement slaps at the Pharisees, whose inferior interpretations are offered only when people have become "drunk" on the Law, which was at least originally superior to what the Pharisees offer.

The chiasm comes around again with the second reference to Cana in verse 11, with the additional narrative comment that what Jesus did was "the beginning of the signs" in which "he revealed his glory." The fourth gospel is not interested in "miracles" but in "signs": acts that require interpretation, evoke discussion, demand decision. We are told that the disciples respond to this beginning of signs by believing in him. To this point in the story, we had not even been told that his disciples had seen what had happened. As will be the case in many similar passages, the disciples are named as present in the opening verses, disappear for the main conversation or action, then reappear at the end. Their function is simply to watch and believe the one who has been sent by God to proclaim the reconciliation of God and God's people, those who are given authority to become God's children. The meaning of the additional term "glory" will not begin to be revealed until much later in the story, when the disciples and readers have gone a long way down the road with Jesus.

The passage closes in verse 12 with an apparently parenthetical geographic aside that, however, contains two important details. First, we are told that Jesus went with "his mother and brothers and disciples." For now, we note only that the "brothers" are not included within the category "disciples." Second, for reasons not given, the visit to Capernaum is not a long one: "They remained there only a few days." This passing reference to the Capernaum visit will gain in significance upon their return to that locale in 6:24.

# 4

# "Zeal for Your House Will Consume Me"

## *The First Visit to Jerusalem*

## John 2:13–25

A. **Chiasm:**
   a: 13: Jesus in Jerusalem at Passover
      b: 14–17: disciples remember scripture
         c: 18–21: destroy/I will raise
      b[1]: 22: disciples remember scripture
   a[1]: 23–25: Jesus in Jerusalem at Passover[1]

B. **Location:** Jerusalem, the Temple

C. **Time:** near Passover

D. **Hebrew scripture context:** Psalm 69; Mal 3:1

E. **Social factors:** Galilee vs. Jerusalem; Temple/Passover vs. Jesus' word

F. **Themes:** replacement of Temple with Jesus' body

G. **Key words:** sign, temple (*naon*)

*See, I am sending my messenger to prepare the way before me, and the Lord whom you seek will suddenly come to his temple.* (Mal 3:1)

The narrative transition between the messianic joy of the wedding at Cana and Jesus' dramatic overthrowing of the Temple tables in Jerusalem is extraordinarily sudden. Despite the power of the "sign" at Cana, there has been no suggestion that Jesus is known by anyone outside of the servants, disciples, and

---

1. Ellis (1984, 45).

family at Cana and Capernaum. Out of nowhere, he arrives in Jerusalem "near" the holiest time of year, Passover, and without warning begins to "exorcise" God's Temple. His actions are shocking and his verbal explanation bold and mysterious. How can we not empathize with the Judeans' outraged reaction: Who do you think you are to come in here like this?

The story of the Temple "exorcism" — it is not described in the text as a "cleansing" but as a "throwing out" (*exebalen,* from which the Latinate "exorcise" is derived) — is one of the few found in all four gospels. In the synoptics, though, it is saved for the climactic moment of Jesus' public ministry, during his only visit to the capital city. In the fourth gospel, we find it here at the beginning, fulfilling Malachi's prophecy of the Lord coming suddenly to the Temple. In addition to placing the incident differently, the fourth gospel changes important details to provide its own theological and narrative emphases.

As the scene opens in verse 13, we are given time and place, the first time we have been told both coordinates at the outset: "The Passover of the Judeans was near, and Jesus went up to Jerusalem." The whereabouts of those with Jesus at Capernaum is not disclosed. The image is of a lone figure approaching the centerpiece of Jewish religious and political power.

The Temple at Passover time would have been an unbelievably loud, crowded, and busy place. Pilgrims from throughout Palestine and the Diaspora came to Jerusalem three times a year for prayer, sacrifice, and payment of tithes. Passover was the most holy of these occasions. Joachim Jeremias carefully estimates that the normal population of Jerusalem would triple at Passover from around 50,000 to over 180,000.[2] The Law required that all Passover lambs be slaughtered at Jerusalem, in addition to the innumerable cattle used for ritual purity sacrifice. Accommodations would become scarce, but the cool early spring nights discouraged outdoor sleeping without tents. The normally noisy Jerusalem would at Passover be transformed into a cacophony of caterwauling, as animals, vendors, and money changers trading local coins for the various foreign currencies cried out over the noise coming from the multitudes.

This was the scene into which Jesus proceeded. The description in verse 14 would be no surprise at all: "And he found in the Temple the ones selling cattle and sheep and doves, and the money changers sitting." But his response in verse 15 is totally shocking: "And having made a whip out of ropes, he ejected [*exebalen*] all from the Temple with sheep and cattle, and he poured out the money changers' coins and overturned the tables." For a single person to drive the thousands of sheep and cattle out of the Temple precincts (*hierō*) was not only an awesome act of prophetic boldness but also a miracle of movement amidst the overflowing Temple grounds. Whereas Mark and Matthew mention the money changers and dove sellers, none of the synoptics provides the details about sheep and cattle or about the "whip of ropes."

Having done these outrageous acts of civil disobedience, Jesus speaks in verse 16: "And to the dove sellers he said, 'Take these things from here! Stop

---

2. Jeremias (1969, 75–84).

making my Father's house into a house of commerce [*emporiou*]!'" Jesus' protest in the fourth gospel is not simply against the economics of tithing or the exploitation of the poor represented by the dove sellers (doves were the sacrificial animal of the poor)[3] but also against the Temple sacrificial system itself. Thus, whereas the transformation of water into wine — that is, the introduction of the messianic age — was an effortless event in the hospitable environment of Cana in Galilee, the toppling of the Temple ideology among the Judeans is one of brutal confrontation and resistance.

For the first time, Jesus identifies the God of Israel as his "Father." For the moment, this element of his action goes unnoticed by the Judeans, who ask in verse 18 about his authority, not his paternity. The narrator follows Jesus' speech with the remark in verse 17 that the disciples "called to mind [*emnēsthēsan*] the scripture, 'Zeal for your house will consume me.'" We have not, however, been told that the disciples in fact witnessed this scene, or even that they were in Jerusalem. They do not appear again until 4:27, when Jesus is in Samaria. The text may be suggesting that the disciples, upon *hearing* about this incident, *later* recalled the scripture in interpreting Jesus' actions and words. H. Koester notes that the "term 'remember' [*mnēmoneuein/apomnēmoneuein*] was decisive for the trustworthiness of the oral tradition" and "is part of the controversy with the Gnostics."[4] There is as yet no reason to think that they are as bold as their Rabbi and would be found with him in performing such a dangerous act, although one would expect them, like any good Jews, to come to Jerusalem for the Passover. In any case, their eventual interpretation is cast in the form of a commentary from the sidelines: it is Jesus who is on center stage in the fourth gospel.

The scripture cited appears to be Ps 69:9. The entire psalm is a prayer for deliverance from persecution, and many parts of it form background to Johannine texts (e.g., Jn 15:25, quoting Ps 69:4). For now, the immediate context of the quoted portion includes this verse:

> I have become a stranger to my kin,
> an alien to my mother's children. (Ps 69:8)

Jesus, the one who calls God "Father," is becoming alienated from his own people, just as the prologue predicted in 1:11.

The chiasm reaches its center in the confrontation between the Judeans and Jesus over his authority. As we heard in 1:48, the Johannine Jesus has a penchant for responding to questions with Zen-like sayings. This time, he answers them in verse 19 with a challenge: "Tear down this temple [*naon*] and in three days I shall raise it up." The Judeans' attempt at interpretation in verse 20 is the first instance of the Johannine technique of misunderstanding: "It took forty-six years to build this temple [*naos*], and you in three days will raise it up?" The fact of their challenge contrasts them with Jesus' mother in 2:5: she trusted his

---

3. R. Brown (1966, 115).
4. H. Koester (1990, 34).

word; they do not trust it.[5] As a good teacher, the narrator "gives" us an interpretation in verse 21: "He was speaking about the temple [*naou*] of his body."
In the future, readers will have to figure out the meaning of Jesus' comments for
themselves or risk ending up in the same uncomprehending situation as Jesus'
conversation partners. Here, the Judeans naturally hear Jesus' words as referring to the Temple *buildings,* which took forty-six years to build (and were still
incomplete during Jesus' lifetime). In interpreting *naon* as Jesus' body, the narrator reinforces the growing sense of intimacy between Jesus and God. Not only
can Jesus call God "Father," but God lives within Jesus' own body!

For the puzzled and outraged Judeans, though, no interpretation is provided.
They are left, seemingly unfairly, with the feeling that Jesus must be crazy,
both to drive out the cattle and money changers and to think he can do the
impossible task of rebuilding a demolished Temple in three days. Once again, it
is the disciples' recollection of scripture in verse 22 that fills in the picture for
them, but this time, we are explicitly told that it was not until after Jesus was
raised from the dead that they understood his words. Whatever they thought of
his statement *at the time,* we are not told.

The chiasm closes in verse 23 with a second reference to Passover in Jerusalem. Following the emerging pattern, the result of Jesus' action is to lead some
to faith, but we are told that it was because of "having seen the signs" that
some believe. In verse 24 the narrator says that while they may believe in Jesus,
"Jesus did not believe in them." We might make more sense of this comment
by translating the Greek *episteuen,* the standard word for faith/belief, as "trust."
Jesus did not trust them for two reasons: (1) because he "knew them all," and
(2) because "he did not need any witness about *tou anthrōpou*" (verse 25). This
last phrase is the "title" given to Jesus by Pilate upon presentation of the battered messiah to his unbelieving people in 19:5. It matches the scriptural root by
which Jesus has referred to himself in 1:51, *ton huion tou anthrōpou,* the Son
of Humanity. In this case, it also bears the sense of *all* humanity. Thus, Jesus
both understands how people are *and* does not need their witness about his own
nature. The transition from this declaration of independence from human affirmation forms a carefully stitched segue with the introduction of one of the most
important characters in the story, the Pharisaic ruler, Nicodemus.

---

5. Moloney (1993, 101).

# 5

# To Be Born of Water and Spirit

## Nicodemus's Struggle to Commit

### John 3:1–21

**A. Chiasm:**

    a: 1–2: came to Jesus/night/do . . . with God

        b: 3–9: question: how born again?

            c: 10: are you a teacher?

        $b^1$: 11–18: answer: believe in Son

    $a^1$: 19–21: come to light/darkness/deeds wrought in God[1]

**B. Location:** not given

**C. Time:** night

**D. Hebrew scripture context:** Wisdom

**E. Social factors:** secret disciples and Johannine community

**F. Themes:** baptism into Johannine community

**G. Key words:** born *anōthen* (from above/again); *pneuma* (wind/spirit); water/ spirit

## 1. THE DIFFICULT DIALOGUE OF REBIRTH

**Chiasm: 3:1–10**

a: 1–2: we know you are a teacher

    b: 3–4: unless born *anōthen*; Nicodemus asks, "how can this happen?"

        c: 5–6: unless born of water/spirit

---

1. Ellis (1984, 50).

b¹: 7–9: don't marvel at born *anōthen*; Nicodemus asks, "how can this happen?"

a¹: 10: you are a teacher and don't know

*He knew what was in* to anthrōpō. (2:25)

*There was an* anthrōpos *out of the Pharisees, Nicodemus by name.* (3:1)

Poor Nicodemus! Before he can open his mouth, careful readers of the fourth gospel will likely distrust him deeply. The text has placed several important descriptors in the way of Nicodemus's otherwise bold approach to Jesus in chapter 3. The scene that unfolds expresses much about the Johannine community's simultaneous heartfelt desire to bring the religious leaders into commitment to Jesus and their doubt, based on hard experience, that this was likely to happen. For modern readers, it provides an archetypal encounter challenging a person powerful in the eyes of the world to convert and become powerful in the eyes of God.

As chapter 2 ended, we heard the narrator's omniscient view of Jesus' internal attitudes toward the people around him in Jerusalem at Passover. He does not trust them, does not need their witness, knows them only too well. Out of this distrusting atmosphere steps one of them to speak with Jesus privately. The juxtaposition of *to anthropō* in 2:25 and *anthrōpos* in 3:1 identifies Nicodemus precisely as one of those Jesus knows and does not need witness from. Upon this negative narrative signal is added the identification of Jesus' visitor as a *Pharisee,* one of the party who asked John the hard questions in the wilderness. Is Nicodemus coming to Jesus on a similar mission, having seen the equally illegal acts performed at the Temple? Nicodemus is identified not only as a Pharisee but also as a "ruler of the Judeans," that is, a member of the *Sanhedrin,* the Jewish court that radiated legal authority from Jerusalem throughout Palestine. Finally, the narrator tells us that Nicodemus came "at night," the time of darkness. This does not promise to be a joyous encounter.

With this dark introduction, Nicodemus opens the conversation in verse 2 by addressing Jesus as Rabbi, just as did Jesus' first disciples. Could Nicodemus be coming as a prospective disciple? He continues by speaking in the plural as he gives Jesus precisely the witness that Jesus does not need: "We know that you have come as a teacher from God, for no one is able to do the signs you are doing unless God is with him." Furthermore, Nicodemus's "witness" is based on signs, precisely what Jesus doesn't trust. It is now clear: Nicodemus *is* one — and apparently represents others — of those described in 2:23 who believed in Jesus because they saw the signs he performed in Jerusalem.

Jesus ignores this confession/flattery and puts the challenge directly to Nicodemus in verse 3: "Amen, amen I am saying to you: if anyone is not born *anōthen,* he cannot see the reign of God." How fitting that the Johannine Jesus addresses his own reference to the "reign of God" to a "ruler" of the Judeans! Jesus gives Nicodemus a straight-out, either/or proposition: be born *anōthen* or give up on seeing God's reign. What does Jesus mean by this "born *anōthen*"? The Greek word has the double meaning of "again" and "from above," between which English translations must choose. Nicodemus must figure out the meaning of the term for himself.

Following the pattern begun in the previous *naon* discussion in 2:19–23, Nicodemus chooses only to reject the obvious, but seemingly impossible, interpretation: Can born *anōthen* mean going back into one's mother's womb? Jesus offers his own interpretation in verse 5: "Amen, amen I am saying to you: unless one is born of water and spirit, one is not able to enter the reign of God." He elaborates with a second double entendre in verse 8: "The *pneuma* [wind/spirit] blows where it wills and you hear its sound, but you do not know wherefrom [*pothen*] it is coming and wherefrom it is going." Between these two images, Jesus reemphasizes in verse 6 the radicality of the choice he offers: "What is born of flesh is flesh, and what is born of spirit is spirit." What does all this talk about birth from flesh or spirit say to Nicodemus, the ruler of the Pharisees?

As David Rensberger has clearly shown, the entire dialogue is best seen in terms of the discourse time of the Johannine community rather than the story time of Jesus. All the statements are made in terms of Nicodemus as a representative character. "To be 'born from above' means not so much to have a certain experience as to take a certain action, an action with a definite communal and social dimension."[2] The Johannine Jesus challenges this ruler — and those he represents — to give up their status, their worldly glory, and join the Johannine community by being baptized. Just as Ezekiel had announced God's invitation to be cleansed in water and receive God's spirit and a new heart (Ezek 36:25–27), so the Johannine Jesus proclaims the call to renew one's commitment to the ancient covenant.

This interpretation clarifies the Johannine Jesus' use of the term "reign of God," common in the synoptics but found only here in the fourth gospel. Jesus offers not a "heavenly" metaphor for an otherworldly utopia but an "earthly" ultimatum (cf. 3:12). As Francis Moloney notes: "The kingdom of God refers to a community that professes and attempts to live the Johannine understanding of Jesus."[3] As we will see, Jesus'/God's reign is "not of this world" (18:36) but is precisely where believers have openly gathered in witness to the light (3:20).

Nicodemus apparently hopes he can continue as a secret believer, visiting Jesus at night. But the challenge of the fourth gospel is to walk in the light, to make a commitment to a countercommunity that is so permeated by newness that it is as if one were starting life from scratch, born again (or from above). To perhaps well-intentioned but equally well-established Jerusalem officials such as Nicodemus, such a change in social location seems as impossible as reentering one's mother's womb.

Yet in verse 7 Jesus tells Nicodemus and the others: "Do not wonder [*thaumasēs*] because I said to you people, it is necessary [*dei*] for you to be born

---

2. Rensberger (1988, 56).
3. Moloney (1993, 113).

*anōthen.*" As will be seen clearly at the Bethzatha and Tabernacles encounters in chapters 5 and 7–8, Jesus and the Johannine community see the Judean rulers as having enough background from which to understand this apparent mystery. While the *character* Nicodemus who comes to this barely known "teacher" to inquire about the teacher's ways might not be expected to understand birth from "water and spirit," the Judean rulers *whom the Johannine community encounter two generations later* should know to what this language refers. Nicodemus's implicit "wonder" is the first of several occasions on which Jesus will be critical of a reaction indicating lack of understanding (5:28; 7:15, 21).

The challenge to Nicodemus moves in verse 8 from the call to baptism to the metaphorical description of the spirit-driven community into which his people are invited. That community's relationship to the Temple-religion and its supporters is like the *pneuma*: you hear it, but you don't know where it's from (*pothen*) (above/heaven/God) or where it's going (back to God via the mission to "the world"). Just as God's breath/spirit animates creation, the Johannine community/paraclete will animate Judea, if allowed to blow freely.

In verse 9, Nicodemus is stymied once again: "How can these things come to be?" How can God work so completely outside the very institutions that represent God's presence on earth to believing Judeans? How can this obscure "son of Joseph" from Nazareth be the messiah awaited by the Pharisees?

Jesus answers in verse 10 with an ironic reversal of Nicodemus's honorific greeting in verse 2: "You are a teacher in Israel, and you don't know these things?" While the Sanhedrin official recognized Jesus as a teacher *from God,* the messiah attributes to Nicodemus the lesser authority of teacher of *Israel,* that is, one who holds the office of teacher in the institutional religion. And yet, even as this official teacher, Nicodemus ought to be able to know the truth from the same scriptures that inform Jesus and the Johannine community. The chiasm ends with this unanswered question, leaving the bewildered ruler in the dark.

## 2. GOD SO LOVED THE WORLD

Although the exit of Nicodemus is not narrated, the tone of the speech beginning in verse 10 changes imperceptibly until it seems that the narrator has replaced Jesus as speaker. While many scholars have argued over whether the transition takes place precisely in verse 21, if at all, my view is that the passage is deliberately ambiguous. For the Johannine community, the narrator's voice *is* the voice of Jesus/God (see introduction, B.4.f, above). Any attempt to separate these voices misses a primary message of the entire gospel: *this text* is the word of God, participating in the Word that *was* in the beginning and through which all things have their being. The sacred stories that form, shape, and sustain Johannine Christians are of equal stature with the scripture inherited through the traditions of Israel, books not yet fully canonized until the second century C.E. If this claim was not clear to readers from the prologue, the passage 3:10–21, with its numerous statements about God's will and judgment, establishes it without doubt.

The first-person speech continues through verse 12, then is totally replaced by the narrative third-person voice. Verse 11, recalling the prologue once again (1:11–12), puts the Johannine community in the same position as the light. "We" speak, see, and bear witness, but "you people" do not "receive our witness." Just as the light came into its own during Jesus' earthly sojourn, so it comes again and again in the Johannine community through the ages, but those who prefer earthly glory and power do not receive their witness. It is an example of the "hermeneutical reversal" prefigured in the prologue (1:17–18): the teacher of Israel, having failed to interpret Jesus according to his own tradition, will hear (if he is listening!) Moses interpreted through the Human One and the "grace and truth" present in the Johannine community.

For the first time in the fourth gospel, verse 12 expresses the contrast that has been implicit through much of the story so far: "If I have told you earthly things and you are not believing, how will you believe if I tell you heavenly things?" Flesh-earth/spirit-heaven do not form a Greek or gnostic dualism that denies the value of creation. Rather, they contrast two *attitudes* that pervade human existence. The first focuses on the obvious, the superficial, what "meets the eye"; the second looks deeper, finding meaning and value in things visible only to the heart. These images will gain richness and fullness as the gospel proceeds and readers are drawn into further scenes in which the two attitudes present themselves for decision.

Verses 12–21 are linked not by chiasm but by a *stair-step progression*, in which an important word from one verse links with the following verse, which adds a new thematic word to link it with the succeeding verse. It can be seen in the following chart:

| | | |
|---|---|---|
| 12: heaven | 13: heaven–Human One | 14/15: Human One–eternal life |
| 16: eternal life–world | 17: world–judge | 18/19: judge–light |
| 20/21: light–works | | |

From the reference to heaven in verse 12, the text stair-steps in verse 13 by taking the theme of "heaven" and using it to identify the *pothen* of which Nicodemus and his people do not know. Ascending and descending from heaven is an image from the Wisdom tradition, as seen, for example, in Bar 3:29: "Who has gone up to heaven and got her [Wisdom] and brought her down from the clouds?" As Wayne A. Meeks has pointed out, it serves here as a "warrant" for the claim of knowledge by Jesus, again identified by the apocalyptic *ho huios tou anthrōpou*, the Human One.[4] But as Norman Petersen has shown, the use of the image in the fourth gospel subverts both Wisdom and Mosaic traditions of ascent/descent. For Nicodemus and the Pharisees, Moses' having ascended Mt. Sinai to receive the Torah from God and descended with it was a primary

---

4. Meeks (1972, 53).

sign of the Torah's having come from God. But "Moses" himself denied that a "heavenly journey" was necessary, because God's command is close at hand:

> Surely, this commandment that I am commanding you today is not too hard for you, nor is it too far away. It is not in heaven, that you should say, "Who will go up to heaven for us, and get it for us so that we may hear it and observe it?" Neither is it beyond the sea, that you should say, "Who will cross to the other side of the sea for us, and get it for us so that we may hear it and observe it?" No, the word is very near to you; it is in your mouth and in your heart for you to observe. (Deut 30:11–14)

The passage from Baruch quoted above continues by denying — together with John — that anyone has in fact made such a journey; nor *should* anyone do so. But the fourth gospel goes farther than Baruch in two ways. First, it inverts the terms: the Human One has *first* descended, then will ascend later. Second, whereas the Wisdom literature spoke of God's gift of Sophia as a metaphor for the Law, John incarnates "Wisdom" in Jesus himself.[5]

This theme continues in the next image. Stair-stepping once more, the text takes the title Human One and contrasts it in verse 14 with the "lifting up" of the serpent in the desert by Moses in Num 21:9. Raymond Brown has noted that the word in both the Hebrew and Greek text of Numbers means "placed," not "lifted up."[6] But the fourth gospel is concerned with another element of the contrast. The serpent-on-the-pole was a source of healing in the exodus from both the bite of poisonous snakes and the sin of grumbling against God. In a similar yet more ultimately powerful way, Jesus' "lifting up" on a cross will heal the people from the snakebite of religious oppression and their own paralyzing disbelief. This healing is named through the common Johannine metaphor, used in verses 15–16 for the first times, *zōēn aiōnion*, "eternal life." This term adds a further aspect to the ideological undermining of Moses. If Moses' "raising up" of the serpent gave "life" (Num 21:9), the "raising up" of the Human One gives "*eternal* life."[7]

This is the first of three Johannine "lifting up" passages (8:28; 12:32, 34), parallel to the synoptic Passion predictions. The fourth gospel eschews the synoptic language of suffering and being put to death in favor of the Johannine "lifting up" to emphasize these positive, healing elements of the crucifixion that are in fact God's "glory." Rather than focusing on the evil of the executioners, the fourth gospel brings the readers' attention to the voluntary, loving nature of Jesus' movement toward Golgotha and beyond.

This focus is reinforced in perhaps the most famous verse in the gospel, 3:16. The reason for the "lifting up" is God's intense love for "the world," the place dominated by darkness that rejects the light. Paul S. Minear expresses it powerfully:

---

5. Petersen (1993, 114–119).
6. R. Brown (1966, 133).
7. Petersen (1993, 100–101).

[God] offers life to *his enemies*. This is the "ultimate insanity" of the revelation that this narrator is trying to convey to his readers. To believe in that insanity is what requires a rebirth through the Spirit.[8]

This theme continues in verse 17, with the only reference in the fourth gospel to God's "saving" function. Not for destruction or condemnation, but for life and salvation, has God sent the "only Son" into the world. As one continues through the text and faces the harsh and bitter encounters between Jesus and his opponents in "the world," it is essential to remember this basic premise of the mission of Jesus and the Johannine Christian community.

The twice-heard image of the "only-begotten Son" (*monogenē hoion*, 3:16, 18) in this context recalls its usage at the end of the prologue, where the issue was the relative status of Moses and Jesus (1:17–18). Petersen makes a strong case that the use of that phrase in the fourth gospel "is always found in connection with anti-structural statements about Moses in which the 'Son' assumes the role played by Sophia in Jewish wisdom texts."[9] That is, whereas the Wisdom tradition implicitly includes Moses among the many "sons" of mother-Sophia (e.g., Wis of Sol 10:16; Sir 4:11; 15:2), the fourth gospel insists upon the *exclusive* sonship of Jesus. This also serves to undermine the hope in a Davidic messiah, through which all of Israel's kings, including the messiah, would be enthroned as a "Son of God" (2 Sam 7:12–14). Jesus is *not* simply another in a line of "sons" of either Wisdom or David.

Verses 18–21 move from the "grace" of 14–17 to the "truth." If the Son has not come to judge, it is because those who do not believe are "judged already" (verse 18). The "basis for judgment" stated in verse 19 is the starkest statement of the gospel's view of the problem: "The light has come into the world, but people loved darkness rather than the light, for their works were evil [*ponēra*]." Far from the simplistic "Jesus is my personal Lord and Savior" faith of some fundamentalist interpreters, the fourth gospel makes clear that judgment is a matter of freely chosen attitude *and* behavior.

The preference for "darkness" is no more a matter of private lack of faith than is the challenge to Nicodemus to be born *anōthen* a matter of private confession of faith. This is underscored by the elaboration in verse 20: "Everyone practicing foul things [*phaula*] is hating the light and is not coming to the light, so that their works might be reproved [*elegchthē*]." As we have seen in interpreting the distinction between children of God and children of the devil (see chap. 1.2 above), 1 John amplifies this distinction in terms of justice and love for one's brothers and sisters (1 Jn 3:10). As one commentator has expressed it, the term for "reprove," although rare in the New Testament (but cf. 16:8–11), is part of a biblical tradition going back to Lev 19:17 and was for the rabbis "an integral part of love."[10] To join the Johannine community, then, is to receive the

---

8. Minear (1984, 41).
9. Petersen (1993, 112).
10. F. Buchsel, *TDNT* 2:475.

one sent by God who offers love that leads to eternal life and to allow oneself to be purified within the community by the truthful, correcting aspect of love. Those who do so are "doing the truth," the opposite of doing foul things, and reveal that it is in God that their works are done (verse 21).

Another community existed at the time of the Johannine community that would have found these words harmonious with their way of life: the people at Qumran, who left what we call the Dead Sea Scrolls. Their writings are filled with similar images of doing truth and walking in light as opposed to doing evil and walking in darkness.[11] Although scholars continue to debate strenuously questions of the historical relationship between the fourth gospel and the Qumran writings and community, one important difference is relevant here. Whereas the Qumran community was apart from the world, living in the desert by the Dead Sea away from the corruption of the Jerusalem establishment, the Johannine community heard its call to be deeply involved with the world, even if it meant misunderstanding, persecution, and death. For the fourth gospel, God's love for the world cannot be separated from the community's call to shine light into the places of darkness where evil continues to be practiced.

If Nicodemus is still listening, this speech has made all too clear what he must do to understand Jesus' riddles about new birth and the blowing spirit. His position as Pharisaic ruler is antithetical to his supposed faith in Jesus as a teacher sent from God. No secret discipleship is allowed! Nicodemus and those on whose behalf he speaks must either participate openly in the Johannine mission or remain in the dark.

---

11. See, generally, Charlesworth (1990).

# 6

# John Must Decrease

## John 3:22–4:3

**A. Chiasms:**

a: 3:22–26: baptism/all going to Jesus

  b: 27–28: from heaven/witness

    c: 29–30: increase/decrease

  b[1]: 31–36: from heaven/witness

a[1]: 4:1–3: baptism/Jesus more disciples than John (the Baptist)[1]

**broader chiasm from 1:19 to 4:3**:

a: 1:19–51: John (the Baptist) witness

  b: 2:1–12: water replaced by wine

    c: 2:13–25: Temple exorcism

  b[1]: 3:1–21: water and spirit

a[1]: 3:22–4.3: John (the Baptist) witness[2]

**B. Location:** Judean countryside

**C. Time:** not given

**D. Hebrew scripture context:** "election" as Chosen People

**E. Social factors:** John (the Baptist)'s community vs. Johannine community

**F. Themes:** Jesus is greater than John (the Baptist)

**G. Key words:** baptism

Jesus' initial round of activities has been completed. He has gathered a community of disciples; inaugurated the messianic era at Cana; symbolically

---

1. Ellis (1984, 60–61).
2. Ellis (1984, 29).

overthrown the locus of oppression, the Jerusalem Temple; challenged a quasi-disciple to come forward; and established the purpose of his and his followers' mission in the world. In a sense, the remainder of the fourth gospel is a set of variations on these themes, much as a symphony follows the overture with thematic explication and variation.

It is fitting, then, for there to be a sort of narrative summary at this point. Whether one sees it as a plot function in terms of the completion of Jesus' first "ministry tour" from Galilee to Jerusalem and back[3] or as a structural aspect of the text in terms of completion of a larger chiasm as shown above, it seems clear that the last passage in chapter 3 completes the first portion of the gospel. A comparison of key themes and words used in 1:19–3:21 and repeated in 3:22–4:3 further illustrates this textual feature:

| first passage | theme or word | summary passage |
|---|---|---|
| 1:20 | I am not the Christ | 3:28 |
| 1:23 | the Lord | 4:1 |
| 1:25–26 | baptizing | 3:23 |
| 1:28 | beyond the Jordan | 3:26 |
| 1:35 | John's disciples | 3:25 |
| 1:30 | sent in front | 3:28 |
| 1:43 | Jesus goes to Galilee | 4:3 |
| 2:6 | purification | 3:25 |
| 2:6 | measures | 3:34 |
| 2:9 | bridegroom | 3:29 |
| 2:16–17 | speaking sayings of God | 3:24 |
| 3:1 | dispute with Judean | 3:25 |
| 3:3, 7 | *anōthen* | 3:31 |
| 3:11 | witness not receiving | 3:32 |
| 3:12 | earth/heaven | 3:31 |
| 3:15–16 | eternal life | 3:36 |
| 3:17 | one God sent forth | 3:34 |
| 3:18–19 | faith/lack | 3:36 |

As we pick up the story in 3:22, then, we will not be surprised to begin to experience the Johannine technique of repetition, a process whereby the startling story of Jesus can begin to take root in readers.

The passage begins in a unique geographic location in the fourth gospel: the "Judean countryside." On every other occasion, Jesus when in Judea is found in Jerusalem or its immediate environs (e.g., Bethany). This is his only experience among the "folks" of Judea, and all we are told is that he baptized. Indeed, the narrative shifts attention immediately from Jesus — who is not heard from or seen again until he leaves Judea for Galilee in 4:3 — to John and his disciples.

---

3. Staley (1988, 72).

The almost throwaway reference to Jesus and his disciples' baptismal ministry has aroused much debate among scholars, especially as none of the synoptics suggests that Jesus ever baptized people himself. The fourth gospel itself comes back at the end of this passage to disclaim Jesus' personal participation in this activity (4:2). Commentators have responded to this "inconsistency" with source-oriented theories of redaction (in which the text has allegedly been cut-and-pasted by people with inconsistent historical or theological perspectives) and a discourse-oriented theory of "reader victimization" (in which the "implied author" has tricked the "implied reader" into a false point of view to put the reader off guard).[4] Whatever one's explanation for the apparent paradox, the text is barely concerned with the question, which does not come up again. Instead, it uses the issue of baptism as a means to convince remaining disciples of John that the time has come to leave their master and come to Jesus. Just as Nicodemus is called to leave his establishment position in favor of the Johannine community, so too, the members of John's countercommunity must change their social location in favor of the one established by the man from heaven.

Thus, while Jesus and his disciples are reported to be in the Judean countryside, we are immediately relocated in verse 23 to Aenon near Salim, where John and his own disciples are continuing their ministry. Little is known about the historical location of this site, although a sixth-century church's mosaic floor map locates it on the east bank of the Jordan,[5] which matches the fourth gospel's previous description of John's ministry "on the other side" (1:28). However, shortly in verse 26, John's disciples appear to refer to "the other side of the Jordan" as a place from the past. Wherever they are located, it is apart from Jesus and his disciples. Two separate baptizing communities are at work among the people.

The text then almost parenthetically adds in verse 24 the chilling detail, "for John had not yet been thrown into prison." In the fourth gospel, there is no narrative of John's witness against Herod and his subsequent beheading as in Mark 6:14–29. Indeed, after this scene, John himself does not appear again but is referred to only in the past tense by Jesus (5:33–36) or the narrator (10:40–41). The implication seems to be that the witness John gave to the Jerusalem "apostles" in the opening scene will eventually catch up to him. Unauthorized religious rituals cannot be allowed! It is the first explicit statement in the gospel — apart from Jesus' as yet cryptic reference to being "lifted up" — that the price for faithfulness to God may be official persecution or worse. For now, though, the narrator allows this message to settle into the background.

In verse 25 we come to the heart of the matter at issue in this passage: the dispute between John's disciples and a Judean over "purification." More precisely, John's disciples argue with *Ioudaiou,* a singular but anarthrous term that perhaps bears overtones of a more generic disagreement than that with a particular Judean individual. At the core of John's ministry is the replacement of

---

4. Staley (1988, 98).
5. *HBD* 14.

official Judean purification rituals with his own form of baptismal cleansing. At the same time, Jesus, too, replaces Judean rituals, but with the far more powerful messianic banquet, as we saw at the wedding in Cana. Can both of these "replacements" be equally valid? Which alternative purification should the truly devout Judean seek out instead of the established Temple/Torah system?

The disputants in verse 26 take this question to John, their own rabbi. They recall the prior union of John and Jesus and John's witness to Jesus before noting in a jealous tone: "See! This one is baptizing, and all are going to him!" John, the ever-faithful witness, happily acknowledges in verses 27–30 his reduced role in the presence of the messianic age. By speaking in terms of "receiving" from heaven in verse 27, John reverses his disciples' perspective. They see the question as a competition between two communities to win the most converts: How many can *we* receive? But John sees it with the eyes of the prologue: whoever *receives* the light is given authority to become children of God. The issue is not receiving converts, but receiving God. *This* can only be done if given by heaven.

John then repeats his earlier witness — reinforcing his fidelity and credibility in the mind of readers — and adds a new twist in verse 29 to a previously considered image:

> The one having the bride is the bridegroom, but the friend of the bridegroom, having stood and heard him, rejoices greatly to hear the bridegroom's voice. Therefore, my joy has been fulfilled.

Clearly, John identifies himself as the "friend of the bridegroom" whose "joy has been fulfilled." But from this perspective, *Jesus* is the bridegroom. Who, then, is Jesus' "bride"? The Johannine community. We cannot help but look back at the Cana story and reconsider. The bride and bridegroom were never named, nor even specifically present, except for the bridegroom's implied receipt of the feastmaster's comment about saving the best wine for last (2:10). We now can see more precisely the implication of the verb *eklēthē* in describing Jesus and his disciples' presence at the wedding. The term — sharing the same root as *logos*[6] — carries the rich connotation of the election of God's Chosen People in the Hebrew scriptures. The Cana feast not only replaces the Judean purification rites with the messianic banquet but also celebrates the replacement of the nation of Israel as God's people with the Johannine community.

We must once again be careful not to allow this message to lead to anti-Jewish sentiment in our age. The question with which the fourth gospel struggles throughout is: What makes someone a "child of God"? Whether Jew or Christian, then or now, the primary criterion, according to the fourth gospel, is not membership in a particular group or sharing in an ancestry, but willingness to receive God's representative into our midst and walking in his way. The Johannine community itself apparently foundered on the shoals of internal betrayal

---

6. G. Quell, *TDNT* 4:145–168.

and mistrust, leading the author of 1 John to accuse people formerly within the community of being children of the devil and messengers of the Antichrist (e.g., 1 Jn 4:1–6). But within the context of threatened persecution and excommunication by the Pharisees for their confession of Jesus as messiah, the Johannine community found itself in a deeply polarized situation that brought forth an either/or tone to its interpretation of Jesus. The hope was that the "world" — including their fellow children of Abraham and Moses — would come to share in the messianic joy that the Johannine community experienced and celebrated in sacrament and story. If Jesus was the bridegroom, it was because he identified himself with the God of the covenant, the true God that Israel claimed as its own. If the Johannine community rather than Israel became the bride, it was because they were open to good news that, mysteriously, many of their compatriots were not able to see or hear (cf. 12:37–43). The focus both in the Cana passage and in 3:29, then, is not so much on condemnation of those who do not join the Johannine community but on the universal call — *eklēthē* — to share in the banquet's joy. This is why John, though required to decrease so that Jesus can increase, finds his joy "fulfilled."

Once again, as in the dialogue with Nicodemus, the speaker's voice is gradually effaced by that of the narrator, so that the final verses of the chapter take on a sense of universal discourse.[7] A series of previously used images is repeated to emphasis Jesus' superiority over John: he is the one from above (*anōthen*) and from heaven (verse 31). He has witnessed to what he has seen and heard, but — shockingly — "no one receives his witness" (verse 32). The wholly negative implication of this statement is immediately softened in verse 33: "The one having received his witness has sealed the fact that God is true." The singular suggests that this refers specifically to John, whose ability to receive Jesus is a gift from heaven. Given the imagery in the early Christian communities of baptism as a "seal,"[8] verse 33 reinforces the sense that John's baptism was not so much intended to establish a separate community but to verify one's receipt of his witness, namely, that *Jesus* is the Lamb of God.

In contrast to the bountiful but limited volume of the Judean purification jars in 2:6, the one sent from God "does not give the spirit by measure" (verse 34). This introduction of the theme of "giving the spirit" completes the contrast with John that John himself began in 1:26 and continued in 1:34 with the theme of Jesus baptizing in "holy spirit." Water and spirit will remain in the air, so to speak, through the rest of the gospel.

The speech concludes in verses 35–36 with one of the clearest expressions of the equal and opposite consequences of the choice at issue in the fourth gospel. Those who believe in the Son, who has been given all from the Father, have eternal life; but those who "disobey the Son will not see life, but the wrath of God remains on them." The term "wrath" is extremely rare in the gospels and occurs only here explicitly connected with God. It is perhaps some consolation

---

7. Rensberger (1988, 61).
8. G. Fitzer, *TDNT* 7:953.

to note that this dire consequence is not a direct result of "unbelief," but of "disobedience." But what room there may be in the Johannine conception for one obedient to the Son but lacking in faith is hard to imagine. One must rest in the recognition that, despite the universal call to participate in the messianic community, there are those who will refuse, and we cannot deny the reality of consequences following upon whatever actions we take.

# 7

# The Savior of the World

## Jesus Becomes a Samaritan

## John 4:4–45

A. **Chiasm:**

    a: 4–6: labor (*kekopiakōs*)/field

        b: 7–18: woman surprised at Jesus' words; food

            c: 19–24: spirit/truth

        b[1]: 25–34: disciples surprised at Jesus' words; food

    a[1]: 35–38: labor (*kekopiakasin*)/fields[1]

B. **Location:** Samaria/Galilee

C. **Time:** the sixth hour/two days

D. **Hebrew scripture context:** Gen 24:10–61; 29:1–20; Ex 2:15b–21 (well courtship scenes); Jer 2:1–13

E. **Social factors:** Judeans vs. Samaritans; male vs. female; Jesus vs. Caesar

F. **Themes:** inclusion of outcasts; rejection of patriarchy/monarchy

G. **Key words:** "living" water; labor; food

Although Jesus' words and actions so far in the story have been shocking and radical, they at least have been contained within the social world out of which he arose, the Jewish communities of Judea and Galilee. In chapter 4, the Jewish messiah visits a land virtually forbidden to Judeans and, before he leaves, is proclaimed as one greater than Caesar! The lengthy story of Jesus' encounter with the woman of Samaria and her kinsfolk breaks open new ground for the growing Johannine community, ground even his disciples thought off-limits.

---

1. Ellis (1984, 66–67).

# 1. COMPETING BAPTISMS

A single sentence comprising three verses at the beginning of chapter 4 sets up Jesus' encounter in Samaria. The narrator, exercising his psychological omniscience, informs readers that "the Lord knew that the Pharisees had heard that Jesus was making and baptizing more disciples than John." It is the first of three preresurrection narrative descriptions of Jesus as "Lord" (6:23; 11:2), an odd intrusion of the narrator's discourse-time perspective into the story time of the gospel. It has the effect of reminding readers that the gospel is reporting events from a temporal and theological distance.

As Francis Moloney points out, the "proliferation of baptismal ministries... poses a threat to the established religious authority in Judea."[2] In the background of the scenes in Samaria, Nicodemus's fellow Pharisees are beginning to recognize the threat that these "unauthorized" rites present to their control. Rather than engage in this dispute now, Jesus allows it to ripen while he plants seeds in more fertile ground.

# 2. LIVING WATER

**Chiasm: 4:4–15**

a: 4–7: Jesus asks for a drink; Jacob's well [*pēgē*]

  b: 8–11: division between Judeans/Samaritans; living water

    c: 12: are you greater?

  b¹: 13–14: unity among those who drink living water

a¹: 15: woman asks for a drink: become a fountain [*pēgē*]

*It was necessary for him to go through Samaria.* (4:4)

During the triannual pilgrimage that Galilean Jews would make to Jerusalem, an old feud would be confronted. On the West Bank of the Jordan, between Galilee and Judea, lay the hated land of Samaria. For readers not familiar with this ancient antipathy, the narrator expressly tells us in verse 9 that "Judeans have no dealings with Samaritans." More specifically, this probably refers to the prohibition against sharing utensils, such as drinking cups, for fear of contracting ritual impurity.[3] Behind this wall lay hundreds of years of hostility, the kind of hatred that, like Protestants and Catholics in Northern Ireland, can only come from religious differences combined with a shared (in part) heritage. To feel the depth of what Jesus does in Samaria, it is worth reviewing the history of the split between Judeans and Samaritans.

2. Moloney (1993, 136).
3. Talbert (1992, 113); Thomas (1991, 165–169).

In 722 B.C.E., Assyria conquered Israel, the Northern Kingdom of the United Monarchy of Israel and Judah. This conquest separated the two kingdoms for the first time in some two hundred years since they had first been united under King David. As described in 2 Kgs 17:24–41, the Assyrian king, as was common practice among empires, replaced the inhabitants of Samaria (up until then a portion of Israel) with people from other nations, in order to diffuse the possibility of rebellion. The religious result was a number of hybrid customs, mixing worship of Israel's God with worship of many national gods, including the practice of child sacrifice. As the biblical summary concludes:

> These nations worshiped the Lord, but also served carved images; to this day their children and their children's children continue to do as their ancestors did.

The Babylonians conquered the Southern Kingdom of Judah in 587. Cyrus of Persia converted the resulting exile into colonialization some fifty years later. The population of Samaria had become, according to the book of Ezra, "the adversaries of Judah and Benjamin" (Ezra 4:1). The returned exiles had determined at this point to set about the task of rebuilding the Jerusalem Temple, which had been destroyed by the Babylonians. The mixed nationality Samaritans asked to participate in this rebuilding, claiming, "We worship your God as you do, and we have been sacrificing to him ever since the days of King Esar-haddon of Assyria who brought us here" (Ezra 4:2). However, the Judeans rebuffed this attempt at religious solidarity, finding the history of what they saw as idolatry too defiling to allow participation in the sacred rituals of national rebirth involved in Temple reconstruction.

The rejected Samaritans, in a "sour grapes" pattern too sadly familiar, responded by writing to the Persian king, warning that allowing Judah to rebuild the Temple would rekindle the rebellious nationalism for which Judah had become famous. Although the Samaritan epistle was temporarily effective in withdrawing Persian consent for the project, the stubborn Judeans set about the rebuilding program without approval, appealing to the previous permission granted by Cyrus. This ploy was effective and the Temple was rebuilt, but not without cementing the thick wall of hatred between Jerusalem and Samaria.

By the first century, this hostility meant that pilgrimaging Jews would sometimes cross the Jordan to "the other side" in order to go around Samaria rather than take the obvious route between Galilee and Jerusalem. This was the history into which it was "necessary" for Jesus to enter on his own way from Judea to Galilee. What Temple worship had separated, Jesus would reconcile, but in a manner completely unimaginable to his disciples.

Jesus comes to rest in Sychar, a place mentioned only in Jn 4:5 in the entire Bible. Immediately, we are asked to associate it with powerful symbols: the field Jacob gave his son Joseph (Gen 48:22) and Jacob's "well" (*pēgē*). Jesus, "having labored [*kekopiakos*] on the journey, was sitting on the well." It is the sixth hour, midday, when the heat and light are at their peak.

Into this scene comes a woman of Samaria, to "draw" water. The last time we heard about "drawing" what was expected to be water was at Cana, when Jesus ordered the servants to "draw" the wine from the purification jars. The link with the Cana story will be reinforced by the detail in 4:28 that, upon returning to the city to report what she had heard, the woman left her water jar (*hydrian*, as in 2:6) behind.

By the fact of her arrival at the well at midday, we already suspect she is an outcast. The well in a culture without indoor plumbing or a river or lake at hand is a center of social activity at morning and evening. In the cool of the day, women gather at the well to share stories, complaints, and hopes for the day or night. This woman, though, comes alone during the heat of the day. We are led to wonder: What is it about her that causes her to come at this unsociable hour to the well?

Before we hear another detail from her, Jesus has addressed her, asking simply and directly for a drink. Apart from the Jewish/Samaritan question, this opening of conversation by a man with an unknown woman was a serious violation of the cultural code.[4] In a public setting, it was rare for men and women to speak to one another apart from the necessities of the marketplace.[5] For people of different clans and even different cities, this inclination toward noninteraction was even stronger. For *foreign* men and women, even more of a presumption against discourse existed. For a *Jewish man* and a *Samaritan woman* to speak together was wholly unthinkable! Jesus, with no apparent regard whatsoever for this powerful code, initiates a dialogue with her: "Give me a drink."

The incipient conversation is interrupted with a comic parenthetical narrative comment in 4:8: "His disciples had gone into the city to buy food." In previous scenes where the disciples were not present, we were given no information at all about their whereabouts. The intrusive nature of the explanation of their absence at this point in the story serves several functions. At the structural level, it sets up the chiastic parallel in verses 31–34 where "food" is again the topic of conversation. At the narrative level, it adds suspense by delaying momentarily the readers' awareness of the woman's response to Jesus' inquiry. At the symbolic level, it contrasts Jesus' concern for "drink" with their concern for "food," the deeper meaning of which will unfold as the story is told. Finally, at the socio-theological level, it contrasts how Jesus and his disciples get their respective needs met: while the disciples participate in the established system of things (the marketplace), Jesus initiates new systems by breaking down the cultural codes that limit the opportunities for sharing of resources among people.

In verse 9, the woman expresses her shock at his unthinkable behavior: "How is it that you, despite being a Judean, are asking me, a Samaritan woman, to drink?" Jesus takes both the Samaritan woman and the narrator's assumptions

---

4. Malina (1981, 33).

5. Karris (1990, 75–76), in contrast, cites sources supporting his view that "it is false to make Judaism's view of women so bleak that Jesus' and primitive Christianity's view and praxis are seen as revolutionary." Karris suggests instead that the Johannine story served as a missionary tool to diasporan women who already served as synagogue leaders (p. 78).

about noninteraction and ups the ante considerably in his response to her question in verse 10: "If you had known the gift of God and who is the one saying to you, 'Give me a drink,' you would have asked him, and he would give you living [*zōn*] water." He moves the conversation from the "earthly" level of thirst and ethnic hatred to the "heavenly" level of the "gift of God," the question of his own identity, and the metaphor of "living" water. Further, he reverses the direction of the thirst-quenching: from asking her for a "drink," he challenges her to ask him.

Her response in verses 11–12 is complex, offering several reasons for the impossibility of his offer: "Sir, you have no means for drawing, and the well is deep. Wherefrom [*pothen*], therefore, are you getting this 'living water'? You are not greater than our father Jacob, who gave us the well [*phrear*] and drank out of it with his sons and his cattle, are you?" The first half of her reply focuses only on the third of the new topics introduced by Jesus. As did Nicodemus, she interprets the ambiguous term in Jesus' statement at the obvious (but impossible!) earthly level. "Living" water in her mind, and in common parlance, would be *flowing* water, as opposed to the stagnant well water in front of her. Her words, revealing this interpretation, suggest many possible aspects of her character. Perhaps she is bitter and sarcastic: Give me a break, sir! I'm too tired for this kind of foolish talk! Perhaps sly and laconic: Oh, you think you're pretty clever with your fancy words! So tell me how you're going to pull off this trick! Perhaps sincerely hopeful but naturally doubtful: I'd love to see you do it, sir, but I can't imagine how.

Regardless of how we interpret her character, her words ironically point to the core of the matter, the *pothen* of his living water. Once again, the issue of Jesus' source is raised by an unknowing speaker.

The second half of her statement takes up the middle term of Jesus' own words, the "who it is who speaks to you." At the heart of the chiasm is her ironic questioning of whether this strange Judean is greater than the Samaritan patriarch, Jacob. Note first how her word here and in verse 11 for "well" is different than the narrator's in verse 6 and Jesus' in verse 14. Her term, *phrear*, is more like "cistern," while the narrator's and Jesus' term, *pēgē*, is more like "fountain."[6] What she speaks of in relation to her great "father" is, indeed, not "living" water, but for the narrator and Jesus, both Jacob and Jesus are rooted in the water that flows from God.

The additional details of the humans and animals that drank at the well suggest the woman's patriotic defense of the wealth of what *she* has received from the ancestor she shares with the Judean man who has challenged her.[7] She may be an outcast woman drawing water at midday, but she is *still* a descendant of Jacob and *still* entitled to share in the limited but plentiful bounty of her inheritance. Perhaps her response implies her view that Jesus thinks he's special simply by being a Judean man, in relation to this despised Samaritan who is also

---

6. R. Brown (1966, 170).
7. O'Day (1988, 62).

a woman. Judean men may see themselves as superior to Samaritan women, but he's certainly not superior to Jacob, her "father."

As we have seen before, Jesus ignores her questions, both as to his *pothen* and his greatness, and continues about his own mission, the offering of the "gift of God." He provides in verse 14 a triple parallel statement that sharply contrasts her expectations with his offer:

Everyone drinking from this water will get thirsty again.

But whoever should drink from the water which I shall give to them, will never [*ou mē*] get thirsty at all [*eis ton aiōna*],

For the water which I shall give will become in that one a fountain [*pēgē*] of water bubbling up into eternal [*aiōnion*] life.

Jesus twice uses "heavenly" language about the eternal value of the water that he gives. Further, the imagery in the third line of his statement suggests that his water not only will provide ultimate satisfaction but also will overflow like a fountain, affecting those around the one who has received it.[8] It is a classic Johannine statement of the intimate link between the value of faith-commitment for the believer and its evangelical effect on others.

In powerful contrast with the teacher of Israel who apparently gave up on Jesus at a similar point in the conversation, this Samaritan woman keeps the conversation going. Although she still thinks on an earthly level about being relieved of the exhausting daily task of coming to the well and quenching her bothersome thirst, she does in verse 15 what Jesus invited her to do back in verse 10: "Sir, give me this water." With this positive step forward in the dialogue, the first chiasm closes, and the topic changes dramatically.

## 3. WORSHIP IN SPIRIT AND TRUTH

**Chiasm: 4:16–26**

a: 16–19: Jesus is a prophet

   b: 20–21: worship on mountain/hour is coming

      c: 22: you don't know/we know

   b¹: 23–24: worship in spirit and truth/hour is coming

a¹: 25–26: Jesus is the messiah

From the quenching of thirst, Jesus switches topics in verse 16: "Go and call for your husband [*andra*] and come here." The woman responds in verse 17 to Jesus' command with the bare admission, "I have no husband." Jesus in verse 18 strips away further layers of this woman's vulnerability with his surprising

---

8. Cf. Rev 7:17; 21:6.

awareness of her situation: "You spoke well in saying, 'I have no husband,' for you have had five husbands, and the one with whom you are now is not your husband. You have spoken the truth." We often hear this passage interpreted in terms of marital infidelity, as if Jesus were being both critical of her current extramarital affair and affirming of her willingness to admit the truth. However, nowhere else in the fourth gospel is there expressed a concern with this kind of moralizing.[9] The Johannine Jesus has much larger concerns than the sanctity of marriage, as important as that issue may be to many in the church today. Indeed, the text has no more to say on the subject after this initial exchange; the topic quickly turns to the place and nature of worship, a theme much more consonant with the overall pattern of the gospel than marriage itself. As we saw in the Cana story, weddings and marriage are ancient metaphors for relationship with God, and we are more likely to be in tune with the text by pursuing this line of interpretation in the immediate case.

Why does Jesus ask the woman to call her husband/man to this place? How does he know about her personal life? An excerpt from Jer 2:1–13 may provide a clue:

Thus says the Lord: I remember the devotion of your
    youth,
your love as a bride,
how you followed me in the wilderness. . . .
O house of Jacob, and all the families of the house of
    Israel, thus says the Lord:
What wrong did your ancestors find in me
that they went far from me,
and went after worthless things,
and became worthless themselves? . . .
Those who handle the law did not know me;
the rulers transgressed against me;
the prophets prophesied by Baal. . . .
Has a nation (LXX, *ethnē*) changed its gods
even though they are no gods? . . .
My people have committed two evils:
they have forsaken me,
the fountain (LXX, *pēgēn*) of living water,
and dug out cisterns for themselves,
cracked cisterns that can hold no water.
                    (Jer 2:2, 4–5, 8, 11, 13)

The "house of Jacob" has acted like an unfaithful wife by practicing idolatry, forsaking God, the true "husband" and "fountain of living water." What might

---

9. The beautiful story placed at Jn 8:1–11 of the woman caught in adultery is universally agreed to be a later addition, not found in earlier texts of the fourth gospel.

this prophetic poetry have to say about Jesus' conversation with the Samaritan woman? Recalling the passage from 2 Kings 17 establishing the antipathy between Samaria and Israel, we find that exactly five nations are listed as infecting worship of God with worship of gods (2 Kgs 17:30–31).[10] If we begin to see this anonymous woman of Samaria as the representative of her people, just as Nicodemus was a representative of a group, we find the relationship between her "husbands" and her current "man" to be an expression of Samaria's colonial past and present. As Craig Koester points out, if the five previous husbands are symbolic of Samaria's intermarriage with foreign peoples and the acceptance thereby of their false gods, her current man can be seen as *Rome,* with whom she "lives" but has not married. Koester adds that the Jewish historian Josephus, in his book *The Jewish War,* describes the transformation

> by Herod the Great of the capital of Samaria into the Greco-Roman city named Sebaste, the Greek name for Augustus. Foreign colonists were settled in Sebaste — six thousand of them according to Josephus (J.W. 1.21.I §403) — and the imperial cult was introduced.... The Samaritans lived together with the foreigners, but did not intermarry with the new colonists as extensively as under the Assyrians.[11]

In this context, the woman's response in 4:19, "Sir, I see you are a prophet," and her statement about the place of worship are not attempts to change the topic to avoid further questioning of her personal life[12] but rather indicate a direct acceptance of Jesus' statement of her national history.

The remainder of her response, found in verse 20, shows how clearly she understands Jesus' statement about her "men" as implying the question of nationality and religious loyalty: "Our fathers worshiped in this mountain, and you people are saying that Jerusalem is the place where it is necessary [*dei*] to worship." By introducing the question of "this mountain" versus "Jerusalem," the woman evokes a major point of contention in the history of relations between Samaritans and Judeans. A complex set of biblical and extrabiblical traditions links Mt. Gerizim through Jacob with proper — and improper — worship. According to Koester: "In the first century, Samaritans believed that Moses had hidden the vessels of the tabernacle on Mt. Gerizim, ... but Judeans insisted that the situation was quite different."[13] The opposing view was that, in accordance with Gen 31:19, 34, and 35:4, Jacob had stolen Rachel's father's household gods (i.e., local idols) and buried them beneath a tree near Shechem,[14] in the

---

10. C. Koester (1990b) provides rich background for the interpretation of the woman's husbands as colonial nations.

11. Ibid.

12. E.g., Duke (1985, 103).

13. C. Koester (1990b, 673).

14. Shechem was a center of religious dissidence for centuries, having afforded refuge to Jerusalemites who had been "expelled, despite their protestations of innocence, for violating the dietary laws or the sabbath regulations or for 'any other such sin'" (Ashton [1991, 154], citing Josephus *Ant.* 11.346).

shadow of Mt. Gerizim. Further, Jerome Neyrey cites archaeological evidence that a building identified as the Samaritan temple was on Mt. Gerizim. According to that evidence, that temple was then buried beneath a *Roman* temple to Zeus![15] Neyrey adds that a Samaritan tradition hoped that the "hidden vessels" in the temple — whether Moses' tabernacle vessels or Jacob's household gods — would be recovered by an eschatological prophet who would "restore true worship there as the rightful place."[16] To complicate matters further, other Jewish traditions claimed Jacob as the basis for Mt. *Zion* being the proper site of worship. Throughout all these conflicting traditions lay one predominant theme: "our" ancestors established a place of religious worship, and upon this tradition, our *national* identity is grounded. The woman's question, premised on the proposition that Jesus is a prophet, puts him to the test. She is asking him to resolve this dispute once and for all: Which nation, Samaria or Judea, is the true descendant (and inheritor) of Jacob?

Jesus' answer, as we have come to expect, goes well beyond her either/or nationalistic-religious vision and opens up unforeseen territory for her consideration: "Believe me, woman, the hour is coming when neither on this mountain nor in Jerusalem will you people worship the Father!" Jesus begins his long response by addressing this Samaritan with the same title with which he addressed his mother at Cana (2:4) and with which he will address her again from the cross (19:26): "woman." This outcast water-drawer of Samaria bears the identical dignity as Jesus' own mother! He continues with the eschatological, "the hour is coming," suggesting the ultimate end of geographically localized worship.

At the heart of the chiasm, a new theme is introduced as Jesus continues his speech in verse 22: "You people worship what you do not know, but we worship what we do know, because salvation is out of the Judeans." Again, behind this contrast is the argument over Jacob. In Gen 28:16–18, Jacob awakens from his dream-vision of the ladder between heaven and earth with the exclamation: "The Lord is in this spot, and I did not know it." Neyrey shows how the question of Jacob's knowledge was one disputed by the Samaritan tradition, which claimed that Jacob *did* know the place, that is, Mt. Gerizim.[17] The Judean insistence that Jacob did not know underscored that tradition's denial of Mt. Gerizim as a proper place for worship. Jesus' "we" who do know, though, is more likely a reference to the Johannine community's knowledge, not that of the Judeans, who remain focused on Jerusalem as the holy place. Thus, the Jesus whose every act is witnessed to by and fulfills the Hebrew scriptures (5:39) — which included the Prophets and Wisdom literature, which the Samaritan Pentateuch did not include[18] — can claim that "salvation" is out of the Judeans yet maintain

---

15. Neyrey (1979, 428).
16. Ibid.
17. Ibid., 432–433.
18. E.g., R. Brown (1966, 171).

the contrast with the lack of knowledge of the Judeans, who, like Nicodemus, "do not know these things" (3:10; cf. 7:28; 8:14, 43).

In contrast with the "coming hour," when worship will take place on holy mountains, is the *present* hour, when "true worshipers will worship the Father in spirit and truth, for these are the ones the Father is seeking to worship him" (verse 23). The end of national worship may be an eschatological dream, but the Johannine community exists *now*!

As Jesus insisted to Nicodemus that he and his people could not see the hoped-for "reign of God" without being reborn in water and spirit, so he tells the Samaritan woman and her people in verse 24: "God is spirit, and those worshiping that one must [*dei*] worship in spirit and truth." It was "necessary" (*dei*) for Jesus to go to Samaria; equally necessary for the fulfillment of his mission is the Samaritan response, in contrast with the prevailing Judean ideology that insists it is necessary (*dei*) to worship in Jerusalem (4:20). Where she expects Jesus-the-Judean-prophet to clarify the Gerizim/Jerusalem question, the option he insists on transcends nationalism in favor of "true worship" in "spirit and truth."

The woman neither affirms nor denies Jesus' declaration but probes his credentials for such a statement still further in verse 25: "I know the messiah is coming, the one called 'Christ.' When that one comes, he will announce [*anangelei*] to us all things [*apanta*]." By having her express the expectation of a coming messiah, the author of the fourth gospel is perhaps confused about the details of Samaritan tradition. Scholars have shown that Samaritan sources do not discuss a *messiah* until the sixteenth century.[19] Instead, documents before the time of the Johannine community refer to the expectation of a *taheb,* a more vague concept generalized as a revealer of God's truth. Her idea that the messiah would "announce to us all things" fits with this concept of the *taheb.* However, there is a basis within the Jacob tradition for the supplanting of Jacob by a royal messiah who would also be an official interpreter of Jewish Law and worship.[20] In this context, the woman's statement can be read as an indirect way of asking: Are you really the one to replace our father Jacob?

Jesus' reply, after all the metaphorical speech, is surprisingly direct: "I AM [*egō eimi*], the one speaking to you." It is the only time in the fourth gospel that he expressly acknowledges the title messiah, Christ. He does so in the form of the first of many *egō eimi* statements that link his being with that of the one revealed to Moses at the burning bush (Ex 3:28). It is the fulfillment of the negative witness of John back in the first scene of the narrative, when he offered the solemn confession, "I am not [*egō ouk eimi*] the Christ" (1:20). And it comes not to the Judeans, who will eventually (and murderously) press Jesus for just such a confession (10:24), but to the Samaritans, and to a woman!

19. De Jonge (1972–73, 268–269).
20. Neyrey (1979, 430–431).

## 4. FOOD OF WHICH YOU DO NOT KNOW

**Chiasm:**

a: 27–30: Samaritan woman gets people to come to Jesus

   b: 31: disciples: "eat"

      c: 32: food of which you do not know

   b¹: 33–34: disciples: "eat"

a¹: 35–38: parable of harvest

When the disciples return in verse 27, they are so flabbergasted to find their Rabbi speaking with a woman that they cannot speak. The silence of the disciples, filled in ironically by the narrator, leads readers suddenly to see them as "outsiders" in relation to the Samaritan woman, who has engaged Jesus in deep and meaningful conversation. The first of their unasked questions, "What are you seeking [*zēteis*]?" forms an ironic contrast with Jesus' immediately preceding statement that the Father is "seeking" (*zētei*) true worshipers.[21] Furthermore, whereas the woman is perfectly willing to ask her "foolish" questions and thus expose herself to Jesus' potential criticism, the disciples do not dare to challenge Jesus' shocking intergender discourse, preferring their ignorance and "honor" in the sight of this foreign woman to the risk of growth in knowledge in the sight of the messiah.

The woman apparently takes advantage of the new arrivals to share the news of the mysterious encounter with her kinsfolk: "Therefore, leaving her water jar, the women went into the city and told the people, 'Come see the person who told me all things [*panta*] which I did. This couldn't be the messiah, could it?" The leaving of the jar suggests two interpretive alternatives: (1) she will be returning shortly,[22] or (2) she has no further need for the jar, in fulfillment of Jesus' promise that "whoever drinks from the water I give will never thirst again" (4:14).

Her announcement to the people follows directly from her messianic expectation expressed in verse 25 of being told "all things." Without another word, the people respond to her call and, the narrator tells us in verse 30, "were coming toward him."

As they approach, we are returned by our omnipresent narrator to the well, where Jesus and his disciples are gathered. With their minds on their initial mission to go into the city (the same city the woman went into?) to buy food (verse 8), they offer some to Jesus in the impertinent form of a command in verse 31: "Rabbi, eat!" The previous conversation over thirst and water is modulated to the key of hunger and food, as Jesus for the first time offers his gathered disciples the sort of mysterious double entendre he has already given to the

---

21. O'Day (1988, 74–75).
22. Ibid.

Judeans at the Temple, Nicodemus, and the Samaritan woman. He phrases it in verse 32 in terms of their ignorance, just as he did with Nicodemus (3:8, 10) and the woman (4:10): "I have food to eat of which you do not know." Again afraid to embarrass themselves with the open acknowledgment of their ignorance (of which, ironically, Jesus is already well aware), they ask one another (not Jesus) in verse 33: "No one else has brought him something to eat, have they?" At the heart of their misguided internal questioning is one of the key theological premises of the fourth gospel: Jesus' own disciples do not really know or understand him any better than do "outsiders." Despite their initial enthusiasm replete with powerful titles — none of which Jesus affirmed — the disciples must stumble along in the dark just like everyone else.

Jesus elaborates for the benefit of his community, but we are given no further word on whether the disciples have a clue as to the meaning of the parable he spins for them in 4:35–38. He prefaces the parable in verse 34 with the metaphor: "My food is to do the will of the one who sent me and to complete his work." He is the living embodiment of those who have authority to become God's children (see 1:13), with no other purpose in life than to do God's will. The statement is the first of three "completion" pronouncements Jesus speaks in the fourth gospel (5:36; 17:4).

With this context in mind, Jesus offers the parable of the harvest. He begins in verse 35 with a statement of "earthly" wisdom ("four months and the harvest is coming") and transposes it to the "heavenly" level. The emphasis is on words of "sight": "Look, lift up your eyes, see the fields white for harvest!" If the disciples were to "lift up their eyes," they would see the Samaritans coming toward Jesus from the "field" (*chōras* in verse 36; *chōriou* in verse 5) provided by Jacob for his descendants. The next sentence anticipates Jesus' sending of his disciples on their own "fruitful" mission (15:1–8). He tells them that the one harvesting is already "gathering together" (*synagei*) the fruit into eternal life, thereby "receiving" the reward, so that sower and reaper may rejoice together. As José Miranda points out, these images are familiar eschatological symbols from the prophets, for example, Isa 27:12, Amos 9:13.[23] However, a look at this verse from Isaiah and its successor shows a particular connection with the scene unfolding before the disciples' eyes:

> On that day, the Lord will thresh from the channel of the Euphrates to the Wadi of Egypt, and you will be gathered one by one, O people of Israel. And on that day a great trumpet will be blown and *those who were lost in the land of Assyria* and those who were driven out to the land of Egypt will come and worship the Lord on the holy mountain of Jerusalem.

"Those who were lost in the land of Assyria" include, of course, the very Samaritans who are on their way to Jesus, who supplants the "holy mountain of Jerusalem." The Isaian prophecy expects the reconciliation of Samaritan and

---

23. Miranda (1977, 174–175).

Judean, but the fourth gospel gives it a special twist by expressing its fulfillment in terms of a new "synagogue," the Johannine community, wherein those gathered will rejoice together.

Jesus then quotes another earthly saying: "In this, the word [*logos*] is true, that 'one is sowing and another one harvesting.'" Raymond Brown suggests that the original import of the saying was negative, expressing the unfairness of life.[24] But Jesus reinterprets it as a heavenly word expressing the continuity of the call to do the will of the divine Sender. Jesus sent off (*apesteila*, expressing the future act in the story world as the past act of the discourse world) his disciples to harvest that on which they have not labored (*kekopiakate*). We recall the narrator's description of Jesus' initial state at the beginning of the story as "having labored" (*kekopiakos*). But he then goes on to express it in plural terms in verse 38: "Others have labored [*kekopiakasin*], and you have entered into their labor." Whether this plural refers to the Hebrew prophets from Moses on who have planted the seed of God's covenant or more specifically to the first disciples in the two generations preceding the Johannine audience, the text does not say. Regardless of the specific referent, Jesus' parable makes clear that his unknowing disciples are being sent to participate in an ongoing mission, which has as its object the gathering together of true worshipers for the Father.

## 5. THE SAVIOR OF THE WORLD

    a: 39: Samaritans believe/all that I did

       b: 40–41: two days

          c: 42: Savior of the world

       b¹: 43–44: two days

    a¹: 45: Galileans welcome/all that he had done[25]

After Jesus finishes his parable, the narrator returns us to the observation of the arriving Samaritans, but only after adding a crucial detail: the people from the city are not only coming to check Jesus out, they have *already* believed in him because of the "word [*logon*] of the woman bearing witness, 'He told me all things which I did.'" This outcast foreign woman has joined the privileged circle to which only John belongs at this point, those who have "witnessed" to Jesus. Although the first disciples responded by following and calling others, only this Samaritan has been described in this special way. As John has expressed his "word" to his people, so the woman has also done to her own. The harvest has already begun.

The response of the arriving Samaritans in verse 40 is fitting both for Johannine community members and for descendants of Abraham: "Therefore, the

---

24. R. Brown (1966, 182–183).
25. Ellis (1984, 77).

Samaritans came to him, asking him to remain [*meinai*] with them, and he remained there two days." Their offer is both one of hospitality to the stranger and one of acceptance of him as the messiah. As the spirit *remained* on Jesus (1:32) and as he *remained* with the first two disciples (1:39), so, the narrator tells us, Jesus now remains in the formerly hated country of Samaria. As Gail O'Day has said, this invitation and response bring "the narrative full circle. In verse 9 the Samaritan woman had balked at the idea of social interaction between Samaritans and Judeans; here, as a result of the mediation of the Samaritan woman, the Samaritans are requesting that interaction."[26]

Because of Jesus' "remaining," we discover in verse 41 that "Many more believed because of his word [*logon*]." Their statement to the woman in verse 42 after this experience seems harsh at first: "We no longer believe because of your speech, for we have heard and have known that this one is truly the Savior of the world." Why the need to criticize this woman who has brought them the good news? A closer look reveals two reasons for their reaction to the woman. First, we recall that the news she brought them was actually equivocal: "This couldn't be the Christ, could it?" (verse 29). What she was excited but still uncertain of, they have found out for sure. Perhaps more importantly, what they have discovered is that this one is not only the messiah who supplants their father Jacob but the "Savior of the world."

As Craig Koester has shown in detail, the term "savior" was a common one in the first century for a revered person such as a philosopher or other leader, but the full title "Savior of the world" was one used exclusively for the Roman emperor.[27] The title is only used of Jesus one other time in the entire New Testament, also in the Johannine literature (1 Jn 4:14). Its meaning in 4:42 can only be that the Samaritans have come to see that for them Jesus is the one to replace the emperor.

With this reminder of the marriage imagery seen earlier in verses 16–18, the entire story is revealed to be shaped on a common biblical "type-scene": the well courtship story.[28] Type-scenes are familiar to us all: examples are the detective whodunit where the least suspected person is revealed to be the killer and the western where the white people are the good guys and the Indians the savages. It is familiarity with such a western type-scene that allows for the success of a film like *Dances with Wolves,* where the expected stereotype is reversed.

Such basic story patterns are common in the Bible as well as in modern fiction genres. The Pentateuch contains three examples of the basic plot device of courtship at a well: a man comes to a well, finds a maiden there, asks her for a drink; they converse; she runs home to tell her people what has happened; they return with her to the well and approve of the man; he returns to their home and marries the maiden. This is roughly how Isaac met

---

26. O'Day (1988, 87).

27. C. Koester (1990b, 666–67).

28. Alter (1981, 47–62) discusses the nature and function of "type-scenes" in the Bible; Duke (see below) derives his interpretation from Alter.

Rebekah, how Jacob met Rachel, and how Moses met Zipporah (Gen 24:10–61; 29:1–20; Ex 2:15b–21). Paul D. Duke has shown the ironic function of this type-scene as played out in the Samaritan well story.[29] Jesus meets not a maiden but a five-time married woman. Rather than looking for another husband, our Samaritan woman is just looking for relief. And rather than looking for a wife, Jesus is looking for "worshipers in spirit and truth." The net result, though, is similar to the marriage celebrated at Cana: the messianic joy of God's presence brings back the "bride" whom Jeremiah had lamented for going after false gods. Jesus the bridegroom has bonded himself to the people "lost in the land of Assyria," forming a unity that "remains" far longer than two days.

The story of the Samaritan woman and her people encountering the Savior of the world is also the dramatization of one of the central oppositions in the prologue: not born of the "will of man [andros] but out of God were born." The Samaritans had previously found their identity, their birth, in the will of men: their ancestor Jacob and his well, the Assyrian king who mixed many nationalities in the conquered land of Israel that they occupied, the Caesars who oppressed them and with whom they lived but were not intermarried. They had struggled to maintain their sense of self by claiming earthly "fathers" and a "fatherland," which inevitably pitted them against their neighbors with whom they fought for survival. By receiving Jesus and believing in him, they were reborn by the will of God. As the Nicodemus story reflected the failures of birth from the will of flesh and the unaccepted invitation to be reborn of spirit, this story reveals the possibility of rebirth that transcends nationality and racial identity. In the presence of the true Savior of the world, one no longer needs to rely on one's fatherland to provide knowledge of who one is supposed to be.

After the two-day stay in Samaria, Jesus returns to Galilee, his destination in 4:3. Verses 44–45 are an epilogue to the sojourn through Samaria. The saying in verse 44 is at first ambiguous in the referent of its paraphrase of Jesus' "witness that a prophet is not honored in his own fatherland [patridi]." Is Jesus' patridi Galilee, where Nazareth is located, his supposed birthplace? Or is it Judea, the land of his fathers in faith, the land of Jerusalem and the Temple? There is a basis of support for those scholars who see the Galilean context of 43–45 as implying that Galilee is the place of Jesus' lack of honor. However, the broader context of the gospel suggests that the rejecting fatherland is Judea, especially in light of verse 45, which proclaims that "when he arrived in Galilee, the Galileans received him, having seen all the things he did in Jerusalem at the festival."[30] And yet there is a certain ominous note even in the Galileans' reception, which otherwise seems to echo the call of the prologue in 1:12. They welcome him *because of the things he did at the festival.* We recall that this is almost exactly the description in 2:23 of those whom Jesus did *not* trust!

---

29. Duke (1985, 101).
30. Meeks (1966, 165).

The difference is that in 2:23, it was specifically the "signs" that led to faith; whereas in 4:45, it is "all things" (*panta,* cf. 4:29, 39) that he did. Whether the distinction between faith based on signs and receiving based on "all things" is enough of a difference for the fourth gospel will require continued attention as we proceed through the coming scenes.

# 8

# "His Whole Household Believed"

## *Royal Servanthood Comes to Faith*

## John 4:46–54

**A. Chiasm:**

    a: 44–46: own land/Galilee/water-wine

      b: 47–49: dying/*basilikos*/you will not believe

        c: 50: son lives/believed word

      b¹: 51–53: living/father/believed

    a¹: 54: Judea/Galilee/second sign

        **or**

    a: 46–47: came/Galilee/water-wine

      b: 48–50a: come down/son will live

       c: 50b: person believed

      b¹: 51–53: going down/son will live

    a¹: 54: come/Galilee/second sign[1]

**B. Location:** Cana in Galilee

**C. Time:** seventh hour and following

**D. Hebrew scripture context:** Ex 7:3–4

**E. Social factors:** Galilean royal servant vs. Jerusalem ruler (implied)

**F. Themes:** faith in signs vs. faith in Jesus' word

**G. Key words:** *basilikos,* sign, word

As 2:23–25 provided a narrator's perspective on the interaction between Jesus and the "*anthrōpos* out of the Pharisees" about to unfold, so 4:44–45

---

1. Ellis (1984, 82).

shapes readers' preunderstanding of what will take place in 4:46–54. Although I have included the two transitional verses in the previous chiasm in accordance with Ellis's view, they also overlap to form the first link in the chiasm that comprises this story. It is part of the structural beauty of the fourth gospel — and the theological insight that the structure houses — that these verses fit within both stories, for we can see the activity in Samaria and in Cana as part of a single theme: the rebirth of people by God rather than through the will of men.

As we have seen in the last chapter, 4:44–45 provided an ambiguous comment on the faith of the Galileans who welcome Jesus. Are they like the Jerusalemites who believe only because of signs? Or are they like the Samaritans who believe because of Jesus' word? A phrase in 4:45 leaves this open: "having seen all things which he did..." It is neither expressly because of signs nor expressly because of the word that they believe. Another glimpse into their faith is necessary to understand their commitment to Jesus and the Johannine community.

The scene opens in verse 46 with the return of Jesus to "Cana of Galilee, where he made the water wine." If we read closely, we find that this is really the first express confirmation of the link between Jesus and the water-turned-wine. By reminding us of this happy occasion of messianic celebration, the text leads us to begin with positive feelings about the people from Cana, even if we might harbor gnawing doubts about Galileans in general due to 4:45.

We immediately witness in verse 46b the first encounter between Jesus and someone in need of healing: "And there was a royal official [*basilikos*] whose son was sick in Capernaum." Up until this point, apart from the Samaritan woman's chronic exhaustion, no one has been in physical need in the gospel. Although we have heard Jesus' powerful words and have seen his bold action in the Temple, we have no particular reason to expect him to bear healing power. If we are trying to read this text without the influence of the synoptics, it may come as a surprise that a person has come to Jesus hoping for a healing.

The person bearing this expectation is described as a *basilikos*. The word is usually translated "royal official," but we really have little clue about its specific connotations. At least it carries a sense of connection with royalty, although it is clear that this *basilikos* is not himself a king. Rather, he works for a king in some capacity: he is a royal servant.[2] This function, however, is only one of two defining characteristics: he is also a father of a son who is sick. How do these two features of the man's life interact within him? As a *basilikos,* he is invested with official power and authority, not unlike Nicodemus. His dignity comes from his association with another, a worldly ruler. That is, as a *basilikos,* he is one of those who is born "of the will of man." Such a person is unlikely to come to a lowly person like Jesus for help and, if Nicodemus is any guide, would not be

---

2. Karris (1990, 58–61) suggests "royal functionary," noting that a Jewish Galilean working for the client-king would still be marginalized vis-à-vis Judean royal officials. Moloney (1993, 182–183) notes that the identity of the *basilikos* as a Jew or Gentile is ambiguous. The focus in the passage is not on the man's religion, though, but on his class status and its inability to help him in time of need.

likely to believe in him. However, as a human father, he has another perspective, one that overrides his official viewpoint: his son is sick and in need of help. At the moment of crisis, he instinctively acts with regard for his beloved child, showing no apparent concern with the "honor" of his official rank.

One might expect such a person of power in need of help to *send* for Jesus, but he has no time for that. We are told in verse 47: "Having heard that Jesus is coming from Judea into Galilee, he went toward him and asked him to come down and heal his son, for he was dying." Both the *basilikos*'s intentions and actions are given by the narrator. This has the effect of including verse 47 in the introduction to the scene, which begins in earnest with Jesus' word in verse 48.

His statement is surprisingly bitter: "If you people don't see signs and wonders [*terata*], you will never [*ou mē*] believe." It is a harsh evaluation, ending with the Greek double negative that expresses strong certainty that they will have no "faith" unless there are signs and wonders. We have, of course, heard before about Jesus' distrust of signs-only faith (2:23–24), but this is the first and only time in the fourth gospel we hear about "wonders," expressed in the common synoptic term usually translated as "miracle." To the alert listener, it echoes an ancient doubt of the faith of an earlier royal leader:

> Though I multiply my signs and wonders [LXX, *terata*] in the land of Egypt, Pharaoh will not listen to you. (Ex 7:3–4)[3]

Will this *basilikos* and his people to whom Jesus speaks be as hard of hearing as Pharaoh? We must also ask: Who are the others to whom Jesus addresses his comment? Royalty in general? People of power? The people from Cana? Galileans? At this point, we cannot be sure, but it seems likely that the emphasis here is on all those whose "birth" is out of the "will of man."

The person, again identified as *basilikos,* ignores Jesus' fuming and in verse 49 says: "Sir, come down before my little child dies." It is not dissimilar to the previous Cana encounter, when Jesus' complaint that it was not his "hour" was met with his mother's command to the servants: "Do whatever he tells you" (2:5). The *basilikos* adds the poignant detail that his son is but a "little child," attempting to play on Jesus' compassion.

Jesus' response is as sudden as it is surprising. With no transition or explanation whatsoever, he proclaims simply in verse 50: "Go, your son is living." Despite the initial rebuff, this is enough for the one now described more broadly as "the person," *ho anthrōpos,* whom we are told "believed" in the "word [*logō*] which Jesus said to him." Before he can get home, his slaves meet him with the good news, expressed by the narrator in verse 51 in almost the same words as those used by Jesus: "His boy is living."

Despite the previous expression of faith in Jesus, there remain lingering doubts in the *basilikos* that had not been told to readers but are now revealed as perhaps the basis for Jesus' strong statement. It is not quite enough that the

---

3. R. Brown (1966, 191).

boy is living: "He therefore asked them the hour in which he had become better [*kompsoteron,* the only use of this word in the Bible]." Perhaps the boy recovered on his own, and Jesus' confident word was only a coincidence. But these doubts are immediately dispelled upon the slaves' assurance that the fever left the boy at the "seventh hour," literally early afternoon, and *literarily,* the hour after Jesus was with the Samaritan woman at the well (the "sixth hour," but at least two days earlier). With this extra confirmation, we are told in verse 53: "The father knew, therefore, that it was the hour in which Jesus had said to him, 'Your son is living,' and he believed and his whole household, too." No longer identified with his official position, the believing man from Cana is "reborn" as a father. Just as with the first Cana account, there is not within the story any direct attribution of the healing to the word or action of Jesus. Readers are given only the experience of the father: to put two and two together and decide if it adds up to faith.

The result also offers another parallel with the previous scene in Samaria: as the woman who at first doubted led her townspeople to faith, so this at first doubting *basilikos* leads his "whole household" to believe. Thus, the first Johannine house-community is born.

The chiasm closes in verse 54 with another specific link between the two Cana stories: "This was the second sign which Jesus did having come from Judea into Galilee." Although the recurrence of the word "sign" brings satisfying closure to the chiasm, it stirs once more the doubts raised before the scene began: Are these simply more people who, as Jesus said, believe *because* of the sign? We have been given many varying signals about this believing *basilikos* and his people. As the story ends and the action returns to Jerusalem, all we can know is that faith in Jesus remains mixed with doubt, at least in the land of Cana.

# 9

# "My Father Is Working Now, and I Am Working"

## John 5:1–47

A. **Chiasm:** none for entire section (see subsections)

B. **Location:** Jerusalem Temple

C. **Time:** sabbath

D. **Hebrew scripture context:** Exodus 31 (sabbath); Daniel 12 (raising dead)

E. **Social factors:** Judeans vs. Jesus

F. **Themes:** healing on sabbath; witnesses to Jesus

G. **Key words:** witness, truth, resurrection, sent forth

## 1. HEALING ON THE SABBATH

**Chiasm: 5:1–18**

a: 1–10: Judeans challenge sabbath healing

    b: 11–13: Judeans ask who healed

        c: 14: Jesus and man in Temple

    b¹: 15: man tells Judeans who healed

a¹: 16–18: Judeans persecute Jesus because of sabbath healing[1]

**Chiasm: 5:1–13**

a: 1–3: multitude

    b: 5–9a: healed (*hygiēs*)/pick up your mat and walk

        c: 9b–10: sabbath

    b¹: 11–12: healed (*hygiē*)/pick up your mat and walk

a¹: 13: crowd

---

1. Ellis (1984, 86–87).

The fourth gospel pictures Jesus moving rapidly from province to province; this contrasts with the synoptics, which portray him as largely in Galilee until the climactic journey to Jerusalem for Holy Week. He went from Cana to Jerusalem in chapter 2, spent time in the Judean countryside at the end of chapter 3, passed through Samaria and back to Galilee in chapter 4, and now at the beginning of chapter 5 has returned for the second visit to Jerusalem. Readers might gain several different impressions of this constant movement. At one level, it shows a Jesus not confined to a given place, not bound by a particular "home." He is one who crosses boundaries easily, refusing to be limited by the culture's perspective on where one ought to go. But at the same time, each visit to Jerusalem is accompanied by the narrator's prefatory comment that there was at that time a "feast of the Judeans" (2:13; 5:1). From this perspective, Jesus' travels to Jerusalem are simply the expected behavior of an observant Jew. Another impression is that we are being given only "highlights" of his "dwelling among us" (1:14), a highly selective set of stories that is designed to accomplish the purpose of the storyteller, an impression reinforced by the narrator's comments at the end of chapter 20. Finally, we get the sense that a substantial amount of time is passing as the story unfolds. Although the text never specifies the *movement* of seasons or years — preferring to emphasize the *present* religious season rather than the passage from one season to another — it conveys the feeling that Jesus has been speaking and acting in Palestine for quite a while. As we listen to the story of Jesus' activities in the capital city in chapter 5, we might wonder whether those he encounters remember the necessarily notorious incident of the overturning of the Temple tables and casting out of the sacrificial animals on an earlier Passover visit.

Verse 1 begins the change of scene: "After these things, there was a festival of the Judeans, and Jesus went up to Jerusalem." We are not told *which* festival it was or even that Jesus went *because* of the festival. The time and Jesus' movement are simply juxtaposed, leaving us to draw the inference of connection. Verse 2, like a camera moving in from an aerial view to ground level, describes a specific location in the capital, again without suggesting a link with Jesus: "In Jerusalem there was at the sheepgate a pool, called in Hebrew, 'Bethzatha,' having five porticos." The details suggest personal familiarity with a city totally destroyed by the time the gospel was written. The pool named Bethzatha or Bethesda (in contrast with the Hebrew of 1:38, 41, and Aramaic of 1:42, readers are given no translation of this expressly Hebrew name, which means "house of olives")[2] at the sheepgate is mentioned only here in the Bible. The inclusion of the detail that the gate had "five porticos" suggests a purpose more meaningful than simply picturesque description. Given the Jerusalem site, it is not a leap to associate the porticos with the five books of Moses, the Pentateuch. The city built on the Law would have been likely to contain such numerical symbols, just as Washington, D.C., contains images built on the thirteen states.

---

2. *HBD* 109. The entry notes that an 1871 archaeological team rediscovered the site, complete with the five porticos described.

This initial feeling of royal grandeur is immediately contrasted in verse 3 with the dark side of the Torah-state: "Lying there was a multitude of those sick, blind, lame, and withered." Just as the street-grate sleepers and bag people in the shadow of the White House are a national disgrace that U.S. politicians and other government workers learn to ignore, so these marginalized wounded have come to be a fact of life in the city whose precious Torah promises hospitality and comfort to the poor (e.g., Ex 23:11). But anyone with a sense of the living covenant between God and humanity would be outraged at this sad spectacle of a shuffled-aside multitude.

If the Jerusalem crowds do not remember Jesus' last visit to the capital, readers certainly will. If the presence of sacrificial animals and money changers provoked Jesus' sense of injustice crying for correction, we might expect this pathetic scene to spark a similar reaction. The text will not keep us in suspense for long.

Immediately upon hearing the description of the general scene, the narrator focuses in verse 5 on a particular person in the crowd: "There was one who had been sick for thirty-eight years." The specific ailment is not named, nor even described. It might be inferred to be a handicap that prevents walking, but many illnesses would slow one down enough to prevent a quick trip to the pool. It is enough for the gospel to number this one among the "sick," allowing a more general empathy to develop in readers.

Is there a special meaning to the fact that *is* given about the man's condition: it has lasted for "thirty-eight years"? While historical-critical commentators like Raymond Brown deride the attempt to find symbolism in the number thirty-eight as "unnecessary,"[3] it seems even less likely that such a specific number would be given in this precisely worded text without *some* meaning apart from a supposed "fact" about the person in question. If we search the scriptures (a procedure the Johannine community repeatedly engaged in to figure out what God's word was about [e.g., 2:22; 20:9]), we find this use of the figure in the midst of Moses' summary of the wilderness sojourn, one of only three times it occurs in the Bible:[4]

> And the length of time we had traveled from Kadesh-barnea until we crossed the Wadi Zered was thirty-eight years, until the entire generation of warriors had perished from the camp. (Deut 2:14)

The purpose of Moses' recitation of this bit of history is to emphasize the time required to rid the people of warriors, so that they could enter the land of the Ammonites without communal memory of battle. Without attempting too attenuated a connection, we can say that the number thirty-eight at least has biblical precedent for the span of a generation. The person in focus in Jn 5:5 has been sick longer than anyone (except the narrator) can remember. He is not

---

3. R. Brown (1966, 207).
4. The others are 1 Kgs 16:29 and 2 Kgs 15:8, both indicating kingly succession.

only sick, but also quite old. We might easily imagine such a person with little hope of a life change at this late date.

In verse 6, Jesus suddenly appears on the scene: "Having seen this one lying there and having known that he had been there a long time, he said to him, 'Are you willing [*theleis*] to become healthy [*hygiēs*]?' " The use of the term *theleis* recalls once more the central element in the prologue, the contrast between those of different "wills." Although the sick one cannot consider Jesus' question in these terms, readers may see this as an invitation to rebirth parallel to those preceding it (3:3, 5; 4:10, 14). But which form of negative will is at issue: "bloods" (i.e., violence), "man" (i.e., patriarchy/nationalism), or "flesh" (i.e., dominant cultural attitudes)? The narrator leaves this implicit question suspended for now.

The term *hygiēs,* used here for "healthy," is a rare one in the New Testament. It connotes not healing or cure but the condition of health, something with which the Bible is largely unconcerned.[5] Although its use in connection with "to become" (*genesthai*) associates it with the process of change and not simply a static condition, it is not the usual invitation of a "healer" in ancient Palestine.

The person, identified by the narrator in verse 7 as "the sick one," avoids Jesus' question in favor of what sounds like a stock line he has delivered again and again over the years: "Sir, I have no one when the water is disturbed to throw me into the pool! By the time I am going, another before me is stepping in." The sick one has been counting, for God only knows how long, on a folk tradition of healing waters. His hope is almost a parody of Jesus' offer of "living" (i.e., "moving") water in the previous chapter. Alas, this life-giving pool only serves one at a time, and not a single Judean will help the sick one achieve his pathetic, poignant dream.

Craig Koester provides background by suggesting that the healing-pool setting, although located at the Jerusalem Temple, bears more resemblance to Greco-Roman healing shrines to the gods Asclepius and Serapis, which would have been common in the eastern Mediterranean at that time.[6] Perhaps this is meant as a hint that the Temple's corruption was so deep as to lead the masses to turn to Hellenistic healing practices.

In any event, Jesus has no concern whatsoever for the folk legend. Perhaps no one in thirty-eight years had said the empowering words Jesus pronounces in verse 8: "Rise, pick up your mat and walk!" Three interrelated commands in seven Greek words are enough to invite a reversal of a lifetime of suffering. The narrator in verse 9 describes the response: "And immediately the person became [*egeneto*] healthy [*hygiēs*], and picked up his mat and walked." The command of this stranger produces not only a response but also health.

Just as readers are about to celebrate this victory of curing and empowerment over the stupidity and insensitivity of urban numbness, the mood shifts dramatically, with the narrator's understated but darkly troubling afterword in verse 9b: "The day was the sabbath." It is the great day of God's rest from cre-

---

5. U. Luck, *TDNT* 8:308–313.
6. C. Koester (1994, chap. 2).

ation, the weekly feast day intended religiously to honor God and socially to prevent Israelites from overwork. It is hard to overestimate in our modern ethos of perpetual activity the seriousness with which this sacred feast was held:

> The Lord said to Moses, "You must also tell the Israelites: take care to keep my sabbaths, for that is to be the token between you and me through-out the generations to show that it is I, the Lord [LXX, *egō eimi*], who makes you holy. Therefore, you must keep the sabbath as something sa-cred. Whoever desecrates it shall be put to death. If anyone does work on that day, he must be rooted out of his people. Six days there are for doing work, but the seventh day is the sabbath of complete rest, sacred to the Lord. Anyone who does work on the sabbath day shall be put to death. (Ex 31:12–15)

The threat of expulsion and death is suddenly in the air, replacing the celebra-tory mood with a great ominous tone. Did anybody see Jesus speak to this man the unlawful command? Will anyone at the pool report the man walking with the mat to the authorities? Before we can stop to consider the depth of the threat, the second question is answered in verse 10: "Therefore, the Judeans were say-ing to the one who had been cured [*tetherapeumenō*], 'It is the sabbath, and it is not lawful for you to pick up the mat.'" The walking man, now described by the narrator as the "one having been *cured,*" is suddenly confronted with the abrupt reality of the Law. We are not told who these Judeans are, whether Phar-isees, priests, members of the Sanhedrin, or just folks in the vicinity. Regardless of their particular authority, they bear the weight of tremendous cultural pres-sure; their statement might as well be a command to stop. Note also a subtle implication of their words: whereas Jesus' words expressed the link between the sick one and the sign of his affliction ("*your* mat"), the Judeans do not rec-ognize this connection, focusing on the object only as an implement of illegality ("*the* mat").

We are not told, now or later, whether the cured man either put the mat down or stopped walking. Instead, we hear his ambiguous response in verse 11: "The one who made me healthy [*poiēsas me hygiē*] is the one who said, 'Pick up your mat and walk.'" Is the man passing the buck or witnessing? Commenta-tors formerly agreed that this man was a negative character in the fourth gospel, a "tattletale" blaming Jesus for his problems. Recently, this consensus has been shaken by a reading that sees the man differently, as one who obeys the un-lawful command of a stranger and speaks the truth to his challengers.[7] At this point in the narrative, he remains ambiguous, much as the Samaritan woman who wonders about Jesus' messiahship (4:29) and the *basilikos* who checks the time (4:52). His response expresses a positive link between his health and the man who spoke with him, but he does not take responsibility for his own empowerment.

---

7. Staley (1991, 63–64).

His response, though, is certainly a surprise to the Judeans. They have no reason to know about the cure; it is not of concern to them at all, focused as they are on the violation of the sacred sabbath. It shifts their attention slightly, away from the cured man and to the healer. Picking up his words, we hear in verse 12 for the third time the unlawful phrase, "Pick up and walk." However, the Judeans only imperfectly repeat what the man has told them: "They asked him, 'Who is the person having said to you, 'Pick up and walk'?'" Their paraphrase again omits the "your," which the cured one had reinserted into the topic of conversation. Furthermore, the cured one's own attempt to quote Jesus was already an imperfect repetition of Jesus' command, "*Rise,* pick up your mat and walk." While the latter two imperatives establish the illegality, it is the first one that invites rebirth. Readers, like the cured man, might be excused for not understanding the precise significance of Jesus' words at this stage of the narrative, perhaps seeing "rise" and "walk" as two parts of the same movement. However, in light of the resurrection connotations of the term "rise," we may find ourselves looking back at this passage from a later vantage point and reconsidering the character of the cured man.

Rather than allowing us to hear from the cured man, the narrator steps in to speak for him in verse 13: "But the healed one [*iatheis*] had not known who it was, for Jesus had turned away, there being a crowd in the place." The narrator now changes from speaking of cure to *healing.* The term has even stronger connotations than *therapeuo,* used in verse 10. The latter, although used in the New Testament many times for a sense of divine healing, is used only here in the fourth gospel. But *iaomai,* although used fewer times in the New Testament generally, is a common Septuagint term for God's act of restoring one to right relationship with God.[8] As we shall see, the fourth gospel will also use it in this sense in quoting Isaiah at the end of the first part of the gospel (12:40). Thus, as the pressure over the sabbath violation builds in the conversation between the healed one and the Judeans, readers become increasingly aware that what has happened is not an "earthly" cure but a "heavenly" healing.

The narrator's statement also provides authentication for the man's lack of knowledge, something we might have reason to question if he had spoken for himself in this pressure situation. The statement also provokes retrospective curiosity: *When* did Jesus disappear into the crowd? Just at this moment? Did he overhear the conversation, or was he already on to other business? Also: *Why* did he leave? Did he simply abandon the poor man to the wolves of the Law, or was it a test of the man's fidelity? Was he just busy curing other people gathered around the pool? The text leaves this gap open to readers' imaginations, with substantial questions about Jesus' character — and the burden of discipleship — left hanging in the balance.

In verse 14, the time and place change, although the "scene" continues: "After these things, Jesus found [*euriskei*] him in the Temple." The physical relationship between the pool of suffering/healing and the Temple is unspeci-

---

8. A. Oepke, *TDNT* 3:194–215.

fied, as is the amount of time that has passed. Whether a few minutes later or
a different day altogether, we are not told. But again, it is Jesus who has taken
the initiative by "finding" the man, inverting the process described by Andrew
to his brother Simon in 1:41 ("We have found [eurēkamen] the messiah") but
continuing the established relationship between Jesus and the cured man.

Jesus' words to the man start with a restatement of the obvious but jump suddenly to a very surprising topic: "See, you have become healthy, but don't be
sinning, so that something worse does not happen to you." Why the sudden introduction of the claim that the man has been sinning? What is he doing wrong?
As Jeff Staley points out, the words are a statement of a present condition —
the man is sinning now![9] Jesus is certainly not concerned with his carrying his
mat on the sabbath. In addition to the statement of the man's condition is a dire
warning. What "worse" thing than spending thirty-eight years with an illness
might there be? The only clue the gospel has provided so far lies in the ominous conclusion to chapter 3: "The wrath of God remains" upon the one who
disobeys the Son (3:36). Just as the man's initial illness is left unspecified, so
is his sin. But we are left watching the man closely to see if his behavior will
offer any clues to satisfy our sense of curiosity about him.

In verse 15, we are allowed to observe the healed one's response: "The person went and told the Judeans that Jesus is the one who made him healthy."
Is this act "witness" or "betrayal"? The line is revealed to be finer than we
might have expected. The evidence for and against the man is balanced carefully, preventing an easy judgment about him. In a gospel of light and dark,
the cured man of Bethzatha seems to live in a land of dappled shadow. However, as R. Alan Culpepper points out, when we view this encounter as a unit,
we find contrasts with the previous "signs stories" that suggest a negative conclusion about the healed one.[10] Both Cana incidents — expressly noted by the
narrator as "signs" (2:11; 4:54) — establish the pattern, from which the current
story varies. Whereas at Cana, a supplicant presents Jesus with a request, here
Jesus asks about the person's will to be healed. In the first two episodes, Jesus
rebuffs the request, and the person persists; here, the one by the pool is evasive
while Jesus persists. Finally, at Cana, there is a response of faith and rejoicing;
here, there are a doubtful response and condemnation. Thus, taken as a whole,
the healed one seems to symbolize those who are "drawn" by Jesus to become
children of God but who are unwilling to be born anōthen.

Regardless of his character, the disposition of the Judeans is made crystal
clear in verse 16: "Because of this, the Judeans were persecuting [ediōkon]
Jesus, because he was doing these things on the sabbath." The Judeans' attitude about Jesus on his first trip to Jerusalem was left open (2:20–25). They
may be in the dark for lack of full understanding, as exemplified by Nicodemus and those who believe "because of the signs" only, but the ramifications
for Jesus' ministry have been unstated. Now it is clear: they not only have cho-

---

9. Staley (1991, 62).
10. Culpepper (1993b, 8–11, 17–18).

sen the sacred sabbath over the lawbreaker but also have taken up "persecuting" him. The verb *diōkō* has the double meaning of "to persecute" as well as "to follow zealously" or "to pursue or promote a cause."[11] The narrator's term expresses both implications of the Judeans' choice: to pursue the cause of the Law is to persecute Jesus, the one whose mission leads him to violate, indeed, to ignore, the Law.

How they went about their mission is not told, but it is public enough to provoke a response from Jesus in verse 17: "My Father is still working, and I am working." Jesus has claimed God as "my Father" in the Temple before (2:16), but the Judeans either did not hear or missed the implication at the time. Now, his proclamation immediately ups the ante in verse 18: "Because of this, therefore, the Judeans were seeking to kill him, because not only was he tearing down [*elye*] the sabbath, but he was also saying God was his own Father, making himself equal to God." From "persecuting" Jesus, the Judeans began "seeking to kill" him. Jesus earlier asked his first disciples what they were "seeking" (1:38), but there is no need to ask the Judeans this question. For the rest of the fourth gospel, they will pursue this "seeking" mission with a vengeance. The narrator's closing comments on the scene express the double charge against him: (1) violation of the sabbath and (2) "making himself equal to God." For the reader of the prologue, there is a subtle but crucial mistake in their charge. Their complaint is that, although a human, he is *making himself* something he is "obviously" not. But readers are in on the secret: the one who is the living Logos is not making himself anything that he has not been from "the beginning."

The verb *lyō,* translated here as "tearing down" the sabbath, is the same used by Jesus in his metaphor about "tearing down" the Temple (2:19). With this remark, the battle lines are drawn: Jesus' messianic mission involves tearing down the twin pillars of the Judean state. There is no disagreement about these goals. The only question is the one for which the Judeans assume they know the answer: Is Jesus just another criminal deserving death or is he the one sent by God deserving discipleship?

## 2. "THE HOUR IS COMING... AND IS HERE NOW"

### Chiasm: 5: 19–30

a: 19–23: Son can do nothing on own; judgment; Jesus' "will"

   b: 24–25: hour is coming when dead hear voice

      c: 26–27: Father gives Son authority to judge

   b¹: 28–29: hour is coming when those in tombs hear voice

a¹: 30: I can do nothing on own/judgment; Jesus' "will"[12]

---

11. A. Oepke, *TDNT* 2:229–230.

12. Ellis (1984, 90–91) notes this chiasm. I have noted further details that reinforce the parallels, namely, Jesus' "will."

The following chiastic section begins the first "public" discourse of Jesus in the fourth gospel. Previously, we recall, he has spoken only to individuals or his disciples as a group. Now, in Jerusalem at an unnamed feast — but on the sabbath — Jesus proclaims in verse 19 for "them" to hear.

The form of the "sabbath discourse" is that of a trial defense. Repeatedly, we hear the language of judgment and witnesses, as Jesus takes up his response to the twin charges of civil disobedience, focusing in verses 19–29 on the accusation of "making himself equal to God."

Jerome Neyrey has clearly shown the forensic nature of the confrontation beginning back in verse 10 with the Judeans' charge of a violation of the Law.[13] The declaration of a crime and questioning leading to the accusation against Jesus generate the first part of the ongoing trial narrative that will continue until Jesus' burial in chapter 19. From the social perspective of first-century Judaism, a trial was not so much an "investigation of facts" as a "declaration on the admissibility and competence of witnesses."[14] Paul S. Minear points out the dual nature of the courtroom: from the Judean perspective (i.e., the "earthly" courtroom), Jesus is on trial as a lawbreaker and blasphemer. But from Jesus' perspective (i.e., the "heavenly" courtroom), his accusers are on trial for preferring human glory to God's glory (5:41–44).[15] Both of these perspectives reflect the story world. But in the discourse world, the trial reveals the Johannine community's perspective on *their* persecutors as being themselves "accused" by Moses (5:45) of disbelieving the scriptures. As the trials proceed, these various viewpoints are interwoven into the words of Jesus.

Neyrey claims that the first part of the discourse reflects a two-part defense "strategy" of showing Jesus' relationship to the two powers traditionally attributed to God: creation and judgment, the powers of the "beginning" and the "end."[16] Philo of Alexandria, a Jewish philosopher of the first century, describes these two aspects of God as the *dynamis poiētikē* and *dynamis basilikē,* the creative power and the royal power.[17] Philo expressly relates these powers to symbols important to Johannine theology:

> And from the divine Logos as from a spring, there divide and break forth two powers. One is the creative power through which the Artificer placed and ordered all things: this is named "God." And the other is the royal

---

13. Neyrey (1988, 9–35, esp. 10). Neyrey provides valuable background on the forensic context of the discourse, although his exegesis is limited by his use of historical methodology that insists on focusing on the text as a series of redactional "layers," failing to take seriously the text as an integrated literary whole. See also Harvey (1972).

14. Neyrey (1988, 11).

15. Minear (1984, 96).

16. Neyrey (1988, 23–27). Neyrey divides the discourse at verse 29, claiming verse 30 as the beginning of the defense against the sabbath-violation charge. However, this separation totally ignores the chiastic structure of the discourse, which clearly links verse 30 with the preceding verses, as well as the language of judgment that, according to Neyrey's own argument, is part of the "eschatological" defense against the charge of claiming to be "equal to God" and not part of the defense against the charge of sabbath violation.

17. Cited in Neyrey (1988, 25–27).

power, since through it the Creator rules over created things; this is called "Lord."[18]

These two powers reflect the traditional scriptural image of God's often paradoxical nature as merciful and just, or, as taken up in Johannine discourse, God's "grace and truth" (1:17), on the one hand, and God's "wrath" (3:36), on the other. Jesus has already expressed his unity with God's creative power in 5:17, in terms of the shared continuity of his and his Father's "work," a term understood by many early Jewish commentators as an expression of God's creative activity *not* interrupted by the sabbath.[19] In 5:19–29, the defense of "equal to God" is expressed in terms of Jesus' participation in God's eschatological/royal power.

Commentators have traditionally divided this section of the discourse into two components, 5:19–25 and 26–30, seeing the first as an example of "realized eschatology" and the latter as an expression of "final eschatology."[20] These terms signify what is a popular scholarly distinction in the fourth gospel distinguishing it from the synoptics and the Pauline literature. Whereas the synoptics and Paul sometimes picture a future return of Jesus in judgment (the so-called Second Coming), upon which the early church eagerly awaited (e.g., Mt 24:29–31), the fourth gospel portrays both a final judgment *and* a present judgment (e.g., Jn 16:11, 33). However, José Miranda, who, as a liberation theologian, is concerned with finding a scriptural message that offers hope *now* to a suffering people, provides a different hermeneutical perspective. Whereas traditional scholarship, seeing these as two inconsistent eschatological messages, has argued over which viewpoint came first in terms of the editorial history of the text, Miranda claims that "there is absolutely no literary basis for holding that the content of Jn 5:21–25 differs from that of Jn 5:26–30."[21]

What is the "content" of the defense set out in these verses? The chiastic centerpiece focuses the surrounding verses. In harmony with the "two-powers" perspective, verses 25–26 expressly claim that Jesus has received both powers from God. In verse 25, Jesus as "Son" (without a qualifier such as "of God") has the same power of "life in himself" as does his Father. In verse 26, as "Human One" or "Son of Humanity," Jesus claims the receipt of God's authority to judge. In this interpretation, the ideological and literary elements of our method combine in a way that the tools of traditional scholarship have not. As Miranda's and Neyrey's social analysis reveals the purpose of the defense as providing support to the Johannine community's claim of Jesus' divine authority in response to Judean charges of blasphemy, so Peter Ellis's chiastic literary analysis points to both the unity of the passage and its interpretive center in verses 25–26.

---

18. Philo *Q. Ex.* 2.68, cited in Neyrey (1988, 26).
19. Neyrey (1988, 21).
20. E.g., R. Brown (1966, 219).
21. Miranda (1977, 182).

Having gained our bearings from a look at the passage as a whole, we can return to verse 19 to see how it unfolds. Jesus begins with a double-amen saying indicating the seriousness of his following words: "Amen, amen I am saying to you: the Son is not able [*dynatai*] to do [*poiein*] anything from himself, but only what he sees the Father doing [*poiounta*]. What that one may do [*poiē*], these things the Son also is doing [*poiei*]." The statement takes the form of what Miranda calls a simple parable of apprenticeship: "The parable is simply saying that an artisan teaches his son the skills of his trade."[22] It is an expression of Jesus' imitation of his Father's *creative power*, as seen through the use in verse 19 of the terms used by Philo, *dynatai* and *poiounta/poiē/poiei*. Lying subtly in this verse is a confirmation of the prologue's claim about the unique perspective of Jesus as the one who has "seen" God (1:18). It is Jesus' *observation* of the creative activity of his Father that enables him to imitate what he sees.

In verse 20, the defense gives a surprising justification for God's grant of authority to Jesus: "For the Father has affection [*philei*] for the Son, and is showing him all things [*panta*] which he is doing." This is the first statement by Jesus of his emotional relationship with God, and it is provided in the relatively weak language of *philea* rather than the stronger language of *agapē*. God seemingly has *agapē* for the world (3:16) but only *philea* for the Son! The text will eventually express God's *agapē* for Jesus (10:17), but at this point, it provides only *philea* as a justification for God's revelation to Jesus.

The verse continues as a segue between the creativity and judgment elements of Jesus' defense: "And he will show him greater works than these, so that you may wonder." The reference to "these" is ambiguous and creates a reading gap: Is Jesus comparing the relatively minor act of empowering a sick person to walk with the announcement of his power to raise the dead in the following verse? Are the "works" the violations of the sabbath Law that will be exceeded by the eventual rejection of the Law altogether? Is Jesus comparing the claim to continue working as his Father does with the text's (but not Jesus') claim that Jesus is the messiah himself? By leaving the gap unfilled, the text creates an expectation that any or all of these deeds and words of Jesus may be exceeded by things revealed to Jesus but not as yet to the audience or readers.

Jesus says that the response of the observers of his actions will be to "wonder" (*thaumazēte*). This word, associated in the synoptics with the crowd's response to a miracle (e.g., Mk 5:20; Lk 11:14), has only negative connotations in the fourth gospel. In 3:7, Jesus told Nicodemus's people *not* to wonder about being born *anōthen,* and in 4:27, the narrator uses the term to describe Jesus' disciples' response to his conversation with a woman. In 5:20, then, it expresses the uncomprehending surprise that Jesus predicts will be the response of the Judeans to the "greater" works that the Father will show to the Son.

Suddenly, the discourse shifts magnitude in verse 21: "For even as the Father is raising the dead and making them alive [*zōopoiei*], so also the Son is making

---

22. Ibid., 141–142.

alive those whom he wills [*thelei*]." Not only power to heal but power to "raise the dead" and "make alive" belongs to the Son! To a modern Christian audience, this is, of course, familiar enough doctrine. But to Jesus' audience within the story world, no more shocking claim can be imagined. The very expectation of a resurrection of judgment was a relatively new concept in the Hebrew scriptures, first appearing in Dan 12:2–3, verses clearly underlying the entire thrust of Jesus' eschatological claim:[23]

> Many of those who sleep
> in the dust of the earth shall awake;
> some shall live forever;
> others shall be an everlasting horror and disgrace.
> But the wise shall shine brightly
> like the splendor of the firmament,
> and those who lead the many to justice
> shall be like the stars forever.

The term *zōopoiei* is not found in the other gospels.[24] But in this Johannine context, it serves to bridge the themes of the Father's and Son's "doing" and the ultimate creative power of giving life. It adds to the more common "raising the dead" by suggesting the completion of a two-part process. *First* one is raised, and *then* one can be given life again.

Verse 22 amplifies the claim with an even more surprising statement: "For the Father judges no one, but has given all judgment to the Son." This moves beyond the apprenticeship metaphor of verses 19–20 into the claim of an absolute donation of power. Jesus does not judge *as* he sees the Father judging, but *instead* of the Father! At first, this appears to contradict what we have heard in 3:17 about the Son's mission *not* to judge but to save the world. But a careful reading of the entirety of 5:21–30 shows that its claims are in fact consistent with 3:17–21. *Authority to judge* is given to the Son, but *judgment itself* is a self-imposed reality, based on the preference of people for darkness rather than light, for the covering up of foul deeds rather than the gradual movement toward light and truth (3:19–21). The issue in chapter 5, we remember, is not the fact of judgment but the defense of Jesus' deeds and words. And the specific issue in the chiasm of verses 19–30 is the justification in terms of Jesus' bipartite sharing of God's powers. Verse 23 makes this clear: the purpose of the grant of authority is "so that all may honor the Son just as they honor the Father . . . who sent him."

Verse 23 uses the term for "honoring" (*timōsi*) four times. Although the term "honor" represents an extremely complex aspect of the implicit social code of ordinary life in New Testament times,[25] it also bears the specific biblical conno-

---

23. R. Brown (1966, 220).
24. It is, though, found in the Pauline literature approximately twelve times.
25. See, generally, Malina (1981, 25–48).

tation of God's royal dignity.[26] It is a first implicit expression of Jesus' kingly nature, a theme that will be emphasized in the trial before Pilate.

The passage continues in verse 24 with a second double-amen saying, one that shifts from the visual metaphor of 5:19 to an auditory image: "the one hearing my word [*logon*] and believing in the one who sent me has life everlasting and is not coming into judgment but has gone from death into life." The emphasis throughout the verse is on a *present* state of things. Again, the reference is to the action of the hearer as avoiding judgment rather than to a nonjudgment or positive judgment by the Son. Note also that, although the fourth gospel will eventually focus on the issue of faith in Jesus (20:31), the focus now is on *hearing* Jesus and believing in the *one who sent him.* Finally, in contrast with those who conceive of "eternal life" as something following death, the text has Jesus clearly offer this mysterious gift as an aspect of the current reality of his hearers. The hearer who believes has passed *now* from death to life!

The auditory image continues in verse 25, as Jesus offers his third double-amen saying in seven verses. The "hour is coming and is now when the dead will hear the voice of the Son of God and the ones having heard will live." The first phrase is identical to the one expressed to the Samaritan woman in 4:23 about true worshipers: "the hour is coming and is now!" As Jesus announced to the Samaritans the imminence of the new community, so he also offers this news to the Judeans.

Implicit within this imagery is a question: Is Jesus literally talking about dead people, or is this simply another Johannine double entendre, like being born *anōthen* or receiving living water? To the extent that Jesus' discourse invites his current listeners (and readers) to hear, believe, and pass from death to life, it is clearly metaphorical. "Death" from this perspective consists of all the elements of a person's earthly life that block the flow of *God's* life within that person and within a community. Jesus invites the believer to leave these dead elements behind so that he or she can be reborn. But, of course, this is not simply an invitation to individual transformation. Jesus in the story world is speaking to an audience of *Judeans,* those committed to the Temple/Torah system. The "death" in their lives is the elevation of the Law over "eternal life." For the reading audience, this is a challenge to be reborn from commitment to slavish loyalty to dead social systems that, although perhaps once well-intended, have, like Judean purification jars, run out of life-giving power. The alternative is to be found in Johannine community, that is, discipleship gatherings centered on the life-giving power of Jesus. Thus, the discourse continues in verses 26–27, at the chiastic center, by reinforcing the presence both of God's creative life power and of God's royal power of judgment in Jesus.

As we cross to the other side of the chiasm, we reach in verse 28 the nonmetaphorical connotation of the power of resurrection: "Do not wonder [*thaumazete*] at this, because the hour is coming in which all those *in the tombs* will also hear the voice, because he is the Human One!" While scholarship has

---

26. J. Schneider, *TDNT* 8:170.

usually focused on the temporal contrast between verses 25 and 28, it has not given sufficient attention to the addition in verse 28 of this concrete reference to the seemingly impenetrable enclosure of death, the tomb. Again, we hear the term *thaumazete* used negatively with regard to the audience's reaction to Jesus' double claim of God's power in verses 26–27. If they are mystified by the metaphorical giving of life to the dead, wait until they experience the literal! While we heard in verse 25 of the present movement from death to life, in verse 28, this is given only in future terms. But, with Miranda, we note that the fourth gospel is not attempting to postpone the eschaton into some infinite future.[27] It is only putting it off until the narration of the raising of Lazarus in chapter 11.

Recalling the language of 3:19–21, the current passage characterizes in verse 29 the contrast between the "resurrection of life" and the "resurrection of judgment" in terms of "good deeds" (*hagatha*) and "foul deeds" (*phaula*). The surprising aspect of the description is not so much the split between good and foul deeds, but the claim that "*all* will hear his voice." Among the living, judgment is avoided by those who are hearing Jesus' voice. Among the dead, all will *hear,* but only those whose lives were oriented toward God will be raised to *life*. Interestingly, the living who believe are given "eternal life," while those in the tombs come out "only" to "life"! The point is not a comparative devaluing of "mere" life, but simply the emphasis on "eternal life" as an aspect of present reality.

The chiasm closes with a summary repetition in verse 30: Jesus from himself "can do nothing" (*ou dynamai egō poiein*), but judges as he hears, linking the royal-auditory power with the creative-visual power in 5:19. Recalling the Danielic theme, Jesus characterizes his judgment as "just." The final phrase adds a note of ambiguity that leaves open what might otherwise seem closed, that is, the identity of Jesus' "will" and that of God's. Although phrased in terms of Jesus "seeking" not his will but the will of the one who sent him, it suggests the *possibility* that Jesus' will might be different than God's *if* he was not constantly watching and listening to what God does and says. But the fourth gospel is not interested in theoretical questions about Jesus and his Father; rather, it is concerned with the practical implications for discipleship of what in fact Jesus says and does. Reflecting this emphasis, one might paraphrase Jesus' words: "*If* I were seeking my own will, my judgment would not necessarily be just, *but* as it is, it *is* just." In other words, the justice of Jesus' judgment does not have to do with an appropriate decision about a particular situation or person. Rather, the point is that the *basis* of the judgment is focused on moral behavior, not (as the Judeans would have it) on obedience to the Law and its sabbath regulations. The Judeans had believed that these were always one and the same. But confronted with the question of healing on the sabbath, they faced the judgment — the *krisis* — that determined their religious affiliation and their future relation-

---

27. Miranda (1977, 179–180).

ship with God. The chiasm closes, then, with opposing standards of judgment upon which each party to the trial will judge the other.

### 3. THE WITNESSES TO JESUS

**Chiasm: 5:31–47**

a: 31–32: another witnesses to me

   b: 34–35: not receive witness from humans

      c: 36–40: works, Father, scripture as witnesses

   b¹: 41–44: not receive glory from humans

a¹: 45–47: Moses wrote of me[28]

### a. *"So That You Might Be Saved"*

**Chiasm: 5:31–38**

a: 31–32: another witnessing to me

   b: 33–34a: you sent forth to John (the Baptist); John (the Baptist) bore witness; not accept witness from humans

      c: 34b: I say these things so that you may be saved

   b¹: 35–36: witness greater than John (the Baptist) = works of Father; Father sent forth Jesus

a¹: 37–38: Father witnesses to me

The opening argument of the trial is over. As the Judeans stated their charge and basis for judgment in 5:10, 16, 18, now Jesus has stated his version of the charge and basis. Whereas their *charge* was a violation of the sabbath Law and blasphemy (really a single charge against the Torah) and their *judgment* the mandate of the Torah (that sabbath violators should be put to death), Jesus' *charge* against them is that they do not hear the voice of God, and the basis for *judgment* is their doing of foul deeds. We can now see the entire passage of verses 19–47 as an integrated trial narrative. The first chiasm opened the case with a summary of what each side wished to prove; the second chiasm sets forth the witnesses for Jesus and his summary of his case against the Judeans. Their own witnesses will get their turn in 7:15–24, when the trial continues. The change in the phase of the trial is expressed verbally by the use of some form of the key word "witness" *eleven times* in verses 31–39.

Structurally, Jesus' witnesses overlap the smaller chiasms I have noted but are all contained within the larger chiastic unit of 5:31–47. The first witness, Jesus himself, is introduced in verse 31: "If I bear witness about myself, my witness is not true." He acknowledges that his own testimony is not only insufficient but "not true" if unsubstantiated. Like the previous statement about

---

28. Ellis (1984, 93–94).

Jesus and the Father's will, the sentence expresses a contrafactual situation that reinforces the truth of the reality. Jesus is *not* a lone witness!

The first substantiating witness is offered in verse 32: "Another is witnessing about me, and I have known that his witness about me is true witness." Having established suspense in this introduction, Jesus continues in verse 33 by naming this second witness: "You have sent forth people to John, and he has borne witness to the truth." The validity of John's testimony is underscored by Jesus' repeated linkage between his witness and "truth." Not only does Jesus "know" that John's witness is true (verse 32), but the Judeans themselves have heard it from John's own mouth. This is the first time Jesus' current audience is expressly revealed as more than simply a gathering of ordinary Judeans in the Temple for the feast. They are the same ones who sent forth priests and Levites into the desert to question John in the opening scene of the gospel (1:19). In case readers had any doubt about the seriousness of the trial, it is now clear that Jesus' persecutors and threatening killers are members of the Sanhedrin itself, the highest Judean authority in Jerusalem.

But having established the validity of John's witness, Jesus disclaims his need for it in verse 34: "But I do not receive [*lambanō*] witness from people, but I am saying these things so that you might be saved." Jesus has not called John "to the stand" to prove his innocence, but so that his hearers "might be saved." The judgment that the Judeans threaten to render *on themselves* with the "foul deed" of persecuting and killing Jesus is not inevitable. If they would only put two and two together and acknowledge the truth of what they hear!

The use of *lambanō* recalls the contrasting negative in 3:32, that the one from above bears witness, but "no one receives" (*lambanei*) it. The proper direction of receiving is from above to below, from heaven to earth, from God's voice to human ears and hearts. The nonhearers are wrong to fail to receive Jesus' word from above, but Jesus is right not to "receive" witness from below, even the witness of John.

Another surprising piece of information about John is provided in verse 35: "That one was a burning and shining [*phaniōn*] lamp, and you were willing to exult [*agalliathēnai*] in his light for an hour." John was not "the light" (1:8) but was still a revelatory lamp, perhaps evoking Ps 132:17: "There I will cause a horn to sprout up for David; I have prepared a lamp for my anointed one." The word *phaniōn* shares a root with *phaneroō*, to reveal, which John described as his function in 1:31. But John was only a temporary illumination in the darkness. This reinforcement of both the narrator's and John's self-description of his role is not itself surprising. What is unexpected is that Jesus' audience once *was* "willing" to "exult" for an "hour" in his light. The word *agalliathēnai* is rare in the New Testament and in the Bible generally, being used in a cultic sense to express the eschatological joy of God's definitive presence (e.g., Lk 1:44, 58). Could it be that the members of the Sanhedrin were once this excited about this John whom they would eventually throw in prison (3:24)?

When was this period of their exultation? Before they sent priests and Levites to question him? Or did it occur after their emissaries returned and as a *result* of what they reported? The latter seems impossible, yet the former is equally surprising. It suggests, perhaps, that John once spoke and acted in Judea, even in Jerusalem, but retreated to the desert once his ministry became too threatening to the authorities. It is a possibility no other gospel considers. The meaning for the fourth gospel is that the process from John to Jesus is more gradual than readers might otherwise have thought. First, they exulted in John for "an hour." Then, John moved to the desert to start a separate community, which led the Judeans to seek him and challenge him there. This led John to witness to the advent of Jesus and to the transfer of the loyalty of some of John's disciples to Jesus. After this, the authorities condemned John to prison (but we are not told in the fourth gospel whether he was "persecuted" or killed — perhaps readers are expected to know of this tradition without being told). Finally, Jesus arrives and his activities lead to an eschatological *krisis* in Judea, which will eventually lead to his own "hour." Readers are left with the image of Sanhedrin members who are not perpetually blind and deaf but who grow gradually more rigid and murderous as God's surprising will unfolds in their midst.

If these erstwhile rejoicers in John are not convinced of the truth by this, then Jesus has a "greater" witness to introduce in verse 36: "the works which the Father has given me to complete." What "works" have they seen so far? Only two have been generally visible to the Judeans: the expulsion of the money changers and animals from the Temple and the very healing at issue here. Perhaps word of Jesus' activities in Galilee might have made it to the present audience, especially via the *basilikos*. Perhaps Jesus is inviting his listeners to wait and see what will happen next, to withhold their judgment until they have the bigger picture. Whatever the intended scope of reference of his "works,"[29] Jesus expects the Judeans to be able to base their judgment in part on what they see Jesus saying and doing, not simply on the human witness of John.

Jesus now pulls out the trump card in verse 37. Not only are John's and Jesus' works witnesses for Jesus, but "the Father who sent me has himself borne witness about me." How has this taken place? Jesus does not answer this question but instead continues by echoing the conclusion of the prologue for the second time: "You have never heard his voice nor seen his figure..." (verse 37b). Jesus does what he sees the Father doing (5:19) and judges as he hears (5:30), but the Judeans have *never* heard nor seen God. As Raymond Brown has pointed out, Jesus' claim runs directly in the face of the exodus tradition that God made the divine voice and countenance known to the people on behalf of Moses so that they would trust Moses "forever" (Ex 19:9, 11).[30] The Johannine Jesus not only claims his own direct experience of God as Father but also denies that of the Judeans! The Judeans with whom Jesus is contending, of course, were not at Mt. Sinai themselves, but would claim their ancestors'

---

29. In order to resolve the tension in the naming of unspecified "works" as a witness for Jesus, many scholars have attempted to reduce this witness to either the words of Jesus (Von Wahlde [1981], 390–391]) or the witness of God directly (Neyrey [1988], 13]). This, however, denies the narrative power of ambiguity and its effect on the readers.

30. R. Brown (1966, 225).

experience as their own. As we have seen and will continue to see, Jesus' argument is not over the veracity of the exodus experience or the sanctity of the Torah itself, but with the hypocrisy of those who claim holiness simply by having descended from their revered ancestors. It is as if he is saying, "Your — and my — ancestors may well have seen God as I have, but you have not!" His objection goes to the heart of one's relationship with a religious tradition. Does each generation of the community *inherit* the covenant as an established entity, or does each generation *forge its own* covenant with God out of the common symbols and stories from the past?

The implications of their lack of experience of God are made clear in verse 38: "You do not have his word [*logon*] remaining in you, because the one whom that one sent forth you do not believe." This statement is an ironic double entendre, lost on his Judean audience but clear enough to the Johannine community. Jesus *is* God's word, the one who "remains" with his disciples, and the Judeans' failure to believe in him as the one sent from God proves what they are missing. For the Judeans, though, Jesus' words suggest an even deeper lack, going to the heart of the Deuteronomic discourse given by Moses on the edge of the Promised Land:

> The word is very near to you; it is in your mouth and in your heart for you to observe. (Deut 30:14)

Whether taken as the word spoken of by Moses or incarnated by Jesus, the charge that the Judeans lack it is a grave challenge indeed.

### b. *"Moses Wrote about Me"*

**Chiasm: 5:39–47**

a: 39–40: scriptures you search; you are not willing
   b: 41–42: not glory from humans
      c: 43: I come in Father's name
   b$^1$: 44: you receive glory from one another
a$^1$: 45–47: Moses wrote of me, you are not believing

The final chiasm in the discourse takes up this theme of God's presence in word in verse 39: "You are searching [*eraunate*] the scriptures, because you think that in them you have eternal life." Jesus begins by conceding the good intentions of the Judeans. Brown suggests that the Greek word for "searching" translates the Hebrew *daras,* the rabbinical term for scripture study.[31] They are not simply finding proof texts in a legal case but are trying to find "eternal life." The problem from Jesus' perspective (and that of the Johannine community) is that if they were *really* looking for eternal life in the scriptures, they would recognize its presence in Jesus.

---

31. Ibid.

The mystery of the Judeans' sincere search but refusal to acknowledge the fruit when they find it was one of the greatest puzzles the Johannine community had to face, one that surfaces again and again in the fourth gospel (e.g., 12:37–43). It is similarly a problem that haunts discipleship communities in our own day: Why are so many religious leaders who claim to follow Jesus and who quote the Bible regularly so unwilling to recognize God's presence in the works of justice and peace? Why can so many ordinary Christians not hear the call to serve the poor and establish the beloved community together? It is not a question of moral superiority, of "holier than thou." Jesus' disciples in the fourth gospel are hardly portrayed as pious saints! But, despite their stumbling and despite their sinfulness, despite their fears and doubts and confusions, they do *hear* God's word in Jesus calling them to live differently. Although they may not live it out any better than others, the Johannine community members do not deny the truth of what they see and hear. And yet, so many today are like those to whom Jesus speaks in verse 40: "And you are not willing [*thelete*] to come to me that you may have life," preferring to remain locked up in the dark palaces of worldly comfort and privilege.

This is what Jesus contrasts with his own mind-set in verses 41–44. Jesus does not "receive" human glory (verse 41), but his audience is "receiving [*lambanontes*] glory from one another" (verse 44, filling the opposite chiastic pair). In the Johannine ideology, these "glories" are mutually exclusive, representing what the liberation theologians call the "fundamental option." Just as Jesus has contrasted the way of earth and heaven, the way of flesh and spirit, the way of darkness and light, now he contrasts the glory of "one another" with the glory of God. The person seeking one cannot receive the other. This stark reality may seem too dualistic in our liberal, pluralistic world, but it expresses a truth for the Johannine community that seems absolute. It is not that people in ordinary life do not participate in seeking and accepting both types of glory, but that in the moments in life when one is actually seeking God's glory, one becomes in fact disinterested in human glory, and vice versa. Rather than seeing Jesus' words as harshly judgmental, one might find them an accurate and astute psychological assessment of how people really are.

Jesus tells them not only that they do not have God's word in them but also that they are lacking in God's love (*agapēn,* verse 42). It is really saying the same thing, for as 1 Jn 4:16 adds, "God *is* love." Jesus continues in verse 43 by expressly placing his audience in the category of those named in the prologue (1:11): "I have come in the name of my Father, and you are not receiving me. But if another comes in their own name, you will receive that one." Who might the one coming in their own name be? Maybe it is simply a rhetorical question that means: "If someone were to come in their own name, you would receive him." But perhaps it bears a specific reference that will not be revealed until the final moments of the lifetime of Jesus. For the moment, the text leaves this gap open, perhaps unnoticed, awaiting the "hour" in which all will be revealed.

Jesus' argument has changed from a defense to a prosecution. Whereas he was occupied in verses 31–37 with naming witnesses on his behalf, he has since gathered witnesses *against* the Judeans. The Father not only bears witness about Jesus; the *absence of his word* bears witness against the Judeans. Similarly two-edged is the witness of scripture. In verse 45, Jesus expressly speaks about playing the "accuser" (*katēgoron*) to the Father against the Judeans. But in an incredible, last moment, courtroom flash, Jesus brings in a surprise prosecutor: "Moses, in whom you have hoped"! What more shocking turn of events can be imagined? The Judeans certainly have seen the issue as Moses versus Jesus, the Law versus "equal to God." To Jesus, though, anyone who hears or sees God is on Jesus' side in this case. The Judeans have misframed the case. If they had believed Moses, they would believe Jesus, for "that one wrote about me" (5:46). Moses has instead become a *katēgoron,* the root from which the Hebrew term *satan* is derived. The tables have turned completely around. The Judeans have all the evidence they need to believe in Jesus, but are on the edge of catastrophic self-judgment. Nowhere does Jesus exercise judgment himself in this courtroom scene. He is speaking not to judge, but to save (5:34). There is still time to respond, but the clock is ticking toward the onset of night.

# 10

# The New Exodus

## *Munching the Bread of Life*

## John 6:1–71

### 1. FEEDING WITH GOD'S BREAD: JOHN 6:1–15

**A. Chiasm: 6:1–15**

    a: 1–3: multitude/Jesus to mountain; signs

      b: 4–9: loaves/fish: hunger

        c: 10: seating

      b¹: 11–13: loaves/fish: filled

    a¹: 14–15: people/Jesus to mountain; signs[1]

**B. Location:** a mountain on "the other side of the sea" (Galilee)

**C. Time:** near Passover

**D. Hebrew scripture context:** Ex 16:16; Num 11:13; Psalm 107

**E. Social factors:** the "crowd" and the community

**F. Themes:** Jesus is greater than Moses

**G. Key words:** loaves/fish, signs

Jesus completes his closing trial argument at the end of chapter 5, but we are told nothing of how his outrageous claims are heard by his audience. Readers cannot help but anticipate that these Judeans who were prepared to kill Jesus for the simple statement of the continuity of his own work

---

1. Ellis (1984, 100). I have added the parallel detail of the "signs."

with his Father's work are *really* angry now. Far from acquitting himself in their eyes, he has compounded the problem by denying the Judeans' own relationship with God. The scene closes with electric tension permeating the "courtroom."

At the beginning of chapter 6, the scene changes instantly from Jerusalem at sabbath to Galilee "near Passover." Jesus' second "ministry tour" is on its return trip.[2] We might immediately recall the ambiguous signals about "Galilee" at the end of chapter 4, signals that left us wondering whether the festival/sign-based faith of the Galileans was sufficient. In case we have forgotten, the narrator "reminds" us indirectly in 6:2 with the statement that the "great crowd was following him because they saw the signs he was doing upon the sick." But despite the ambiguity, this response certainly seems more positive than what Jesus left behind in Jerusalem.

The entire chapter illustrates a Johannine faith-building and faith-challenging technique that we have already seen in the Nicodemus and Samaritan woman episodes. Jesus takes his hearers/observers where they are and, using symbols and metaphors from their own tradition, leads them steadily to a life-determining choice, a *krisis* that they cannot avoid. Nicodemus began with the startling yet still acceptable notion of Jesus as a "teacher come from God" and was challenged with the demand to be born *anōthen*. The Samaritan woman sought an end to water-gathering and wound up with a question about the messiah. Here, the Galilean crowd proclaims Jesus "the prophet" but find themselves faced with the "impossible" challenge to "munch flesh" and "drink blood." As Wayne A. Meeks has expressed it:

> In the chapter as a whole, the movement is from a concept familiar to Jews (something which comes down from heaven is given by the hand of a prophet), but doubted in the specific instance of Jesus, to their total alienation by his outrageous claim to be himself that which comes down from heaven — and returns thither.[3]

This opening scene bears many parallel details to the core of the conversation in 4:6–25:

| | |
|---|---|
| 4:6/6:3: | Jesus sat |
| 4:8/6:5b: | buy food/bread |
| 4:11b/6:5b: | "where from" [*pothen*] water/bread |
| 4:18/6:9: | five husbands/loaves |
| 4:19/6:14b: | prophet |
| 4:31/6:5b: | eat |
| 4:20/6:3: | mountain |
| 4:25/6:15: | messiah/king[4] |

---

2. Staley (1988, 72–73).
3. Meeks (1972, 59).
4. Ellis (1984, 105–106).

As Jesus left Judea for Samaria in 4:3–4, now he similarly leaves Judea for Galilee. The unfolding text creates the expectation of challenge and the possibility of messianic faith.

The scene opens in verse 1 with Jesus crossing to the "other side of the sea [*thalassēs*] of Galilee of Tiberias." This is the first reference in the fourth gospel to this important body of water, generally known outside the gospels as a "lake" and not a "sea." The image of "sea" is mentioned 289 times in the Hebrew scriptures, almost always in reference to the primal sea of crossing, the Red (Reed) Sea, the transversal of which marked the beginning of the exodus journey in Exodus 11.

The specific naming of this sea as "of Galilee of Tiberias" is fraught with social significance. The name "Tiberias" occurs in the Bible only in the fourth gospel (also at 6:23 and 21:1, where it is used without "Galilee"). It associates the sea/lake with the city of Tiberias mentioned later in 6:23.[5] The city, named for Tiberius Caesar, was founded by the Jewish tetrarch Herod Antipas around 18 C.E. to replace Sepphoris as the capital of Galilee. It was apparently founded upon a necropolis — a city of the dead — which made it unclean under the Torah. However, the wealthy were nevertheless attracted to it by its location on a popular trade route linking Syria with Egypt and its government offices. This in turn also attracted the poor with the promise of land and housing. It developed a certain degree of sovereignty under Roman rule, electing its own *archōn* (the title given to Nicodemus in 3:1) and minting its own coins. During the Jewish War with Rome in 66–70, it was captured by Josephus (before he retired to become a historian) and was surrendered to the Roman general Vespasian, averting destruction and leading to its continuity under Jewish rule at the time of the Johannine community, despite the destruction of Jerusalem. In the second century, despite its impure origins, the city became the home of a powerful rabbinical school, whose influence lasted for one thousand years.

Thus, the "great crowd" that follows Jesus in 6:2 is likely comprised of the poor who are "unclean" under the Law just by the fact of their residence. In their pursuit of basic economic security, they had chosen to let go of the religious security of Torah obedience. In the world of the Johannine community, these people were not a historical relic like the Jerusalem priests, but a thriving mass of humanity in search of satisfaction of their hunger.

The narrator tells us in verse 2 that "a large crowd was following him, because they saw the signs which he was doing upon the sick." Whether this includes the healing stories readers have witnessed (the *basilikos*'s son and the man at the pool), we are not told. The important signal is the reference to "signs." We recall 2:23–24, where we were first told that Jesus did not trust those who believed because of the signs. What will Jesus do with this hungry crowd?

---

5. Information about Tiberias is from *HBD* 1069–1070.

The exodus imagery comes every few words in the next verses. In verse 3, we find out that "Jesus went up the mountain, and was sitting there with his disciples." The image is similar to Exodus 19. The reappearance of the disciples is their first time on stage since the harvest parable in 4:31–38. We might suddenly notice that there is no mention that they went with Jesus to Jerusalem in chapter 5; perhaps they have remained in Galilee while their master confronted the Judeans and faced persecution and murderous threats. Whether or not readers imagine them as present on the last ministry tour or not, they *are* with Jesus on the mountain.

In the manner of the fourth gospel's increasingly familiar narrative style, the fact that it is "near Passover" is injected into the plot in verse 4 after the scene has begun to unfold (cf. 5:9b). The fact that the members of this Jewish Galilean crowd choose to pursue Jesus in Galilee rather than go to Jerusalem for the feast is powerful evidence of their disaffection from the dominant Judean ethos.[6] Might Jesus the healer be the one to liberate them from the oppression the Judean Temple-state has imposed?

As if in a single motion, several actions are described in verse 5: "Having lifted up his eyes, Jesus saw that a large crowd was coming toward him, and he said to Philip, 'Wherefrom [*pothen*] might we buy loaves for these to eat?'" Before we can consider the implications of this surprising question, we are given the information by the narrator in verse 6 that Jesus' question is "testing" Philip, "for he [Jesus] already knew what he was about to do." The idea of God "testing" the people carries powerful exodus overtones:

> Moses said to the people, "Do not be afraid; for God has come only to test you and to put the fear of him upon you so that you do not sin." (Ex 20:20)

> Remember the long way that the Lord your God has led you these forty years in the wilderness, in order to humble you, testing you to know what was in your heart, whether or not you would keep his commandments. He humbled you by letting you hunger, then by feeding you with manna, with which neither you nor your ancestors were acquainted, in order to make you understand that one does not live by bread alone, but by every word that comes from the mouth of the Lord. (Deut 8:2–3)

Jesus has placed the question of feeding with loaves in terms of "buying" to see whether his disciple would succumb to the temptation of accepting the "earthly" way of providing food (as the disciples have already done in 4:8, 31–33) or would remember what both Moses had taught so long ago and Jesus had taught in his very last (narrated) conversation with the disciples. Readers might well object to this trick: it is hardly fair for Jesus to entrap his own disciple like this! While our sympathy goes out to Philip, we also are called to recognize

---

6. Hendricks (1992, 49–50).

the teaching value of Jesus' lesson in faith and economics. By leading Philip to give the "fleshly" answer, Jesus makes certain that what he does will become that much more deeply imbedded in his disciple's consciousness. At least, that's the pedagogical theory.

Philip's answer in verse 7 is not only spoken in terms of worldly methods but sadly expresses the depth of his despair at the question: "Two hundred denarii worth of loaves are not enough for each one to receive a little piece." The proposition is surely a hyperbolic way of expressing Philip's doubt: two hundred denarii equaled two hundred days' wages, far more money than this band of disciples was likely to have available. Also, given the relatively low cost of bread, his answer tells us how huge the crowd is. How many people might we feed on ten thousand dollars or so worth of bread! When Philip looks out across this hungry sea of humanity, his religious imagination fails him. With a humorous mixture of ludicrousness and hope, Andrew, identified for the second time as the brother of Simon Peter, jumps in with the information that a "little boy has five barley loaves and two small fishes, but what are these to so many?" (verse 8). In the face of this massive hunger, they are looking to a child for help. The little boy's supplies are both bountiful for one his age and ridiculously small. The detail that the loaves are "barley" emphasizes the poverty of the crowd, as this kind of bread was even cheaper than the more common wheat.[7] It also recalls 2 Kgs 4:42, wherein the prophet Elisha "miraculously" feeds a hundred people on barley loaves. With this intertextual reference, alert readers are prepared for the possibility that Jesus' "plan" might resemble Elisha's, if not Moses'.

With the disciples' expressions of doubt and incredulity in the air, Jesus acts. In verse 10, he begins by issuing a command (presumably to his disciples) to have the people recline as at a meal. The people are not simply to "eat" but to share in a *meal,* which includes the sense of being a people, not simply a crowd. Verse 10b adds a seemingly extraneous detail about there being "much grass in the place." What can this pastoral imagery mean in this highly symbolic re-creation of the exodus? If we examine Hebrew scripture, we find grass to be a common image in the Psalms and elsewhere for the transitory nature of life (Pss 37:2; 58:7). It is also a common metaphor for the bounty of God's gift of life (Job 5:25; Ps 72:16). But in the context of the exodus, we find this particular word on the lips of Moses at the beginning of a song of celebration and recollection of the completed journey through the wilderness: "May my teaching drop like the rain, my speech condense like the dew; like gentle rain on grass, like showers on new growth" (Deut 32:2). Whether symbolic of the quantity of people covering the hillside like grass or of the word of God that is both rain on grass and bread, we cannot decide for sure. At the purely descriptive level, the plentiful grass suggests a fertile place, unlike the desert wilderness through which the Israelites traveled.

---

7. R. Brown (1966, 233).

In one of the fourth gospel's rare references to male persons, verse 10 continues by narrating the obedience of "five thousand men" to Jesus' command to recline. The figure "five thousand men" is found in each of the four gospels' recitation of the wilderness feeding, despite the variation among them in many other details. Although without a particular symbolic link to Hebrew scripture, the number is perhaps meaningful as representative of a thousand for each of the books of the Pentateuch. But from a plot perspective, the figure shows the enormity of the following that Jesus has generated from the seashore towns around Tiberias. Persecuted and conspired against in Judea, Jesus has brought forth a huge multitude of hungry Galilean pilgrims seeking the one who performs signs. D. A. Carson suggests the specification of men "is a way of drawing attention to a potential guerrilla force of eager recruits willing and able to serve the right leader."[8]

While the little boy's meager provisions that Andrew called attention to in verse 9 seemed pathetically absurd as a source from which to feed this multitude, they are enough for Jesus to work with in verse 11. His action comes through three verbs: "received," "thanked" (*eucharistēsas*), and "distributed" (*diedōken*, the only occurrence of this verb in the fourth gospel). The actions are the paradigm of how Johannine disciples are to treat Jesus in turn. To receive and then hand back out to many is a form of the harvest parable Jesus told the disciples at the end of chapter 4. Inserted between these actions is the pregnant Christian term *eucharistēsas*. At this point in the story, it carries little meaning beyond its obvious sense of giving thanks to God, the traditional preface to a meal in the Israelite tradition. But as the chapter unfolds, the term will take on a particular meaning for the Johannine community and its audience.

The actions are followed by the narrator's observation that they had "as much as they willed [*ēthelon*]." The narrator continues in verse 12 by noting the people's being "filled" as an expected given! As with previous "miracle" stories, the fourth gospel is not as interested in the fact of the occurrence as in the interpretation of the event by Jesus and others. Just as the water-turned-wine and the sick child of the *basilikos* and the sick man by the pool made well are reported plainly and directly, so too this reenactment of the exodus feeding is told in a straightforward style that belies the modern readers' sense of "such things don't happen."

Jesus' words in verse 12b similarly take the satisfaction of the people's hunger for granted: "Gather together [*synagagete*] the abundant fragments, so that nothing should be lost [*apolētai*]." The command to "gather together" recalls Ex 16:16, Moses' command to "gather together" the manna: "It is the bread that the Lord has given you to eat. This is what the Lord has commanded: 'Gather together [LXX, *synagagete*] as much of it as each of you needs.'" However, the manna story ends on a sour note: "And Moses said to them, 'Let no one leave any of it over until morning.' But they did not listen to Moses; some

---

8. Carson (1991, 270).

left part of it until morning, and it bred worms and became foul. And Moses was angry with them" (Ex 16:19–20). In contrast, Jesus' disciples *do* gather the messianic quantities of bread in verse 13 — matching the quantity of Cana wine in abundance — "filling twelve baskets of fragments from the five barley loaves." If the symbolism of the "five thousand men" is obscure, the symbolism of the twelve baskets and five barley loaves is not: out of the meager fare of the Torah, Jesus' actions fill people and leave enough leftovers for a basket apiece for each of the tribes of Israel. Once again, Jesus has surpassed Moses at his own "game." For the Tiberian crowd of "unclean" poor, Jesus has provided an overabundant feast.

Although Jesus' act is never characterized as a "miracle," the narrator continues in verse 14 by noting the people's (no longer referred to as "men") response to "the signs he did: they began to say, 'This one is truly the prophet who is to come into the world.'" Their proclamation superficially resembles the Samaritan response in 4:42: "This one is truly the Savior of the world." How different, though, is Jesus' response to the two titles! Whereas he "remained" with the Samaritans for two days, in verse 15 he now withdraws alone to the mountain. The narrator provides the crucial distinction for us: "Jesus, having known they were about to come and seize him to make him king…" Ironically, Jesus has been accused by the Judeans of "making himself equal to God," but he refuses to be "made king" by force. The demeanor of the crowd had changed dramatically because of the "signs" they have seen. Whereas at the beginning of the scene they were "following" Jesus but quietly obeyed the command to recline, now, with powerful verbs, they are described as a violent mass of humanity,[9] desperate for a king. Of course, their proposal is unpatriotic if not downright treasonous: they already have "kings" in the form of Herod Antipas, the client king who established Tiberias, and his boss, Caesar.

This, of course, is precisely the problem. The Jewish desire to be rid of Roman rule overrode nearly every other goal in the minds and hearts of Palestinians from Galilee to Judea. As Craig Koester notes, "Roman rulers regularly placated the populace with distributions of bread or grain."[10] The Roman "feeding" has been replaced with a Jewish "meal"! This multitude responds to Jesus' actions with the "correct" interpretation: he is the messiah, the one who will set Israel free! This is the meaning of the "prophet who is to come into the world" — the one predicted by Moses (Deut 18:18) to speak God's word as Moses' successor. The crowd is right about Jesus, but also terribly wrong. He will not be "made" into anything that is not the will of the one who sent him. Instead of allowing himself to become a tool of the masses' desperation, he withdraws to await the "hour" when he *will* accept his kingship, on his own terms.

---

9. R. Brown (1966, 235).
10. C. Koester (1994, chap. 2).

## 2. "I AM, HAVE NO FEAR!": JOHN 6:16–21

**A. Chiasms:**

**6:16–21**

a: 16–17a: begin sea crossing

  b: 17b: disciples alone

    c: 18: strong wind

  b$^1$: 19–20: Jesus comes

a$^1$: 21: finish sea crossing[11]

**6:16–24**

a: 16–17a: Capernaum

  b: 17b–18: Jesus absent

    c: 19–20: fear: *egō eimi*: don't fear

  b$^1$: 21–23: Jesus absent

a$^1$: 24: Capernaum

**B. Location:** on the sea

**C. Time:** evening

**D. Hebrew scripture context:** the exodus; Genesis 1

**E. Social factors:** the Johannine community's relationship with Jesus

**F. Themes:** Jesus as new Moses; Jesus as master of chaos

**G. Key words:** sea, "came to be" (*egeneto*)

From the mountain to the sea, verse 16 narrates a dramatic change in geography that reflects a powerful continuity in theology. The movement echoes images from Psalm 107:

> Some wandered in desert wastes, finding no way to an
>     inhabited town;
> hungry and thirsty, their soul fainted within them.
> Then they cried to the Lord in their trouble,
> and he delivered them from their distress. . . .
> For he satisfies the thirsty,
> and the hungry he fills with good things. (verses 4–5, 9)
>
> Some went down to the sea in ships,
> doing business on the mighty waters;
> they saw the deeds of the Lord,
> his wondrous works in the deep.
> For he commanded and raised the stormy wind,
> which lifted up the waves of the sea. . . .

---

11. Ellis (1984, 109).

> He made the storm be still,
> and the waves of the sea were hushed.
> Then they were glad because they had quiet,
> and he brought them to their desired haven.
>
> (verses 23–25, 29–30)

This poetic summary of God's exodus activity joins with Jesus' activity on the mountain and the sea to underscore the narrative's subversive, messianic theme: Moses was a messenger of God's word and works, but Jesus *is* God's word and works.

The scene on the sea in 6:16–21 also provides verbal echoes of the fourth gospel's own reworking of the creation story through the use of two themes from the prologue: the overcoming of "darkness" (verse 17) and the repetition of the Greek *egeneto,* "came to be." Careful reading of the way the narrator tells the story will show how Jesus, the one who "is" — *egō eimi* — overcomes what merely "comes to be."

Structurally, alternative chiasms link the scene on the water with the following long conversation in Capernaum that continues through the remainder of chapter 6. Whether we see the passage extending from "sea to sea" (6:16–21) or from "Capernaum to Capernaum" (6:16–24) depends on whether the center is the chaotic force of wind in verse 18 or Jesus' calm *egō eimi* in verse 20. As befits the intricacy of Johannine discourse, this is largely a false choice, as each of the overlapping chiasms helps focus an important aspect of this archetypal episode. Peter Ellis's chiastic breakdown of the entire gospel places this short scene at the center of the text, drawing a parallel with the exodus story as the center of the Pentateuch.[12]

Verse 16 launches the passage with a long sentence that fully establishes the scene: "As evening came to be ... " brings readers into the world of becoming, the transitory place of ordinary life in which nothing is certain and everything changes. It continues: "His disciples went down to the sea." Is Jesus still on the mountain? If so, why are his disciples on their way somewhere else? Are they afraid of the multitude who want to seize their master for their own designs? Has Jesus forbidden them from joining him so he can be alone to think and pray? This reading gap between our awareness of Jesus' and his disciples' location and intentions suddenly yawns wide. The only other time in which we were told that Jesus and his disciples were not together, we were given the specific reason by the narrator (4:8). In contrast, here we are only informed of the bare reality of the separation of master from disciples.

The sentence continues in verse 17 by adding that they had "entered a boat." The Greek phrase, though, is anarthrous, perhaps suggesting that the term "boat" connotes more than a particular boat. The sentence then narrates the current situation: "They were coming to the other side of the sea, into Capernaum." The next sentence intensifies the introduction to the previous one: "And darkness

---

12. Ibid., 107–108.

[*skotia*] already had come to be." "Evening" is a transitory period of shadow between day and night, but "darkness" brings us directly back to the language of the prologue. What will happen to these sea-journeying disciples in the midst of darkness? Why are they out traveling in the dark? As we consider these unanswered questions, the foreboding atmosphere deepens with the grim narration in verse 18: "And not yet had Jesus come to them, and the sea was blowing with a great wind and was awakened [*diegeireto*]." Almost as if linked by cause and effect, Jesus' absence and the rousing of the sea follow one another. It is not simply that Jesus is not with them; the narrator expresses it in terms of anticipated but unrealized presence, as if they had been waiting for him to come but had given up and started on the voyage without him. The verb *diegeireto* used to describe the condition of the sea comes from a root meaning "to awaken from sleep." The sea takes on an archetypal sense of the antagonist, the evil monster waiting to trap these unsuspecting and unprotected disciples of Jesus in its jaws.

Whatever the disciples are feeling in the midst of this stormy sea, we are not told. Similarly, whether the wind is with or against them is not narrated. It is the simple fact of the wind-driven sea that concerns the text, and the Jesus-less disciples out in the midst of it. All we are told is that they continued rowing across this primal chaos until they were out in the middle of it.

Suddenly in verse 19, the narrator adds in typical low-key style: "They saw Jesus walking on the sea and *coming to be* near the boat." At this point, when their salvation is at hand, we are told surprisingly: "They grew fearful." The stormy sea may not have frightened them, but the presence of Jesus walking on the water does! What is the precise nature of their fear? Is it holy awe in the presence of this impossible experience? Is it sheer terror at the implications of what they are witnessing for who Jesus really is? Is it simply concern for their master's safety out on the sea without a boat? Stubbornly, the narrator again refuses to answer these questions, keeping the disciples' thoughts hidden beyond fearful silence. There is more important business at hand — Jesus' crucial words in verse 20 to his band of followers amidst this terrible scene: "*Egō eimi*, be not afraid!" While the identification of Jesus with the words signifying the sacred name of God is familiar to readers from 4:26 — we recall that his disciples were off buying food at the time — they have not had this reality revealed to them previously in the story. It comes to them not in a calm conversation or even in heated debate (as it will come to others later in the chapter), but at the moment of life and death, when hope seeks its response in faith. It comes associated with the simplest yet most powerful assurance God can offer fragile created beings: do not be afraid. To the disciples in the boat, Jesus is revealed as more than a holy teacher or even the messiah. He comes to them bearing identity with the beingness of God, just as the primal dark waters of chaos in Genesis 1 are ordered into beauty and goodness by the Creator.

What possible response can they make? In one of the only "proper" responses of these oft-confused disciples in the fourth gospel, the narrator tells us in verse 21: "They were willing therefore to receive him into the boat." *Willing to receive him*, two prologue themes recalled once again: "Into his own he came, but his own did not receive him, but as many as did receive him, he gave authority to become God's children, . . . those not . . . of the will of flesh nor the will of man" (1:11–12). The result of their willingness is "immediately the boat *came to be* on the earth to which they were going." Their salvation comes immediately upon receiving Jesus into the boat.

For the fourth gospel, this scene offers the basic model of what it means to become a Johannine community "in the boat." Without Jesus, life is darkness, chaotic, stormy, out of control. With Jesus' presence within the community, the possibility of living through to the other side of fear is revealed. In an incredibly compact six verses, the fourth gospel has expressed in powerful images the reenactment of the voyage from bondage to freedom, from being a ragtag bunch of frightened escapees to becoming a community of God's children, from seeing Jesus as a teacher whom the crowd wants to make a worldly king to the epiphany of Jesus as the one who incarnates the Holy One.

### 3. EUCHARIST AS PUBLIC COMMITMENT TO JESUS: JOHN 6:22–71

A. **Chiasm:**

> a: 22–24: Capernaum/disciples
>> b: 25–40: bread of life/eternal life
>>> c: 41–42: Judeans murmur
>> b[1]: 43–58: bread of life/eternal life
> a[1]: 59–71: Capernaum/disciples[13]

B. **Location:** on "the other side of the sea" in Capernaum in Galilee: in *synagōgē*

C. **Time:** the next day

D. **Hebrew scripture context:** the exodus (esp Exodus 16) and prophetic recollection

E. **Social factors:** Galilean *Ioudaioi* and Johannine community

F. **Themes:** Jesus' "bread" is from God

G. **Key words:** bread, murmuring, eternal life, "munching flesh"

### a. Testing the Prospective King: "What Sign Do You Give?"

**Chiasm: 6:22–25**

> a: 22a: people on other side of sea
>> b: 22b: Jesus had not entered boat with disciples
>>> c: 23: boats came after *eucharistēsantos* bread
>> b[1]: 24: Jesus not there nor his disciples; enter boat
> a[1]: 25: they . . . on other side of sea

---

13. Ibid., 114–115.

The little chiasm from 6:22–25 returns the context of the narrative from Jesus and the disciples to the "crowd." The geographic movement is ambiguous and confusing. In 6:1, we were given the first direction: Jesus went "to the other side of the sea." One implication of "other side" in the exodus context is across the Jordan, that is, a west-to-east journey, from the direction of Tiberias (see map). The next stop is "a mountain," which might refer to any of the hills around the lake. In verses 16–21, the disciples travel to "the other side of the sea into Capernaum," which is located in the northwest lake region. But in verse 22, we hear of a "crowd, the one having stood on the other side of the sea," finding a "little boat" but knowing that Jesus had not entered the boat with his disciples. The first puzzle is: If this crowd was on the side of the sea where the meal took place — that is, the crowd who tried to seize Jesus to make him king — how did they know who crossed the sea at night? Are they now in Capernaum observing the little boat in which the disciples arrived? If so, when did they come: later that night, amidst the storm, or after the storm subsided? Early the same morning? And if they knew that Jesus was not with the disciples, why have they left the place where they expect Jesus — whom they seek — to go where his disciples are?

Verse 23 only adds to the confusion. It tells us that "boats from Tiberias [i.e., on the same side of the Jordan as Capernaum, but conceivably still 'the other side' of the sea from Capernaum] came near the place where they ate the *eucharistēsantos* bread of the Lord." Are these newly arriving boats coming now to the place where the meal took place — on the other side of the sea from Capernaum? Or is this simply a late description of those who experienced the mountainside eucharist? Finally, to cap it all, verse 24 speaks of the "crowd," which sees neither Jesus nor his disciples, now entering "little boats" and coming to Capernaum "seeking Jesus." If this is the same crowd as in verse 22, then that verse must be speaking of the people who, on the "meal side" of the sea, find a lone "little boat" not taken by the disciples and somehow know that the disciples crossed without Jesus. If so, these people now board "little boats" that were not there in verse 22!

Perhaps we can make sense of it this way: the crowd on the "meal side" finds a lone boat, sees boats arrive from Tiberias, and joins these boats for the journey to Capernaum. (How five thousand people fit into these quaintly described "little boats" is another question.) Then, once they find him in verse 25, the place is referred to again as "the other side of the sea," suggesting the possibility that they did *not* find Jesus in Capernaum, but continued looking until they *did* find him. This last ambiguity, mercifully, will be clarified at the end of the conversation, in verse 59. But by reserving the specific location until that point, the fourth gospel allows the dialogue to seem to take place more generally on "the other side," the place where John baptized, the place of otherness, of the unknown, outside the "Promised Land," where the Israelites wandered with Moses for forty years, wondering if they would ever arrive, wondering if the whole journey was a terrible mistake.

Amidst this mixed-up description — surprising for the otherwise precisely

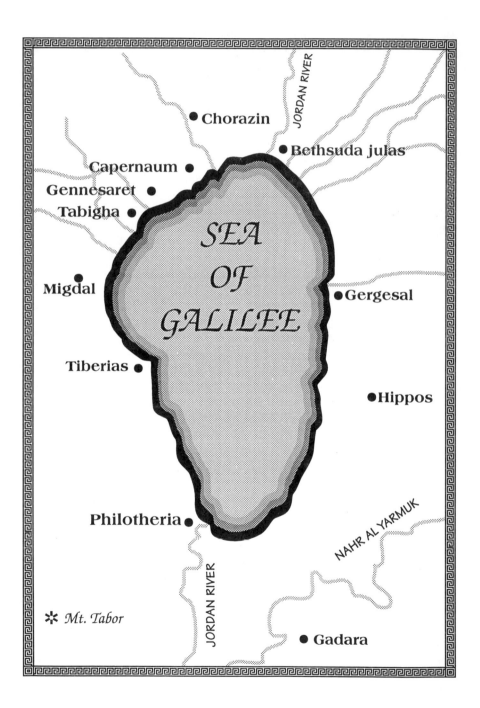

Chorazin

Bethsuda julas

Capernaum

Gennesaret

Tabigha

SEA
OF
GALILEE

Migdal

Gergesal

Tiberias

Hippos

Philotheria

JORDAN RIVER

JORDAN RIVER

NAHR AL YARMUK

✳ Mt. Tabor

Gadara

worded fourth gospel — a few narrative details *are* clear. The crowd that now arrives in Capernaum consists at least partly of people who shared in the meal, but it seems unlikely that any of them saw Jesus walk on the sea or speak to the disciples the revelatory words. Further, they are "seeking" Jesus, presumably to continue about their mission of making him king. Finally, at least some of this entourage consists of Tiberians (even if those who ate the meal were not), those unclean people of relatively recent conversion to Judaism whose home city is a cosmopolitan blend of Hellenism, Roman colonialism, Jewish rule, and international trade. They have come to the place of the "*eucharistesantos* bread of the Lord," one of the only times in the fourth gospel where the ambiguous Greek word *kyrios* (meaning both "sir" and "Lord") clearly refers to Jesus as Lord. While this phrase (which is in fact missing from many early manuscripts)[14] is usually translated "bread, after the Lord had given thanks," in light of the subsequent discussion in chapter 6, it seems unduly literal to deny the theological import of the term "eucharist" in connection with both "bread" and "Lord." What has taken place, in the voice of the narrator at least, is not simply a "feeding," but a eucharistic meal, with all the implications for community commitment which that central Christian feast entails. The crowd might or might not see it this way, but the Johannine narrator makes clear for readers that this is in fact what has happened.

From this point on in the scene, this multitude is referred to simply as "they" and speak with a single voice, as if they are engaged in a small-group conversation with Jesus rather than being the mass gathering that appears to be forming in Capernaum. Not until 6:41 does Jesus' conversation partner take on a new descriptive term. By that time, the subject matter will have changed substantially, and so will the challenge to remain with Jesus and his disciples.

### Chiasm: 6:26–35

a: 26–27: loaves/food/fill/eternal life

   b: 28–29: what are works of God?

      c: 30–31: what sign? our fathers ate

   b¹: 32–34: bread from heaven

a¹: 35: I AM bread, no hunger/thirst

The conversation begins in verse 25 with the sort of statement that is typical of the fourth gospel; it is mundane on an "earthly" level but decisive on a "heavenly" one: "Rabbi, when did you *come to be* here?" At the level of plot, it answers one small ambiguity from the preceding verses: the crowd clearly did *not* witness the nighttime epiphany. The tone of the question seems almost exasperated, as if, out of breath from seeking him everywhere, they are now peeved for having had to work so hard to find him. But at the more profound level, the question asks Jesus about his relationship with creation itself: "here" refers to

---

14. R. Brown (1966, 258).

the world-of-becoming, the place in which the Word pitched its tent (1:14). Is it possible that this crowd intends this depth of meaning? They have proclaimed him "truly the prophet who is to come into the world" and seek to make him their king. No doubt they are filled with high hopes after the experience of the eucharistic meal, even without the vision of the sea-walk. Perhaps their question does attempt to penetrate the messianic mystery.

At whatever level they ask it, Jesus does not answer their question, but goes directly to the heart of the ambiguity of their purpose in seeking him. In other words, the question is not *when Jesus* arrived here, but *why they* have.[15] Jesus' answer is one of the rare occasions in the fourth gospel when he seems to speak in contradiction to the narrator. In 6:2 and 6:14, the narrator had expressly stated that the people were responding to "the signs," but in verse 26, Jesus proclaims, "Amen, amen I am saying to you: you are seeking me *not* because you saw signs but because you ate from the loaves and were filled." If we review these references to "signs" carefully, we find that rather than being contradictory, they are evolutionary. In 6:2, the signs were specified as those "done on the sick." The crowd was curious, watching to see what this "miracle worker" would do next. In 6:14, the reference is without a limiting qualifier, and the crowd has decided that Jesus is "the prophet" who will be made king. Now in 6:26, Jesus tells them (and us) that the signs have been abandoned altogether as a source of meaning in favor of the practical satisfaction of full bellies!

Jesus proceeds to offer them a challenge in verse 27: "Be working not for the food that perishes [*apollymenēn*] but for the food that remains into eternal life, which the Human One will give to you. This is the one whom the Father, God, has sealed." The implications of this invitation will occupy the next forty-four verses.

The initial sense of Jesus' saying is in the context of an audience comprised largely of the poor from Tiberias and the surrounding region. Their "work" is day labor in the city, fishing, farming, perhaps even small-scale artisanry, all with the primary purpose of putting bread on the table. Their attraction to the one they have proclaimed as prophet would consist largely in his apparent ability to end this ceaseless cycle of labor by providing them their "fill." In this regard, they are precisely like the Samaritan woman, whose main purpose in questioning Jesus was to end her daily visits to the well (4:15). As he did with the woman, Jesus challenges this "fleshly" perspective through double entendre and metaphor.

The first metaphorical contrast he offers is between "food that perishes" and "food that remains into eternal life." The concern for "perishing" was first heard in 3:16: "that everyone who believes in him might not perish [*apolētai*] but have eternal life." Again at the mountainside meal, Jesus ordered his disciples to gather the fragments so that "nothing would perish [*apolētai*]." Interestingly, this image is not mentioned again throughout the present discourse, either by Jesus or by his audience.

---

15. O'Day (1988, 98).

Similarly, "food" itself is not again discussed. "Loaves" (*artōn*) and "bread" (*arton*) become the central metaphors, while the more generic "food" disappears. However, its initial use by Jesus does recall the parable of the harvest (4:31–38) and his disciples' misunderstanding about Jesus' "food," which he clarified for them when he said, "My food is to do the will of the one who sent me and to finish his work" (4:34). Of course, this Galilean crowd did not hear that conversation, but perhaps his disciples remember it. Certainly readers should be alert to it, having the privileged knowledge vis-à-vis the Galileans that "working . . . for food that remains" refers to Jesus' carrying out of his mission from God.

In light of these intratextual references and differences in knowledge, it is interesting that the question Jesus' statement evokes in verse 28 is phrased in terms of "working the works of God." They have caught the meaning of the metaphor: to "work for food that remains into eternal life" equals "to work the works of God." Their question accepts both Jesus' challenge to think beyond full stomachs and his authority to speak about things of God, as expressed in terms of being "sealed" by God (as in 3:33). The opening of the conversation is hopeful; they have calmed down from the violent urge to make Jesus a king and are now patiently listening to him, asking the "right" question. Will Jesus succeed in gathering in this harvest in fulfillment of God's will? The drama of the scene hinges on this suspenseful prospect.

In verse 29, Jesus gets specific. The question was in terms of "works," the good deeds that make up the ethical life. By even asking it this way, the members of the crowd reveal their lack of loyalty both to the Torah, which, of course, makes very specific what is required, and to the Pharisees, whose embrace of oral Torah brought the question of "works" even closer to everyday life. They seem to expect a new set of commandments, like the Israelites in the wilderness, awaiting the words of God. But the Johannine Jesus offers no Sermon on the Mount or Plain as in Matthew or Luke. Instead, "works" is reduced in verse 29 to a single "work": "to believe in the one sent forth."[16] As we will see, this "simple" faith-requirement bears its own challenging implications for discipleship.

This challenge produces in verse 30 another question, one that casts a large shadow over the sense of imminent enlightenment that readers might have been hoping for based on the previous exchange. "What sign, therefore, are you doing, so that we might see and believe? What are you working?" The ambiguous reality of sign-faith has crept back in, along with the recollection of Jesus' angry admonition on his last visit to Galilee: "You people will never believe unless you see signs and wonders" (4:48). Their second question suggests a tit for tat: "They will do God's work only if Jesus does God's work first."[17] Sadly, as their response to Jesus continues, the situation seems to get even worse. They recall in verse 31 the act of God on the exodus sojourn:

---

16. Ibid., 99.
17. Ibid., 100.

"Our fathers ate manna in the desert, as it is written, 'He gave them bread from heaven to eat [*phagein*].'" They are asking for the very sign that they have just witnessed! Raymond Brown points out that second-century Jewish documents reveal an expectation that the messiah would perform just such a sign at Passover.[18] Thus, they are still "in the ballpark" in trying to understand who Jesus is. But what can account for their *now* requesting this sign when the previous day they had already decided that Jesus was the prophet who would become their king?

Within the *story* world, this backsliding makes no sense at all. Why should this crowd, which has gone to all this trouble to find Jesus and seek his guidance about the "works of God," suddenly become stubborn and forgetful? But from the perspective of the *discourse* world — that is, the world of the Johannine community — the scene is transformed into the drama that has been their life experience. Their Galilean compatriots, unlike their Judean counterparts, were at least willing to pursue Jesus this far. But they have been thinking about the relationship in terms of what Jesus might do for *them,* that is, set them free from Rome. By the time of the fourth gospel, this hope has been thoroughly dispelled both by the crucifixion of Jesus and by the destruction of Palestine and crushing of the Jewish rebellion by the Romans a generation later. The Johannine community has built its faith in Jesus not on this messianic hope, but on an entirely different kind of messiah. The crowd was perfectly willing to follow the prospective military liberator-king, but has a few tough questions to ask before it will follow *this* messiah!

The change is signaled by the question of Jesus' "work." He may have orchestrated a mountainside meal, but what *lasting* difference will it make to these poor Galileans? Specifically, how can the Johannine *Christian* community prove that its eucharistic meal is from God in the same way that Moses' manna was? The rest of the chapter will express the basic objections that the Jewish Galileans had to this Johannine claim.

In verse 32, Jesus begins to address the question in terms of the scriptural paraphrase that they introduce.[19] Many commentators have seen the following section from 6:31–50 in terms of the structure of a rabbinical midrash.[20] This entails the recitation of the passage to be exegeted, followed by commentary on each important word, and concluded by the repetition of the passage. In the context of our reading, it suggests also the engagement by Jesus (and the Johannine community) of the battle of myths over the meaning of this crucial scriptural phrase. Upon the meaning of this phrase, the contrast between Pharisaic Judaism and Johannine Christianity rests.

---

18. R. Brown (1966, 265).

19. R. Brown (1966, 262) points out that the phrase is an amalgam of several verses from Hebrew scripture: (1) Ex 16:4: "rain loaves from heaven"; (2) Ex 16:15: "bread which the Lord has given you to eat"; (3) Ps 77:24: "gave them the bread of heaven"; and (4) Wis 16:20: "sent them from heaven, bread that took no labor."

20. R. Brown (1966, 262); O'Day (1988, 101–102). The suggestion originated with Borgen (1965).

Jesus starts in verse 32 by clarifying the meaning of "he": "Amen, amen I am saying to you: it was not Moses who gave you bread from heaven, but my Father is giving you the true bread from heaven." Schematically, we can see three contrasts in Jesus' statement:

| Moses | my Father |
|---|---|
| did not give | is giving |
| bread from heaven | true bread from heaven |

All three parts imply that the questioners are concerned (incorrectly) with the past, while Jesus is concerned with the present and future. Implicit is the Deut 8:3 reference that first came up *within* the Johannine community with Jesus' testing of Philip in 6:5. The questioners, like their ancestors, misunderstood the meaning of the manna. As Moses had to explain to them the difference between living on "bread alone" and "every word that comes from the mouth of God," so Jesus distinguishes manna from "true bread."

Jesus goes on in verse 33 to split the image of "bread from heaven," inserting himself in the middle: "The *bread* of God is the one who comes down from *heaven* and is giving life to the world." The object of the life-giving effect of this bread is not limited to the Israelites/Judeans as was the manna, but extends to "the world."

Do the Galileans understand? Their request in verse 34 can be taken either way: "*Kyrie,* give us this bread always." In form it is virtually identical to the Samaritan woman's request for water in 4:15, except she qualified her request with the explicit *misunderstanding* of the living water as ending her trips to the well. The Galileans may be asking, like her, simply for "bread that perishes," or they may be asking Jesus for "the one who comes down from heaven." The ambiguity of their request is underscored by the subtle use of *kyrie.* Is Jesus simply one worthy of respect ("sir") who can help them or the one from heaven ("Lord") to whom they rightfully owe allegiance? The next section of the conversation will clarify both the meaning of Jesus' "bread" and their response to it.

### b. Bread=Flesh=Life=Johannine Community

#### Chiasms 6:35–58: pattern one

#### Chiasm 1: 6:35–48

a: 35–38: I AM bread of life: seen me/comes to me

   b: 39–40: raise on last day

      c: 41–43: murmuring: son of Joseph

   b¹: 44: raise on last day

a¹: 45–48: heard Father/comes to me; I AM bread of life

### Chiasm 2: 6:49–58

a: 49–51a: ancestors; bread from heaven

  b: 51b–52: my flesh; life of world

    c: 53: amen, amen: munch/drink

  b[1]: 54–57: flesh, everlasting life

a[1]: 58: bread from heaven; ancestors

### Chiasms 6:36–58: pattern two
### Chiasm 1: 6:36–40 (R. Brown)

a: 36: you see, don't believe

  b: 37: come, not cast out

    c: 38: I come from heaven, will of sender

  b[1]: 39: not lose but raise (on last day)

a[1]: 40: sees, believes [21]

### Chiasm 2: 6:43–58 (Ellis)

a: 43–50: Father; raise up on last day; fathers died, eat and not die

  b: 51: flesh

    c: 52: how give us flesh?

  b[1]: 53: flesh

a[1]: 54–58: Father; raise up on last day; fathers died, eat and not die[22]

As the above alternative chiastic patterns show, commentators have found several different ways to group the following verses in the "bread of life" discourse. The first pattern seems stronger to me for two reasons. First, the two parts are both contiguous with one another and with the surrounding sections. Second, the parallels not only are more numerous but also demarcate clearer changes in topic within the conversation between Jesus and his audience. Readers may find other patterns as well if the verses are scoured hard enough. What is important about any chiastic pattern is whether it frames and centers the crucial elements of the narrative. In the first pattern, the central components are the murmuring of the Judeans and the double-amen statement insisting upon "munching the flesh of the Human One and drinking his blood." In the second pattern, the emphases are reversed. First is the affirmation of Jesus as doing the will of his sender, and second is the contentious question challenging Jesus' ability to give his flesh to eat. In either case, the central demand and the central opposition are essentially the same. The entire section from 6:35–58 will confront both Jesus' audience and the fourth gospel's readers with the most difficult and bewildering challenge in the New Testament: the undeniably cannibalistic-sounding requirement of "munching flesh" in order to receive life.

---

21. R. Brown (1966, 276).
22. Ellis (1984, 126–127).

The section begins in verse 35 with the first metaphor-linked *egō eimi* statement in the gospel: "I AM the bread of life." Previously, to the Samaritan woman and to his wave-swept disciples, Jesus proclaimed the great "I AM." Now, a new Johannine technique appears: the joining of the divine identity with an "earthly" image. In these statements, heaven and earth, being and becoming, and God and humanity form inextricable bonds. In this opening example, Jesus has continued the gradual transposition of the conversation from "food that remains," to "the work of God," to "true bread from heaven," and now to "bread of life." This last phrase, so familiar to modern Christians, was a biblical innovation of the fourth gospel. Despite the thick exodus atmosphere and its theme of bread that permeates the entire chapter, the particular association of "bread" and "life" in this way is not found in the Hebrew scripture. Jesus has moved into new territory. The Galilean audience can no longer interpret his words through the filter of the Torah and the various biblical narratives recalling the exodus. They are left on their own to either accept or reject Jesus on his own terms.

The next part of his proclamation in verse 35 links two strong parallel lines: "The one coming to me will never hunger, the one believing in me will never thirst." The Greek is absolutely emphatic, using the double "not" structure in both halves of the statement. Is there a particular reason for the linkage, coming/not hunger, believing/not thirst? Also, why the introduction of "thirst" at all when the discussion is focused on bread (water is not mentioned in the entire passage)? Thirst, of course, recalls the story of the Samaritan woman at the well and its almost identical statement, "Whoever drinks of the water I shall give will never thirst" (4:14). Given the six previous intratextual links between chapter 6 and the Samaritan episode, it should not be too surprising to find Jesus linking hunger and thirst in this way. Both hunger and thirst are basic demands of daily life. The Johannine Jesus, considering the deeper hunger and thirst that drive humanity's quest, claims to supply the satisfaction sought to meet these needs forever.

Once the issue of "thirst" is joined, we can look at the different ways the two stories are told to see how the different metaphorical pairs function in each. The Samaritans had nowhere to "go" to join Jesus — he, on behalf of his "future" laborers, comes to them to gather in the ripe field awaiting harvest that they represent. They need not "come" to Jesus because he (and his community) has come to them. In contrast, the Galilean Jews have a long journey to make: they must leave the Torah and synagogue system and find their way into the Johannine community. As the Samaritan episode ends with the proclamation of their *faith* in Jesus (4:39–42), so this passage will end with the question of whether the Galilean Jews will *"come"* to Jesus or *"go back"* (6:65–66). Each pair provides the basic image through which the respective social group is challenged to become a Johannine Christian community.

All of this is for the benefit of disciples and readers, though, as the story-world audience cannot be expected to make the connection between what they are being told and what Jesus said and did in Samaria. The "insider" message underscores the gospel's purpose in relating a story from the past in order to affect the affiliation of readers in the readers' own present, a point that will eventually be made explicit by the narrator's direct address to readers themselves (20:31).

In verse 36, Jesus gives his second evaluation of his audience. In verse 26, he told them about their purpose in seeking him. Now he adds: "But you have seen me and yet you are not believing." Despite the hopeful possibility of their request for bread in verse 34, Jesus, who knows "what was in a person" (2:25), sees their superficiality. Perhaps it is the body language of the crowd growing uncomfortable with the implications of his *egō eimi* claim. However he knows, he speaks of the crowd in the singular, as a unit that will either believe or not believe.

Jesus continues by beginning to lay a foundation for the long Tabernacles discourse/conversation in chapters 7–8. It flows from the question with which many in the Johannine community struggled: *Why* won't their fellow Jews believe in this one who offers eternal life? Verse 37 offers a hint: "All which the Father is giving me will come to me." If these Galileans will not come to Jesus, it must be because the Father has not given them to him! We must await further discussion before getting a closer look at the contours of this issue. The second half of this sentence contains a hidden barb, which may not be obvious to modern readers at this point in the story, but would be clear enough to the Johannine community. Jesus will "certainly not cast out" the one coming to him. Commitment to the Johannine community faced one with the consequence described later in 9:22: "If anyone should confess him as messiah, they would be expelled from the synagogue." In sharp contrast, those who come to Jesus will *not* be cast out. Jesus states the reason in verse 38: "because I have come down from heaven not to do my will but the will of the one who sent me." The opposition of "my will" and "the will of the one who sent me" appears to suggest a paradox: that Jesus' "will" is different from God's will. But the purpose of the statement at this point in the increasingly polemical discourse is not to contrast Jesus' will with God's, but to contrast his *obedience* to God's will with the *disobedience* to God of those who do cast out Johannine believers. Phrased another way, Jesus is saying, "*I* do *God's* will and therefore keep safe those whom God has given me, but *you* do *your own* will and therefore cast out those whom God has given you!"

This interpretation is reinforced by the follow-up in verse 39: "This is the will of the one who sent me: that all which he has given me I should not destroy [*apolesō*] but should resurrect it on the last day [*eschatē hēmera*]." Again, the implicit contrast is apparent: God's will is to "resurrect" on "the last day," whereas the will of those who oppose Jesus is to "destroy." It is the same word used to contrast the food that "remains" and that which "perishes" in verse 27.

The comparison also introduces a new Johannine theme that reveals the scope of Jesus' authority: the *eschaton*, or end-time. As the prologue presents Jesus as with God "in the beginning," now he presents himself acting out God's will on the "last day." The one who comes down from heaven is, indeed, much greater than Moses, who would never have dreamed of claiming such authority.

Verse 40 repeats the thought with the other half of the metaphorical pair introduced in verse 35. As verse 39 matched "given to me" with "resurrection on the last day," verse 40 links "believing in him" with the *eschaton.*

Jesus has now completed the first part of his "homily" on the "he gave them bread from heaven to eat" quotation by associating the identity of his will with that of the one who sent him, namely, to resurrect on the last day all who have come to him. This is the meaning of "he gave them bread from heaven." Before he can explain the meaning of "to eat," we hear the reaction of his audience to what he has claimed so far.

With verse 41, the identity of Jesus' conversation partner changes. Those who had been named in verse 24 simply as "the crowd" and in 25–35 as "they" or "them" now suddenly are identified as *Ioudaioi,* that is, Jews or Judeans. Up to this point in the gospel, we have seen a fairly distinct division between Galilee as a place of faith in Jesus and Judea as a place of loyalty to Temple and Torah. Yet the Galilean group with whom Jesus speaks in this dialogue has been revealed as not believing in Jesus (verse 36). Geographically, they are not "Judeans," so at first glance it seems that the term *Ioudaioi* suggests unbelieving Galilean "Jews." However, this sudden renaming in connection with lack of faith and "murmuring" suggests a more theological/symbolic meaning of *Ioudaioi.* As Jouette Bassler has put it, "Once people reject Jesus, regardless of their geographic location, they become classified as *Ioudaioi*[23] (see, generally, Introduction, B.4.c.i)." We will see further examples of this theological demographics later in the fourth gospel, when the question of whether a person may be a "Samaritan" or a "Judean" even if that is not their physical origin is raised in 8:48 and 18:35. Given this perspective, we recall that the only reference in the text so far (and indeed, in the entire gospel) to "Galileans" is to those who "received him" at 4:45. While I have used that name to indicate their geographic home, from the fourth gospel's viewpoint, the crowd was a "them" waiting to be named, depending on whether they made the move toward Jesus and the Johannine community or not. With verse 41, the narrator declares his evaluation of "them" in line with that of Jesus in verse 36.

In the Greek word order, we are actually told that these people were "murmuring" before they are named as *Ioudaioi.* It suggests cause and effect: *because* they are murmuring, they are accurately characterized as *Ioudaioi.* The murmuring is in turn directly associated with a particular aspect of Jesus' word to them: "He said, 'I AM the bread that came down from heaven.'" The connection between murmuring and this phrase bears two implications. First, although this statement does sum up the gist of what Jesus spoke, in fact, it is *not* a phrase he used. He said in verse 33, "The bread of God is the one who comes down from heaven," and in 35, "I am the bread of life." Given Meir Sternberg's admonition to pay careful attention to biblical repetition of direct speech,[24] this misquotation has more significance than our weak American attention to words might

23. Bassler (1981, 254).
24. Sternberg (1985, 393–440).

suggest. The words of God that Moses quoted in the wilderness were not to be loosely remembered! Each precise turn of phrase in the Torah became grist for the rabbinical mill of analysis and reflection. To misquote Jesus is to give his words less than full divine authority. It is proof that the audience is not really listening to him and does not believe he does the will of God.

Second, their focus on the first part of Jesus' statement extending from 32 to 40 suggests that, since they murmur in response to a paraphrase of his words in 33–35, they have not heard at all what he has said since verse 35. They have been busily murmuring, like the Israelites in the desert in Ex 16:2, 7, 8.

The content of their disgruntled discussion among themselves in verse 42 is the apparent conflict between Jesus' parentage and his claim: "Is this not Jesus, the son of Joseph, whose father and mother we know?" Although it was traditional in the strongly patriarchal Hebrew culture to name a man as the son of his father (but cf. Mk 6:3), this second naming of Jesus' father (see 1:45) is pointedly in contrast with the nonnaming in 2:2–3 of his mother. The usual presumption that important people are named and unimportant people left anonymous is reversed once more in the fourth gospel, just as Nicodemus was named but the Samaritan woman was not (and as Peter is named but the "Beloved Disciple" is not in John 13–21). Joseph has no role to play in the entire text except as the object of other people's naming in association with his son.

Their murmuring also reveals another detail about their relationship with Jesus: they "know" his father and mother. The implication is more than simply the naming of Jesus as "son of Joseph," which suggests only that they have heard of his father. To know *both* his father and mother is to claim actual personal awareness of these people, for "knowledge" of a person's mother would not be claimed of a casual acquaintance. The submission of women outside the home would imply that to know Jesus' mother, the speakers have been in his parental home, or at least his village or town of origin. This place had been named in 1:45 by Philip to Nathanael as Nazareth, also in association with Joseph as Jesus' father. These two pieces fit together here to suggest that at least some of these "Judeans" are actually Jesus' disciples! This suggestion will be confirmed in 6:60 and 6:66, but at this point, it is simply a dark hint that Jesus' claims are generating controversy even among those who seemingly "know" him. It is, of course, an ironic "knowledge," given how many times Jesus has emphasized that *God* is truly his "Father."

Jesus responds in verses 43–44 to their murmuring with the command to stop, and repeats what he has already said — but which they have not heard — while they were murmuring "among themselves." His repetition includes two new nuances: not only has the Father given everything that comes to Jesus, the corollary is also true: that is, the *only* way they can come to Jesus is if the Father "draws" them. The term "draws" suggests the paradoxical nature of God's call in the fourth gospel: it is like a magnetic pull upon a person that exerts a strong influence but can still be resisted. It also carries an implication of nonuniversality: some people *may not* be "drawn" to Jesus. Again, the Johannine community through this text finds explanatory room for the (at least partial) failure of its salvific mission to "the world."

Jesus follows his repetition with a quotation from "the prophets" (Isa 54:13) in verse 45, "And all will be taught by God." Of the various citations of scripture in the text, this is the first attributed specifically to "the prophets." It is apparently a change in source from the incessant exodus/Pentateuch context of chapter 6. But the broader Isaian context shows that this brief quotation draws together several themes. The text is Isa 54:13-15; 55:1-3 (with the Johannine verses cited in brackets):

> All your children shall be taught by the Lord,
> and great shall be the prosperity of your children.
> In justice you shall be established;
> you shall be far from oppression, for you shall not fear;
>     [cf. Jn 6:20]
> and from terror, for it shall not come near you.
> If anyone stirs up strife, it is not from me. . . .
> Ho, everyone who thirsts, come to the waters;
> and you that have no money, come, buy and eat [LXX,
>     *phagete*]! . . . [cf. Jn 6:5, 35]
> Why do you spend your money for that which is not
>     bread, [cf. Jn 6:27]
> and your labor for that which does not satisfy?
> Listen carefully to me, and eat what is good,
> and delight yourselves in rich food.
> Incline your ear, and come to me; [cf. Jn 6:37, 44, 45]
> listen, so that you may live. [Jn 6:40]

The second half of verse 45 picks up both the theme of listening/hearing and "come to me" from Isa 55:3, reinforcing the link between Jesus' quotation and the following Isaian verses. It is as if to say to these Judeans: you have heard this all before, so pay attention *now* so that you may live!

Jesus continues in verse 46 by telling this audience what he has already told the Judeans in Jerusalem: "No one has seen the Father but the one who is from God" (cf. 5:19, 37). Thus, to be taught by God is to listen to Jesus, the only one who has seen the Father. Their murmuring is preventing them from catching on to what is being offered to them, but it is not too late to hear and have eternal life!

The preferred chiastic section comes to a close with the repetition in verse 48 of what we heard in 35. The new chiasm opens by introducing the second part of the midrash on the scripture quoted in verse 31. The issue now is: What does it mean "to eat" the bread from heaven? Jesus begins in 49–50 by contrasting the manna that their ancestors ate with the bread from heaven: the former led eventually to death; the latter leads not to death but to eternal life. This contrast should not surprise readers, given what Jesus has already said about "food that perishes" and "food that remains" in verse 27. But the sharpening of the contrast takes a dramatic step with the image Jesus offers in verse 51: "The bread that I shall give is my flesh for the life of the world."

It is not surprising that this shocking metaphor leads to argument. But what is surprising is that the argument is not between the Judeans and Jesus, but among the Judeans themselves. The narrator tells us in verse 52 that they were "fighting [*emachonto*] with one another" over the possibility of "this one giving to us his flesh to eat." Raymond Brown interprets *emachonto* as implying a violent dispute.[25] The initial part of their disbelieving question ("How is it possible?") precisely echoes Nicodemus's words in response to Jesus' challenge to be born *anōthen* in 3:3–4. But whereas Nicodemus's words were directed to Jesus (and those he represents, i.e., the Johannine community), these disputants aim their unbelief at one another. For this to make sense, we must imagine either that some of these people believe what Jesus is saying or that there are at least two interpretations among the Judeans of Jesus' mysterious statement.

The prospect that some of them are believers is belied by both Jesus' statement in verse 36 and the naming of them as Judeans. If we focus on the alternative, what might the multiple interpretations be? To get at this takes us to the heart of the dispute over eucharist in the early days of Christianity. Long before such now-standard Catholic theological terms as "real presence" and "transubstantiation" came into use, Christians struggled over the early and traditional belief that Jesus had identified himself with bread and wine and commanded his followers to remember him in the breaking of bread at mealtime (e.g., 1 Cor 10:16–17; Lk 24:35; Acts 2:42). While the synoptics and Paul each remember this command, they provide no record of theological debate over its meaning. In contrast with the other eucharistic texts, which introduce the command to eat Jesus' body (*soma*), the fourth gospel commands followers to eat Jesus' "flesh" (*sarx*). It is eucharist in this graphic form that the Judeans are fighting over.

As Brown points out, to consume one's "body and blood" in Hebrew idiom could mean something as simple as accepting the whole person.[26] From this perspective, participation in the eucharistic meal is a sign of a community member's acceptance of Jesus' teaching and life. But to "eat flesh" is an entirely different story. This term in Hebrew idiom has quite a different connotation: it is the work of vultures (Ezek 39:17) and evildoers (Ps 27:2; Zech 11:9). Thus, apart from the distasteful cannibalistic overtones, the Johannine Jesus' association of his eaten flesh with "life" is a complete non sequitur for the scripturally aware listener. Similarly, drinking blood was forbidden by the Law, or even the eating of meat with blood still in it (e.g., Lev 7:26–27). Might the whole flesh-and-blood business simply be an "impossible" metaphor, like being "born *anōthen*," which Nicodemus foolishly tries to take literally? Perhaps the entire ugly side of the tradition's association with eating flesh and drinking blood can

25. R. Brown (1966, 282).
26. Ibid.

be cast aside in this context as a ridiculously literal understanding of what Jesus is saying. Such an interpretive pattern would, of course, fit the several examples we have already heard where Jesus speaks on a "heavenly" level while his hearers are stuck on the "earthly."

Yet in the face of this path out of this most natural and biblically based confusion, Jesus intensifies the command in verse 53 even further: "Amen, amen I say to you: *unless* you eat the flesh of the Human One *and* drink his blood, you do not have life in yourselves!" The word "flesh" is repeated six times and "blood" four times in verses 51–56, just in case there is any doubt that Jesus is not simply talking about his "body." "Flesh" is only used eight times in the synoptic gospels, and not once in the context of eucharist. Jesus is now holding nothing back; the moment for decision is at hand.

In verse 54, Jesus adds the final element to his statement of the demand on his hearers: "The one munching [*trōgōn*] my flesh and drinking my blood is having eternal life." If the word "eat" (*phagein,* as used in the LXX for the Isaian quote above) left room for interpreting Jesus' word metaphorically, his use of *trōgōn* — Greek for "munch" — withdraws that interpretive space. The word connotes a graphic sort of eating done by an animal — not an image to consider "spiritually" like Ezekiel's consumption of Torah (Ezek 3:1–3). Jesus' unequivocal command is to "munch his flesh."

The graphic language of verse 54 is completed with the third repetition of the promise: "I will resurrect him on the last day." If we put the three uses of this phrase together as parallel lines, we have the following:

*believing in the Son (40)=come to me (44)=munch my flesh and drink my blood (54)*

Now, the Johannine message becomes clear: to believe in the Son is to come to him, that is, to join the Johannine community, and the evidence that one has done this is participation in the eucharistic meal which that community celebrates. This is the "true food" and "true drink" that Jesus offers, that which satisfies every hunger and thirst (6:35), the "food which remains" (6:27). The one who does this "remains in me and I in that one" (6:56).

The bread=flesh statement, therefore, is not *merely* a metaphor — the first Christians believed that in a mysterious way, Jesus was physically present to them in the bread of the eucharist. But, of course, it is not a simplistically literal equation either, as the flesh of Jesus departed with the cross and resurrection experience that preceded the "coming to be" of the fourth gospel. It is rather a hybrid image, more literal than that of returning to one's mother's womb to be born *anōthen,* but not as purely "spiritual" as the image of "living water." The command to "munch" *is* literal, but the flesh that is eaten is not.

For the "Judeans" struggling between loyalty to Temple and Torah and the "drawing" of them by the Father toward Jesus, the command to "munch flesh and drink blood" makes unequivocal the demand to take the risk of openly joining Jesus in the community that lives in his spirit. If the first stage in this journey was the invitation to Nicodemus to be "born *anōthen*" and commit oneself, the second stage is to be willing to celebrate that commitment for all to see by taking part in this life-giving but paradoxically life-threatening sacred feast. For the price of making this regular and open statement of new loyalty is to be rejected by the Judeans, those who are persecuting Jesus and threatening to kill him for obeying the one who sent him. It is to give up one's entire social reality for a new one, one from which one will *not* be "cast out" (6:37). As David Rensberger has said, "Participation in the eucharist is here made a criterion for inclusion in or exclusion from 'life' in a manner that brings its function as a boundary to prominence."[27] As the gospel continues, it will show and tell us exactly what these consequences are. For now, the dark side is hidden by the brilliant light of the invitation to share in eternal life, but it is not so hidden as to prevent the Judeans listening to Jesus from being aware of what the choice really is.

In verse 58, Jesus sums up the contrast: "*This* is the bread that came down from heaven. It is *not* like what your ancestors ate — they died. The one who munches on this bread will live forever." Not only did the ancestors in Moses' day die, but those who think they are following in his footsteps but who are not really listening or seeing the ways of God in Jesus' day are also in danger of dying. But the invitation to life, not the prospect of death, is the emphasis as the chiasm (and Jesus' homily) closes.

### c. Betrayal from amongst the "Twelve"

**Chiasm: 6:59–71**

a: 59–64: one will betray

  b: 65: no one can come

    c: 66: many withdrew to "the things behind"

  b[1]: 67–69: to whom shall we go?

a[1]: 70–1: one will betray[28]

The narrator enters in verse 59 to add a surprising bit of information: "He said these things in the synagogue, teaching in Capernaum." Up to this point, readers knew only that the location was Capernaum, but given the apparent size of the crowd on the mountain and the sense of a swarm seeking Jesus "on the other side," one might have imagined an open field or other public place in the city. But to find that Jesus has been speaking this way in the *synagogue* makes his speech even more shocking. It is the first time this place of Jewish religious assembly has been mentioned in the fourth gospel, although the verb from which it is derived, *synagogein,* meaning "to gather together," has been used in 4:36 (the harvest) and 6:12 (the fragments of bread). The contrast is clear: for

---

27. Rensberger (1988, 78).

28. Ellis (1984, 132).

the Judeans, the synagogue is a *place,* but for the Johannine community, *synagogein* is an active verb, a command central to the mission of discipleship. The contrast is similar to that of "apostle," the religious office, and *apestelein,* "to be sent." As with *synagogein,* only the verb appears with respect to the Johannine community.

In addition to establishing this difference between the Judean and Johannine sense of gathering, the naming of the location in this way leads us back over the entire dialogue to hear how it sounds when imagined in *this* location. No wonder the Judeans dispute among themselves over Jesus' words! It is a slice of the experience of the Johannine community, as those who eventually became a separate faith group argued with their brothers in tradition (women apparently had little part in the life of the synagogue) over the meaning of Jesus' life and words.

The reaction of many in this synagogue could not be more clearly stated than in verse 60: "This is a hard word [*skleros logos*] — who is able to hear it?" But another surprise accompanies this reaction: it is spoken by many of "his disciples." Only among people already committed at some level to following Jesus would the subject even be worth arguing about. For the Judeans in Jerusalem, Jesus is already a condemned man, whose words are unworthy of serious attention. The crowd that has come this far to seek Jesus is the multitude who acknowledged him as the prophet and wished to make him king. They want the sign that finally convinces, the bread that Jesus offers. Well, now they have it — and it's too hard to swallow!

In the face of this understandable but life-negating resistance, Jesus tries once more in verses 61–62. He "knows" that even his disciples are "murmuring," and asks them, "Does this scandalize you? What if, therefore, you saw the Human One ascending [*anabainonta*] to where he was before?" Twice before in the face of wavering unbelief, Jesus pulled out the trump card of the "ascending" Human One (1:51, Nathanael; 3:13, Nicodemus). However, here Jesus does not expressly link the verb with heaven, but with the more ambiguous "where he was before." Given the previous use of the verb by the narrator in its more ordinary sense of "going up" (i.e., to Jerusalem for a feast, 2:13; 5:1; also, 7:8, 10, 14; 11:55; 12:20; cf. 20:17), it is unclear whether Jesus is now proposing a vision of the "one from heaven" or a return to Jerusalem for further confrontation with the authorities and other Judeans. In either case, the offer is the same: the one who "goes up" to Jerusalem with authority to speak truth to power can only be one who is sent from God. However it is heard, it has the effect of saying: Lift up your minds and hearts! Get your minds off your "earthly" ways of thinking and consider God's thoughts! Nathanael's "scandal" was Jesus' origin in Nazareth. Nicodemus's was the challenge to be born *anothen.* Now, Jesus tries to raise his audience's mind from the scandal of flesh-eating "up" to the power of the spirit, which gives life (verse 63). The "flesh," in the prologue sense of the ways of earthly cultural thinking (1:13), "profits nothing," but "the sayings I have spoken to you are spirit and life." The command to "munch" Jesus' "flesh" is followed by the comment that the flesh is good for nothing! How far can Jesus' words take us into the labyrinthine chambers of God? The contrast seems to be between two meanings of flesh: what is useless is the "low" way of thinking, the path that gets us caught up in our mental categories and blocks out new ideas; what Jesus' flesh offers, though, is the path to him, which is the path to God, via open and committed membership in the Johannine community.

But, the narrator tells us in verse 64, "Jesus knew from the beginning which are the ones not believing and who is the one about to betray him." For the first time, the darkest possibility of all enters the story. Not only will some in Jerusalem persecute and kill him, but Jesus will be the subject of *betrayal* from *within* his discipleship community. It is not only the life of the unbeliever that is at stake but also the life of Jesus — and hence, of all who follow him. The mission to witness to God's truth is not only a selfless one for love of the world but also one of self-preservation. And yet this betrayal is known to Jesus "from the beginning." Even though he will not be able to prevent this ultimate act of unbelief, Jesus persists in doing the will of the one who sent him until it is completed. Amidst the murmurers is one to whom it has not been "given by the Father" to come to Jesus.

### Chiasm: 6:66–71

a: 66: disciples leave Jesus

    b: 67: twelve: Jesus: not you also go away?

        c: 68–69: Peter: you have the words

    b¹: 70: twelve: Jesus: one is a devil

a¹: 71: Judas will betray

At the center of one chiasm and the beginning of the next in verse 66 is the sad statement: "Because of this, many of his disciples went back into the things of the past [*eis ta opisō*] and would not walk with him any more." The opposite of following is withdrawing, retreating, returning to what "was" rather than continuing on the path of what is "coming to be."

Now, in verse 67, Jesus speaks to a select group familiar to synoptic readers but not mentioned until this point in the fourth gospel: "the twelve." While this gospel generally refers to "his disciples" to speak of Jesus' community of believers, the use of this specific term brings to mind the relationship of the Johannine community with the Christian communities founded on the authority of one of the twelve. The movement from "the crowd" to "the Judeans" to "his disciples" to "the twelve" has continually narrowed the focus until the question of faith reaches its most basic challenge: Do those who have started communities in Jesus' name really believe?

Simon Peter, always the spokesman for that group, speaks in verse 68 the classic line of the faithful remnant: "Lord, toward whom shall we go? You have the sayings of eternal life." How many times within a fragile community of Christian faith and resistance in our modern world have we said these words to one another? When times are difficult, when the demands seem too great, when the work of just not betraying one another weighs heavily and the temptation to quit looms large, we ask: Where else shall we go? As impossible as it may seem at times in our privatized, consumerized, death-dealing culture, the intimate life of the small Christian community is where eternal life is preached and lived. For all our sinfulness and lack of faith, our efforts to bond our lives with one another through the mystery of Jesus' flesh and blood find no counterpart in the secular world. In the world of the text, Simon Peter, speaking for all the apostolic Christian communities of the first century, expresses the wonderfully ironic "Where else?" faith upon which the reign of God is to be built. In the face of those who disbelieve, he affirms in verse 69: "We have believed, and we have known that you are the Holy One of God."

Among all the various titles given to Jesus in the fourth gospel, "the Holy One of God" appears only here. It is offered without explanation by Peter or response by Jesus.[29] Given this bare pronouncement, it is hard to draw any conclusions on its positive or negative connotations. It is not the title affirmed by the narrator at the summary point of the entire text (20:31) nor one used by Jesus about himself. And yet in the context of Peter's "whom else" affirmation of Jesus in the face of doubt, dissension, and betrayal, it cannot be completely rejected as an honest and accurate theological evaluation of who Jesus has come to be for the twelve, upon whose behalf Peter speaks.

The mystery of the call to discipleship deepens with Jesus' response to Peter in verse 70: "I chose [*exelexamēn*] you twelve, didn't I? Yet one of you is a devil [*diabolos*]." The theme of Jesus' "election" of his disciples will recur in the Last Supper discourse in the context of Judas and betrayal. By introducing it here, the fourth gospel emphasizes the paradoxical link between being called and still being a potential "devil." The narrator has prepared us for this in verse 64 by informing us of Jesus' "knowledge from the beginning" that one would betray, but the description of this one by Jesus as a "devil" intensifies the sense of foreignness of this "elected one" amongst the discipleship community. Why would Jesus have intentionally chosen a person he knew would betray him, one who is a devil? Was it to "enable" the eventual "lifting up"? There seems little likelihood that Jesus would avoid this prospect even without a devil in the circle around him. Was it to show God's love for the world? Perhaps it was meant as a lesson for the Johannine community and its successors: that we should be willing to share the sacred meal even with those who seem oriented around a different center than we, so long as *they* choose to participate. The text offers no clue for discerning among these (or other) possibilities, leaving the gap open for our reflection and prayer.

The narrator's naming of this devil as Judas, son of Simon Iscariot, gives readers crucial inside information that will remain unknown to the disciples until the moment of Jesus' arrest. The specific naming of Judas and his person and place of origin adds the kind of detail that we have come to expect to bear par-

---

29. R. Brown (1966, 298) points out its usage in Hebrew scripture for consecrated persons (Judg 13:7 [Samson]; Ps 106:16 [Aaron]); but cf. Myers (1988, 142) regarding its negative connotations in Mark.

ticular meaning in the fourth gospel. At one level, it contrasts the two "Simons": one who stays, and one whose son betrays.

The other detail is more obscure. The derivation of "Iscariot" remains a subject of scholarly debate, but a strong possibility is Ish-Kerioth, Hebrew for "man from Kerioth," a city in southern Judea. As Brown notes, "It would make Judas a Judean disciple of Jesus, whereas the other members of the Twelve of whom we know were Galileans."[30] Such an interpretation would not be far-fetched given what we have seen of Galileans and Judeans thus far, although chapter 6 itself makes clear that geographic *origin* is not as precise a measure of faith as geographic *identity*. In any event, as chapter 6 ends, we have moved from the context of Jesus and the masses of those seeking a king to the mysterious mixture of faith and betrayal at the heart of Jesus' closest community. The journey outward leads back to the journey inward, as we are called to reflect on our own response to the shocking call to public munching of flesh and drinking of blood.

---

30. R. Brown (1966, 298).

# 11

# Tabernacles

## Crying Out to Quench Thirst

## John 7:1–52

**A. Chiasm: 7:1–52; 8:12–59**

    a: 7:1–36: Jesus comes out of hiding from Judeans seeking to kill him

        b: 7:37–44: living water and spirit

            c: 7:45–52: failure to arrest Jesus

        $b^1$: 8:12–20: light and Father

    $a^1$: 8:21–59: Jesus hides from Judeans seeking to kill him[1]

**B. Location:** Jerusalem (except 7:1–9)

**C. Time:** Tabernacles

**D. Hebrew scripture context:** Leviticus 23; Zechariah 14

**E. Social factors:** Abraham and Moses as basis for nationality/God and Jesus as basis for community

**F. Themes:** Jesus replaces Tabernacles

## 1. STRUCTURE OF 7:1–10:42:
## THE THIRD "MINISTRY TOUR"

After the period around the "sea" in chapter 6, we are given a narrative pause at the beginning of chapter 7. Once the opening scene has unfolded, though, Jesus returns to Jerusalem, the place where the Judeans are seeking to kill him, and remains there until the end of chapter 10. This entire section forms what Jeff Staley calls Jesus' third "ministry tour," his third of four circuits between

---

1. Ellis (1984, 135).

Galilee and Judea.[2] Within this larger unit is the section from 7:1 through 10:22, when the time switches from Tabernacles to Dedication. Although the drama of the healed blind person in chapter 9 is clearly a separate episode from the heated arguments in chapters 7 and 8, it also appears to take place within the Tabernacles feast, as does the "epilogue" to the drama in 10:1–21 (concluding with the reference to the opening of the blind person's eyes).

Within these broad sweeps of activity and dialogue, though, the discourse within 7 and 8 clearly forms a unit as the chiastic structure indicates. Throughout, Jesus argues at length with the Judeans over the meaning of his presence among them, in keeping with the Tabernacles theme of God's presence both on the exodus journey and in the Jerusalem Temple.

Within this section, chapter 7 in turn forms a unit marked by the narrator's three mentions of the passing feast of Tabernacles (7:2, "near"; 7:14, "in the middle"; 7:37, "the last great day") and the response of the authorities to Jesus' proclamation. In the midst of a murderous conspiracy, Jesus boldly, even recklessly, speaks the way few of even the most radical of modern-day disciples would dare to do.

## 2. SEEKING BUT NOT FINDING

### Chiasm: 7:1–36

a: 1–11: where is he?/seeks

   b: 12–13: murmuring

      c: 14–30: Jesus in Temple in middle of feast

   b[1]: 31–32: murmuring

a[1]: 33–36: where is he going?/seek[3]

## *a. The Kairos: 7:1–9*

**A. Chiasm:**

   a: 1–3: Galilee, feast/going up

      b: 4–5: world/works

         c: 6: my time vs. your time

      b[1]: 7: world/works

   a[1]: 8–9: Galilee, feast/going up

**B. Location:** Galilee

**C. Time:** near the feast of Tabernacles

**D. Hebrew scripture context:** Lev 23:33–43; Deut 16:13; Zechariah 14

**E. Social factors:** Jesus vs. his "brothers"

---

2. Staley (1988, 64–65).
3. Ellis (1984, 140–142).

**F. Themes:** Jesus' "time" and his brothers' "time"

**G. Key words:** *kairos*

Chapter 7 begins with one of the strongest arguments for interpreting *Ioudaioi* as "Judeans" rather than "Jews" (see, generally, Introduction, B.4.c.i). The narrator starts off in verse 1, "And after these things, . . ." a variation on a common Johannine bridge phrase, "After these things . . ." (*meta tauta*), that both segues to the next scene and through the "and" links the preceding and subsequent Galilee passages. Jesus, we are told, "was walking in Galilee, for he was not willing to walk in Judea, because the Judeans were seeking to kill him." Jesus' geographic preference would make little sense if the issue were simply "Jews" seeking to kill him, for as we have seen, there are plenty of *Ioudaioi* in Galilee. Only if the killers are *Judeans* would it follow that Jesus now continues to walk in Galilee.

Immediately, we are given a new temporal note in verse 2: "The feast of the Judeans, Tabernacles, was near." For modern readers this Jewish feast is not as well known as Passover or Chanukah (Dedication), but the fourth gospel gives it a prominence unknown to the synoptics. Indeed, this verse is the only place in the New Testament where the word for Tabernacles, *skēnopēgia,* occurs, although its verbal relative, *eskēnōsen,* describes the Word's presence "in us" in the prologue (1:14). Without some understanding of the symbolics and origin of this feast, the following scenes in the fourth gospel will make little sense.

Tabernacles was one of the three main feasts of ancient Jerusalem that required pilgrimage to the Holy City (the others being Passover and Weeks, also known as Pentecost).[4] All three were adopted from eastern neighbors of Israel and originated as agricultural festivals. As the traditions developed, each became associated with a particular aspect of the movement from Egypt to the Promised Land: Passover with the exodus itself, Weeks with the Torah, and Tabernacles with the period in the wilderness.

Tabernacles, in its agricultural aspect, was a joyous fall festival celebrating the grape and olive harvests. As such, it was accompanied by the drinking of new wine and dancing. It became identified with the "booths" or "tents" used as temporary shelters in the desert, as described in Deut 16:13. This also matched the harvest practice, when temporary workers lived in similar shelters in the fields.

The cultic aspects of Tabernacles can be seen in Lev 23:39–43:

On the first day you shall take the fruit of majestic trees, branches of palm trees, boughs of leafy trees, and willows of the brook; and you shall rejoice before YHWH your God for seven days. You shall keep it as a festival to YHWH seven days in the year; you shall keep it in the seventh month as a statute forever throughout your generations. You shall live in

---

4. Yee (1989, 70–82) provides excellent background on the relationship between the feast of Tabernacles and the fourth gospel.

booths [LXX, *skēnais*] for seven days; all that are citizens in Israel shall
live in booths, so that your generations may know that I made the people
of Israel live in booths when I brought them out of the land of Egypt: I
am YHWH your God.

By the postexilic period, the feast became associated with the end-times, the
*eschaton.* Zechariah 14, a reading on the first day of the festival, envisions all
nations going up to Jerusalem with "no rain upon them" (14:17). Prayers for
rain were likely a part of the fall festival, to bring on the season following
the hot summer and provide water for the coming months. The image of "no
rain" anticipates the end of time, in which there would be no worry for the
next season.

The Zechariah passage also associated the feast with light, as the prophet
painted a picture of "continuous day,... not day and not night, for at evening
time there shall be light. On that day living waters shall flow out from
Jerusalem" (Zech 14:7, 8).

In the postbiblical period — and probably during the time of Jesus — tradition specified that the four trees of Lev 23:40 be carried in procession in the
Temple throughout the seven days, while the chanting of Psalms 113–118 accompanied the procession. A water-libation ceremony also took place. Gale Yee
describes it:

> Each day a procession from the Temple would make its way down to the
> pool of Siloam and draw up a golden flagon of water. Journeying back to
> the temple, the cortege would pass through the Water Gate accompanied
> by blasts of the *shofar.* The Water Gate had special eschatological signif-
> icance. R. Eliezer b. Jacob identified it as the south gate envisioned in
> Ezek 47:1–5 through which waters of life would flow.... With the golden
> flagon in hand, a priest would proceed up the ramp to the altar and pour
> the water into one of the two silver bowls positioned there.... Into the
> other bowl, the priest would pour a libation of wine. Spouts in each of the
> two bowls allowed the water and wine to flow out onto the altar.[5]

Finally, there was the light ceremony, in which four golden candlesticks were
set up in the Court of the Women in the Temple. As Yee says:

> Atop each candlestick, which could only be reached by ladders, were
> golden bowls holding oil. Wicks floated in the oil, which were made from
> the drawers and girdles of the priests. The Mishnah went on to state that,
> when these wicks were lit, "there was not a courtyard in Jerusalem that did
> not reflect the light of the House of the Water Drawing." The illumination
> represented God's own light.[6]

---

5. Ibid., 75.
6. Ibid., 76.

### Chiasm: 7:3–5

a: 7:3a: his brothers

  b: 7:3b–3d: works you are doing

    c: 7:4a–b: secretly/publicly

  b¹: 7:4c–d: you do these things

a¹: 7:5: his brothers

It is into this highly charged cultic, historical, and earth-cyclical atmosphere that Jesus is invited to go by his "brothers" in verse 3. The "brothers" were last mentioned in 2:12, as accompanying Jesus, his mother, and his disciples from Cana to Capernaum. Recollection of this first reference should make us immediately suspicious: the "brothers" are noted as distinct from "disciples." Further, the preceding sentence in 2:11 stated that "his disciples believed in him," but makes no mention of any faith of the brothers (or his mother for that matter, whose faith-description will await her presence at the foot of the cross). As they begin to speak now in 7:3, we cannot be sure of their motivation in commanding Jesus, "Go from here into Judea so that your disciples may see the works you are doing, for no one who does things in secret is seeking to be known openly. If you are doing these things, reveal yourself to the world."

What do the brothers have in mind? What is the tone of their "invitation"? Is it sarcasm, suggesting that Jesus would have just as much "success" in Judea as he just had in Galilee?[7] Is it honest encouragement, hoping that Jesus will win more converts in the royal city than in the hick backwaters of Galilee? Or is it an attempt to make a "star" out of their "brother" so that they can bask in his reflected light? Raymond Brown sees the "question" as the third put to Jesus in the Johannine version of the synoptic "temptation in the wilderness" story: first, to become king (6:15); second, to provide bread (6:31); and, third, to show power (7:3).[8] The narrator's own interpretation in verse 5 adds weight to this interpretation: "In fact, his brothers didn't believe in him."

Who are these "brothers" who do not believe in Jesus? The fourth gospel offers no further details about who they are. After this scene, they are not mentioned again until Jesus' command to Mary Magdalene to tell "my brothers" (20:17). Whoever they are, the designation "brothers" suggests extreme closeness of relationship, whether due to blood, common geographic home (i.e., Nazareth), or faith-relationship. The latter is expressly excluded by verse 5. It is another example of those close to Jesus who would lead him the wrong way.

Jesus' response to them in verse 6 is direct and surprisingly harsh: "My time [*kairos*] is not yet here, but your time is always at hand." Other than in the disputed verse 5:4,[9] the word *kairos* is found only in this passage in the fourth gospel. It is one of two Greek words for "time" and is distinguished from *chronos*. The latter is clock time, the passing of hour after hour, day after day.

---

7. Duke (1985, 84).

8. R. Brown (1966, 308).

9. Many early manuscripts omit this verse, and I have not considered it.

*Kairos,* on the other hand, is *the* time, the special moment, as in the statement, "The time is now!" It is another way of referring to Jesus' "hour," the moment in which he is to glorify God. His brothers would push that time up in order to have Jesus be more well known, to give him human glory. They presume that Jesus acts in order to gain fame (and fortune?) and are perhaps hoping to horn in on some of it. But Jesus knows the difference between their *kairos* and his own.

He continues in verse 7: "The world is not able to hate you, but me it is hating, because I bear witness that its works are evil." We recall the challenge in 3:20 to those who do "foul deeds" in darkness to come into the light to be reproved and healed by love. Similarly, 5:29 predicted the resurrection of judgment for those who do foul deeds. Jesus' current description of the "world's" works is even more explicit: they are not only "foul" but "evil" (*ponēra*). These unbelieving brothers *cannot* gain the world's hatred because they *will not* bear witness against the world's evil. To do so as Jesus does indicates not contempt or hatred of the world, but the reverse: it is an expression of God's love for the world (3:16). Those who fit in with the world cannot love the world, because to fit in is to accept the world's evil without challenge. To act like Jesus is to lovingly challenge the world's acts in order to encourage the world into conformance with God's will.

Jesus tells his brothers to go where they fit in: to the festival. He will not be ordered to act against his own sense of the *kairos*. He remains, for the moment, in Galilee.

### b. Murmuring at the Feast: 7:10–36

**A. Chiasm:** 7:10–32

    a: 10–13: crowds murmuring; fear of Judeans

       b: 14–20: taught in Temple; not mine but one who sent; seek to kill, true

          c: 21–24: Moses/sabbath/judgment

       b¹: 25–29: taught in Temple, not mine but one who sent; true; seek to kill

    a¹: 30–32: crowd murmuring; arrest threat from chief priests/Pharisees

**B. Location:** The Temple

**C. Time:** Tabernacles (through the middle of the feast)

**D. Hebrew scripture context:** (see above)

**E. Social factors:** Temple vs. Jesus as source of "water"

**F. Themes:** objections to Jesus

**G. Key words:** murmuring, the Christ

Verse 10 opens with the expected response of the brothers: they go up to the festival. But the second half throws us off guard. The narrator adds, "Then he also went up, not openly [*phanerōs*], but in secret [*krpytō*]." Jesus has just made a big point of distinguishing his own *kairos* from his brothers' *kairos* and expressly said that he was "not yet going up to the feast." Was he lying? Did he change his mind? Was it simply "not yet" his *kairos* when the brothers were going, but was soon thereafter? If so, what has happened in such a short span to change things?

The key is in the words used by the narrator to describe what Jesus has done — and what he has not done. In verse 4, the brothers used three words in telling Jesus what they thought he should do: "No one does anything in secret [*kryptō*] and is seeking to be known openly [*parrhēsia*]. If you are doing these things, reveal [*phanerōson*] yourself to the world." The brothers make a false assumption: that one who seeks to be known *openly* should *reveal* oneself *now.* Jesus does *speak* openly at the feast (7:26) — in contrast with those who do not for fear of the Judeans (7:13). But his revelation is a matter of *deeds,* which are done by Jesus as "signs" (2:11; cf. 9:3; 21:1, 14). The brothers want Jesus to go up to the feast and perform a powerful act — they are looking for a sign, like the crowd Jesus left behind in Galilee (6:30). It is not the *kairos* for Jesus to *act,* but it is the *kairos* to *speak* openly. Jesus remains "hidden" (*kryptō*) in the sense that his power will not be shown at this feast, even though he will speak strongly and openly to the Judeans (16–19), "the crowd" (21–24), the Jerusalemites (28–29), an unspecified audience (33–34), and finally to "anyone" (37–38).

When he arrives, we find in verses 11–12 that he is the object both of "seeking" by the Judeans and of "much murmuring" among the crowds. The "seeking" has ominous overtones, for the last time Jesus was in Jerusalem, the Judeans there were persecuting and "seeking" to kill him (5:18). The Judeans, like police authorities on the prowl, ask among the crowds in verse 11, "Where is that one?" which leads everyone present to be afraid of the Judeans. The narrator tells us in verse 13 that the murmuring crowd is unwilling to speak "openly" (*parrhēsia*) about Jesus, but he is the topic of general conversation nonetheless. It is the third example (6:41, 61) of the continued "murmuring," maintaining the exodus atmosphere, even though the scene has changed from Galilee to Jerusalem.

Their murmuring is the first expression of several specific objections to Jesus voiced at Tabernacles (7:15, 27, 41–43), objections that persist among many non-Christians to this day. The first issue, raised in verse 12, is whether Jesus is "good" or not because "he is making the crowd err [*plana*]." The implication of "good" is not simply a secular sense of moral correctness, but a sense of being associated with God's own qualities (cf. Mk 3:4; 10:18).[10] The opposite is *plana,* to be religiously fraudulent, one who leads people astray into idolatry (LXX: Deut 13:6; 2 Kgs 21:9). The concern, of course, is that following Jesus as if he were God is tantamount to idolatry, *unless* he is, in fact, *good.* The narrator does not comment on this debate, emphasizing instead the unwillingness of anyone to speak openly, even those who think Jesus is "good."

The feast reaches its midpoint in verse 14, and Jesus goes public with a vengeance, entering the Temple and "teaching." The only previous reference to Jesus "teaching" was his presence in the Capernaum synagogue at the end

---

10. W. Grundmann, *TDNT* 1:10–18.

of chapter 6. On earlier occasions, Jesus visited the Temple to cast out sellers at Passover and to heal the man at the pool on the sabbath. But at Tabernacles, Jesus comes to God's house as teacher, to clarify for his hearers what the purpose of this feast is.

The first response to Jesus' teaching presence is the "wonder" (*ethaumazon*) of the Judeans in verse 15. When this word was used earlier, it expressed an element of disbelief or doubt in a hearer of Jesus' challenging words (3:7; 4:27; 5:21, 28). So before the reason for the Judeans' wonder is given, we immediately should suspect that it will reveal a doubt that interferes with faith. In this case, it is the question of Jesus' education in "writings [*grammata*] when he has not studied [*memathēkōs*]." Put another way, the issue is: How can Jesus know what Moses taught (cf. 5:47, *grammasin*) when he has not been a disciple of an acknowledged teacher? The usual way of education among Israelites was to attach oneself to a teacher as a disciple (*mathētes*). Then, once one's apprenticeship was completed, the good student could proceed to teach on his own, gathering his own community of disciples. Thus, the problem at this point is not the content of Jesus' teaching, but his lack of qualification according to the tradition. The implication is that, rather than handing on the teaching of a recognized teacher, he is offering his own (unauthorized) ideas.

Jesus responds to this charge in verse 16: "My teaching is not mine but that of the one who sent me." He goes on in verse 17 to elaborate a principle of great importance to a community living long after Jesus' death and resurrection and trying to discern God's truth amidst many voices claiming to speak from a heavenly perspective: "If anyone wills to do his will, they will know whether the teaching is from God or whether I speak on my own." The play on the word "will" adds a now-familiar echo of the prologue (1:13), indicating the address of Jesus' words to those seeking to be born of the will of God. It is a difficult principle upon which to base a church: if you're trying to do God's will, you'll know God's teaching when you hear it! Time after time, the Johannine Jesus (in contrast with the Matthean Jesus) refuses to give detailed, Torah-like rules for discipleship, insisting instead on a spirit-based sense of communal discernment. But verse 18 does add some small measure of "evidence" by which one can determine whose teaching one is hearing. Those speaking on their own "seek their own glory," while one seeking the glory of the one who sends "is true, and there is no injustice [*adikia*] in that one." While the theme of contrasting glory is already a familiar Johannine image (e.g., 5:44), this verse contains the only use of *adikia* in the fourth gospel.

### Chiasm: 7:18b–24

a: 7:18b: injustice
>   b: 7:19–20: Moses, the Law, accusation that Jesus is possessed
>>      c: 7:21: one deed I did and you wonder
>   b¹: 7:22–23: Moses, the Law, accusation that they are bilious
a¹: 7:24: justice

What does Jesus mean by "injustice" and why does he introduce the concept into this conversation about his credentials for teaching? At the center of the Johannine distinction between light and dark, God's will and the various other wills, lies one criterion: God seeks to give life, while unenlightened humanity seeks to kill. Jesus tells his questioners in verse 19: "Moses gave you the Law, didn't he? But none of you is doing the Law. Why are you seeking to kill me?" Jesus focuses on the teaching that the Judeans *do* recognize as a result of God's will, the Law given to them by Moses. But, according to Jesus, *none* of these Torah-quoters "does" the Law. The proof: the Torah — to the extent it represents God's will — is for giving life (e.g., Deut 30:19), but these Judeans are in the midst of a murderous conspiracy.

Readers, of course, have known of this conspiracy since 5:18. But this is the first time it has been spoken of "openly." The response of "the crowd" to this declaration deepens the evidence of "injustice" against them. They tell Jesus in verse 20: "You have a demon! Who is seeking to kill you?" As it is "the crowd" who speaks and not specifically "the Judeans," one might infer that the masses gathered in Jerusalem for the feast do not know of the plot against Jesus, and that, in their ignorance, they react understandably by suggesting that Jesus is possessed, paranoid, delusional. But to the very extent that the conspiracy is secret, it is even more unjust. An open accusation of blasphemy and the "proper" trial would at least be consistent with the Law. As it is, though, the plotters are engaged in a hidden murder plan, in stark contrast with Jesus' open announcement of the state of things. They are doing foul deeds in the dark; Jesus is doing "good" in the light of day.

Jesus neither refutes the charge of possession nor elaborates on the question of his potential killers. Instead, he refers in verse 21 back to the "one work I did which causes you to be wondering." Which work could it be? Since arriving in Jerusalem for Tabernacles, Jesus has not been reported to have done any work at all. The text creates a moment of suspense, as we must wait to find out if the "work" will be specified.

Once again, Jesus refers back to what has been given by Moses, this time to circumcision in verse 23. This central ritual of Jewish identity Jesus immediately distinguishes as given not actually by Moses, but by "the fathers," although Gen 17:11 reports *God* as giving the command to Abraham. It is not from Moses, and yet the Judeans perform it on the sabbath. It is clear evidence not only of their failure to do the Law but of their hypocrisy. They have previously accused Jesus of violating the Law by telling a person to carry his mat on the sabbath (5:18), but they also violate the sabbath! The legal point is that the rite of circumcision is done even on the sabbath to fulfill God's purpose of marking Israel as a people set apart in covenant with God. Thus, the act, although not from Moses, is described in verse 23 as done to keep the purpose of the Torah, that is, the conditions of the covenant. If you are willing to do one thing beyond the letter of the Law to fulfill the spirit of the Law, Jesus asks, then why "are you bilious [*cholate*] to me because I made a person healthy on the sabbath?"

Now it is crystal clear which "work" is in question: the healing of the man by the pool in chapter 5, the incident that first aroused the Judeans' murderous plot. Jesus' words in verse 23 are the first affirmation that Jesus in fact cured the person by the pool. At the time, we recall, the text quoted Jesus as giving the threefold command to "rise, pick up your mat, and walk" (5:8). Only now is it made certain that this command was what worked the cure. Ironically, Jesus' link between his act of healing and the Judeans' anger misstates the precise nature of their objection at the time. Never did they protest his healing of the man. Rather, they took issue with the carrying of the mat itself, apparently paying no attention to the fact of the cure that the mat-carrying actively expressed. Jesus (and the narrator [5:9, 15]) is the one concerned with healing; the Judeans are simply concerned with the Law.

The word used to describe the Judeans' feelings, *cholate,* occurs only here in the New Testament as a personal adjective. It is a distinctly gut-level term, expressing the idea that the Judeans are not using their hearts (the locus of reason and wisdom for the ancients) but an "unclean" part of themselves instead. It is a Torah joke, suggesting that at the very moment the Judeans are concerned with legal purity, they are themselves acting from impure feelings.

The little chiasm ends in verse 24 with Jesus' exhortation not to judge "according to appearances but judge with just judgment." What has appeared to violate the sabbath has in fact been a fulfillment of it: the providing of rest to the one who has labored with sickness for thirty-eight years. Note that Jesus does not dispute the authority of the Judeans to "judge," but rather the standard upon which their judgment is based. The Johannine community, even at this late date in the proceedings, has not given up on the ability of the Judean establishment to reform itself in the presence of the light.

The response in verse 25 to Jesus' teaching comes from a new character group: the Jerusalemites. In case the crowd speaking in verse 20 was not familiar with the conspiracy against Jesus, this audience *is.* And yet we find a dichotomy between the Jerusalemites and the Judeans, revealed in verse 25: "Isn't this the one whom they are seeking to kill?" The Jerusalemites know that "they" are seeking to kill Jesus but are not part of the plot themselves. Their elaboration in verse 26 makes clear the scope of this distinction, at least from their perspective: "See! He is speaking openly [*parrhēsia*], and they are saying nothing to him. The rulers [*archontes*] have not come to know for sure that this is the Christ, have they?" Their speech confirms the narrator's description in verse 10 about Jesus being at the feast "openly" (*parrhēsia*) but not "manifestly" (*phanerōs*). The Jerusalemites' speech witnesses to the credibility of the narrator, the courage of Jesus, and the place of darkness in which the killers hide their foul deeds from the light.

The reference to the *archontes* begins the trial of the rulers.[11] The trial takes place in four stages, beginning here with the question by the Jerusalemites (7:26, 48, 52; 9:27). We should not be surprised when Nicodemus returns to the stage

---

11. Duke (1985, 80–82).

to embody the rulers who secretly believe but are challenged — first by Jesus, and now by their fellow rulers — to confess their faith openly.

The Jerusalemites' speech seems to characterize them positively, as they speak truthfully about the plot against Jesus, his openness, and the rulers' silence. But in verse 27, they are cast into shadow, as they claim, ironically, "We have known where [*pothen*] he is from, but when the Christ comes, no one is to know where [*pothen*] he is from." We have heard the question of *pothen* so far in connection with wine (2:9), wind/spirit (3:8), water (4:11), and bread (6:5), but now the term is expressly applied to the *pothen* of Jesus. This is the third traditional objection to Jesus, one anticipated by Nathanael's question regarding Jesus' origin in Nazareth (1:46) and the murmuring Judeans' question in Galilee regarding Jesus' parentage by Joseph and his wife (6:42). Now the objection comes in a less specific, and therefore more ironic, form: "We know where." Where *do* the Jerusalemites think Jesus is from? Of course, we know the "real" answer: from God, the one who sent him. Could it be that this is the awareness to which the Jerusalemites object? The question echoes a theme from the Wisdom literature:

But where [LXX, *pothen*] shall wisdom be found? And where is the place of understanding? Mortals do not know the way to it, and it is not found in the land of the living. The deep says, "It is not in me," and the sea says, "It is not with me." (Job 28:12–14)

Where [LXX, *pothen*] then does wisdom come from? And where is the place of understanding? It is hidden from the eyes of all living, and concealed from the birds of the air. (Job 28:20–21)

This expression of the tradition of the "hidden messiah" also fits with John's disclaimer back in 1:33 that "even I did not know him." What separates the Jerusalemites from John is that John recognized and confessed Jesus as the one once Jesus arrived on the scene, but the Jerusalemites confuse their apparent familiarity with Jesus with the expected secrecy of the messiah and are unable to bring these two pieces of "knowledge" together.

The response of Jesus to this confusion is sharp and dramatic. For the first time in the fourth gospel, he is described in verse 28 as "crying out." We are reminded that he is still teaching in the Temple (filling the chiastic parallel line), but now, his teaching becomes infused with urgency and emotion, as he proclaims with sarcastic exasperation, "You know me and you know where [*pothen*] I am from! I have come not on my own, but the one who sent me is true, whom you have *not* known. I know him because I am from him; that one sent me." Whatever the Jerusalemites might have been thinking, now Jesus openly cries out his *pothen* for all to hear. Even more ironically, though, in this little speech, Jesus does not name the one who sent him as either "God" or "my Father." Readers, of course, have heard many times the equation: one who sent=God. But for the crowd gathered for the feast who may be hearing Jesus for the first time, Jesus' loud proclamation tells them nothing at all.

When Jesus makes his claim about those who do not know the true one, he uses the word "you." The question of the referent of this plural "you" is difficult. Is it the entire crowd of Tabernacles worshipers murmuring in verse 12 and challenging Jesus in verse 20? Just the Judeans who wonder in verse 15? The Jerusalemites who claim knowledge in verse 27? All of the above? Perhaps more importantly, who is the "they" in verse 30 who respond to Jesus' proclamation by "seeking to get hold of him"? Presumably, it is the Judeans who were plotting back in 5:18, the "they" whom the Jerusalemites have in mind. But perhaps, after Jesus' loud speech, we are to imagine the entire crowd trying to grab him. Whoever it is, we are told that "no one laid a hand [*epebalen*] on him, because his hour had not yet come." The use of *epebalen,* literally, "to throw upon," is ironic: as those who confess Jesus face being thrown out and Jesus will not throw out those who come to him (*ekbalo,* 6:37), they now try to stop Jesus by the opposite gesture of force.

The narrator's comment provides the first explicit reference to Jesus' "hour" since 2:4 at the wedding in Cana. Just when it might seem that things are getting out of control, we are reminded that the "script" follows Jesus. In this midst of this tight spot filled with violent anger and a threatening crowd, God's power in Jesus reveals its supremacy.

The public discussion on the middle feast day apparently ends with a note of ambiguous hope in verse 31. In spite of the confusion, "many of the crowd believed in him." But the ambiguity is framed once again in terms of "signs": "When the Christ comes, he will not do more signs that this one, will he?" The first part of the question implies that "this one" is *not* the Christ. Further, by measuring the degree of similarity between Jesus and their expected messiah in terms of signs, they fall back into the category of those in 2:23–25, 4:48, and 6:30 who may believe in Jesus at some level but are not in turn trusted by him.

Immediately, though, the scene switches, as the omnipresent narrator takes us in verse 32 into the conversation among the Pharisees themselves. Perhaps surprisingly, it is the first time we have found the Pharisees on stage since the opening scene of the gospel. They will become a common character group from this point on, but they appear suddenly at Tabernacles as those who, along with the chief priests, are in charge. Historically, this is a bit inaccurate, as the Pharisees as a party had no particular authority in Jerusalem except to the extent that some members of the Sanhedrin happened to be Pharisees. But for the Johannine community, this only-surviving group after the destruction of the Temple *is* in charge of official Judaism.

We are told that the Pharisees "heard the crowd murmuring these things about him." Even the possibility of faith in Jesus is too much for them, so they join with the priests to send *hypēretas* to get hold of Jesus. The exact nature of these people "sent forth" (*apesteilan*) from the Pharisees and chief priests is not clear. The term is variously translated as "subordinates," "police," and "officers" and suggests people under hierarchical control of their senders. The irony is thick and contrasts those sent by the Sanhedrin with those sent by God or, eventually, by Jesus. The representatives of Torah (Pharisees) and Temple (priests) are the conspirators who comprise the "they" in verse 25.

Once this new revelation is made, we are brought back to the public forum where Jesus, despite the attempt to grab him, continues to speak. In verse 33 he introduces a new theme, one which will echo many times through the Last Supper discourse: "I am with you just a short time, until I go to the one having sent me. You will seek me and you will not find me; where I am you are not able to come." Raymond Brown points out the Proverbs passage lying behind this proclamation.[12] The entire Proverbs passage sings notes that echo through the Tabernacles discourse:

> Wisdom cries out in the street, in the squares she raises
>     her voice.
> At the busiest corner she cries out, at the entrance of the
>     city gates she speaks:
> "How long, O simple ones, will you love being simple?
> How long will scoffers delight in their scoffing and fools
>     hate knowledge?
> Give heed to my reproof; I will pour out my thoughts to
>     you;
> I will make my words known to you.
> Because I have called you and you refused,
> have stretched out my hand and no one heeded . . .
> Then they will call upon me, but I will not answer;
> they will seek me diligently, but will not find me.
> Because they hated knowledge and did not choose the
>     fear of the Lord,
> would have none of my counsel and despised all my
>     reproof.
> Therefore they shall eat the fruit of their way
> and be sated with their own devices.
> For waywardness kills the simple, and the complacency
>     of fools destroys them;
> but those who listen to me will be secure and will live
>     at ease, without dread of disaster.
>                                         (Prov 1:20–25, 28–33)

This is an apt summary of Jesus' activity at the feast and the response of his hearers. It also provides another occasion for Johannine irony, as the Judeans, speaking once again to one another in verse 35 (cf. 6:43), misinterpret Jesus' "going" as being a mission to the Greek-speaking diasporan Jews in other parts of the empire. And yet they do not believe their own guess, as indicated by their

---

12. R. Brown (1966, 318).

(accurate) quote of Jesus' question to them. At least they heard him correctly this time! Of course, for the Johannine community, their interpretation is also ironically correct, for although Jesus is referring to his "going" to his Father via the cross, he *will* eventually go to the Greeks via the Johannine community. It is the first time in the fourth gospel that the scope of the "world" is expanded beyond the bounds of Palestine. The quest for God's children by the one through whom the world was created will not be limited by national boundaries.

We must give some credit to these Judeans, who are to be distinguished at this point from those who, offstage, send out their agents to arrest him. They are still *trying* to figure out what he is talking about. Given the incomprehension of Jesus' questioning disciples revealed later in the fourth gospel, this is no small matter. To at least be asking questions is not to have abandoned the search for knowledge. Is it not our inquiring ignorance that leads us to do Bible study in the first place?

### 3. THE GREAT DAY OF THE FEAST: 7:37–52

A. **Chiasm:** 7:40–52

    a: 40–41: prophet/Galilee

        b: 42–45: scripture/division among people/Pharisees

            c: 46: no one ever spoke like this one

        b¹: 47–51: Law/Nicodemus vs. others (division among Pharisees)/ Pharisees

    a¹: 52: prophet/Galilee

B. **Location:** Jerusalem

C. **Time:** Tabernacles, the last great day

D. **Hebrew scripture context:** (see above)

E. **Social factors:** the crowds vs. the Pharisees

F. **Themes:** "scripture" vs. "Law"

We now reach what the narrator calls in verse 37 "the last, great day of the feast." The full Temple and Torah pomp and circumstance is at hand: the water and candlestick ceremonies, the array of robed priests and costumed women, the thousands of pilgrims, merchants, and residents of Jerusalem pressed upon one another in joyous celebration. The new wine and cultic water are flowing, as harvest and religion merge into a single symphony of praise. It is like St. Peter's in Rome on Easter, or the Mall in Washington, D.C. on the Fourth of July. Pietists and patriots alike fill every square inch of space with a paradoxical blend of revelry and reverence.

In the midst of this stupendous scene, as the priestly waters pour over the ceremonial altar, the narrator tells us in verse 37: "Jesus stood up and cried out, 'If anyone is thirsty, let them come to me and drink!' " Can we begin to imagine the effect of this shockingly "inappropriate" action? In the history of bold acts of nonviolent resistance, is there any parallel to such an astounding action?

We have heard Jesus proclaim himself the source of thirst-quenching waters before (4:14). But neither his disciples nor this Jerusalem crowd was present at the Samaritan well. The only hint was the solemn word to Nicodemus about being born of water and spirit (3:5). Did Nicodemus tell any of his fellow Pharisees or other Sanhedrin members about this word? Would there be any basis for the crowd to make sense of Jesus' Tabernacles proclamation? Without the clues we have from our "presence" at the well, what might we think Jesus has in mind?

Before we have time to pause and consider, Jesus continues his interruption of the feast in verse 38, in a saying that has baffled scholarly attempts to determine a particular meaning: "The one believing in me, according to scripture, out of his belly [*koilias*] will flow rivers of living water." The basic question is: Whose "belly" is the source of "living water"? Is it Jesus' belly or the belly of the one believing? As Brown explains, the former interpretation has dominated Western Christianity, while the latter has dominated in the East, reflecting an emphasis on either christology or discipleship.[13] Of course, given what we have experienced so far in the fourth gospel, not only is it not surprising to find such an ambiguity, but we also may expect it to be unresolvable. Possible references from Hebrew scripture to interpret the quote in verse 38 are numerous; Brown cites fourteen![14] Among the most fruitful for consideration are the following:

Isa 58:11: You shall be like a watered garden, like a spring of water, whose waters never fail.

Prov 5:15: Drink water from your own cistern, flowing water from your own well.

Ps 105:40–41: He opened the rock, and water gushed out; it flowed through the desert like a river.

Ps 78:15–16: He split rocks open in the wilderness, and gave them drink abundantly as from the deep. He made streams come out of the rock, and caused waters to flow down like rivers.

Isa 43:20: For I give water in the wilderness, rivers in the desert, to give drink to my chosen people.

Deut 8:15: He made water flow for you from flint rock.

Zech 14:8: On that day living waters shall flow out from Jerusalem.

Ezek 47:1–11: (water flowing all around the Temple into all creation).

---

13. Ibid., 320–321.
14. Ibid., 321–323.

Would any of these texts likely be in the minds of Jesus' hearers at the feast of Tabernacles? The first two suggest the believer as the source of water, consistent with one interpretation of Jesus' image. The quotes from Psalms, Isaiah 43, and Deuteronomy would have Jesus presenting himself in opposition to the water found by Moses' splitting of the rock in the wilderness, an apt theme for Tabernacles. The Zechariah quote, as we heard earlier in this chapter, was associated with the eschatological dimension of the feast and would present Jesus in opposition with the Temple/Torah system's expectation of a final gathering of all people in Jerusalem. Similarly, the Ezekiel quote presents an eschatological image of the Temple, which Jesus' statement claims to supersede. The author of the fourth gospel, as we have seen, was fully capable of precisely quoting scripture if that was important. By offering a paraphrastic, thematic summary of several scriptural passages, the text allows us to see Jesus proclaiming himself as a thirst-quenching source greater than the entire Hebrew scriptural tradition, at least as that tradition had been lived out in the Jerusalem of his day.

The word translated above as "belly," *koilia,* was used previously as "womb" in Nicodemus's misunderstanding question about being born *anōthen* (3:4). Given that the two scenes are already linked through the image of water (and that the word is used nowhere else in the fourth gospel), we can see *koilia* here as providing a feminine image for the place from which living water flows. Given also the rich Wisdom (*sophia*) background noted above for Jesus' "crying out" in the public square, we find that the passage as a whole begins to take on a feminine cast. If Jesus on the mountain and in the desert in chapter 6 was a certain type of "king" leading his people through the wilderness, then chapter 7 offers the balancing image of Jesus as the female aspect of God calling to her children.

This notion is enhanced by the narrator's explanatory comment in verse 39 that "he said this about the spirit which those who believed in him were about to receive, for as yet there was no spirit." In both Hebrew and Greek, "spirit" (Heb, *ruah*; Gk, *pneuma*) is distinctly feminine. Of course, the narrator's insight is only for the edification of readers, not listeners in the crowd.

The narrator's comment adds another element that modern Christians may find puzzling. In the view of the fourth gospel, "the spirit" was not an entity coeternal with God and the Word as these are described in the prologue. Rather, it was an aspect of Jesus' completion of his earthly mission, coming to be through Jesus' "glorification." By introducing this notion somewhat parenthetically at this stage, the narrator prepares readers for the more complete discourse in chapters 14 and 16 on the relationship between Jesus and the spirit. This doesn't help the disciples, though!

The crowd's reaction in verse 40 is, in part, almost identical to that of the Galilean crowd who ate from the loaves: "This is truly the prophet" (6:14). However, some in the crowd differ in their interpretation by saying in verse 41, "This is the Christ." Prophet versus messiah is now the question in dispute. Put another way: Is Jesus a "descendant" of Moses (prophet) or of David (messiah)? Thus, the claim of messiahship is countered in verses 41b–42 with the challenge,

"The Christ isn't coming from Galilee, is he? Doesn't scripture say that from the seed of David, from Bethlehem the village of David, is where the Christ is coming from?" This is the core of the battle of myths *within* Israel. As Richard Horsley and John S. Hanson put it:

> There is also little or no literary evidence for any expectations of an eschatological prophet among the Pharisees.... The basic reason... was their firm conviction that the decisive revelation of the will of God had already been given in the Torah. Their principal task, their own *raison d'être*, was to interpret and realize the provisions of the law in the life of the community.[15]

On the other hand, the Eighteen Benedictions, a Jewish text from the late first century, contained the following prayer:

> In thy great mercy, O Yahweh our God, have pity on Israel thy people ... and on thy Temple... and on the kingdom of the house of David, the Messiah of thy righteousness. Let the shoot of David sprout quickly and raise up his horn with thy help.[16]

Thus, while there were general popular hopes for either an eschatological prophet *or* a royal messiah, the Pharisees hoped *only* for the messiah, the shoot of David. The "division" (*schisma*) within the crowd in verse 43 reflects, at least in part, this battle for hearts and minds between the mass of people and the literati. The *schisma* is the first of several that will be reported on in this cluster of chapters describing Jesus' final public encounters with the crowds. It has been implicit throughout the Tabernacles scene, as the various Judean objections to Jesus reach expression (7:12, 15, 26–27, 31).

The particular question of the messiah's origin in Bethlehem is itself a two-edged sword, one that the narrator does not offer further help on. If one assumes general awareness of the tradition of Jesus' birth in Bethlehem recorded by Matthew and Luke, fulfilling the prophecy of Mic 5:2, then the text of the fourth gospel is ironic.[17] It implicitly acknowledges the earthly birthplace of Jesus while emphasizing, as it does throughout, his heavenly origin. On the other hand, Wayne A. Meeks sees it as another example of the Judea/Galilee opposition: Jesus is from Nazareth (Galilee), not from Bethlehem (Judea).[18] Given our interpretation of the geographic issue in terms not of locale (Judea/Galilee) but of identification (Judean/Galilean), Meeks's point is not as convincing. Without appeal to external christological traditions, however, the passage simply represents another misdirected dispute over "earthly" things, not unlike Nathanael's doubts about good coming from Nazareth (1:46).

---

15. Horsley and Hanson (1985, 158).
16. Quoted in ibid., 109.
17. Duke (1985, 67); De Jonge (1972–73, 260).
18. Meeks (1966, 162).

The scene ends in verse 44 with the second attempt to get hold of Jesus, and the second failure. The futility of the conspirators' efforts is darkly comical, as they seemingly stumble like Keystone Kops, unable — or even unwilling — to capture this dramatic would-be leader of the crowd.

The simultaneous drama begun in verse 32 with the sending forth of the Sanhedrin police is now completed beginning in verse 45. We are not surprised when the chief priests and Pharisees challenge the failure of their "apostles" to carry out their orders. As Jesus does the will of *his* sender, these do *not* do the will of theirs. But their excuse offered in verse 46 *is* surprising: "Never has anyone spoken like this!" It is apparently not a question of inability but of *unwillingness* to arrest Jesus. Are the police on the verge of becoming converts? Or were they simply afraid of being outnumbered by the believers in the crowd? Or perhaps they were simply shocked or spellbound by the unexpected drama of Jesus' Tabernacles speech and forgot what their duty was until it was too late! Whether they approve of Jesus' words is not narrated. They simply speak the truth without evaluation: no one has spoken like this before.

Their statement is too much for the Pharisees, who take charge of the situation, while the chief priests remain strangely silent. At this point, the narration in verse 45 is revealed to be ambiguous: it may have been only the Pharisees who asked the first question as well as the one in verse 47. In the fourth gospel, the Pharisees become the de facto "rulers," despite the historical nod to the priests who no longer exist in the discourse world of the Johannine community. The Pharisees' challenge comes in two parts. First, they ask: "You have not also been misled [*peplanēsthe*], have you?" They implicitly refer back to the murmuring early in the feast (7:12), when the crowd argued about whether Jesus was "good" or "misled" (*plana*) the people. Have the Sanhedrin police come to believe that Jesus is "good"? Second, they issue a challenge in verse 48 to the possibility of faith in Jesus on the basis of their authority: "Not one of the rulers or the Pharisees have believed in him, have they?" The question ought to immediately bring to mind the one possible exception of which readers are aware: Nicodemus, the "person of the Pharisees, . . . ruler of the Judeans" (3:1). Yes! we might call out. There is one! Speak up, Nicodemus! Before we find out whether Nicodemus will respond, the Pharisees add in verse 49 another slap at those who might fall for Jesus' errors: "But the crowd not knowing the Law are accursed people." Their harsh statement condemns the crowd on the basis of Deut 27:26: "Cursed be anyone who does not uphold the words of this Law by observing them." In a classic statement of self-righteous intellectual superiority, the Pharisees condemn their own people for their ignorance — those who expect the prophet, those who chase into the wilderness after every miracle worker, powerful speaker, offerer of quick fixes. The Pharisees have put their trust in the tradition of Moses and cannot be helped by any Johnny-come-lately speaker of God's word. Given the eventual outcome of the fourth gospel, it is a terribly ironic curse.

With this angry and bitter mood prevailing, the narrator lets us know that Nicodemus *is* there and will speak. But the introduction in verse 50 is highly ambiguous: "Nicodemus, the one having come to him before, and who was one of them..." The first detail is clear, recalling the previous story in chapter 3. But the second opens a huge gap in the text. Which "them" is he one of? We already know that Nicodemus is both a Pharisee and a ruler. But is he also "one of them," that is, the accursed crowd who errs by believing that Jesus is good? Nicodemus has "confessed" that Jesus is a "teacher come from God" and that "God is with" him (3:2). He is firmly on the fence straddling these unreconcilable positions, apparently one of both "thems." How can he speak without coming down from his lofty neutrality and declare his loyalty to one or the other?

The master of diplomacy, Nicodemus in verse 51 finds a way out of his dilemma by appealing to "due process." "Our Law does not judge a person without first hearing from him and knowing what he is doing, does it?"

The "perfection" of his response is worth dwelling on for those of our age who have found public debate limited by the labels "conservative" and "liberal." Within that anachronistic framework, the questioners are clearly the "conservatives" and Nicodemus the "liberal." His question presumes the basic validity of the system of law upon which Israel (and modern "democracies") are grounded. If "our Law" were applied properly, he claims, we would give this absent accusee full rights to confront his accusers, testify on his own behalf, explain his motives, and so on. The U.S. Bill of Rights is not the first document to provide for such procedures. Many, many well-meaning but naive protesters have found themselves in a U.S. courtroom hoping that if only their "rights" were respected, justice would emerge. I myself have been one of these, raised on the tradition of the 1960s that expected that if "good people" filled the judicial seats and the legislative bodies, the U.S. Constitution would allow for the development of just policies for all people. Thus, we as a nation passed civil rights laws to protect and provide equal opportunity for people of color, women, youth, elderly, and other marginalized persons. However, the experience of subsequent decades put the lie to change through the "liberal" route of assuring equal rights under law. The beating of Rodney King and the subsequent trials, the hearings regarding Clarence Thomas and Anita Hill's allegations, the burying of Iraqis in the desert during the Gulf War, and numerous other events proved that law is an insufficient basis upon which to build justice. What is required instead is the interdependent personal commitment of *community*. If this seems like a new insight, we should have studied our scriptures sooner, because the scene in Jn 7:45–52 powerfully dramatizes this exact conflict in ideologies.

Nicodemus hopes that the precious and beloved Law that he appeals to as "ours" will be enough to vindicate Jesus without Nicodemus's personal witness. It is not. David Rensberger says it was "hardly likely that this timid legal quibble would constitute a confession of faith satisfactory to the Fourth Evangelist."[19] Why? Because, as Mary Margaret Pazden puts it, Nicodemus's "concern about legal precision and being expelled from the group is greater than witnessing on

---

19. Rensberger (1988, 39).

Jesus' behalf."[20] When push comes to shove, the government of laws and the community of persons are irreconcilable. If Nicodemus sides with the Law, he denies Jesus and the Johannine community. If he witnesses for Jesus, he risks being condemned by his fellow Pharisees as "accursed." The "liberal" instinct is inconsistent with commitment to Jesus, for the Law will eventually be the cause of Jesus' death.

Ironically, even this weak attempt to walk the line is harshly ridiculed in verse 52 by the Pharisees, who are not as "liberal" as Nicodemus. Again, their criticism comes in the double form of an ironic rhetorical question and a statement. The question puts Nicodemus to the basic identity test of the fourth gospel: "You're not a Galilean, too, are you?" In the minds of the Pharisees, of course, the accusation suggests that he is part of the illiterate crowd, the country bumpkins so removed from cosmopolitan Judea that they don't know what's what. From the narrator's and readers' viewpoint, though, it is the central faith identification: to be a Galilean is to be among those who "receive" Jesus (4:45). The second half of their challenge is: "Search [*erauneson,* as in 5:39] and see that no prophet is to be raised up out of Galilee." If they are stating that historically no prophet is "raised up" out of Galilee, they are simply wrong: both Jonah and Nahum (Nah 1:1) are from that region.[21] But if they are speaking about the future prophet — the one whom the crowd hopes Jesus is but the Pharisees aren't expecting at all — then they are speaking more from outside the Law, for the Hebrew scriptures do not specify the origin of that prophet. The thickness of this irony is almost too much: here are the rulers who condemn the crowd for its ignorance who themselves make a serious mistake in recalling their tradition.

How will Nicodemus respond to this? They have put the challenge to him just as clearly as did Jesus in chapter 3. Sadly, he once again disappears into silence, as the scene closes without another word from the defender of due process.

---

20. Pazden (1987, 147).
21. Duke (1985, 68).

# 12

# The Trial Continues

*Determining One's Paternity*

## John 8:12–59

**A. Chiasm:** 8:21–59

    a: 21–30: I am

       b: 31–41a: descendants of Abraham

          c: 41b–47: your father the devil

       b[1]: 48–56: your father Abraham

    a[1]: 57–59: I am[1]

**B. Location:** the Temple treasury

**C. Time:** Tabernacles

**D. Hebrew scripture context:** Abraham covenant traditions

**E. Social factors:** the Pharisees vs. the Johannine community

**F. Themes:** determining who God's children are

**G. Key word:** Father

## 1. INTRODUCTION:
## THE WOMAN CAUGHT IN ADULTERY

John 7:53–8:11 contains one of the most famous stories in the New Testament. It offers a beautiful lesson in the dangers of self-righteousness and in the joy of forgiveness. Its vocabulary and themes fit within the basic framework of the fourth gospel.

---

1. Ellis (1984, 150–151).

**191**

Unfortunately, it is not a part of the most reliable ancient manuscripts of the gospel. While many commentators have wasted much ink and paper developing theories of the "displacement" of one part or another of the text in favor of a version that they prefer,[2] there is an entirely different basis for excluding this passage. It is not a matter of imposing an artificial theological or narratological unity on the supposed text and then "rearranging" the gospel to fit one's pre-existing view. Rather, it is an issue of recognizing the material evidence upon which the gospel we *have* is based. Raymond Brown, summarizing the matter, points out that Western commentators do not mention the passage until around the year 900.[3] While there appears to be some evidence from the East for an early version of the story, some manuscripts place it in Luke! From a perspective of biblical poetics, then, we must be faithful to the text of the fourth gospel that has the best likelihood of actually having arisen from the complete experience of the *Johannine* community and not just from the early church generally.

## 2. THE LIGHT SHINES AT TABERNACLES

### Chiasm: 8:12–20

a: 12: *egō eimi*; light of life

   b: 13–14: witness

      c: 15–16: judgment

   b[1]: 17–18: witness

a[1]: 19–20: if you knew me, would know Father (i.e., Father=Jesus=*egō eimi*=light of life)

Just as we might have expected the scene to change from Jerusalem to Galilee or perhaps the wilderness as it did in 3:22 and 6:1 after powerful confrontations between Jesus and the Judeans, we find Jesus in 8:12 speaking "again to them." He either is very courageous and confident of God's protection or is a risk-taker beyond all sense of reasonable prudence. How can he continue to speak in the midst of people trying desperately to get hold of him and to condemn him as an enemy of God?

And as we stop to consider the boldness of his speech, we might even wonder: Where are Jesus' disciples in the midst of all this Tabernacles uproar? The last we heard of them was at the end of chapter 6, back in Galilee. Have they even come up to Jerusalem with their master? Are they hiding out in fear, or overwhelmed by his behavior, or . . . ? Not a clue is provided as to the whereabouts or feelings of Jesus' closest companions. But regardless of whether they

---

2. Rudolf Bultmann was the first to engage in this distrust of both the manuscripts and the final text, but not the last. See Ernst Haenchen's two-volume (1984) commentary for a particularly unhumble attempt to know better how the gospel should have been written.

3. R. Brown (1966, 335–336).

are watching from the sidelines or have left Jesus totally alone in the midst of a pack of wolves, Jesus continues to fulfill his mission.

More dramatic words at the denouement of the feast of Tabernacles are hardly imaginable than those that Jesus proclaims in verse 12: "I AM [*egō eimi*] the light of the world. The one following me will surely not walk in darkness, but will have the light of life." We recall the candlestick ceremony of the feast, in which Jerusalem was totally illuminated with light, representing the very light of God. Either during or soon after this ceremony, Jesus claims to embody that light himself, the light announced to readers first in the prologue.

While we have heard both the narrator and Jesus speak of the light *in* the world (1:9; 3:19), Jesus' statement adds another powerful nuance to the previous passages. Jesus is the light *of* the world. The implication is not only that Jesus is like a torch, offering illumination where there is darkness, but that the *only* light the world has comes from Jesus. His light is not in addition to other lights but is the only light by which the world can truly see.

Furthermore, for the late first-century audience, the Zecharian vision that the Jerusalem Temple would be the eschatological gathering place of all people to the light "was a sham."[4] For the Johannine community and future readers of the fourth gospel, Jesus was the light that the Temple failed to be.

Furthermore, the light is for the purpose of empowering "walking." For those who envision the fourth gospel as a purely mystical tract, this passage offers an antithesis. Jesus is not speaking to people simply *being* in the dark, but to those who are on a journey, an exodus pilgrimage, a liberation passage from death and bondage to life (cf. 11:9–10).

The response of the Pharisees in verse 13 is both oblique and Law-bound. Rather than challenge the truth of his remarkable assertion directly, they re-introduce the forensic theme we saw laid out in chapter 5. Jerome Neyrey offers the following schematic outline of the elements of this version of Jesus' "trial" by the Pharisees:

1. testimony (8:12)

2. basis for testimony: firsthand knowledge (8:14)

3. criteria for judgment (8:15)

4. two witnesses as acceptable testimony (8:16–18)

5. authorized testimony (8:19)

6. setting for dispute (8:20)[5]

It is a much more concise trial scene than 5:19–47, fitting perfectly within the chiastic structure of the passage. It begins in verse 13 with the challenge to

---

4. C. Koester (1994, chap. 4).

5. Neyrey (1988, 38–39) sees this trial as parallel with parts of chapter 7, but the word "witness" (*martyria*) is not found in that chapter at all, except in verse 7, where Jesus "witnesses" against the world.

Jesus' testimony: "You bear witness about yourself." We have heard Jesus refute this exact (implicit) charge in 5:31, where he denied that he in fact did bear
witness about himself, offering in addition several other credible witnesses. In
verse 14, though, he takes an entirely different tack: "Even if I am bearing witness about myself, my witness is true, because I have known where [*pothen*] I
came from and where I am going, but you have *not* known wherefrom [*pothen*]
I am coming or where I am going." From a forensic standpoint, Jesus now
claims that his knowledge of his own *pothen* validates his witness. He has already proven to them that his testimony is backed up by powerful witnesses,
and he has no need to repeat himself. This, of course, is totally unsatisfactory
as Torah trial procedure, but we should not be surprised at this late date to
find Jesus providing a legal standard based on knowing one's source (i.e., God)
rather than simply knowing one's tradition.

In light of the argument earlier in the Tabernacles week about whether, given
the Jerusalemites' "knowledge" of his *pothen,* Jesus could be the Christ, the
present statement by Jesus is heavily ironic and underscores the sarcasm of his
previous response to their own claim (7:27–28). They do *not* know where he
is truly from, which, according to their own messianic ideology, partially qual-
ifies him to be the messiah! His statement is both a rebuke of their claim to
knowledge and a renewed invitation to consider who Jesus is.

Their incorrect sense of Jesus' *pothen* comes, he tells them in verse 15, by
their wrong standard of judgment (cf. 7:24): "You judge according to the flesh;
I am not judging anyone." His announcement reveals their having been born by
"will of flesh" (1:13), that is, the dominant, "earthly" culture. We might expect
the contrast with Jesus' judgment to describe his own as according to "spirit,"
but instead, he offers the somewhat surprising statement that he does not judge
at all. We did hear in 3:17–18 that the Son has come into the world not to judge
but to save and that the one having faith is not judged. But in the previous trial
scene, Jesus claimed that the Father, who judges no one, had given him authority
to judge and that "as I hear, I judge" (5:22, 27–30). Which is it? Does Jesus
judge or doesn't he? Just to confuse matters further, he continues in verse 16
with: "And if I *am* judging, my judgment is true." Mixed messages like these
lead many scholars to throw up their hands and pass it all off as a matter of
sloppy editing or expressions of different stages in the life of the Johannine
community. From a narratological standpoint, we cannot allow ourselves out of
the bind so easily. Is it possible to make sense of these apparently conflicting
signals?

To attempt to find the key, a schematic picture of the various judgment
statements might help sort things out:

**standard**

3:19: this is the basis for the judgment: that the light has come into the
world but *people loved darkness* rather than the light

5:24: the one who *hears* my word and *believes* in the one who sent me has eternal life and is *not* coming into judgment

5:29: those who *practiced foul deeds* to a resurrection of judgment

5:30: as I *hear,* I judge, and my judgment is *just*

7:51: our Law does not judge a person without a *hearing,* does it?

7:24: stop judging by *appearances*

8:15: you judge according to the *flesh*

**who does the judging**

5:22: the Father judges no one but has given all judgment to the *Son*

5:27: he has given authority for judgment to *him,* because he is the Human One

5:30: as I hear, *I* judge, and my judgment is just

8:15: *I do not* judge any one

8:16: *if I do* judge, my judgment is true

8:26: *I* have many things about you to be speaking and judging

8:50: there is *one* seeking and judging

The first group of sayings does not offer any difficulty; the basis for judgment and nonjudgment is clear. But the second group is irreconcilable except as a "both/and" paradox. The Father judges no one (5:22) and is judging (8:50); Jesus judges no one (8:15) and is judging (5:30). What later theology came to express via the tension between justice and mercy, righteous condemnation and compassionate forgiveness, the fourth gospel allows to remain under an "illogical" simultaneous no *and* yes. Just when the community's experience of persecution and injustice leads it to declare God's judgment upon its enemies, the challenge to "save" crops up. And at the same time that unconditional love appears, the need to chastise for the sake of growth arises. The tension is unavoidable and irreconcilable.

Returning to the basis for Jesus' "defense" against those who clearly *do* judge, though, he claims in verse 16b that the reason for the truth of his judgment is that "I am not alone, but the Father who sent me is with me." Here we find Jesus' "witness" and "judgment" blending together, as the simultaneous trials continue to merge. Both the Father and Jesus testify, and that is also the basis for the truth of their combined judgment, even under the standard of "your" Law.[6]

---

6. R. Brown (1966, 341), though, points out that the usual Torah standard required two witnesses in addition to the one testifying, except in the case of a parent on behalf of a child.

When this argument provokes the retort in verse 19, "Where is your Father?" readers do not know whether to laugh or to cry. This question comes from the people who have been tormenting Jesus at least since the previous Passover precisely because he claimed that *God* was his Father (5:18)! What kind of people is Jesus dealing with? Are they zealous partisans of a Law and its apparent source for which Jesus shows little respect? Or are they simply blind and deaf murderers bent on destruction and condemnation? Up until this point, the former view at least allowed generous readers to consider them as misguided but sincere. Now, it seems almost impossible to have sympathy for them.

And yet, strangely, we note that the term "Father" was used eleven times in chapter 5 and ten in chapter 6 but did not occur once in chapter 7. Further, we note that of the various arguments against Jesus in chapter 7, none refers directly to this issue of his paternity. Does this suggest that the "they"/Pharisees who inquire in 8:19 but were not expressly mentioned in the previous encounters have never before heard this claim? Can the Judeans be so divided among themselves that those who persecuted him and sought to kill him after 5:18 have not spoken with these Pharisees at all about Jesus? If we are not to take the Pharisees' question as part of an absurd caricature, we must at least consider these possibilities.

This amended picture portrays the Pharisees as removed from the entire situation since their first (implicit) appearance as the senders of the inquirers of John in chapter 1. They are so disdainful of the crowd who does not know the Law that they have nothing to do with them or their popular arguments about the latest prophets and messiahs. Their attention was not drawn to Jesus by his action in the Temple in chapter 2 because the Temple is not their particular precinct. And in retrospect, we see that the "trial" in chapter 5 was not necessarily one that drew wide-scale public notice. But when Jesus stood up so outrageously at Tabernacles that the entire crowd began to "murmur," the Pharisees stand up and begin their own inquiry. From this perspective, the current trial is not so much a repetition of the one in chapter 5 but a new one by a different group of prosecutors. This perspective calls us to look back at the Pharisees' attempts to arrest Jesus starting in 7:32 not necessarily as tantamount to his murder, but as (perhaps) an attempt simply to bring him in for questioning, as Nicodemus's own question suggests. The "they" who the Jerusalemites suspect of seeking to kill him are not necessarily these Pharisees at all, but the "Judeans" who question him in 7:15.

What becomes apparent as it unfolds, then, is that this trial is precisely the "hearing" that Nicodemus claimed the Law required before it judges someone. If, as I have suggested, the Pharisees are engaging in their first dialogue with Jesus here, then we have no basis for assuming that they have already judged him, other than in their sarcastic and angry response to Nicodemus in 7:52.

---

Thus, Jesus claims the special case of the Father's lone support for his Son as sufficient under the Law. Note also that Jesus' case hanging on his sole witness would be insufficient in the court of Qumran as well (see, e.g., 11QT 51).

Their *presumption* is that Jesus is just another self-appointed messianic or pro-phetic teacher who is leading the accursed crowd astray. But they *will* grant him a hearing, in accordance with the Torah. From this perspective, they may be wrong about their history or too quick to assume the worst (Which one of us would recognize Jesus if we heard him on the street corner?), but they are faithful to the Law, at least to this extent. As the scene plays out in chapter 8, then, we should not confuse the Pharisees' reactions with those of the previous prosecutors in chapter 5, who had already condemned Jesus before the trial began.

Just as we begin from scratch to ask these questions of who knows what about Jesus, he offers the Pharisees in verse 19b what turns out to be his final word to them about his relationship with his Father: "Neither me nor my Father have you known. If you had known me, you would know my Father, too." Since they apparently do not know who his Father is, we expect that they do not catch the depth of his statement of their ignorance, but readers cannot miss the meaning: the very God whom they claim to represent is unknown to them.

The chiastic trial ends in verse 20 with the characteristic after-the-fact narrative detail that this scene took place in the "treasury," the only reference to this location in the fourth gospel. In Mark and Luke, the treasury is the place of Jesus' comments on the widow's coins (Mk 12:41–44; Lk 21:1–4), a tale not found in John. Nonetheless, the financial reference conjures up memories of Jesus' earlier condemnation of the behavior that had turned his "Father's house" into an "emporium" (2:16). Although the Pharisees were not traditionally associated with the money functions of the Temple, in the fourth gospel they have recently been linked with the chief priests (7:32, 45), who did have such responsibility. It is at least an implicit explanation for their ignorance of God: they have their minds on earthly rather than heavenly things.

The scene closes in verse 20b with the third Tabernacles reference to the impossibility of arresting Jesus before his "hour" has come (7:30, 44).

### 3. "WHY AM I SPEAKING TO YOU AT ALL?"

**Chiasm: 8:21–30**

a: 21: where I am going, you cannot come (they are separated from Jesus)

    b: 22–24: kill himself; world, *egō eimi*

        c: 25: who are you + Jesus' response

    b[1]: 26–28: lifted up, world, *egō eimi*

a[1]: 29–30: not left me alone (Jesus and Father are united)[7]

---

7. Neyrey (1988, 40) suggests the chiasm from 8:21–28, but this leaves verses 30–31 hanging, not an unprecedented structural possibility in the fourth gospel, but one that gives way in the face of the better chiastic "fit" indicated.

The narrator introduces Jesus' next provocative statement in verse 21: "Therefore, he said to them again, 'I am going and you will seek me, and in your sin you will die. Where I am going you are not able to come.'" The first question for readers is the meaning of "them again." If "them" refers to the Pharisees, it may be a simple addition to his previous words to them, that is, "continued speaking to them." However, the phrase he says has in part been narrated before but not to the Pharisees (7:33–34). Thus, the text remains ambiguous.

The repetition also contains a crucial difference. The two statements contain the following elements:

| *7:33–34* | *8:21* |
|---|---|
| 1. *a little time I am with you* | |
| 2. I am going to the one who sent me | 1. I am going |
| 3. you will seek me | 2. you will seek me |
| 4. *you will not find me* | 3. *you will die in your sin* |
| 5. where I am you are not able to come | 4. where I am *going* you are not able to come |

What was previously a statement primarily about Jesus' *own* future is now directed at *theirs* by the inclusion of the first use in the fourth gospel of the word "sin" (*hamartia*). His statement ought to lead his hearers to wonder about the relationship between his going and their own sin-ridden death. Instead, they are either blind or unwilling to hear the personal challenge, asking instead about the meaning of Jesus' going where they cannot come.

And in the constant shift of characters that we may be getting used to, verse 22 finds the respondents once more to be the Judeans, not the Pharisees. This makes sense out of the ambiguity in verse 21 as to "them again," for the Judeans were the audience on the previous occasion. Another possibility is that the Pharisees, as their doubts and confusions about Jesus are revealed, have merged into the broader category of unbelievers called "Judeans," just as did the Galileans who sought Jesus in chapter 6. Whether we are to think of the conversation beginning in 8:21 as a continuation of the trial scene with the Pharisees or of the Tabernacles discourse with the Judeans in chapter 7 is unclear, and leaves open several possible interpretations of the following dialogue. If it is in continuity with chapter 7, we see a contrast between the two interpretations of Jesus' "going." Whereas last time the Judeans ironically suspected a diasporan mission as the meaning, now at least they come to link Jesus' going with death, suggesting he might kill himself. As Paul Duke points out, their question is doubly ironic: he *will* in fact lay down his life, but *they* will be the primary cause of his death.[8]

Jesus returns the focus from a question of detached curiosity to one of urgent life-and-death decision making. In the fourth gospel's only use of a double

---

8. Duke (1985, 86).

parallel metaphor, Jesus starkly states the nature of things in verse 23: "You are from the things below; I am from the things above. You are of this world; I am not of this world." He follows in verse 24 with a repetitive (mis)quote of himself: "This is why I said to you, 'You will die in your sins.' For if you do not believe that I AM, you will die in your sins." From *sin* to *sins,* Jesus' rhetoric is inclusive of the one sin (unbelief) and its numerous manifestations (foul deeds done in darkness).

It is the first time Jesus has referred to himself in Judea with the unmetaphorical use of *egō eimi.* Talk about speaking "openly"! The challenge and the consequences of an insufficient response could not be clearer: Jesus is the very one identified to Moses at the burning bush, the one upon whose authority the Torah is based. Failure to accept this reality will result in a dark death.

The response in verse 25 illustrates precisely the contrasts Jesus set forth in verse 23: "Therefore, they said to him, 'Who are you?' " They take *egō eimi* in its ordinary meaning of "I am" and wonder who Jesus is, not grasping that when heard "from above," the simple words contained their own predicate. Their question asks for a definitive answer from Jesus' own mouth regarding the various murmurings of the crowd. The options include "prophet" or "messiah," but "I AM" is not one of the choices they are expecting.

Jesus' reply in verse 25b is one of the most difficult translation exercises in the fourth gospel. The Greek words do not form a sentence and may be fit together in several very different ways. Raymond Brown summarizes the main theories:[9]

1. as an affirmation: "[F]rom the beginning I have been speaking to you"

2. as a question: "[H]ow is it that I speak to you?"

3. as an exclamation: "Why am I speaking with you!"

The first option pays attention to the important Johannine phrase, "the beginning" (*tēn archēn*), which starts the word string. It suggests the answer to the question as a calm but insistent prologue-affirmation: "I am the word you have heard from the beginning." The second and third options contain more emotion, suggesting exasperation in the face of a question the answer to which could not be more obvious at this point in the story. Both are along the line of, "What's the use? You're impossibly deaf to what I'm telling you." José Miranda, though, offers a nuance favoring the middle option, a nuance based on Hellenistic parallels with the Greek phrase *hoti soi kai lalō,* literally, "and that I am speaking." He says:

> The power of Jesus' answer lies in the word "that." The Judeans were anticipating a predicate or an attribute, something reducible to a con-

---

9. R. Brown (1966, 347–348).

cept. Reduction to a concept is our most useful device for suppressing the otherness of the one who speaks.... He is the word as word.[10]

From this perspective, the scene is a reenactment of the burning-bush encounter: the Judeans, like Moses, wish to pin down the identity of the other, so as to gain control and mastery. But the other remains just that, mysteriously powerful and unable to be grasped, either intellectually or physically.

The prologue imagery continues with Jesus' words in verse 26: "I have many things about you to be speaking and to be judging. But the one having sent me is true, and what I heard beside him, these things I am speaking to the world." But for an audience that has not heard Jesus speak like this before, his words remain mysterious, which the narrator points out in verse 27: "They did not know that he was speaking to them about the Father." It is the first clear occasion on which the narrator has spoken of the Father (cf. 3:35), and the statement has the effect of affirming the privileged knowledge of readers in the midst of the characters' ignorance.

And yet in verses 16–18, Jesus had spoken explicitly to the Pharisees of the identity between "the one who sent" and "the Father." And if we think of the current audience as the broader group of Judeans, then we see that they have been after Jesus since chapter 5 precisely because of this claim. How then to explain the ignorance of Jesus' audience in 8:26–27? The question is at the heart of the Johannine community's frustrating experience of the unwillingness or inability of their compatriots to share in their understanding of who Jesus is. Throughout the remainder of this scene, we will find Jesus saying things that we have heard before but that continue to go misunderstood. Meeks offers an anthropological explanation based on the theory of "noise":

> If a message is to be conveyed in the face of pervasive distractions — "noise," or, in the case of myth, the overwhelming complexity of the total social matrix — then the communicator must resort to "redundance." He must repeat the signal as many times as possible, in different ways.[11]

Jesus is repetitive, and his Judean hearers do not get the message because of the power of the dominant myth to exclude other possible truths. We see this phenomenon every day in our own culture, as the mainstream media and political pundits refuse to see the evidence before their eyes that the U.S. myth is intellectually and morally bankrupt and cannot generate a life-giving and life-sustaining communal reality. Peace and justice groups find themselves repeatedly saying the same old things on their banners and at their demonstrations: violence begets violence; racism tears at the fabric of our society; justice requires that the homeless and people with AIDS obtain a full place at our national banquet, and so on. We ask: Why don't they get it? Why is there one war

---

10. Miranda (1977, 116).
11. Meeks (1972, 48).

after another, one racist denunciation of poor people after another? No matter how much we try to explain the "deafness" we experience logically in terms of social structures of power and control or spiritual structures of evil, there is an element of our experience that remains in the realm of the mystery of impenetrable stubbornness. When reality has been carefully created by long-term socialization, it is almost impossible to generate new consciousness.[12] As Jesus has said, one must be born *anōthen,* completely leaving behind the old ways of thinking and experiencing. The alternative, from a Johannine perspective, is to die in one's sins.

Jesus goes on in verse 28 to offer another way in which his audience may come to know who he is: "When you have lifted up the Human One, then you will know that I AM...." It is the second of the three Johannine "lifted up" sayings, parallel to the synoptic Passion predictions (3:14; 12:32–34). In this context, it offers a look in the other temporal direction. One way to understand who Jesus is is to consider things from "the beginning," while the other looks to the future (in the story world) event of the "lifting up," that is, the crucifixion. The latter saying fills the center of a minichiasm comprising verses 26b–29a:

a: 26b: the one having sent me is true

   b: 26c: what I heard beside him, these things I am speaking

      c: 27–28a: they did not know; when you lift up, you will know

   b¹: 28b: as the Father has taught me, these things I am speaking

a¹: 29a: the one having sent me is with me

The minichiasm closes with a repetition of Jesus' statement in verse 16 that the one who sent him has not left him alone, but it offers a unique reason for Jesus' permanent accompaniment by the Father: "because I always am doing the things that please [*aresta*] him." The word for "please" is found in the gospels only here. It also occurs in 1 Jn 3:22 to indicate that the disciple's function is that of the master: "His commandments we keep, and the things that are pleasing [*aresta*] in his sight we are doing." For a Johannine community that was constantly feeling a sense of abandonment by the dominant culture, this sense of assurance of God's presence on the way so long as they do what pleases God was a powerful encouragement.

Perhaps surprisingly in the face of the apparent resistance and ignorance that Jesus is experiencing in this scene, the narrator tells us in verse 30: "As he was speaking these things, many believed in him." What is it that has led some of this audience to convert? It is the first time that a general audience in Judea has believed in Jesus *not* because of signs (cf. 4:39, 50, the Samaritans). In the absence of the kind of sign-based faith of which Jesus is suspicious, what has been the turning point in this conversation? The narrator gives no particular clue

---

12. Berger and Luckmann (1966); Kuhn (1970).

at this point, and, as the scene continues to unfold and the mind-set of these so-called believers is revealed, we must wonder whether the narrator has made a mistake.

### 4. "WE ARE ABRAHAM'S SEED . . . "

#### Chiasm: 8:31–37

a: 31: if you remain in my word, you are truly my disciples

    b: 32: truth will make you free

        c: 33: we are from Abraham

    b¹: 34–36: Son sets you free

a¹: 37: my word finds no place in you

Verse 31 starts with Jesus addressing those who are, in Johannine terminology, a living oxymoron: "the Judeans who believed in him." It is the narrator's judgment on the depth of faith actually present in those who in verse 30 are said to believe. We should not expect much evidence of faith as this chiasm plays out, given this characterization of the conversation partners as "Judeans," even if qualified by "having believed."

Their situation is the Johannine equivalent of the synoptic image of the seed that falls on rocky ground, springs up immediately, and then withers for lack of roots (Mk 4:5–6). Jesus begins in verse 31 by encouraging just this sort of rootedness: "If you remain in my word, you are truly my disciples." When the Samaritans believed because of the woman's witness, they asked Jesus to "remain beside them." Because of this remaining, their faith is deepened so that they come to know for a certainty that Jesus is "the Savior of the world" (4:39–42). The invitation here is parallel: if the Judeans who believe would remain with Jesus, their faith would have a chance of developing roots that will not be withered by the scorching sun of the dominant Judean myth. They will experience two consequences of this commitment, named in verse 32: "You will know the truth, and the truth will free you."

As Brown points out, the idea of being freed by truth has no precedent in Hebrew scripture, although it is a notion that the Qumran community expressed.[13] Jesus is inviting his new believers into a new paradigm, one for which the Torah has given no preparation.

Their reply in verse 33 indicates that they are far from ready for this kind of leap of faith, as they, predictably yet sadly, prove their home in the regions "below" by taking Jesus' words literally: "We are the seed of Abraham and have never been slaves to anybody!" They want to affirm Jesus without giving up their privileged status of membership in the Chosen People by virtue of their ancestry. This conflict occupies the rest of the chapter and is at the very core of

---

13. R. Brown (1966, 355).

the fourth gospel's challenge. Just as the Samaritan woman was told that true worship took place on neither Samaria's nor Judea's "holy mountain," now the believing Judeans face the most difficult implication of Johannine discipleship: to give up their claim to inherited national pride in favor of receiving the authority to become God's children by means of belonging to a loving community of discipleship. It is the same choice that Nicodemus faced in chapter 3, the same one that few modern-day North American Christians realize we also face in trying to claim loyalty as children both of the Founding Fathers and of the Father of Jesus.

Paradoxically, it is precisely the Judeans' claim never to have been slaves that binds them. They claim not to have been slaves to people (which, of course, is patently and absurdly wrong as a matter of history), but Jesus explains in verse 34 that their slavery is not to people but to sin itself. By linking their identity to their national heritage, they admit their association with the sinful unbelief that manifests itself in the hatred of Samaritans, the corruption of the Temple, the oppression of the poor stemming from greed-based interpretations of Torah, and, finally, the plot to kill Jesus.

Jesus gives them an example in verse 35 from their own experience as a parable to illustrate the consequence of being slaves. "The slave is not remaining in the house forever, but the son does remain forever." That is, the slave, as one who is simply a functional element of the household, is cast out when the function is completed or when the task can no longer be performed. In contrast, one who is, like a son, an actual member of the household "remains" because of the deeper unity that binds kin. In spinning this little parable, Jesus turns their paternity principle against them. Whereas they claim that their status as Abraham's children is enough to assure a permanent place in God's house, Jesus tells them that this would be true *if* they were truly children of Abraham, but instead, they are slaves of sin. The freedom he offers is not the mere effect of national pride but the "essence" (*ontos,* the only use of this word in the fourth gospel) of freedom (verse 36).

The chiasm closes in verse 37 with the repeated emphasis on *ho logos,* with a different twist. If the Judeans are threatened with finding no place in the house of God, it is because Jesus' word "finds no room in you."

## 5. "... THEN DO THE WORKS OF ABRAHAM!"

**Chiasm: 8:38–42**

a: 38: my Father/your father

   b: 39: Abraham/what Abraham did

      c: 40a: you seek to kill me

   b¹: 40b: not what Abraham did

a¹: 41–42: your father; I came forth from God

Despite the threatening tone of Jesus' words about sin, slavery, and death in the preceding verses, there is still a sense that his audience of believers might come to understand the implication of his speech and leap across the chasm that divides them from him. But in verse 38, Jesus introduces a new theme with frightening implications that reverberate into our own time and place.

The first part of the verse covers very familiar territory, that Jesus acts and speaks in accordance with what he sees of his Father (5:19; 6:46). But the second part sounds ominous in the ears of both characters and readers: "You are doing what you have heard from your father."[14] What can Jesus mean by contrasting his Father with theirs? Their predictable and understandable retort in verse 39, "Abraham is our father," shows that they don't have a clue as to the implication of Jesus' word.

Jesus responds in verses 39b–40 by underscoring the functional rather than hereditary nature of the status of "children of Abraham": "*If* you are children of Abraham, *do* the works of Abraham." Seeking to kill one who speaks God's truth is most emphatically *not* a work of Abraham!

The Judeans in verse 41 can draw only one inference from Jesus' words: he is telling us that we are illegitimate, "born of fornication" (*porneias*)! Their righteous indignation at such a suggestion also bears an element of bitter sarcasm: we, *unlike you,* have God for our father (cf. 7:27). Their interpretation also bears implications that echo Hos 2:4, in which the prophet spins an allegory of a whoring mother whose children are born of *porneia* (LXX). The allegory concludes by condemning the mother's devotion to her "lovers" who turn out to be the false gods of the neighboring peoples (Hos 2:13). Thus, the Judeans' own words suggest that Jesus is accusing them of being idolaters.

Their words provide a new variation on the prologue's contrast between different sources of birth. For the moment, they have moved beyond their claim of birth of the will of a man (Abraham) and deny the claim that they are born of the will of the flesh/*porneias,* equivalent metaphors for birth by the dominant spirit of idolatry. But one of the unholy trinity remains to be considered: birth from blood, that is, violence. Jesus has already twice indicated that the main evidence against their claim of freedom due to their descent from Abraham is their "seeking to kill" him (8:37, 40). It should not surprise us when this becomes the theme of the following chiastic section of the dialogue.

As the current chiasm comes to its close, we hear Jesus in verse 42 willing once more to allow the Judeans to control the terms of debate. If they claim the fatherhood of Abraham, they should do what Abraham did. If they claim the fatherhood of God, they should love Jesus, for he has come from God as a messenger. The suspense begun in verse 38 has built throughout this section as Jesus denies both of their claims of paternity but has yet to suggest an alternative. Who can their father be?

---

14. R. Brown (1966, 356) notes that variant textual readings harmonize the "seen" and "heard," so that we cannot be sure whether sensory identity or contrast is meant.

## 6. A LIAR AND MURDERER FROM THE BEGINNING

### Chiasm: 8:43–49

a: 43–44: you cannot hear my word; your father is the devil

   b: 45: I am speaking the truth, but you don't believe me

      c: 46a: which of you convicts me of sin?

   b[1]: 46b: if I am speaking the truth, why don't you believe me?

a[1]: 47–49: one who hears words of God; you are a Samaritan and have a
       demon

The trial begun in verse 13 is coming to the last phases. Both parties have presented their evidence, their witnesses, and their basis for judgment. Now, Jesus offers his closing argument and his verdict. He claims in verse 43 that the members of his audience do not know what he is saying because they "are not able to hear my word." Their slavery to sin has totally disabled them from comprehending the life-giving message Jesus proffers. The verdict comes in verse 44: "You are from your father the devil [*diabolou*], and you will to do your father's desire [*epithymias*]." The cat is out of the bag! These Judeans, who claim both Abraham and God as their father, are revealed, according to Jesus, to have the most terrible father imaginable.

Who was the "devil" for Jesus' audience? The Hebrew word *satan* refers to a heavenly accuser, one who prosecutes wrongdoers on behalf of God. He became a dreaded enemy because of the role of pointing out sinfulness and alienating humanity from God. The clearest example of this role is in the book of Job, where Satan attempts repeatedly to show how Job will not retain his loyalty to God under the pressure of intense suffering (Job 1:11; 2:5). Over time, this notion was expanded to cast Satan in the role of instigator of evil, rather than simply one who names the evil that already exists.[15] The later Christian notion of Satan as a "fallen angel" had no part in the Johannine conception. Thus, the Greek equivalent, the *diabolos* (literally, *dia-bolos,* the one who casts apart), is the one who accuses and even causes human evildoing.[16] Thus, Jesus accuses them of being children of the accuser, a fittingly ironic conclusion to his own prosecution!

The term *epithymia* translated as "desire" underscores the element of the devil's willfulness that is inherited by his children. It occurs only here in the fourth gospel but is associated otherwise with lust and carnality that stem not from irrationality but from disobedience.[17]

Jesus offers his own reason in verse 44b for naming the devil as his audience's father: "That one was a murderer from the beginning, and does not stand

---

15. G. Von Rad, *TDNT* 2:73–75.

16. In gnostic thought, this notion underwent the further development that led the embodied principle of evil to be considered as a separate entity from God altogether.

17. F. Buchsel, *TDNT* 3:167–172.

in the truth, because truth is not in him. When he speaks lies, he is speaking from his own way, because he is a liar and the father of lies." This focus is different from seeing the devil simply as one who accuses or incites evil. This devil has two particular characteristics: killing and lying. The first underscores the "fulfillment" of the prologue's contrast of the children of God with those born "out of blood." It is specifically their seeking to kill Jesus (and later, the members of the Johannine community) that proves this aspect of their paternity. This association is also used in 1 Jn 3:10–12:

> The children of God and the children of the devil are revealed [*phanera*] by this: every one not doing justice is not out of God, nor does that one love his brother [or sister]. Because this is the message which you heard from the beginning: that we should love one another, not according to Cain, who is from the evil one [*ponērou*], who killed his brother. And why did he kill him? Because his works were evil [*ponērou*], but those of his brother were just.

But why has Jesus added the further element of "not standing in truth" to the devil's nature? How has *lying* been a crucial characteristic of the Judeans — those who believed in him — to whom Jesus is speaking in this passage? Is it because they "lied" about being free people due to their descent from Abraham? This claim seems more the result of stubbornness or what the Bible often calls "hard-heartedness" than direct fabrication. Can we associate these Judeans who seek to kill him with the "crowd" in 7:20 who accused Jesus of having a demon because he alleged that someone intended to kill him? Asking the question from the social standpoint: What in the experience of the Johannine community might have led them to experience the Judeans who once believed in Jesus to be liars "from the beginning"?

The word for "liar," *pseustēs,* does not occur in the synoptics and occurs rarely in the entire New Testament. However, it is used five times in 1 John, and each time has to do with claiming faith without living it justly (1 Jn 1:10; 2:4, 22; 4:20; 5:10). The clearest parallel to Jn 8:44 is 1 Jn 2:4:

> The one saying, "I have known him," and not keeping his commandments is a liar [*pseustēs*], and the truth is not in this one.

Thus, although the immediate context within the fourth gospel itself leaves the meaning of 8:44b somewhat ambiguous, it seems that the Johannine community used the term almost technically to indicate a person who had appeared to be a true follower of Jesus (according to Johannine ideology) but turned out not to be.

Their "ancestry" turns out to be as ancient as Jesus' own, going back beyond Abraham and Moses to "the beginning." Johannine theology saw sinfulness not as a matter of "falling" but as an aspect of a person's (or community's) character that, although perhaps latent, is revealed under the pressure of circumstances to be what it has always been. For modern people such as ourselves whose basic metaphors are those of change (e.g., evolution, growth, life journey, etc.), such a notion may strike a sour note. But for a persecuted community struggling to figure out why their "own" rejected them and their leader so bitterly and violently, such an explanation offers much comfort. As Jesus says in verse 45: "I tell you the truth, but you are not believing me." It is hard for those of us who have lived comfortably within a general consensus of common opinion about the world (no matter how much we might differ from our neighbors on "strategies") to imagine being in such an alienated place. But for people in the United States or other places who have tried for years to speak of love and peace only to be met by family or neighbors with patronizing acceptance at best or hostile resistance at worst, the Johannine explanation may perhaps contain a ring of accuracy.

Having announced his own "verdict" on his accusers, Jesus continues in verse 46 by asserting his own innocence: "Who of you convicts [*elegchei*] me of sin?" He uses the expressly forensic term, *elegchei,* which we heard in 3:20 used about those who remain in the darkness to avoid being "convicted" of their foul deeds. It is the central element of this chiasm, the point of contention that proves the entire official response to Jesus to be grounded in injustice and falsehood. For a community built around a person executed by the authorities as a common criminal, the claim of Jesus' innocence is crucial.

The chiasm closes in verse 47 with the summary of the case: "The one from God hears the sayings of God. You are not hearing because you are not from God."

What must the Judeans be thinking or feeling as this explosion of dire accusation pours forth from Jesus? These proud Judeans, whose entire ethnic identity is based on being God's Chosen People, are now told by an upstart teacher that they are children of the devil! It seems almost mild when they respond in verse 48 by saying, "We're clearly right in saying that you are a Samaritan and have a demon!" Although these two pejorative terms are as strong as their culture can muster, "having a demon" is hardly as deadly a charge as being children of the master of demons. The naming of Jesus as a Samaritan is an ethnic slur not unlike a white person calling another white "nigger." Jesus is "nuts," wacko, out of touch with reality. How could they possibly take such accusations as his seriously?

We must pause, though, to note two more subtle aspects of their response. First, they do not deny the charges directly. Instead, they stand on their previous "testimony" about Abraham and turn to vilifying the accuser as a defense strategy. Second, they do their best to respond in kind: as Jesus has refuted their claim to God's paternity, so they refute his by offering his supposed Samaritan background. However, while Jesus' charge is a serious one, theirs is simply name-calling. Or is it?

In verse 49, Jesus denies half of their accusation: "I do not have a demon, but I am honoring my father and you are dishonoring me." However, he does *not* deny being a Samaritan! The crowd from Galilee in chapter 6 became "Judeans" as they proved their lack of faith in Jesus. Similarly, the Pharisees earlier in chapter 8 seem to have merged into Judeans. Now Jesus, who has been associated previously with being from either Galilee (Nazareth, 1:46) or Judea (Bethlehem, 7:42) but is "really" from "above," accepts the "charge" of being a Samaritan.[18] Although this audience has not witnessed the "marriage" of Jesus to the woman at the well and her townsfolk, they have correctly named Jesus as a person identified with the most outcast and marginalized people in their social reality. As Paul Duke has put it, "For Christians of every era weary of elitist and bigoted religion... this intended insult, accepted by Jesus with wonderful silence, elicits the smile of irony."[19] But although he accepts the designation "Samaritan," Jesus is most assuredly not possessed by a demon!

Jesus introduces a new term to the debate in verse 49: the question of "honor." In 5:23, the only previous use of the term, Jesus told the Judeans that the transmittal of the authority to judge was given to the Son so that "all may honor the Son just as they are honoring the Father," and he added that "the one not honoring the Son is not honoring the Father who sent him." Thus, in accusing Jesus of having a demon, they cast dishonor on not only the Son but also the Father, the very one whom Jesus honors by doing his will and carrying out his work.

## 7. "WHO DO YOU CLAIM TO BE?"

### Chiasm: 8:50–55

a: 50–51: don't seek my own glory/keep my word

   b: 52a: Abraham died/prophets died

      c: 52b: you say: keep my word/never taste death

   b¹: 53: Abraham died/prophets died

a¹: 54–55: Father glorifies me/I keep his word

The mutual judgment having been declared, the trial turns to the passing of sentence. Immediately in verse 50, though, Jesus forgoes this "right," asserting that there is another one who "is seeking and judging." As on earlier occasions, Jesus denies that his words are for his own glory (5:41–44; 7:18). But before these questions of honor or glory can be pursued, in verse 51 Jesus changes the focus again, offering profound hope just when all seems anger and mutual condemnation: "Amen, amen I am saying to you: if anyone keeps my word, they will never see death."

If they weren't justified in believing Jesus "possessed" before, now in verse 52 the Judeans are sure of it! His claim is absurd on its face; death was as commonplace in their world as the cycle of seasons and the passing of generations. If he's not crazy, what could Jesus possibly mean by such a statement?

---

18. Karris (1990, 71).
19. Duke (1985, 75).

From the readers' standpoint, is there anything we have heard so far in the fourth gospel to prepare us for such a proposition? The closest we have is 5:24, in which Jesus told the Judeans that "the one hearing my word and believing in the one who sent me has eternal life, and is not coming into judgment but has passed over from death to life." In the present context of judgment and sentence, this earlier statement suggests that Jesus' words here contain an element of metaphor: one who has eternal life *now* will not "see" death but will look out at the world and see only life. This is not a matter of wearing rose colored glasses or being a naive optimist but of clear-eyed recognition that, despite the *fact* of death, life's power cannot be crushed for those who believe. If faith in Jesus purported to offer the literal prospect of nondeath, few people who have spent many years in this world would maintain faith for long. Instead, Jesus tells his hearers that to "keep his word" is to accept the less magical but deeper comfort that God's creative, life-giving power is stronger than the devil's power of death-dealing.

The Judeans in verse 52, like so many before them in the fourth gospel, argue with Jesus by taking him literally and then misquote him to boot! They offer the bare fact of the deaths of Abraham and the prophets — other people blessed by God's presence — as evidence against their misquote of him, "If anyone keeps my word, they will never *taste* death." Their error proves that they are not among those who "hear the sayings of God." The implication of "tasting" death as opposed to "seeing" it is that "tasting" suggests the actual personal experience. They can only hear the absurd proposition that believers will not die.

And yet there is still a small crack in the door of their hearts' locked room. Despite having accused Jesus of being a Samaritan and possessed, they ask in verse 53: "You are not greater than our father Abraham, who died, are you? And the prophets died. Who are you making yourself to be?" Their first question echoes the Samaritan woman's almost identical inquiry in 4:12 about their father, Jacob. In that case, Jesus answered with the divine, I AM.

Their second question echoes the narrator's summary of the reason for the earlier Judean decision to persecute and seek to kill him: "He was saying that God was his own Father, *making* himself equal to God" (5:18). Is it too charitable to interpret this loaded question as bearing an iota of openness? Are they simply waiting to hear Jesus condemn himself out of his own mouth by "making himself" God's Son? What will he tell them? Will the answer to the Judeans be the same as to the Samaritan woman?

Jesus keeps the suspense going in verses 54–55 for a few moments longer by once more assuring them that, whomever he tells them he is, it is for God's glory, "the one whom you say is your God," not his own. Just as they are liars for claiming to know God, Jesus would be a liar if he denied his relationship with the Holy One.

He then offers in verse 56 one more oblique opportunity for them to "get" it: "Your father Abraham rejoiced at the prospect of seeing my day, and he saw it and was glad." Just as the Judeans once "rejoiced" at seeing John (the

Baptist [5:35]), so Abraham rejoiced at seeing Jesus' day. This is maddening lunacy for those who don't understand who Jesus is! Jesus almost seems to be taunting them, revealing everything but the centerpiece. No wonder they take him literally again in verse 57: "You are not yet fifty years old and you have seen Abraham?"

For late first-century readers, the idea of Abraham seeing Jesus' day may have evoked an image from the pseudepigraphical Apocalypse of Abraham, which was likely written around the same time as the fourth gospel. That text, which was apparently composed to explain the destruction of the Temple as caused by Israel's violation of the covenant and by the "opportunistic politics of the leaders,"[20] offers hope to the survivors through an appearance to Abraham by "an angel" sent "in the likeness of a man" (*Apoc. Ab.* 10:4). The heavenly visitor says to Abraham, "Fear not, for I am Before-the-World and Mighty, the God who created previously, before the light of the age," and "I will show you the things which were made by the ages and by my word" (9:4, 10).[21] Such a text would likely have been circulated in dissident Jewish circles, not unlike the Johannine community, but probably far removed from the Judean milieu of either Jesus' opponents in the story or those who persecuted the Johannine community.[22] Thus, even if the image of Abraham's experience made sense to "insiders," Jesus' current opponents would have been unlikely to understand the reference at all.

The time to put the cards on the table comes in verse 58. There are no more metaphors, no more tricky statements: "Amen, amen I am saying to you: before Abraham came to be, I AM." Although he has told them this in 8:24 and 8:28, it still carries a wallop. Perhaps in the first situation, they heard *egō eimi* in its everyday sense, missing the import of Jesus' challenge. But now, there can be no further doubt as to what Jesus claims about himself. Their ancestor is of the world of "becoming," but Jesus *is*. The Johannine community is grounded not in the ancient — although constantly renewed — covenant between one man and God, but on the very presence of God in their midst in the person of Jesus. With these words, the sentence to be meted out by the Judeans is certain: such a person making himself God must die (verse 59).

One more time, Jesus escapes from the would-be stone-throwers, leaving the Temple. As he went up to the Temple "secretly" (*kryptō*) for the feast of Tabernacles (7:10), now he exits the same way (*ekrybē*).

---

20. H. G. Lunt in Charlesworth (1983, 685).
21. The text has survived only in Slavonic manuscripts, so we cannot compare either Hebrew or Greek biblical language to the language of the apocalypse.
22. Ashton (1991, 141–144).

# *13*

# Healing Humanity's Blindness and Witnessing to One's Re-creation

## John 9:1–41

A. **Chiasm:**

  a: 1–5: introduction: Jesus and his disciples and the question of "sin" and blindness: Jesus and the world

  b: 6–7: Jesus and the blind one: the physical healing: invitation to community

  c: 8–17: neighbors and bystanders/Pharisees and healed one: first testimony

  d: 18–23: Judeans and parents: refusal of testimony

  c¹: 24–34: "they" and healed one: Moses and second testimony

  b¹: 35–38: Jesus and healed one: spiritual healing: acceptance into community

  a¹: 39–41: conclusion: Jesus and Pharisees "with him": question of sin and blindness: Jesus and the world

B. **Location:** near the pool of Siloam (Jerusalem, Temple environs)

C. **Time:** sabbath

D. **Hebrew scripture context:** Genesis 2–3

E. **Social factors:** synagogue vs. Johannine community

F. **Themes:** modeling discipleship through faithful witness to the world

G. **Key words:** blind/seeing, sin, hearing

211

## 1. SETTING THE STAGE FOR HUMANITY'S HEALING

What will Jesus do in hiding from the Judeans who seek to kill him? Will he return to Galilee as on previous occasions? Will he dare to make himself visible again to the Judeans? And what of his absent disciples, whom we have not heard from since the end of chapter 6? Have they, too, merged into the Judeans who once believed in Jesus but have most recently picked up stones against him?

These are but a few of the questions we might have as the dramatic confrontation at Tabernacles comes to a conclusion at the end of chapter 8. It seems that Jesus has told the Judeans all he can tell them, has done powerful works of healing, feeding, and witnessing to back up his claims of divine authority, and has generated an uproar of controversy within all Palestine over the question of who he is. How can the fourth gospel continue from here without breaking the tension or simply repeating itself? What more is there to be said or done?

Were the fourth gospel written only to show the greatness of Jesus — that is, for "christological" reasons — it might well skip from Tabernacles to the Passion. But once we follow its internal logic from the beginning all the way through to the end, we find that the "high" christology is not proclaimed for its own sake but for its power to generate and sustain a community of discipleship. That is, the gospel is not for the glory of Jesus but for the glory of God. What good would it do to put Jesus on a pedestal if it didn't lead humanity to the healing of its divisions and the doing of the will of the one who sends?

For the original Johannine community, the gospel takes ten chapters to get from Tabernacles to the final Passover in order to provide hope and nourishment for people struggling between the "rock" of the Temple and the "hard place" of Roman persecution. Chapter 9 reveals both the hope for humanity's healing and the response required of those who form the community of the healed.

## 2. STRUCTURING DRAMA INTO DISCIPLESHIP

Chapter 9 forms a dramatic unity unlike anything we have previously encountered in the fourth gospel. It is a tragic irony that in the name of historically verifiable truth, this chapter has been reduced by many scholars to a "core" story of but a few verses piled over by "incorrect" theology, as if the "core" were somehow more "real" than the "additions."[1] But seen from a narratological perspective, the chapter forms a tightly structured unity in which each word is in its proper place and each subscene advances the dramatic tension of the plot until the final section provides a deeply ironic twist. Many historical critics have also recognized the powerful structural unity of the text, even if they insist

---

1. Most extreme in this rewriting of the gospel is Haenchen (1984 Vol. 2, 41), who sees only verses 4 and 39–41 as from the "evangelist."

on seeing it as the result of layers of editorial rewriting.[2] Recent literary studies have agreed on the basic unity, but differed in the delineation of the sections. For example, Peter Ellis sees a chiasm in the following sections:

> a: 1–7: Jesus gives physical sight to man
> > b: 8–17: Pharisees reject man's testimony
> > > (how open eyes?/not from God/sinner)
> > > c: 18–23: Pharisees reject parents' testimony
> > b[1]: 24–34: Pharisees reject man's testimony
> > > (how open eyes?/not from God/sinner)
> a[1]: 35–38: Jesus gives spiritual sight to man[3]

However, by excluding the final three verses from the chiasm, Ellis's proposal fails to account for the crucial confrontation between Jesus and the Pharisees. Another try is by Paul Duke and George W. MacRae, who divide the chapter this way:

> a: 1–7: Jesus and man: blindness gains sight
> > b: 8–12: man and neighbors: where is Jesus/*ho anthrōpos*
> > > c: 13–17: man and Pharisees: not from God
> > > > d: 18–23: Pharisees and parents: consequences
> > > c[1]: 24–34: man and Pharisees: from God
> > b[1]: 35–38: man and Jesus: Jesus outside/Son of Man
> a[1]: 39–41: Jesus and Pharisees: seeing lose sight[4]

This proposal improves upon Ellis's in two ways. First, it acknowledges the importance of the final verses. Second, it finds seven parts, not just five, corresponding to the basic changes in scene. But there are flaws with this approach, too. Verses 1–7 are no more a unit than are 35–41, as 1–7 contain both the discussion between Jesus and the disciples and the physical healing of the person by Jesus while 35–41 contain both the spiritual healing of the person by Jesus and the discussion between Jesus and the Pharisees.

If we simply divide both 1–7 and 35–41 into two sections each, we end up with *eight* sections and no center, whereas the confrontation between the Pharisees and the parents will be shown clearly to be the focal point. My proposal to link the scene with the neighbors in verses 8–12 and the first discussion between the once-blind one and the Pharisees is based in part on the apparent continuity in ideological interest between the neighbors and the Pharisees, as will be discussed as we get to those verses.[5] Furthermore, the social role of the

---

2. E.g., R. Brown (1966, 376–378).
3. Ellis (1984, 158–159).
4. Duke (1985, 118); MacRae (1978, 124).
5. Staley (1991, 66) gives good literary-critical reasons for seeing the neighbors and Pharisees as ideologically united in their questioning, but he does not reach the matter of invitation/acceptance into the Johannine community.

text provides another basis for this division of scenes. The seven parts show a movement back and forth between alienation/misunderstanding of Jesus and acceptance/commitment — with the central section making the main point clear:

a: 1–5: Jesus' disciples: ask a question that alienates them from Jesus

    b: 6–7: blind one: accepts invitation to wash (baptism) and sees

        c: 8–17: neighbors/Pharisees: ask questions that show their lack of faith

            d: 18–23: parents: refuse to tell what they know for fear of being expelled

        $c^1$: 24–34: Pharisees: again ask questions that show their lack of faith

    $b^1$: 35–38: healed one: accepts invitation to believe in Human One (commitment)

$a^1$: 39–41: Pharisees "with him": ask a question that alienates them from Jesus

From this perspective, the entire chapter tells three interdependent stories simultaneously: (1) the bittersweet tale of perfect discipleship's experience of invitation and acceptance by Jesus and simultaneous rejection by "the world"; (2) the sad story of betrayal by one's closest relations because of fear of the world's authority; and (3) the classic biblical narrative of the increasingly hard hearts and blind eyes of those in positions of worldly power who refuse to recognize God at work among the poor and rejected in their midst.

## 3. ASKING WHY VERSUS DOING GOD'S WORK

The shift in tone from the end of chapter 8 to the beginning of chapter 9 is remarkable: from the tension and drama of Tabernacles to an apparently calm, philosophical/theological discussion between Jesus and his disciples. But the shift is only apparent and in the eyes of the disciples. *They* ask questions; *Jesus* acts.

The scene is opened in verse 1 by the narrator with the description of a poignant aspect of human reality: "And as he was going along, he saw *anthrōpon* blind from birth." It is an unusual construction in Greek, and forces us to pause before jumping to the obvious translation of *anthrōpon* as "a man" or "a person." The sentence omits the usual Greek article, *ho*, for "a," or *tis*, for "the." John Painter has interpreted it to mean: "The man is everyman.... The omission of *tis* takes the emphasis off the particularity of the individual, as does the use of *anthrōpos* rather than *anēr* [male]."[6] Duke draws the inference one step deeper, suggesting that the omission of *ho* or *tis* has the effect of "de-emphasizing [the person's] particularity and hinting that for John all humankind is born blind."[7] Thus, we can fairly translate the opening sentence as "And as

---

6. Painter (1986, 42).
7. Duke (1985, 118).

he was going along, he saw *humanity,* blind from birth." We all share in the condition of the *anthrōpon* by the side of the road!

The disciples respond collectively in verse 2 to this universal fact of existence with an interesting but misguided question: "Rabbi, who sinned, this one or his parents, so that he was born blind?" They presume that lifelong blindness is caused by sinfulness, a common notion about the origin of ill health in the ancient world. And given this presumption, only two choices seem possible. The first is that the person has felt the inherited effects of his ancestors' sins, a notion to which the prophets objected, but which was still prevalent in Jesus' day.[8] The second, which is apparently an unprecedented notion in scriptural or rabbinical sources, is that the person himself has sinned. But how could a person have sinned so as to cause blindness at *birth?* What sort of notion of *in utero* responsibility can the disciples have in mind? Or are they just mouthing standard "wisdom" and offering the only other possibility they can think of as an option without considering the absurdity of their premise?

These aspects of the disciples' question cast them in a negative light at the outset of the story. And as we will see, they will not appear again until 11:3, when they set up another scene with a similar misunderstanding of what the situation calls for. Jesus' disciples are hardly a model at this point in the story for what it means to follow Jesus!

Where does their question come from? Why has the fourth gospel placed this question at this point in the narrative? If we consider the implications of the previous Tabernacles discussions, we can draw several conclusions that shed some light on these questions. If we can assume that the disciples either were present at the feast to hear the conversation or at least heard about it upon their reunion with Jesus, then they might have found themselves shocked with the implications of the outcome of the "trial." Those who have been held up all the disciples' lives as those most knowledgeable about the ways of Torah and the nature of God have now been accused of being children of the devil. Those who claim the inheritance of the covenant of Abraham and the Law of Moses now are revealed to be "faithful" to the evil desires of murder and falsehood. How could such a terrible thing have happened? The previous discourse suggests not a "fall" but a permanent condition resulting from birth from the wrong "father." If these paragons have a faulty birth, how can we know who has not? Aren't we all in the same boat? In other words, doesn't the revelation of the Judeans' paternity suggest that we are all "blind from birth"?

From this perspective, their proposed options take on new meaning. In other words, their question comes down to: Are we blind because of our ancestors' faults or because of our own? Have we simply inherited a bad situation or have we made it bad ourselves?

This is a difficult moral and theological dilemma, one that we struggle with frequently in our own day. Why are so many apparently good people, respected leaders, and upholders of society's virtues so concerned with worldly glory and

---

8. Jer 31:29–30/Ezek 18:1–4; Lieu (1988, 84).

power? At a simpler level, why don't people treat each other with basic dignity and respect instead of killing and deceiving one another every day? In modern lingo, the choices come down to: Is it personal responsibility or structural evil that makes the world the way it is?

Jesus' response to this universal query is: stop asking abstract moral questions and get about the business of healing! As David Rensberger has put it, "Theodicy here is the disciples' interest.... They see suffering as an occasion for moralizing about the victim. Jesus sees it as an occasion for doing the works of God, that is, for relieving the suffering."[9] In verse 3, he refutes both options the disciples offer in explanation in favor of another reason for the situation: "so that the works of God might be revealed [*phanerōthē*] in him." What would not be "revealed" at the feast of Tabernacles (7:1–10) *will* be now.

Jesus continues in verse 4 by linking two themes last united in Samaria: "we" and "must" (*dei*). Rarely has Jesus spoken in the first-person plural (although frequently in the second-person plural) in the fourth gospel, generally speaking only of his own call and witness. But here, he responds to the disciples' collective question by including them among those whose call it is to "work the works of the one who sent me while it is day." Furthermore, the call is not an option but a requirement. Few times has Jesus asserted a strict requirement; not even the "amen, amen" sayings about munching his flesh and drinking his blood carry this particular form (3:7 [born *anōthen*]; 3:14 [Human One lifted up]; 3:30 [John decrease, Jesus increase]; 4:20, 24 [worship on this mountain or in spirit/truth]). Doing the works of God, not developing moral theology, is essential to discipleship.

The time to work is now, while it is day, not at "night, when no one is able to work." The only previous reference to the time of darkness was in 3:2, when the narrator told us the time of Nicodemus's arrival on the scene. It is an image that will grow in importance as the day of Jesus' ministry comes to a close. Although no particular time of day is given, it seems that in the course of the single symbolic day of Jesus that began in Cana, it is now somewhat later than the "sixth hour" in which Jesus stayed in Samaria. It is the afternoon, when the light is beginning to recede. Thus, we have the first mention of the idea that Jesus' day will eventually come to a close with the advent of night. Accompanying this thought is Jesus' first hint (verse 5) that the coming of night will be the time of his own departure: "*As long as* I am in the world, I am the light of the world."

## 4. THE INVITATION TO BE BORN AGAIN ACCEPTED

Having verbally set the scene, Jesus goes to work. Note that there has been no conversation with the blind one at all to this point. We have no idea whether he has even heard the discussion between Jesus and his disciples (or how many

---

9. Rensberger (1988, 44).

times he had heard himself used as an example for moralizing discourse) or dared to hope for healing. Jesus' action is a free gift of God, parallel to that proffered to the woman at the well (4:10), an example of the pure grace that contrasts with the well-measured Law (1:16–17).

The act of healing narrated in verse 6 is simple but wholly unprecedented, and in blatant violation of the Torah: "After saying these things, he spat on the ground and made clay [*pēlon*] of the spit, and he put his clay on the eyes." Saliva, like any bodily fluid, was considered unclean (e.g., Lev 15:8). But the combination of spittle and soil making clay bears powerful scriptural overtones:

> And now, O Lord, you are our Father, and we are clay [LXX, *pēlos*], all of us the work of your hands. Be not very angry with us, and remember not our sins forever, but now look on us, for we are all your people. The city of your holiness has become desolate, Zion has become a wilderness, Jerusalem a curse. The house, our sanctuary, ... has been burnt with fire, and all our glorious things have gone to ruin. (Isa 64:8–11)

The narrator has already told us that the "living water" that flows from the belly of Jesus is the spirit (7:38–39). Thus, the spittle and soil are symbols of spirit and earth, the primal elements from which God made humanity in the beginning (Gen 2:7). Raymond Brown points out that the interpretation of the healing as a re-creation goes back to the early church.[10]

Jesus puts clay on the person's dead eyes, and the act is completed. The invitation follows in verse 7: "Go, wash yourself in the pool of Siloam," a name that the narrator says means "sent forth." The words suggest engaging in the very act that Nicodemus could not do: to be born *anōthen* in water and spirit (3:5). The command echoes Elisha's command to Naaman to heal his leprosy: "Go, wash in the Jordan seven times, and your flesh shall be restored and you shall be clean" (2 Kgs 5:10).

The notation of the name of the pool as Siloam and its translated meaning provides a reference to both the Tabernacles water ceremony (Isa 8:6; see 12.a.2, above) and the deeper reality that it signifies but that has apparently been lost on the Judeans. The pool exists to remind Israel of its mission as a people sent forth, but has instead become a tool of the corrupt Temple status quo. Jesus re-creates the pool as well as the person, restoring its original function as the launching pad for discipleship. Craig Koester also suggests that "Siloam," sometimes written as "Shiloah," in turn similar to Shiloh, carried messianic overtones (cf. Gen 49:10).[11]

Without the slightest hesitation, the narrator tells us in verse 7b: "Therefore, he went, and he washed, and he came seeing." What could the blind one have expected? A stranger, whom the person had no reason to suspect was a man of renown (for better or worse) in Jerusalem, comes up to him without a word and

---

10. R. Brown (1966, 380–381).
11. C. Koester (1994, chap. 3).

puts clay on his atrophied eyes, and gives the command to wash. Should we imagine him expecting a healing? If we had not heard the story before, would we expect a healing? Have we heard narratives of Jesus' healing the blind so many times that we cannot imagine what it would be like *not* to expect that such an unprecedented event could actually happen? After all, it is not an occurrence that happens frequently in the modern world! What kind of power would this most economical narrative have had for the first audience?

The narrator provides no clues to help imagine either the person's expectations or his reaction. Obedience to God's command — even when we don't know that what we are doing *is* God's command — produces its own fruits.

## 5. WITNESSING TO THE TRUTH:  ROUND 1

Immediately in verse 8, the scene becomes populated by new characters. Not a word is given about the whereabouts or thoughts of Jesus or his disciples throughout the rest of the chapter, until the healed one finds Jesus on the "outside" in verse 35. The one who can see is on his own, to fend for himself before the various questioners who make up his "world."

The narrator tells us that the "neighbors and those who used to see that he was a beggar" began to question his identity. Virtually all commentators collapse these two character groups into the single category of "neighbors," despite the clear distinction in the narrator's introduction. It is true that the inquisitors in verses 8–12 are referred to after this introduction simply as "they," without further elaboration. However, a close reading suggests that the narrator is telling us something additional. The word for "neighbors," *geitones,* occurs only here in the fourth gospel and otherwise in the New Testament only in Luke (14:12; 15:6, 9), where it means those who share the same piece of earth.[12] Unless we think of these people as fellow beggars who are "neighbors" sitting on the ground (which would make the second named group wholly redundant), it must refer to people who were his neighbors when he still had a home, that is, while living with his parents. The second group, then, are people who have only seen him in his current state as a roadside beggar. The neighbors presumably are aware of his blind *birth,* but the others know only of his being a blind *beggar.*

Their questioning among themselves addresses only his former identity as a beggar: "Isn't this the one who used to sit and beg?" The words of both narrator and questioners indicate that this is an element of his past, not his present. As the narrator did not describe the person initially as a beggar at all but rather as born blind, we cannot know whether it is the healing that has led him to give up begging or whether he had given it up beforehand. Regardless, it is his status as a sitting beggar that names him to these questioners. He has no name, no anything, just an association with poverty and dependence. People have not

---

12. The more common biblical Greek word translated as "neighbor" in the sense of Lev 19:18's duty to one's neighbor is *plēsion*; e.g., Mk 12:31; Rom 13:8.

paid enough attention to him to even be sure that the person who can now see is even the same one who once begged. Robert Karris suggests that the status of "beggar" is the "narrative expression" of 7:49 and refers to those who, in the eyes of the Pharisees, do not know the Law.[13]

They have also not even paid him the courtesy of asking him about his own situation. He boldly intrudes in verse 9 on their debate with the bare words, "I am [*egō eimi*]." It is the only place in the fourth gospel in which someone other than Jesus utters the sacred words. While they appear to be nothing more than a statement of self-identity, the specific use of this term when the more ordinary *eimi* alone would have sufficed cannot be accidental. In the context of discipleship already established by the initial dialogue and the "we" of verse 4, we can only see this phrase expressing the acceptance by this now-seeing person of the very authority of Jesus to speak the truth. He, like his healer, is "sent forth" as one re-created in earth and God's spirit.

With this briefest yet most powerful of statements, the questioners turn in verse 10 from their internal dialogue to speak to the person directly. Their question to him contains a snide tone: "How, then, were your eyes opened?" It is obviously impossible that one born blind can now see, but he claims that he is the former beggar who was definitely blind. If we are to believe your *egō eimi*, then tell us how you came to see?

The person's response to them in verse 11 is carefully and precisely worded: "The person [*ho anthrōpos*] called Jesus made clay and anointed my eyes and said to me, 'go to Siloam and wash.' I went, therefore, and washed and can see." As Jeff Staley has observed, his description of the healing is almost identical with the narrator's.[14] However, the "minor" differences are telling. First, by describing Jesus as *ho anthrōpos,* he provides the very particularity about Jesus that the narrator did not give about the blind one himself in verse 1. The healed are universal, but the healer is specific. Second, by naming the *anthrōpos* as "Jesus," the person indicates that he has been listening to other people's talk about Jesus, for the immediate passage did not recite Jesus' name in the person's presence. He is therefore in contrast with the Judeans at Tabernacles, whom Jesus said "do not listen because you are not from God" (8:47). Third, the healed one mentions the "clay" but does not say that Jesus formed the clay from his own saliva, which will have implications we shall see below. Fourth, the narrator described the action with the clay as "put" (*epethēken*), while the man says that Jesus "anointed" (*epechrisen*) his eyes. While the narrator may have thought of the clay event as only a prosaic "putting," the blind one understood it as much more. With the act, the former beggar becomes one chosen, if not yet perceived as such by God, at least by one with holy authority of some sort. *That* is why he can boldly proclaim, *"Egō eimi."* Finally, he refers simply to "Siloam" rather than the narrator's "pool of Siloam." The empha-

---

13. Karris (1990, 48).
14. Staley (1991, 65).

sis is on the "sent forth"; the fact that there is a pool involved has no further relevance to him.

The questioners do not comment on the remarkable story they have just been told other than to ask in verse 12: "Where is that one?" Why do they want to know? Are they impressed with the "miracle"? Are they just curious? Not a clue is provided to discern at this point whether they are friends or foes.

The healed one's response that he does not know *where* his healer is places him in a similar position with the man healed by the pool in chapter 5, who initially suffered from the further ignorance of not knowing *who* his healer was (5:13). But what unfolds from this point forward could hardly be more different.

In verse 13, the narrator tells us that the questioners "led the once-blind one to the Pharisees." The narrator's description of the man is in marked contrast with that given in connection with the initial questioners: "the former beggar." It shows how the emphasis in questioning has changed from the person's sheer identity to the fact of the healing. We can expect from this that the new questioners will not challenge *who* he is (and avoid provoking another *egō eimi*) but *how* he is.

If we were unsure of the perspective of the neighbors and fellow observers from their questions, the fact that they respond by bringing the man to the *Pharisees* casts a shadow over their character. At the least, it indicates that they see the Pharisees as authorities who, for better or worse, ought to be informed of this unusual event. But it also suggests that they understand that something may be wrong with what has taken place. This reader suspicion is confirmed in verse 14 when the narrator adds in the usual after-the-fact manner, "It was the sabbath day on which Jesus made clay and opened his eyes." It is the first sabbath since 5:9, the previous account of a healing by a pool. Once again, it is given to us as a surprise, but perhaps not as much of a surprise as the first time. While we do not hear another word from the initial questioners, their bringing the person to the Pharisees *on the sabbath* bears undoubtedly ominous overtones.

The narrator's summary in verse 14 is consistent with the earlier description of the incident in verse 6 in terms of "putting," but thereby establishes an even stronger contrast with the man's interpretation of the action as "anointing." Are we to hear this difference as suggesting that the blind man was wrong in his understanding? Or has our reliable narrator suddenly become subject to question? Furthermore, the narrator has dropped the instructions to "go and wash" and replaced them with the more unilateral, "Jesus opened his eyes." The change has the effect of shifting the emphasis, at least for the moment, from the call to discipleship to the fact of vision.

The narrator provides in verse 15 an indirect account of the Pharisees' questioning how it is that the man can see, allowing for the direct response of the man: "He put [*epethēken*] clay on my eyes, I washed, and I see." The phrasing is again different; it is shorter and more circumspect. "Anointing" is replaced with the narrator's "putting"; Jesus' name is not mentioned; the "making" of clay is gone; and Siloam is omitted. Staley suggests that the differences are intended to shield Jesus from a charge of sabbath violation, now that the man has caught on to the drift of the questioning.[15] The acts of anointing and making clay would each be contrary to the sabbath rules, but as it is recited, no violations are named. Nonetheless, the Pharisees sense a violation anyway and respond in verse 16 to the "miracle" with doubts about Jesus' authority: "This one is not a person from God because he does not keep the sabbath." Perhaps, as Staley suspects, those who brought Jesus to the Pharisees have told them more than what the man has. Otherwise, why would they begin to question him about his experience at all?[16] In that case, their exclamation indicates that they were asking the man to confirm what those who brought him in had already said, but, even though he provides no evidence of a violation, they trust the questioners rather than the one who has had the experience himself!

This scene has profound implications from the perspective of the Johannine community. The once-blind man acts out their own experience of having their witness doubted in favor of the word of those who are invested more in the "integrity" of the Law than in the possibility of God's newness in their midst.[17] For prospective Johannine Christians of our day, the passage to this stage offers, if not hope, at least a consoling precedent for those who find their witness doubted by institutional defenders of various stripes.

But those among the Pharisees who assume the worst about the healer do not totally dominate the group in verse 16b: "Others were saying, 'How is a person who is a sinner able to do such signs?' And there was a split [*schisma*] among them." Whereas the disciples in the opening verses assumed that blindness was caused by sin, now the question is raised about whether "signs" can be done by a sinner. It is the second schism in response to Jesus (7:43). Whether this second group consists of the "we" represented by Nicodemus in chapter 3 who would like to give Jesus the benefit of the doubt, we cannot know for sure.[18]

But the division is enough to provoke further questioning in verse 17, as the Pharisees change their focus from a search for fact to a request for opinion: "What do you say, since he opened your eyes?" The narrator prefaces their question with a surprising description of the person as "the blind one." Is it to contrast the Pharisees' perspective on the person as still blind to the "reality" of his healer's sinfulness? Certainly the narrator does not consider the person still blind. The shift adds further suspicion to the purpose of the questioning. Are the Pharisees asking because they want to learn or because they are looking for evidence with which to convict? In other words, is this an educational forum or a trial?

Consistent with the character we have observed so far, the man answers simply and directly in verse 17b, with a relatively modest yet still bold title: "He is prophet." The term *prophētēs,* like *anthrōpos* in verse 1, is anarthrous and leaves open the question of whether the man is suggesting that he perceives Jesus as "a" prophet or as completely embodying the prophetic reality (as in

---

15. Ibid., 67.
16. Ibid.
17. R. Brown (1979, 72).
18. Rensberger (1988, 43).

4:19). It is distinct from the negative proclamation in Galilee of Jesus as the prophet (6:14), an announcement that leads to the attempt to force kingship upon him. But precisely what the man means is left unclear, as is the reaction of the Pharisees.

## 6. THE SIN OF THE PARENTS VISITED ON THE CHILD

As the tension between the once-blind one and his inquisitors mounts with the proclamation that the healer is "prophet," the stage suddenly shifts to present new characters. In verse 18, we reach the center of the story, in which none of the previous personages is present. In this scene, we find the Judeans — who are introduced by the narrator as persons who have "not believed" — calling for testimony from the man's parents.

Why have the Judeans called for the parents? There is no hint that the once-blind one is a minor; indeed, in a few verses, the parents will use his age to shield themselves from further inquiry. What is the fourth gospel trying to get us to consider in shifting our attention so sharply from the conversation between the healed one and the Pharisees to this "aside"?

The first clue is in the use of the word "parents." It is a rare usage in the gospels,[19] and, with the exception of the infancy narrative in Luke, is almost wholly negative (e.g., Mt 10:21; Mk 13:1; Lk 2:41). In the fourth gospel, it is used only in this passage, first at the beginning as a possible explanation of the source of the sin that has caused blindness, and four times from verses 18–23, just after the question of sin has been raised again. In all other references to a person's parents, one or the other or both are mentioned, but never as "parents" (Jesus' mother in 2:3–5; father and mother in 6:42; Father/father throughout).

I suggest that in the context of the re-creation theme of the man's healing, the calling of his parents links the creation of humanity with the Genesis account of the first parents' sin. As the child is given a chance to recover from his blindness, so are the parents provided an opportunity to be redeemed by speaking the truth when questioned. Are they up for this challenge?

The Judeans ask two questions at once of the parents in verse 19 without waiting for an answer to the first. They get right to the heart of the matter, assuming that the parents will acknowledge the identity of the person in question as their son. Their first question, besides expecting a positive response, implies that someone has already spoken to the parents and gained an answer: "Is this your son, *who you are saying* was born blind?" The second question ("How, therefore, is he seeing now?") puts the parents directly on the spot, threatening consequences with which the Johannine community was certainly familiar but that require "extra" information for the outsider-reader in the upcoming verses.

---

19. Paul uses it for a wholly different purpose than the gospel writers, namely, as an example of respect that is either lacking or due one's elders; e.g., Rom 1:30; Eph 6:1.

Their answer appears at first consideration as straightforward as the testimony of their son. Speaking with a single voice in verses 20–21, they say: "We know that this is our son and that he was born blind. But how he is now seeing we do not know, or who opened his eyes we do not know." Their volunteered negative response as to *who* opened their son's eyes indicates that they suspect that this is what the Judeans are really after. After this response, which would have been sufficient to answer the questions asked, they add, "Ask him. He is of age and will speak for himself."

Why did they go on to put their son back on the spot? It is obvious that the Judeans are not asking these questions so that they can clap the healer on the back and offer thanks! Why not just answer the questions asked and leave well enough alone?

The narrator does not allow this gap to remain open for long. In verses 22–23, he explains the entire strategy of the parents: "His parents said these things because they were afraid of the Judeans, who had already agreed that if anyone should confess him as Christ, they would be expelled from the synagogue. This is why his parents said, 'He is of age, ask him.'" This narrative explanation is the longest attribution of intention in the fourth gospel to this point. Of all the possible gaps in intention that might have been at least partially filled, the narrator chooses this one to fill in great detail, even repeating the offending statement. It implies that what the parents have said is of the essence of what the fourth gospel is struggling with and what the Johannine community experienced in its difficult journey from the synagogue to the church.

With this explanation in mind, we must go back and reread the passage starting in verse 18. The Judeans now can be seen clearly not as curious unbelievers perhaps looking for a sign but as prosecutors on a witch-hunt. As Staley has put it, the narrator's comment "turns an unnecessary and rude conversation into a courtroom drama."[20] The questions put to the parents dare them to do what their son has already begun the process of doing before the Pharisees: confessing Jesus as the doer of messianic acts. As Isaiah expressed it in a passage that is preceded by a reference to "the clay" and the potter:

On that day the deaf shall hear the words of a scroll, and out of their gloom and darkness the eyes of the blind shall see. (Isa 29:18)

Do the parents believe that this person who healed their son's blindness on the sabbath is the messiah? They will not say one way or another. But their behavior reveals more than simply refusal to "name names." As Rensberger says, the "parents have not only tried to shield themselves from scrutiny, they have deliberately turned the inquisitors' attention back upon their own son, knowing...that he will be subject to the very sentence that they themselves are afraid to face."[21] This is the emphasis of the narrator's comment in repeat-

---

20. Staley (1991, 68).
21. Rensberger (1988, 47).

ing this phrase. It is not just their denial of knowledge, but their passing the buck to their son that is their "sin."

From the Johannine community's perspective, the narrator's comments bring to the very center of the passage just what they faced: the terrible either/or of denying Jesus or being expelled from their world. Many commentators criticize the fourth gospel for its "dualism" in painting the world as darkness and Jesus as light. But it must be seen that if the Johannine community developed a perspective that admits of little gray, it was out of the experience of being treated in terms of extremes by their own people. What must have at first seemed like a logical both/and situation — keep the Torah and acknowledge Jesus as God's emissary — was rejected completely by their compatriots. And not only was the message rejected, but anyone bearing the message was completely removed from their social universe. It is almost impossible for us living in the land of "live and let live," of largely uncritical pluralism, to imagine the consequences of speaking an unacceptable message in such a culture. Whereas those of us who attempt to bring God's word of justice and love to the United States are largely ignored or ridiculed, the Johannine community faced the most difficult of choices in believing that Jesus was sent by God to save the world from its own sinfulness: repress the message, or lose everything. That, of course, is the choice Nicodemus would not make, as well as those who could not accept the demand to participate in publicly known eucharistic celebrations (6:60). "Fear of the Judeans" becomes Johannine code for unwillingness to take the risk of public faith. Perhaps predictably, but still sadly, the healed one's parents also cannot muster the courage to leap the chasm from the "world" to Jesus.

## 7. WITNESSING TO THE TRUTH:  ROUND 2

**Chiasm: 9:24–34**

a: 24–25: sinner

   b: 26: how open your eyes?

      c: 27–29: disciples of Moses; don't know where he's from

   $b^1$: 30: opened my eyes

$a^1$: 31–34a: sinners

The dialogue between the Judeans and the parents is left hanging, as was the preceding one between the once-blind one and the Pharisees, with many plot questions left unanswered. What happened to the parents after this? For that matter, what was the Judeans' response to their mixed answer to the Judeans' questions? These gaps are left for readers to ponder.

Instead of following this conversation, the text returns us in verse 24 to the interrogation of the one who was blind by a group referred to obliquely as "they." By starting the scene with the phrase, "They called, therefore, a second time for the one who was blind," the only apparent inference is that the inquisitors are the Pharisees who first questioned him in verses 15–17. However, on that occasion, we had been informed only that the neighbors and street observers had brought the man to the Pharisees on their own initiative. Putting these clues together, verse 24 suggests that the initial visit to the Pharisees was actually initiated by the Pharisees themselves! Given the apparent harmony of interest among the inquirers in verses 8–17 (and the chiastic structure that results from seeing that section as a unit), we find that the Pharisees have been directing the action all along, with the exception of the central scene.

Is the reason for their second call — the "therefore" in verse 24 — the conversation between the Judeans and parents? As we left the Pharisaic inquiry in verse 17, the once-blind man was still with the Pharisees, but now they call for him again. The text implies that some time has passed in which the Pharisees considered what they had heard so far, perhaps in conjunction with the results of the apparently simultaneous Judean questioning of the parents. Where the once-blind man was during this interval is left unstated, but now, the court is reconvened for a new purpose: the destruction of the credibility of the healer.

The scene in 9:24–34 parallels the discussion in 7:45–49 in three thematic ways: (1) the issue of the Pharisees' attitude toward loyalty to Moses and the Law, (2) the choice between security in the Law or in Jesus and (3) their superior attitude toward those ignorant of the Law.[22] Jesus' followers must face the same cultural challenge as did the master, a theme that will be made explicit in the Last Supper discourse (13:16; 15:20).

The inquirers begin here not with a question but with a statement that demands affirmation: "Give glory to God: we know that this person is a sinner." Duke observes the irony within their comment: by accusing Jesus of being a sinner — that is, a person with a bad attitude in relation to the Torah — they make him an outsider, which, in fact, he is.[23] The opening phrase, "Give glory to God," is the equivalent of putting him under solemn oath, a typical courtroom procedure.

What answer are they expecting from the healed one? "I agree, he is a sinner" seems the logical option, and yet there he is, a person who was born blind and now can see. The Pharisees no longer dispute either the healed one's identity or the fact of the healing, focusing now only on the character of the one who has performed the messianic act. They "know" that he must be a sinner to make clay on the sabbath. Does the man know the Law or is he one of the "accursed" previously reviled by the Pharisees (7:49)?

The once-blind one does not accept their premise but speaks in verse 25 only to his experience: "If he is a sinner, I do not know. One thing I do know: I was blind and now I see." As Rensberger has said, "The blind man sets the one thing he is certain of, his own experience, against the standards with which the

---

22. Karris (1990, 49).
23. Duke (1985, 78).

Pharisees confront him. . . . The blind man's God does not live in a book . . . but in the act of mercy."[24]

In verse 26, the interrogation takes a farcical turn, as the flustered Pharisees are reduced to repeating the questions implied in verse 15: "Therefore, they said to him, 'What did he do to you? How did he open your eyes?' " Are they hoping again that the man will give a piece of information that will convict Jesus of being a sinner? Or are they truly mystified as to how this "impossible" action of doing God's work on the sabbath could have happened?

The man's response in verse 27 is remarkable for its boldness and sarcasm: "I told you already but you did not hear. Why are you willing to hear it again? You're not willing to become his disciples, too, are you?" It is as if his confidence is growing as he comes to "see" just how stubborn his religious leaders are. His lines are humorous even to our remote ears, and must have been outrageously funny to the Johannine community. His insistence that he has told them but they have not listened underscores the parallel between the disciple's experience and the master's (8:47). But his impudent remark suggesting that their inquiry stems from their own desire for discipleship goes beyond witness to sheer wit. Implicit in his "you, too" is the possibility of his own commitment to discipleship, although "too" might imply only their joining Jesus' other disciples. The inclusion of this remark may have had the effect of emboldening Johannine witness beyond the simple requirement of speaking one's own truth to the further aspect of creative denouncement of the hypocrisy of the inquisitors. For all those of our era who have felt inspired to engage in imaginative courtroom speech or action that points out the foibles of the so-called justice system, the once-blind man's words are a powerful precedent.

It should not surprise us that the Pharisees respond in verses 28–29 to this little speech with anger and abuse. They present two oppositions in inverse parallelism that form the center of the chiasm:

1a: you are a disciple of that one

2a: we are disciples of Moses

2b: we know God spoke to Moses

1b: but this one, we do not know where he is from (*pothen*)

Up to this point, despite the scene with the parents, it has not been clear that the blind man was facing the threat of expulsion, but the Pharisees' retort puts this possibility in the air. Now they challenge his loyalty directly, basing his commitment on his answer to their implicit question of Jesus' *pothen*. Their claim of ignorance of this *pothen* is, of course, heavily ironic, given their previous certainty that he was from Galilee (7:41, 52)! It also is ironic at another level: by acknowledging their ignorance, they imply that he fulfills the messianic condition stated by the Jerusalemites at Tabernacles: "When the Christ comes, no one is to know where he is from [*pothen*]" (7:27).

---

24. Rensberger (1988, 45).

The increasingly empowered man continues his bold witness in verses 30–33, turning the tables on the questioners in the longest speech in the chapter. In the fourth gospel's final "wonder," he begins by expressing surprise about their inability to put two and two together to see the irony of the situation: "Now this is a wonder [*thaumaston*]!" The educated officials do not know the healer's *pothen*, but this former beggar has had his eyes opened!

For the first time, the once-blind one speaks in the plural in verse 31: "We know that God does not hear sinners, but if anyone fears God and does his will, God hears that one." As Brown has observed, the "we know" picks up the format of Jesus' discussion with Nicodemus in 3:10, contrasting the knowledge of the Judean officials with that of the Johannine community.[25] His statement reverses the premise of the link between hearing, sin, and God that was considered earlier. In 8:46–47 and 9:27, the issue is whether sinners hear God; now the man inverts it by stating that "we know" God does not hear sinners. Of course, there is an element of sarcasm in this, too, for the Psalter is filled with cries to God from self-confessed "sinners" who expect to be heard (e.g., Ps 25:7, 18). The man suggests ironically that "we" refers to him and the Pharisees together: "We know this, don't we?" He is challenging their theology head on, in an unmistakable tone of doubt that they in fact understand the ways of God, something he is coming to see more clearly as the interrogation proceeds.

In verse 32, he adds a historical fact to the chain of evidence: "It has never been heard of for anyone to open the eyes of a person born blind." The conclusion in verse 33, therefore, is clear: "If this one were not from God, he would not be able to do anything." That is, according to *their* premise, Jesus would not be able to call on God to give him the power to heal blindness if he were a sinner. The fact that he has indeed performed this unprecedented action *must* mean that he is from God, mustn't it? They have forced him to think through the implications of his own experience in light of prevailing theology to reach a new understanding, precisely the experience of the Johannine community under persecution in reaching its own "high christology."

The scene comes to a beautifully poetic complete circle in verse 34, as the Pharisees indignantly and ironically denounce him on the same basis as the disciples' initial presumption: "You were born totally in sin and you are teaching us?" The final straw for religious officials is for those defined by the institution as outsiders to claim the authority to be teachers. Whether women challenging religious patriarchy or the economically or politically oppressed challenging the church's complicity with dictators and the interests of greed, people from the perspective of the bottom have persistently shared in the once-blind man's experience of being rejected for not having the authority to teach. As Jesus' credentials to teach were questioned, so are those of his disciples.

And the consequences of presuming that one's experience is sufficient basis for "teaching" are extreme: being "thrown outside." The man comes under just the sentence the threat of which prevented his parents from acting. The cycle

---

25. R. Brown (1966, 375).

of inherited sin is broken: the child does not follow in the fear of his parents. Change *is* possible; people *can* be born *anōthen*! *This* is the glory of God that Jesus told his disciples would be revealed by the works of God done through the blind one. It is not the physical healing that is the focus of the story but the new sight that allows the man to see beyond the narrow strictures of his upbringing and culture, to grasp both the dark truth of his society's weakness and evil and the bright truth of Jesus' power and God's glory that works through "sinners." Humanity, born into blindness for reasons not named, is capable of learning to see, of being sent forth to witness to God's healing power. But there is a price to be paid.

## 8. FINDING JESUS ON THE OUTSIDE

The theme of "hearing" takes on another aspect in verse 35: "Jesus heard that they threw him outside and having found him said..." It is an interesting element of this story about blindness and sight that the primary sensory form of awareness throughout is audition. Apart from the description of the healing and its repetitions, there are no visual clues at all to the activity, until the image of "throwing outside." The action proceeds through conversation that is "heard" to varying degrees. Both Judeans and Pharisees "call" (literally, "sound," *ephōnēsan*) for witnesses. The issue of "sin" revolves around the theme of what God hears and who hears God. Now, on the outside, Jesus hears of the expulsion of the healed one. It is the first time the name "Jesus" has been heard since verse 11; neither Pharisees or Judeans will utter his name.

The narrator's connection of healer and healed evokes the image of Wisdom:

> She makes her own rounds, seeking those worthy of her,
> and graciously appears to them in the ways
> and meets them with all solicitude. (Wis 6:16)

Jesus' presence on the outside ends the ignorance that the man expressed in verse 12 about Jesus' whereabouts. As Duke says, "Jesus is outside the synagogue, at the side of those who are cast out."[26]

Having found the excommunicated one, Jesus in verse 35b invites the confession of faith, but in different terms than those rejected by the synagogue Judeans: "Are you believing in the Human One?" The title that Jesus repeatedly chooses for himself in the fourth gospel shifts the emphasis away from the expected royal military leader and to the one who will be "lifted up" in glory (3:14; 8:28). The seeing one has not associated the title with Jesus, but the question he asks in verse 36 in response is totally open to faith: "And who is he, sir [*kyrie*], that I should believe in him?"

---

26. Duke (1985, 124).

Considering how many times Jesus has spoken directly of *egō eimi,* the circumlocution he expresses in verse 37 is interesting. It invites just what the Pharisees will not accept: to consider one's own sensory experience as a basis for truth: "You have seen him and the one speaking with you is the one." Seeing and hearing come together.

The "confession" in verse 38 is as direct and simple as possible: "I am believing, Lord [*kyrie*]." Curiously, the verbal acknowledgment is joined with a gesture otherwise unprecedented in the fourth gospel: "And he worshiped [*prosekynēsen*] him." The only previous occurrence of the term was in 4:20–24, the discussion between Jesus and the Samaritan woman about the place and nature of true worship. It does not occur elsewhere in connection with an act toward a person and was not used this way by contemporary Judaism, but rather referred to attitudes of respect and reverence toward the Temple and Torah.[27] In light of the replacement themes in the gospel, the act seems to fulfill the idea that Jesus himself will take the place of both Temple and Torah as the site of respect and honor.

## 9. ARE WE BLIND?

The final scene is an ironic mirror of the opening discussion between Jesus and his disciples, who are apparently *not* with their master to welcome their new community member. As the first scene ended with a proclamation about Jesus' presence in the world as light, the final scene begins in verse 39 with: "For this judgment I came into the world." In the beginning are light and birth, and in the end are judgment and separation. The chapter neatly summarizes the entire scope of discipleship.

The judgment is "that the ones not seeing may see and those seeing should become blind." Eschatological reversal is a prevalent biblical theme, whether expressed in the terms of Mary's Magnificat in Luke or the prophetic oracles predicting the exaltation of lowly Israel. In Johannine terms, it follows the imagery of light/dark, day/night, seeing/blindness.

Just as it seems that the passage might end with this proclamation, the narrator keeps the story open with a surprising bit of information in verse 40: "The Pharisees who were with him *heard* these things." We had not anticipated that any Pharisees were "with him" at all. Are these eavesdroppers, spies, or secret disciples? Are they simply overhearing as a result of the momentum of throwing out the "sinner," or have they chosen to be with Jesus for some reason? The phrase "with him" leaves the distinct impression that these are indeed people who, at this point, have chosen Jesus at some level, contrary to the usual sense that they are the ones who kicked out the seeing man from the synagogue (cf. "with *them,*" 18:5, 18). In light of the division over Jesus described in verse 16

---

27. Josephus *J.W.* 5.402.

and the irony of 7:48, it is not unreasonable to read this verse as a question and answer between Jesus and *secret believers* from among the Pharisees.

From this perspective, their question has a different tone than when considered as spoken by the expelling inquisitors: "We are not blind, too, are we?" Their attitude suggests a degree of "holier than thou" in relation to the completely blind inquisitors that comes from having accepted. The chapter started with the image of all humanity being born blind; surely we who are "with you" are not blind, are we? Just as the disciples at the outset tried to distance themselves from the blind one whom they discuss from a superior, moralistic viewpoint, these Pharisees wish to exclude themselves from a condition that is common to all humanity.

Jesus' response in verse 41 is precise and clear, but often misunderstood: "If you were blind, you would have no sin; but now that you say, 'We are seeing,' your sin is remaining." That is, they are *not* blind. If they were blind, like the inquisitors, there would be no sin. Despite the stubbornness of the interrogating Pharisees, Jesus will not condemn them simply for being blind — although their eventual participation in the plot to kill him is another matter for judgment. But these Pharisees *do* see — they are "with" Jesus. But because of this, their sin remains. If they are indeed seeing, what, then, is their sin? The refusal to commit openly and allow themselves also to be thrown out! As Brown puts it, to Jewish Christians who want it both ways, "the gospel appeals to them to allow themselves to be excommunicated, for Jesus will seek them out as he sought out the blind man in v. 35 and bring them to complete faith."[28] They cannot continue to be both "Pharisees" and "with him." Just as Nicodemus remained in darkness, they remain in sin, so long as their faith is a matter between themselves and Jesus alone. To the Johannine community, the public confession and witness of faith that pays the price of being thrown out of the world are the basis for being fully accepted into the loving embrace of the community of discipleship.

---

28. R. Brown (1966, 380).

# 14

# "The Shepherd
# Lays Down His Life
# for His Sheep"

## John 10:1-39

A. **Chiasm:** (see below)

B. **Location:** Jerusalem

C. **Time:** 10:1–21: unstated; 22–39: Dedication/winter

D. **Hebrew scripture context:** Jeremiah 23 and other "shepherd" passages cited

E. **Social factors:** Judean leadership vs. Johannine community leadership

F. **Themes:** shepherding as life-giving

G. **Key words:** shepherd, lay down life

## 1. THE QUESTION OF SETTING
## AND CONTINUITY

Although the story of the blind one forms a remarkably sharp structural unit within the bounds of chapter 9, the beginning of chapter 10 does not announce any transition to a new time or place, as do most other segues in the fourth gospel. If there were no chapter marker — which, of course, there was not for the first thousand years — we would have no narrative reason to read this as a new scene. Rather, it appears as a monologue by Jesus to the Pharisees who were "with him" — those whom the members of the Johannine community have the most reason to persuade to join them openly. The next temporal marker is in verse 22, when the narrator tells us that "it was then the feast of Dedication

231

in Jerusalem; it was winter." Whether this includes the previous verses — following the common Johannine technique of announcing the time part-way into the scene — or refers only to what follows is not clear. Certainly until we get to that place in the narrative, we have no reason to believe that the time or place has changed at all.

Following this sense of continuity, Peter Ellis proposes a chiasm extending from 9:39 to 10:21 as follows:[1]

> a: 9:39–41: blind/heard
>> b: 10:1–5: amen, amen; sheep/shepherd; thief/robber; voice
>>> c: 10:6: did not understand
>> b¹: 10:7–18: amen, amen; sheep/shepherd; thief/robber; voice
> a¹: 19–21: why listen? blind

These parallels are impressive and cannot be easily dismissed, except for the clear sense of completion of the preceding story (and chiasm) that comes in verse 41. While it is not impossible for chiasms to overlap, the smaller ones shown below definitely use 10:1 as a starting point. Given also the sharp change in metaphor from blindness/sight to shepherd/sheep, it seems to make more sense to see chapter 10 as beginning a new unit, even with the continuity of time and place.

Recent attempts to read this passage from a "literary perspective," by reading as if the text were written in our time and with our sense of modern narrative, have failed to uncover the narrative role of the metaphors Jesus offers.[2] If we start our reading with the understanding that the chapter is making a life-or-death appeal to the secret believers among the Pharisees to recognize the exclusive authority of Jesus' leadership vis-à-vis the Judean officials, we reach a very different conclusion than if we simply read as twentieth-century Americans trained in novel and poetry reading.

As we precede, we will find an interlocking and "illogical" set of metaphors of immediate power to an audience in first-century Palestine. Throughout, the challenge is to convince readers of the evil motives of the official leaders in contrast with the loving purpose of Jesus, the good shepherd.

---

1. Ellis (1984, 166).

2. E.g, Kysar (1991) and Reinhartz (1992). The latter effort, expressly from a "reader-response" perspective, focuses on the so-called cosmological tale that abstracts from the "historical" and "ecclesiological" stories within the gospel to focus on the "universal" plot. However, my reading throughout the gospel emphasizes that the "cosmological" aspects of the text (e.g., "God," "Satan," "heaven," etc.) are used only to provide legitimation for the concrete call to discipleship, whether of first- or twentieth-century followers of Jesus. Reinhartz makes passing reference to the discipleship discourse implicit in the gospel (pp. 101–102) but does not link it with her interpretation of the good shepherd discourse.

## 2. CALLING THE SHEEP BY NAME

**Chiasm: 10:1–5**

a: 1: thief/plunderer

  b: 2: shepherd

    c: 3: open, listen, call, lead out

  b$^1$: 4: shepherd

a$^1$: 5: strangers

In verse 1, Jesus introduces two new images with a solemn double-amen saying: "The one not entering through the gate into the sheepfold but going up from another place is a thief [*kleptēs*] and a robber [*lēstēs*]." Immediately, readers are challenged to consider each aspect of this startling statement in relation to the preceding discussion with the Pharisees who were "with him." Is this an allegory or a metaphor? If the former, what do the "gate" and "sheepfold" represent, and what other options for "entering" are there? What are the *kleptēs* or *lēstēs* trying to gain by nefarious means? The shift in vocabulary from the "standard" Johannine language catches us off guard and leaves the otherwise "inside" readers surprisingly on the outside of understanding. This has the effect of warning readers who think they "see" that perhaps they, like the Pharisees who are with Jesus, should not be so fast to claim exemption!

In the broader context of the narrative, the negative image is easily associated with the Judeans/Pharisees who have treated the healed one and, by implication, Jesus, so harshly and unjustly. Hebrew scripture helps us fill in some of the implicit background that gives the image coherence:

> Moses spoke to the Lord, saying, "Let the Lord, the God of the spirits of all flesh, appoint someone over the congregation who shall go out before them and come in before them, who shall lead them out and bring them in, so that the congregation of the Lord may not be like sheep without a shepherd." So the Lord said to Moses, "Take Joshua...." (Num 27:16–18)

>> Know that the Lord is God.
>> It is he that made us, and we are his.
>> We are his people, and the sheep of his pasture. (Ps 100:3)

> Woe to the shepherds who destroy and scatter the sheep of my pasture! says the Lord. Therefore thus says the Lord, the God of Israel, concerning the shepherds who shepherd my people: It is you who have scattered my flock, and have driven them away, and you have not attended to them. So I will attend to you for your evil doings, says the Lord. I will raise up shepherds over them who will shepherd them, and they shall not fear any longer. (Jer 23:1–4)

Thus says the Lord God: Ah, you shepherds of Israel who have been feeding yourselves! Should not shepherds feed the sheep?...I am against the
shepherds; and I will demand my sheep at their hand....I myself will
search for my sheep, and will seek them out....I will rescue them from all
the places to which they have been scattered on a day of clouds and thick
darkness....I myself shall be the shepherd of my sheep. (Ezek 34:2–15;
also, Micah 3; Zechariah 10)

The criticisms of the prophets against Israel's shepherds who got fat themselves rather than feeding the sheep would ring resonantly in the ears of
Palestinian Jewish peasants whose land was lost and whose families had huge
debts because of the corruption of the Jerusalem Temple officials and the Pharisees who bypassed criticizing their misdeeds in favor of establishing "liberal"
reforms. But how would these still valid jabs at greedy officialdom fit with the
image of "entering by some other place"?

While readers ponder the possibilities, Jesus offers in verses 2–4 a positive
counterpart to the first negative image: "The one entering through the door is
shepherd of the sheep. The gatekeeper opens to this one, and the sheep hear
his voice. He calls his own sheep by name and is leading them out. When his
own are all out, he goes in front of them, and his sheep follow, because they
know his voice." Adding to readers' struggle to comprehend is the image of the
*gatekeeper.* But having mentioned this figure, Jesus does not again include the
gatekeeper among the images offered.

Instead, he tells how and why the shepherd who enters through the gate shepherds the sheep: (1) he calls "his own" by name; (2) the sheep hear his "voice";
(3) he leads them "out"; (4) he goes before them; and (5) they "follow." Suddenly, the direction of the movement is reversed. Whereas verses 1–2 spoke
of "entering" the sheepfold, the place of protection, verses 3–4 speak of going
"out." The new image of hearing the voice and coming out recalls 5:28–29,
when those in the grave will hear the voice of the Son of God and come out.
From this perspective, "in" is a place of death and "out" is a place of eternal
life! It is the shepherd who enters, but the sheep who go out when they hear
their shepherd's voice.

The chiasm ends in verse 5 with the second negative image: "They will never
follow a stranger but will flee from him, because they have not known the voice
of strangers." The word for "strangers," *allotriōn,* is rare in the New Testament
and occurs only here in the fourth gospel. It has the connotation of something
alien or belonging to another, even something hostile. It is certainly a hostile
term here, for the sheep not only do not hear the strangers' voice but actively
flee from them.

We therefore have two positive images (shepherd and gate) and three negative images (thief, robber, and stranger) that Jesus poses as a means to challenge
the Pharisees with him to leave their world behind and join the Johannine community openly. It should not surprise us too much when, in verse 6, the narrator

tells us that "they did not know what it was he was saying to them." Can we do better in solving the riddle?

Taking the negative images first, we find that "thief" accurately describes the economic practice of the Judean officials. "Robber," though, has a different connotation. The term *lēstēs* is used in the synoptics and in Josephus to refer to the revolutionary guerrillas who attempt to change things by force through acts of terrorism (e.g., Mk 14:48; cf. Jn 18:40). Interestingly, in the synoptics, but not in John, it is used by Jesus in his criticism of the Temple elite at the "cleansing": "You have made it a robber's [*lēstōn*] den" (Mk 11:17). Whether of insiders or outsiders, the term has a connotation not only of economic malpractice but of violence as well. This is why the sheep "flee" at the voice of "strangers" — they are life-threatening as well as harmful to the pocketbook!

That the opponents at issue here are the Judeans will be underscored later in the chapter when Jesus tells them that they do not believe "because you are not my sheep" (10:26). That is, the thief/plunderer does not try to persuade Jesus' followers by entering the Johannine community but comes in to find the sheep "by another place," that is, through the Temple-state system and its successor, the synagogue/Torah-based rabbinical community.

On the positive side, the images are more cryptic. It is easy enough for readers from the evidence of chapter 5 — but not necessarily for the Pharisees with Jesus, whom we have no basis to believe heard that speech — to understand Jesus as the shepherd, and the "doorkeeper" as his Father, God. Sheep cannot follow two shepherds calling in different directions. The Pharisees must choose: the thieves and robbers or the shepherd who calls his own by name.

The image of the "gate" does not offer so simple a solution. If we try to think logically about the relationship among the positive images, then seeing Jesus as the shepherd might suggest that the gate is the message Jesus offers about discipleship, the place through which sheep follow the shepherd out. But if we have not caught on yet, we will momentarily: understanding the ways of God is not a matter of logical thinking!

## 3. THE DOOR OF THE SHEEP

**Chiasm: 10:7–10**

a: 7: I am the door

  b: 8: thieves

    c: 9: I am the door: anyone entering through me will be saved

  b¹: 10a: thief

a¹: 10b: I come so they have life

In keeping with the manner of speaking of the Johannine Jesus, verses 7–18 offer not so much an "explanation" of the metaphor as more metaphor. And the first new metaphor is one that might surprise us: "I AM [*egō eimi*] the door of the sheep" (verse 7). If Jesus is the *door* through which the sheep pass, who is the shepherd?

Before we can consider that, he goes on in verse 8 to offer another angle on the thieves and robbers from verse 1. In addition to being those who enter the wrong way, they are "all those who came before me." Jesus is different both spatially and temporally from the "others." Who are the "all others" intended by this apparently sweeping statement? Is *everyone* who came before Jesus a thief and robber? Just the "all others" who have performed the function of "shepherds"? Does this include Moses, Aaron, and Joshua as well as the latecomers criticized by the prophets? Or does he mean more specifically those who have come before Jesus to lead the people in their current captivity to Rome? If so, does this include John (the Baptist)?

A small clue is given in the second half of verse 8. The false doors are those whom "the sheep have not heard." But again, this clue is subject to several interpretations. Are the sheep referred to simply the members of the Johannine community and, thus, those who do not hear Judean "doors"? Or are the false doors those who have not been listened to by the general population, that is, the false messiahs and false prophets warned of in the synoptics (e.g., Mk 13:22)? So far, Jesus' additional speech only raises more questions.

The center of the chiasm in verse 9 repeats the *egō eimi* statement (dropping the phrase "of the sheep") and adds two more details: "Anyone entering through me will be saved and will go in and out and find pasture." We have heard Jesus refer to his "saving" mission before (5:34; cf. 3:17), but the image of "pasture" is unique here in all the gospels. However, it is a very common image among the prophets for the restoration by God of Israel to a place of harmony under the guidance of good shepherds. In particular, Micah speaks of pasture in ways echoed in the fourth gospel passage:

> I will surely gather all of you, O Jacob,
> I will gather the survivors of Israel;
> I will set them together like sheep in a fold, like a flock
>     in its pasture;
> it will resound with people.
> With a leader to break open the path and go before them,
> they will break out and pass through the door, going out
>     by it.
> Their king will pass on before them, the Lord at their
>     head. (Mic 2:12–13)

The prophetic image casts God as the one who gathers sheep in the fold but the leader as the one who "breaks open" the path to get out into the pasture. This passage makes sense of the double movement in verses 1–4 and suggests the cyclic pattern of the gathering in of the community and going out in mission that the fourth gospel presents as the paradigm of Christian life. To the Pharisees who are secret disciples, it proclaims that Jesus is the leader who does God's work in leading the people to pasture.

As the details in verse 9 shed light on the meaning of Jesus as "the door," verse 10 offers three interconnected images that give us a fuller picture of the "thief," who "is not coming unless to steal and kill and destroy." "Steal" is clear enough from our understanding of the economic reality of the Judean dependence on the Temple and its theft from Jews coming there from throughout the world. The word for "kill" used here, *thyō*, is different from that used by Jesus at Tabernacles in reference to the plot against his own life, *apokteinai*. The latter term connotes the act of ending life, but *thyō* connotes *sacrifice*. Raymond Brown suggests the use here may connote a sly reference to the priestly authorities.[3] As spoken to the Pharisees who have already been linked with the priests in the fourth gospel (7:32, 45), this would offer the specific challenge to break up their unholy alliance in favor of union with the Johannine community. Of course, it also carries the overtone of the death of Jesus (and the Johannine martyrs) as sacrifices (cf. Jn 16:2). Linguistically, it forms a play on words with *thyra*, "door," emphasizing the contrast between Jesus and the "thieves."

Finally, "destroy," *apolesē*, recalls the several uses of the term earlier in which Jesus emphasized both God's call and the disciple's duty not to let anyone or anything "perish" (3:16; 6:12, 27, 39). The "thief," in contrast, has "destroying" as a goal. This seems to recall the agreement to expel those confessing Jesus as messiah, "destroying" them by intending to put them outside what the leaders believe to be God's life-giving community.

These death-dealing purposes could not be in sharper contrast with Jesus' own purpose stated in verse 10b: "I have come so that they may have life and have it to abundance [*perisson*]." The only previous use of the root for *perisson* was in the description of the "extra" (*perisseusanta*) fragments that Jesus ordered the disciples to "gather together [*synagagete*] so that nothing would be lost [*apolētai*]" (6:12). The duty of disciples is to gather together the abundance that Jesus-the-door has given, so that the "thieves" will not allow it/them to be destroyed.

### 4. "THE GOOD SHEPHERD LAYS DOWN HIS LIFE FOR THE SHEEP"

**Chiasm: 10:10–30**

a: 10–15: destroy, life in abundance, snatching sheep, Father knows me and I know Father

   b: 16–18: other sheep/one sheep herd, lay down/receive life as commandment

      c: 19–23: division: demon vs. opening eyes of blind

---

3. R. Brown (1966, 386). As will be seen, this suggestion is consistent with the warning in Jn 16:2, where *apoktenas* is linked with *latreian*, the term for religiously obedient service.

> b¹: 24–26: none of you are my sheep; I told you: the works I do in Father's
> name witness
> a¹: 27–30: destroy, eternal life, snatching sheep, Father and I are one

The chiastic structure of chapter 10 does not follow the precise lines of some previous units but overlaps smaller units with the larger ones. While verses 10–30 are shaped as delineated above, within that section are smaller chiasms that do not necessarily match the overall structure. It is an example of the gospel's unwillingness to be completely bound by any particular categories, just as Jesus cannot be fully grasped by any text or any reader.

With the center of the larger piece as the division among the Judeans, we find the plot moving more toward the central reality of the gospel: Jesus' witness to God's truth will generate a deep split among those who claim God as their Creator and covenant partner. It is a split that, despite God's overwhelming desire for the breach to be healed, persists to this day both between Jews and Christians and among the uncountable splinters of the Christian community. The chiasm begins with a contrast that brings to light one of the primary reasons for this division: the coexistence of irreconcilably opposite styles of leadership.

### a. The Hired Ones

**Chiasm: 10:11–16**

a: 11: I AM good shepherd; lay down life for sheep
  b: 12a: hireling not a shepherd
    c: 12b: wolf comes and scatters
  b¹: 13: hireling cares not for sheep
a¹: 14–16: I AM good shepherd; lay down life for sheep

Having offered a stark, if metaphoric, contrast between the "door" and the "thief," Jesus continues with the "explanation" of the "shepherd." Verses 7–14 offer the densest collection of *egō eimi* statements in the gospel, using the sacred phrase four times. In verse 11, Jesus introduces the section by linking *egō eimi* with "good shepherd." We are probably not surprised to find out that Jesus is the shepherd, but it wreaks havoc on the idea that the shepherd and the "door" are separate entities. Jesus is both the shepherd and the door, perhaps an illogical image but one that is consistent with the very notion of Jesus as *egō eimi,* the one who *is.* The adjective "good," *kalos,* was previously used to describe the abundant wine at Cana, the very picture of messianic bounty.

But this expectable image is followed by one wholly unprecedented in either Hebrew scripture or the pastoral practice of human leaders or literal shepherds: "The good shepherd lays down [*tithēsin*] his life for the sheep." Again, logically it makes no sense: if the shepherd lays down his life, what will become of the sheep? This, of course, is a question that will plague Jesus' disciples throughout the Last Supper discourse, as they ponder the meaning of his "going away" and their own fate without him. But as a sign of absolute selflessness, it is perfectly clear. Whether the standard television news story of the parent jumping in the icy water or into the burning building to save a child or the militarist myth of the "good soldier" who throws himself on the grenade for his buddies, people the world over instinctively recognize the powerful commitment expressed by the willingness to give up one's life for another.

The contrast here is not with the "thief" but with another economically based image: the "hired one" (*misthōtos*). It is used only here in the fourth gospel, but in the synoptics, it connotes a sense of being an outsider (e.g., Mk 1:20; Lk 15:15–19). In Hebrew scripture, it is very common as a description of the lowly members of the household but also carries occasional mercenary overtones. A particularly apt example is in Nehemiah 6. There, Nehemiah, having narrated both the story of the building of a wall around Jerusalem and the perception among the nations that this wall-building is part of a plot to rebel against the Persians, tells of receiving a letter warning him of a plot to kill him for building the wall. A man named Shemaiah warns Nehemiah to hide with him in the Temple to avoid the murderers, and Nehemiah answers:

> "Should a man like me run away to save his life? I will not go in!" Then I perceived and saw that God had not sent him at all, but he had pronounced the prophecy against me because Tobiah and Sanballat had hired [LXX, *emisthōsanto*] him. He was hired for this purpose, to intimidate me and make me sin by acting in this way, and so they could give me a bad name, in order to taunt me. (Neh 6:11–13)

The brave and faithful Nehemiah is a perfect contrast with the hireling in verses 12–13 who "is no shepherd and to whom the sheep do not belong as their own; he sees the wolf coming and abandons the sheep and flees, and the wolf snatches them and scatters them, because he is a hireling and is not concerned with the sheep." For the Johannine community and the listening Pharisees, this willingness to abandon the sheep rings true about those leaders who, during the war with Rome in the late 60s, chose to collaborate with the empire to save their lives rather than be willing to remain with the people (and with God) until the end. From Herod down to the Sanhedrin members of the Johannine community's day — and even to our own time — leaders had calculated the political odds and made the worldly-wise choice to do what was "possible." For church leaders who accommodate imperial oppressors on the theory that doing some good in a bad situation is better than dying altogether, the fourth gospel speaks a word of warning.

The outcome of the hired person's bad shepherding is the attack by the "wolf." It is an image used by Jeremiah to portray the fate of those who have abandoned God's ways to take up idolatry and other evil ways (Jer 5:6). It is used in Matthew as an image of the false prophets (Mt 7:16), and both Matthew and Luke offer it as the environment into which lamb-like disciples will be sent (Mt 10:3; Lk 10:16). It is used only here in the fourth gospel. It is a threat from elsewhere than the hired shepherds themselves, one from which the shepherds are to protect the sheep. In the context of being hired to assure the wolf's access to "snatch and scatter," the image may be thought of concretely as Rome or perhaps more abstractly as the "devil" who fathers murderous and deceitful children. In either case, the wolf clearly presents a violent and horrible fate to which the hired help have exposed the sheep.

The chiasm reaches the final segment in verses 14b–15: "I know my sheep and my sheep know me, just as the Father knows me and I know the Father." It is the quintessence of the intimacy to which the Johannine community is called, and to which Jesus calls these Pharisees who are "with him" but not nearly closely enough. Why should they be linked with hired help when they can be intimate with the one who is close to the Father? The theme of mutual "knowledge" among sheep and shepherd introduced almost in passing here will reach full development as Jesus continues his walk toward the night and his Father.

Verse 15 ends on the seemingly disconnected repetition of the example in verse 11 of the shepherd's self-sacrificing love. Its function here is to emphasize that the laying down of life is not simply an expression of love for the sheep but also an expression of the intimacy between Father and Son. Throughout the gospel, Jesus reminds us directly and indirectly (as here) that he does not do his will but the will of the one who sent him.

The theme shifts in verse 16 with the inclusion of the "other sheep not of this fold; it is necessary [*dei*] that I lead these, and my voice they will hear, and they will become one sheep herd, one shepherd." Who are these "other sheep not of this fold" and why are they mentioned at this point in the discourse? If the "fold" is the Johannine community, then those not of this fold may refer to the other Christian communities to which the fourth gospel speaks a word of challenge and invitation. To the listening Pharisees, it suggests that the new place to which Jesus calls them out of the fold of the Judeans will include not only those who confess their faith in and commitment to Jesus, but also others. Where the "thieves" are willing to allow some to perish, Jesus calls all his hearers into one "sheep herd" (*poimnē*) under one "shepherd" (*poimēn*).

### b. *"This Is Why the Father Loves Me"*

#### Chiasm: 10:17–18

a: 17a: Father loves me

   b: 17b: lay down my life, take it up again

      c: 18a: no one took it from me

   b[1]: 18b: authority to lay down, and authority to take it up again

a[1]: 18c: Father's commandment (commandment=love, as in 15:10,12,17)

Jesus' speech to the Pharisees "with him" ends with a tightly knit chiasm that establishes an aspect of Jesus' death and resurrection very different from those developed from the synoptic viewpoint. It begins in verse 17 with a phrase that may sound a dissonant note to Christians raised on the idea of God's *unconditional* love: *"This is why* the Father loves me: because I lay down my life so that I can receive it again." For the fourth gospel, neither God's love for the Son nor Jesus' love for his disciples is unconditional. It is expressly and clearly grounded in the willingness of the beloved to witness to their faith by laying down their lives and trusting that they will be received again.

The center of the unit makes a claim essential to Christian argument against those who saw Jesus as simply another "failed" messiah or prophet, wiped out by the very powers that he sought to overthrow. "No one has taken it from me, but I lay it down by myself." The image of Jesus' death as "laying down life" rather than being killed, of being "lifted up" rather than forcibly taken to the cross, of being "glorified" rather than mocked paints a very different picture than the synoptic version. Whereas the synoptics show Jesus struggling with but eventually accepting his fate, the fourth gospel portrays Jesus as voluntarily laying down his life as one might lay down a cloak (cf. 13:4). While this may make no sense to Romans or perhaps even to some elements of Judean officialdom, it made a lot of sense to many faithful Jews, whom Josephus records as willingly putting their necks before the sword rather than allowing desecration of the Temple by the presence of the Roman golden eagle.[4] Jesus is not suggesting anything to the Pharisees of the late first century that they have not already seen lived out among their own, but he is ever more sharply distinguishing himself from the "hired hands."

The chiasm ends with an additional difference from other New Testament theology. Whereas the synoptics and Paul speak of the resurrection as something that God did to Jesus (i.e., "He was raised up" [Mk 14:28; Acts 2:24]), the fourth gospel has Jesus emphasize his own "authority" both to lay his life down and to "receive it again." It is a "commandment I received from my Father" and, thus, is derived from the highest possible source.

Of course, in the story world, all this talk about death and resurrection is before the fact and would be hardly coherent to an audience of Pharisees. Although the Pharisees were distinguished from the more conservative groups like the Sadducees in part on the basis of their belief in resurrection, they would have been unlikely to expect Jesus to express this "doctrine" in terms of authority from his Father to lay down and receive his life back again! Throughout this speech, they are utterly silent. Whether in awe, or shock, or simple unwillingness to get drawn into the issues further, we cannot be sure. It is, sadly though, the last time Jesus will speak directly to this group, whose last words to him are the question in 9:40 asking about their own state of sight. From now on, they will discuss him only behind his back or through their police force. The only additional encounter between Jesus and a Pharisee will be Nicodemus's retrieval of the lifeless body on the cross.

---

4. Josephus *Ant.* 18.3.1

## c. Division at Dedication

We should not be surprised to find in verse 19 that the reaction to Jesus' challenging and even threatening words is again "division" (*schisma*). But we may be caught off guard when the narrator tells us that the division is among the *Judeans*. Whether this is like the previous occasions when prospective disciples who cannot follow after hard conversation become "Judeans" (6:41, Galileans; 7:35, Pharisees) or whether others have been listening to the conversation all along is not precisely clear. But given the failure of any Pharisees to make the break openly and the narrator's summary in 12:42–43 about the limits of the faith of the "rulers," it seems likely that this is a "conversion" scene, albeit one in the wrong direction. Just as many of the Galilean disciples could no longer follow Jesus after his hard words about eucharist (6:66), so too the Pharisees who had been "with him" are no longer able to do so.

Even the terms of the schism reflect doubts among those who are most "for" Jesus in the debate in verses 20–21. The first group, understandably but wrongly, hears this talk about laying down life and the corruption of the shepherds as the words of a demon, someone who is "raving" (*mainetai*). The term is used only here in the fourth gospel and rarely in the Bible, but in the Septuagint it describes "the raging of the nations under the terror of the divine judgment of war."[5] Since the Judeans had already concluded that Jesus has a demon (8:48), this new accusation (substituted for the earlier "Samaritan") suggests that Jesus' words come from a place of opposition to God. The two pejorative labels function as parallels to Jesus' calling the leaders "thieves" and "robbers." Neither side thinks very highly of the other.

As for the Judeans who are divided from this group, their "supportive" opinion refutes the possibility of one possessed by a demon opening blind people's (*typhlōn*, plural) eyes, but has no apparent argument with the idea that he is "raving." For these hearers, Jesus' words make no sense, but they cannot find fault with his works. They may be recalling Ps 146:8: "The Lord opens the eyes of the blind [LXX, *typhlous*, plural]." Their use of the plural suggests that they see Jesus' act in chapter 9 as having wider symbolic value than simply that of an individual healing. Jesus has done the work of God but speaks as one possessed. How can these two realities be reconciled?

In verses 22–23, the narrator breaks in with an unexpected temporal notice: "The feast of Dedication happened then in Jerusalem. It was winter, and Jesus was walking in the Temple in Solomon's colonnade." The late-developed feast of Dedication (Chanukah) is mentioned nowhere else in the New Testament nor at all in the Hebrew scripture and played only a minor role in the Jewish calendar. But in Jerusalem, it was a major focus of celebration during the winter respite from agricultural chores and the burdens of hosting pilgrims from the broader Jewish world. To understand why the fourth gospel adds this bit of

---

5. H. Preisker, *TDNT* 4:360–361.

information, it is helpful to understand something of the background of this feast.

Unlike feasts like Passover and Tabernacles that invoked images from the primal founding experience of Israel in the desert, Dedication was grounded in a relatively recent event: the successful military defeat of the Seleucid leader Antiochus by the Jewish hero Judas Maccabeus in 164 B.C.E.. As an aspect of his rule over Israel, Antiochus had enlisted the help of corrupt elements of the Jewish aristocracy and priesthood to take over the Temple priesthood and buy the high priest's office for his brother. This led to the perpetration of many acts horribly offensive to the Jewish mind, including encouraging sporting events in the Hellenistic gymnasium-style that involved nude competition. Eventually, Antiochus sacked the Temple and stripped the wealth, setting up a military fortress against the remaining Judeans loyal to Torah and Temple. Judas Maccabeus defeated Antiochus after a series of battles and set about rededicating the Temple after it had been desecrated by the "desolating sacrilege," a pagan altar to Zeus, set up by Antiochus (see Dan 11:31; 1 Macc 1:59).

The rededication was celebrated by an eight-day feast modeled on the feast of Tabernacles (1 Macc 4:52–59; 2 Macc 10:5–8). As Gale Yee has said, "Throughout this joyous celebration lurked the memory of the Temple's desecration and the nightmare that it could happen again."[6]

A temporal question arises with the mention of this feast in John: Is Dedication a feast that marks only the narrative to follow, or is it one of the typical Johannine "late" time signals that tells us about what has just been narrated? All of chapter 9 took place in the shadow of Tabernacles, but without a specific time reference of its own. A new scene is suggested in 9:1, but it but did not tell us that any gap in time should be understood. We might therefore see 9:1–10:21 as a part of Tabernacles, with 10:22–23 marking a new scene at Dedication. Or the Dedication period may have started back in 9:1, that fact being withheld from readers' awareness like the knowledge of sabbath in 5:9 and 9:14. The Dedication theme would fit very well with Jesus' critique of the Judean leaders in 10:1–13, recalling the corrupt leaders who allowed the Temple to be desecrated. As it stands, the narrator leaves it ambiguous, allowing the preceding section to float between Tabernacles and Dedication, letting the symbols of both feasts permeate the action and dialogue.

The spatial marker of Solomon's portico is also unique in the gospels, although in Acts it is mentioned as the site of preaching and healing activity by Peter and other apostles (Acts 3:11; 5:12). It is believed to have been on the sheltered east side of the Temple, which allowed protection from the winter wind.[7] It was totally destroyed during the sack of Jerusalem in 70 C.E., so whatever physical associations it may have had were but memories by the time the fourth gospel was written. However, because of its name, it also recalls the glorious first establishment of the Temple. Between the spatial and tempo-

---

6. Yee (1989, 88).
7. Ibid., 89; *HBD* 977.

ral notations, then, the narrator has evoked the entire history of the Jerusalem Temple.

We might pause for a moment to wonder what Jesus is doing in the Temple given the threats against him at Tabernacles (e.g., 8:59). After the terrible dispute about paternity, here he is, walking around as if everything was normal, with no apparent fear whatsoever. The bold Jesus will not long find himself undisturbed, however.

### d. "If You Are the Christ, Tell Us Openly!"

The enemies "encircle" Jesus in verse 24, asking him, "How long will you keep us in suspense? If you are the Christ, tell us openly [*parrhēsia*]!" The demand on Jesus is darkly ironic. Jesus has only acknowledged himself as messiah to a Samaritan woman, referring to himself as the Human One or Son of God to the Judeans. Yet he has always spoken openly, even when his disciples are nowhere to be found, while the crowds have *not* spoken openly for fear of the Judeans (7:13). This gathering of vultures is not one seeking faith but a conviction: Jesus' "confession" that he considers himself the Christ would be enough to justify his death. They have put the question directly to him, hoping to end this nonsense one way or another. What will Jesus say in response? Will he deny it and become a "liar" like his inquisitors and thus confirm their suspicion that he is not from God? Or will he "admit" it and face their stones?

Another piece of the irony lays in the idiomatic phrase translated as "How long will you keep us in suspense?" Literally, they ask, "Until when will you lift up [i.e., take away] our souls?" As Raymond Brown says, "although Jesus lays down his own life for those who follow him, he also provokes judgment and thus takes away the life of those who reject him."[8] They threaten his life by asking when he will take away theirs!

Always in charge, the Johannine Jesus chooses his own path in verse 25: "I have told you, and you are not believing. The works I am doing in the name of my Father, these things bear witness about me." His answer is another maddening conundrum. What exactly *has* he told them? Enough to give birth to faith if they were open, but not enough to subject himself to their "justice." And the works carry precisely the same ambiguity for the Judeans: they may not be the works of one possessed of a demon, but how could the true messiah break the sabbath? For the unbeliever, his response is a nonanswer.

In verse 26, Jesus continues by explaining the reason for their lack of faith in terms of the metaphor used in the first part of the chapter: "You are not of my sheep." Now the temporal evidence for the entire section from 9:1 through 10:39 taking place at Dedication is increased. Jesus apparently expects the audience (whom he knows does not hear him!) to be familiar with the shepherd parable he spun earlier. Otherwise, his image seems to come out of nowhere and is dropped as soon as it is introduced. But if we hear verses 26–29 as using images

---

8. R. Brown (1966, 402–403).

given just recently (sheep, destroyed, snatch), his remark indicates that these encircling Judeans are those loyal to the hired shepherds, and, hearing *those* voices, are trying to kill Jesus rather than believe in him.

### e. "The Father and I Are One"

Jesus goes on in verses 28–30 to complete the contrast left partially open in verses 12–13. In contrast to the hired hand who abandons the sheep, Jesus has said that he lays down his life for the sheep (10:15). Similarly, as the wolf then "snatches" the sheep and scatters them, no one "snatches them" out of Jesus' hand (verse 28).

In verse 29, Jesus sets up the "clincher" coming in verse 30: "What the Father has given me is greater than all, and no one can snatch from the Father's hand." Jesus' "hand" is just as safe a place as the Father's "hand" because of the mysterious something that the Father has given Jesus. What has Jesus been given? Readers and audience become curious to know. We know already that he has been given "all things" (3:35), authority to judge (5:22), and "life in himself" (5:27). Is Jesus referring to any of these gifts, or to something else?

Before we can answer, Jesus speaks as "openly" as is possible in verse 30: "The Father and I are one." This statement should come as no surprise to either readers or Judean hearers. It is as close as they will get to their demand in verse 24, and they are ready to act on it.

### 5. "YOU ARE GODS"

**Chiasm: 10:31–39**

a: 31–32: took up stones again; works/Father

    b: 33: blasphemy; make yourself God

        c: 34–35: is it not written?

    b¹: 36: blasphemy; I am the Son of God

a¹: 37–39: works/Father; again tried to arrest

For the second time (8:58), the Judeans in verse 31 attempt to stone Jesus. In case there was any doubt, it is now clear that their intentions have not changed an iota since Tabernacles. Jesus responds in verse 32 to this doomed-to-fail effort with a piece of brutal sarcasm that mocks their supposed loyalty to the Torah: "I have shown you many good works from the Father; for which of these works are you stoning me?" It is certainly not the kind of remark one would expect from someone in fear of imminent death!

One might begin to empathize just a bit with the Judeans, who are understandably angry at this "uncalled-for" bit of bitter humor. "Obviously," they are not intending to kill Jesus for a "good" work! From their perspective, his claim is blasphemy of the most blatant sort, "because although you are a person, you are making yourself God" (verse 33). For the first time, they vocalize what the narrator told us back in 5:18 was the basis for their plot, but with the additional legal categorization of the "making" as "blasphemy." Even though Jesus has just told them that what he has is "given" by the Father and not a result of his own "making," they insist on interpreting his claim in the way any rational unbeliever would. A person who sees herself or himself as one with God must be either an egotist of the worst kind or simply crazy. If Jesus does not accept the latter charge, then the only option is that he has completely lost track of his own status as "clay" in the hands of the potter (Isa 29:16; 64:8).

Jesus engages the battle of myths with them at a level that goes to the heart of what it means to be both an Israelite and a child of God. Quoting Ps 82:6, he asks them in verse 34, "Is it not written in your Law, 'I said, "You are gods" ' ?'" A closer look at this short psalm reveals much:

> God has taken his place in the divine council;
> in the midst of the gods he holds judgment:
> "How long will you judge unjustly and show partiality
>     to the wicked?
> Give justice to the weak and the orphan;
> maintain the right of the lowly and the destitute.
> Rescue the weak and the needy;
> deliver them from the hand of the wicked."
>
> They have neither knowledge nor understanding,
> they walk around in darkness;
> all the foundations of the earth are shaken.
>
> I say, "You are gods, children of the Most High, all of
>     you;
> nevertheless, you shall die like mortals, and fall like any
>     prince."
>
> Rise up, O God, judge the earth;
> for all the nations belong to you!

The psalm offers the same condemnation of Israel's bad judges as Jesus does of the bad shepherds, and in imagery fitting easily within the Johannine worldview. Those who exercise the power of God's Law are acting as gods, yet they will "die like mortals." At the moment when Jesus is threatened with death for apparently claiming to be more than a mortal, he invokes a psalm calculated to remind these would-be judges of their own mortality!

And yet by quoting just the short phrase from the psalm, Jesus focuses more specifically on the scriptural warrant for human beings being thought of as gods. In the heat of the moment, Jesus coolly gives them in verses 35–36 an exegetical challenge as clever as that of any Pharisaic rabbi: "If he called 'gods' those to whom the word of God came, and scripture cannot be loosened, then why are you saying to the one whom the Father has sanctified [*hēgiasen*] and sent forth into the world, 'You are blaspheming' because I said, 'I am God's Son'?" Either they base their case against him in *all* the scripture, and not just the texts that fit their predisposed disbelief in him, thereby acknowledging his right to claim to be God's Son, or they admit that they are not themselves faithful to the "Law"!

Jesus' argument establishes a wonderful paradigm for those modern-day Christians who find their discipleship practice and prophetic speech challenged by church leaders and others who proof-text against them. Before one begins quoting scripture, one had better be familiar with the entire Bible, or else be willing to change one's viewpoint when the power of other texts not necessarily fitting one's position becomes known. The lesson, of course, cuts both ways: we who see the Bible as setting out God's call to peace and justice for all creation need also to become intimate with as many scriptural texts as possible, and not allow our "favorites" to blind us to the entire message of the word of God.

Interestingly, Jesus uses the argument not to justify the specific claim of being one with the Father but to support his calling himself "God's Son" (5:25). It is a long way to go back into the trial between Jesus and the Judeans just when they are about to execute judgment against him!

Once more in verses 37–38, Jesus appeals to his works to evoke faith, this time specifically in his unity with the Father. But the narrator tells us in verse 39 that rather than argue scripture with him, the Judeans tried again to "seize him, but he went out from their hand." The chiasm closes with a humorous irony: no one can "snatch" the sheep from either Jesus' or the Father's "hand," but Jesus escapes from the "hand" of those who allow the wolf to snatch their own sheep.

# 15

# "Come Out!"

## *Confronting the Final Fear*

## John 10:40–12:11

A. **Chiasm:** 10:40–12:11

    a: 10:40–42: in Bethany beyond Jordan, many believe in Jesus

        b: 11:1–44: Jesus raises Lazarus after his burial

            c: 11:45–47: plot to kill Jesus

        b[1]: 12:1–8: Mary anoints Jesus before burial

    a[1]: 12:9–11: in Bethany near Jerusalem, many believe in Jesus[1]

B. **Locations:** "the other side," just outside of Bethany, Jerusalem, Ephraim, Bethany

C. **Time:** late in the day

D. **Hebrew scripture context:** 1 Kings 18 (Elijah); 1 Samuel 8 ("nation")

E. **Social factors:** Johannine community vs. Sanhedrin

F. **Themes:** fear of death; community

G. **Key words:** resurrection, nation/people

### 1. A RESPITE ON "THE OTHER SIDE"

The time for trying to convince the Judeans to come to faith in Jesus expired with their insistence on carrying out the death sentence for his "crime" of blasphemy. No more will Jesus interact directly with the "Judeans." His words and works are reserved now first for those whom he loves and then for his final

---

1. Ellis (1984, 177–178).

248

judges during the Passion narrative. His discourse on sheep and shepherds seems to have convinced no one to come forward and join him openly. Instead, it ironically made "open" the murderous intent that had simmered since chapter 5.

And so in verse 40, we are told that Jesus took a retreat on "the other side of the Jordan, in the place where John was baptizing at first, and was remaining there." As John told his own disciples in 3:30, he must decrease while Jesus continued to increase. Thus, this final mention of John is the briefest of all his "appearances" in the gospel, a literary living out of his "decrease."

While on the other side in verses 41–42, Jesus finds the faith that was lacking on the side of the "Promised Land." It is a bitter irony that true believers are found in the fourth gospel outside of the place where the tradition understood God to live in great glory. As in the original exodus, "many" found faith in the desert, apart from the institutions of government and cult.

The final word about John in verse 41 crystalizes our image of his successful ministry and distinguishes it definitively from Jesus' own ministry: "John, indeed, did no signs, but everything John said about this one was true." For remaining partisans of the Baptist, the "many" who believe during this visit of Jesus emphasize the lesser role of speaking the truth about another and also underscore that John allowed himself to disappear into the message he had delivered. John himself is absent from the scene. The only ones who speak are his disciples who have done what the Judeans could not or would not do.

## 2. CONQUERING THE FEAR OF DEATH

**Chiasm: 11:1–44**

a: 1–19: Lazarus, love, four days in tomb, Judeans

   b: 20–22: Martha meets Jesus

      c: 23–27: I AM the resurrection and life: do you believe?

   b[1]: 28–32: Mary meets Jesus

a[1]: 33–44: Lazarus, love, four days dead, Judeans[2]

### a. "There Are Twelve Hours of Day, Aren't There?"

**Chiasm: 11:1–19**

a: 1–2: Mary, Martha, Lazarus; Bethany

   b: 3–6: illness/death; glory

      c: 7–10: day/night

   b[1]: 11–16: sleep/death; "die with him"

a[1]: 17–19: Mary, Martha, Lazarus; Bethany

---

2. Ibid., 182–183.

The beginning of chapter 11 presents the strongest narrative break since the start of chapter 7, when Jesus argued with his "brothers" about whether to return to Judea from Galilee. After four chapters in Jerusalem spanning the period from Tabernacles (autumn) to Dedication (winter), Jesus has returned to the other side. The narrator starts off in 11:1 as if telling a completely different story: "There was one who was sick, Lazarus from Bethany, the village of Mary and Martha her sister." None of these characters has been heard from before, nor has the place where they live. Before we are even given their names, we are told that one is ill. The introduction recalls the previous "sickness" narratives, in which the ill person is introduced and the place named before Jesus enters the scene (4:46; 5:1–5). Given what happened in those cases, it does not take much imagination on readers' part to expect that Jesus will arrive and cure the ailment.

This expectation is increased by the root meaning of the sick one's name: "Lazarus," from the Hebrew *eleazer,* "God helps."[3] Furthermore, the specific variant "Lazarus" is, according to O. Obery Hendricks, Jr., "a distinctively Galilean pronunciation" of Eleazar. Hendricks further notes that Eleazar "was one of the two most common priestly names in Jewish antiquity."[4] Thus, there is a suggestion in the introduction of Lazarus that this character "serves as a conscious parody of the urban pretensions" of the Judean priests. Given the role of Caiaphas at the center of the chiasm from 10:40–12:11 and the narrator's emphasis on his holding of the priestly office (11:49–52), this possibility rings true and gives the scene from its first words an ambience of symbol and satire.

In the first verse, there is no information to connect Lazarus with the other named characters, other than that they live in the same village. It is almost as if the narrator expects the identification of Bethany as the place of Mary and Martha to be something familiar to readers: "Oh, we see, Lazarus is from *their* city." But, of course, we know nothing of the sort. The story thus opens with a tricky sort of insider/outsider perspective that throws us off guard.

If the first verse tilts our stance of comfortable knowledge, the second knocks us over completely: "It was the Mary who had anointed the Lord with myrrh and wiped his feet dry with her hair whose brother Lazarus was sick." For the first time in the fourth gospel, the narrator speaks as if we have already read the entire story — the scene referred to as if past is not narrated until 12:1–8. If we have not read ahead — or at least continue to engage in the reading fiction that the story is unfolding before us in a particular direction — then this information throws us completely out of our inside position and leaves us unsure whether we are even in the same gospel. Our only anchor is the narrator's use of "Lord" to refer (presumably!) to Jesus, although it is a rare usage (4:1; 6:23) at that.

As a structural matter, the verse links the Lazarus scene tightly with the anointing scene at the siblings' house and the aftermath in 12:9–11 and will force readers to see that the giving of life is inextricably bound to its taking. As counsel will be taken to kill Jesus because of what he does for Lazarus

---

3. R. Brown (1966, 422).
4. Hendricks (1992, 72).

(11:53), so counsel is taken to kill Lazarus because of what Mary does for Jesus (12:10). But for now, the verse functions as a monkey wrench in readers' sense of clear plot direction and challenges complacent readers to sit up and pay close attention or risk being left behind.

With verse 2, we have at least learned that Mary, Martha, and Lazarus are siblings. Thus, after this rocky start, we are not surprised when the sisters "sent forth [*apesteilan*] toward him, saying, 'Lord, the one you are friends with [*phileis*] is sick." The narrator continues in somewhat cryptic style, allowing the indeterminate "him" and "Lord" to substitute for the specific reference to "Jesus." It adds an element of mystery and stealth, as does the way in which the message is seemingly sent without mention of messengers. They *know* where their Lord is on the other side and manage to communicate with him across the distance. No names are needed or advised. Those who know do not need to allow extra information to circulate in case there are eavesdroppers. The implication is of an intimate discipleship community, which is in touch with one another despite threats from the dominant culture's representatives. The narrator paints a picture similar to what we might have found in El Salvador during the war years or in other locales in our world where Christians meet in secret under risk of persecution and death.

The relationship between Jesus and Lazarus is described with a term previously unused in the fourth gospel, with the exception of 5:20: *phileō*. Although the term is usually translated simply as "love," we risk missing an important distinction if we allow *phileō* the same translation as the stronger and deeper *agapaō*. Whereas the former denotes the emotional bond of friendly affection, the latter denotes the self-sacrificing and morally perfect love that Jesus will demand of his disciples for one another (e.g., 13:34–35). The sisters collectively understand Jesus to have the lesser but still powerful relationship with their brother and send a message to let their brother's friend know about the illness.

The message reaches its goal in verse 4, but Jesus responds with an unexpected remark: "This sickness is not for death but for the glory of God, so that the Son of God might be glorified through it." Who had said anything about ending in death? The degree of illness was unstated by both the narrator and the sisters, unlike 4:49, where the *basilikos* warned Jesus that the end for his son was apparently near. But at the same moment that Jesus introduces the idea that Lazarus might be suffering from a more serious illness, he replaces the thought of death with the ultimate goal, the "glory of God," and further, the glory of the "Son of God." We have heard about Jesus' "glory" periodically, starting with the narrator's summary of the events at Cana, then at Tabernacles (2:11; 7:39; 8:54). But it has remained a mysterious quantity, not being linked with either words or works that might give content for readers. Will we now find out what Jesus means by it?

Furthermore, we may wonder: Who is Jesus' remark spoken to? Is it just a comment to the air, an out-loud thought recorded by the omniscient and omnipresent narrator simply to express Jesus' mind-set? Or are those who believe in him on the other side listening? If so, what might they think about this cryptic comment? The narrator offers no help on these questions.

Before we can find out whether Jesus intends to respond further to the message about his ill friend, the narrator corrects the record: "Jesus was loving [*ēgapa*] Martha and her sister and Lazarus. . . ." His commitment to their brother is even greater than they know. It suggests at the outset that even these close friends are not "one with" their Lord as deeply as they might be. A curious point might also be observed: Why does the narrator name Martha and Lazarus but refer only indirectly to Mary as "her sister"? Is it simply to provide a measure of symmetry with verse 1, which mentions Mary first and then "Martha her sister"? Or might it be a way of suggesting a different level of relationship, despite the common *agapē* Jesus has for all three? Perhaps the ensuing dialogue will illuminate this question for readers.

In verse 6, the narrator gives us a shocking follow-up to the statement of Jesus' *agapē*. The word would lead us to expect Jesus to do the loving thing, that is, race to the village to be with and, perhaps, to heal Lazarus. Instead, the narrator tells us, "When he heard, therefore, that he was sick, he actually remained in the place where he was for two days." The "remaining for two days" recalls Jesus' stay in Samaria (4:40), during which many people came to faith. Similarly, here Jesus is on the other side where people are believing in him. That much meets our expectation. But why would Jesus continue to develop a faith community "on the other side" when his beloved friends are calling for him in Bethany? How do we put together the "glory of God," Jesus' love, and his remaining on the other side? This reading gap will remain a yawning chasm throughout much of the remainder of the fourth gospel.

As we reach the chiastic center of the opening sequence of the story, we may feel confused, uncomfortable, and anxious in ways we have not previously experienced in our sojourn through the gospel. Verse 7 finds a discipleship community with similar feelings. The disciples suddenly reenter the plot for the first time since their brief appearance on stage in 9:1–2, as Jesus tells them, "Let us be going into Judea again." After all that happened on the last visit, after the near brush with death, Jesus "invites" his followers back to the place of conspiracy and lies! Do the disciples know about Lazarus's illness? For that matter, do they even know Lazarus at all? We have no reason to think that they do, as the narrator has carefully based the scene on a message sent and received only between Jesus and the three siblings. But even if they do know, the proposal of going into the threatening environment of Judea is not likely to sound like a good suggestion for the next stop on their journey.

The disciples express these very thoughts in verse 8, with one minor but telling difference: "Rabbi, the Judeans are seeking to stone you, and you are going there again?" He has invited them along, but they respond only in terms of *Jesus'* travel plans. Either they are not subject to the same hostility he is (because they are not yet engaged in the same works/words) or they do not plan on accompanying their Rabbi on this risky journey. Their incredulity reveals how little they understand about Jesus' mission. Their fear of death — or at least their fear of their Rabbi's death — blinds them to any other reason for which one might be willing to engage the powers on their own turf.

Jesus' response in verses 9–10 in terms of the contrast between day and night recalls the last dialogue between master and disciples in 9:1–5. As the blindness was for the purpose of "revealing the works of God," so this illness is for God's glory and that of God's Son. There, Jesus contrasted working in the day with the inability to work at night; here, he contrasts "bumping" (*proskoptō*) at night with the absence of obstacles to walking in the daylight. The image of "bumping" is unique here in the fourth gospel and rare in the New Testament. It builds on the earlier image by suggesting not only that "work" is impossible at night but that even continuing on the discipleship journey has great risks in the dark. But there are "twelve hours of day" in which to walk; night will come later.

The "twelve hours" serves a triple function. In the ancient world, it was the basic division of the day, with the sixth hour as our "noon." But in the context of the conversation with disciples and the specific Johannine sense of "hour," it also implies an hour for each of the "twelve." As Jesus moves through his day toward the "hour" of his glory, so all disciples may expect their own hour, as will be discussed in the Last Supper discourse. Finally, it marks the progression of Jesus' journey throughout the story: as the Samaritan episode was at the sixth hour and the healing of the *basilikos*'s son was at the seventh hour (4:52), so the time is much later now, although not precisely specified. But there is still time for Jesus to walk, so the journey back to Judea is appropriate.

Unlike the scene in chapter 9, this conversation with the disciples does not end here. Jesus tells them the purpose of his journey in verse 11: "Lazarus our friend [*philos*] has laid down to rest, but I am going to awaken him." Now it is clear that the disciples share *phileō* with Lazarus also, but perhaps not *agapē*. Jesus speaks only in terms of his own mission, leaving open for the moment whether the disciples continue to be invited to join him.

Whether they know about Lazarus's illness, though, remains open, for Jesus uses the metaphor of sleep/waking to describe the situation of their friend. The disciples, like so many of their predecessors when faced with a double entendre spoken by Jesus, take the wrong route in verse 12 in interpreting his metaphor: "Lord, if he has rested, he will be saved [*sōthēsetai*]." The Greek verb *sōzō* is a common term for recovering from illness or affliction in the synoptics, but has been used in the fourth gospel only in the sense of religious salvation (3:17; 5:34; 10:9). There is no indication, though, that the disciples were hearers of any of these speeches by Jesus, so we might imagine that they are using the term only in the ordinary sense of being made well. Readers, therefore, have special knowledge that their statement is ironic: the disciples think only in terms of physical recovery, but we have already heard that the illness is for the glory of God *and* that salvation involves much more than physical well-being.

While readers may suspect that Jesus' remark about rest and awakening suggests that Lazarus has died, there is no specific reason for drawing this inference until the narrator makes it plain in verse 13 that "Jesus had spoken about his death." It is the only time in the gospel that the narrator directly explains the different interpretations of the conversation partners involved in misunderstanding. Ironically, Jesus' actual meaning is even more "earthly" than theirs, although not the literal message of the words. So if the "lesson" from the earlier examples of being born *anōthen,* drinking living water, and eating the bread of life has been to think not of the physical meaning but of the spiritual, the disciples are crossed up by Jesus' very physical message of their friend's demise.

After informing us of the conflict in interpretation, the narrator gives Jesus' "open" (*parrhēsia*) statement in verse 14: "Lazarus died, and I am rejoicing for your sake that I was not there so that you might believe. But let us be going to him." What was a possible consequence in verse 6 is now a paradoxical fact: Jesus' "remaining" on the other side has allowed Lazarus to die for the faith of his disciples. It is a shocking and disturbing statement. It seems to suggest that Jesus would toy with the life and death of a friend in order to make a point for his apparently unbelieving disciples. What is going on here? Why do Jesus' own disciples need something shown to them to generate faith? What is it that they are having trouble believing? Up to this point, the passage has revealed a strange and troubling set of circumstances, putting both disciples and readers in a confused and perhaps anxious state of mind.

In the midst of this turmoil, Thomas, "whose name means 'twin,' " a disciple who has not been mentioned before, responds in verse 16 with a surprising statement to his fellow disciples: "Let us go too so that we might die with him." Is this a show of bravado or cynical sarcasm in the face of likely persecution at the hands of the Judeans? Does this previously invisible character have a deep sense of understanding of the call of discipleship, or is he simply "one with an eye for the grim facts, but no perception of the glory"?[5] Whatever his intention, we are given neither the disciples' response nor a further explanation from Thomas. Instead, we are told simply in verse 17 that Jesus arrived four days after Lazarus was placed in the tomb. Whether the others — including Thomas — went with him or not is a gap left completely open, for the next mention of the disciples is in verse 54, when they are said to be in Ephraim near the wilderness.

With the mention of the "tomb" in verse 17, we might recall the previous use of that term in 5:28 and its context. Jesus said then that "the hour is coming and is here now when the dead will hear the voice of the Son of God, and those who have heard will live" (5:25); *and* "the hour is coming in which all those in the tombs will hear his voice and will come out, the ones having done good into a resurrection of life and the ones having done foul deeds to a resurrection of judgment." In turn, this recollection might trigger our memory of the more recent statement that the sheep will "hear his voice, and he calls his own sheep by name and leads them out" (10:3; cf. 10:27). These were powerful words by Jesus that, if believed, would suggest that Jesus has the power over life and death. Putting the various clues together ought to lead us to expect that Jesus will call Lazarus, his friend whom he loves, by name out of the tomb.

---

5. Duke (1985, 59).

Although this expectation is increased tremendously for modern Christians who take for granted Jesus' power to raise the dead, it is important to read this story if we can from the realistic perspective that neither the original audience *nor* we have any experience of such a phenomenon taking place. While we may "see" resurrection in the seasonal cycles of nature or in the irregular movements in our lives between despair and hope, burnout and being energized, the concrete act of calling dead bodies out of the tomb is, I presume, not something any of us has witnessed. Yet this possibility, not a metaphorical sense of the rhythms of life and death, is what the previous narratives have proposed.[6] And now, it is what the four-days-dead Lazarus presents as a challenge to the faith of the disciples and those who experience the events narrated in the rest of chapter 11.

Having introduced these expectations, the narrator shifts suddenly in verse 18 to geography, telling us that Bethany was about two miles from Jerusalem. The juxtaposition of death and life takes another turn with the mention of the capital city, because it means that "Judeans had come to Martha and Mary to console them about their brother" (verse 19). Lazarus is in the tomb, and the Judeans have been threatening to put Jesus there, too! The disciples' fearful sense of impending stoning in verse 8 finds ironic embodiment in people come to Bethany as mourners.

We might pause to consider the role of coming and going in this passage in linking ideology and faith:

1.  The sisters sent a message from Bethany to the other side to express affection
2.  Jesus goes from the other side to Bethany for God's glory
3.  Thomas offers to go on the same journey "to die with him"
4.  Judeans go from Jerusalem to Bethany to console
5.  Martha goes from Bethany to where Jesus is to express mixed hope and unbelief
6.  Mary imitates Martha's journey
7.  The Judeans follow Mary outside the village to where Jesus is
8.  Lazarus hears Jesus' voice and comes "out"
9.  Some Judeans go the Pharisees to report what Jesus has done
10. The Sanhedrin remain where they are to condemn Jesus
11. The "scattered children of God" will be gathered as one

As the passage unfolds, paying attention to these markers will help us understand how the text continues to enrich the subtle yet important link between one's place and movement and one's perspective.

---

6. However, cf. Hendricks (1992, 74), suggesting several metaphorical possibilities for "resurrection" in this context, including the restoring to hope of Galilean "sociopolitical reconscientization" or "ideological reempowerment."

Returning to the scene in verse 19, we find the sisters gathered with mourners engaging in the normal cultural ritual of mourning. The usual process included a thirty-day period of consolation, including "loud wailing and dramatic expressions of grief,"[7] usually provided at least in part by professional mourners.[8] Just as we might hire musicians and a caterer for a funeral, so people of means in Palestine provided for the "appropriate" help after death. But professional mourners, in line with the Judean tradition, could not provide true hope for the sisters, whose grief was all too real.

### b. *"I AM the Resurrection and the Life"*

**Chiasm: 11:20–32**

a: 20–21: Martha: "Lord, if you had been here . . . "

　　b: 22–24: Martha and "rise"

　　　　c: 25–27: I AM the resurrection and the life

　　b¹: 28–31: Mary and "rise"

a¹: 32: Mary: "Lord, if you had been here . . . "

While verse 17 seemed to suggest that Jesus has actually arrived in Bethany, verse 20 paints a different picture: "Therefore, when Martha heard that Jesus was coming she met him, but Mary was sitting in the house." In a passage already riddled with gaps, we find new ones here, as there is no explanation of how Martha heard about Jesus' presence, where she met him, or why she went out but Mary "was sitting" (*ekathezeto*). The only previous "sitting" in the fourth gospel was when Jesus was sitting on the well in Samaria (4:6). Here, it seems to suggest that Mary is continuing to engage in the mourning procedure, sitting with the Judeans, while her sister, consistent with the Lukan portrayal of them, is more active (Lk 10:38–41). However, whereas in Luke, Martha's activity is criticized as generating worry that distracts her from the important faith practice of contemplation, in John, her activity implies a measure of discipleship, as she leaves her culture behind to go to Jesus.

When Martha finds him, she speaks with a mixture of anger, disappointment, and hope in verses 21–22: "Lord, if you had been here, my brother would not have died. But even now I know that whatever you ask God for, God will give you." What was the hope she expected Jesus to fulfill? Does her statement express the impossible dream that Jesus could give life to a man four days dead? She claims to "know" something about Jesus that neither he nor the narrator has claimed: that Jesus could "ask" (*aitēsē*) God for something and have it done. The only previous use of the term was in Samaria in reference to "asking" for a drink (4:9, 10). In the Last Supper discourse, there will be much discussion about "asking." But regardless of the eventual conversation between Jesus and

---

7. R. Brown (1966, 424).

8. Carson (1991, 415).

those gathered at supper, Martha has heard none recorded in the text, so her knowledge is either intuitive or based on unreported conversations, as, of course, the entirety of the siblings' relationship with Jesus is unrecorded until now.

In verse 23, Jesus seems to ignore both her disappointment in his previous absence and her knowledge, offering what the culture would consider a trite answer: "Your brother will rise." That Martha hears it as such is clear from her impatient response in verse 24, about the "resurrection on the last day." From her perspective, Jesus' words are about as comforting as the common graveside offering, "Your loved one is with God." That may be fine for the loved one, but not for the lonely mourner! Martha's affirmation of the Pharisaic belief in the resurrection shows both her at least partial alignment with the dominant theology as well as the limitations of that theology. The "last day" is a long way off, a very distant locus of hope for human beings whose sojourn on earth is but a moment in the sweep of time. With the reference to "tomb" in mind from 5:28, readers know, however, that Jesus has promised to call people forth from the tomb at an hour that is "now." Does Martha's hope in Jesus' power to ask God for anything include the prospect of *immediate* resurrection?

At the heart of the small chiasm from verse 20 to 32 as well as the larger one from verse 1 to 44 lie those verses (25–27) in which the most powerful and demanding Christian hope is expressed by Jesus. It is well worth our focusing on its internal structure to grasp what it claims. Jesus makes three interrelated yet separate statements and asks Martha if she believes:

1. that I AM (*egō eimi*) the resurrection and the life
2. that the one believing in me, even though that one should die, will live
3. that everyone living and believing in me will never die at all

Here is the central challenge of the passage and perhaps of the entire gospel. It is one thing to believe that Jesus is "a good man," a "teacher come from God," a prophet or even a messiah. People have placed their faith in all kinds of leaders through the ages because of the power of their words or the saintliness of their acts. But Jesus' statement presents a much narrower door through which faith is called to travel than following a teacher or prophet. The first part presents in the familiar metaphorical form the equation of *egō eimi* with two things: resurrection and life itself. The former involves the restoration of life to those already dead and is explicated in the second line. The latter part of the metaphor involves the very fact of life's reality and is explicated in the third line. But is the third line itself another metaphor, or does it dare us to take it literally?

Clearly, the statement cannot claim with any expectation of belief the notion that disciples will not experience physical death. The cessation of bodily functions after a time and the decay of the body did not stop with the birth of Christianity, even for those with the utmost faith. And yet the statement's very specificity and insistence demand us to take it more seriously than a too easy spiritualizing response might. Is there another alternative between the facilely literal and the purely metaphorical?

To find this middle option, we should stop to consider the plot function that the passage plays in the overall structure of the text. Why at this point in the story, after blind humanity has been offered sight, is it important for the fourth gospel to present to both characters and readers this supreme challenge? Up until now, we have seen that the risk of faith in Jesus for a synagogue Jew included misunderstanding, ridicule, hostility, and even excommunication. But there has not been an explicit suggestion that anything worse might happen. For the once-blind one, the loss of one community was the invitation to another. The abandonment by hired shepherds was replaced by the love and fidelity of the good shepherd.

But for the Johannine community, the risk of faith was eventually much greater. As Jesus will warn his disciples in the Last Supper discourse, "If they have persecuted me, they will persecute you, too" (15:20); in fact, "The hour is coming when everyone who kills you will think they are rendering worship to God" (16:2). Although these predictions come later in the story, the hint is already in the air with Thomas's remark in 11:16. The cost of discipleship in a hostile and unbelieving world may well include persecution and death, as Dietrich Bonhoeffer understood nineteen centuries later. This was indeed the fate of Christians late in the first century, as even the Roman historian Tacitus recorded in his only reference to the "cult" of "Christus":

> Nero looked around for a scapegoat, and inflicted the most fiendish tortures on a group of persons already hated by the people for their crimes. This was the sect known as Christians. Their founder, one Christus, had been put to death by the procurator Pontius Pilate in the reign of Tiberius. This checked the abominable superstition for a while, but it broke out again and spread, not merely through Judea, where it originated, but even to Rome itself, the great reservoir and collecting ground for every kind of depravity and filth. Those who confessed to being Christians were at once arrested, but on their testimony a great crowd of people were convicted...of hatred of the entire human race. They were put to death amid every kind of mockery. Dressed in the skins of wild beasts, they were torn to pieces by dogs, or were crucified, or burned to death: when night came, they served as human torches to provide lights. Nero threw open his gardens for this entertainment....These Christians were guilty, and well deserved their fate.[9]

To follow a controversial teacher and face ridicule is one thing; to serve as a human torch is quite another. While such consequences may seem remote and primitive to some of us in the United States, for people in El Salvador, Malawi, or many other places in which confessing one's allegiance to Jesus the liberator may mean torture and midnight death, the early Christians' fate provides a powerful precedent that cries out for just the sort of promise that

---

9. Tacitus *Ann.* 353–354 (Dudley, trans.).

Jesus offers Martha. In other words, will death separate the disciple from the community and from God? And the corollary: Will the fear of death prevent discipleship from taking root in the first place? This is the social situation in which the Johannine community told the story of Lazarus and his sisters.

Of course, the death of Lazarus was due to illness, not torture. There is no reference in the text so far that implies that Martha is mourning a martyr. But when the "happy ending" to the story unfolds, the raised Lazarus *does* become the subject of the same murderous conspiracy as is Jesus (12:10). The chiasm does not close until Lazarus's fate is bound up with that of his shepherd.

With this social setting in mind, we can return to the question of the meaning of the third part of Jesus' statement. It recalls his comment to the Judeans in 8:51 that "if anyone keeps my word, they will never see death." The two statements are highly parallel: both are built on the double negative (*ou mē*) and the phrase for unlimited time, "into the age" (*eis ton aiōna*). Thus, the challenge to Martha is: if you have life through me, neither Judean stoning nor Roman torture and execution can separate you from me.

Her response in verse 27 is excruciatingly ambiguous. She begins with the simple and direct, "Yes, Lord, I have believed," which evokes an immediate readerly sense of relief that she is apparently not another would-be disciple who either cannot respond or gives the wrong answer to one of Jesus' demands. She continues, though, not with an affirmation of Jesus' statements about life and death, but with a sequence of three titles: "You are the Christ, the Son of God, the one coming into the world." Eventually, the narrator will affirm acclamation of the first two of these titles as the basic purpose of the gospel (20:31). But these titles, as valid as they may be as some measure of understanding who Jesus is, do not respond to the question he asked Martha. As Paul S. Minear has said, "She is unable to say, 'Lord, I believe that whoever lives and believes in you shall never die.... Like her, they [the Johannine community] were ready to join in confessing Jesus as the Messiah, ... [but they] also did not fully believe that Jesus is himself the resurrection and the life."[10]

From another perspective, the very fact that Jesus is asking this question of *Martha* and receiving the sort of "confession" he does says a lot about the fourth gospel's attitude toward women and discipleship. The interaction has many similarities with the synoptic account of Jesus' conversation with Peter in which the lead apostle expresses who he believes Jesus is: "You are the Christ, the Son of the living God" (Mt 16:16). Although the Matthean Jesus starts off affirming Peter's answer, he soon turns to rebuke Peter's "Satan"-like behavior. In Mark, Peter's confession that Jesus is the messiah receives an immediate rebuke (Mk 8:29–30). Thus, even if Martha's answer may be seen as "imperfect," the fact that it is she who gives it rather than Peter is a strong affirmation of the right of women to participate in the community and of the importance of their opinions and commitment. Peter, as one of the twelve, has already had his opportunity

---

10. Minear (1977, 119).

to "confess" in the fourth gospel (6:69). Now, a beloved woman shares equally in that role.

Unlike the synoptic confessional scenes, this one continues without further comment by either the characters or the narrator. Whatever evaluation is to be made of Martha's response is left completely up to readers until the scene reveals more. For now, the narrator in verse 28 breaks in with the description of Martha's return to "call" her sister Mary, "saying secretly [*lathra*], 'The teacher is near and is calling you.'" This sense of secretness is slightly different from the clandestine nature of Jesus' Tabernacles appearance in 7:10 (*kryptō*). The term used here is found only in this place in the fourth gospel and is used elsewhere in the New Testament with the connotation of surreptitiousness (e.g., Mt 1:19; 2:7). In this context, it seems clear that Martha speaks this way to her sister to try to prevent the Judeans from knowing that Jesus is near.

Twice verse 28 used the verb *phōneō*, "to call," first for Martha's calling of Mary and then for Jesus' call. Previously, this term has referred to the summoning to give testimony or has been used in the religious sense of calling (1:48; 2:9; 4:16; 9:18, 24). We can, therefore, expect that Mary will be asked to respond in a way perhaps similar to her sister. Mary, for her part, we are informed in verse 29, "when she heard, rose quickly and went toward him."

The narrator, as has been his style, adds in verse 30 a piece of information that challenges us to go back and reconsider the scene in light of the new fact: "Jesus had not yet come into the village, but was still in the place where Martha had met him." While we already knew from verse 20 that Martha had left the house to meet her Lord, it had not been clear that Jesus had not even entered the village. In combination with the secret call, it deepens the sense of suspense in Jesus' and the sisters' attempt to keep his presence a secret from the Judeans. However, the cat gets partly out of the bag in verse 31 when we are informed that "the Judeans who were with her in the house consoling her, having seen Mary quickly rise and go out, followed her, thinking that she was going to the tomb to weep there." They do not yet know the reason but are aroused by Mary's sudden departure. The positive sense we might have felt to Mary's immediate response to the call is now balanced by the fact that it will likely give away Jesus' presence to the Judeans and lead to his confrontation with those who are anxious to stone him to death. How precarious is the line between discipleship and betrayal!

Mary in verse 32 arrived at the place where Jesus is and, seeing him, "fell at his feet, saying, 'Lord, if you had been here, my brother would not have died.'" It is a verbatim repetition of Martha's plea, but there is no reason to think that Mary knew what her sister had said to Jesus. This implies either that the remark is a cliché that people might be expected to say to an absent friend lately arrived or that the sisters had discussed among themselves what Jesus' presence would have meant during Lazarus's illness and had reached a common conclusion.

It is an interesting aspect of Mary's character that she is continually pictured while with Jesus as being "at his feet" (see 11:2; 12:3; cf. 20:16–17). No other character is found with Jesus in this degree of physical intimacy and humility.

The particular element of "feet," as proleptically "recalled" in 11:2 and in 12:1–8 and 13:1–20, becomes a symbol of the link between discipleship and death. In 11:32, though, it is overshadowed by the poignancy of the second sister's greater concern with what *wasn't* than with what *is*.

## c. Groaning Deep in the Spirit

### Chiasm: 11:33–45

a: 33–36: Judeans "having come with" Mary

   b: 37–39: eyes; dead man; stone

      c: 40: see the glory of God

   b¹: 41–44: eyes; dead man; stone

a¹: 45: Judeans "come toward" Mary

The stage is now set. Jesus has come and surveyed the scene and found two beloved friends wondering why he had "remained" on the other side; in verse 33, he sees "her [Mary] weeping and the Judeans having come with her weeping." It is all mourning and impossible hope, with the exception of Martha's "knowledge" about Jesus' power to ask God anything *now*. The narrator provides an enigmatic yet powerful statement of Jesus' response to this situation: Jesus "groaned [*enebrimēsato*] in the spirit and was deeply troubled [*etaraxen*] in himself." The two emotion-describing verbs are almost untranslatable but extremely important to consider for what they reveal about Jesus' state of mind and heart at this crucial moment. The first is used only here and in verse 38 in the fourth gospel. In the synoptics, it is also rare, used to describe Jesus' rebuke of healed persons against telling about him (Mt 9:30; Mk 1:44) and for the disciples' anger at the anonymous woman who anoints Jesus' head with costly perfume (Mk 14:3–5), a story with strong affinities to the anointing in Jn 12:1–8. It has its root in the sound of a horse snorting and clearly expresses deep anger. The second word, *tarasso*, is used in the synoptics to convey deep fear (e.g., Mk 6:50; Lk 24:38); in the fourth gospel it has not occurred until now as an expression of human emotions, but only in its more literal meaning of stirring up water (5:7). Together, they show a side of Jesus we have not seen before in this gospel, a deeply emotional internal stirring that is enraged and perhaps fearful about some aspect of what is presented before him. What is it that has evoked these powerful feelings in Jesus?

Before we try to answer this question, it will be helpful to wait to see how the emotions continue to unfold in the next few verses. Filled with these feelings, Jesus says in verse 34: "Where have you [plural] laid him?" Suddenly, it is no longer a one-on-one discussion but the all-too-familiar conversation between Jesus and the "they" who respond. It is not clear whether this "they" refers to the sisters or to the Judeans whom Jesus has seen weeping with Mary. Whichever combination it may be, "they" say, "Lord, come and see." The idea that the Judeans might call Jesus "Lord" is unlikely, unless we translate *kyrie* here as the more generic "sir" (cf. 6:34). The sisters have used this term to address Jesus more consistently than any other characters in the story (11:3, 21, 27, 32). Thus, the title does not really help us identify the "they" any more precisely.

But the "come and see" is darkly ironic. It was used previously as a call to experience Jesus (1:39, 46; 4:29), but here it is a summons to experience a dead body. This "come and see" leads the narrator to tell us in verse 35: "Jesus shed tears." While many readers share the Judeans' interpretation of these tears as a sign of Jesus' affection for his dead friend, in the context of the angry and fearful emotions Jesus expresses, they must mean more than simply the normal grief for the dead. Indeed, given that Jesus has actively set up Lazarus's death by his delay and claimed that it would be for the glory of God, it misses the point of the entire story to attribute Jesus' tears to the ordinary experience of death. Indeed, allowing this interpretation to be put in the mouth of Judeans greatly undercuts its likelihood. It is as if the narrator *expects* readers to come up with this interpretation and refutes it through the ironic role of the Judeans. Another clue to the prospect of a deeper meaning is that the Judeans speak of Jesus' "affection" (*ephilei*) as something from the past, while the narrator tells us that Jesus' love for all three siblings is ongoing (11:5). Finally, even those among the Judeans who acknowledge in verse 37 Jesus' previous opening of the blind one's eyes only think of his ability to help Lazarus as an opportunity whose time had passed: "Wasn't this one able ... to prevent this one from dying?"

Given all these factors, it seems that Jesus' feelings and tears come not from grief at the fact of death but at the *unbelief* that accompanies it. The traditional mourning practices, the disappointment about Jesus' absence, even the hope for an eschatological resurrection all bespeak an unwillingness or inability to believe that death does not have the last word. Jesus *is* life, but all those around him see nothing but the finality of death. After everything he has said and done, both these dear friends and the Judeans have missed the basic message of his incarnation: that the God who creates and sustains all that has come to be is fully present in the one some proclaim as Christ.

Both Judean statements rooted in the past lead Jesus to groan again in verse 38 as he goes to the tomb. The narrator describes it as "a cave with a stone lying on it." This form of burial indicates that the family had a certain amount of wealth, for not everyone could afford a burial cave. Jesus speaks another short, direct command in verse 39: "Lift up the stone." Looking back we see that since his *egō eimi* statement in verses 25–26, he has vocalized only the question in verse 34 and this command. His sole intent is to carry out the work that first led him to remain on the other side and then led him to risk the Judeans' wrath: to "awaken" their friend Lazarus.

Martha, though, is still focused on the graphic reality of death in verse 39. The narrator alters the description of her slightly by calling her "the sister of the dead one" as she gives voice to her famous line, "Lord, already it is smelling, for it is the fourth day." It is the second time we have been told that Lazarus is four days dead (11:17), which serves a double function. In the Jewish mindset of the time, the soul remained with the body until the third day, when it was finally released. By the fourth day, it was therefore absolutely certain that a person was irretrievably gone. It also shows how focused Martha is, despite her "knowledge," on the "earthly" nature of death. No other gospel portrays as harshly the repulsiveness of physical death or its ability to overwhelm human hope in the continuity of life.

Jesus confronts this "thinking from below" in verse 40: "Did I not tell you that if you believe you will see the glory of God?" Although there is no narration of this specific promise by Jesus to Martha, it was hinted at by the narrator's description of the disciples' reaction to the Cana experience in 2:11, where seeing Jesus' glory led them to faith.

Whether Martha recalls or understands Jesus' statement now is not told, for the story is now ready for the decisive action. Verse 41 contains a poignant contrast: "They therefore lifted up [*ēran*] the stone, but Jesus lifted up [*ēren*] his eyes and said..." "They" are focused on the earthly stone, but Jesus is focused on his heavenly Father. For the first time in the fourth gospel, Jesus speaks directly to God: "Father, I thank [*eucharistō*] you for hearing me. I know that you are always hearing me, but for the sake of the crowd standing here, I say this so that they might believe that you sent [*apesteilas*] me." The prayer echoes the prayer of Elijah in 1 Kgs 18:37:

> Answer me, O Lord, so that this people may know that you, O Lord, are God, and that you have turned their hearts back.

Unlike Elijah, though, Jesus knows before he speaks that God hears him. It is not the prayer that Martha had hoped for, in which Jesus would "ask" God something. Instead, Jesus simply offers thanks "for the sake of the crowd." Similarly, the plan does not arise from the circumstances or from Martha's petition but is now revealed as fully formed from at least the moment of the message's arrival on the other side, if not from "the beginning."

The moment has finally come in verse 43: "Having said these things, he cried out in a great voice, 'Lazarus, come out!'" The shepherd has called his sheep by name; will the one in the tomb hear his voice?

The narrator describes the scene in verse 44 in a highly symbolic way: "The one having died came out, having been bound in feet and hands with wrappings, and with his face covered with a cloth." It is almost impossible to picture the scene. Are we to imagine the tightly bound Lazarus floating out of the tomb?

The triple binding of feet, hands, and face dramatically underscores the inability of the dead one to become free without help, even after being called forth by Jesus. Thus, Jesus' final command is: "Unbind him and let him go." It is not addressed to anyone in particular, nor is obedience to the command narrated. But it is a clearly stated aspect of Jesus' mission that the life he has given that extends beyond the stone wall of death is not fully restored *unless* human beings untie the bonds that they have created for themselves. The burial cloths are the work of human tradition and culture, which, in this case, see death as something to be shrouded from sight, hidden away in a dark hole, and not looked on again.

Jesus is indeed the resurrection and the life that cannot be destroyed, but human beings must do their own work to remove the binding cloths, just as the one born blind was required to wash away the clay from his own eyes. God's grace is an unasked for gift that provides sight and life to the blind and dead, but *only if* the recipients cooperate by doing the work that follows.

The scene comes to a dramatic and screeching halt after verse 44, as the curtain drops with many questions left wide open, crying out for answers. What was the reaction of Martha and Mary to this unprecedented experience? What did Lazarus feel and think? Who unbound Lazarus? Did he "smell," or was he somehow preserved from death's decay? None of these questions, so seemingly important to us as readers, is given the slightest attention by the text. Instead, the narrator moves on to what is important to the Johannine community: the reaction of the Judeans and those to whom they give allegiance.

Verse 45 gives the first part of the reaction: "Many of the Judeans having come to Mary and having seen what he did believed in him." Is it possible that "Judeans" will truly believe? Or perhaps more realistically given what has happened, is it possible that any observers could *not* believe? As far as we know, it was not the sabbath, and Jesus violated no Torah prohibitions. Could anyone, no matter how committed to the established system and dominant culture, witness a dead person leaving the tomb and not be converted?

## 3. "YOU HAVE NOT KNOWN ANYTHING!"

### Chiasm: 11:45–12:11

a: 11.45–47: many Judeans believe; chief priests and Pharisees

    b: 48–53: preparation for Jesus' death; questionable concern for "nation"

        c: 54–57: Jesus retreats; threat of arrest

    b[1]: 12:1–8: preparation for Jesus' death; questionable concern for "poor"

a[1]: 9–11: many Judeans believe; chief priests plan Lazarus's death

### Chiasm: 11:46–57

a: 46–47: Pharisees and chief priests: "what are we doing?"

    b: 48–50: Romans will come: one person should die

        c: 51–52: Jesus to die for children of God to be gathered

    b[1]: 53–55: they took counsel to kill him; many come to Jerusalem

a[1]: 56–57: chief priests and Pharisees; "what are you thinking?"

One chiasm ends with apparent faith, while the next begins in verse 46 with apparent doubt: "But some of them went off to the Pharisees and told them what Jesus did." Have they gone to report a miracle or simply to let the Pharisees know that their nemesis is back in the neighborhood and up to his old "tricks"? We are told nothing further about the intention of the Judeans, but instead, the narrator shifts our intention in verse 47 to the "gathering" (*synēgagon*) of the Sanhedrin by "the chief priests and the Pharisees."

Historically speaking, these would not be the two groups comprising or having the power to gather the official council of Jerusalem. In fact, the priests and Pharisees were groups often at odds, as the former focused on Temple worship led exclusively by the Levites while the latter advocated lay holiness centered in the home and daily life. That the fourth gospel pictures them operating together here is symbolic of the union of Temple and Torah against the Johannine community, named in the center of this passage as "the children of God who are scattered" and are "led together" (*synagagē*) (11:52). Of course, by the time of the fourth gospel, the priests were history, while the Pharisees remained as the primary exponents of Jewish orthodoxy.

It is the only reference to the Sanhedrin in the fourth gospel and begins with the asking of the crucial question: "What are we doing because of the many signs this person is doing? If we let him go like this, all will believe in him, and the Romans will come and take away [literally, 'lift up,' *arousin*] our place and the nation." The question is pregnant with meaning and summarizes for the first time the true reason for the conspiracy against Jesus. It is not concern for the sabbath or blasphemy that motivates the Sanhedrin but *fear of the Romans,* who are mentioned here for the first time in the gospel. Their fear is that the "signs" that *ho anthrōpos* does will lead "all" to believe. We have already seen Jesus' negative attitude toward those who believe because of signs, yet it is certainly clear that those who do represent a formidable threat to the power of the Sanhedrin (6:14–15). They are concerned not simply with a messianic following but that "*all* will believe in him."

The fear is that this universal belief will arouse the Romans, with whom the Sanhedrin has made a compromised peace, to "lift up" their "place" and "the nation." The "lifting up" is another form of the verb recently used in relation to the tombstone and to Jesus' eyes. It is ironic that these supposed children of God (but whom readers know to be children of the devil) express their concern in very "earthly" terms. "Place" (*topon*), referring to the Temple, is the most secular possible way to describe God's house, called earlier by the name *naos,* a divine place or habitation (2:21). Further, they are afraid of losing their "nation" (*ethnos*). In the Septuagint, *ethnos* translates the Hebrew word *goy,* which we speak as "Gentile." In the Hebrew Bible, the Gentiles are distinguished regularly from Israel as foreign nations worshiping false gods or no god. The *worst* sin for Israel is to want to be "like the nations [*ethnē*]" (e.g., 1 Sam 8:19), for, as God says to Samuel, "they have not rejected you, but they have rejected me from being king over them" (1 Sam 8:7). By stating their concern about Jesus in terms of place and nation, the Sanhedrin make clear that, at least among themselves, they have abandoned any pretense of serving God.

More particularly, their fearful exclamation expresses their concern over the potential loss of their power as leaders. For, as the elite of Israel learned through the experience of the exile six centuries before, destruction of the official religious machinery forced the people to learn how to develop an egalitarian religious community.[11] The removal of "our place" and "the nation" would not (and, historically, did not) destroy faith in the God of the covenant but would certainly demolish priestly control over the practice of that faith.

The problem, therefore, that Caiaphas — described in verse 49 as "chief priest that year" — addresses is not the way they have named their fear but their lack of certainty of what to do about it. In his only line in all of scripture, he speaks one of the most richly ironic truths in the New Testament:

> You people know nothing! You have not figured out that it is more expedient [*sympherei*] to you that one person should die for the people [*laou*] and that the whole nation [*ethnos*] not be destroyed [*apolētai*].

How many powerful statements are packed into this short but conclusive speech! Caiaphas begins by correctly assessing the state of knowledge of the Sanhedrin. They have completely misunderstood Jesus and his mission and, therefore, are faced with utter confusion over what to do about his presence in their midst. Second, they are so busy worrying and reacting to each word and action by Jesus one at a time that they have not taken the time to "figure out" (*logizesthe*, the only use of the word in the fourth gospel) anything. Their giving in to their murderous instincts, "inherited" from their father, has prevented them from determining calmly what the situation calls for, as Jesus will do when he declares what is "expedient" (*sympherei*) for his disciples (16:7). What Caiaphas and Jesus find expedient is precisely the same: that Jesus die/"go away" for the sake of the people. By contrasting the *laos* and the *ethnos,* Caiaphas attempts to find a "both/and" position in relation to the concerns voiced by the San-hedrin in the preceding verse, for in the Septuagint, *laos* refers to the "people of God."[12] Thus, Caiaphas correctly argues that one person should die for the sake of the *laos.* However, while he means the people of *Judea* who also com-prise the Sanhedrin's *ethnos,* Jesus' death will truly be for the *laos* comprising the "scattered children of God." Caiaphas unconsciously sees the situation as re-quiring application of the scapegoat principle,[13] but Jesus sees it as enacting the love of the good shepherd. Finally, Caiaphas sees the single death as prevent-ing the "destroying" of the "whole nation," whereas in reality, Jesus' death will gather together people who would otherwise risk destruction, or "perishing," at the hands of the hired shepherds (10:10, 28).

The result of the "gathering" of the Sanhedrin will be the "gathering" in of the scattered children of God (verse 52). The previous "gathering" was of the fragments left over from the wilderness feeding in 6:12, 13. We can now look back on that command, where Jesus voiced his intention that nothing would "perish" (*apolētai*), as the symbolic beginning of the gathering that will flow from Jesus' impending death. It is a mission that his disciples will carry out in his absence.

---

11. Gottwald (1985, 425).
12. Duke (1985, 88).
13. Girard (1986, 113).

The narrator, while naming the central conclusion that Jesus' death will be for more than the "nation," attributes in verse 51 Caiaphas's "prophesy" to his holding of the office of "chief priest that year." Many have noted that as a matter of history, the office of chief priest was held for life, not annually, so the narrator must be referring to the fact that *that* year Caiaphas was chief priest. But it is still a baffling comment in a gospel that has repeatedly gone out of its way to refute the idea that Israel's religious offices came endowed with inherent authority. It is as if the narrator still wants readers to know that *if* the shepherds had been good and loving rather than thieves and robbers, Israel as a holy nation, complete with Temple and Torah structure, *would have* been blessed by God and the entire tragic story avoided. But as it is, the chief priest's "truth" is wholly ironic. The authorities will stop him from going on in this way; Jesus will die for the people. *And* "all will believe in him, *and* the Romans will come and take away our place *and* the nation." They have tried again and again to kill Jesus and he repeatedly got away. Now they successfully will "stop" him, and their worst nightmares will face the light of day.

What has up until now been the persecution and conspiracy by the "Judeans" now becomes a result of the "council" (*ebouleusanto*) of the Sanhedrin (verse 53). Mob violence has given way to the organized, "civilized," "reasoned" violence of government. It is a bitter pill for the Johannine community to swallow that the leadership of their own nation has "baptized" the foul plans of the crowds.

Therefore, the narrator tells us in verse 54: "Jesus no longer went about openly [*parrhēsia*] among the Judeans, but went from there into the country near the wilderness, to the city called Ephraim, and remained there with the disciples." Jesus, who knows even the internal workings of the Sanhedrin, recognizes that, despite the faith of some of those who witnessed the raising of Lazarus, his final public deed has been done in Judea. The time for conversion must give way to walking the final part of his journey back to God.

Why does the narrator specify the retreat location as the wilderness city of Ephraim? Although this is the only reference to this locale in the New Testament, it is a place rich with history in the Hebrew scripture. Explained in Gen 41:52 as meaning "fruitful place," it was the name of Joseph's younger son (Gen 48:1–20). Through the centuries of Israel's development, it became an important worship center in the Northern Kingdom of Israel, which eventually separated from the Southern Kingdom of Judah in 722 B.C.E. It was the birthplace of Samuel (1 Sam 1:1) and Jeroboam (1 Kgs 11:26), two important opponents of the southern view of monarchy that focused on the importance of the Jerusalem Temple. Thus, Jesus leaves Jerusalem for a place in which his views would be much less suspect, yet a place still a part of historic Israel.

Once more, the narrator tells us that Passover was near (verse 55). For the first time, though, we are given the detail that "many people went up to Jerusalem from the country before the Passover to purify themselves." The first Passover's sacrificial animals (2:14) are now implicitly linked with their purpose. The idea of sacrifice is in the air.

Having generated this mood, the narrator in verse 56 focuses in on the conversation among the people who were arriving in the capital, who were "seeking" Jesus and "saying to one another as they stood in the Temple, 'What do you think? He certainly won't come to the feast, will he?'" Their second question, strongly assuming a negative answer, provides still another irony. They assume that Jesus will avoid returning to Jerusalem because of the death threats against him, which are obvious even to the people from the country. In making this assumption, they imply that he will be willing to break the Torah (by not observing the Passover) in order to save his own life. Of course, he *will* come to Jerusalem, not to keep the Torah but to keep the commandment of the one who sent him, and in so doing, will give up his own life. The chiasm ends in verse 57 with the news that the "chief priests and Pharisees had given commands that if anyone should know where he is, they should disclose it, so that they might arrest him." The Sanhedrin have made their will the will of the people by imposing a legal requirement to become a tattletale.

## 4. "LEAVE HER ALONE!"

**Chiasm: 12:1–11**

a: 1–2: Lazarus, whom Jesus raised from the dead

   b: 3: Mary anoints Jesus

      c: 4–6: Judas: why?

   $b^1$: 7–8: she has done in view of my burial day

$a^1$: 9–11: Lazarus, whom Jesus raised from the dead

"Therefore, six days before the Passover..." Chapter 12 begins the final week of Jesus' life, just as 1:19–2:11 narrated the first week.[14] Things are starting to come around for the last time. The light is starting to depart; night is approaching.

The narrator provides details in verse 1 that we could not easily have forgotten so soon but that both provide the parallels that structure the "a" parts of the chiasm and provide the reason for what will take place in the scene: "...came to Bethany, where Lazarus was, whom Jesus raised from the dead." While the synoptics do not recount the Lazarus story at all, the fourth gospel gives it not only as the ultimate act of Jesus' divine power and as a decisive sign of hope for the Johannine community but also to show the proximate reason for his approaching death. Not only did Jesus call his beloved friend back from the grave, but he sits down to share table fellowship with him.

Once again, the characterization of the sisters in verse 2 is consistent with the Lukan view of busy Martha and prayerful Mary, beginning with the description of Martha as "serving" (*diēkonei*). But although the Lukan image contains

---

14. R. Brown (1966, 452).

the negative element of distracted task-mindedness, the fourth gospel paints the scene in terms of the discipleship verb, *diakoneo* (Mt 4:11; 25:44; Rom 15:25; cf. 1 Tim 3:10). It may suggest that the "meal" (*deipnon*) is not an ordinary supper but a eucharistic celebration (cf. 1 Cor 11:20, *deipnon* of the Lord), in which Martha is the "minister." This possibility is enhanced by the unspecified referent of the "they" who are said to have made the meal[15] and the notation that Lazarus "was one of those reclining with him." One implication is that there are many people present at Martha and Mary's house beyond the family themselves, including, as we will find out momentarily, at least one of his disciples.

Whether simple supper or special celebration, the focus shifts dramatically in verse 3 away from Martha who serves and Lazarus who reclines, to the other sister: "Mary, having received a pound of perfumed oil, made of genuine nard of high price, anointed Jesus' feet and wiped his feet with her hair." The tale of a woman anointing Jesus with oil is found in all four gospels, but only John attributes it to a known character and works it so completely into the fabric of the plot (cf. Mk 14:3–9; Mt 26:6–13; Lk 7:37–50). Mark and Matthew both portray the location as Bethany, but in the house of Simon the leper, and name the anointer simply as "a woman." Luke has the anointing take place in a Pharisee's house, but the woman is "a sinner" who is forgiven. In our traditional way of mixing and matching scripture stories from the different gospels, many imagine the story as recounting an act of Mary Magdalene, who they think is a prostitute! It is one of the best examples of how different an interpretation we reach when we allow each gospel to tell its own story from beginning to end.

Although we are informed right away that the perfume was made of an exotic substance (nard) and is very valuable (*polytimou,* literally meaning "much honor"), the specific value is withheld for the moment in favor of the description of her use of it. Mary anoints Jesus *feet,* just as we were "foretold" in 11:2. There is no immediate precedent for such an action in Jewish practice; the usual place of anointing was the head, and it was done as a mark of royalty or other special qualities. The bodies of the dead were also anointed, but, of course, Jesus is quite alive during this scene.[16] The intimacy of the drying of Jesus' feet with Mary's hair not only was unprecedented but was a shocking violation of the normal distance women and men kept from one another except during the privacy of marriage. And in the antithesis of privacy, the narrator adds that "the house became filled with the scent [*osmēs*] of the perfume." This scent contrasts dramatically with the smell that Martha feared, the stench of death of the four-days-dead Lazarus (11:39, *ozei,* same root as *osmēs*). Although Lazarus's smell is feared, its fact is never narrated as is that of the perfume, one of the only smells described in the New Testament. In antiquity, "odors are regarded as exhalations of mist and air that have the power to give either life or death."[17] Also, in ancient theophanies, "an inscription speaks about a deified boy giv-

---

15. Carson (1991, 427–428).
16. Ibid., 454.
17. G. Delling, *TDNT* 5:493–495.

ing off sweet scents that give life to flowers growing out of his grave."[18] Thus, the scent of Mary's perfume emanating from the feet of Jesus may well have provided associations with powerful forces of life and death, even before Jesus expressly linked the action with his burial in verse 7.

The description of the scent as filling "the whole house" suggests the breadth of effect of Mary's anointing. As Herold Weiss puts it, "That the act of Mary affected the whole house refers to the fact that she, in a way, was the first one to identify truly with the dead Messiah, but her act of faith and devotion . . . serves as a model for others who must also tie their destiny to that of the dead Messiah."[19] To the extent that we envision this scene as a eucharistic celebration (from the time perspective of the Johannine community), "the whole house" suggests that the entire community (i.e., house church) was affected by Mary's prophetic and proleptic act.

Given these overtones of death, devotion, and holiness, the intervening remark of Judas in verse 5 — his only spoken line in the fourth gospel — comes partially as a rude surprise: "Why was this perfume not sold for three hundred denarii and given to the poor?" We have heard about him only once before, in association with his eventual role as betrayer (6:71), as he is immediately identified here, too.

His comment, although an interruption of the beautifully poignant, shocking, committed act by Mary, nonetheless provides a detail that may evoke a measure of sympathy for his point of view. Not only is the pound of perfume now running across the floor valuable, it is, according to Judas's estimation, worth three hundred denarii, or three hundred days' wages for ordinary folks! How might *we* respond to the "waste" of many thousands of dollars of perfume, even in the most beloved act of adoration? It is as if someone threw a gallon of Chanel No. 5 around — Wouldn't a few ounces of something more economical have made the same point and left some funds behind for the needs of others? Wouldn't Jesus also want to feed the crowds, provide shelter, or otherwise see the money go to a "good cause"?

Just when we might find ourselves wondering with Judas about this "waste" and how we might react in similar circumstances, the narrator breaks in again in verse 6 to add another characteristic of Judas omitted by the synoptics: "He said this not because he was concerned about the poor, but because he was a thief, and had the money box and carried off what was in it." Rather than refute the basic "justice" of Judas's statement, the narrator stoops to impugning his motives, not unlike what the Judeans do to Jesus! Okay, we might say, so even if Judas is a betrayer and a thief — an image otherwise reserved for the bad "shepherds"[20] — isn't it still true that Mary's act was an extravagant waste?

---

18. Ibid.

19. Weiss (1979, 314).

20. Karris (1990, 25) notes that the word for "care" (*melō*) used by the narrator in 12:6 matches that used in 10:13 to describe the indifference of the bad shepherds for the welfare of the people.

In addition to leading us to question the propriety of her act — now challengeable on the several different grounds of male/female relations, choice of inappropriate body part, and extravagance — Judas's comments lead us to go back and wonder about Mary: Where did she get such an incredibly valuable pound of perfume? The narrator had told us only that she "received it." Did it come from a wealthy patron of Mary, perhaps a rich disciple of Jesus? Or was it a family heirloom, something waiting for generations for the *kairos* in which to anoint the messiah?

Neither the narrator nor Jesus addresses these questions, turning instead in verse 7 to Jesus' response both to Judas and to Mary: "Leave her alone! She has done this to observe [*tērēsē*] the day of my burial; the poor you always have with you, but me you will not always have." In spite of all the reasons to stop her, Jesus affirms her act, extravagance and all. For the first time, he mentions the frightening yet imminent prospect of "the day of my burial." Although the narrator's earlier proleptic reference to the act focused on the anointing and wiping of his feet with her hair, it did not add this interpretation by Jesus of the act. Now, the cat is out of the bag: Mary has anticipated correctly what the result of Jesus' act upon her brother will be. She had, in a sense, "traded" some extended time with Lazarus for the continued presence of Jesus. For better or worse, this is the way it is, and her recognition of and preparation for it are commended by Jesus.

With the association of her act with the burial, we can, with Weiss, go back and see the Sanhedrin gathering as the first step in the "symbolic passion" account that continues through the triumphal entry into Jerusalem in a few verses. Weiss notes four stages of the "preview" that match the final enactment:

1. Sanhedrin decision to kill Jesus=crucifixion
2. the anointing=the burial
3. the identification of the betrayer=judgment upon evil
4. the entry into Jerusalem=resurrection[21]

If the disciples are afraid of losing Jesus because of his talk about death and departure, then the entry into Jerusalem should help them understand his eventual return. However, "should" does not necessarily equal "does," as we have seen many times already.

Jesus' response, in addition to affirming Mary despite the odds against her, does so with a remark that has been used over the centuries as an excuse to ignore the needs of the poor by those who claim to follow Jesus. But to understand why Jesus frames his response this way, we need to examine the traditional attitudes toward the poor found both in Hebrew scripture and in Jewish practice at the time of the Johannine community. One of the clearest places in which the duty to take care of the poor is noted and its failure castigated is in Psalm 82,

---

21. Weiss (1979, 311).

cited by Jesus against the Pharisees in 10:34 and quoted in full above (p. 246). Thus, Judas is arguing against Mary from the same source (or at least a similar one) that Jesus used in arguing against the Pharisees! Of course, the entire Temple tithing system was established ostensibly to care for both the priests and their families as well as the "widows and orphans" and other poor people who populated Jerusalem and other parts of Judea in great numbers. By the time of the Johannine community, though, the Temple was destroyed, and the Pharisees had taken over the duty within the synagogue system of collecting alms and distributing them to the poor.[22] From this perspective, *Judas's statement identifies with the synagogue practice*, which he implicitly advocates should be binding on the Johannine community as well.

Jesus' words do not reveal a disinterest for the poor but, instead, a practice more radical than the collecting and distribution of charity. He tells Judas and the others that "you always have the poor *with you*." That is, the poor should not simply be objects of charity but are to be an integral and permanent part of the discipleship community. However, the physical presence of Jesus will not be a permanent feature of the Johannine community, and, thus, it is appropriate for Mary to recognize this and do what she can now while he is still there in body as well as in spirit.

No further comment is provided by any of the characters, as the narrator immediately switches in verse 9 to the reaction of the "crowd of Judeans," who come to know Jesus is there *because* of the anointing. Whether it is because of the scandal of Mary's outrageous act, the waft of the scent, or simply the ongoing presence of Lazarus and Jesus at table, the crowds have come "to see Lazarus whom he raised from the dead." Poor Lazarus! Disturbed from his rest in the tomb, where he was *not* separated from God, he has now become an object of gawkers. And, in the supreme irony, in verse 10 he is bonded with Jesus as an object of the chief priests' murderous plans, too. Jesus would not let him rest in the tomb, and now the priests will not let him rest at the table of his own house! The reason, not surprisingly, for the priests' expanded death sentence is that "many of the Judeans were going there and believing in Jesus" (verse 11). Like the Mafia at work, all witnesses must be disposed of by the Sanhedrin.

---

22. E. Bammel, *TDNT* 6:892–894.

# 16

# "The Hour Has Come"

*"Father, Glorify Your Name!"*

## John 12:12–50

**A. Chiasm:**
> a: 12–19: Jesus comes and is greeted as "messiah"
>> b: 20–22: Greeks want to see Jesus
>>> c: 23–36: Jesus' hour arrives
>> b¹: 37–43: Judeans refuse to see
> a¹: 44–50: Jesus comes as God's emissary

**B. Location:** Jerusalem

**C. Time:** near Passover

**D. Hebrew scripture context:** Psalm 118; Zechariah 9; Isaiah 6, 53

**E. Social factors:** the opening to the Gentiles

**F. Themes:** Jesus' "hour" has come; the reason for the disbelief of the Judeans

**G. Key words:** glory

## 1. THE ENTRY UPON A YOUNG ASS: THE BATTLE OF MESSIANIC MYTHS

**Chiasm: 12:9–19**
> a: 9–11: chief priests react to crowd going to Jesus
>> b: 12–13: crowd "meets" Jesus because of raising from dead
>>> c: 14–16: Jesus' messianic counterwitness
>> b¹: 17–18: crowd "meets" Jesus because of raising from dead
> a¹: 19: Pharisees react to crowd going to Jesus

The story of "Palm Sunday" in the fourth gospel gains a very different perspective from the synoptic accounts because of the narrative power and consequences of the Lazarus passage. Whereas each of the synoptics builds its unique stories around Jesus' symbolic initiative upon his *first and only* entry into Jerusalem (Mt 21:1–9; Mk 11:1–10; Lk 19:28–44), John's version starts with the initiative of the "great crowd" that reacts to the raising of Lazarus upon Jesus' *fourth* visit to the capital. Although each of the synoptics narrates an expectation that Jesus will face official hostility when he arrives in Jerusalem and persecution and death at the hands of the Judeans, there is no buildup of pressure anything like the already narrated attempts to kill Jesus in the fourth gospel.

The chiasm emphasizes how the gathering of the great crowd who come to see Lazarus is directly linked with their messianic greeting of Jesus in verses 12–13. That verses 9–11 overlap both the preceding and subsequent chiastic units underscores the connection the fourth gospel makes between these two crucial events.

The crowd's greeting in verse 13 is a liturgical direct action consisting of both symbolic ritual and powerful words. The narrator tells us that "having heard that Jesus is coming into Jerusalem, they took palm [*phoinikōn*] branches and went out to meet him." Of the four gospels, only John specifically describes the branches as palms. Palm branches had several associations in Hebrew scripture. They were one of the four types of branches specified to be waved as part of the Tabernacles rites (Lev 23:40; cf. Neh 8:15). Because they were signs of fertility and life, Solomon had their image inscribed in several places on the Temple itself (1 Kgs 6:29, 32, 35, etc.; cf. Ezekiel 41). Isaiah used the image as a metaphor for Israel's "head," with the stalk as the "tail," both of which are cut down by God for failure to provide rest for the people (Isa 9:14–16). The prophet expressly explains the image of palm branch/head as referring to the elders and leaders who have let the people down. Finally, on the basis of these prior usages, particularly the Tabernacles association, palm branches became a symbol of the Maccabean triumph in restoring the Temple (2 Macc 10:7). So strong was the symbolic link between palm branches and triumphant celebration among the oppressed of Israel that they were used on the coins of the temporarily freed Judeans during the second revolt period, a generation after the writing of the fourth gospel.[1] To welcome Jesus with palm branches was to proclaim him a new Judas Maccabeus, a new national liberator.

The words of the crowd match their gesture in several ways. Their shout of "Hosanna!" expresses a prayer for liberation, as the Hebrew root indicates.[2] It, too, was specifically associated with Tabernacles in Ps 118:25–27:

> Save us [MT, *hosanna*], O Lord!
> O Lord, we beseech you, give us success!
> Blessed is the one who comes in the name of the Lord.

---

1. R. Brown (1966, 461).
2. E. Lohse, *TDNT* 9:682–684.

We bless you from the house of the Lord.
The Lord is God, and he has given us light.
Bind the festal procession with branches, up to the horns
of the altar.

The crowd's conclusion that they are welcoming "the king of Israel" is also unique to the fourth gospel. It is the first mention of Israel since Jesus accused Nicodemus, "thc tcacher of Israel," of not understanding (3:10). Nathanael also used this title for Jesus (1:49), but Jesus' response was in terms of the Human One. Given the Sanhedrin's discussion about the relationship between the "people" and the "nation," readers can easily hear this royal title as an expression of the crowd's hope for a *national* leader rather than one to gather the scattered children of God.

On the previous occasion when Jesus was confronted by a crowd attempting to makc him "king," he responded by retreating alone (6:15). Now, however, he engages in countersymbolics. If the crowd's expectations are based on Psalm 118, Jesus offers his own text in the battle of myths, Zech 9:9–10, at least in the interpretation of his disciples:

Rejoice greatly, O daughter Zion!
Shout aloud, O daughter Jerusalem!
Lo, your king comes to you, triumphant and victorious
is he,
humble and riding on a donkey; on a colt, the foal of a
donkcy.
He will cut off the chariot from Ephraim
and the war horse from Jerusalem;
and the battle bow shall be cut off,
and he shall command peace to the nations;
his dominion shall be from sea to sea.

All four gospels portray Jesus incarnating this image from Zechariah, but only the fourth gospel shows it as a response to the crowd's own messianic text. Further, the narrator's scripture quotation in verse 15 alters the Zechariah text in important ways: "Have no fear, daughter of Zion! Look, your king is coming, riding on a foal of a donkey." The substitution of "have no fear" for "rejoice greatly" indicates that the Johannine community was not yet able to rejoice,[3] a theme that will recur in the Last Supper discourse (14:27–28; 16:20, 22). It also invokes another countertext from Isa 40:9–11:

Get you up to a high mountain, O Zion, herald of good tidings; lift up your voice with strength, O Jerusalem, herald of good tidings, lift it up, do not fear; say to the cities of Judah, "Here is your God!" See, the Lord God

---

3. Cf. Minear (1984, 79).

comes with strength, and his arm rules for him; his reward is with him, and his recompense before him. He will feed his flock like a shepherd; he will gather the lambs in his arms, and carry them in his bosom, and gently lead the mother sheep.

The entry is messianic, but as a gentle shepherd-messiah who stands willing to lay down his life for the sheep. What the crowd sees as a triumphant launching of a royal liberation, the disciples (and narrator) interpret (later) as the terrifying beginning of Jesus' march toward death.

The narrator's interesting "admission" in verse 16 that "these things the disciples did not know at first, but when Jesus was glorified, they remembered that these things were written about him and that they did these things to him" notifies us of the disciples' presence at the entry into Jerusalem, an accompaniment of which we otherwise would not know. Only Judas (!) was described as present at the supper in Bethany, and we had not been given further information about the whereabouts of the disciples since Jesus remained with them in Ephraim (11:54). So focused is the text on the actions and words of Jesus that the disciples continue to exist only as confused bystanders, asking "wrong" questions and failing to understand what they are seeing. According to the narrator, they not only did not interpret Jesus' action as enacting the Zechariah passage but also did not even notice that the crowd had welcomed him triumphantly with palm branches! Given the description of the crowd as "great" and the fear that must have been in the disciples' hearts upon seeing a huge mass of Judeans and others who had come to Jerusalem for Passover approaching Jesus, it is almost beyond credibility to imagine them missing the event altogether. Perhaps it is simply the specifics of the *palm* branches that they missed, a detail "missed" by the synoptic writers, too. If we hear the narrator's comment in this way, we need not imagine totally oblivious disciples, but simply people whose education in the deeper meaning of scripture had to await the sending of the paraclete to "teach them all things and remind them of all things" (14:26).

These symbolics and countersymbolics are joined by what appears to be a different crowd in verse 17: "the crowd that was with him when he called Lazarus out of the tomb and raised him up from the dead." This crowd "witnesses" to the Palm Sunday crowd about Lazarus. Verse 18 offers a response that ambiguously joins the two crowds and their respective experiences into one: "Because of this, the crowd also met him, because they heard that he had done this sign." The confusion comes from the issue of the reference to "this" at the beginning of the sentence and "sign" at the end. One possibility is that the "this" is the witnessing of the "Lazarus crowd," who, because of their telling about the raising from the dead to the "Palm Sunday crowd," hear about the "sign" of riding on the young donkey. The other possibility is that the "this" is the raising of Lazarus, which leads the Palm Sunday crowd to meet him, having heard about the "sign" of raising Lazarus. However, as the Palm Sunday crowd has already met him, the first possibility seems the better interpretation.

In any event, the reaction is for an even larger crowd to form, causing the

Pharisees in verse 19 to "say among themselves, 'You see that you are ac-
complishing nothing [*ōpheleite ouden*]! The world has gone after him.'" Their
comment ironically confirms Jesus' word in 6:63 that "the flesh is useless
[*ōphelei ouden*]." The ways of the Pharisees are the ways of the flesh and have
no power over either Jesus' life or his mission. Their words are also ironic in
naming those who follow Jesus as "the world." Throughout the fourth gospel,
we have repeatedly heard Jesus use this term for the place of those who do not
know God, yet which Jesus has come to save. The Pharisees, fully a part of
this "world," see themselves losing power before their eyes, as their "domain"
seems to slip into Jesus' hands regardless of their efforts to stop him.

The final irony comes from the chiastic structure of the passage. At the beginning, we are told that the "chief priests" alone take counsel to kill Lazarus,
and now, the "Pharisees" alone remark on the futility of their entire scheme.
Where these two groups were gathered together in 11:47 to judge Jesus at the
beginning of the symbolic Passion account, here at the end, as Jesus' symbolic
resurrection is narrated, they have been separated, with the huge crowd following Jesus "separating" them. Their *synēgogon* has been interrupted by the
humble messianic mission of Jesus.

## 2. THE GRAIN OF WHEAT MUST FALL: SUBVERSIVE AGRICULTURE

**Chiasm: 12:23–36**

a: 23–24: hour for Son of Man to be glorified; dies

   b: 25–26: this world

      c: 27–30: voice

   b[1]: 31: this world

a[1]: 32–36: Son of Man to be lifted up; die[4]

As the Pharisees observe the world going after Jesus, the narrator zooms in
for a close-up view in verses 20–21: "There were some Greeks [*Hellēnes*] who
had come up to the festival to worship. These, therefore, approached Philip, the
one from Bethsaida in Galilee, and requested of him, saying, 'Sir, we are willing
to see Jesus.'" As Raymond Brown points out, *Hellēnes* refers to Gentiles, not
the Greek-speaking Jews called *Hellēnistas* (e.g., Acts 9:29).[5] These non-Jews
have come up to Jerusalem to worship at the feast but would have been excluded
from the inner courts of the Temple, which were open only to Jews and gentile
proselytes.[6] But what they seek is to see Jesus the good shepherd who welcomes
the sheep of other folds (10:16), not to participate in the nationalistic Judean
Passover rituals. It is the first time that non-Jews other than the part-Jewish

---

4. Ellis (1984, 202).

5. R. Brown (1966, 466).

6. Carson (1991, 436).

Samaritans and the Romans mentioned in 11:48 have taken the stage in the fourth gospel. They are part of "the world" that follows Jesus, despite the efforts to stop him.

Their approach is indirect, yet very specifically described, an unusual manner of narration that draws our attention and curiosity. Other than Judas's objection to Mary's anointing, we have not heard a disciple mentioned by name (the Bethany siblings, though clearly "beloved," are never expressly named as "disciples") since Thomas's invitation to "die with him" in 11:16, and not before that since Peter and Judas in 6:66–71. The gospel has shown little interest in the specific characters among the disciples, but when it has focused on individuals, it has been to illustrate some particular facet of their character rather than simply in the role of conversation partners or observers. Here, the narrator not only tells us that the Greeks came to Philip but also reminds us that Philip is from Bethsaida in Galilee, a detail we were first told of in 1:44. These are the only references to that location in the entire gospel. Philip himself is mentioned among the lists of disciples in all the gospels but has no part to play outside John except in the book of Acts, where he is evangelist to the Samaritans and the gentile Ethiopian eunuch in Acts 8. Earlier in the fourth gospel, we may recall, Philip was the object of Jesus' "test" about where to find bread to feed the crowd (6:5, 7).

Before we try to discern the reason for Philip's sudden insertion into the narrative, it is important to consider the additional detail the narrator provides about the angle of approach of the Greeks to Jesus: "Philip came and told Andrew, and Andrew and Philip came and told Jesus." Andrew is also mentioned in all the gospels, always as the brother of Simon Peter, but with little other characterization in the face of the importance of his sibling. In the fourth gospel, he is always associated with Philip, either directly or indirectly. In 1:44, Philip's origin in Bethsaida is named as "the city of Andrew and Peter," surprisingly listing Andrew first. Andrew was the first named disciple in 1:41, who then "found" Simon and brought him to Jesus. In 6:8, following Jesus' exchange with Philip, Andrew comes forward to share the information about the boy with five loaves and two fish.

Both these disciples also share another feature in common: Greek names.[7] If we can imagine that the reputation of Philip as a gatherer of non-Jewish disciples was known to the fourth gospel — an admittedly tricky assumption given our reading method — we can see Philip as bringing these non-Jewish Greek disciples to Jesus "through" the presence of the first disciple, who brought the Jewish Simon to Jesus. The fact that they come together suggests the Johannine community's vision of the blending of Jewish and non-Jewish disciples who are scattered into a single family of God's children.

These verses appear to fall between the cracks of the chiasms that surround them. They are an interlude that opens the door to Jesus beyond the confines of "his own" and to the broader community of those who "are willing" to receive

---

7. Beutler (1990a, 341).

him. As such, they echo the Septuagint words of Isa 52:15 about the Suffering
Servant:

> Thus shall many nations wonder at him, and kings shall
>     hold their tongues.
> For they to whom no report was brought about him shall
>     see,
> and they who have not heard, shall consider.

As Johannes Beutler puts it, "The sense in the Septuagint becomes: those
who had not yet come to knowledge of the Servant will see, and those who had
not yet heard (about him) will hear."[8]

As the next chiasm begins in verse 23, Jesus responds to this news from his
disciples: "The hour has come for the Human One to be glorified!" After the
long wait, the confusion about the *kairos,* the many signs and teachings and
arguments: Jesus' moment is at hand. As the scene shifts from the approach of
the Greeks to Jesus' speech and the reaction of the crowd in verse 29, we find
that the Greeks never do encounter the one they seek within the story! Their
desire to see Jesus is enough to trigger the "hour." The actual "harvest" will
be done by the Johannine community later on, as they reap what others have
labored over (4:38).

Jesus introduces the presence of his hour with a parabolic saying in verse 24:
"Amen, amen I am saying to you: unless the grain of wheat [*kokkos tou sitou*]
falls to the earth and dies, it remains alone; but if it dies, it bears much fruit
[*karpon*]." It is one of the rare agricultural images in the fourth gospel, and it
immediately links with the sense of reaping the harvest of non-Jewish disciples
in the similar image in chapter 4. To appreciate the power of the metaphor, we
must stop to gain some understanding of the social context of wheat farming
among Palestinian peasants of Jesus' day.

Anthony Gittins provides much helpful background on the meaning of wheat
to the ancients.[9] The primary distinction he draws to our attention is between
wild and domesticated wheat. Whereas nomadic peoples had long been able to
gain some sustenance from wild wheat, "more settled groups — people who
had learned to domesticate wheat and to produce harvests to feed large aggre-
gates of people — quite naturally looked with great respect to the earth as the
bountiful provider; and they focused their religious worship largely on a Mother
of the Earth."[10] The wild wheat, also known as "emmer" wheat, blew its seed
freely through the air and produced a crop without human assistance, but it was
thin and of little economic or nutritional value. Domesticated or "bread" wheat,
on the other hand, produced a bountiful crop in good conditions but was so
heavy and tight in the head that it required assistance in order to scatter the

---

8. Ibid., 342.

9. Gittins (1990).

10. Ibid., 201.

seed, or risk simply falling where it was and failing to grow at all. This function of breaking up and distributing bread wheat grains fell to women: "Cereal cultivation has, in a unique way, been the legacy of women.... [It] demands knowledge of cycles and seasons, moons and meteorology,... knowledge and activities originating with and residing in women par excellence."[11] Thus, in two essential ways, the image of wheat farming was a feminine metaphor.

Gittins also notes that the Greek phrase *kokkos tou sitou* used in Jn 12:24 refers not to a single grain but to a harvestable quantity of already sifted grain.[12] With this background in mind, we can see that Jesus' parable describes the reality of bread wheat: if it is not harvested, it "remains alone" and bears no fruit; but if it *does* "die" by being broken up and planted, it does bear much fruit. As Jesus told his disciples in 4:36: "The one harvesting is receiving the reward and is gathering [*synagei*] fruit [*karpon*] into eternal life." The hour has indeed come for the Johannine community to enter into Jesus' labor unto death by gathering the new "synagogue" that includes Samaritans and Greeks, the fruit of eternal life.

And startlingly, Jesus uses a metaphor of women's work as the main image for the mission of discipleship. It should not surprise us, then, to find in our own day that church offices may be largely held by men but that the work of spreading the good news in word and deed is largely done by women or men who are not afraid to identify with the "feminine" qualities in all persons.

The plural nature of *kokkos tou sitou* suggests also that the fruitful death of Jesus is not a unique act but will be imitated by many who follow. This sense was recognized early in Christian history in Tertullian's phrase, "The blood of the martyrs is the seed of the church."[13] Whether Archbishop Romero or the Salvadoran Jesuits, whether the Johannine community members burned as Nero's lamps or the masses slaughtered by death squads, Christian witness that is willing to die for truth and love has always borne much fruit.

That Jesus intends his parable to apply not just to himself but to his followers is supported by his saying in verse 25: "The one who is fond of [*philōn*] his life is losing [*apollyei*] it, and the one hating his life in this world will safeguard it for eternal life." It is not an antilife statement, but an anti-"world" statement, when the "world" is seen not as those who come to Jesus but as the home of death and lies ruled over by Satan. The Lazarus story ought to assure us that death itself is no enemy, despite our often fearful approach to its unknown gate. Rather, fondness for the life the world offers is what causes us to perish. Those who become stuck within cultural bounds of community, who limit their sense of sister or brother to those of their generation, ethnicity, class, gender, or other narrow group, are allowing their participation in eternal life to be destroyed.

Jesus completes this discipleship message by linking it in verse 26 with service and presence: "If anyone would serve [*diakonē*] me, let them follow, and

---

11. Ibid., 199.
12. Ibid., 204.
13. Cited in Chadwick (1967, 29).

where I am, there also will my servant [*diakonos*] be; and if anyone serves [*diakonē*] me, the Father will honor them." Three times in one verse, Jesus speaks of service and servanthood, a term otherwise used only in 2:5, 9 in the fourth gospel. If Jesus' willingness extends to the point of death, his "deacons" must follow him there. It is a hard place to go, and Jesus will spend much of the Last Supper discourse trying to bolster the Johannine community's courage to take this step on the way. But if it is taken, it is rewarded with a great gift: "honor" from the Father. Although our modern ears may not resonate to the power of receiving "honor," to the contemporaries of the gospel, honor was the primary social value to which one might aspire.[14] To receive honor from God would be greater than any earthly reward. To a mind focused on the "world," this makes little sense in the face of the glory human beings bestow on one another in terms of wealth, power, prestige, or comfort. But for those who aspire to be servants of Jesus and to follow in his footsteps, the Father's honor is enough.

Suddenly in verse 27, Jesus shifts from exhortation of his community to attention to the meaning for him of the presence of the "hour": "Now my soul [*psychē*] is troubled [*tetaraktai*], and what shall I say? 'Father, save me from this hour?' But for this hour I came! Father, glorify your name!" The literal words that Jesus speaks link his troubled soul both with his earlier emotion in the presence of the unbelief of his beloved friends and the Judeans at Lazarus's graveside (*etaraxen*, 11:33) and with the warning about being bonded to one's life (*psychēn*) in verse 25. It is as close as the Johannine Jesus comes to "temptation," the Gethsemane experience that the synoptics, especially Mk 14:42–46, describe in painful detail. He struggles with the very human characteristic that he urges his disciples to resist, to cling to his soul/life. However, it is but a momentary crisis, for before the sentence is completed, he has resolved against calling out to his Father to be "saved," precisely what the Palm Sunday crowd had prayed for. This "hour" is the moment in which he has been saying all along that both the Father and Son would be glorified. It is not to be resisted, but to be walked through in faith.[15]

By addressing his final words as a direct prayer to the Father, Jesus evokes an unexpected response in verse 28: "Therefore, a voice out of heaven came, 'I glorified it and again I will glorify it.'" A possible background text to this voice is found in the apocalyptic book the Testament of Levi, which would likely have been available to the Johannine community: "The skies shall be opened, and sanctification shall come upon him from the Temple of glory with the Father's voice, as from Abraham to Isaac; and the glory of the Most High shall be uttered over him" (18:6–7).[16] It is an event familiar from the synoptic baptismal and Transfiguration accounts, but in a wholly different context. Where the baptismal voice was a private revelation for Jesus and the Transfiguration voice was for

---

14. Malina (1981, 27–28).

15. Carson (1991, 440) reads "Father, save me from this hour" not as a rhetorical question but as an actual prayer revealing Jesus' full agony. Either option reaches the same result: Jesus' will, despite his troubled soul, remains united with the will of the one who sent him.

16. R. Brown (1966, 468).

the inner circle of disciples, the Johannine heavenly voice speaks for all the crowd to hear. Further, the synoptic voice speaks of "beloved Son" and "listen to him," not of glorification. Once again, the fourth gospel has taken an element of the common tradition and modified it to fit within its own narrative structure and ideology.

Theological speculation has wondered about the two different times of the glorifying referred to by the heavenly voice. Brown notes the basic options:

1. preexistence/postresurrection
2. ministry/death-resurrection-ascension
3. entire ministry/exalted Christ drawing all[17]

Whether one feels the need to choose among these options or prefers to see it simply as the glorious embrace by heaven of Jesus from "beginning" to "end," the fact of the voice emphasizes for all who hear it that Jesus has been speaking the truth all along. The witness he has claimed since chapter 5 would testify for him has now done so. At the hour of glory, the "defense" electrifies the crowd with the last-minute, star witness whose testimony should remove any further doubt from the minds of jurors and judges.

But, alas, the fourth gospel's irony goes on, as verse 29 reports the various ways in which the voice is heard: "Therefore the crowd which stood by and heard was saying it was thunder; others were saying an angel has spoken with him." Up to this point, we might have thought that only Philip and Andrew were present for Jesus' words, but now we find that this is a public gathering in which both earthly and heavenly perspectives persist. Because the group is described as a "crowd" and not as Judeans, readers might imagine them to be the crowd that came together on Palm Sunday. For some of these people, the sound was merely a natural, albeit powerful, "earthly" phenomenon. For others, it was indeed a voice from heaven.

None seems to have heard the words, though, for even those who attribute the sound to the voice of an angel can only assert that it was speaking "to him." The message does not penetrate the crowd without Jesus' help, just as readers require the narrator's help to "hear" and understand the voice from heaven. So in verse 30 Jesus makes clear for the story-world audience the purpose of the controversial sound: "Not for me has this voice happened, but for you people." For those who wish to follow Jesus and hope to experience a political revolution through him that will restore the glory of Israel (or at least provide freedom from Roman and Temple taxes), the fact of the voice "proves" that Jesus' own path is the way of heaven. But if they are like the Tabernacles Judeans whom Jesus accused of not listening to the sayings of God (8:47), they will miss the point, both now and when Jesus is glorified before their eyes on the cross. Still, Jesus does not repeat the voice's words for the crowd, leaving only readers and perhaps silently comprehending members of the crowd aware of the glory at hand.

---

17. Ibid., 476.

Thus, Jesus continues in verse 31 by linking the occurrence of the voice with the present judgment of the world: "Now the ruler [*archōn*] of this world will be cast out!" Previously, *archōn* was used exclusively to refer to Nicodemus and the rulers of Judea (3:1; 7:26, 48). While we might think of *archōn* in terms of *the* ruler, that is, Satan or the devil, the phrase "ruler of the world" was not used in rabbinical literature with such a referent,[18] and we should not be too quick to assume such a meaning here. For the Johannine community, the specific incarnation of that power was the *Sanhedrin*, who "cast out" both Jesus and the members of their own community (e.g., 9:34). In contrast in verse 32 is the "drawing" of "all people to myself" that will be the result of Jesus' being "lifted up out of the earth." As the drawing of water at Cana and Samaria promised to quench thirst, so Jesus' lifting up will provide satisfaction by "drawing."

After the third "lifting up" statement by Jesus (cf. 3:14; 8:28), the narrator in verse 33 finally makes clear what the metaphor means: "This he was saying to signify [*sēmainōn*] what kind of death he was about to be dying." The lifting up of Jesus is the final "sign" upon which faith will be determined. Linked with the theme of glory, it evokes Isa 52:13 (LXX): "See, my Servant shall prosper and be lifted up, and glorified greatly." Isaiah goes on to describe the sufferings of the Servant, which match to a terrible degree those of Jesus. The Isaian passage immediately preceding will be used in just a few verses to explain the crowd's lack of faith.

The crowd, though, does not have this inside knowledge provided to readers. Instead, in verse 34 they make still another challenge based on the prevailing ideology: "We heard from the Law that the Christ is remaining forever. How are you saying that it is necessary [*dei*] for the Human One to be lifted up? Who is this Human One?" The latter is a pathetic question at this stage of Jesus' ministry and reveals a complete lack of understanding of what he has been saying to them. They make several assumptions that show how easy it is to miss the point when one does not follow carefully what has been said.

First, they speak about the Law's understanding of the "Christ" remaining. Jesus has not spoken at all about the Christ, but their very presence with him now — especially if we see this as the Palm Sunday crowd — indicates that "the Christ" is who *they* think he is, according to their own messianic ideology. Their assumption, supposedly based in the Law, is not found in the Hebrew scriptures. However, Ps 89:36 speaks of the "seed of David" remaining forever, in a psalm that contains two messianic references (89:38, 51). In the context of the psalm, though, the "messiah" refers simply to the anointed king of Israel. In fact, it expresses in verse 38 God's "wrath" against the anointed!

Second, they assume that to be "lifted up" is somehow in contrast with "remaining." Why would the crowd, without the narrator's explanation of the metaphor, come to this conclusion? Was "lifting up" a common term for crucifixion? If so, why does the narrator need to name it for readers? This is a gap that is left open and makes even more ironic the combination of powerful

18. Carson (1991, 443).

insight and misunderstanding that the crowd's statement expresses. Of course, they are right in a way that "lifting up" will remove the Human One from them, but terribly wrong if they interpret the lifting up as a permanent absence.

Third, they make the surprising connection between Jesus' use of "Human One" at the outset of his speech in verse 23 and his statement about his own fate in verse 32 as suggesting that the Human One will be lifted up. But then they *don't* see it as applying to Jesus.[19] They pick and choose both from Hebrew scripture and Jesus' words, and their exercise in "proof-texting" ends up tying them in terrible knots of misunderstanding. It is a powerful example of what can go wrong when one uses a flawed method of exegesis.

Jesus refuses to engage their questions. It is clear that their confusion will not be unraveled with explanatory words. Instead, he invokes in verses 35–36 the imagery of the prologue once again: "The light will be in you for just a little time [*mikron chronon*]. Walk in the light while you have it, so that darkness will not overpower [*katalabē*] you. The one walking in the darkness does not know where he is going. While you have the light, believe in the light, so that children of light you might become." Light, darkness, and the threat of being overpowered are all familiar Johannine themes. Rather than get into squabbles about the Law, Jesus offers the basic choice, the fourth gospel's version of the Deuteronomic option presented by Moses: to choose life rather than death in order to continue as God's children (Deut 30:19). It is the only use in the gospel of the common Qumranic phrase, "children of light."[20] It suggests that the crowd gathered for the Passover but now tantalized by Jesus' powerful works into hoping for the Torah's messiah are caught up in the dappled shadow of two conflicting worlds, but have the choice to join the Johannine community and leave the darkness of Jerusalem behind.

But rather than wait to find out what they choose, the narrator tells us in verse 36b: "Having spoken these things, Jesus went off and hid from them." The light departs from their midst for the moment, just as he did previously when faced with a disbelieving crowd (8:59). The action suggests that the crowd might attempt the same act that led Jesus to hide before, that is, stoning him for "blasphemy." Rather than give them a chance to prove their loyalty to the Law of Judea, Jesus removes himself from the scene.

### 3. CALLING ISAIAH AS THE FINAL WITNESS

**Chiasm: 12:37–43**

a: 37: did not believe

   b: 38–39: Isaiah: arm of the Lord revealed

      c: 40: blinded, hardened

---

19. De Jonge (1972–73, 260–261).
20. Charlesworth (1990, 101).

b¹: 41: Isaiah: saw his glory

a¹: 42–43: believed but did not confess

What was the experience like for the Johannine community to find their message of hope and love repeatedly rejected and misunderstood by both Sanhedrin and crowd? How could they explain to themselves and to people they exhorted so strongly to join them that the one sent from God in whom they had put their faith had been executed as a common criminal? And worse, those who caused the execution to take place were the very people trained in the tradition that Jesus proclaimed as fulfilled in his person and mission. How do we justify *our own* allegiance to the biblical tradition of nonviolent resistance in the face of institutional churches and millions of Christians who proclaim just wars, condemn "Marxist" theologians and popular leaders, and practice patriotic capitalism as if it were one of the Ten Commandments?

The Christian community that formed around the fourth gospel was, in many ways, no different in this respect than the apostolic communities of Peter, Paul, or James. They had each gathered together in the name of the Crucified One, the Human One from Galilee who had invited them on a path that, despite its challenges and difficulties, offered more life than was provided by the mainstream religion. To justify their decision did not take them outside the tradition but rather more deeply into its core. They learned to focus not on the messianic passages in scripture that proclaimed a new warrior-liberator like David but on those that described God's Suffering Servant. In particular, they found comfort and support in Isaiah 53, a Servant Song that is frequently quoted today in Holy Week liturgies (cf. Mt 8:17; Rom 10:16).

The fourth gospel presents as a final witness in favor of Jesus the prophet Isaiah and, in particular, the Servant Song of chapter 53 and the prophetic mission passage of Isaiah 6. The narrator introduces these passages in verse 37 in familiar Johannine terms: "Although he did so many signs before [*emprosthen*] them, they were not believing in him." The term *emprosthen* previously referred to the vanguard movements of John (the Baptist) (1:27, 30; 3:28) and the shepherd (10:4). Thus, the immediate connotation of *in front of* should be supplemented by the earlier temporal sense of *before,* to suggest that the signs happened *before* Jesus was "glorified" for all to see and raised from the dead.

To explain how this could happen without insight on the part of the Judeans, the narrator in verse 38 calls on Isaiah, whose "word" (*logos*) is "fulfilled" through the lack of faith: "Lord, who has believed the thing we have heard? And to whom has the arm of the Lord been revealed?" It is a near verbatim quote from the Septuagint version of Isa 53:1, which, in accordance with the literary code of the time, implied the witness of the entire passage. The chapter goes on to show how the one with "no form of majesty that we should look at him... was despised and rejected by others,... was wounded for our transgressions" because "like sheep we have all gone astray." The people are like leaderless sheep, but the Servant is "like a lamb that is led to slaughter."

The references to "before," Isaiah, and "lamb" all form an *inclusio* with the

John passages in chapter 1, and help close what many call the "book of signs" extending from chapter 1 to chapter 12.

The narrator continues in verse 39 by expressly linking the citation of the prophet with the explanation of Judean unbelief: "The reason why they were not able to believe was that, as Isaiah again said, 'He has blinded their eyes, and hardened their hearts, so that they might not see with their eyes and understand with their hearts and be turned and I should heal them.' " This quotation from Isaiah 6 is also what Brown calls a "stock text used by Christians,"[21] found in Acts 28:26–27, Rom 11:8, and Mk 4:12. However, Isaiah also includes ears/ hearing along with eyes and heart, as do the other New Testament passages outside the fourth gospel. Thus, the narrator emphasizes the link between the healing/invitation in chapter 9 and subsequent rejection of God by those who cannot see.

Although the text from Isaiah was frequently used as an explanation, it is a difficult basis for us to accept, for it suggests that the blindness and hardness of heart of unbelievers are *caused by God.* Brown attributes it to a "primitive causality,"[22] but given the sophistication of the fourth gospel's use of language, irony, and symbolism, it seems too easy to pass off this theological viewpoint as something "primitive." Instead, we might see it as part of the metaphorical teaching style of the entire fourth gospel, in which the narrator and Jesus use figures of speech, sarcasm, and other dramatic literary techniques to force readers to rethink traditional "wisdom." In this case, one might read the Isaiah quotation in its Johannine context as suggesting that *even if* we "blame" God for what has happened, Jesus has invited us all to be healed of our blindness, even those who claim to see. We have already been warned through Jesus' response to the disciples' question about the blindness of the beggar in 9:1–3 not to spend too much time engaged in pointless moral speculation, when the purpose of our discipleship mission is to be about the business of healing.

Another effect of the explanation is to underscore the repeated Johannine theme of judgment as something that God does because of our own choices (e.g., 3:19; 5:24–29). Jesus' presence creates a *krisis* in which people's eyes and hearts are forced to side with the truth that they claim. Thus, humans make the decision, and God "ratifies" it either through healing or condemnation.

The narrator's final comment about Isaiah in verse 41 (i.e., that Isaiah has "seen his [Jesus'] glory") is provided to justify the narrator's own statements. Although the gospel has twice made clear that no one has ever seen God (1:18; 6:46), the narrator now claims that the prophet has seen "his glory, and spoke about him." The only consistent way to interpret these passages is to understand the subject not as God but Jesus, just as Jesus affirmed that Abraham had seen him (8:56). To see his "glory" does not necessarily imply that Isaiah physically saw the person of Jesus eight hundred years before his birth, but that his glory is his acceptance of his mission from God, his identification of himself as *egō eimi.*

---

21. R. Brown (1966, 485).
22. Ibid.

Indeed, Isaiah makes just this self-affirmation in response to God's call to send someone: "I am, send me!" (LXX, 6:8, *egō eimi, apestelein me*). Anyone who can claim to be sent by God, who becomes a spokesperson for God's Word, thereby sees God's glory, as did Isaiah. Thus, the affirmation of the prophet's experience is also an exhortation to the Johannine community to continue in its turn the tradition of saying *egō eimi,* just as did the once-blind one at the beginning of his own truth-telling mission (9:9).

The summary passage gets specific in verses 42–43, as the narrator concludes his role in the first part of the gospel by focusing on the reason for the ambivalence of Nicodemus and "the Pharisees who were with" Jesus: "All the same, of course, many of the rulers [*archontōn*] believed in him, but because of the Pharisees, would not confess so that they should not be expelled from the synagogue, for they loved [*egapēsan*] the glory of humanity rather than the glory of God." The blind person's acceptance of healing and prophetic mission is contrasted with the choice made by his parents, now attributed as well to the rulers. To believe but remain within the synagogue could only be explained as being the result of the preference for human glory over God's glory. It summarizes the consequence of the prologue's "wrong" choice of being born of the "will of the flesh," that is, of human cultural patterns rather than God's will. It is, indeed, a choice we make every day when we protect our status in the eyes of our families, neighbors, church, nation, and so on. To be a "secret believer" is both the most basic temptation and the worst sin for the fourth gospel. Better not to have seen at all than to claim to see but remain in sin (9:41)! Thus, the final witness is not simply against "them" but also against "us" each time we are tempted to put ourselves outside the situation of those who continue to be in need of God's healing power.

## 4. THE CLOSING ARGUMENT

### Chiasm: 12:44–50

a: 44–45: sent me: unity of Jesus/Father

   b: 46–47a: light-belief; not judge

      c: 47b: not judge but save world

   b[1]: 48: not believe; judge

a[1]: 49–50: sent me: unity of Father/Jesus

The final verses of chapter 12 present what source-oriented critics understandably see as a "disconnected" discourse of Jesus, a "leftover" speech pasted into the gospel here for lack of a better place to put it. Certainly from a dramatic standpoint, it opens a question of location and time, as we had been told in verse 36b just before the narrator's Isaian summary that Jesus had "gone off and hid from them." However, if our narrative reading is to continue to seek consistency, it is not hard to imagine this final statement as directed by Jesus not at the characters whom he has left behind but directly to readers and hearers within the Johannine community. The spotlight shines on an empty stage, and there is Jesus, making one more "public" plea, one final summation of his "defense" in the face of the charges that will momentarily lead to his arrest, formal trial, and execution. No new themes are introduced in these closing verses. Rather, a host of Johannine themes are knitted together, just as an attorney would tie up the loose ends of evidence at the close of a trial to show the jury and court the "obvious" conclusion that should be reached based on what they have seen and heard. These themes can be schematically listed to show how they summarize previously "proven" points:

| theme | verse | earlier "proof" |
|---|---|---|
| 1. faith in me=faith in one who sent me | 12:44 | 6:29; 6:57 |
| 2. seeing me=seeing one who sent me | 12:45 | 6:40 |
| 3. come as light into the world | 12:46 | 3:19; 8:12; 9:5 |
| 4. not remain in darkness | 12:46 | 3:19; 8:12; 12:35 |
| 5. hear my words/not judge | 12:47 | 8:15 |
| 6. not to judge, but to save the world | 12:47 | 3:17; 5:34 |
| 7. not receiving my words | 12:48 | 3:11 |
| 8. word will judge on last day | 12:48 | 5:24, 29; 6:40 |
| 9. I speak not on my own | 12:49 | 7:17–18; 8:28 |
| 10. Father gave me commandment | 12:49 | 8:28; 10:18 |
| 11. commandment=eternal life | 12:50 | 5:24; 6:40 |
| 12. as the Father speaks, I am speaking | 12:50 | 8:28, 38 |

The only word in the seven verses not used before in the fourth gospel is *athetōn* in verse 48, a legal term for disregarding or annulling a command. It is fitting in this final forensic speech for Jesus to claim that it is the annulment of words that is the judge. As the authorities have accused him of disregarding the Torah's word about the sabbath, now he concludes by condemning those who disregard his words that have come from God.

With this summary, the curtain comes down for the last time on Jesus' public ministry. The next seven chapters will take place in the short span of Jesus' last day, as his "hour" reveals his glory for those with eyes to see.

# 17

# "I Have Set the Example"

## *The Final Initiation into the Johannine Community*

## John 13:1–30

**A. Chiasm for Entire Last Supper Discourse:**

  a: 13:1–32: hour, mission, glory

    b: 13:33–14:31: going away, paraclete, asking in Jesus' name, peace

      c: 15:1–25: vine

    b¹: 15:26–16:33: going away, paraclete, asking in Jesus' name, peace

  a¹: 17:1–26: hour, glory, mission[1]

**B. Location:** unspecified

**C. Time:** near Passover, at an evening meal

**D. Hebrew scripture context:** Genesis 47–49; Deuteronomy 29–34

**E. Social factors:** Jesus' "own" vs. the "world"

**F. Themes:** loving one another as Jesus/Father loves

## 1. INTRODUCTION TO THE LAST SUPPER DISCOURSE: THE NARRATIVE MOSAIC OF INHERITANCE

When the curtain rises again, the mood and setting of the fourth gospel have changed completely. No longer are Jesus and his disciples arguing with Judeans or the crowd. The death threats are being held in abeyance, and the frenetic festivities of Passover preparation are off in the distance. A most remarkable

---

1. Ellis (1984, 210–211).

narrative sequence will unfold in John 13–17, unique in the New Testament. For five chapters, Jesus will speak to "his own" of his fate and theirs, of his relationship with the Father and theirs, of a new Advocate who will teach them "all things."

For some readers, the Last Supper discourse is repetitive, boring, and static. There is virtually no action — except the decisive acts in chapter 13 — and no change of scene or setting. Surprisingly perhaps, there is no eucharistic talk at all, in contrast with the unanimous testimony of the synoptics and Paul about the important sayings emanating from this final meal.

Scholars have spent immense energies analyzing the supposed sources for the discourse, breaking it up into various cut-and-paste units that they claim show the stages of composition and editing. From this source-oriented perspective, the Last Supper discourse becomes a sloppy pastiche of quips and quotes, a potpourri of collected sayings of Jesus, all thrown together under the auspices of his final gathering with his disciples.

As we will see, whatever the compositional history of these chapters may have been, what we actually have is a precisely worded, beautifully structured, powerfully prophetic exhortation to a discipleship community. Just as in the preceding twelve chapters, each word is in its place for a specific reason, built on the twin pillars of chiastic parallelism and the social need to bolster the community facing the death of its master.

The Johannine community found themselves in the midst of an impossibly complex matrix of social messages. Caught up in belief in Jesus, they had to negotiate the competing *mythos* of synagogue Judaism, various Christian gnostic alternatives, the radical Jewish Qumran ideology, Roman imperialism, and other messianic and prophetic voices (see Introduction, B.3). As Wayne A. Meeks has said, the fourth gospel's repetitious quality, especially in the Last Supper discourse, helped the Johannine community immensely in charting a course through this maze (see p. 200 above).

Another important aspect of the entire Last Supper discourse is its atemporal and aspatial quality. Although it has a vital and coherent function in its precise place in the fourth gospel's narrative structure, it has also been written to stand apart from the plot. Raymond Brown notes that Jesus is "speaking from heaven.... His words are directed to Christians of all times.... It is meant to be read after he has left the earth."[2] By omitting any spatial referent whatsoever, the discourse breaks the bounds of the remainder of the story to express Jesus' discipleship message to a universal audience. From a temporal perspective, chapters 13–17 "bring the future and the present together in one narrative moment."[3]

Although unique to New Testament literature, the basic genre of the Last Supper discourse has several precedents in Hebrew scripture and intertestamental writings. The best-known parallel "farewell" discourses are those of Joseph

---

2. R. Brown (1970, 582).
3. O'Day (1991, 156).

in Genesis 47–49, Joshua in Joshua 22–24, and Moses in Deuteronomy 29–34. Brown lists the following elements found in each instance of the genre:

1. announcement of imminent departure
2. sorrow/reassurance
3. recall of past life
4. directive to keep God's commands
5. love/unity among "children"
6. future fate of children
7. promise of God's presence
8. promise of a successor[4]

More specifically, Paul S. Minear offers the following elements found in the Last Supper discourse and Moses' departure speech:

1. "prophet's death is understood as necessary to God's design"
2. farewell discourse form
3. "poignant testimony to the community's dullness and ignorance"
4. people entrusted with mission
5. people reminded of signs
6. promise of inclusion of other nations
7. blessing prayer at conclusion[5]

As we work our way through the Last Supper discourse, it may be helpful to refer back to these elements to see how the fourth gospel shapes its narrative to meet the particularities of the Johannine community's needs and its claims about Jesus.

The other ancient genre that has certain features in common with the Last Supper discourse is that of *apocalyptic*. Mark 13 and its parallels in Matthew and Luke are the clearest examples of this form in the gospels. In that genre, a speaker warns the hearers about dire events about to take place and exhorts them to expect joy after a period of intense trial.[6] In particular, note the following parallels between Mark 13 and John 13–17:

---

4. R. Brown (1966, 598–600). The pseudepigraphical *Testaments of the Twelve Patriarchs* (Charlesworth [1983]) in its final form, dating probably from the early second century C.E., bears many structural and thematic similarities to the Johannine Last Supper discourse (e.g., spirit of truth versus spirit of darkness; command to love one another). However, its underlying hope in the efficacy of the Mosaic Law and its specific ethical concerns (e.g., the alleged evil of women) position its exhortations far afield from that of John's gospel. During the second century, it may well have been another religious ideology competing for the hearts and minds of Jewish followers of Jesus.

5. Minear (1977, 108–109).

6. R. Brown (1970, 601). See also Collins (1984).

1. "the end" (Mk 13:7, 13; Jn 13:1)
2. private speech between Jesus and disciples (Mk 13:2="Peter, James, and John"; Jn 13:1="his own")
3. birth-pang metaphor (Mk 13:8; Jn 16:21)
4. persecution by synagogue (Mk 13:9; Jn 15:20; 16:2)
5. the disciples' "hour" (Mk 13:11; Jn 16:2, 4)
6. holy spirit will speak for you in court (Mk 13:11; Jn 14:16; 16:8)
7. disciples as objects of hatred (Mk 13:13; Jn 15:18–25)
8. Jesus tells disciples before it happens (Mk 13:23; Jn 14:29)

The fourth gospel has used these existing genres of the farewell discourse of the revered leader and apocalyptic speech to shape a narrative that prepares hearers for both the departure of Jesus as well as their own disruptive and threatening future.

## 2. SETTING THE EXAMPLE: JOHN 13:1–30

A. **Chiasm:**
  a: 1: hour
    b: 2–11: devil; Peter; not all clean
      c: 12–17: footwashing as example
    b[1]: 18–27: Peter, Satan, Judas
  a[1]: 28–32: now . . . glorified[7]
B. **Location:** unspecified
C. **Time:** before Passover, at evening meal
D. **Hebrew scripture context:** Exodus 30; 2 Macc 6:28, 31
E. **Social factors:** Jesus' "own" vs. the "devil's" own
F. **Themes:** laying down life for friends; community intimacy
G. **Key words:** know; lay down/receive; love (*agapē*); clean

### *a. Becoming Clean*

**Chiasm: 13:2–11**
a: 2: Judas/betray
  b: 3–6: Simon Peter; footwash
    c: 7: you don't know . . . you will know
  b[1]: 8–9: Simon Peter; footwash
a[1]: 10–11: not all clean/betray

---

7. Ellis (1984, 211–212).

If the entire Last Supper discourse is unique in the New Testament as a lengthy speech, so is the action in chapter 13 unique as a *sacramental* sign. Nowhere else does Christian tradition record Jesus washing feet and offering the act as an "example" to follow. But before the action itself is narrated, the scene is carefully set in verses 1–3.

The opening verses are structured to show Jesus "surrounding" the devil, as each leader prepares his own to follow. That is, verses 1 and 3 speak of Jesus' knowledge and planning, while verse 2 speaks of the devil's own activity. This pattern will be repeated in 18:4–8, as Judas, the one "sent forth" by the devil, finds himself surrounded by *egō eimi* at Jesus' arrest. It is the enactment of the first stage in the judgment of this world, the casting out of its ruler described in 12:31.

As verse 1 starts, we find for the first time the juxtaposition of "sacred" and "profane" time, but with a Johannine twist. The Judean calendar tells us that it is near Passover, the central feast of Israel's covenant with God, while "Johannine time" tells us that it is Jesus' "hour to pass out of this world to the Father."[8] From an "earthly" perspective, "Passover" is sacred time and an "hour" is very ordinary. However, from the Johannine community's "heavenly" viewpoint, reality is just the opposite. Passover has become a *national* celebration of Judea, while the "hour" is the focal point of the messiah's sojourn among humanity. The former involves the sacrifice of lambs, but the latter the sacrifice of "the Lamb of God." Further, the narrator highlights Jesus' "knowledge" of the hour, which takes place at Passover. Just as for Christians, Good Friday and Easter supplant their Passover roots, so for the Johannine community, the hour supplants the traditional seder meal.

For the first time, the narrator has disclosed what the "glory" of the hour is: for Jesus "to pass from the world to the Father." The earthly reality of death as the means for the movement is enshadowed by the bright illumination of Jesus' return to the one who sent him. It will be for Jesus a moment of reunion, of celebration, of glory, not one of despair or pain. At least, this is the message of the narrator.

With awareness of the *kairos,* the narrator tells us that Jesus "loved his own [*idious*] in the world; to the end [*eis telos*] he loved them." "His own" recalls once more the center of the prologue: "Into his own [*idioi*] he came, but his own did not receive him" (1:11). It also contrasts the devil's "own" (8:44) with the good shepherd's "own" who are led out by name (10:3, 4; cf. 10:12). Are Jesus' "own" in 13:1 those from the prologue who do not receive him, or those led out by the shepherd? Their being "in the world" does not necessarily help clarify the matter, for Jesus will contrast being *in* the world with being *of* the world later in the Last Supper discourse (17:11–18). For now, the narrator focuses not on the identity of Jesus' "own" but on the fact of his persistent love for them. *Eis telos* has several meanings, suggesting both the totality of Jesus' love and

---

8. Culpepper (1990, 135).

its permanence.[9] It also bears the sense of "until completion," as in the earlier uses of a form of *telos* in 4:44 and 5:36 in reference to Jesus' completion of his Father's work. It is the first of the links with the apocalyptic rhetoric of Mark 13 listed above and helps set the discourse in a temporal mode inclusive of all history.

In the midst of this multilayered time setting, the narrator adds another, more specific note, at the beginning of verse 2: "And supper was taking place." It is the second "supper" in two chapters, the only ones in the fourth gospel. Because the previous one involved preparation of Jesus by Mary for his death and burial, readers' curiosity may be stirred to wonder what *this* supper will hold in store. Almost before one can form this thought, the verse continues with disclosure of the most ominous fact possible: "The devil had already thrust into [*beblēkotos*] the heart that he should betray him: Judas, son of Simon Iscariot." The first phrase is a Semitic idiom meaning "to decide."[10] It is a done deed, apparently irrevocable. The mysterious link between Judas the betrayer and the devil is mentioned only here, and in violent terms. The verb often weakly translated as "put" shares its root with the word for the action that casts out the once-blind one (*exebalon*, 9:34), an action that Jesus promises he will *not* do to those the Father has given him (6:37). It also matches the "throwing" of stones at Jesus by those Jesus accuses of having the devil for their father (*balōsin*, 8:59). In like manner, the violence of the devil has already entered Judas, although the specific moment of this crucial event is not narrated. Whether we should understand this as meaning that the devil forced his way into Judas or whether Judas was somehow open to this violent entry is not clear. What *is* clear is that this supper takes place in the midst of imminent betrayal, a betrayal that we know will lead to Jesus' death.

Verse 3 continues to describe the consciousness of Jesus as if the cold reality of verse 2 had not penetrated the scene: "Having known that all things were given into his hands by the Father, and that from God he came out and toward God he was going..." As always, Jesus and the Father are one mind and one spirit. The narrator reminds us of this not as if it were a new awareness within Jesus or us but to complete the introduction of the action to follow with *our* knowledge refreshed.[11] Everything that will be said and done at this supper by Jesus will be with this consciousness. No matter how confusing things may appear or sound, no matter how many times we may have to go back and read again to catch the depth of meaning, the scene unfolds with awareness that the source and goal of Jesus' life is God.

The table set, the narrator shifts to describe the action in verse 4: "He rose [*egeiretai*] from the supper and laid down [*tithēsin*] his outer garments and took [*labōn*] a towel and girded [*diezōsen*] himself." Each verb in this verse is pregnant with Johannine meaning and is worthy of consideration. Jesus is described

---

9. R. Brown (1970, 550).
10. Culpepper (1983, 24 n. 25).
11. Cf. Tolmie (1991, 280).

first as "rising," a verb used almost exclusively in the fourth gospel to mean resurrection (2:19, 20, 22; 5:8, 21; 12:1, 9, 17). It is in a sense the risen Jesus who acts and speaks throughout the Last Supper discourse, even though the story world has not yet reached his death.

Next, he "lays down" his outer garments, a verb used in 2:10 but that gains its clearest meaning in its quadruple appearance in the good shepherd speech as to Jesus' "laying down" of his *life* (10:11, 15, 17, 18; cf. 11:34). As he will lay down his life freely, so he lays down his cloak, his outer garment, symbolic from a Hellenistic (and perhaps gnostic) perspective of the shell that is his physical body. Although a Hebrew mentality would see body and spirit as a single entity, the Greeks have now joined the family of God's children, and it is appropriate for Jesus' action to be expressed in a way fitting with their anthropology. It is an ironic reversal: Jesus first "rises," *then* "lays down" his cloak/life!

The "taking" of the towel is also carefully molded into the Johannine vocabulary. The verb here is *lambanō,* which occurs forty-five times in the fourth gospel, usually as "receive" or "accept." It is also a prologue verb, expressing the opposition between his own who do not receive him and the children of God who do (1:12).

Finally, the "girding" is a new verb here but will eventually be associated with Peter's actions after Jesus has been raised (21:7, 18). For now, it simply expresses Jesus' taking of the towel to himself and preparing for the action that is to follow.

Verse 5 expresses the action with three more verb phrases: "After this, he threw [*ballei*] water into a basin and started to wash [*niptein*] his disciples' feet, and to wipe [*ekmassein*] them with the towel with which he was girded." Once more, each verb links the action to what has gone before. The "throwing" of the water contrasts with the throwing of stones: the latter is to *cause* death, while the former will be shown to be *preparation* for death. The "washing" is connected to the previous washing in Siloam that led the blind one to see (9:7, 11, 15), the only other washing in the fourth gospel. Finally, the "wiping" ties this action to that of Mary's wiping of Jesus' feet with her hair (12:3). Putting the verbs in verses 4 and 5 together, we find the risen Jesus, who lays down his life for his own, girding himself to prepare his disciples to see their own deaths that are approaching!

This interpretation comes not only from the intratextual verb use but also from intertextual meanings of washing feet. Herold Weiss points out that in the Hellenistic synagogue — a context already invoked with the symbol of the cloak/life — "there was speculation about footwashing as providing sanctification by the divine spirit and opening up the soul to the divine manifestation."[12] In other words, "Washing of the feet was a preparation for meeting God."[13] This link is also found in Philo, a Hellenistic Jewish philosopher of the first century. In commenting on the instructions given to Moses in Ex 30:19 to place a basin

---

12. Weiss (1979, 304).
13. Ibid.

of water between the altar and the sanctuary for Aaron and his sons to wash their feet, Philo says:

> One should not enter with unwashed feet on the pavement of the temple of God.

Elsewhere, in commenting on a levitical law regarding washing the feet of animals in preparation for sacrifice, Philo explains:

> By the washing of the feet is meant that his steps should be no longer on earth but tread the upper air. For the soul of the lover of God does in truth leap from earth to heaven.[14]

Philo's comments on Ex 30:19 lead us to see how that passage also links the Johannine footwashing with preparation for death. In the Exodus passage, God directs Moses not only to place the washing basin but also to prepare an expensive blend of myrrh and spices to anoint the tabernacle and the basin, as well as Aaron and his sons, "in order that they may serve me as priests" (Ex 30:30). The imagery of washing and anointing in Exodus matches Mary's anointing of Jesus' feet for his burial with Jesus' washing of his disciples' feet for their own approach to God. Just as Jesus' death is referred to obliquely in 13:1, 3 with the metaphor of moving from this world to the Father, so the disciples' death is implicitly described as preparing to meet God.

Whether any of those present understood these connections is not narrated, except for the reticence of Simon Peter, who stops the action in verse 6 by questioning the obvious, that his "Lord" is about to wash his feet. Jesus' response in verse 7 makes clear that Peter's question is grounded in ignorance, but that "after these things" (*meta tauta*), he will know. The ordinary words *meta tauta* are deeply ambiguous: Are the "these things" simply the words of the Last Supper discourse, the completed journey of Jesus to God, Peter's own experience of his lack of self-knowledge, or the experience of the risen Jesus and the paraclete? *Tauta* will echo like a refrain throughout the discourse, gathering meaning as we continue. At this point, it expresses the greatest possible distance between Jesus' knowledge and Peter's and helps prepare readers to hear Peter's other comments in the Last Supper discourse as coming from the very human but crucially limited place of "not knowing."

Given Peter's lack of knowledge, we can understand his strong reaction expressed in verse 8: "You will never [*ou mē*] wash my feet!" His abhorrence is not of the prospect of his own death (which he doesn't understand is the meaning of the act) but of the humiliating behavior of his Lord. Which of us would not be embarrassed to have someone we respect and admire bend over and treat us in this way? Palestinian peasant feet were certainly crustier and filthier than our own relatively pampered toes and heels. To accept such a "gift" would make

---

14. Philo *Q. Ex.* 1.2 and *De. Spec. Leg.* 1.206, 207, cited in Weiss (1979, 304).

us cringe and would have been unheard of in the much more strictly regulated culture of the Johannine community's age.

In addition, to allow someone to wash our feet is to open ourselves to an intimacy beyond the scope of most relationships. As a nurse friend has told me, many people in the hospital will willingly undress for an examination or treatment but will hesitate to take their socks off! Feet are hidden, far from our usual visual intercourse even when sandal-clad. To be close enough to wash a foot is to "know" its nooks and crannies, its callouses, cracks, and curves. For Peter to allow Jesus into this most personal space was beyond his ability to be vulnerable at that moment. It is in poignant contrast with Jesus' own invitation — which Peter accepted — to receive his flesh and blood into his body (6:52–69).

Where Peter denies Jesus his feet, his Lord responds by claiming his entire being[15] in verse 8b: "If I don't wash you, you have no share [*meros*] with me." Brown points out that the term *meros* is used in the Septuagint to translate the Hebrew *heleq,* the God-given heritage of Israel, in which each tribe shares.[16] Jesus' statement makes receipt of the footwashing an absolute condition of participation in the Johannine community, which is the heritage of those who follow Jesus.

With typical exuberance, Simon Peter overresponds in verse 9, but in a way that provides light-hearted comic relief at an otherwise extremely tense moment: "Lord, not only my feet, but my hands and head, too!" In addition to this function, Peter's line, according to Weiss, is a "clear polemic" against the prevailing Pharisaic practice of wearing phylacteries as a sign of sharing in the inheritance of the tribes.[17] If Peter is to become a member of Jesus' "tribe," he wants to be marked just as the Pharisees are marked! Of course, a washing would leave no visible trace for people to see, so his demand is humorously ironic as well as socially critical.

Jesus responds in verse 10 by developing a contrast that Peter's comment implicitly missed, that between "washing" and "bathing": "The one who has bathed [*leloumenos*] has no need to wash [*nipsasthai*] except for his feet,[18] but is wholly clean [*katharos*]." To be bathed (*louein*) is to have one's entire body washed, referring both to the ordinary cleansing activity as well as the Jewish ritual bath that cleansed a person of legal impurity. To wash (*niptein*) is to participate in an act parallel to that of the blind man in 9:7. That is, the issue is neither physical cleansing nor legal cleansing but rather is Jesus' *foot*washing that makes one "clean." Earlier, we saw that the Judean "purification" (*katharismos*) jars had lost their power to produce celebration (2:6). Also, we heard disciples of John (the Baptist) arguing with a Judean over "purification" (*katharismou*; 3:25), which resulted in an emphasis on the "increase" of

---

15. Weiss (1979, 317).
16. R. Brown (1970, 565).
17. Weiss (1979, 317).
18. Although many ancient manuscripts omit the phrase "except for his feet," most retain it, as do most modern versions.

Jesus. Now, the moment has come to show what has replaced both Judean ritual purification and John's baptism: Jesus' footwashing.

The discussion gets personal and ominous, though, as Jesus completes his thought: "You people are clean, but not all." The narrator underscores the meaning of the contrast in verse 11: "He knew which one would betray him; this is why he said, 'Not all of you people are clean.'" Note that Jesus declares all present — except one — "clean," even though he has not yet washed Peter's feet. It is not the physical act that is important in the fourth gospel but the *commitment* expressed by willingness to undergo the act. John's gospel develops no new cultic rituals but rather true *sacraments*: physical/verbal acts that signify the presence of grace. Peter's "reborn" acceptance of the need for Jesus to wash his feet is what is important, not the actual washing itself. At the same time, Judas's willingness to be physically washed — no exception is stated when the narrator describes what Jesus does — is *not* enough to declare him clean. Peter may be ignorant, but he is still oriented around doing what Jesus commands. Judas, on the other hand, is committed to his own "father's" will, even if he is present at the supper and footwashing.

### b. *"Happy Are You if You Do This!"*

**Chiasm: 13:12–17**

a: 12: do you know?

   b: 13–14: teacher/Lord

      c: 15: give you an example

   b$^1$: 16: servant/master

a$^1$: 17: if you know

**Chiasm: 13:12b–14**

a: 12b: what I have done for you

   b: 13a: teacher, Lord

      c: 13b: you speak well, for I am that

   b$^1$: 14a: Lord, teacher

a$^1$: 14b: you do for one another

In this context of cleanliness and betrayal, the narrator describes the completion of Jesus' act in verse 12: "When, therefore, he washed their feet, he took up [*elaben*] his outer garments and sat down." Just as the removal of his outer garments was symbolic of laying down his life, so the replacement of the garments matches his authority to "receive" his life again (*labein*; 10:18). Ironically, it is the risen Jesus who "sits down" to explain the meaning of his act to the bewildered disciples.

The question he asks them in 12b is purely rhetorical: "Do you know what I have done to you?" We know for sure that Peter *does not* know; if any other disciples have been able to put the pieces together, they are not given a chance to say so. Rather than allowing them either to admit their ignorance or to feign knowledge, Jesus changes topics abruptly to one he has not yet addressed, the question of "titles": "You call me 'the teacher' and 'the Lord' and you speak well, for I am that." Of all the titles Jesus has been given throughout the fourth gospel, he has never affirmed or criticized any directly, preferring to speak of himself as "the Son" or "the Human One" instead. Now, he expressly commends the disciples for two titles: teacher and Lord.

But the point is not so much to emphasize the "correct" titles as to show the implications of giving Jesus these titles for their own discipleship: "Therefore, if I washed your feet and am 'the Lord' and 'the teacher,' you also should be washing one another's [*allēlōn*] feet." It is the first of six times in the Last Supper discourse where Jesus will tell the disciples what they should be doing for "one another." Earlier, *allēlōn* was used negatively to express the context of confusion, murmuring, dispute, or incorrect "glory" (4:33; 5:44; 6:43, 52; 11:56). Jesus begins the process of replacing these "worldly" ways in which people act toward one another with his "heavenly" ways. The world's relationships breed contention, distrust, and self-importance, but those within the Johannine community are to encourage sharing, self-sacrifice, intimacy, and love. In this first instance, Jesus focuses on the call to wash each other's feet, that is, to prepare one another to face suffering and death.

Jesus goes on to explain that what he has done is an "example" (*hypodeigma*) for them "so that as I did to you, you may also do." R. Alan Culpepper has shown how the word *hypodeigma* is used in the Septuagint specifically as an "example" of a noble death.[19] A good instance is in 2 Macc 6:28, 31, where Eleazer describes his own impending demise:

> "Therefore, by manfully giving up my life now, I will prove myself worthy of my old age, and I will leave to the young a noble example [*hypodeigma*] of how to die willingly and generously for the revered and holy laws." ... This is how he died, leaving in his death a model of courage and an unforgettable example [*hypodeigma*] of virtue not only for the young but for the whole nation.

As Jesus replaced the feast of Dedication established by Eleazar, so his preparation for death provides the new *hypodeigma* for God's people to imitate.

He follows this with a double-amen saying that "limits" his disciples' authority: "A slave is not greater than his lord, nor is one sent [*apostolos*] greater than the one who sends." This statement is the usual basis for the normal misreading of the footwashing as an example of "humble service." How many Holy Thursday services and homilies have put priest and bowl before the congregation as an "example" of "lowering oneself like Jesus" to do the dirty work of washing feet! How easy it is for relatively safe and secure middle-class Christians

---

19. Culpepper (1990, 142–143). He also notes 4 Macc 17:22–23 (mother/sons' martyrdom) and Sir 44:16 (Enoch's death).

to deny the call to death in favor of charity work! The prevailing interpretation is a function of both the chasm between the position of the interpreter and that of the Johannine community as well as the folly of taking passages out of context. If readers are comfortable, it is enough of a challenge to call them to serve the poor (or even "one another") by humble actions. But if readers are like the Johannine community — as people in El Salvador, Malawi, and other places are where proclaiming God's truth is to risk one's life — "humble service" is a commonplace that requires no exhortation at all. It is the call to help one another face death that is both the challenge and comfort of the gospel.

Further, the "normal" interpretation does an injustice to the words that Jesus speaks. As Graydon Snyder puts it, "If the footwashing narrative were a paradigm of humble service, ... the logion would be reversed ... 'a master is not greater than his slave.' ... *That* would be radical humility."[20] Jesus, instead, tells them that they as slaves are no greater than he as master: if he cannot avoid death, neither can they. He continues in verse 17 with one of the two "beatitudes" in the fourth gospel: "If you know these things [*tauta*], blessed are you if you do them." Action follows knowledge, and the reward of right action is God's blessing. In this way, the fourth gospel again distinguishes itself from gnosticism, where knowledge alone is often enough. For the Johannine community, the life of faith requires activity that transforms relationships, producing the "fruit" of "eternal life" in the midst of betrayal and death.

### c. *"Lord, Who Is It?"*

**Chiasm: 13:18–30**

a: 18–19: ate my bread, lifted heel; tell you now (betrayal/ignorance)

> b: 20: receiving you, me, one who sent (intimacy of disciples, Jesus, Father)

>> c: 21: one among you will betray

> b¹: 22–25: one at bosom; intimacy of disciples, Beloved Disciple/Peter, Jesus

a¹: 26–30: ate morsel; no one knew why (betrayal/ignorance)

In spite of its death context, the first part of the footwashing episode is a highly positive scene. Jesus has shown his love for his own and given them an example of what that means. He has encouraged them to support one another in the most difficult moments of their lives and has offered those who do a blessing. He has taught them how to find life in the midst of the inevitability of death.

Now, though, the scene gets darker, as the moment of night approaches. Their ignorance will have its price. In verse 18, Jesus returns to the theme left behind at the end of the chiasm from 13:2 to 13:11: that is, the presence of the betrayer

---

20. Snyder (1971, 7).

in their midst. At first blush, his statement seems to suggest that the betrayer is not one of the chosen: "I am not talking about all of you; I know whom I chose." However, in 6:70, Jesus expressly included the "devil" within the "twelve" as among those Jesus has chosen. It is not that Judas is not *chosen*, but that he *is known* by Jesus. The intimacy between them is emphasized with the quotation from scripture that is "fulfilled" (*plerōthē*) by this internal darkness within the community: "The one eating [*trōgōn*] my bread has lifted up his heel to me." The quotation is from Ps 41:9, but in the Septuagint, the verb for "eat" is *esthiōn*, not *trōgōn*. The eucharistic discourse may have taken place in Galilee long ago in the Johannine story world, but it has strong echoes in its familiar setting at the Last Supper. *Trōgōn* recalls the powerful challenge to "munch my flesh," the call to participate in the publicly known agape meal that identified one to the world as a Christian. Judas has indeed been a part of the community. He is *not* an interloper, a "plant," or a spy, but one of Jesus' own who has not known Jesus as he himself has been known. The betrayal is genuine, in that a person who had turned toward Jesus has now turned away. The image of the raised heel, in addition to expressing a terrible insult in Middle Eastern cultures to this day,[21] is an ironic twist on the "example" Jesus has given to wash one another's feet. Just as King David, the traditional author of Psalm 41, was not exempt from betrayal by friends, neither is Jesus the king.[22]

Jesus clarifies for the disciples in verse 19 that he is "saying this to you now before it happens, so that when it does happen, you may believe that I AM [*egō eimi*]." It introduces a major theme of the Last Supper discourse: Jesus telling them things "before" in order to instill faith. For the Johannine community living two generations after Jesus' death and resurrection, an essential element of Jesus' authority and integrity of mission was that he knew what would happen and walked through it in fulfillment of God's will. The messiah's death was not a mistake or accident. It was not a failure, but God's glory in fulfillment of scripture. Those who imagine Jesus intending to start a new religion should take note here that his emphasis on how his actions are in accordance with the Hebrew scriptures underscores his continuity with the tradition. If the Johannine community ended up establishing a separate existence, it was not because Jesus taught them to reject the world as did those who formed the Qumran community, but because they had been expelled first. This theme will be illuminated more specifically later in the discourse. For now, the "before" invites readers to "observe" one of Jesus' predictions come true and allow the upcoming "befores" to be fulfilled at more of a narrative distance.

In addition to the Psalm quoted, Jesus' own words also fulfill scripture. In Ezek 24:24, God says: "When these things [LXX, *tauta*] come about, you will know that I am the Lord." And in Isa 43:10, we find God making this proclamation: "You are my witnesses and my servant whom I have chosen; so that you may know and believe that I AM [LXX, *egō eimi*]." Although the Judeans and

---

21. R. Brown (1970, 554).
22. Carson (1991, 470).

Pharisees in particular claim the authority of scripture as a basis to reject Jesus, his disciples are taught that, as Jesus told the Judeans in 5:39, the scriptures "are the ones that bear witness about me."

At first, the saying that follows in verse 20 seems unconnected with the theme of fulfillment of scripture. But within the structure of the scene, it parallels the saying in verse 16 that followed abruptly from Jesus' "example." As the double-amen saying in verse 16 "limited" the authority of the "slave" to that of the "master" who has set the example, so the double-amen saying in verse 20 "expands" the authority of the one sent by Jesus to that of God: "The one receiving anyone I send is receiving me; the one receiving me is receiving the one who sent me." If the scope of the disciples' *responsibility* is as broad as that of Jesus, so is the scope of their *status*. Those who are slaves are also representatives of God. As Jesus will "prove" his divine sonship by his obedience to the call to lay down his life, so will the disciples who follow in Jesus' footsteps participate in the intimacy of that relationship.

Whatever the disciples may be thinking or feeling throughout this speech is left open for one more verse. Before we get a glimpse into their reaction to all this, the narrator in verse 21 breaks in to tell us of Jesus' own feelings: "After saying these things [*tauta*], Jesus became troubled in spirit [*etaraxthē tō pneumati*] and bore witness, saying, 'Amen, amen I am saying to you: one of you will betray me.'" For the third time, we are told of Jesus' deep internal emotional struggle (11:33; 12:27). Each occurrence has been in the context of death, the consequence of the betrayal that Jesus informs his disciples is about to take place. Although readers have known about the fact of betrayal and the identity of the betrayer since 6:71, it comes as shocking news to the gathered disciples. In case they have not understood the meaning of the Psalm quoted or the statement that not all of them are clean, Jesus clarifies the situation for them just as he did about Lazarus's death (11:14).

Can we imagine what it was like for the disciples to hear this news? The narrator tells us that "the disciples were looking at [literally, 'into'] one another, at a loss [*aporoumenoi*] as to whom he was speaking about." How much of their collective character is revealed by this simple statement! Here they are, a group of disciples who have traveled with Jesus and one another for some time in close quarters. They have apparently given up their old ways of life to be together on this new journey. They have seen Jesus do many signs, have sensed death in the air, have made the commitments to be born *anōthen* and to munch his flesh. And yet they stand in a position not too different from the Sanhedrin condemned by Caiaphas as not knowing anything, at least not what counts in this crucial moment of community testing and faith.

We may tend to hear the word "know" in our modern scientific sense of empirical evidence, facts, data. To "know" something or someone is to have information about them. But in the ancient world, especially in the Hebraic mind-set, knowledge equalled *intimacy*. As "to know" someone is a famous biblical metaphor from Genesis for sexual intercourse, knowledge means the deep awareness of a person that comes from being close, vulnerable, open. Jesus' "knowledge" of his Father has been described in the fourth gospel many times not as awareness of theological concepts about the Trinity or similar propositional or intellectual awareness, but as the "oneness" that comes from constant watching and listening to the other. *This* is the knowledge that Jesus has of his own fate at the beginning of this scene. This is the knowledge he has of Judas, the one he has chosen. The disciples, in ironic and poignant contrast, do not know each other at all! Not only do they not know that anyone in their midst is a betrayer, but they are "at a loss" as to which one it might be once the fact of the betrayer is made plain. As the scene continues, the depth of their ignorance will be even more clearly revealed, an ignorance that is the antithesis of what the gnostic communities purport to remedy with their own brands of esoteric knowledge.

For those of us who have taken the risk at one time or another to experiment in community with others, how might we feel to be reliably informed of the presence of a betrayer in our midst? Would we "know" each other well enough to look around and name the one? Would betrayal likely bear as serious consequences for us as it did for Jesus and for the Johannine community? We find in 1 John that the community's experience did indeed parallel that of the first disciples. For example, we hear in 1 Jn 2:18–19:

> Little children, it is the last hour, and as you have heard that the Antichrist is coming, now many Antichrists have come to be, which is how we know that it is the last hour. They came out of us, but they were not out of us, for if they were out of us, they would have *remained* with us. But so that it might be revealed that they are not out of us, they have gone.

Brown has argued that this internal betrayal eventually resulted in the destruction of the Johannine community in a terrible fit of accusation and hatred.[23] And what community do we know that could withstand this sort of schism? Once a single betrayer is revealed, how could the members continue to have any trust at all? A deep paranoia would be a natural result of such an experience, one that could easily scar a person for life.

But for Jesus, the presence of betrayal presents the challenge to draw the intimacy of the community even deeper. As the discourse continues, the interrelated themes of knowledge and unity will become refrains. Contrary to our human impulse, Jesus calls us to walk through the experience of his betrayal and our own and allow it to lead those of us who remain into even more vulnerability and personal risk.

At this moment of high tension, we meet a key character for the first time in verse 23: "There was one of the disciples leaning against the bosom [*kolpō*] of Jesus, whom Jesus loved." This so-called Beloved Disciple, who is otherwise completely anonymous, appears here as the antithesis of the betrayer. It is

---

23. R. Brown (1979). However, cf. the recent work of Talbert (1992, 61–63), who argues that the Johannine epistles cannot be conclusively dated later than the gospel itself.

a much needed narrative antidote, which maintains the thread of hope just as faith might seem to stretch beyond its limit. His position in relation to Jesus is identical to that of the Word in relation to God: at the bosom (1:18). If one of the chosen will lift his heel, this one is in a place of wonderful intimacy.

And then, a surprising event takes place in verse 24: "Simon Peter nodded therefore to this one, saying to him, 'Ask who it is he is talking about.' " Simon Peter, the last one other than Jesus to speak, dares to try again, but rather than revealing his ignorance to the whole group or to Jesus, he signals the Beloved Disciple to ask the question. For the first time, Peter is not the lead disciple as he was in 6:66–71. Instead, he goes through the mediation of the Beloved Disciple, the one whom the Johannine community sees as its central authority about Jesus. For the remainder of the fourth gospel, the relationship between these two characters will ebb and flow, but always the Beloved Disciple will come out as at least an equal. If we see Peter as the "apostle" upon whom the synoptics build the church and to whom even Paul offers a degree of deference, then the whispered request to the Beloved Disciple to ask a question to Jesus bears powerful overtones for the relationship between differing Christian communities. We will see in detail how these differences are expressed later in the gospel. For now, the narrator is content with introducing the theme by showing the Beloved Disciple as in a closer relationship with Jesus than is Peter.

But before we get too excited about the superiority of the Beloved Disciple, the narrator tells us that "he leaned back against Jesus' breast [*stēthos*] and said to him, 'Lord, who is it?' " Suddenly, the disciple is not at the "bosom" but at the "breast." While physically identical, the difference is as great as heaven and earth. "Bosom" expressed deep intimacy, but "breast" is simply physical closeness, for this disciple does not know the betrayer either! Whether he has been so focused on his Lord that he has not gotten to know his fellow disciples, or whether he is simply no different than the others, we cannot conclude one way or another. But the result is that all the disciples are "in the dark."

Rather than simply answering the question, Jesus responds with a signal that we can only be sure will be known to the Beloved Disciple, for we are not informed that he shared the information with Peter: "That one to whom I shall dip [*bapsō*] the morsel that I shall give to him." It is an ironic "baptism," for Jesus' act of dipping will lead the recipient to be entered by Satan, not God. The time sequence is narrated very carefully in verses 26–30:

1. the one to whom I will dip (*bapsō*) the morsel (26a)

2. having dipped (*bapsas*) the morsel, he is taking (*lambanei*) and is giving to Judas, son of Simon Iscariot (26b)

3. and after the morsel, then Satan entered into that one (27a)

4. what you are doing, do quickly (27b)

5. having received (*labōn*) the morsel, therefore, that one went out at once (30)

From prediction, to action, to exhortation to further immediate action, to completion, the gospel moves us through the dire moment with rapt attention. Did Judas feel the change? Could the disciples have noticed the difference? This wide gap is left completely to our imaginations to fill in.

Whatever the effect on Judas, the narrator portrays the devil as acting in two steps upon his own "chosen" one. First, the devil decided upon Judas (13:2) but did not "enter" him. Only now, with the morsel given by Jesus, can the devil's disciple be possessed. Even Satan cannot act until Jesus gives the signal! Furthermore, the Satan-filled Judas must await Jesus' "permission" in order to respond to his own master's call. It is an extreme irony that Jesus orders Judas to obey the devil's command quickly, and Judas complies with Jesus' order!

Another mystery is the meaning of the "morsel" (*psōmion*). It is a word not found elsewhere in the New Testament, but it is repeated four times in five verses here. The literal meaning is of a crumb, a bit of bread broken off from a loaf. But in the context of the Last Supper and Jesus' carefully worded scripture quotation in verse 18, it is hard not to conceive of the morsel as *eucharistic* bread, the very flesh of Jesus that the disciples are to eat.[24] In this most intimate of moments at an intimate meal, we discover in verses 28–29 that there is not only a lack of shared knowledge but a communication problem as well. Those gathered at table hear Jesus' remark to *Judas* but must *not* have heard his remark to the *Beloved Disciple,* for, according to the narrator, they completely misunderstand what Jesus has told the betrayer. Instead, we are informed in verse 29: "Some were thinking that since Judas had the money box, Jesus was telling him, 'Buy what we need for the feast,' or that he should give something to the poor." The ironies reach tragicomic proportions at this point in the story, for the disciples have not heard Jesus, have not known Judas, *and* have not understood what the moment calls for!

Readers have already been told expressly that Judas was "a thief" and helped himself to the collection, but the disciples apparently have no knowledge of this (or think that Jesus doesn't!) if they expect Jesus to order Judas to do money deeds, whether for their own sakes or for the sake of the poor. And the specific deeds that they think of have both been negatively associated earlier: "buying" as the test of Philip at the wilderness feeding (6:5–7) and giving to the poor while Jesus "remains" with them at the anointing by Mary, where *we* learned that Judas was a thief (12:5–8).

And how can they imagine that, at this moment of the announcement of betrayal, Jesus could be sending Judas out on one mundane task or another? The disciples have been reduced to caricatures, comic book figures who don't know which end is up. Whether we attribute this confusion to their being distraught at the news of an internal betrayer or simply the gospel's need to contrast Jesus with his followers in extreme terms, their misunderstanding of what is happening in their midst makes us not sure whether to laugh or to cry.

---

24. Moloney (1991, 250–255).

The narrator sums up the state of affairs with an exquisitely simple and precise remark at the end of verse 30: "It was night." The time to work is past (9:4); the time to walk in the light is eclipsed for now (11:9–10). The disciples have many lessons to learn during this time of darkness, lessons upon which their lives depend.

# 18

# "We Don't Know Where
# You Are Going"

*Teaching the Disciples the Way*

**John 13:31–14:31**

**A. Chiasm:**

　　a: 13:33–14:4: commandments, not hearts be troubled, *monai*

　　　b: 5–14: I am in the Father

　　　　c: 15–17: paraclete

　　　b¹: 18–20: I am in the Father

　　a¹: 21–31: commandments, not hearts be troubled, *monēn*[1]

**B. Location:** unspecified

**C. Time:** near Passover

**D. Social factors:** community faith in Jesus' absence

**E. Themes:** sending of paraclete; the nature of love

**F. Key words:** dwelling(s) (*monai*), paraclete/holy spirit, commandment

## 1. THE INTRICATE INTERWEAVING OF THEMES

With the advent of night, the Last Supper discourse enters a new phase. The "action," such as it has been, is over. Now, the soon to be glorified Jesus teaches his disciples — and all who are called to follow throughout the ages — the lessons required to live a life of communal love in a hostile world of hatred and persecution.

---

1. Ellis (1984, 216–217).

Although we have become familiar as we have journeyed through the fourth gospel with the Johannine style of repetition and interwoven themes, this literary art form reaches its climax in the remaining chapters of the Last Supper discourse. It is a subtle ballet that connects the major themes into a unified message of hope:

1. the commandment to love one another ("bearing fruit"; "laying down life")
2. the unity of Father, Son, and disciples ("remaining"; being "one"/"in"; not being "alone"/"orphans")
3. asking in Jesus' name
4. Jesus' departure ("a little while"; "going to Father"; "going away")
5. the paraclete ("spirit of truth"; "holy spirit")
6. the disciples' mission ("I send them")
7. the hostility of the world ("hate"; "persecution"; the disciples' "hour"; labor pains)
8. God's ultimate victory ("joy"; "glory"; "judgment" on world)

This web of themes is woven with overlapping chiasms, where the beginning and end of one come in the midst of others, just as the disciples' mission begins partly while Jesus is still in the world but continues after he has returned to the Father. The combination of the usual linear structure with more "spiral" elements replicates the path of discipleship, as growth in knowledge of God, the world, and one another takes two steps forward and one back, one sideways, and haltingly moves forward again.

## 2. ASKING QUESTIONS:
## DARING TO STATE COMMUNITY NEEDS

### Chiasm: 13:34–14:15

a: 13:34–35: love/commandment

   b: 13:36–14:4: Peter says, "Lord"; lack of faith

      c: 14:5–7: I AM the way, truth, life

   b¹: 14:8–14: Philip says, "Lord"; lack of faith

a¹: 15: love; commandment

Although verses 31–32 were listed in the previous chapter as the end of the chiasm that began in 13:1 because of the parallel between Jesus' return to the Father and his "glory," it is clear from a narrative point of view that the departure of Judas and the arrival of night signal a new stage and a new scene. R. Alan Culpepper and others have argued for treating 13:1–38 as a single passage, which may help the reader link the two discussions between Peter and

Jesus.[2] Although Culpepper somewhat arbitrarily divides verses 1–38 into six units,[3] one might approach the section chiastically as follows:

a: 1–11: Jesus will give up his life; Peter questions his role and reveals his ignorance

b: 12–20: as I have done, so you should do for one another

c: 21–30: the betrayal and lack of intimacy in the community

b¹: 31–35: love one another as I have loved you

a¹: 36–38: Peter offers to give up his life; Jesus questions Peter's role and reveals Peter's ignorance

It is unreasonable to claim that one perspective or another on the organization of the Last Supper discourse is "right" or "wrong," as the text supports many different structural lenses.[4] I have chosen the breakdown I have primarily because seeing 13:1–38 as a unit leaves us to consider a new section beginning at 14:1, which, if not for the artificial division of chapters, contains no narrative signals marking a new unit. But I heartily encourage readers to consider these questions for themselves and see if they discern a different pattern altogether.

Thus, we continue with verse 31, which the narrator introduces by emphasizing that the betrayer had "gone out" (*exēlthen*). As the chapter began with the narrator's remark that Jesus had "come out [*exēlthen*] from God" (13:3), so now Judas goes out from Jesus, but to do Satan's work, not God's. And as Judas goes out "at once" (*euthys*), so now Jesus is glorified "at once" (*euthys*). The contrast underscores both the different "fundamental option" that each one takes and the cause-and-effect relationship between them. Jesus' knowledge of his relationship with God leads him to give the morsel to Judas to set the devil's work in motion, and Judas's departure leads to the glorification of both God and the Human One.

Jesus begins his "post-Judas" teaching with a cascade of glory: "Now the Human One is glorified, and God is glorified in him, and God will glorify him in himself, and will glorify him at once." The sentence exemplifies the discourse's style of expressing unity by overlapping personhood and time. It is almost impossible to sort out the acts and objects of glory between the Human One and God. Further, the Greek contains an even more complex time relationship than most English translations. The sentence literally begins with a temporal paradox: *nyn edoxasthē,* "now was glorified." The end is almost as mysterious: *euthys doxasei,* "at once will glorify." To swirl time and glory around a bit more, we recall the previous statement about the imminence of Jesus' glory in 12:23, 28:

---

2. Culpepper (1990).

3. Ibid., 134.

4. Segovia (1991a) surveys the attempts and offers his own painstaking effort at discerning the structure of the discourse, but in the end he is no more convincing, perhaps even to himself, in characterizing his book as "a reading" (p. 328). It is odd that Segovia, a self-proclaimed liberation theologian committed to the importance of social location for interpretation, expressly brackets out the implications of his own social location in offering his reading of John 13–16.

> The hour has come that the Human One might be
> glorified [*doxasthē*].
> I glorified [*edoxasa*] and again I will glorify [*doxasō*].

Without delving into the intricacies of Greek grammar, one can see that several different tenses of the verb *doxazō* have been mixed up with the time-markers "now," "at once," and "the hour has come." Given the highly abstract nature of the term "glory" in the first place, how can we make sense of these various signals? What is the text trying to communicate to us with this confusing rhetoric?

One basic pattern between both 12:23, 28 and 13:31 is the idea that two different occasions of glory are being described, one noted in the story world as completed and one about to take place. The four verbs in 13:31 form two pairs: *edoxasthē* ("was glorified," twice) and *doxasei* ("will glorify," twice). This parallels the usage in 12:28 noted above. The second point is that, within the story world, the two moments are not far apart, as indicated by "at once." If we can think of the darkness falling in two moments — the acceptance of the morsel and the going out "at once" — then the light similarly is glorified in the two moments of Jesus' death and resurrection. Jesus will "leave the world" in the first moment of glory, on the cross. Then he will "go to the Father" "at once" in the second moment of glory, the resurrection. Although the narrator will tell us that it was the "first day of the week" when Mary Magdalene discovers the empty tomb, the third day since the crucifixion (20:1), nowhere does the fourth gospel suggest that it took three days for Jesus to rise. In this gospel's theology, death and resurrection is a continuous movement, even if it takes three days for Jesus' disciples to recover enough from the shock of his death to go to his tomb.

Thus, at the very outset of the nighttime discourse, Jesus has told his disciples, albeit in highly coded language, that his death will not be the conclusion of the story, for him or for them. The remainder of the discourse involves Jesus' struggle to get this message across and the disciples' struggle to come to grips with the way in which this truth will be revealed.

As Jesus has spoken of his filial relationship with God, so in verse 33 he transfers that image to the relationship between himself and the disciples: "Little children, yet a little time [*mikron*] am I with you." It is a tender title with which Jesus addresses those gathered with him at supper, the only time in the fourth gospel he calls them this (cf. 21:5, "children"). While the synoptics speak of children frequently, even putting them at the center of the community (e.g., Mk 10:13–15), the fourth gospel has, up to this point, been largely a text for and about adults. However, the image of adults-as-children has been a focal point of the Johannine call since the prologue's central proclamation about receiving "authority to become God's children" (1:12). To be born *anōthen* is to become a new child. These infants in "the Way" are named as such by their "father," as Jesus teaches them what they need to know to go out into the world. It is a phrase that 1 John will pick up and use seven times in its short span of five chapters, suggesting that it became an important symbol for the relationship between master and disciple within the Johannine community.

The *mikron* within which Jesus will continue to be with the disciples echoes prophetic images of the approach of God's moment of salvation. For example, in Isa 10:25, 27, we hear:

> In a very little while [LXX, *mikron*] my indignation will come to an end, and my anger will be directed to their destruction.... On that day his [the king of Assyria's] burden will be removed from your shoulder, and his yoke will be destroyed from your neck.

And in Jer 51:33:

> Daughter Babylon is like a threshing floor at the time
>     when it is trodden;
> yet a little while [LXX, *mikron*] and the time of her
>     harvest will come.

Thus, while the disciples may be hearing only the frightening fact of their Lord's imminent absence, the deeper message is of their impending release from bondage.

But after this hidden hope is expressed, Jesus goes on to associate them with a group that has otherwise been the antithesis of the discipleship community Jesus seeks to form: "You will seek me, and as I said to the Judeans, 'Where I am going you are not able to come,' so I say to you now." To "seek" Jesus has been associated with the conspiracy against him (5:18; 7:1, 11; etc.), especially in the Tabernacles context to which Jesus expressly refers (7:34). Could he possibly be suggesting that the disciples are of the same mind-set as the Judeans? Why else would he specifically say that his words to them are the same as his words to the Judeans? The image the remark leaves behind is of disciples and Judeans both seeking Jesus but being unable to find him. Perhaps the sense is that even though the disciples' intention is not the same as the Judeans', the result of Jesus' going will be the same for both: bewildered inability to achieve the goal. Both his enemies and his friends will have to continue without his physical presence. For the Johannine community two generations later, this had been their lifetime experience, as synagogue and Christian community continued their search for Jesus but could not go where he is.

How much consolation is there for the disciples when Jesus in verse 34 gives them "a new commandment: that you love one another. As I loved you, so should you love one another"? For the second time, Jesus has turned from his relationship with them to their relationship with "one another." Footwashing and love are their communal responsibility, both of which Jesus has modeled for them. They have just been informed that there was a betrayer in their midst — only the Beloved Disciple knows who it is — and yet they are commanded to love one another! How can they love people whom they are not sure they can trust? What does it mean in practice to love those among us whom we don't really "know"?

If any of these questions can be imagined to be passing through the disciples' minds, Jesus clarifies in verse 35 that the purpose of the commandment is not so much consolation as evangelization: "In this they will all know that you are my disciples: if you have love for one another." Although the sentiment of this famous line has often been trivialized in our world, where "love" is thrown around on Hallmark cards and as a description of our feelings about food or cars, it bears the core challenge to the churches. For all the missionary efforts of two thousand years of Christianity, whether the violence of the Crusades and conquistadores or the hard sell of today's television preachers and Bible beaters, no "strategy" would be as successful in bringing people within Jesus' sheepfold as the concrete witness of communities of mutual love. How ironic it is that the fourth gospel in particular has been used more than the synoptics as a basis for anti-Semitism, "born-again" religious imperialism, and other vicious and destructive campaigns against those who, for whatever reasons, have not felt called to follow Jesus!

Perhaps the problem lies in part in the fact that many Christians, like Simon Peter in verse 36, have so focused on the logistics of heaven that they have not heard the commandment. When Peter asks his question, "Lord, where are you going?" it is clear that his attention became stuck on the prospect of losing his master rather than learning what he should be doing to follow. Therefore, Jesus' answer is not so much a prohibition as a description of Peter's state of spiritual awareness: "Where I am going, you are not able to follow me now, but you will follow later." As Culpepper puts it, "He cannot follow — that is, he cannot discharge his duty as a disciple — because he does not understand the meaning of Jesus' death."[5]

Despite the centrality of the image of "following" to the practice of discipleship, it has actually been only rarely used in the fourth gospel (1:43; 10:4, 5, 27; 12:26) and occurs only once more after this scene, where it is used three times in four verses (21:19–22). That Peter accepts its importance but is not ready to live the call is underscored in verses 37–38. Peter does not know why he cannot follow but seems to understand that following has something to do with laying down his life, which he offers to do for Jesus' sake. And yet at this point in the narrative, the association suggests a misunderstanding of the good shepherd discourse, in which Jesus spoke of the *shepherd* laying down his life for the sheep, but the sheep as the ones who are to *follow*.

More importantly, Peter does not know himself, as Jesus embarrassingly notes in verse 38 for all the disciples to hear: "Will you lay down your life for me? Amen, amen I am saying to you: a cock will surely not crow until you have denied [*arnēsē*] me three times." The tradition of Jesus' prediction of Peter's denial is very strong, for the verb used here is not found elsewhere in the fourth gospel and is used in the synoptics almost exclusively for Peter's denial

---

5. Culpepper (1990, 147).

of Jesus and Jesus' challenge to his followers to deny themselves. In the Johannine context, it completes the circle of ignorance: the disciples do not know the betrayer, they do not know each other, and Peter does not know himself!

As a matter of characterization and plot, it is the second time in thirty verses where Peter has made a fool of himself in front of his fellow disciples and the third time he has shown that he does not know what is going on. While even the synoptics portray a pompous Peter whose balloon Jesus repeatedly pops, the Johannine juxtaposition of Peter with the Beloved Disciple gives this particular scene a connotation of criticism of the apostolic churches, founded on Peter. As the gospel continues, this characterization of the lead "apostle" will grow steadily more cartoonish, which must have provided a bit of satirical relief to a Johannine community struggling to discern its relationship with other, more "mainstream" Christian communities.

From a scenic perspective, we might imagine Peter first leaping forward to proclaim his allegiance and then shrinking back as Jesus makes his solemn double-amen proclamation. It should not surprise us that Peter has nothing more to say during the Last Supper discourse! The time for bravado is long past. What is required is attention to Jesus' words and a willingness to obey his commandments.

How the other disciples reacted to Peter's comeuppance is not recorded, but we might infer a hint of it from Jesus' words to them in 14:1: "Do not let your [plural] heart be troubled [*tarassesthō*]." Raymond Brown points out that the Greek text follows Hebrew and Aramaic practice, in contrast with normal Greek grammar, in treating the community's heart as a single entity.[6] Despite the insistence of some commentators on the supposed "individualism" of the fourth gospel on the basis of its many one-on-one conversations between Jesus and his disciples, the text could hardly emphasize more strongly the communal nature of discipleship. In this instance, it takes the form of speaking to the "heart" of the community.

As Jesus was "troubled" at the absence of faith at Lazarus' tomb (11:33), the arrival of his own "hour" (12:26), and the consideration of Judas' imminent betrayal (13:21), now the same emotion is found in the heart of the Johannine community. But Jesus urges them past this deep feeling by exhorting them to "believe in God and believe in me." Although it may appear to us a trite remark, in the gospel context it summons them to put in perspective the smallness of their "troubles" in the face of God's power in Jesus to overcome the darkness. As Mark has Jesus say nearly the same thing to the disciples in the face of the prospect of the collapse of the Temple (Mk 11:21–22), so the Johannine Jesus urges the disciples not to fear even the prospect of Peter's denial.

As another promise of hope, Jesus offers them this image in verse 2: "In my Father's house, there are many dwellings [*monai*]. If there were not, I would have told you, because I am going to prepare a place [*topon*] for you." The individualistic approach to the fourth gospel has traditionally heard this statement as

---

6. R. Brown (1970, 618).

if Jesus were promising each disciple a separate heavenly hotel suite. However, a closer look will reveal a meaning much more in harmony with the context of the Last Supper discourse, which is focused not on "heaven" but on the mission of the disciples in the world.

"My Father's house," has, of course, been used previously to refer to the Jerusalem Temple (2:16). By the time of the Johannine community, this physical entity was a pile of rubble, and certainly Jesus cannot be making reference to the disciples' finding a home there. As we have heard, the "house of God" — that is, the place of true worship (see 4:20–24) — is not a building but a *relationship* among those who hear God and do God's will. Jesus has systematically dismantled the symbolic structure upon which the Temple-state rested, replacing purification jars with footwashing, the Temple with his own body, Moses' manna with Jesus' flesh and blood, Tabernacles with his own living water and light of the world, and so on. Now, "my Father's house" is transformed from the Temple building to the *Christian community,* the place in which worshipers gather "in spirit and truth."

The word translated as "dwellings," *monai,* comes from a secular Greek term for a traveler's temporary resting spot, a place to go at night.[7] Far from the older English connotation of "mansion," *monai* were places of comfort in the dark, where one might find communal welcoming and a meal. Putting these ideas together, we find that Jesus may be telling the Johannine community that in the Christian family, there are many places of welcome, many house churches, a variety of acceptable forms of community. That is, in spite of the hostility and misunderstanding the Johannine community may feel from the apostolic churches, there is room for their own style of shared life. Each of these is but a temporary stop on the journey to God that Jesus is taking now but the disciples are unable to do just yet. Even the Johannine ideal is but a short-term goal, for eventually Jesus will "receive you to myself, so that where I am, you also may be" (verse 3).

The promise to "prepare a place" in verses 2 and 3 echoes Moses' own farewell discourse in the Septuagint version of Deut 1:33:

> . . . the Lord our God, who goes before you in the way [*hodō*] to choose a place [*topon*], guiding you in fire by night, showing you the way [*hodon*] by which you go, and a cloud by day.

As God empowered Moses to lead the twelve tribes into the Promised Land to become a single people, so God empowered Jesus to lead the various discipleship communities into a shared place in God's "house." And as the Deuteronomic text describes God showing the people "the way," so Jesus for the only time in the fourth gospel turns to speak of "the way" in verse 4: "And where I am going, you [plural] have known the way [*hodon*]." It is another traveler's image, reinforcing the sense of *monai* as temporary stops that provide

---

7. F. Hauck, *TDNT* 4:577.

rest until the community is reunited with Jesus after death. For the Torah, the Promised Land is the final destination. It is the basis for many Zionist views of Israel to this day, which has led to untold misery for Jews and Arabs alike as the unending battle for a patch of land continues to shed blood and tears. For the fourth gospel, the earthly goal is but a stop along the way, for the Christian community is not to focus on building a sacred place or nation but on establishing a living channel of love between heaven and earth.

Pathetically, all of this is lost for the moment on the disciples, or at least on Thomas, who voices the sad plaint in verse 5: "Lord, we don't know where you are going — how can we know the way?" Thomas, unlike Peter, reveals his ignorance in the first-person plural. Whether it is because of a greater sense of community or a lesser willingness to be vulnerable and claim his own thoughts and feelings, we cannot be sure. Thomas, we recall, is the disciple who urged his fellows to go with Jesus to Jerusalem to "die with him" (11:16). He seemed to know *then* where Jesus was going! But "the Way" is completely lost to him now. Given the use of the term "the way" in the early churches as a general metaphor for discipleship (Acts 9:2; 18:25), Thomas's "confession" could not be more plain. They have been watching Jesus do his Father's work but have not yet caught on to what it means for them when he is gone. For that matter, the reality that he is leaving has not sunk in either. Isn't the messiah supposed to "remain" — or at least get rid of the Romans first? All Jesus seems to have done is put himself in the jaws of death and drag his disciples behind him into the same sharp teeth!

With this confusion prevailing, Jesus in verse 6 tries another image to get his message across: "I AM the way and the truth and the life — no one is coming to the Father except through me." The way of Jesus *is* Jesus, just as "munching" his "flesh" is necessary to having life (6:53). Whether in contrast with the Hebrew tradition that referred to the Torah as "the way" (e.g., Ps 119:29–34) or the Qumran community that spoke of its own interpretation of Torah as "the way,"[8] for the Johannine community, the path is a person, not a doctrine or set of laws.

Jesus has spoken many times about speaking the truth or worshiping in spirit and truth, but only the prologue has suggested that he *embodies* truth (1:14, 17). The third element has been expressed before, in the previous *egō eimi* statement in 11:25, "I AM the resurrection and the life." But we should not allow our Western, analytical mind-sets to control our interpretation of these three attributes as distinct and separable. Jesus states them as a single reality: I AM=way=truth=life. It is more of a mantra than a theological proposition, something for the disciples and readers to meditate on and ponder in their hearts.

The immediate emphasis, though, is on Jesus as the self-revelation of God, which he puts to them in verse 7: "If you had known me, you also would have known my Father. From now on, you are knowing him and you have seen."

---

8. 1QS 8.12–16.

The first part tells the disciples plainly what readers have already figured out: that the disciples do *not* know Jesus. Even at this point in Jesus' systematic exposing of the disciples' ignorance and fears, it is a shocking statement. What have they been doing all this time if not getting to know the one they are following, whom some acclaimed at the beginning as "messiah" and "king of Israel"? They are revealed as hardly different in awareness from the Judeans, just as blind as the roadside beggar. And yet they *are* still with him. For the fourth gospel, this is practically the only distinction between Jesus' friends and enemies: while remaining an enigma to all, his friends at least have chosen to follow rather than exhibit the all-too-human tendency to destroy what they don't understand.

But *now,* Jesus tells them, they *are* knowing and seeing the Father in Jesus. What has happened between verse 7a and 7b to provide this sudden consciousness? Or is the "now" the broader moment of the Last Supper discourse, in which Jesus teaches them what they need to know? Or is the "now" the reading moment of either the Johannine community or modern readers who share in the benefits of intervening history and faith experience?

Lest we imagine an epiphany taking place before the disciples' eyes, Philip's demand in verse 8 bursts that bubble completely: "Lord, show us the Father, and it is enough [*arkei*] for us." In a subtle bit of ironic characterization, we find that Philip's last recorded statement was also about getting "enough": "Two hundred denarii in loaves is not enough [*arkousin*] for them" (6:7). First concerned with an earthly "enough" and now with a heavenly "enough," Philip has not perceived that Jesus *himself* is enough to satisfy both kinds of need.

Once again, we find a named disciple speaking in the plural. One might imagine that while Jesus is speaking, the disciples are busily talking to one another, trying desperately to figure out what he means. In that case, they are much like the Judeans, who "dialogued among themselves" (6:52) to discern the mystery of munching flesh. On the other hand, the gap in description might also be filled by picturing Philip speaking amidst a silent and befuddled group, offering a plural demand to hide his own vulnerable ignorance. In either case, it is a sad testimony that even one disciple who has been with Jesus since the start has not understood the central reality of the Word made flesh.

Jesus expresses his own exasperation to this effect in verse 9, wrapping the straightforward declaration in critical rhetorical sentences: "So much time I am with you people and you have not known me, Philip? The one seeing me has seen the Father. How are you saying, 'Show us the Father'?" Jesus' words emphasize Philip's unique limitation by directing his answer to him by name and in singular verbs. Another disciple finds himself wanting to slink under the table in embarrassment! He continues with this one-on-one challenge in 10a: "Are you [singular] not believing that I am in the Father and the Father is in me?" Throughout the gospel, we have been left wondering whether the disciples were even present during the confrontations between Jesus and the Judeans, in particular during the "trials" of chapters 5 and 7–8 and the speech to the "Pharisees who were with him" in chapter 10. Philip's ignorance is possible evidence of his previous absence. Otherwise, how do we explain his failure to understand such clear statements as "the Father and I are one" (10:30)?

But beneath the frustration, Jesus remains the patient teacher and continues to speak to the group of disciples about the relationship that they have not perceived. His relationship with his people in this manner parallels the pattern of God's patience with Israel, despite the recurrent covenant breaking that Israel exhibited. Once again, he shifts images, this time focusing on the relationship between faith and "works." Verses 10b–12 reveal a "downward" movement that culminates with a surprise:

> (1) The sayings I tell you I am not saying from myself, but the *Father* who remains in me is *doing his works. Believe me* that I am in the Father and the Father is in me; (2) but if not, *believe through the works.* (3) Amen, amen I say to you, the *one believing in me, the works I am doing that one will also do, and will do greater than these,* because I am going to the Father.

Jesus starts by telling them that his words equal the *Father's works,* and they should believe this. Next, he turns to *his own works,* which they should believe even if they cannot believe simply on the basis of his words. Finally, he turns to the *disciples' works,* which, startlingly, he tells them will be "greater than these" if they believe in him. Statements (1) and (2) contain things that readers have heard before, even if the disciples have not. In fact, the particular exhortation to believe in Jesus' works to understand the unity of Father and Son, even if one cannot believe in Jesus' words, was heard in 10:37–38, the same speech that would have taught Philip that "the Father and I are one." Whether as repetition or as a first-time declaration to his disciples, Jesus speaks to them just as he spoke to the "Pharisees who were with him," reinforcing the parallel between the disciples in 9:1–5 and the Pharisees in 9:40–41. Both groups who wished to distance themselves from those who are blind are equally in the dark. But in spite of all this, the result of faith — if they can muster it — is to do works "greater" than those of Jesus! What possible greater works are left to do? Jesus has healed the sick, given sight to the blind, and raised the dead. He has overturned the Temple tables, replaced the entire spectrum of Judean rituals, and spoken truth to power. He has broken open the bounds of "God's people" to include Samaritans and Greeks. The one work he has not done yet is *to establish a continuing community of faith to follow in his footsteps* when he has departed. At Jesus' death, there will be few left, and even after his resurrection, the disciples remain scattered and scared. It will be *their* job to reap the harvest (4:38). By the time of the gospel, of course, this "greater" work was already partly in the past, although the long-term existence of the Johannine community and the wider Christian family remained in great doubt. This is indeed a greater work than any individual healing or short-term institutional challenge, for it is the necessary step in assuring that Jesus' life and teaching will be remembered.

To assure them that they have the authority to accomplish this work, Jesus gives them in verses 13–14 one of the strongest promises in the fourth gospel, repeated twice and wrapped around the reason for its giving in a minichiasm:

> Whatever you ask in my name, this I will do,
> so that the Father might be glorified in the Son.
> Whatever you ask in my name, this I will do.

It introduces a theme that will recur five more times in the Last Supper discourse: asking in Jesus' name. As Brown points out, it is not a matter of a magic talisman, but that the "Christian prays in Jesus' name in the sense that he is in union with Jesus."[9] To ask in Jesus' name is to ask what Jesus would ask, to think like Jesus thinks, just as he does what he sees the Father doing. What a triviality this profound challenge has been reduced to by fundamentalists and others who imagine that simply saying the word "Jesus" will get them whatever they want! We are often distracted from daring to ask in Jesus' name by the obscenity of prayers in Jesus' name for winning the lottery, for victory in football or war, or for similar culturally encouraged goals. What have we witnessed Jesus praying for? That those "standing around" would "believe that you sent me" (11:42) and that God's name be glorified through Jesus' faithfulness in the "hour" (12:28). The purpose of the promise is precisely this, that "the Father may be glorified in the Son." But to align their wills with the will of Jesus in this way, they (and we) need help. It is just the provision of this help to which Jesus now turns.

### 3. NOT LEAVING THEM ORPHANS: THE PROMISE OF THE PARACLETE

**Chiasm: 14:15–21a**

a: 15: love/commandments

   b: 16–17: behold/spirit remains/is with you/know

      c: 18: not leave you orphans

   $b^1$: 19–20: behold/Jesus lives/is in you/know

$a^1$: 21a: commandments/love

**Chiasm: 14:16–26**

a: 16–18: paraclete/spirit of truth

   b: 19–21: keep my commandments; loves me, loved by Father, Jesus loves

      c: 22: Judas: show yourself

   $b^1$: 23–24: keep my word; Father loves, not love me

$a^1$: 25–26: paraclete/holy spirit

---

9. R. Brown (1970, 636).

**Chiasm: 14:21–31**

a: 21: keep my commandments; loved by Father, Jesus loves disciples

  b: 22–24: Judas's question; not my word but Father's

    c: 25–27: paraclete; peace as gifts from Jesus

  b¹: 28–30: answer to Judas's question; Father is greater than I

a¹: 31: I am doing Father's commandment; Jesus loves the Father

As one can see from the overlapping chiasms listed above, the remainder of chapter 14 forms a unified fabric that highlights three things: the gift of the paraclete so that the disciples will not be left orphans, the question of why the disciples are in a privileged position vis-à-vis the world, and the gift of Jesus' peace. Throughout, the unifying force is love.

Just as Jesus will do whatever is asked in his name, so he places in verse 15 a reciprocal responsibility on those who do the asking: "If you love me, you will keep [*tērēsete*] my commandments." He loves them, so he will do what they ask; if they love him, they will do what he asks. Jesus' "commandment" was clearly stated in 13:34, to love one another as he has loved them. But now, he speaks in the plural of *commandments.* Nowhere in the fourth gospel has Jesus given nor will he give any more commandments. Why, then, is the call to loving obedience stated in the plural, as it will be again on the other side of the small chiasm in verse 21? Perhaps it is because in the model of Moses' farewell discourse comprising the book of Deuteronomy, he speaks of "keeping the commandments" over thirty times! In particular, Moses three times associates loving God with keeping God's commandments (5:10, 7:9, 11:1). Thus, even if Jesus' "torah" can be reduced to a single precept, the covenant between him and those who love him is stated in Mosaic terms.

The notion of "keeping" or observing (*tēreo*) has come up five times before but will be used eleven more times in the Last Supper discourse, always in reference to commandments or one's word. It bears the sense of religious observance and, in looking back, shows the battle of myths engaged in struggling to decide what is to be "kept." In 2:10, the theme was "keeping" the good wine until now: the new commandment has been reserved in the wine cellar! At Tabernacles, Jesus first raised the issue of keeping his or God's word (8:51, 55). Jesus was accused through the witness of the once-blind man of not keeping the sabbath (9:16). Finally, Mary was praised for "keeping" the perfumed oil for the day of Jesus' burial (12:7). All of these "keepings" coalesce in the single commandment to love one another with God's own love.

Such a commandment would be impossible to keep were it not for the gift that Jesus now promises in verses 16–17:

> I will pray to the Father, and he will give you another paraclete, to be with you forever, the spirit of the truth, which the world is not able to receive, because it is not seeing it or knowing it; you are knowing it, because it is remaining with you and is in you.

Amazingly, this central gift of the fourth gospel is not mentioned anywhere else in the New Testament, not even in 1 John, which uses the term "paraclete" expressly to refer to Jesus himself. Where does this idea come from and why is it introduced at this crucial moment in the Last Supper discourse?

The word *paraklētos* is not found in the Septuagint at all, but the verbs *paraklēsis* and *parakaleō* are used primarily for the Hebrew term *hacham,* meaning "to comfort."[10] The contexts of this sense of comfort are many but focus especially on mourning a death or absence. In nonbiblical ancient sources, those who are dying provide comfort to survivors through parting words or writings about themselves.[11]

Several Hebrew scripture passages provide illuminating background for the use of *paraklētos* in the fourth gospel. For example, in the book of Job, we find both criticism of ineffective comfort and this metaphor for good comfort: "I lived like a king among his troops, like one who comforts [*hacham*] mourners" (Job 29:25). A famous passage in a context not unlike the Last Supper discourse is Ps 23:4:

> Even though I walk through the valley of the shadow of
> death,
> I fear no evil for you are with me.
> Your rod and your staff — they comfort [*hacham*] me.

Similar is Ps 86:17:

> Show me a sign of your favor,
> so that those who hate me may see it and be put to
> shame,
> because you, Lord, have helped me and comforted
> [*hacham*] me.

Thus, the Hebrew scriptures put trust in God to comfort but do not refer to God as a *paraklētos.* That term comes from the secular Greek context of one who helps in court, which was adapted by both rabbinical writings and Philo to mean an *advocate* before God.[12] This sense rather than "comforter" also fits well with the alternative title provided in Jn 14:16, "the spirit of the truth." The similar phrase "spirit of truth" was a common one in Qumran documents for the angelic figure who would lead Israel's final battle against the prince of darkness.[13] The fourth gospel combines these various notions into a single figure, the *paraklētos,* who both comforts and advocates, who defends and leads the battle, on behalf of Jesus' disciples.

But Jesus says that he will pray to the Father for *"another* paraclete." If the one to come is at least the second, the first can only be Jesus, the one who

---

10. O. Schmitz, *TDNT* 5:793–799.
11. G. Stählin, *TDNT* 5:779–788.
12. J. Behm, *TDNT* 5:800–814.
13. A. R. C. Leaney, in Charlesworth (1990, 43–44).

has gone to battle for them in the court of the Judeans and Pharisees. He has comforted them so far, but another will comfort them after he returns to the Father. This one is not simply *a* spirit but is "*the* spirit of *the* truth." In Johannine ideology, there is only one spirit of one truth, just as there is one messiah and one Human One.

It should not surprise us to hear that the world neither sees nor knows this spirit, given the darkness in which the world stumbles along its path. But it *is* surprising to hear that, given their carefully and clearly revealed ignorance, the disciples "know" it already, because "it is remaining and is in you." At first, Jesus speaks of something he will do in the future, but by the end of the sentence, it is accomplished! It is an example of the several simultaneous temporal perspectives of the Last Supper discourse, which can describe Jesus' lifetime, the time of the Johannine community, and the unfolding future of readers of the fourth gospel all at once.

At the center of the 14:15–21 chiasm lies the reason for this powerful promise: "I will not leave you orphans: I am coming to you." Although none of the disciples has been vulnerable enough to say it directly, Jesus' speech indicates that their primary concern is that he will leave them alone in a hostile world. Peter's desire to follow, Thomas's ignorance of Jesus' destination and the way, Philip's request to see the Father, all express indirectly their fears, which will be named by the narrator as they huddle beind locked doors after Jesus' death (20:19, 26). But Jesus promises that they will have a new paraclete *and* that they will "see me, because I live and you will live" (verse 19). The world will see neither, but the disciples will "know" the paraclete and "see" Jesus. Despite their limitations and doubts, Jesus, the divine comforter, gives them assurances that will guide them through the dark days ahead.

The switch from the paraclete to Jesus also involves a subtle switch in time: the paraclete they know and have *now*, but Jesus they "*will* see." This difference is highlighted at the beginning of verse 20, with the first of three instances in the fourth gospel of the phrase "in that day." In the Hebrew scriptures, the term is used hundreds of times for the moment of God's powerful actions, for better or worse, in Israel. In the fourth gospel, it carries the meaning of the moment of definitive understanding of Jesus' life and message, the day on which "you will know that I am in my Father and you in me and I in you."

For the first time, Jesus tells the disciples that their relationship with him is identical to that of Jesus with his Father. Some consider the Johannine Jesus to be portrayed with a "high christology" that emphasizes Jesus' divinity, but we must also consider it to have a "high humanity," or at least a "high discipleship." Whether as a matter of essential unity or functional activity, those who believe in Jesus are empowered to do what Jesus does and be where Jesus is. It is very important to note that this assurance is given *collectively*, not individually. Jesus is "in" the Johannine community, just as is the paraclete. All of the statements in verses 15–20 are addressed to a collective "you."

If we do not pay attention to this feature of the discourse, we will miss the change that takes place in verse 21, which is addressed to individuals: "The one who has my commandments and keeps them is the one loving me; the one loving me will be loved by my Father, and I will love that one and will reveal myself to that one." Johannine love is both collective and individual but is primarily an aspect of the communal life.

The second half of verse 21 expresses an idea that many Christians may at first glance find disturbing: the Father's and Jesus' love comes to those who love Jesus. It is *not necessarily* universal *or* unconditional but is an aspect of *mutuality* in relationship. Love that finds no reciprocity is not love in the Johannine sense. Although we heard that "God so loved the world that he gave his only Son" (3:16), that act is completed and past. Whether God *still* loves the world is a gap that the fourth gospel does not fill. In fact, one can read the phrase in 5:42, "You people [the Judeans] do not have the love of God in you," as pointing to not simply the Judeans' lack of love but also the *absence of God's love* in them. The sequence seems to run like this: God *did* love the world, and gave his Son. *Now,* God and the Son await the love of those who have been empowered to become God's children, and *will* love them. *To these,* Jesus will be revealed. The event of the incarnation has changed forever the relationship between humanity and divinity. From now on, God's love is a response, not an initiative. The fact that God first calls or "draws" people (6:44; 12:32) does not necessarily imply the gift of love.

The talk of unity and love is not as interesting to the disciples, at least to the "other" Judas, as is the mystery of "insider" revelation. In verse 22, we hear from a character nowhere else mentioned in the fourth gospel, named negatively as "Judas, not Iscariot." This may or not be the Judas referred to in the synoptics as Judas son of James (Mt 13:55; Lk 6:3). For the fourth gospel, the focus is simply on differentiating him from the infamous Judas whose characterization has, to this day, removed the appellation from the general lot of male names.

His question focuses on the need to figure out why the disciples are apparently being offered a special revelation: "Lord, what has happened that you are going to reveal yourself to us and not to the world?" Given the general lack of awareness of Jesus' destination among those gathered, it seems likely that Judas's inquiry shows his expectation of something like the synoptic Transfiguration, a dazzling vision that will provide certainty and hope. But we readers know that Jesus' revelation is his glorification, that is, his being "lifted up" on the cross. The disciples will see this event *as* a revelation: it will eventually teach them what it means to be God's messiah, the one sent forth. To the world, which does not see the spirit of truth, the event is just another execution, a regrettable but necessary disposal of a dangerous, self-proclaimed prophet whose presence is a risk to nation and empire (11:50). Jesus has already told Judas the answer to the question: only those who keep the commandments and therefore are themselves revealed to be lovers of Jesus will understand the cross in the way Jesus does.

Although the narrator's introduction in verse 23 suggests that Jesus' subsequent words are an "answer" to the question, the specific response to the "what has happened" part is delayed so that Jesus can continue to focus on what he wants to tell them. First, Judas's question assumes that "us" comprises the bounds of the inside group, an assumption that Jesus refutes immediately: "If *anyone* is loving me, they will keep my word, and the Father will love that one." Although Jesus was specifically addressing "you" in verses 15–20, Judas has missed the broader invitation of verse 21, which Jesus clarifies in verse 23. It is a warning against one of the creeping temptations of any religious group: to think that "we" are the elect, and "they" are the enemy, the lost, or the ignorant. As much as the fourth gospel emphasizes relationship and community, the boundaries of that community are not coterminous with those whom the disciples think are on the "inside."

Jesus continues by using another image to describe the loving unity of Father, Son, and disciple: "We will come and make our dwelling [*monēn*] with that one." As Jesus promised in 14:2 that there were many *monai* in his Father's house, now he brings even a deeper degree of intimacy to the relationship. If the "resting places" in verse 2 referred to the various Christian communities, now Jesus tells them that whoever keeps his word (*logon*) becomes a community of sorts from that very fact.[14] As the Word dwelt in Jesus, so the Father and Jesus together dwell in the believer, whose faith is evidenced by his or her practice of love. Thus, although it appears at one level to express an individualistic mysticism of God's indwelling in a person, the statement cannot be separated from the emphasis throughout the Last Supper discourse on the inherently communal nature of Jesus' "commandments" and "word." To Judas, though, it underscores Jesus' refutation of the assumption that God and Jesus will be found exclusively in the Johannine community.

The flip side of this is expressed in verse 24a: "The one not loving me is not keeping my words." It offers a practical principle for distinguishing insiders from outsiders. Just as Jesus told them that their mutual love will make them visible to all as his disciples (13:35), so now nondisciples are visible by their not keeping his words. Later, in 1 John, much use will be made of this principle when the community finds itself torn by internal dissension among those who are and those who are not keeping Jesus' words (e.g., 1 Jn 2:4–5). The principle is so important that Jesus emphasizes that it is not his word "you [plural] are hearing" but is from "the Father who sent me."

Jesus begins the central section of the 14:16–26 chiasm by providing a lynchpin for the fourth gospel's authoritative nature even when it contains reports and speeches not otherwise part of the Christian tradition. "These things [*tauta*] I have said to you while I am remaining with you; but the paraclete, the holy spirit which the Father will send in my name, that one will teach you all things [*panta*] and will remind [*hypomnēsei*] you of all things [*panta*] which I said to you." It is not difficult for us to imagine how the disciples during Jesus' lifetime did not "get" the message. Which one of us, without substantial immersion in the stories, poetry, and other elements of our tradition, would be able to make

---

14. Cf. Oliver and Van Aarde (1991, 398).

sense out of Jesus? Which of us, *even with* two thousand years of reflection behind us, can really claim to understand what Jesus wants us to know? For them and for us, Jesus promises that the paraclete will help by "teaching" and "reminding" us of "all things" that Jesus said.

To seek a handle on the implications of this promise leads us into a look at the difference in mind-sets between the ancient world and our own when it comes to attributing words or thoughts to someone. For us, a quotation is a "fact": either the person said it — and we can prove it by pointing to the specific tape transcript, writing, or personal knowledge of one who heard it — or the person did not. By putting words inside those little typographical marks, we associate them with the dichotomous notion of truth/untruth. If we have modified the original words, we call it a paraphrase or a summary and take the quote marks away. To do otherwise is to "lie," to engage in a morally repugnant behavior that gets journalists, historians, and other writers of "nonfiction" into serious ethical and professional trouble.

But the ancient world not only had no quote marks, it had no scruples against putting words into other people's mouths. An obvious example is the writing of Plato, "spoken" in the voice of Socrates, but clearly expressing the writer's philosophy through the *character* of the famous teacher. Similarly, noncanonical writings such as the so-called Pseudepigrapha are given that name precisely because they "falsely" give an epigraph that suggests a speaker or writer from a much earlier period. An important example of this is the book of 1 Enoch, which attributes its words to the descendant of Adam and Eve mentioned in Gen 5:24, even though it was not written until roughly the beginning of the Christian era.[15] It is not a matter of ancient people being more gullible than we "sophisticated" moderns (or ultrasophisticated "postmoderns") but of a different literary convention governing attribution. To speak in the voice of Enoch is to set the story being told in a particular viewpoint, one that has observed humankind since nearly the beginning of our history.

In a similar way, to speak in Jesus' voice is not so much to claim transcript-accurate reporting as it is to attribute to the speaker's way of thinking and acting all that is being said. We refer to this process theologically as *inspiration*: the ability of God to communicate God's thoughts through human agents. And very literally, this is what is being claimed in Jn 14:25–26: the holy spirit has taught and reminded the disciples of things Jesus said but of which they otherwise had no direct recollection. Whether or not Jesus physically voiced these words is not the point. Whether these words express what Jesus wanted his disciples to know is precisely the point.

The word used to describe the "reminding" part of this process is rare in the gospels, occurring only in Luke 22:61 to describe Peter's remembering of Jesus' prediction that the cock would crow. Otherwise in the New Testament, it is found only in the later writings (e.g., 2 Tim 2:14), suggesting that as the Christian communities grew and developed, they "remembered" teachings of

---

15. Charlesworth (1983, 6–8).

Jesus that helped in given situations but that had not been recorded up until that point. Such is exactly the situation of the Johannine community writing at least two generations after the first eyewitnesses. In this sense, the entire Last Supper discourse is a product of this reminding, which gives hope and courage to people in situations not faced directly by the communities of the earlier gospel writers and Pauline communities.

"The holy spirit" is used as a title for the paraclete only here in the fourth gospel, paralleling the title "spirit of truth" in 14:16. Although some scholars argue that the specificity of "*the* holy spirit" is a result of later editing,[16] as usual, we take the gospel as we have found it and accept the term as used in the text. It is important for now simply to note that we should not confuse later trinitarian doctrines about "the holy spirit" with what is being discussed in the fourth gospel. Jesus is clearly referring to an entity that *does not yet exist* at the moment being narrated. In 7:37–39, the narrator explained Jesus' statement about "living water" as referring to "the spirit which those who believed in him were about to receive, for as yet there was no spirit, because Jesus was not yet glorified." In Johannine thinking, the "Word" was there at "the beginning" to participate in creation, but "the spirit" comes to be as a result of Jesus' "glorification," that is, his death and resurrection. Under whatever name — paraclete, the spirit of truth, or the holy spirit — this "other" advocate comes to the disciples after Jesus is gone.

In verse 26, the masculine reference word *ekeinos* ("that one") replaces the more neutral reference in verse 16. The paraclete is now personalized, both positively as linked with Jesus' own (masculine) person, and negatively, as a divine being in battle with the demonic one whose presence will soon be announced, "the ruler of the world" (14:30).[17]

But in the meantime, in verse 27 Jesus leaves his disciples "peace." Although the Greek word *eirēnēn* certainly is intended to translate the Hebrew *shalom*, there is much more to Jesus' gift than simply the everyday offering that matches our "good-bye," with its root of "God-be-with-ye." *Shalom* is one of the richest concepts in Hebrew, giving expression to the yearning for ultimate totality and wholeness with self, creation, and God that is at the heart of human reality. The specific usage in Hebrew scripture associated God's gift of *shalom* with the messianic moment, the time of completion when the lion and lamb would lie down and swords would be turned into plowshares. An example is found in Zech 9:10:

And I will cut off the chariot from Ephraim, and the horse from Jerusalem. And the battle bow shall be cut off, and he shall speak peace [*shalom*] to the nations. And his dominion will be from sea to sea, and from the river to the ends of the earth.

---

16. E.g., Leaney, in Charlesworth (1990, 44–47). The issue arises from comparing the term in 20:22, which is the anarthrous "holy spirit" (*pneuma hagion*).

17. Draper (1992, 24).

This is the peace that people expected from the messiah — a peace clearly not experienced by the Johannine community or by ourselves. It was the failure of Jesus to bring this sort of peace that has led many Jews to this day to find the Christian claim that Jesus fulfilled the messianic expectation preposterous. What good is a messiah who does not end war and strife?

But as we know, Jesus' messiahship is grounded in very different expectations and practices. One earlier "messiah" in the literal sense of an anointed king of Israel who brought a sort of peace was Solomon. His reign is described as follows in 1 Kings 4:24: "For he had dominion in every region,... and he had peace [*shalom*] on all sides." But the surrounding verses tell how the king achieved this *shalom*: through forced tribute, slave labor, and "forty thousand stalls for chariot horses and twelve thousand horsemen" (1 Kgs 4:26). Walter Brueggemann has suggested that the author's juxtaposition of the description of *shalom* with the measure of military might and royal oppression was meant as a subtle but strong criticism of the king.[18] Solomon's peace corresponds in this way to the "way the world gives it," which Jesus distinguishes from his own kind of peace. If the messiah was supposed to be a military "peacemaker" like David and Solomon, then Jesus certainly failed in the mission. But Jesus' peace does not end war directly; rather, it allows one to live through it without succumbing to the temptation to live according to its own logic and necessities. As Paul S. Minear puts it:

> The world's power, and hence its peace, depended on its readiness to use violence.... Jesus' gift... is made available in the midst of intense hatred and violent persecution, where it enables the disciples to continue their struggle against the world.[19]

The Sanhedrin, just like Solomon before them, attempt to bring *shalom* by destroying their enemies and subjugating those who would dissent. Jesus, in contrast, engages enemies and encourages dissent, so that differences can be reconciled in the power of nonviolent love rather than merely repressed.

This whole business is clearly disturbing to the disciples. Jesus is speaking the language of true messianic power to members of a community who are beginning to suspect that their own "hour" must not be far behind. The "paraclete" and "peace" are nice sentiments, they might think, but how are they going to help us face the Sanhedrin or the Romans? For the Johannine community, these were not abstract questions about the future, of course. Their "hours" had already come. This is why Jesus repeats in verse 27 the identical "Do not let your heart be troubled" as in verse 1, adding to it, "nor let it be afraid." Minear, once again, states the situation well:

> "Let not your hearts [*sic*] be troubled" means "Don't be frightened by the authority and power of your adversaries. Don't be discouraged by the

---

18. Brueggemann (1981, 195–196).
19. Minear (1984, 67).

apparent futility of resisting them. Don't try to buy security by betraying me. Don't let your fear of death prompt compromises with my enemies."[20]

Although I think Minear is right on the point, this is another example of a discipleship instruction that is easy to say and hard to do! Jesus again goes into the "comforter" role by reminding them of what he told them in verses 2–3, but which they apparently did not really hear, that he is going away and coming back. There seems to be an element of hurt in Jesus' tone when he goes on in verse 28 to say, "If you were loving me, you would have rejoiced that I am going to the Father, because the Father is greater than I." As it is, though, they are troubled and fearful, thinking more of their loss than of Jesus' reunion with the one who sent him. One of the major goals of the Last Supper discourse is to convert this sorrow into joy, their suffering into celebration.

Many commentators have found the last part of Jesus' statement as evidence of "redaction" or other means of explaining what they see as the conflict between the claim that "The Father is greater than I" and the earlier statement that "The Father and I are one" (10:30). However, Jesus has acknowledged — even proclaimed — throughout the fourth gospel that his words, actions, and thoughts are not his own, but those of God/Father/one who sent (e.g., 5:19; 7:28; 8:42; 10:18; 14:24). To see Jesus is to see the Father, but the Father remains greater, for Jesus' particularity cannot encompass God's universality. What could be greater cause for joy than to return to the one who is the source and destination of all that has come to be, including Jesus?

Finally, in verse 29, Judas gets the "answer" to the question asked in verse 22. Just as in 13:19 Jesus told them about the imminent betrayal "before it happens so that when it does happen, you may believe," so now he has told them about his departure/return. The answer to Judas is that nothing "has happened" (*genonen*) yet to distinguish their experience of Jesus from that of the world. But because they are informed "before it occurs" (*genesthai*), they will have a different "revelation" when Jesus leaves via the cross.

Minute by minute, the hour progresses. In verse 30, Jesus inverts his earlier comment to the Judeans that "I have many things to say to you" (8:26): "Not for long will I have many things to say to you; the ruler of the world is coming." With great care, the fourth gospel ticks off the time, increasing the urgency that the disciples/readers pay attention. There will not be too many more chances to ask questions!

The reason is that the "ruler of the world is coming." We already know from 12:31 that this ruler will be "cast out," but it is an ominous sign nonetheless of the imminence and scope of the confrontation about to take place. Jesus hastens to add, for his fearful disciples, that "in me he does not have anything," a colloquialism for absence of control or dominance. Jesus' death is not a triumph of evil but of love, as he states in verse 31: "But so that the world should know that I am loving the Father, just as the commandment the Father gave to me, I

---

20. Ibid., 60.

am doing." Just as the deaths of modern followers of Jesus such as Archbishop Romero or the Salvadoran Jesuits, the countless crushed reeds slaughtered by the powers to try to repress their message of truth and hope, the death of Jesus is proof of the inverse of the world's power: that it *is* possible to remain nonviolent in the face of the amassed forces of evil and destruction.

And with that word, Jesus issues an abrupt command: "Rise, let us go from here." Source-oriented writers see this as the clearest proof of the stitching together of different pieces to make up the Last Supper discourse. It certainly does appear to mark the end of the discussion — except that Jesus keeps talking for three more chapters! The earliest commentators, however, unencumbered by source-oriented notions, offered several contextual interpretations of Jesus' command, including the suggestion that Jesus and the disciples leave the world (via death).[21]

From our narrative perspective, Jesus' command is an exhortation to the troubled disciples not to remain in their despair. They are to "rise" from their gloom and continue in discipleship. How many songs and sermons call us to "get up" or "walk" without us taking them literally and leaving that moment? It is not hard to read verse 31b as this type of figurative encouragement, which will eventually become a call to immediate action when chapter 17 is finished. For now, Jesus completes the first part of the Last Supper discourse with a powerful yet still rhetorical challenge not to be cowed by the powers, not to let fear of the world snuff out the light that Jesus continues to trust is still in them.

---

21. Bammel (1991, 205).

# 19

# The Vine and the Branches

## *The Johannine Community's Model of Church*

## John 15:1–25

A. **Chiasm:**
   a: 1–6: true vine: Johannine community
     b: 7–10: commandment: love; fruit
       c: 11: joy made full
     b[1]: 12–17: commandment: love; fruit
   a[1]: 18–25: false vine: synagogue[1]
B. **Location:** unspecified
C. **Time:** near Passover
D. **Hebrew scripture context:** prophetic images of vine/fruitfulness
E. **Social factors:** Johannine community vs. apostolic churches and synagogue
F. **Themes:** egalitarian community; bearing fruit
G. **Key words:** fruit, clean, remain, love, hate

### 1. BEARING FRUIT AND BEING CLEANED

**Chiasm: 15:1–6**
a: 1–2a: I am the vine; branches not bearing fruit are taken away
   b: 2b: branches bearing fruit are cleaned
     c: 3: clean because of word
   b[1]: 4: branch cannot bear fruit from itself
a[1]: 5–6: I am the vine; branches not remaining are cast out

---

1. Ellis (1984, 225–226).

At the very heart of the Last Supper discourse, its chiastic center, lies the basic image that provides the model for the shape and life of the Johannine community: "I AM the true vine,...and you are the branches." Through the explication of this image, Jesus challenges his disciples to build through their relationship with him a loving community different in style from both the synagogues and the apostolic churches.

To appreciate the power of this image, we need to consider the role of the "vine" in Hebrew scripture and in Israel's memory. Beginning in Gen 9:20 with Noah, the "first one to plant a vineyard," the image of vines and vineyards is used over two hundred times in the Bible. For a nomadic people, a vineyard is a natural symbol of settling down, calling a place home. To this day, villages in France and Italy proudly measure their longevity by the age of their vines. A healthy vine is a multifaceted source of joy, providing fruit to eat, economic sustenance, and wine for celebration.

It is not surprising that many of the biblical writers found this image a useful one in speaking of God's promise to Israel, as well as of Israel's failure to live according to the covenant. A sampling of these passages gives us the flavor:

> You brought a vine out of Egypt, you drove out the
>     nations and planted it....
> Turn again, O God of hosts; look down from heaven and
>     see,
> have regard for this vine, the stock that your right hand
>     planted. (Ps 80:8, 14)

> Let me sing for my beloved my love-song about his
>     vineyard:
> My beloved had a vineyard on a very fertile hill....
> He expected it to yield grapes, but it yielded wild
>     grapes....
> For the vineyard of the Lord of hosts is the house of
>     Israel,
> and the people of Judah are his pleasant planting;
> he expected justice, but saw bloodshed;
> justice, but heard a cry! (Isa 5:1, 2, 7)

> A pleasant vineyard, sing about it!
> I, the Lord, am its keeper; every moment I water it.
> I guard it night and day so that no one can harm it;
> I have no wrath.
> If it gives me thorns and briers, I will march to battle
>     against it; I will burn it up.
> Or else let it cling to me for protection, let it make peace
>     with me. (Isa 27:2–5)

> Yet I planted you as a fruitful [LXX, *karpophoron*] vine
> from the truest [LXX, *alithēnēn*] stock.
> How then did you turn degenerate and become a wild
>     vine? (Jer 2:21)

> Many shepherds have destroyed my vineyard, they have
>     trampled down my portion. (Jer 12:10)

> Then he took a seed from the land, placed it in fertile
>     soil;
> A plant by abundant waters, he set it like a willow twig.
> It sprouted and became a vine, spreading out, but low;
> Its branches turned toward him, its roots remained
>     where it stood. (Ezek 17:5–6)

For there shall be a sowing of peace; the vine shall yield its fruit....
O house of Judah and house of Israel, so I will save you and you shall be
a blessing. Do not be afraid, but let your hands be strong. (Zech 8:12–13)

As we can see, for better or worse, the prophets in particular frequently
thought of Israel as a vine and its fruitfulness as a measure of fidelity to the
Lord, the vine "keeper." This image took concrete form as a ubiquitous decora-
tion on the Temple and was used as a sign of hope on the short-lived coins of
the first revolt period in the late 60s.[2]
For Jesus to tell his disciples that "I AM the true [*alēthinē*] vine, and my
Father is the vine grower [*geōrgos*]" is once again to place himself in the position of Israel as the one closest to the bosom of God. The adjective "true"
recalls in particular the Jer 2:21 passage cited above and turns the statement
into a polemic against what was *supposed* to be the true vine. For readers of
the fourth gospel, this proclamation also recalls the first scene of fruitfulness in
Cana. There, Jesus, despite the fact that it was not yet his "hour," proved to be
the "source" (*pōthen*) of messianic wine, unknown to all but the servants (2:9).
Now it *is* his hour, and the link between Jesus and the source of celebration can
be stated openly. The Cana wine was not a magic trick but a manifestation of
what Jesus *is*: the source of God's life for humanity.

The phrasing of 15:1 reinforces the superiority of the Father, though, just
as Jesus claims *egō eimi*. The vine is only a source of life *if* it has a vine
grower. Otherwise, it brings forth "wild grapes" and thorns, as the prophets
characterized the vine of Israel when the people had turned away from God.

The purpose of the proclamation is not so much to emphasize Jesus' relationship with God for its own sake as to express the basis for the relationships
within the discipleship community. In verse 2, Jesus turns to this theme: "Every
branch in me not bearing fruit [*karpon*] he takes away [*airei*], and every one
bearing fruit he cleans [*kathairei*] so that it may bear more fruit." The vine may

---

2. R. Brown (1970, 674).

be pretty to look at, but for a people constantly struggling to find sufficient sustenance, beauty alone is an unaffordable luxury. What is important is the bearing of fruit. The image is clear to anyone who gardens, either in the ancient world or today. What is not fruitful is cut off. But even what *is* fruitful is "cleaned," so that its yield may increase.

What does this message say to followers of Jesus? It is a word addressed only to those who are "in" Jesus; the Judeans and others who reject the entire prospect of Jesus' messiahship and way of discipleship are not part of the vine at all. Those who are "branches" come in two types, fruit bearers and non–fruit bearers. The latter are "taken away" from the vine. For those who think of the Christian church as an all-inclusive body that welcomes and embraces people unconditionally, this is a jarring message. While all may be welcomed into the Johannine community, only those who bear fruit are allowed to stay. In a situation of persecution, betrayal, and suffering, there is no room for the purely contemplative or those who find simplistic salvation in calling oneself a Christian. It is not a place for bystanders but for those whose connection to the vine brings life to others.

For those who do bear fruit, the prospect is of being "cleaned." As Raymond Brown points out, while the images of cutting and pruning fit the gardening metaphor, the Greek words used are not natural to the context but are chosen for their wordplay: *airei* and *kathairei*.[3] Being cleaned also recalls 13:10–11, where Jesus told them that they were "clean" (*katharoi*) "but not all." To be cleaned is to have one's feet washed, to commit oneself to the Johannine community until death does you part. Thus, Jesus goes on in verse 3 to repeat that "already you are clean through the word which I have spoken to you." To be in this relationship is to "remain in me and I in you" (verse 4). The image of the vineless branch sharply expresses how dependent the disciples are to be on their relationship with Jesus, something that will be challenged by every authority and competing religious leader around, whether Judean or Roman, Qumranian or gnostic.

When the *egō eimi* statement is repeated in verse 5 (the only time in the gospel that an *egō eimi* image is repeated), it provides a subtle but important variation on these themes. Jesus tells them that "the one remaining in me and I in that one *is* bearing much fruit...." If one is *truly* connected with Jesus, it is as impossible not to bear fruit as it is to bear fruit "apart" (*chōris*) from him. As we heard in the prologue that nothing came to be "apart" (*chōris*) from the Word (1:3), so the disciples can do nothing apart from Jesus.

Verse 6 picks up the theme of the non-fruit-bearing branch: "If anyone is not remaining in me, that one is thrown out [*eblēthē exō*] as a branch and is dried up, and they are gathering them together [*synagousin*] and throwing [*ballousin*] them into the fire and it is burned." This is an undeniably harsh image, one that has fueled hellfire and damnation sermons for centuries. But what is it trying

---

3. Ibid., 660.

to tell readers in the context of this parable and the Last Supper discourse as a whole?

Another Hebrew scripture image provides background:

> Go up through her vine-rows and destroy, but do not
>     make a full end;
> strip away her branches, for they are not the Lord's.
> For the house of Israel and the house of Judah
> have been utterly faithless to me, says the Lord. . . .
> The prophets are nothing but wind, for the word [LXX,
>     *logos*] is not in them. (Jer 5:10–11, 13)

As in Israel, so in the Johannine community: there is no room for fruitless branches that suck up energy for no return.

The verbs of "throwing out" and "throwing" recall the Pharisees' treatment of the once-blind one, who was "thrown out" (*exebalon outon exō,* 9:35), and the devil's treatment of Judas, into whom was "thrown" the idea of betraying Jesus (*beblēkotos,* 13:2). The style may be discomforting in our "polite" culture, but to people trying to form a resistance community in the face of overwhelming odds, there can be no compromise with potential betrayers. Of course, this is a very dangerous course of action, as the Johannine community discovered, which we hear in 1 John. It is not always easy to tell the fruit bearers from the others, or whether a branch that is fallow one season might, if left alone, bloom the next. But this is the message of the fourth gospel's Jesus, and our cultural differences cannot allow us to soften the word to suit our tastes.

In the midst of the violence of throwing out and on the fire is a poignant irony: those who do the throwing out "gather together" (*synagousin*) the fruitless branches. As the Sanhedrin was gathered together (*synēgagon,* 11:47) and as the scattered children of God will be gathered together (*synagagē,* 11:52), so the lifeless branches are treated. The branches die because they remain alone, but in their death, they are gathered with others of their type. It is a darkly comic reversal of Jesus' mission and a verbal joust at the synagogues that throw out Johannine believers.

The image of being "thrown into the fire and burned" certainly is likely to conjure up notions of hell and damnation for Christians raised on post-Dantean cosmology. And we cannot deny the sense both in the fourth gospel and in many contemporaneous writings that judgment would involve eternal suffering and separation for those who practiced injustice and oppression. Our North American liberal theology of universal salvation would seem nonsense to the Johannine community and others of that day, for it makes a mockery of the justice of God.[4] Without softening the force of this image, we can find solace only

---

4. Cf. Schüssler Fiorenza (1991, 64), who, in responding to Revelation's similar imagery aimed at the imperial powers, notes: "Exegetes, who generally do not suffer unbearable oppression and are not tormented by God's apparent toleration of injustice, tend to label this outcry for justice

in noting that Jesus does not dwell on this topic but simply announces it and moves back to his preferred mode of encouragement rather than judgment.

## 2. "YOU ARE MY FRIENDS IF . . . "

**Chiasm 15:7–17**

a: 7–12: if you remain in me, and my words in you, ask; bear fruit; love one
              another, commandments

  b: 13–14: friends

    c: 15a: not slaves any longer

  b¹: 15b: friends

a¹: 16–17: bear fruit that remains; ask; love one another/command

**Chiasm: 15:12–17**

a: 12: command . . . love one another

  b: 13–14: lay down life for friends

    c: 15a: not servants

  b¹: 15b–16: friends, bear fruit

a¹: 17: command . . . love one another

As he did in 14:13 in relation to doing "greater works," so Jesus does in 15:7 in relation to bearing fruit: assuring his disciples that "if you remain in me and my sayings remain in you, whatever you are willing [*thelēte*], ask and it will happen to you." Throughout the "trial" narrative of chapters 5–8, Jesus focused on doing the "will" of the one who sent him and urging his hearers to a decision on whose will theirs was aligned with (e.g., 5:40; 6:67; 7:17). Now, this challenge takes the form of a powerful affirmation: to remain in Jesus is to align one's will with his; and to align one's will with that of Jesus is to have whatever one seeks happen. Just as Jesus is nowhere subject to the powers but is totally in charge of his destiny, so the disciples who remain in him are totally empowered to shape their future.

The reason is again like in 14:13: for the glory of "my Father." But the shift between past, present, and future in the Last Supper discourse adds an interesting twist after this phrase, where Jesus tells them that the glory is shown by "you bearing much fruit and *becoming* my disciples." In spite of the promises and assurances Jesus has given them that they are "already clean" and already "know" and "see" the spirit of truth, they remain on the way *to* discipleship. Their response to Jesus' own glorification will make clear that they cannot really claim at this point to be "my disciples," even though they are *with* Jesus now.

---

as unchristian." But, she continues, when one does experience or at least envisions such a social context, such harsh proscriptions can be understood.

Verses 9–10 form a minichiasm that highlights the centrality of keeping Jesus' commandments as the key to remaining:

a: as the Father has loved me, and I have loved you

  b: remain in my love

    c: if you keep my commandments

  b¹: you will remain in my love

a¹: just as I have kept the Father's commandments and remain in his love

For the third (and final) time — all since 14:15! — Jesus urges them to "keep my commandments." It is easy for modern readers to become exasperated at Jesus and the fourth gospel by this stage, thinking, "Enough of this already — we get the message!" But alas, the problem is that we *do not* get the message, for if people kept the commandment to love one another, what a different world we would live in! The fourth gospel and Paul's letters ring the gong of "love" loudly and clearly, yet, in one of the great ironies of Christian history, the church has largely not been a model of what its own founder preached so many times that we get bored with hearing it.

Although we will not hear again about "keeping" the love commandment, Jesus is far from finished with announcing its importance. Verse 11 provides a narrative pause, with the familiar *tauta* refrain: "These things [*tauta*] I have said to you so that my joy may be in you and your joy might be fulfilled [*plērōthē*]." Readers — although perhaps not the disciples — heard John (the Baptist) speak of his joy being fulfilled at the voice of the bridegroom in 3:29. Now, Jesus implores his listeners to the same experience as John's. Despite the difficulty of Jesus' message, it is meant not to be one of grim determination — an attitude we all too often betray in our efforts at countercultural discipleship practice — but of fulfilled joy.

In the intricate structure of the fourth gospel, verses 12–17 (and verse 8) repeat themes found in 13:34–35 and with those verses form bookends around the four questions asked by the disciples. In fact, the phrase in verse 12 is identical to that in 13:34: *hina agapate allēlous kathōs ēgapēsa hymas* ("so that you may be loving one another as I loved you"). But the new twist is in verse 13: "Greater love than this no one has: to lay down one's life for one's friends." Previously, Jesus has spoken of his own call to lay down his life for the sheep, and we have seen the symbolic fulfillment of this in the narrative details of the footwashing. But now, for the first time, Jesus makes explicit that this description of love applies to his disciples as well. Thomas has called his fellow disciples to die with Jesus (11:16), and Peter has impetuously and prematurely vowed to lay down his life for Jesus, but no one has yet suggested that to "love one another" would be expressed by willingness to lay down lives for one another. As Brown states it, "15:12–13, with its command to carry love to the point of laying down one's life for others, is an excellent commentary on what

Jesus means in 13:15."[5] It is for the disciples an unprecedented idea, one that the Torah did not suggest and that remains foreign to mainstream Jewish thinking. But for a community amidst active persecution, Jesus must make clear that love means more than what David Rensberger calls "general kindliness." As Rensberger says further:

> "Love" would mean not only affection and a general kindliness but standing with others in the community against betrayal by outsiders and participating actively in creating the new communal bonds that must take the place of the lost synagogue fellowship.[6]

The laying down of life is not an abstract model of general self-sacrifice, then, but an expression of commitment that flows directly from the relationship among "friends." Only twice before have we heard this term in the fourth gospel. The first time was when John (the Baptist) spoke of himself as "friend of the bridegroom," in the same context as his fulfilled joy (3:29). Also, Jesus spoke of Lazarus as "our friend" (11:11). But now, the notion deepens into the primary description of the bond of discipleship. As Jesus tells them in verse 14: "You are my friends *if* you are doing what I am commanding you." John is already in this relationship. Given the proleptic reference in 3:24 to John not yet having been "thrown into prison," one can infer that the Johannine community and readers of the fourth gospel ought to be familiar with the tradition of John's death as a martyr. Thus, he can claim to be a friend of the bridegroom *because* he was willing to lay down his life both in the figurative sense of "decreasing" in favor of Jesus' "increasing" and also literally through his truthful witness before the powers. Jesus invites his disciples to share in this intimacy by "doing" what he commands.

In verse 15, as if commissioning them to a new phase, Jesus marks the transition in their call: "I am no longer calling you slaves, because the slave does not know what his lord [*kyrios*] is doing. But you I called 'friends' because all things [*panta*] which I heard from my Father I have made known to you." It will require the holy spirit to teach the disciples "all things" and remind them of "all things" (14:26), but Jesus has told them now and called them friends now.

The sense of impending mission is made explicit in verse 16: "You did not choose [*exelexasthe*] me, but I chose [*exelexamēn*] you, and I appointed you to go and bear fruit, fruit that will remain." Jesus reminds them of what he told them in 6:70, but now in Judas's absence: that he *chose* them. The verb for "appointed" is the same as that for "lay down," *tithemai,* and provides a wordplay in Greek that is lost in English between verses 13 and 16: if they are willing to "lay down" (*thē*) their lives for one another, they become Jesus' friends whom he has appointed (*ethēka*) to bear fruit.[7] As with the tension around Judas's betrayal, it is the best that language can do to express the mysterious relationship

---

5. R. Brown (1970, 569).
6. Rensberger (1988, 79–80).
7. R. Brown (1970, 664–665).

between God's will and human will. *They* must choose to lay down their lives, but *Jesus* has chosen and appointed them to do just that!

Another mystery is spoken of in this way in verse 16c, that is, the relationship between Jesus' "doing" and the Father's "doing." In 14:13, he told them, "Whatever you ask in my name, *I* will do," while in 15:16c, Jesus tells them, "Whatever you ask the Father in my name, *he* will give you." It is not meant to arouse theological trinitarian speculation but to assure the disciples (and readers) in the fourth gospel's own way that the Father and Jesus in fact do the same thing.

As if closing a song refrain, Jesus ends this part of his discourse with another *tauta* phrase: "These things [*tauta*] I am commanding you: that you love one another."

## 3. "FOR THIS THE WORLD HATES YOU"

**Chiasm: 15:18–25**

a: 18: hated me

   b: 19–20a: you

      c: 20b–21: you/they antitheses

   b¹: 22–24: they

a¹: 25: hated me

Suddenly, without any warning whatsoever, Jesus reverses the terms of discussion dramatically in verse 18: "If the world is hating you, know that it has hated me first." From love among the disciples-as-friends to hatred from the world — the transition could not be more abrupt. Eight times in the next eight verses, the term "hate" (*miseō*) is used. In our modern age, many people mouth the sentiment of wanting to get along with everyone, and thus many of us are very uncomfortable with the idea of "hate." The word conjures up a sense of deep anger, hostility, and opposition that does not feel good and that we would like to avoid. To get an idea of why Jesus uses such a harsh term so many times in so brief a span, we must pause to consider the role of "hate" in the mind-set of the Bible.

The stories of the first families contain powerful lessons about the effect of hating one's brothers. Esau hated Jacob and plotted to kill him (Gen 27:41), ending up forever separated from him and, ultimately, from the people of Israel, who descended from Jacob alone. Joseph's brothers hated him because of Jacob's preference for him and because of his dream (Gen 37:5–8), but they end up starving while Joseph prospers. In the Torah, Israel is enjoined against hatred, "or you will incur guilt in yourselves" (Lev 19:17).

The primary literary context of the theme of hatred in the Hebrew scriptures, though, is in the Psalms. Hate expresses the opposition between those who love God and those who do not, between those who do what is right and those who do evil. God hates those who do evil and act with violence (Ps 11:5; 26:5), who practice idolatry and injustice (Ps 31:6). The one who loves God also is to hate these (Ps 139:21). Hate also comes in the other direction. The evildoers hate God's ways and law (Ps 81:15). Another element of the hatred of God is that it is without cause, for in the mentality of the Psalms, God cannot be an object of just hatred (Ps 35:19; 38:19; 69:4). This causeless hatred of God is manifested in hatred for God's people, an experience that characterized much of Israel's history and continues to define modern Jewish history after the Holocaust.

For the Johannine community, this experience of being hated without cause paradoxically fulfilled scripture just as it placed them outside the synagogue in which that scripture was proclaimed and celebrated. Jesus places himself in the position of the psalmist and of God, the one who is unjustly hated, and "comforts" his hated community by linking their fate to his.

The section contains two themes. First, in verses 18–20, Jesus relates their experience of hatred and persecution to his own. Then in verses 21–25, he connects their experience to the Father. As they are all to remain together in mutual love, so they are bonded in the shared pain of hatred. After stating the initial premise in verse 18, Jesus makes a distinction that is central to Johannine symbolism and ideology but has been misinterpreted by those who insist on seeing the fourth gospel as "detached." "If you were part of the world, the world would be friendly [*ephilei*] to what is its own [*idion*]. But because you are not part of the world, but have been chosen by me out of the world, the world is hating you because of it." To hear this as a denial of the call of discipleship *in* the world is to miss the point altogether. The Johannine community is not *part of* the world because it responds to what is for the glory of God, not the glory of human beings (5:44; 12:43). It consists of members born of God, not of violence, the will of flesh, or the will of man (1:12–13), the ways in which "the world" bears its children. The contrast is underscored by ironically comparing the world's "friendship" with what it means to be a friend of Jesus. While the world embraces "its own," Jesus was rejected by his own (1:11, *idia*).

For the Johannine community, there is no comfortable path of "Christ in culture." The way of the world and the way of Jesus are radically opposed. To be "chosen" by Jesus is to be chosen "out of the world," to be called to follow a path that the world neither knows nor sees, yet that it finds threatening when others choose it. To the apostolic churches who practiced a "both/and" spirituality as described in Acts with synagogue worship in the morning and eucharistic celebration in the evening (Acts 2:46), the Johannine Jesus gives a solemn warning: you cannot be my followers if you are "of" the world at all. The consequences for our modern church relationship with governments and culturally acceptable practices are all too clear: each time we stand as Christians in support of the violence of war, racism, or nationalism, we betray the call to which Jesus has chosen us to answer.

However, the consequences of not betraying the call are none too pleasant to consider, either. In verse 20, Jesus makes it plain: "Remember [*mnēmoneuete*] the word which I told you, 'A slave is not greater than his lord.' If they persecuted me, they will also persecute you. If they kept my word, they will also keep yours." Fifteen times in his farewell discourse in Deuteronomy, Moses tells his hearers to "remember." The centerpiece of the Mosaic call to memory is God's act of liberation in forming Israel as a people and calling them out of slavery in Egypt. Here, Jesus challenges his audience to remember the lowliness of a slave, of which he had told them in 13:16 in connection with their duty to wash one another's feet. It is a little surprising in this narrative spot, though, for Jesus has just told them that he "no longer calls" them "slaves" but "friends" (15:15). The apparent contradiction struggles to express a paradox parallel to that of Jesus' relationship with his Father. The disciples are *both* Jesus' equals as friends who do his works and greater ones *and* his slaves who have life only if they remain in union with him. At least they are equal in being mistreated and ignored by the world! The last part of Jesus' admonition is, of course, sarcastic: "they" have *not* kept Jesus' word (cf. 5:38; 8:37) and therefore will not keep the disciples' word, either.

How might the disciples be feeling at this point? We have not heard a word from them or been given a shred of narrative description of them since Judas's question in 14:22, other than the implicit sense of their fear and "troubled heart" in 14:27. Jesus has said many things to them, and not even the narrator has dared to interrupt. It is not hard to imagine that they were less than thrilled to hear Jesus predict this fate for them. Only the masochist or martyr-complexed could be glad to be told that they will be hated, persecuted, and ignored. We have no reason to think of these disciples as overly heroic, despite Peter's false bravado in 13:37. They are seeking God's messiah and are told of their own suffering; wanting comfort and are warned of hatred and hostility. How many of our churches would be filled on Sundays if this were the message we were given?

But for the Johannine community that was already experiencing "these things," Jesus' words offer the support of reminding it that it is not the fault of the disciples but the sin of the world that causes them to be persecuted. This is Jesus' focus in verses 21–25. Starting in verse 21, he tells them, "But all these things [*panta tauta*] they will do to you on account of my name, because they have not known the one who sent me." "All these things" has previously referred to what Jesus and the paraclete teach the disciples from the Father (14:26; 15:11, 15). Now, the disciples will experience what the world's father has taught it, precisely because the world does not know Jesus' Father. As Raymond Brown observes, persecution is linked to "my name" not so much through the word "Jesus" as through the word "messiah" for the Judeans and "Lord" for the Romans.[8] Proclaiming Jesus in these ways directly challenges the world's rulers and their own power commitments and announces the Johannine community's freedom from obedience to either synagogue or empire.

Just as Jesus told the Pharisees who were "with him" in 9:41, he tells his disciples in verse 22 that the world's sin is not simply a question of "foul deeds" (3:20) but a result of their not listening to the word of God. This implicitly

---

8. Ibid., 696–697.

fulfills a Mosaic prediction in Deut 18:18–19: "I shall put my words in his mouth. . . . I shall hold responsible anyone who will not listen to my words which he shall speak in my name."

They have no "pretext" (*prophasin*) for their sin. *Prophasin* is used only here in the fourth gospel, and rarely in the New Testament, but has the clear connotation of a false story, a cover, an attempt to conceal true motives. Thus, to have a *prophasin* is itself questionable behavior (cf. Mk 12:40; Phil 1:18), but because of Jesus' word, the world is stripped even of doubtful excuses.

Continuing to link with the biblical sense of hate, Jesus notes in verse 23 that to hate him is to hate his Father. Then in verse 24, he offers a statement linguistically parallel to verse 22, so that we must hear them as a diptych:

22: If I had not come and *spoken* with them, they would have no sin [*hamartian ouk eichosan*].

24: If I did not do *works* in them which no one else did, they would have no sin [*hamartian ouk eichosan*].

Word and works are opposite sides of a single coin in Jesus' mission as well as that of his followers. Either is a basis for recognizing God's presence and knowing sin when one sees it. The refusal to change in the face of either is evidence of hatred of God, no matter what one claims as one's religious allegiance.

All of this, Jesus tells the disciples, is to "fulfill the word in their Law, which is written, 'They hated me without cause.'" The citation is to a phrase found in several psalms (e.g., 35:19; 69:4). But in addition to expressing a sense of fulfillment, Jesus' words bitterly note the cited text as being "*their*" Law." It is terribly ironic that the Judeans are said to fulfill by their hatred of the Johannine community psalms that had originally referred to Israel's enemies' hatred of the Chosen People.

# 20

# "Courage! I Have Conquered the World!"

## John 15:26–16:33

**A. Chiasm:**

    a: 15:26–16:4: hour is coming

        b: 5–15: going to Father

            c: 16–22: a little while...

        b¹: 23–30: going to Father

    a¹: 31–33: hour is coming[1]

**B. Location:** unspecified

**C. Time:** near Passover

**D. Social factors:** persecution of the Johannine community by the Judeans and Romans

**E. Themes:** spirit of truth; grief turned to joy

**F. Key words:** paraclete, convict (*elegchei*), little while (*mikron*)

## 1. THE PAINFUL TRUTH

**Chiasm: 15:26–16:15**

    a: 15:26–27: paraclete/spirit of truth, I shall send, you are with me, beginning; witness; "about"

        b: 16:1–2: I have said these things to you so that/hour

            c: 3: know neither me nor Father

        b¹: 4a: I have said these things to you so that/hour

    a¹: 4b–15: paraclete, I shall send, I was with you, beginning; evidence; "about"; spirit of truth

---

1. Ellis (1984, 231–233).

**341**

**Chiasm: 15:26–16:7**

a: 15:26–27: paraclete; truth, I will send

    b: 16:1–3: I have spoken these things to you: expelled from synagogue; killed (causes of grief)

        c: 4: when the hour comes, you may remember

    b¹: 5–6: I have spoken these things to you: your heart is filled with grief

a¹: 7: paraclete; truth; I will send

In 14:16, 26, Jesus promised that the disciples would have a paraclete to replace him as their source of wisdom and truth. His concern was that they not be left "orphans" (14:18). Now, though, when the promise of the paraclete is repeated, the focus is not so much on replacement of Jesus as holy teacher but on the disciples' need for help in the face of the world's hatred. The apparently open-ended command to "love one another" to the point of being willing to "lay down one's life for one's friends" takes on shockingly concrete and specific form in the passage starting with 15:26.

Verse 26, once again calling the paraclete "the spirit of the truth," emphasizes the role of "bearing witness [*martyrēsei*] about me." It is Jesus' first use of this trial-setting word since his confrontation with the Judeans at Tabernacles in 8:18, where he told them that the Father would witness for him. The world's hate for the Father, Jesus, and the disciples will result in putting Jesus on trial in absentia by bringing the disciples into the courtroom.

Jesus says in verse 26 that he will send the paraclete "from the Father." The subtle contrast with the earlier paraclete passages in which Jesus told them that the Father would send the paraclete "in my name" (14:26) or that Jesus would ask and the Father would give the paraclete (14:16) reinforces the unity of purpose and action that exists between Jesus and the Father. As Raymond Brown points out about the description of the paraclete's "proceeding" from the Father, "The writer is not speculating about the interior life of God; he is concerned with the disciples in the world."[2] Trinitarian mysticism might be a powerful form of meditation for those ensconced in a monastery, but for a community in the midst of active persecution by the world, the need is for strong assurance that God is with them in their time of pain.

The paraclete's job is to inspire the disciples themselves to act: "And you are bearing witness, because you are with me from the beginning [*archēs*]" (verse 27). As the Word was with God "in the beginning [*archē*]" (1:1), so the disciples have been with Jesus since the beginning of his time in the world. From a narrative perspective, this is the case: from the moment of John's pointing out of "the Lamb of God," disciples left John to follow Jesus (1:36–37). But it also suggests something important about the function of the messiah in the world: although Jesus obviously existed as a person before the disciples came

---

2. R. Brown (1970, 689).

along, "the beginning" for him is the moment of the formation of the community that will follow, both in discipleship and in time.

As Jesus said "I have spoken these things to you so that" (*tauta lelalēka hymin hina*) in 15:11 to emphasize the fullness of joy, mutual love, and the call to true friendship, he repeats the phrase in 16:1 to expose the dark side of discipleship. Whereas the "so that" in 15:11 was Jesus' joy in the disciples, now it is "you might not be scandalized [*skandalisthēte*]." The only previous use in the fourth gospel of this term denoting a barrier to faith is in 6:61, when Jesus questioned whether the challenge to "munch my flesh" scandalized the disciples. There, the scandal was engaging in an act that would likely lead to persecution and expulsion. Now, the scandal is the consequences themselves.

Verse 2 offers two frightening predictions: "They will excommunicate you from the synagogue. Indeed, an hour is coming when everyone who kills you will think that they are offering [*prospherein*] service [*latreian*] to God." Both Greek words bear the strong sense of offering sacrifice, making a religious gift or act.[3] Thus, the irony is deep and bitter. Those who think they are serving God are, by doing this terrible violence, serving the devil. At the same time, the Johannine community members who suffer this fate become in the act true sacrifices, offerings to God by their willingness to lay down their lives for their friends. The statement also links the warning with the earlier hint that the priests/Pharisees are the "thieves" whose purpose is to kill (*thysē*, 10:10).

The consequences for following Jesus are never stated more clearly in the New Testament. To be hated is one thing; to be expelled from one's faith community and killed is quite another! As Jesus faces his "hour," so will the disciples face theirs.

The consequences for the separation of the Johannine community from the synagogue have similarly never been clearer. While the story of the once-blind person in chapter 9 acted out this drama as a paradigm of discipleship, now Jesus expressly tells those who would follow him that what that one experienced will be the experience of all. The language of verse 2, like so much of the Last Supper discourse, is in the collective plural. This will not simply be the fate of some individuals within the community but will be the fate of the community as a whole. Obviously, not every Christian will be killed, but the idea that killing Christians is a service to God will become a popular idea among both Judeans and Romans. And the expectation will affect all, for even those who escape death will find it surrounding them in the deaths of friends and loved ones.

The *tauta* that Jesus has done and said could not be in sharper contrast with the *tauta* that the opponents of the Johannine community do. Verse 3 states clearly the reason for the difference: "And these things [*tauta*] they will do because they knew neither the Father nor me."

---

3. K. Weiss, *TDNT* 9:65–68 (*prosphero*); H. Strathmann, *TDNT* 4:58–65 (*latreia*).

The center of the first chiasm in verse 4 provides the reason for this terrible talk: "I have spoken these things [*tauta*] to you so that when the hour for them comes, you may remember [*mnēmoneuēte*] that I told you." For the second time in a dozen verses (15:20), Jesus calls on the power of *remembering* as a teaching tool. The various temporal levels of the Last Supper discourse bend and spiral around one another in this verse. For the characters in the story, the hour and the remembering are in the future. For the Johannine community, the events are *now*. For us, the time sequence depends upon our life situation. Most modern disciples have never experienced the wrenching pain of ostracism or excommunication, and fewer still in North America have faced sacrificial deaths. But for the faithful readers of the fourth gospel, those who dare to accept the text's claim to be the word of God, the creeping feeling that the hour for us *will* come *if* we "keep the commandments" is hard to avoid.

The second part of verse 4 suggests that these experiences were not expected outcomes of discipleship for the Johannine community: "These things [*tauta*] I did not say in the beginning [*archēs*], because I was with you." As Herold Weiss puts it, "[The] contradiction [between the prediction of the disciples' 'hour' and the failure of Jesus to speak about it during his lifetime] clearly indicates that the need to face martyrdom had caught the community by surprise, and, having to face it, the reaction of the disciples varied."[4] The Last Supper discourse, as mentioned earlier, provides the community with Jesus' words of hope from "above," through the vehicle of the paraclete. Within the story world, Jesus speaks as if he is already gone, noting the time of his presence in the past.

And yet in verse 5 he speaks in the present of his "going now to the one who sent me." What is important is not to try to separate these swirling temporal shifts into "logical" relationships but to accept the intentionality of the text, which is to present Jesus speaking *both* to "them" and to us, both acting in the past and in the present/future.

The remainder of Jesus' statement in verse 5 injects a surprising tone of pique at what Jesus claims is the disciples' lack of interest in his future: "No one from you is asking me, 'Where are you going?'" But, of course, Simon Peter asked precisely this question in 13:36, and Jesus refused to answer it directly! What can the implications of Jesus' statement in 16:5 be in light of Peter's earlier question? It certainly cannot be that Jesus did not hear the question, for his next words flow directly from Peter's words. Can it suggest that Peter is not one of the "you" to whom Jesus is currently speaking? Or might it imply that, although Peter asked earlier in the discourse, there is some reason to think that the disciples should be asking the question *again* now in light of what Jesus has spoken to them in the intervening chapters?

However one chooses to resolve this apparent contradiction, it is clear that the thrust of Jesus' concern is that the disciples are so concerned with their own painful future that they have completely forgotten to pay attention to Jesus' continuing journey back to the Father. For if they "remember" that Jesus is going to

---

4. Weiss (1979, 307).

God to prepare a place for them (14:2–3), their own fear might be mitigated. But as it is, the thought of persecution and death has enveloped them and clouded their sense of connection between Jesus' *ultimate* fate and their own.

In verse 6, Jesus names the problem: "But because I have spoken these things [*tauta*] to you, grief [*lypē*] has filled [*peplērōken*] your heart." Precisely the opposite of Jesus' intention has taken place. In 15:11, he told them that "I have spoken these things to you so that . . . your joy might be fulfilled [*plērōthē*]." Instead of being filled with joy, they are filled with grief.

Whereas the synoptics only speak once of *lypē* (Lk 22:45), the fourth gospel uses the term four times in this chapter (see 16:20–22). It is interesting to observe how it comes into play in verse 5. The narrator and characters are totally effaced, but Jesus shares with readers some image of the disciples' (and our!) feelings by naming them himself. Each time in the Last Supper discourse that Jesus does this, it is with reference to their collective "heart" (14:1, 27; 16:22). They have shifted from being "troubled" to being filled with grief, as their own concern has shifted from being left orphans to being killed.

He continues in verse 7 by noting a struggle that every human must deal with: whether to learn the painful truth or to remain blissfully ignorant. Do we really *want* to know what the cost of discipleship is? Would we rather be surprised when trouble from the world comes our way for keeping Jesus' commandments? Jesus clearly opts for the former, although only through the vehicle of the paraclete. Thus, he tells them, "But I am speaking the truth to you. It is for your benefit [*sympherei hymin*] that I go. If I were not to go, the paraclete would never come to you. But if I do go, I shall send that one to you."

Just as Caiaphas told the Sanhedrin it was "for your benefit [*sympherei hymin*] that one person should die for the people" (11:50), so Jesus "agrees." The irony, of course, is that Caiaphas expected that Jesus' death would put an end to the discipleship community and the pressure it puts on Jerusalem, but Jesus assures his audience that his death will enable the community to go on through the gift of the paraclete. The language of verse 7 is absolute in its insistence that they cannot have both Jesus and the paraclete simultaneously, or at least not until after Jesus has "gone." It is an essential point of Johannine theology: what the world sees as the evidence of failure, Jesus has "foretold" to be evidence of God's continuing love and support.

The role of the paraclete vis-à-vis the disciples has been stated in 14:26. Now, Jesus tells his hearers the paraclete's function vis-à-vis the world. Verses 8–11 must be examined very carefully, or we can easily misunderstand their powerful import.

D. A. Carson's article on these verses does more than any other work I know to illuminate this seemingly cryptic text.[5] To start, we must look at the three parallel topics introduced in verse 8 and then referred to sequentially in verses 9–11, paying attention to the key words that determine the meaning:

---

5. Carson (1979).

And having come, that one will:

1. convict [*elegchei*] the world about sin [*hamartias*] (8)...because [*hoti*] they are not believing in me (9)

2. convict the world about justice [*dikaiosynēs*] (8)...because I am going to the Father and you will not see me any more (10)

3. convict the world about judgment [*kriseōs*] (8)...because the ruler of this world has been judged (11)

The key to understanding the entire passage is to interpret *elegchei* and *hoti* so that all three parts form a coherent whole. Carson carefully shows the possibilities and the flaws in various interpretive options, reaching the following conclusions. First, *elegchei* can have a number of related meanings, including "to convict," "to convince," "to reprove," or "to expose."[6] The best in this context is a sense of bringing the world "to self-conscious 'conviction' "; that is, to both show the world's wrongness *and* to convince the world of that wrongness.[7] It is not simply a matter of convincing the *disciples* of the world's fault but of witnessing about this *to the world* itself.

Next is the question of *hoti*. In this passage, there are two basic options. The clauses can *explain* the convictions or *cause* them. That is, we might interpret *hoti* as in each case telling *what* the world's problem is, or as telling *why* the paraclete has the function of convicting/convincing the world of each situation. Carson opts for the latter.[8] Thus, each part takes on the form *"convicts of...because..."*

Each topic bears a substantial role in helping the disciples understand why Jesus must go and be replaced by the paraclete. First, the paraclete convinces the world of its sin, bringing the world to "self-conscious recognition of guilt."[9] As in 3:20, "Everyone who practices foul deeds...is not coming to the light so that their works might be reproved [*elegchthē*]." Just as the Son has been sent into the world because of God's love that hopes to bring people to faith to prevent their destruction (3:16), so the paraclete continues this role. The world will be convicted of its sin *because* it has *not* believed.

Second, the paraclete convicts the world of its "justice." Carson points out the ironic sense of this term in the argument. In the Septuagint translation of Isa 64:6, the prophet compares the *dikaiosynē* of the people with a menstrual cloth; that is, it is "unclean" in God's eyes.[10] Although the term is not used elsewhere in the fourth gospel, this precedent suggests that Jesus is telling his disciples that what the world *thinks* is justice is not. In particular, the world's justice expels and persecutes the disciples. In 15:22, 24, Jesus had told them

---

6. Ibid., 550–557.
7. Ibid., 558.
8. Ibid., 561.
9. Ibid., 558.
10. Ibid., 559.

that his words and works took away any excuses the world might have for its sin. Now, because Jesus is going to the Father and the disciples will no longer see him, this function is handed on to the paraclete, who will also convict the world because what it thinks is justice is its opposite.

Finally, the paraclete will convince/convict the world about its judgment, which is that Jesus is a "Samaritan" and has a "demon" and is otherwise a "sinner." Likewise, the world's judgment is that the disciples are worthy objects of hatred and execution. This incorrect judgment *must* be changed *because* the ruler of the world *has been* judged. The time is now; the judgment against the "ruler" has already taken place. Those who continue to practice wrong judgment face a terrible condemnation, *unless* the paraclete can convince them of their error.

Thus, the paraclete will completely replace Jesus in his role of supporting the disciples in their mission to the world. It is urgent that the truth be spoken and that transformation take place. To the grieving disciples who can think only of their apparent abandonment and prospective suffering, Jesus offers the assurance that the paraclete will act just as Jesus has acted on their behalf.

Are the disciples within the story world grasping all of this? Several times in the gospel, Jesus or the narrator has noted that they cannot understand now but will understand later (2:22; 13:7; 14:26; cf. 16:4). In verse 12, Jesus speaks with a clear sense that they have heard all they can handle for the moment: "I still have many things to say to you, but you are not able to bear [*bastazein*] them right now." Earlier uses of the verb *bastazo* give this compassionate statement an interesting nuance. In 10:31, the narrator describes the Judeans as "carrying" (*ebastasan*) stones against Jesus. Later, in 12:6, we are told that Judas "carried" (*ebastazen*) the money away as an act of theft. Now, Jesus tells the disciples that they are unable to bear/carry the things he has to say to them. Does it suggest that, like the Judeans and Judas, the disciples might misuse Jesus' further thoughts in a violent or otherwise un-Godly way? What is it that Jesus cannot tell them now that might be so misused?

Verse 13 provides some clue: "When that one comes, the spirit of the truth, that one will guide [*hodēgēsei*] you into all truth, for that one will not speak with originality, but whatever is heard, will be spoken, and the things coming will announce [*anangelei*] to you." Nowhere else in the fourth gospel and only four other times in the New Testament is the verb *hodēgeō* used. Its literal sense is to lead in "the way" (*hodos*). Given that Jesus has expressly stated that he is the way and the truth (14:6), it seems clear that he is telling the disciples that the spirit of the truth will also replace Jesus in this function. Just as Jesus spoke only what he heard from his Father (8:28; 12:49), so the spirit of the truth will speak what that one has heard.

The duty to "announce the things to come" belongs to God. As Brown points out, "Declaring of things to come is a privilege of Yahweh that false gods do not possess (Is 48:14)."[11] The verb *anangellō* is used fifty-seven times in Isaiah,

---

11. R. Brown (1970, 708).

associated with the declaration of God's truth. The Samaritan woman's expectation of the messiah included the function of announcing all things (4:25). Thus, what the disciples cannot bear to hear now but that will be announced by the paraclete starts with the "things to come." As in Isaiah, this is a basic "proof" of a spirit's divinity (Isa 41:21–23). In this way, Jesus assures the disciples that the spirit he will give has God's own authorization.

Verses 14–15 state this case in terms of the paraclete's "glorifying" of Jesus. What the paraclete "receives" is from Jesus, and what Jesus receives is "all things" (*panta*) from the Father. Three consecutive verses end with the refrain, "will announce to you" (*anangelei hymin*). This structure enables us to see verses 13–15 as parallel with 9–11. The paraclete will convict/convince the world of sin, justice, and judgment *by* announcing God's truth to the disciples, who in turn are to bear witness to what they hear (15:27). The disciples are not yet able to "carry" these truths with them but will be able to once Jesus has gone and been replaced by the paraclete.

## 2. "ON THAT DAY, YOU WILL ASK NO MORE QUESTIONS"

### Chiasm: 16:16–33

a: 16–20: a little while, etc. [disciples confused]

   b: 21–22: figure of woman in childbirth

      c: 23–24: in that day: ask nothing/ask

   b$^1$: 25–30: not in figures!

a$^1$: 31–3: hour is coming; disciples scattered

### a. *"We Don't Know What He's Talking About!"*

### Chiasm: 16:16–19

a: 16: in a little while you will not see me, and again in a little while, you will see me

   b: 17: disciples question him

      c: 18: we don't know what he's talking about

   b$^1$: 19a: Jesus knew they wanted to question him

a$^1$: 19b: in a little while you will not see me, and again in a little while, you will see me

After all this talk about Jesus being replaced by the paraclete when he leaves, he offers a surprising statement in verse 16: "In a little while [*mikron*] you will not see me, and again in a little while, you will see me." In 13:33, he told the disciples that he would only be with them for a *mikron*; in 14:19, he told them that in a *mikron* the world would not see him but that the disciples are seeing him. Throughout the Last Supper discourse, he has repeatedly said that he was going away but focused on the paraclete who would keep the disciples from being orphans. Now, he baffles them completely with the notion that one *mikron* he's gone, and the next *mikron* he's back!

No wonder the disciples are totally confused. It is a comic relief in verses 17–18 when the disciples finally speak for the first time since Judas's question in 14:2. Indeed, we have not heard of them relating to "one another" since the confusion about the identity of the betrayer, when we were told that they "looked at one another" (13:22). The irony is found in the contrast between, on the one hand, Jesus' repeated command that what they should do with and for "one another" is *love* and, on the other hand, their speaking of their common ignorance.

When the disciples finally dare to break their silence and interrupt the master, the whole sad state of affairs comes pouring out. Not only do they not know what he means by his last statement about not seeing and seeing, but they also do not get his message about "because I am going to the Father" (verse 10). And after the narrator adds a few words to allow the facts of this confusion to sink in to the readers, the disciples add, "What is this *mikron* he is talking about?" Then, from the specific to the general, "We don't know what he is talking about!"

And who among readers can place much distance between the disciples situation and their/our own? Despite our attempts to unravel some of the crisscrossed threads of the Last Supper discourse, the Johannine Jesus' way of speaking remains mysterious, metaphorical, and confusing. Part of the problem, of course, is that the characters in the story — along with superficial readers — cannot possibly digest Jesus' words at the pace at which he speaks them. What is required is study, meditation, and, most importantly, *experience* that illuminates his message. The disciples have not yet undergone either the pain of Jesus' death or the joy of his resurrection. They have not yet felt the sting of their own persecution or the comfort of their mutual love and the support of the paraclete. In the absence of these experiences, Jesus' words seem totally confusing. But once they *have* had those experiences — once they have been transformed from the disciples in the story to the Johannine community — the words, if always partially opaque, do begin to reveal meanings that explain what has happened to them as being within God's will.

The situation is the same for modern readers. For Christians who sit comfortably in middle-class churches in the United States, all this talk about persecution and paracletes may seem distant and unconnected with our lives. But for those who have dared to respond to the call to witness to the world about sin, justice and judgment, Jesus' words, although still confusing, provide encouragement that comes directly from God.

Jesus, with the narrator's subtle help, responds to their confusion, starting in verse 19. Although the disciples are described by the narrator in verse 17 as speaking "to one another," the narrator tells us that "Jesus knew that they wanted to question him." Given how little they have understood of his discourse, it is not surprising that they are afraid to ask him directly to explain! Jesus, as usual, knows what is going on, but his words underscore the direction of their inquiry: "Are you seeking with one another because I said, 'A little time and you will not see me and again in a little time, you will see me'?" It is the third time in four verses that Jesus' exact words are repeated, the only such repetition in the fourth gospel.

But the preparaclete disciples will never understand as long as they only "seek" among themselves, just as people who look to human wisdom for guidance will stumble in the dark. Rather than explain directly what he means by this apparently crucial statement, he offers them a metaphor from women's experience.

### b. *"Grief Will Become Joy"*

#### Chiasm: 16:20–22

a: 20: you will weep/grieve; world will rejoice: grief will become joy

   b: 21a: woman has grief

      c: 21b: hour has come/suffering

   $b^1$: 21c: woman has joy

$a^1$: 22: you have grief; you will rejoice

In the first double-amen saying since 14:12, Jesus offers in verse 20 the assurance of both pain and joy to the disciples: "Amen, amen I am saying to you: you will weep [*klausete*] and you will wail, but the world will rejoice [*charēsetai*]. You will be grieved [*lypēthēsesthe*], but your grief will become joy [*charan*]." The "weeping" recalls the weeping at Lazarus' tomb (11:31, 33), which led Jesus to be deeply troubled. The "wailing" is unique here in the fourth gospel, but is used in Luke 23:27 to describe the reaction of the women to Jesus' way of the cross. It is clear, then, that these reactions are linked with the observance of death. But whose death: Jesus' or the disciples' own? At this point, either interpretation is possible.

The reaction of the world to either event is to rejoice. It is ironic in that Jesus has chastised the disciples for *not* rejoicing at the prospect of his return to the Father (14:28), but the world's rejoicing is clearly because of the death of trouble, not the triumphant return to God.

The prediction that they will be grieved links this passage with 16:6, where Jesus acknowledged that the disciples are filled with grief *now*. Again, it is ambiguous whether their grief is over Jesus' death or that of their community members. In either case, their grief will become joy. Suffering will not have the last word, even if it is a necessary phase of their experience.

Having stated this emotional transformation in direct terms, Jesus offers a powerful metaphor in verse 21: "The woman, when she gives birth, is having grief because her hour has come. But when she has become a parent [*gennēsē*] of a little child, she no longer remembers her suffering [*thlipseōs*] because of the joy that a person has been born into the world." Twice Isaiah offers similar imagery:

> As the woman about to give birth writhes and cries out
> in her pains,
> so were we in your presence, O Lord.
> We conceived and writhed in pain, giving birth to wind.
> Salvation we have not achieved for the earth.
> The inhabitants of the land cannot bring it forth.
> But your dead shall live, those in the tombs shall rise.
>
> (Isa 26:17–19)

> Before she came to labor, she gives birth;
> before the pains come upon her, she gives birth to a
> child.
> Who ever heard of such a thing, or saw the like?
> Can a country be brought forth in one day,
> or a nation be born in a moment?
> Yet Zion is scarcely in labor
> when she gives birth to her children....
> Rejoice with Jerusalem and be glad because of her.
>
> (Isa 66:7–8, 10)

These passages make clear that Jesus' metaphor is linked both with the need to depend totally on God for salvation and with the assurance of resurrection that leads not simply to individual continuity but also to the birth of a people. Since Jesus' words are addressed to the disciples collectively, his metaphor suggests that so long as they depend on themselves, they will weep and wail, believing that death has had the final word, like the Judeans weeping at Lazarus' tomb. But if they turn themselves over to the paraclete for guidance, their grief will become joy in the giving birth of a new people, that is, the Johannine community.

The ambiguity of the cause of their grief is clarified in verse 22 in light of the Isaian background of verse 21: "You, also, are indeed having grief now, but again I will see you, and your heart will rejoice, and your joy no one will take from you." The meaning of their not seeing and again seeing Jesus is inextricably linked with their own "hour." That is, in their life on earth, Jesus' absence will be compensated for by the advocacy of the paraclete. But they will see Jesus again when *their* hour has led them to rejoin him in the place he has prepared for them with the Father. The suffering of their own deaths will be turned to joy by their reunion with Jesus in their own resurrections. The woman's pain is not from observing the suffering of another but from the arrival of her *own* hour. Similarly, while Jesus' death will certainly cause them pain, it is their own death that will allow them to see Jesus again, giving them joy that no one can take away.

## c. *"The Day of Joy and Peace Is Coming"*

### Chiasm: 16:23–33

a: 23–24: you will not question me; joy
   b: 25–27: said in figures
      c: 28: came out from Father/going to Father
   b[1]: 29: not in figures
a[1]: 30–33: no one to question you; peace[12]

In the face of this prospect of grief-turned-joy, of death-become-resurrection, of absence-become-presence, Jesus focuses the disciples' attention on the depth of what their union with Jesus means, both now and in the end. As in 14:20, Jesus begins with the eschatological phrase "on that day," signaling that his words speak of the time of ultimate revelation. In this case, the promise is that "you will not question [*erōtēsete*] me about anything." Only on the other side of death can this promise be fulfilled, for the human journey in the world never ceases its restless questioning.

But immediately upon this assurance of internal peace when there are no more questions, comes the challenge to ask: "Amen, amen I am saying to you: if you should ask [*aitēsēte*] anything of the Father, he will give it to you in my name." The Greek plays on the contrast between *erōtaō* and *aiteō,* to question and to ask. The former is generally (but not always, see 14:16) used to gain information or to challenge, while the latter is generally (but not always, see 4:9) used for requests of God. Roughly speaking, *erōtaō* seeks to fulfill one's own desires, while *aiteō* seeks to align one's will with that of God. The exception is Jesus' use of *erōtaō,* because his will is the same as the will of God. Here, Jesus urges the disciples not to focus on *erōtaō* but on *aiteō.*

What Jesus invites the disciples to ask for "the Father will give you in my name." Does it make a difference that in 15:16 Jesus told them that "whatever you might ask [*aitēsēte*] the Father in my name, he will give you"? Is it the same thing to ask the Father in Jesus' name as for the Father to give them in Jesus' name? Brown notes that "nowhere else in John or in the New Testament is it said that things will be given in Jesus' name."[13] In both cases, the focus is on Jesus' name, which has been rejected by the world but becomes the key for the disciples to their friendship with God.

Despite the numerous invitations to "ask" in the Last Supper discourse (14:13, 14; 15:7, 16; 16:23), Jesus points out in verse 24 something certainly known to the disciples but not necessarily picked up by readers: "Until this moment, you have not asked for anything in my name." If we look back, we find that the disciples not only have not asked in Jesus' name within the story but have not *called* him by name except for the initial identification in 1:45

---

12. Ellis (1984, 237) limits the chiasm to 16:23–30, not seeing the parallel between "joy" and "peace" that extends the chiasm to the end of the speech in verse 33.

13. R. Brown (1970, 723).

by Philip. Indeed, of the 252 times that the name "Jesus" is used in the fourth gospel, only at most eight times is it used by characters other than the narrator (1:45 [Philip]; 4:1 [rumors]; 6:42 [Judeans murmuring]; 9:11 [the once-blind man]; 12:21 [the Greeks]; 18:5, 7 [those who arrest him]; 19:19 [Pilate's sign]).

Is it a question of respect (like the Jewish reticence to pronounce the name YHWH) or fear or powerlessness? Although there is certainly some measure of respect suggested by the various titles by which disciples and friends address Jesus rather than by his name, it also suggests a distance that Jesus seeks to remove. They continue to see Jesus as an elevated "Lord" rather than as a friend they can count on and call on for help and support. Indeed, this attitude has persisted throughout the centuries, as evidenced by the pious seeking of the mediation of Mary and the saints that has arisen in part because of the fear of asking directly in the name of Jesus. While it is certainly a good thing to call on the spirits of ancestors and particularly of the woman Mary — whose feminine holiness complements the masculine holiness of Jesus — when it happens because of fear of engagement with Jesus, it becomes a form of idolatry. The Johannine Jesus urges his disciples not to be afraid to use his name in prayer, and hence show their friendship with him.

Again in verse 24b, Jesus puts the focus of asking on its joyous consequences: "Ask and you will receive, so that your joy may be fulfilled [*peplērōmenē*]." In the literary structure of the gospel, Jesus' desire to see the disciples' joy fulfilled "surrounds" their being filled with grief (15:11 [joy]; 16:6 [grief]; 16:24 [joy]). While there may be pain and suffering in the middle, both beginning and end are to be times of joy for the Johannine community.

In one of the rare self-reflections on the mode with which he speaks, Jesus changes topics to tell his hearers in verse 25 about the before and after of his speech form: "These things [*tauta*] I have spoken to you in proverbs [*paroimiais*]; the hour is coming when I will no longer speak to you in proverbs but will report [*apangelō*] to you openly [*parrhēsia*] about the Father." The announcement begins like the familiar Last Supper discourse refrain, "These things I have spoken to you..." (15:11; 16:1, 4). But the specification that he has spoken in *paroimiais* but will cease that mode soon challenges the disciples and readers to reconsider all that has been said so far.

The word *paroimiais* is unique in the gospels to John and has been used outside this verse only by the narrator to describe the good shepherd metaphor that the disciples did not understand (10:6). Its only other occurrence in the New Testament is in 2 Ptr 2:22, where it clearly bears the meaning "proverb." But does "proverb" fully capture the meaning of *paroimiais* here? The question then becomes: To which prior statements is Jesus referring? Some scholars have interpreted the reference to include Jesus' mode of speaking throughout the fourth gospel.[14] But given the usage in 10:6, it seems to be more narrowly focused on a particular aspect of Jesus' speech that is especially difficult to understand.

---

14. Dewey (1980); O'Day (1988, 105).

One clue may be found in one of the rare uses of the term in the Septuagint. In the book of Sirach, the speaker sets out a contrast between the vocations of scribe and craftsperson. The latter is doing "God's ancient handiwork" (38:34) but is so focused on the materials and tools of the trade that there is no time or energy left for "wisdom." The scribe, on the other hand, is described in part as follows:

> How different the one who devotes himself to the study
>     of the law of the Most High!
> That one seeks out the wisdom of the ancients, and is
>     occupied in prophecies.
> That one will keep the sayings of the famous ones, and
>     where subtle parables are,
> that one will be also.
> That one will seek out the secrets of obscure proverbs
>     [*paroimion*],
> and is busied with the meanings of dark parables.
> That one shall serve among the great, and appear before
>     rulers....
> If he dies, he shall leave a greater name than a thousand,
>     and if he lives, he shall increase it.
>
>                                     (Sir 39:1–4, 11)

Given the rarity of the term in both the Septuagint and New Testament, it is not far-fetched to consider this passage as background for verse 25. If so, it suggests that Jesus casts himself in the role of the wise sage whose *paroimiais* scribes study to shape themselves in accordance with God's will. The disciples, under the guidance of the paraclete, are to become such scribes, in that they are to meditate on these obscure words in order to be united with Jesus and his Father.

The question remains, however: What specifically is Jesus referring to by his *paroimiais?* Many scholars have long argued that the most original aspects of the historical Jesus' speech pattern are found in his parables. In the synoptic narratives, the parables seem to provide a parallel function to the *paraoimian* in 10:1–5, that is, to note the disciples' lack of understanding and to give Jesus a chance to "explain" (e.g., Mk 4:1–20). The term "parable" (*parabolen*) is not used at all in the fourth gospel; nor does Jesus use the particular form of speech to which the term refers. I suggest that the speech type to which the Johannine Jesus refers is not simply "proverbs" but the unique *egō eimi* statements that are the closest Johannine equivalents to the synoptic parables. Although the good shepherd *egō eimi* statement comes in 10:7 *after* the reference to *paroimian,* the figure given in 10:1–5 sets up the "interpretation" that Jesus *is* the good shepherd.

And indeed, Jesus will make no further *egō eimi* comparisons in the fourth gospel, using the term only in the absolute sense of identification (18:5, 8). The "hour" is a time for speaking "openly," which Jesus does with his unadorned *egō eimi*. The Judeans demanded that Jesus tell them "openly" (*parrhēsia*) whether he was the messiah in order to entrap him into a "confession" that would justify their stoning him (10:24). In the end, his speaking not in *paroimiais* but *parrhēsia* indeed *will* lead to his execution. That "declaration" (*anangellō*), which Jesus told them would be given to the disciples through the guidance of the paraclete (16:12, 14, 15), will teach them that what is "joy" to the world will lead to the "*fullness* of joy" for the Johannine community, because it is the pathway by which Jesus goes to the Father and leads to the paraclete's conviction of the world about its own kind of justice (16:10). In other words, everything that Jesus has told them so far in *paroimiais* will be clarified by the lifting up/glorification of Jesus on the cross, the moment when his "hour" arrives.

When that moment comes, Jesus tells them in verse 26, their intimacy with the Father will be forged in a new way: "On that day, you will ask [*aitēsesthe*] in my name, and I am *not* saying to you that I will ask [*erōtēsō*] the Father on your behalf." This time, Jesus contrasts their asking (*aiteō*) with his own nonasking (*ou...erōtao*). At first glance, it seems to suggest a negative: that the disciples will finally do what Jesus has said that they have not done until now, and he will refuse to help them! But the completion of the thought in verse 27 makes it clear that there is another basis for Jesus' refusal to ask on their behalf: "For the Father is friendly [*philei*] with you, because you have been friendly [*pephilēkate*] with me, and you have believed that I came out from the Father." It is surprising that Jesus refers to the relationship between the Father, himself, and the disciples in terms of *phileō* rather than *agapē,* as he has been doing throughout the Last Supper discourse. *Agapē* involves self-sacrifice and has been used as the ultimate measure of intimacy and commitment. But up to this point, the disciples have not shown that sort of relationship with Jesus. Indeed, he has told them that "*if* you were loving [*ēgapate*] me, you would have rejoiced because I am going to the Father" (14:28). So Jesus cannot honestly affirm the Father's *agapē* for the disciples as grounded in theirs for Jesus, because it does not exist, and Jesus only speaks truth. However, their *philea* for Jesus, by which he has called them "friends" (*philous,* 15:15), does justify a reciprocal relationship with the Father on *that* basis. Thus, the disciples and the Father are "friends," and the disciples therefore do not need Jesus to intervene on their behalf but can "ask" the Father directly in Jesus' name.

Verses 26–28 reveal a word-chain structure that we saw previously in 3:12–21. Here, the linkages are as follows:

26: ask–Father
27a: Father–friendly
27b: friendly–I came out from the Father
28a: I came out from the Father–come into the world
28b: leaving the world–going to Father

It is a mnemonic device that will help the Johannine community "remember" what Jesus has told them. The paraclete may provide divine guidance, but a helpful verbal pattern is also a good tool!

In verse 28, Jesus uses this structure to summarize the parabolic course of his journey: out from the Father, into the world, out of the world, and back to the Father.

And suddenly, in verses 29–30 the disciples proclaim their understanding: "The disciples said to him, 'Look! Now you are speaking openly [*parrhēsia*], and you are using no proverb [*paroimian*]! Now we have known that you know all things [*panta*] and that you have no need for anyone to question [*erōta*] you! Through this, we are believing that you came out from God.' " What possibly could have provoked this sudden outburst of understanding and enthusiasm? The disciples communal speech — the only time they speak to him collectively in the Last Supper discourse — is hilariously ironic. For Jesus has just told them that "the hour is *coming*" when *parrhēsia* will replace *paroimian*. But it is *not* now! And there is nothing about the way Jesus has spoken between their utter confusion in verses 17–18 and now that is so different to make their claim credible. In fact, there is hardly a word in these verses that Jesus has not spoken to them before. As Paul Duke concisely states the matter, the "disciples build faulty confession [by this we believe] upon faulty claim [we know you know] upon faulty assumption [now you are speaking plainly]." In shifting the time of Jesus' reference from the cross to the comfort of the supper table, "the necessary death and resurrection are neatly swept away."[15] How many of us would like to proclaim our understanding of Jesus without having to face the reality of the cross? The collective character of the disciples, used so sparingly but powerfully in the Last Supper discourse, now highlights one of the primary *barriers* to discipleship.

Jesus makes this point himself in verses 31–33. He begins by questioning their instant conversion: "Do you believe now? Look! The hour is coming — and has come — in which you will be scattered [*skorpisthēte*], each one into their own [*idia*], and you will leave me alone." He mocks their enthusiastic "Look!" with a "Look!" of his own. It is not the hour of understanding but the hour of scattering and desertion. In the third implicit reference to the good shepherd discourse, Jesus tells them that the hour of the wolf has arrived (10:12, *skorpizei*), the time in which the hired help abandons the sheep. But in a bitterly ironic prediction, Jesus tells them that although they are the sheep and he the good shepherd, *they* will abandon *him*. And in another contrast, while the shepherd takes care of his "own" by calling them by name and leading them out into pasturage (10:3, 4, *idia*), the disciples will retreat into their "own." It will put the disciples to the test: Are they part of the world's "own" who will welcome them back (15:19)? That is: Are they Jesus' "own," who, the prologue foretold, did not receive him (1:11)? Or will they become Jesus' lovers who will be willing in the end to lay down their lives for their friends? The hope lies in the other use of

---

15. Duke (1985, 58).

the verb *skorpizō* in 11:52, that Jesus' death will take place "so that the children of God who are scattered [*dieskorpismena*] might be led together into one."

It is a brutal truth with which Jesus confronts them, but a necessary one in light of their false claim of knowledge. As such, it parallels for the Johannine community what Jesus did for Simon Peter, the only disciple to speak as an individual in the Last Supper discourse (13:37–38). In both places, he responds to a bold claim with a doubting question, followed by a statement of the true nature of things.

But regardless of how things will turn out for the disciples, Jesus will not be alone, "because the Father is with me." Ultimately, the Johannine Jesus does not need the disciples to complete his mission.

But all "these things [*tauta*] I have spoken to you so that in me you may have peace. In the world, you have suffering [*thlipsin*], but have courage! I have conquered [*nenikēka*] the world." Verse 33 summarizes all that Jesus has told them, completing the chiasms with the offer of peace. Joy and peace are parallel realities, the "bookends" that bind the troubles that both Jesus and those who follow him face in the world. Their "suffering" is like the woman in childbirth, who must undergo pain in order to generate new life. As Brown points out, the word *thlipsis* is in the Septuagint "a word that is used almost technically to describe the tribulation that will precede God's eschatological action" (e.g., Dan 12:1; Zeph 1:14–15; Hab 3:16).[16] Thus, the disciples' suffering is for the sake of bringing forth the reign of God, the messianic age that Jesus can proclaim and introduce but that only the disciples can live out and make fully real. That is the joy and peace that Jesus offers: a kind of living completely different from the way of the world, in which friendship and love replace violence and lies. It is a difficult road between here and there, as anyone who has taken the first step knows only too well.

But Jesus assures them that the victory is already won. It is the only place in the fourth gospel that victory is proclaimed, although "victory" is a common term in apocalyptic literature such as the book of Revelation (fifteen times). Just as the disciples' "work" is not to plant seeds but to gather the harvest (4:38), so it is not theirs to achieve the victory but rather to live in the light which that victory casts on the world around them. In place of their fear, Jesus commands "courage," the only time in the fourth gospel for this term as well. These are the final words that Jesus speaks to his fragile, confused, struggling community before the moment of his cross. What remains is a prayer, direct communication between Jesus and his Father, which both the disciples and we are privileged to hear.

---

16. R. Brown (1970, 732). Cf. Rev 1:9; 2:9; 7:14.

# 21

# "Keep Them from the Evil One"

## *Jesus' Prayer for the Community*

### John 17:1–26

A. **Chiasm:**

   a: 1–5: glory before world was made; completion (*teleiōsas*) of Jesus' work

     b: 6–10: given your word

       c: 11–13: prayer for disciples

     b[1]: 14–19: given your word

   a[1]: 20–26: glory before foundation of world; completion (*teteleiōmenoi*) of disciples' unity[1]

B. **Location:** not specified

C. **Time:** near Passover

D. **Social factors:** Johannine community vs. world

E. **Themes:** Passing of the mission from Jesus to the disciples; "in" the world but not "of" the world

F. **Key words:** glory, the world, sent/send, one

---

1. Ellis (1984, 239–240) notes the divisions as 1–5, 6–8, 9–13, 14–19, 20–26, but he does not note the smaller internal chiasms. Given the fit between the smaller chiasms and the thematic parallels in the larger structure of chapter 17, I have divided the passage as shown. Malatesta (1970) offers a different five-part division (plus introduction), each part of which he sees comprising either a three- or five-part chiasm (1a,b,c [intro]; 1d,e,f–5; 6–8; 9–19; 20–24; 25–26). His analysis pays closer attention to the poetic composition of each line than does my own and has much to commend it. Clearly, the text's intricate and delicate interweaving of language and themes supports multiple perspectives on its organizational unity. I chose the pattern shown because it maintains the five-part structure throughout, which is consistent with the chiastic pattern found in the entire gospel.

## 1. "THIS IS ETERNAL LIFE:  TO KNOW YOU AND THE ONE WHOM YOU SENT"

### Chiasm: 17:1–5

a: 1: Father, glorify Son

   b: 2: power over flesh, give life

      c: 3: this is eternal life...

   b¹: 4: on earth [=flesh], finished work [=give life]

a¹: 5: Father, glorify me

Having completed his farewell speech to his disciples, Jesus makes his "farewell" speech to his Father in chapter 17. It is, of course, not a true farewell (nor is the speech preceding it, for that matter) because Jesus is going to the one to whom he speaks. But as with the previous prayer overheard by those gathered around Lazarus' tomb, Jesus speaks for the sake of those listening (11:41–42). The prayer places both disciples and readers in a privileged position, overhearing a piece of the ongoing word between God and Son. It allows us to listen in as Jesus "reports" to his sender on what he has accomplished and what the sender must do to complete the task at hand. As Wayne A. Meeks says, the prayer "as a whole is only intelligible within the descent/ascent framework, for it is the summary 'de-briefing' of the messenger."[2]

The structure and language of chapter 17 are clearly poetic, paralleling the prologue. Yet its poetic pattern serves precisely the opposite function of modern poetry. As E. R. Wendland puts it, "Most poetry depends in large measure upon the principle termed 'defamiliarisation' " in order to prolong the process of perception and invite readers to a meditative interaction with the text. In contrast, John 17 manifests "the technique of 're-familiarisation,' a many-tiered reiteration of sound, sense and syntax the rhetorical purpose of which is to consolidate as well as to motivate [readers] with what they already (should) know."[3] Thus, Jesus' prayer is a summary of summaries, the grand culmination of his teaching to the Johannine community.

Both Johannine prayers begin with the same gesture, although described slightly differently in each case. In 11:41, the narrator told us that "Jesus lifted his eyes upward [*ano*]," whereas in 17:1, he says, "Jesus, having lifted his eyes into heaven [*ouranon*]. . . ." Just as above/below and heaven/earth are interchangeable metaphors in the fourth gospel, so are these small differences in the description of Jesus' locus of attention.

Both prayers continue with the simple introduction, "Father." But where the graveside prayer begins with thanksgiving, the prayer in chapter 17 begins with a petition: "The hour has come: glorify your Son, so that the Son should glorify

---

2. Meeks (1972, 66).
3. Wendland (1992, 77–78).

you." The theme of glory, which completed the chiasm in 13:1–32, now begins the chiasm in 17:1–26. Of the various nuances that the theme undergoes, this usage most closely parallels 13:31, where Jesus speaks of the interconnected glory of God and the Human One. Jesus responded in 12:23 to the coming of the Greeks with the announcement that "the hour has come so that the Human One might be glorified [*doxasthē*]." Now, what *might* be *is* to be. The opening to the Gentiles of the covenant between God and God's children signaled the hour in which Jesus' glory would be revealed. Now, with the community prepared for Jesus' departure, all that remains is for Jesus to summarize his mission and walk into the moment of glory itself.

The summary of the accomplishment of the mission begins in verse 2: "As you gave to him authority [*exousian*] over all flesh, so to all whom you have given to him he will give eternal life to them." Jesus' authority over "flesh" describes his power over the world's dominant culture, just as the prologue contrasted those born of "the will of the flesh" with those born of God to whom Jesus gave "authority" (*exousian*) to become God's children (1:12–13). As the gospel has contrasted the glory that comes from God with the glory people give one another (5:44, 12:43), equating human-given glory with the way of "flesh" (8:15), so now Jesus' moment of divine glory is linked with his superiority over "flesh." As this authority is given to Jesus by God, so Jesus in turn will give his community "eternal life."

And lest we lapse into the temptation to consider this a promise for the afterlife, the narrator intervenes to expressly declare in verse 3 the meaning of the term: "This is 'eternal life': that they may be knowing you, the one true God, and the one whom you sent, Jesus Christ." Just as Jesus previously offered eternal life as a present reality focused on faith (3:36; 5:24; 6:40, 47), so now its presence is affirmed in those who participate in the intimacy with God and Jesus to which Jesus has invited them. It is important to note that the verb for "know," *ginōskō*, describes a *relationship* between knower and known, not knowledge as intellectual awareness of something, as in gnosticism. As we observed throughout the parallel section of the Last Supper discourse at the footwashing, the disciples' "knowledge" or lack thereof has to do with their intimacy with each other and with Jesus. Eternal life is what Jesus gives to those whose relationship with him and with God allows them to live "above" the dominant culture's enticements of human glory.

It is a theme rich in Hebrew scripture background. Jeremiah speaks of the coming days in this way:

> I will give them a heart to know that I AM [LXX, *egō eimi*] the Lord. They shall be my people and I will be their God, for they shall return to me with their whole heart. (24:7)

> I will place my law within them, and write it upon their hearts; I will be their God, and they shall be my people. No longer will they have need to teach their friends and kinspeople how to know the Lord. All, from the

least to greatest, shall know me, says the Lord, for I will forgive their evildoing and remember their sin no more. (31:33–34)

The relationship that God hoped for in the exilic days of Jeremiah has been fulfilled in the Johannine community.

The prayer continues in verses 4–5 with an intimate quid pro quo between Son and Father: "I glorified you on the earth, having completed [*teleiōsas*] the work which you have given me to do. Now, Father, you glorify me in yourself [*para seautō*] with the glory which I had with you [*para soi*] before the world came to be." Jesus has done his part; now it is the Father's turn. Jesus' part, as he noted earlier during its course (4:34; 5:36), was to "complete" the work he had been given. Heaven's will has been done on earth, a Johannine version of one of the petitions of the Lord's Prayer. The second half of the statement, God's part in the "deal," is expressed in language difficult to translate. The phrase *para seautō* is literally "beside yourself," as *para soi* is "beside you." Further complicating the issue, the verb translated "came to be," *einai,* is different than the verb used in the prologue for came to be, *ginomai.* The literal language of verse 5 simply says "before the world to be" (*pro tou ton kosmon einai*). However we translate this uncharacteristically awkward phrase, the meaning seems to be that Jesus is petitioning God for the glory that the preexistent Word shared with God, as in 1:2. As Jesus' work brought God from heaven to earth, so now Jesus asks God to bring him back home.

## 2. THEY RECEIVED, THEY KNEW, AND THEY BELIEVED

**Chiasm: 17:6–10**

a: 6: yours they were

  b: 7: you have given me

    c: 8: know/believe

  b¹: 9: you have given me

a¹: 10: mine are yours

As the first chiasm summarized Jesus completion of the Father's work, the following chiasms continue to describe point-by-point what that work consisted of. Verse 6 expresses the first element: "I revealed [*ephanerōsa*] your name to the people whom you gave me out of the world." Ever since Moses' encounter with the theretofore unnamed God at the burning bush, the revelation of God's name has been a key element of the covenant between God and Israel (Ex 3:14–15). Hundreds of times in the Hebrew scripture, people proclaim the power and holiness of God's name. For the scribes, that name became too sacred to pronounce, or even to write, as the transliterated YHWH was replaced by the neutral *adonai* in scriptural texts. To this day, even many New Testament translations use "Lord" where "YHWH" was the original text, out of deference to God's name.

While there is something powerful about refusing to reduce the infinite God to the apparently common name "Yahweh," the Johannine Jesus refuses to give up the importance of the revelation of the name. In the Septuagint, of course, YHWH became *egō eimi,* the closest the Greek could come to the unfathomable meaning of YHWH. As the Septuagint version of Isa 52:6 puts it, "Therefore shall my people know my name on that day, because *egō eimi* is the one who speaks." *This* is the name Jesus has revealed, restoring its accessibility to those who become his disciples. Just as calling God "Father" brought God out of the sky and into relationship with people's hearts, so the revelation of *egō eimi* puts people back in touch with the power of God's name. And, as we saw in 9:9, the name becomes claimable by disciples *for themselves* as well. The power of God's name, as revealed by Jesus, is available to all who call on it in faith and love.

Those to whom Jesus has revealed God's name are those given "out of the world [*ek tou kosmou*]." The struggle to be "in the world" (*en to kosmou*) and at the same time "out of the world" is a basic theme in Jesus' prayer for his disciples. It is introduced in verse 6 by noting that these people given to Jesus by God are by that giving no longer part of the world, that is, the dominant culture of darkness ruled over by the devil (e.g., 8:44).

But before we can consider the implications of being "out of the world," Jesus focuses instead on the element of the giving: "They were yours and you gave them to me." It is obviously not as if by giving people to Jesus they are no longer God's people. Rather, it is that those who *are* Jesus' people — the Johannine community and other Christian communities — became that through God's giving. The act of committing oneself to the "lifted up" one is to live with the flow of God's will. To a persecuted community feeling alone in the world, the assurance that their link with the "vine" is mandated by God is a powerful aspect of the Johannine story.

It is in this way that the last phrase of verse 6 makes sense: "They have kept your word." While the disciples have been pitilessly portrayed as bumblers and stumblers, they *have* remained true to the most central "word" of the fourth gospel: to believe that Jesus is the one sent by God.

But the prayer continues in verses 7–8 by claiming a depth of understanding for the disciples that readers have not experienced: "Now they have known that all things [*panta*] which you gave to me are from you, because the words which you gave to me, I have given to them, and they received and truly knew that I came from you, and they believed that you sent me." It is one of the longest sentences in the gospel, and seems to flow out of Jesus' mouth as a single thought. To grasp the surprising scope of what it claims, we can look at its parts schematically:

*Now*:

1. they *have known that all things* which you gave me are from you
   (because the words which you gave to me I have given to them)

2. and they *received*

3. and they *truly knew* that I came out from you

4. and they *believed* that you sent me

Is it possible that the "now" is the story world "now" of the Last Supper discourse, a short time before Passover? The disciples, for all their human foibles, have indeed "received" this basic premise. At this late date in the story, they "remain" with Jesus, even in the midst of their confusion, pain, and fear. Lines 3 and 4 set out above exhibit Johannine parallelism, saying basically the same thing: to truly know is to believe; that Jesus came from God means that God sent him. Their understanding of their own call to discipleship may be blocked by their fears now, but they have not lost sight of the central truth, the telling of which Jesus tells his Father has been completed during his sojourn on earth. Their acceptance of what Jesus has given them will lead them to continue to struggle to discern its meaning for their own lives, just as we look to the scriptures to gain deeper insight into what the God we claim to know and believe in wants *us* to do.

These stumbling but faithful people are the ones for whom Jesus "prays" beginning in verse 9: "About them I am asking [*erōtō*]; I am not asking about the world, but about the ones you have given me." The now familiar term for "asking" takes on the sense of entreating or praying, as Jesus gives an example for the disciples of how to "ask the Father." Lest the division between those for whom Jesus prays and those he expressly does not pray for seem too harsh, we must remember that the invitation remains open to all people to leave the world and become included within Jesus' prayer. And, in a way, Jesus' apparently "exclusive" prayer could not be different. How can Jesus honestly pray for those who do not see him as sent from God? God does not work by coercion but by "drawing" people (6:44; 12:32). A prayer that God act in the lives of people who have not chosen to be oriented toward God would be a violent prayer, an insistence that God save people who are not looking to be saved.

The chiasm closes with a return to the opening theme of the unity of "possession" of God and Jesus: "They are yours, and all [*panta*] that is mine is yours, and yours mine, and I have been glorified in them." The last phrase opens an interesting ambiguity that is unresolvable because both possibilities are true. Jesus is glorified "in them" in the sense of "among them"; that is, within the Johannine community, he is glorified. At the same time, he is glorified "in them" in the sense that his glory is seen in the lives of his followers (cf. 13:35). It is a fitting polyvalence following on the symmetry of "yours" and "mine."

## 3. "I AM NO LONGER IN THE WORLD, BUT THEY ARE IN THE WORLD"

**Chiasm: 17:11–13**

a: 11a: world/coming to you

   b: 11b: keep in your name/you gave

      c: 11c: they=one/we=one

   b¹: 12: kept in your name/you have given

a¹: 13: coming to you/world

After noting the separation of his own from the world, Jesus continues the prayer in verse 11 by noting the separation of himself from the disciples: "And no longer am I in the world, but they are in the world, and I am coming to you." It is not a matter of speaking from beyond death but of one's locus of mission and ministry. Jesus no longer acts "in the world" but only here among his disciples. The upcoming Passion will be the ultimate confrontation with the world, but Jesus will remain throughout it apart from the world that finally appears to succeed in destroying him. The terrible trials awaiting Jesus are not part of the sojourn announced in 1:14 but are, as he says in verse 11, part of the process of "coming to" God.

But for the disciples who are in the world, Jesus expresses the petition to which verse 9 referred: "Holy Father, keep them in your name which you have given me, so that they may be one as we are." It is the only place in the Bible that God is addressed or described in this way, although the Lord's Prayer tradition includes the idea of the Father's holy name (Mt 6:9; Lk 11:2). But whereas the synoptics use the notion to proclaim the coming of the kingdom, the Johannine Jesus' purpose is the unity of the disciples. The name *egō eimi* has been given to Jesus, and those who live in commitment to that reality *are* one in that faith.

Verse 12 finds Jesus speaking of his role in the past, appropriate to one whose work is completed: "When I was with them, I kept [*etēroun*] them in your name which you have given to me, and I watched [*ephylaxa*], and none of them were destroyed [*apōleto*], except the son of destruction [*apōleias*], so that the scripture should be fulfilled." The combination of keeping and watching recalls a particular Septuagint verse from the book of Wisdom:

> She, in the midst of the nations' widespread evil [*ponērias*], found the just one, and kept [*etērēsen*] that one blameless before God, and watched [*ephylaxen*] that one against compassion for his child. (10:5)

Just as verse 5 prayed for God to continue glorifying as Jesus did, now he prays that the Father continue the "keeping" that Jesus did. The note that only one was "destroyed" recalls the several other juxtapositions in the fourth gospel between protection and destruction (3:16; 6:12, 27, 39; 10:10, 28; 11:50; 12:25). In particular, Jesus had announced earlier that "this is the will of the one who sent me: that all which he has given to me I should not destroy [*apōleso*] but should raise up on the last day" (6:39). While verse 12 seems at first to suggest an imperfect performance by Jesus in allowing one to be destroyed, we see that by noting the lost one as the "son of destruction," Jesus makes clear that that one was not in fact given to Jesus by the Father but was given by the devil, the father of lies and murder (8:44; cf. 13:1). We have already heard how this betrayal fulfills scripture (13:17), but Jesus notes it again to remind the bystanding listeners that the loss of Judas was part of the risk taken in the incarnation.

Once again, Jesus shifts the focus in verse 13 from the necessity of pain to the fulfillment of joy (15:11; 16:24). "Fulfillment" is a two-edged sword, depending on where one's allegiance lies. For Judas, it means condemnation, but for those who remain with Jesus while they are in the world, it means joy.

## 4. "THEY ARE NOT OF THE WORLD, JUST AS I AM NOT OF THE WORLD"

**Chiasm: 17:14–19**

a: 14a: your word

   b: 14b–15a: they are not out of the world, as I am not out of the world

      c: 15b: keep them from the evil one

   b$^1$: 16–18: they are not out of the world, as I am not out of the world

a$^1$: 19: truth (17b: your word is truth)

Jesus began the prayer for his disciples by noting their separation from the way of the world and continued by noting his own imminent absence from the world. Now, he focuses on the fate of those he leaves behind in the world but not of it: "I have given to them your word, and the world hated them, because they are not of the world [*ek tou kosmou*], just as I am not of the world." While 15:18–25 warned the disciples about the impending experience of hatred, verse 14 speaks of it as an ongoing reality already begun. It is clear that Jesus is speaking here of the Johannine community rather than the story-world disciples, who have not as yet given the world any reason to hate them. The word that these disciples bring into the world inevitably causes those who choose the world's ways to hate the messengers, because the word calls them "out of the world" in which they are comfortably ensconced.

Although *ek tou kosmou* earlier suggested that the disciples were apart from the world (17:6), the literal language of verse 14 says the opposite: "They are not out of the world [*ouk eisin ek tou kosmou*]." It must fit with the language of verse 11, that they are "in the world." That is, their mission is *in* the world, but their allegiance is to God, *not* to the world. It is the most difficult of tasks, one truly requiring divine help. The Qumran community chose not to attempt it: they left the world by moving to the desert and attempting to live a "pure" relationship with God there. The Sanhedrin and other Judeans were called to it by the Torah but could not manage it, succumbing to the ancient temptation that if you can't beat 'em, join 'em. The Johannine community is called to walk the knife's edge between these relatively easy options: to remain in the world but not of it.

Rather than "keep" them by putting them in a safe place, Jesus prays for God's continued protection for them: "I am not asking that you should take them out of the world, but that you should keep them from the evil one [*ponērou*]." The chiastic parallelism between 13:1–32 and 17:1–26 suggests that "the evil one" is the same as "Satan" or the "devil" mentioned in 13:1 and 13:27.[4] Although this is the only occurrence of the term in the fourth gospel, it is a common title in Matthew (e.g., Mt. 6:13; 13:19, 38) and is used in the Lord's Prayer in a similar way as in Jn 17:15. This prayer for protection emphasizes the need for the Johannine community to remain immersed in the devil's kingdom because of God's love for the world.

Verse 16 underscores once more that the disciples are *in* but not *of* the place of evil: "They are not *ek tou kosmou* just as I am not *ek tou kosmou*." Verses 14–16 are indisputably clear about the relationship between the discipleship community and the world, leaving it impossible for later Christians to deny (at least on the basis of the fourth gospel!) the challenge to forge a way of life not in accord with the world.

The prayer takes the form of a commissioning in verses 17–19. Now that it is clear that the mission is in the world and that the disciples will be protected by God while they are there, Jesus prays for their consecration: "Sanctify [*hagiason*] them in the truth; your word [*logos*] is truth." As the Father is "holy" (*hagie*), so Jesus prays that the disciples can be made *hagiason* by means of the *logos,* that is, by Jesus who is the *logos* incarnate. It is a poetic, circular sort of prayer, already accomplished by the work that Jesus has completed. And it is also redolent of the Septuagint:

> For I [*egō eimi*], the Lord your God am holy [*hagiasthēsesthe*], and you shall be holy [*hagioi*], because holy [*hagios*] is [*eimi egō*] the Lord your God. (Lev 11:44)

> And you shall be holy [*hagioi*] to me, because I the Lord am holy [*hagios*], who separated [*aphorisas*] you from all nations, to be mine. (Lev 20:26)

The beautiful chiastic symmetry in Lev 11:44 and the note of God's "separation" of the holy people from the nations form an ironically fitting background for verse 17. The irony lies in the Greek word for "who separated," *aphorisas,*

---

4. Ellis (1984, 243).

from which the *Pharisees* got both their name and their ideology. Now it is the Johannine community that is separated for the sake of holiness, but by consecration, not by removal.

The consecration prepares them for the mission in verse 18: "Just as you sent me into the world, so I sent them into the world." The call is identical, as the precisely parallel phrasing suggests. Further, the "surrounding" of the mission with holiness in verse 19 paints a remarkable word picture of the location of discipleship: "And I am sanctifying [*hagiazo*] myself over [*hyper*] them, so that they may be sanctified in truth." Raymond Brown suggests that the image of "over" recalls the fourth gospel's way of speaking about Jesus' death in 10:11; 11:51; and 15:13.[5] Thus, Jesus' death is the act that begins the process of leading his community into the holiness they need to be protected from the evil one, to carry out the mission to be among those sent by God into the world, armed only with the truth.

### 5. "I IN THEM AND YOU IN ME": PERFECTED IN UNITY

**Chiasm: 17:20–26**

a: 20–21: faith that you sent me

   b: 22: glory you gave me

      c: 23: perfect unity

   b¹: 24: glory you have given me

a¹: 25–26: know that you sent me

Having prayed for the Father's assistance in preparing the disciples for their mission to the world, Jesus turns in verses 20–26 to prayers for "the ones believing in me through their word." It is the Johannine community and its successors that are the objects of Jesus' concern. The central theme is unity, especially in verses 21–23. The speech achieves its effect through the interplay of the Greek words for "one" (*hen*) and "in" (*en*), linked by "so that" (*hina*) and "as" (*kathos*). To appreciate the poetic recurrence and interweaving of these words, it may be helpful to look at the three verses together with the Greek noted:

(21) So that [*hina*] they may all be one [*hen*], as [*kathos*] you, Father, are in [*en*] me and I in [*en*] you, so that [*hina*] they also may be in [*en*] us, so that [*hina*] the world may believe that you sent me.

(22) And the glory which you have given to me I have given to them, so that [*hina*] they may be one [*hen*] as [*kathos*] we are one [*hen*];

(23) I in [*en*] them and you in [*en*] me, so that [*hina*] they may be completed into one [*hen*], so that [*hina*] the world may know that you sent me and you loved them as [*kathos*] you loved me.

---

5. R. Brown (1970, 766).

It is important to note several features emphasized by these verses about the nature and purpose of the unity for which Jesus prays. First, while the depth of interpenetration among God, Jesus, and the Johannine community is certainly supportive of a mystical interpretation, it is a *communal* mysticism that is highlighted. Nowhere is Jesus concerned with the individual believer's unity with him or with the Father; he is concerned, rather, with the disciples as a believing community.

Second, this unity is not simply for the edification or support of the community itself but is an essential element determining the quality of its mission to the world. In the three-part chiasm that the verses comprise, the concluding *hina* clauses in the parallel segments focus on the effect of the oneness on the world. The life of the Johannine community is its most powerful witness to the world, that which has the capacity to bring the world to the faith and knowledge that *are* eternal life (17:3, 8).

Finally, this unity is not a matter of moral or doctrinal agreement but of the intimacy of faith and shared purpose to which the previous sections of the prayer and the entire Last Supper discourse have called them. It is to be a "completed" (*teteleiōmenoi*) unity, which inherits its being from the "completion" of Jesus' work (17:4). In the face of persecution, the willingness of the discipleship community to remain bonded in the mutual love given by the Father through Jesus will speak volumes to a world built around distrust, deceit, and death-dealing. How many Christians have been made or sustained by the witness of Salvadoran communities of faith that practiced this way of life during years of bloodshed and fratricide! What a difference it would make in the United States if more discipleship communities walked this path together into courtrooms or churches!

At the center of this part of Jesus' prayer is his gift of glory to the community. It is a somewhat ironic gift, for as we have been warned and will soon see, the glory that God gives is very different from what people bestow on one another. It is a glory seen and understood as such only by God and God's children. But in the end, it is a glory far surpassing the mere bestowal of wealth and power that are the gifts of those beholden to the Temple-state or the Roman empire.

The prayer and the enormous sweep of the Last Supper discourse come to a crescendo in the final verses, as Jesus offers his prayer in verse 24 that the disciples "may be with me where I am, so that [*hina*] they may see my glory which you have given to me." When the mission is completed, Jesus will rejoin his sheep in the unity that death cannot divide. It is a fitting reprise of the theme in 5:21, when Jesus announced that "the Son is willing [*thelei*] to make alive" those who have died, just as the Father does. In verse 24, Jesus "is willing" (*thelō*) that the future disciples may join him where he is.

While the "gift" of God's glory may look like suffering on this side of life, Jesus prays that the disciples may see it in its true form on the other side. It is a glory that has resulted from God's love for Jesus since "before the foundation [*katabolēs*] of the world." The phrase used has no background in Hebrew scripture but was taken up by several New Testament writers from secular Greek usage.[6] But in the Johannine context, it conveys a subtle nuance different from secular use. The word *katabolē* comes from the root *kataballō,* to throw down. As the Last Supper discourse began with the narrator's comment that the devil "had thrown [*beblēkotos*] into the heart of Judas" the idea of betrayal, so it now ends with a reminder of the "other" Father's love for Jesus from before the world was "thrown" into being.

Jesus addresses God in verse 25 as "Just Father" (*patēr dikaie*), a title nowhere else found in the New Testament. As God's holiness was emphasized in verse 11 to explain Jesus' return to God, so God's justice is used now to explain the separation between the Johannine community and the world: "The world has not known you, but I knew you, and also these knew that you sent me."

The final note is the triumphant return to the theme of unity in verse 26: "I have made known to them your name, and I shall make it known, so that [*hina*] the love with which you loved me may be in [*en*] them and I in [*en*] them." The ultimate expression of Jesus' mission is to share God's name in order to fill people with God's love. God's name is not money or militarism or macho. It is The One Who Is, the one upon whom the foundation of the world rests, the one whose love permeates all that lives and calls it to bear fruit, fruit that will last into eternal life.

---

6. BAG 409.

# 22

# "Whom Are You Looking For?"

## *The Arrest of Jesus*

### John 18:1–12

**A. Chiasm:**

    a: 1–3: band of soldiers/Judean officers to arrest

      b: 4–5: whom do you seek?/ I AM

        c: 6: I AM: fall to ground

      b[1]: 7–9: whom do you seek?/ I AM

    a[1]: 10–12: band of soldiers/Judean officers arrest[1]

**B. Location:** A garden, across the Kidron Valley

**C. Time:** near Passover

**D. Hebrew scripture context:** Genesis 2; Jeremiah 24; 31; various Kings verses about "Kidron"

**E. Social factors:** the combined powers of "the world" vs. Jesus

**F. Themes:** darkness comes to the light

**G. Key words:** *egō eimi,* Nazarene; coming/going

## 1. "HAVING SAID THESE THINGS, JESUS CAME OUT...": INTRODUCTION TO THE JOHANNINE PASSION NARRATIVE

From the slow, even perhaps sleep-inducing suppertime scene in chapters 13–17, the narrator takes us abruptly out of the protection of the indoors and out across the Kidron Valley to a garden. After the longest set of speeches in the

---

1. Ellis (1984, 249–250).

gospels, we are immediately immersed in the force and action of arrest, trial, condemnation, and crucifixion.

For readers familiar with the synoptic accounts of Jesus' Passion, a close look at the Johannine version can be highly disturbing. If we read with an eye toward historical "information," the credibility of the fourth gospel is at its low point in chapters 18–19. Only the most sure-minded literalist can affirm this narrative as providing an eyewitness account of the words and acts of those involved with this dark hour in the life of Jesus and the first disciples. From beginning to end, artistry and ideology have consciously shaped traditions grounded in historical memory for purposes unique to this particular story of Jesus. Numerous details have been included that are nowhere else mentioned in the New Testament. Precise descriptions and electrifying dialogue merge to produce one of the most compelling and powerful stories of courage and commitment, betrayal and fear, politics and passion known to humankind.

If we have not learned to find the importance of each word and phrase by this point in our reading, we will largely miss the carefully nuanced message of the Johannine Passion narrative. But if we do pay close attention, the story will lead us to the heart of humanity's most compelling questions, to a forked road down which we must choose our own path.

The final chapters of John's gospel are neatly divided into two about death and two about resurrection. As we might expect, each pair of chapters forms an overall chiasm in which several smaller chiastic units mark off the scenes. Chapters 18 and 19 can be viewed chiastically as follows:

**Chiasm: 18:1–19:42**

a: 18:1–12: *arrest*: a garden; Jesus is bound; Simon Peter treats Jesus as "worldly" king

  b: 18:13–27: *first (Judean) trial*: Jesus as "high priest"; Beloved Disciple witnesses (with Simon Peter, who denies his discipleship)

    c: 18:28–19:16: *second (Roman) trial*: Jesus the king judged

  b$^1$: 19:17–30: *crucifixion*: Jesus as "high priest"; Beloved Disciple witnesses (with Jesus' mother, who begins her discipleship)

a$^1$: 19:31–42: *burial*: a garden; Jesus is bound; Nicodemus and Joseph treat Jesus as "worldly" king[2]

From the beginning of the story, it is clear that two sets of trials and judgments are taking place simultaneously, just as in chapters 5 and 7–8. Jesus is judged by the Judean and Roman authorities to be worthy of death, which is, paradoxically, Jesus' moment of "glory" and the completion of his mission in the world. At the same time, an astounding array of characters, and perhaps the social worlds they represent — the soldiers and Temple police, Simon Peter, Annas, Caiaphas, Pilate, the chief priests, the Judeans, the Beloved Disciple, the women, Jesus' mother, Joseph, Nicodemus — come face-to-face with their

---

2. Ellis (1984, 247) notes the structure, to which I have added further details.

own loyalties and are tried in the court of the Father, who sees and knows all. For many of these people, this is a moment of apparent triumph or cruel sport, but paradoxically, it is revealed to readers as the characters' moment of condemnation. Jesus versus the world: his beloved ones challenged to watch and to witness and to choose between life and death.

## 2. "I TOLD YOU, 'I AM!'"

The transition from speech to action is made linguistically by the segue from the Last Supper discourse word *tauta* to the Passion word *erchomai,* "to come" or "to go." *Tauta* symbolized Jesus as Word, speaking to his disciples, to his Father, and to future generations. *Erchomai* symbolizes the movement of Jesus back to God, as well as the various other character movements in response to Jesus. Verse 1 begins with this verbal changeover: "Having said these things [*tauta*], Jesus went out [*exēlthen*] with his disciples to the other side of the Kidron Valley." It marks the first of seventeen comings and goings in the Passion narrative.[3]

In addition to the verbal transition, verse 1 also provides the first geographic reference since 12:12, the narrator's notation of the entrance into Jerusalem. Immediately, readers are drawn out of the reflective, prayerful mode of chapter 17 and into visualizing Jesus and his band of disciples moving across the valley. Literally, the description is of a passage across a winter riverbed (*cheimarrou*), common in the Middle East where the year is divided into two seasons of wet (winter) and dry (summer). At Passover in the spring, the passage might well involve fording a creek, on the other side of which is Jerusalem.

The Kidron Valley also recalls Hebrew scripture. David and his men, fleeing from Absalom, traveled the route across the Kidron (2 Sam 15:23). Also, Solomon offered this warning to Shimei: "On the day you go out across the Kidron Valley, know for certain you shall die" (1 Kgs 2:37). In the last moment of Israel's monarchical glory, the reforming king Josiah tore down altars to the idols built by the people and ordered the rubble thrown into the Kidron River (2 Kgs 23:4–12), as had Asa, an earlier reforming king (1 Kgs 15:13). Thus, the Kidron bore memories of threatened death and destruction of idols that had kept the people from fulfilling their covenant with God, fitting themes to mark Jesus' final entrance into Jerusalem.

Having described this symbolic crossing, the narrator goes on to tell us that "there was a garden there, into which he entered [*eisēlthen*], he and his disciples." Despite the common association in Christian memory with the "garden of Gethsemane," such a place is never mentioned in the New Testament! Matthew and Mark mention a "place called Gethsemane" (Mt 26:36; Mk 14:32), but only

---

3. 18:1: *exēlthen/eisēlthen*; 18:4: *exēlthen*; 18:6: *apēlthan*; 18:15: *syneisēlthen*; 18:16: *exēlthen*; 18:28: *eisēlthon*; 18:29: *exēlthen*; 18:33: *eisēlthen*; 18:38: *exēlthen*; 19:4: *exēlthen*; 19:5: *exēlthen*; 19:9: *eisēlthen*; 19:17: *exēlthen*; 19:34: *exēlthen*; 19:38: *ēlthen*; 19:39: *ēlthen*.

the fourth gospel mentions the "garden." The specification of a "garden" associates the scene with the primal location of the first humans in Genesis 2–3. The Hebrew word for "garden" is used twelve times in the Genesis story. It is one of the primary images in the Bible of both the original state of innocence in which humans were created and our collapse into sin and expulsion from paradise. In John, it serves to present Jesus and his disciples as beginning this new stage of their shared journey in the ambiguity of paradise and sinfulness.

Mark Stibbe has noted that the "garden" marks the first of several "narrative echo effects" from the good shepherd discourse (10:1–21) that are found in Jn 18:1–27.[4] He notes the parallel between the walled enclosure of the "sheepfold" and the garden, in which the shepherd protects his sheep. Judas — already noted by the narrator as a *kleptēs* (12:6) — plays the part of the "thief" (*kleptēs*) who comes "only to steal, and kill and destroy" (10:10). Given these parallels, we should not be surprised when Jesus begins in this scene the process of laying down his life on behalf of his sheep (10:15).

Immediately, innocence is lost in verse 2: "Judas, the one betraying him, also knew the place, because many times Jesus led together [*synēchthē*] his disciples there." It comes as a surprise to us that this garden has "many times" previously been a meeting place for the group, for none has been narrated in the story. But with this new bit of information, the garden takes on associations not only with Genesis but with a place of retreat for the discipleship community, a fresh and cool spot in which to be with the Lord, apart from the troubles of the world.[5] Unfortunately, this pastoral picture is preceded by the revelation that Judas also had been with them on those occasions. The tension builds as we cannot help but await the moment in which Judas will burst into the quiet scene and carry out his diabolical mission.

Before we can get a moment with the gathered group in the garden, Judas arrives in verse 3, but with another surprise accompanying him: "Therefore, Judas, having taken the cohort [*speiran*] and the officers [*hypēretas*] from the chief priests and the Pharisees, came there with torches and lamps and weapons." Each word of this sentence is worth considering to appreciate the magnitude of what is being described.

To begin with, Judas is in charge.[6] He has not merely guided the arresting party to the spot; he has "taken" them there. The one appointed by the devil to betray the one sent from God has his moment of power, as he leads the world's forces in dubious battle against Jesus.

And what a combination of forces he has mustered! The first component is described as a *speiran,* an expressly Roman term for a soldier band.[7] And not only a band, but a unit of between two hundred and six hundred men! It is likely the entire force at the command of the Roman governor of Judea, who remains absent physically and by reference at this stage. The interest of Rome in Jesus

4. Stibbe (1992, 101–104).
5. Giblin (1984, 218).
6. Ibid., 216.
7. R. Brown (1970, 807–808).

comes wholly as a surprise at this point in the gospel, for there has been no hint of official concern on the part of the empire about this obscure would-be messiah, other than in the minds of the Sanhedrin (11:48). But it makes clear the Johannine theme that Jesus' message is both a call to the Gentiles (12:20–23) and a threat to the gentile rulers, no less than to the Judeans. The uniqueness of the Johannine account is to show this Roman interest in Jesus *right from the beginning,* in contrast with the synoptics, which present Rome's involvement as developing only after the Sanhedrin turn Jesus over to Pilate.[8]

Also brought by Judas are the *hypēretas,* the Sanhedrin officers sent out first in 7:32 to arrest Jesus, which they were unable or unwilling to do (7:45). They are described as sent by the same conspirators as in 11:47 and 11:57, the uniquely Johannine combination of high priests and Pharisees. As Raymond Brown points out, only the fourth gospel associates the Pharisees with the Passion, and only in this place in the story.[9] Thus, Roman and Judean authorities have *already collaborated* in arranging this most political of arrests, refuting any sense that Jesus was a purely "religious" concern. What the narrator of the fourth gospel makes crystal clear is that religion and politics are, in the end, the same thing. Both claim the availability of ultimate power to shape people's lives. The only question for either is whether the power claimed is of life or of death, of God or of Satan. There is, no matter what official mythologies may claim, no separation of church and state except in the constitutional fantasies of latter-day liberals. It is a notion that would have made no sense to the first Christians and particularly to the Johannine community, who suffered persecution equally at the hands of Temple and empire.

This mammoth force of the world's power comes into the quiet garden with three specific implements: "torches [*phanōs*] and lamps [*lampadōn*] and weapons [*hoplōn*]." Many commentators have noted the irony of the carrying of artificial lights to meet the one who is the light of the world.[10] Only the fourth gospel mentions this detail. In fact, no other gospel mentions either torches or lamps at all, except for Matthew's parable of the bridesmaids (Mt 25:1–8 [*lampas*]). Is there significance to the peculiar notation of two types of artificial lights? Both, of course, involved fire, but one invokes the image of contained flame and the other of more exposed fire. Perhaps the narrator is using the words to suggest something about the *mood* of the arresting party. The open flames suggest a more wild anger at Jesus, while the lanterns a more "sophisticated" approach. In any case, the crowd is in the dark without the assistance of these temporary vehicles of illumination, stumbling around at night.

The final implement is *hoplōn,* weapons. No other gospel uses this term, but it is interesting to note a Pauline passage in which it is found: "The night is far along, but the day has drawn near. We should put aside, then, the works of the darkness, and put on the weapons [*hopla*] of the light" (Rom 13:12).

---

8. Rensberger (1988, 90).

9. R. Brown (1970, 809).

10. E.g., Giblin (1984, 217–218).

Similar is the use of "weapons [*hoplōn*] of justice" in 2 Cor 6:7. If *hoplōn* had metaphorical currency as used by Paul in these passages, then the Johannine use in 18:3 might carry this nuance of contrast between the world's *hoplōn* and Jesus' weapons of truth and love.

With this precise and rich introduction, the confrontation is set. On one side is Jesus and his frightened discipleship community; on the other are the representatives of the aligned powers of the world. The narrator sets the scene with one further detail in verse 4: "Jesus, therefore, knowing all [*panta*] things that were coming upon him, came out [*exēlthen*]." Just as at the beginning of the Last Supper discourse the narrator began by reminding us of Jesus' abiding knowledge (13:1, 3, *panta*), so now we are to remember that all we will witness takes place with Jesus' complete awareness of how things are. The soldiers, officials, and Judas are arrayed in wait, but Jesus takes the step toward them, out from the disciples, to confront the arresting party.

And as he speaks, all eyes and ears are upon him, awaiting what he might have to say at this most tension-filled of moments. What could be more surprising than what he asks in verse 4b: "Whom are you seeking?" As if there was anyone present, including the readers, who don't already know the answer! But the particular form of Jesus' words recalls the earlier occurrence of the question in 1:38 to his disciples. The question was the same then as now, involving as it does the Deuteronomic choice of life or death. Their combined answer — are we to hear the hundreds of soldiers speaking in unison? — is simple and direct: "Jesus the Nazarean."

When Jesus asked the question of the two disciples of John (the Baptist), he got an answer in the form of another question: "Rabbi, where are you remaining?" Now, those questioned *do* answer, but what they say makes clear that what they are seeking is not the one from God but a person from Galilee. Or is it? Upon closer inspection, we find that the precise way in which they name Jesus — the *Nazōraion* — has several possible meanings. Brown notes the following options beyond the straightforward geographic reference:

1. from the Hebrew root *nsr* as "observants," that is, a member of a pre-Christian Jewish sect

2. from Hebrew *nazir,* those consecrated to YHWH by vow (Judg 13:5)

3. from Hebrew *neser* as "messianic branch" (Isa 11:1)

4. passive of Hebrew verb *nasar,* to preserve; that is, *nasur,* the preserved[11]

Of these several Hebrew words possibly linking with "Nazareth," the second option, *nazir,* also bears a meaning with particularly Johannine implications. The Nazirites were Israelites who separated from the body of the people to be consecrated to God (Num 6:1–21). The root of the word, the noun *nezer,* means "separation." Thus, as used to identify Jesus, it is an ironic suggestion that,

---

11. R. Brown (1970, 809–810).

while the Pharisees are the political party of "separatists," Jesus the Nazirite/
Nazorean is separate because of his consecration to God. He is sought after
precisely as one who refuses to go along with the ways of "the world."

Another Hebrew scripture use of the term contains a Johannine flavor as
well. In the description of the requirements of the sabbath and jubilee years,
God tells Moses:

> You shall not reap the aftergrowth of your harvest or gather the grapes of
> your unpruned vine [*nazir*]...." That fiftieth year shall be a jubilee for
> you: you shall not sow, or reap the aftergrowth, or harvest the unpruned
> vines [*nazir*]. (Lev 25:5, 11)

The use of *nazir* for the unpruned vine comes from the sense that the vine is
"separated" by not being cut during the special times.[12] Given the word of Jesus
that the Father cuts/cleans the vine to produce more fruit (15:2) and keeps working even on the sabbath (5:17), the reference to Jesus as a Nazirite/Nazorean
ironically shows the arresting party's distance from Jesus in so misunderstanding
his work and mission as being subject to the Law.

The arresting party's identification of Jesus is one of the very rare occasions
in which the name "Jesus" is used by a character other than the narrator in the
fourth gospel. It recalls another aspect of the first stories regarding the call to
discipleship, where in 1:45 Philip told Nathanael that they had found "Jesus, son
of Joseph, from Nazareth [*Nazaret,* the specifically geographic location]." The
combined flashbacks of Jesus' question, the naming of him as "Jesus," and the
reference to Nazareth suggest that the arrest scene is another beginning of the
mission. As chapter 1 narrated the challenge to individual people on the margins
of society to follow Jesus, now the invitation is made to the representatives of
the world's powers. Of course, the soldiers and Temple officers are themselves
servants, relatively lowly persons doing the will of the ones who sent them.
They are implicitly challenged by Jesus to renounce their allegiance and become
part of the alternative society that is the Johannine community. Their response
makes clear that they are not seeking a messiah, however, but simply the person
required by their senders to appear in court.

Jesus' response to them in verse 5b could not be more powerful: "He said to
them, '*Egō eimi.*' " With no metaphorical extension at all, just the plain "fact"
of his identity, Jesus offers the counterclaim to "Jesus the *Nazōraion.*" At this
point, the narrator intrudes with the telling comment, "Judas, the one betraying
him, was standing with them." In contrast with the Pharisees who were "with
him" in 9:40, Judas the disciple is now pictured standing with the nonbelievers.
At this powerful moment in the narrative, with Jesus facing off the huge crowd
by himself, having "come out" from the garden where the other disciples presumably remain for the moment, we are informed about the sad decision of the

---

12. *TWOT* 2:568.

betrayer. By naming him this way, the narrator emphasizes the opposition between the child of God and the child of Satan, standing apart from one another at the moment of decision.

Having drawn our attention to Judas, the narrator immediately switches back in verse 6 to the interaction between Jesus and the seekers: "Therefore, when he said to them, '*Egō eimi,*' they retreated [*apēlthan eis ta opisō*] and fell [*epesan*] on the ground." By repeating Jesus' all-powerful phrase, the narrator "surrounds" Judas with *egō eimi,* a fittingly ironic contrast to the apparently overwhelming power advantage in Judas's favor. Satan's representative has amassed soldiers, police, and weapons, but God's representative is the one who does the capturing, simply by the power of God's name. It is one of the strongest models of nonviolent resistance in the New Testament and presents the most difficult challenge to those faced with the world's power. Do we *really* believe that God's name is stronger than weapons and military forces? Jesus *does* believe it.

And remarkably, at some level, so do the soldiers and police! His "mere" words lead hundreds of people to fall to the ground! More precisely, the phrase *apēlthan eis ta opisō* literally means "go back to the things behind" and was used earlier in 6:66 to describe the negative response of some of the disciples to the call to "munch" Jesus' flesh. As Charles Giblin says, its usage here

> underscores...the division between disciples and hostile non-disciples. The passion further actualizes the divided reactions to the Bread of Life discourse....What then appeared as revulsion from Jesus' invitation and self-identification is here demonstrated as impotence before the Lord.[13]

The reaction also fulfills scriptural predictions about God's power. For example, the Septuagint version of Ps 56:9 says: "My enemies will retreat [*eis ta opisō*], on the day when I call on you." Also, Daniel reports the reaction of King Nebuchadnezzar to the prophet's interpretation of the king's dreams, that the king "fell [*epesen*] on his face and worshiped Daniel" (Dan 2:46). Thus, the combined elements of the arresting party's reaction indicate that, whether consciously or unconsciously, they recognize the Nazarean as embodying the power of God.

After this dramatic interchange, Jesus asks the question *again*. It is as if he is saying, "I understand that you said 'Jesus the Nazarean' because you were following orders. But *now you know who I am,* so I'll give you another chance to respond differently." But, sadly, their answer is precisely the same, despite their experience of Jesus' power. He reminds them in verse 8 of what they had just heard and reacted so strongly to: "I told you, '*egō eimi!*' If, therefore, you are seeking me, let go of these others." His statement operates at whatever level they can hear it. As the simple "admission" that he is Jesus the Nazarean, it tells them that they have their man and need not bother the disciples. But as the

---

13. Giblin (1984, 219–220).

claim that he has told them of his divine identity, it challenges them once more to decide whether they are seeking *egō eimi* or not.

The narrator gives them time to think about it by interrupting the action to tell us in verse 9 that these things had happened "so that the word [*logos*] might be fulfilled which he said: 'Of those you have given me, not one of them was destroyed [*apōlesa*].' " Now it is *Jesus' word* that achieves fulfillment. It is scripture, *logos,* equivalent to the Prophets, Psalms, and other sacred writings whose fulfillment has been noted throughout the narrative. It fulfills the word in 17:12 by protecting the disciples from the threat of the arresting party. It also confirms Jesus as a good shepherd, who does not abandon the sheep when the wolf arrives but instead lays down his life for them (10:10–15).

Suddenly in verse 10, the narrator shifts gears to tell us about the response of one of the disciples whom Jesus left behind in the garden: "Simon Peter, therefore, having a sword, drew it and struck the slave of the chief priest and cut off his right ear. The name of the slave was Malchus." While all the gospels report the cutting off of the high priest's slave's ear (Mt 26:51; Mk 14:47; Lk 22:50), the fourth gospel adds three telling details. First, it names *Simon Peter* as the one who performs the deed. Second, it specifies that it was the *right* ear that was cut off. Finally, it names the slave as *Malchus.* Why are these particulars mentioned? What Johannine messages are conveyed through each one?

By naming the attacker as Simon Peter, the narrator changes the focus of the story from the general response of one with Jesus to the particular action of a familiar character. The last we heard of Peter, he had been told that his promise to follow Jesus to death was premature (13:36–38). Throughout the footwashing episode, Peter was portrayed as bold but uncomprehending. Now, his behavior is consistent with this picture, as he lunges forward to attack with a sword. What is he doing with a sword, anyway? He is acting like the soldiers, meeting force with force, absurdly, under the circumstances. He understands neither the battle of myths taking place before him nor good military strategy!

Further, Peter represents the militaristic tradition of Israel, which foresaw the messiah as a new David, one to lead them in battle against the Gentiles. In Peter's eyes, the moment has come. But if it is the *kairos* for the messianic war against Israel's oppressors, why strike the first blow against the *high priest's* slave? Wouldn't a Roman soldier be the more appropriate target? Can it mean that Peter, although misunderstanding the nature of Jesus' messiahship, *has* understood the nature of the enemy? Or is it just that this bold partisan of swordsmanship has chosen the weakest link in the chain, the probably unarmed slave rather than the armored Roman soldier? From this perspective, the text becomes a biting satire of the royal tradition, with Peter as the caricature of David.

The detail of the right ear reinforces this comical portrayal of Peter. According to Brown, under indemnity laws of the time, the right ear was a more valuable part of the body than the left ear.[14] Indeed, the right side of the body

---

14. R. Brown (1970, 812).

was generally considered positively, and the left side negatively. Hence, left-handedness was (and in some places remains today) seen as a curse. But this begs the question: Why would the narrator bother in the midst of this tense action to tell us that Peter cut off the slave's right ear?

If we try to picture the scene, what options can we imagine? How would a person with a sword cut off someone's right ear? Two possibilities exist. First, the attacker could be *left-handed*. Hebrew scripture records the story of an earlier left-handed swordsman, Ehud, in Judg 3:15–30. Ehud's left-handedness allowed him to deceive the enemy king into thinking his mission was benign, when its true intent (and result) was to murder the king and thus free Israel from Moabite oppression. Might the narrator's notation in Jn 18:10 be a sly satire on Peter's attempt to recreate Ehud's heroism?

The other possibility is that a right-handed attacker could *strike from behind*. In this case, Peter is not only a violent disciple but a cowardly one as well, picking on a slave whose back is turned. There is obviously no way to distinguish between these two alternatives, but neither paints a pretty picture of Simon Peter.

What about the curious naming of the slave as Malchus? As we have seen, names and naming play a very important role in the fourth gospel. Several important characters are unnamed (Jesus' mother, the Samaritan woman, the Beloved Disciple) while others are named here but not in other gospels (Caiaphas, Nicodemus, Malchus). Naming draws attention to the particularity of a character, just as specifying Simon Peter as the swordsman has done in this scene. But Malchus himself plays no direct role in the story. Could the answer be in an association with the name "Malchus" itself?

It is not a name otherwise attested to in the Bible, but it does occur in other ancient documents. Josephus mentions "Malchus, king of Arabia."[15] As such, it is a *foreign* name, one not found in Israel itself. As the name of the *chief priest's* slave, therefore, it suggests that there is racial impurity within the house of the purest of the pure! Thus, at the same time that the narrator lampoons Peter, he also throws in a barb against the chief priest. It is a subtle reminder of the less-than-pure motives of the Judean authorities whose slaves arrest Jesus, and it prepares us to doubt their sincerity during the mockery of a trial that will soon unfold.

Jesus, for his part, responds to all this with direct criticism not of Peter's violence as such but of its attempt to interfere with Jesus' carrying out of his mission: "Thrust [*bale*] the sword into the sheath; I must drink the cup the Father has given to me, mustn't I?" It is the only time in the fourth gospel that the powerful synoptic symbol of the *cup* is used to refer to the way of the cross. It should not be understood as suggesting that the Father *wants* Jesus to die, but that he wants Jesus to be willing to let go of everything that has been given *except* the relationship with God itself. Peter's action attempts to prevent Jesus from walking the way he has been willing to walk all along. Jesus insists

---

15. Josephus *Ant.* 14.370.

(emphasized in the Greek by the double negative, *ou mē*) that the Father's will be done.

After the interruptions about fulfillment and swords, the narrator returns in verse 12 to the arresting party's response to Jesus' challenge in verse 8. Without another word, they act: "Therefore, the soldiers and their commander [*chiliarchos*] and the Judean officers took Jesus and bound [*edēsan*] him." When the group arrived on the outskirts of the garden, Judas the betrayer was in charge. Now, at the moment of power, he has been replaced by the *chiliarchos*, the Roman troop commander. The commander's presence comes as a surprise, as the narrator withholds announcing him until this last moment in the scene. His presence is further underplayed by putting him between the soldiers and the officers, as if he is just another in the mass of people arresting this one person.

As for Judas, he has been cast aside as a no longer needed tool of the powers. We do not hear about him again in the fourth gospel. The last image of the betrayer is of him "standing with them," yet surrounded by *egō eimi*. There is no escape for him from God's presence, despite his commitment to Satan. His final fate is left to the readers' imagination, and the recollection of the frightening image in 15:6 of what is to happen to the branch that does not remain in Jesus.

The description of the actual arrest of Jesus is dark comedy, as it is clear that one or two officers would suffice to arrest Jesus rather than having the entire cohort swoop down upon him. Indeed, Jesus is ready to go without being subdued at all, so the overkill of binding him adds to the absurdity of the scene. The note of this detail does, however, recall the bound Lazarus (*periededeto,* 11:44, same root as *edēsan* in 18:12). The act of calling for the unbinding of Lazarus has led to the binding of Jesus. The theme of binding/unbinding will play a powerful part in the passage from life to death and back again for both Jesus and those who, in the end, are called to follow in his footsteps.

# 23

# The First Trials

## *Jesus and Peter Put to the Test*

## John 18:13–27

**A. Chiasm:** 18:13–27

    a: 13–18: Annas; Caiaphas; Peter's denial

      b: 19: high priest questions Jesus

        c: 20: Jesus: I have spoken openly

      b$^1$: 21–23: Jesus questions high priest

    a$^1$: 24–27: Annas; Caiaphas; Peter's denial[1]

**B. Location:** in and around the high priest's house in Jerusalem

**C. Time:** night, near Passover

**D. Social factors:** Jesus vs. Sanhedrin; Peter vs. "them"

**E. Themes:** high priesthood

**F. Key words:** standing, *ouk eimi*

Just as the fourth gospel presents the arrest of Jesus consistent with its own purpose and theology, so the trial before the Judean authorities has been shaped in every detail from a Johannine point of view. The narrative key throughout this passage is the role of the omnipresent narrator, who reports simultaneously from *inside* the chief priest's house and *outside* in the courtyard, tightly weaving together the contrasting responses of Jesus and Peter to their respective questioners. When it is over, readers are led to ask where they find themselves in this powerful drama of witness and denial.

The scene begins in verse 13 with the narration that the arresting party "led him to Annas first, who was father-in-law of Caiaphas, who was chief priest

---

1. Ellis (1984, 253).

that year." None of the other gospels reports this interrogation before Annas. In fact, Annas's only appearance in the New Testament outside this scene is as background to Luke's story of the birth of John the Baptist (Lk 3:2) and the story in Acts of the arrest of John and Peter (Acts 4:6). What do we know of these two people from other sources? Why does the author of the fourth gospel mention them and their relationship?

The Jewish historian Josephus has this to say:

> Cyrenius, a Roman senator, . . . being sent by Caesar to be a judge of that nation [Syria], . . . came into Judea, which was now added to the province of Syria. . . .
>
> [H]e deprived Joazar of the high priesthood, which dignity had been conferred on him by the multitude, and he appointed Ananus [Annas], the son of Seth, to be high priest. . . .
>
> Tiberius Nero [many years later] deprived Ananus of the high priesthood, and appointed Ismael. . . . He also deprived him in a little time, and ordained Eleazar, the son of Ananus, . . . which office, when he had held for a year, Gratus deprived him of it, and give the high priesthood to Simon, . . . and when he had possessed that dignity no longer than a year, Joseph Caiaphas was made his successor. When Gratus had done those things, he went back to Rome, after he had tarried in Judea eleven years, when Pontius Pilate came as his successor.[2]

If Josephus's history is to be trusted (and, despite his many biases, there is no reason to question him on these matters), one can infer several aspects of the situation from the above quotation. First, the Judean priesthood was subject to constant political toying by the Roman officials and had little connection with the traditional means of passage from within the control of the priestly families. Second, Annas served many years as high priest, after which a series of replacements filled the office, leading eventually to Caiaphas, who held office for a number of years before Pilate arrived as governor. Finally, by the time of Jesus' arrest and trial, Annas had been officially deposed from office for many years.

Luke, for his part, states that Annas and Caiaphas were high priests *simultaneously,* a situation contrary to the known practice of individual high priesthood and Josephus's historical narrative. In Luke's companion work of Acts, he changes the description somewhat, noting Annas as high priest at the time of Peter and John's arrest and Caiaphas as simply "of the high priestly family" (Acts 4:6). Neither Josephus nor Luke mentions the Johannine detail about the marital interrelationship between the two figures.

What are we to make of this conflict? We obviously cannot resolve the question of the historical accuracy among these reports. But as the Johannine scene

---

2. Josephus *Ant.* 18.1, 26, 33–35.

unfolds, we might pay attention to this background as a way to figure out why the story has been told the way it has.

Although Jesus is first led to Annas, the narrator bypasses the elder priest to remind readers in verse 14 of the prior role of Caiaphas, "high priest that year": "Caiaphas was the one who counseled the Judeans that it is to their benefit for one person to die on behalf of the people." In paraphrasing Caiaphas's only spoken line, the narrator has conspicuously omitted the final part of the sentence, "and not that the whole nation should be destroyed." This restatement expresses the narrator's point of view on the matter. Caiaphas accurately, though ironically, stated the purpose of Jesus' death: for the benefit of the people. But Caiaphas's hope — that Jesus' death would thereby protect Judea's status as a *nation* — was dashed against the fallen rocks of the demolished Temple between the time of Jesus' death and the writing of the gospel. This experience led the Johannine community to interpret Jesus' message as opposing the idea of nations altogether, consistent with the ancient prophetic response to Israel's original monarchy (1 Sam 8:5–22; see commentary on Jn 4:21). Therefore, the narrator quotes the "high priest that year" — already noted for the purpose of explaining Caiaphas's "prophetic" power (11:51) — only for the part of his statement that proved both historically accurate and theologically "correct."

Having set up the scene of Jesus' trial before Annas, the narrator immediately switches our attention in verse 15 to a different setting: "Following Jesus was Simon Peter and another disciple." If we can possibly imagine not already being thoroughly familiar with the stories of Peter's denial, what feelings might flow through us as the narrator brings this character on the stage once again? All we have seen of Peter on this longest of evenings is misunderstanding and rash action that threatened to undermine Jesus' mission. He has been left behind at Jesus' arrest, certainly bewildered and embarrassed by Jesus' rebuke of his swordplay with the high priest's slave. The master has been removed and the disciples left behind, just as Jesus had told them with painstaking detail and repetition all supper long. What can be Peter's intention in following Jesus to the high priest's house? More violent bravado? Silent observation? Are we afraid for him, suspecting that his previous pattern of behavior may lead him to do something rash? Or is there a possibility that he may come out of this the hero, saving Jesus from a terrible fate at the last minute?

And what about his companion, the oddly described "another disciple"? Is this the same person as the Beloved Disciple who was at Peter's side throughout the Last Supper discourse? If so, why this dispassionate description of one whose very existence is defined as being the object of Jesus' love?

These questions might fill our minds as we try to picture the scene being painted by the narrator. Verses 15b–16a add surprising details to the description: "This other disciple was known to the high priest, and he went in with [*syneisēlthen*] Jesus into the courtyard [*aulēn*] of the high priest, but Peter was standing toward the door, outside." The two followers are divided by the "other disciple's" familiarity to the high priest, as the Passion theme of coming and going continues. What are we to make of this relationship between a disciple and the high priest? Nowhere else in the narrative is any disciple described in any relationship at all with the Judeans, let alone with the Sanhedrin members or priestly officials. There is only one character who possibly fits the bill: Nicodemus. The narrator makes a point of not naming this other disciple, and we should not be too quick to fill in a gap that has been intentionally left open. However, Nicodemus or someone like him would be the only type of person to bridge the worlds of discipleship and priesthood in the fourth gospel. This is not to exclude the possibility that the Beloved Disciple himself falls into this category. Having just met him at the Last Supper, we hardly can be sure that the Beloved Disciple was not a (former?) Pharisee or otherwise familiar figure to the high priest. All of this speculation is simply to alert readers to how the narrator subtly allows boundaries to be crossed in the Passion narrative that seemed earlier in the story to be high brick walls. The Passion is the moment in which the messiah will be raised up for all to see. Human-made categories of division must give way to the universality of God's love.

Having established the distance between the other disciple and Peter, the narrator immediately removes it in verse 16b: "Therefore, the other disciple known to the high priest went out [*exēlthen*] and spoke to the portress [*te thyrōro*] and led Peter in." Peter's role is suddenly totally passive, a dramatic shift in character. His ability to follow Jesus is wholly dependent on a disciple familiar to the high priest and a *woman* doorkeeper! People from the social peak (the high priest) and pit (a woman servant) must conspire through the mediation of this mysterious other disciple for Peter's discipleship journey to continue. How far this head "apostle" has fallen in the course of the fourth gospel!

The presence of the doorkeeper is also an ironic recollection of Jesus' good shepherd discourse. There, he noted that "the doorkeeper [*ho thyrōros*, male] opens to this one [the shepherd], and the sheep hear his voice . . . and he leads them out." Now, the *female* doorkeeper opens not to the shepherd but to a disciple of the shepherd, so that the one who will eventually be given the authority of shepherd (Peter, 21:16) can be led *in* to the place of the bad shepherds (the Sanhedrin)!

In addition to the doorkeeper, there are other details that recall the good shepherd discourse. As Mark Stibbe points out, the high priest's courtyard is designated with the same term as was the sheepfold in 10:1, *aulē*, while the "other disciple" goes in and out through the "door" of the *aulē* (cf. 10:9). Stibbe suggests that this description leaves the impression that the "other disciple" plays the role of the shepherd to Peter's "hired hand who flees in the hour of danger" (10:12).[3] This possibility adds even deeper irony to Jesus' postresurrection command to *Peter* to "shepherd my sheep" (21:15–17).

Returning to the political aspects of the trial, we see that the fact that the doorkeeper is female also implies that the trial is taking place, illicitly, at the high priest's house, for only men had such assignments in the temple precincts.[4]

---

3. Stibbe (1992, 103–104).
4. Carson (1991, 582).

The evidence continues to build that those who are apparently concerned with the Law are willing to put it aside when it is inconvenient.

A subtle gap is left open in the narrative by this sly discourse about entrance to the courtyard: Did Peter *want* to go in? The narrator tells us that the other disciple "led" him in, which might be interpreted as taking Peter where he *should* go but is understandably reticent to go. It is part of the ironic characterization of Peter in the Passion narrative that all he can do after his initial decision to be "following" in verse 15 is react to what happens around him. Does he have any inkling of what he is about to experience?

In verse 17, the portress, now also described as a "servant girl" (*paidiskē*), ignores the other disciple to speak directly to Peter: "You're not also [*mē kai su*] out of the disciples of this person?" As Charles Giblin points out, the question "on the lips of the maid tending the door . . . is rather: 'Not another one?!' — a remark befitting an inconvenienced concierge."[5] It is not so much demanding a "confession" as it is expressing her own exasperation at having to let another one through the door. The question is also framed in terms of Peter's membership in a collective. She asks literally, as the above translation suggests, if Peter is from Jesus' community, *ek tōn mathētōn*. As Jesus repeatedly spoke in the Last Supper discourse of his disciples being "out of the world" (*ek tou kosmou*), now the servant girl/portress who is *in* the world wants to know if Peter is "out of the disciples."

It is a straightforward question and hardly seems to contain an element of risk in being answered truthfully. The other disciple has already gone in — although we do not know if the high priest knows that this one is himself "out of the disciples" — and Jesus has promised that none of those he has been given from the Father will be lost (18:9). Thus, it comes as a rude shock when Peter answers, "I am not [*ouk eimi*]." What mixed-up levels of truth and falsehood swirl around these two words! The narrator's twice-repeated reference to Peter's companion as "another" disciple certainly suggests that, in the narrator's point of view, Peter *is* a disciple, and his answer in verse 17 is therefore false. However, it is not difficult to infer from Peter's mistakes and misunderstandings on this long evening that he is in fact not a disciple, in that he does not yet know what it means to follow Jesus. From this perspective, his statement is *true*. But is it true in Peter's mind or only ironically true given the readers' perspective? Does he think he is denying his association with Jesus or admitting his unworthiness to be identified as a member of the discipleship community?

We cannot help but feel sorry for Peter at this stage in his journey. He has come a long way from Galilee to find himself questioned at night by a servant girl outside the high priest's house while his master has been taken into custody. Jesus has been taken away, and the paraclete must await the completion of Jesus' glorification. There is no one to help him. He is totally on his own, in the dark, alone. His answer to the simple question is the exact opposite of Jesus' triumphant *egō eimi* that caused hundreds of Rome's finest to fall flat

---

5. Giblin (1984, 226).

on their faces. Peter *is not*: nonexistent, a nonentity, helpless at the hands of a servant girl.

As if what has transpired is not painful enough, the narrator slows down the pace of events even more, lingering in this difficult moment. In verse 18, more detail is added to the scene: "The slaves and officers had been standing by a charcoal fire [*anthrakian*] which they made, because it was cold, and they were warming themselves." As we might imagine, the servant girl is not alone in the high priest's courtyard but is accompanied by a full entourage of priestly servants. The notation that "it was cold" is an incredibly potent detail, befitting both the Passover season evening weather in Jerusalem and the situation of having the light of the world under the apparent control of the world's powers. The charcoal fire provides the third artificial light in chapter 18, reemphasizing the darkness of the scene. Huddled in the firelight are this crowd of palace guards, and, in 18b, the narrator adds, "Peter was also with them [*met auton*], having stood by, warming himself." Horror of horrors! A phrase previously used only of Judas's alliance with the arresting party (18:6), *met auton,* is now applied to Peter's presence at the fire. The other disciple has presumably moved on to continue following Jesus, but Peter, even after the embarrassing confrontation with the servant girl, is found "with them." And his behavior matches theirs precisely, as he is described as "standing ... warming himself." For the moment, we are left with this sad image of the chilled rock of the apostolic church standing around the courtyard, unable to do anything except try to stay warm.

Finally, the narrator returns us in verse 19 to the scene we have been awaiting, the trial of Jesus before the Judean authorities. The likelihood that we are not surprised by a nighttime trial indicates the degree to which we have grown accustomed to the hypocrisy of the Sanhedrin. They operate in the dark, in keeping both with Jesus' warning that those who walk at night stumble (11:10) and with the far earlier statement that "those who practice foul deeds hate the light ... so that [their] works will not be reproved" (3:20). But even with this expectation of ugliness, we must wonder: Why are they questioning Jesus at all? Haven't their minds been made up since at least 11:53? Are they curious? Mocking? Or just so caught up in their hypocrisy that it seems important to find "legal" grounds for condemning him?

The narrator avoids providing answers to any of these questions (cf. Mk 14:55, 63–64), preferring to leave the interrogators' motives open at this point. Instead, the scene is introduced in verse 19 with: "Therefore the high priest questioned [*erōtēsen*] Jesus about his disciples and about his teaching." After the Last Supper discourse's emphasis on "asking" Jesus and the Father, the high priest's "questioning" of Jesus contains a note of irony. *If* he believed, he could ask Jesus anything and expect it to be answered. But as it is, his questions will only lead to frustration.

The scope of inquiry is twofold: about the disciples and Jesus' teaching. What might the high priest want to know about the disciples? How many are there? Where are they hiding? What are their plans? The scene is all too familiar to those who have been asked to "name names" or otherwise provide information to the authorities about one's partners in "crime." Whether the underlying intent is curiosity or threat, the high priest's questioning challenges Jesus first to provide evidence against those he has been associating with.

The inquiry about Jesus' teaching has similar implications. Is Jesus teaching people to violate the Law? Or is he just another self-appointed prophet or messiah, like the dozens of others who regularly preach to the "ignorant" crowds in Jerusalem and in the countryside? How much of a threat are his teachings to the Sanhedrin? All this and more is hidden away by the narrator in the spare summary of the high priest's interrogation of Jesus.

The narrator's technique also has the effect of effacing the particular character of the high priest. In contrast with the colorful portrayals of Nicodemus, Caiaphas, and, eventually, Pilate, Annas is not allowed to get a word of his own "on the record." Instead, the narrator, having brought Jesus into his presence, pushes him into the background, so that Jesus' response does not have to compete for readers' attention. Another reason for this choice of approaches is to emphasize that regardless of the specific purposes for the inquiry, Jesus' response will be the same, because what he has to say is independent of the particular questions the high priest has to ask.

In verse 20, we are given the first part of Jesus' response: "I have spoken openly [*parrhēsia*] to the world. I always taught in synagogue and in the Temple, where all the Judeans are coming together [*synerchontai*]. In secret [*kryptō*] I spoke nothing." More so than in any other gospel, the Johannine Jesus has indeed spoken in public places and with no withheld messages or secret agenda. His words recall the surprised response of the crowd in 7:26 to his willingness to speak *parrhēsia* despite the threats to kill him that fill the air. And although the narrator has twice noted Jesus' decision to "hide" (*kryptō*, 8:59, 12:36), he said nothing during those periods of seclusion that is reported in the story. Lest one consider the entire Last Supper discourse "hidden" speech, we must remember that anyone *could have* come to that apparently private meal. The fact that the "world" did not hear it was not a result of Jesus' choice but of the world's choices.

His statement to the high priest contains an ironic pun on the Greek word for synagogue. Previously, the text has used the verb form, *synago,* to express the "gathering together" of both people and things (4:36; 6:12, 13; 11:47, 52; 15:2, 6) and only once the noun form *synagōgē* to refer to the specific Jewish religious forum (6:59). The root, of course, is the same: the synagogue was (and is to this day) the place where Jews gather together in prayer and ritual. Now, Jesus refers to the *synagōgē* as a place in which his speech was openly heard but describes the "coming together" (*synerchontai*) rather than the "gathering together" (*synagō*) of the Judeans. Once before (11:33), the narrator had described Judeans as "coming together," to weep with Mary over her dead brother. The implication is that Judeans *come together just like any other people*, that is, like Gentiles, the people of the "nations." The distinction of being gathered together by God has been replaced by the mere being in one place at the same time.

Jesus' statement focuses on the second part of the high priest's questioning, "protecting" his disciples for the moment from the brunt of the inquisition. But in verse 21, he does come around to speaking about his disciples: "Why do you question me? Question the ones who have heard what I said to them. See! These have known what I said!" The first part of his response challenges the high priest's apparent attempt to obtain a "confession" from Jesus, in violation of Jewish law.[6] He then suggests that if the high priest wants a witness "against" the accused, those who heard his open speech have the evidence he seeks. These people, of course, are the disciples and their successors, the Johannine community. Jesus will not incriminate them, but he will also not protect them from taking their own turn in the dock. As he told them in 16:27, "And you are to bear witness, that from the beginning you are with me." Peter, standing outside, is already the first disciple to fail in this assignment!

We modern Christians are probably not surprised by Jesus' willingness to speak these simple but strong statements to the high priest. But as Raymond Brown says, "Self-assurance before authority was probably startling; Josephus tells us that the normal attitude before a judge was one of humility, timidity and mercy-seeking."[7] The text from Josephus to which Brown refers is worth quoting in its own right. The passage involves the bold testimony of *Herod,* on trial for ordering the murder of a number of people without authority from the Sanhedrin. In response to Herod's fearless speech before the court, one Sameas responds:

> I neither have ever myself known such a case, nor do I suppose that any one of you can name its parallel, that one who is called to take his trial by us ever stood in such a manner before us; but everyone, whosoever he be, that comes to be tried by this Sanhedrin, presents himself in a submissive manner, and like one that is in fear of himself, and that endeavors to move us to compassion, with his hair dishevelled, and in a black and mourning garment.[8]

Cowering before the authority of the court is an ancient practice among those accused, and, based on my observation of U.S. courtrooms, it seems the practice is still prevalent today. The "legitimate" power of the state to condemn a person to prison or to death stands robed in black, calmly exercising this divine privilege on behalf of the status quo. And similarly, when modern defendants dare to speak truth to these powers, they are often met with the same reactions of shock, disbelief, anger, and threats. Jesus' brief testimony models for his disciples throughout the ages the Christian way to respond to official accusations, especially those that reveal the injustice and hypocrisy of the court itself.

This is part of the explanation for the violent and immediate response in verse 22: "One of the officers standing alongside gave Jesus a slap and said, 'Is

---

6. Ellis (1984, 257).
7. R. Brown (1970, 826).
8. Josephus *Ant.* 14.172.

this the way to answer the high priest?' " But there is another aspect of Jesus'
response in addition to its bold style that evokes the anger of the official. Paul S.
Minear shows the A-B-B-A structure of verse 20 and its implication:

A: spoken openly to world

B: taught in synagogue/[T]emple

B¹: where all Judeans come together

A¹: said nothing secretly

"The answer given by Jesus equates the world in line A to the synagogue and
[T]emple in line B.... It is *they* who constitute the world — an unthinkable insult. The officer who immediately struck Jesus recognized the insult."[9] Modern
defendants, charged with violating the law for engaging in acts of nonviolent
political resistance, often find themselves challenged to name the court's similarity to the kinds of people it itself would find abhorrent, for example, Nazi
judges. This practice continues Jesus' example of stripping away the court's
pretension to justice and distinction from "others" who are less "civilized." The
Sanhedrin — and certainly the high priest — thought of themselves as grounded
in the superior law of Israel, just as U.S. courts constantly wax pseudopoeti-
cally about the joys of incarnating the constitutional system of justice. In the
end, all these courts are equally "the world," the place that achieves its ends
through lies and violence. The officer ironically proves this to be the case with
his impromptu slap, which is not criticized by the high priest as Jesus criticized
Peter's sword attack.

Jesus responds in verse 23 directly to the officer, who has now engaged
himself in the encounter with Jesus.[10] He puts him to the test of testifying himself: "If I spoke badly [*kakōs*], bear witness about the bad. But if I spoke well
[*kalōs*], why are you thrashing me?" Several times, the issue of speaking *kalōs*
has arisen, with the Samaritan woman and disciples acknowledged by Jesus as
doing so (4:17; 13:13) and the Judeans failing to gain such a concession (8:48).
Previously, Jesus sarcastically challenged the Judeans who were about to stone
him to name the *kalōs* work for which he was to receive that treatment (10:32).
Now, he puts the officer to the same test, to put up or shut up, or, more precisely,
to put up or keep his hands to himself.

But no response is forthcoming from the officer. The gap thus left open suggests, of course, that the officer had no evidence of "bad" speech and that Jesus
has silenced him with his challenge. Not a word is heard from the high priest
himself throughout the scene, nor any reaction at all to Jesus' powerful witness.
Instead, the narrator simply tells us in verse 24: "Therefore, Annas sent him
[*apesteilen*] bound to Caiaphas, the high priest."

It is highly ironic that the one sent from God is now sent by the one holding
the office of God's priest to another described as holding the same office. The

---

9. Minear (1984, 32–33).
10. Giblin (1984, 225).

narrator seems to describe both Annas and Caiaphas as holding the office simultaneously, a version of history different from the other witnesses noted above. However, the fourth gospel's purpose here as throughout the text is not history but theology. Annas and Caiaphas share equal responsibility for the Judean treatment of Jesus. They are partners in crime. And yet, despite their show of force in keeping Jesus bound, his truth cannot be bound and has come forth to testify against them and the entire system of Judean injustice.

Having experienced the grand power of the self-assured Jesus amidst the authorities, the narrator turns our attention once more to the pathetic Peter. The scene is refreshed with the repetition in verse 25 that "Simon Peter was standing and warming himself." It is a startling reminder of the physical and spiritual distance between master and would-be disciple. Before we can dwell on this contrast, though, "they" collectively question him for the second time: "Aren't you out of his disciples?"

Despite the second chance, we are not likely surprised by Peter's repeated *"ouk eimi."* The narrator, however, prefaces Peter's words with the explicit condemnation, "That one denied it, saying..." The mention of "denied" immediately calls to mind Jesus' prediction in 13:38. If we somehow had missed the point of the first *ouk eimi,* the narrator has now given away the mystery. All we can do is watch helplessly as the third opportunity comes and goes in verse 26. But the narrator has one more surprise to offer, in the form of the third questioner: "One of the high priest's slaves, a relative of the one whose ear Peter cut off, said, 'Didn't I see you with him in the garden?' " Ah, how one reaps what one sows! The comic note of Peter being caught by Malchus's kin at least takes a small bit of the pain out of anticipating Peter's third denial. By drawing attention to himself with his misguided effort to defend Jesus with violence, Peter planted the seed of his own condemnation at the hands of the slave.

The contrast between these two simultaneous trials could not be more complete. High priest and slaves, comfortable inner chamber and cold fireside, powerful witness and cowardly denial. The final irony lies in the mention of the garden, the biblical symbol of both paradise and fall. Peter had been with Jesus in the place of joyous peace, but it becomes the basis for the complete collapse of his discipleship, at least for now. It is indeed anticlimactic when the narrator adds in verse 27, "Immediately a cock crowed."

# 24

# "My Kingdom Is Not of This World"

## *The Roman Trial of Jesus*

### John 18:28–19:16a

**A. Chiasm:**

  a: 18:28–32: *outside*: Pilate asked by Judeans to condemn Jesus

    b: 33–38a: *inside*: Pilate questions Jesus

      c: 38b–40: *outside*: find no crime

        d: 19:1–3: *inside*: Jesus scourged/mocked as king

      $c^1$: 4–8: *outside*: find no crime

    $b^1$: 9–11: *inside*: Pilate questions Jesus

  $a^1$: 12–16a: *outside*: Pilate condemns Jesus for Judeans[1]

**B. Location:** in and around the praetorium, in Jerusalem

**C. Time:** early in the morning, the day before the sabbath and Passover

**D. Hebrew scripture context:** 1 Samuel 8

**E. Social factors:** Johannine community vs. Rome and the "world"

**F. Themes:** the nature of Jesus' kingship

**G. Key words:** king/kingdom, no cause

## 1. THE "NONSCENE" BEFORE CAIAPHAS AND THE RESULTS OF THE JUDEAN "TRIAL"

When the narration of Peter's predicted denial is completed in verse 27, we might expect the narrator to return to the second part of Jesus' trial be-

---

1. Ellis (1984, 258–260); R. Brown (1970, 859).

fore the Judean authorities suggested by verse 24. However, the narrator instead in verse 28a skips completely over the encounter between Jesus and Caiaphas: "Therefore, they led Jesus from Caiaphas into the praetorium." Given the powerful image of Caiaphas presented during the Sanhedrin gathering in 11:47–53, we might find ourselves disappointed not to be allowed in on what promised to be a dramatic interaction between two strong figures. Having set up the scene in verse 24, why might the narrator have chosen to skip over this part of the story?

Of the four gospels, only Matthew narrates a trial scene before Caiaphas (Mt 26:57–66). The main thrust of that narrative is the establishment of the official Sanhedrin condemnation of Jesus on the charge of blasphemy. Caiaphas is the spokesman, but the judgment is the result of the consensus of the entire body. In contrast, we find that the fourth gospel does not present either a hearing before the Sanhedrin at this point in the story or a formal condemnation by the Judeans. Instead, we have seen the informal interrogation by Annas and the *sub silentio* encounter with Caiaphas alone. By skipping over the latter scene, the narrator leaves readers to imagine what happened between Jesus and Caiaphas. The result is that the Johannine Jesus is never formally charged or condemned by the Judeans during the Passion narrative. Instead, readers are called to go back to the previous encounters between Jesus and the Judean authorities to find the charges and judgment elsewhere in the story.

If we do this, we are reminded of two things. First, the Sanhedrin — in the form of the chief priests and Pharisees — had already sent the police out to arrest Jesus in 7:32. When the officers return empty-handed to the disgust of the Sanhedrin, one of the leaders, Nicodemus, insists on the propriety of providing a hearing before pronouncing judgment (7:51). Although the others revile him, the following passage turns out to be just the trial-like hearing demanded by Nicodemus (8:12–20, et seq.). Their "judgment" comes in 8:48 when they announce their belief that Jesus is a "Samaritan" and has a "demon" and in 8:59 when they first attempt to carry out the sentence as they try to stone him.

Second, there is a "rehearing" at the feast of Dedication when they challenge him to speak openly (*parrhēsia*) about his messiahship and attempt once more to stone him (10:22–39). Their demand in 10:24 bears a striking resemblance to Caiaphas's challenge in Mt 26:63: "I put you under oath by the living God to tell us if you are the Christ [*ei su ei ho christos*, identical to Jn 10:24], the Son of God!" Thus, we find that the fourth gospel does not provide a Passion-setting narration of the hearing before Caiaphas and the Sanhedrin or condemnation of Jesus because it has *already happened* in chapters 7, 8, and 10.

Just as the fourth gospel puts the Temple-exorcism passage near the beginning of Jesus' ministry and narrates several trips to Jerusalem in contrast with the synoptic pattern, so it treats Jesus' trial by the Judean authorities as an ongoing facet of his encounter with them. There is no need for the Sanhedrin to meet again to hear Jesus; they have already heard him, judged him, and rationalized his death (11:47–53).

Thus, Annas's interrogation can be seen not as a formal trial but as simply an attempt to find out a few more "helpful" things about Jesus before they hand him over to the Romans for execution. Similarly, the scene between Jesus and Caiaphas, in this context, would be anticlimactic. Rather than providing conversational fireworks, it would likely be another dreary attempt to extract information that would assist the authorities in their efforts to stamp out not only Jesus but his followers as well. The narrator saves readers the trouble of listening to this redundant session and moves directly on to the more promising interaction between Jesus and the Roman governor.

## 2. "I AM NOT A JUDEAN, AM I?": THE SAVIOR OF THE WORLD CONFRONTS THE POWER OF THE EMPIRE

### a. The Structure of the Trial before Pilate

As shown at the beginning of this chapter, the trial scene between Jesus and Pilate is in the form of a seven-part chiasm rather than the usual five-part chiasm. With the healing and trial of the person born blind, this passage shares the privilege of being marked by the additional parallel sections. One might speculate on whether this is symbolic of the "seven hills of Rome"[2] or has other numerological significance. But regardless of the reason for the specifics of seven, it is clear that this scene has been stylistically crafted and shaped perhaps more than any other episode in the fourth gospel. The careful alternation of inside and outside leads readers through a dense thicket of political power and theological revelation.

In addition, Paul Duke notes the four simultaneous plot progressions that unfold during the superficially single-focused effort to get Jesus to the cross:

1. fall of Pilate

2. self-destruction of Judeans

3. elevation of Jesus

4. specificity of accusation against Jesus[3]

Like an M. C. Escher print, the narrative twists and turns in on itself until the defendant becomes judge, the accusers the condemned, and the lofty imperial judge just another conspirator. Throughout the story, the ironies run thick as honey, yet are bittersweet in the extreme. When it is over, both characters and readers are challenged to reconsider everything they/we have ever thought about their allegiances to God and country, law and society.

---

2. Ellis (1984, 260).

3. Duke (1985, 127–128).

## b. Coming Outside to Meet the Judeans: 18:28–32

We should not be too surprised to find Jesus handed over to the Romans, given the huge contingent of soldiers sent out with the Sanhedrin officers to arrest him. Jesus' threat to the imperial government has been waiting in the wings of the story at least since the end of the journey of Jesus through Samaria, at which he was proclaimed "savior of the world," a title properly reserved for Caesar (4:42). The power of the empire is expressed in verse 28 by the description of the movement of Jesus from a *person* (Caiaphas) to a *building* (the praetorium). For the Johannine community, Israel's powerful architecture has already been torn down and its official authority reduced to the stature of the persons holding legal offices. But Rome's stature loomed just as large at the end of the first century as in the middle. The praetorium symbolized the ability of the distant imperial government to radiate its power into every land it held in colonial subjugation.

Immediately, the narrator follows with the first temporal marker since "it was night" (13:30): "It was early [*prōi*]." Raymond Brown points out that *prōi* was the last of four Roman divisions of the day, indicating the time just before dawn.[4] The term operates at two levels: it moves the narrative out of Judean and into Roman time, and it signals the coming return of light, the approaching end of the long night through which Jesus and his disciples have traveled.

But having introduced this Roman context, the narrator goes on in 28c to juxtapose it with the Judean one: "And they did not enter [*ouk eisēlthon*] into the praetorium, so that they would not be defiled [*mianthōsin*] but could eat the Passover." This "they" who transfer Jesus from Caiaphas to the praetorium and fastidiously (and hypocritically) avoid contact with the pagan house are left undefined. In verse 24, the narrator had specified that it was Annas who sent Jesus to Caiaphas. Now, Jesus is in the hands of the more ominous and somewhat more universal "they." One can easily equate "they" with the Sanhedrin or at least the *hypēretai* under orders from that body. But by choosing to leave the issue open, the text has the effect of portraying Jesus under the worldly control of a faceless enemy, albeit one concerned with the details of ritual purity.

The description of their concern is in terms of *miainō,* or ritual uncleanness. It is a term not elsewhere found in the gospels but common in the Septuagint, where it refers to violating prohibitions of the Torah.[5] It is a bitter sarcasm here, for those who are so worried about this legal technicality are anxiously attempting to have a man of their own covenant killed. By noting the specific ground of their worry as the ability to eat the Passover meal, the narrator thrusts the entire trial passage into the powerful symbolic milieu of the exodus journey and its annual re-creation in ritual and story.

The narrator continues in verse 29 by noting: "Therefore, Pilate went out [*exēlthen*] outside [*exō*] toward [*pros*] them." The movement of the Roman

---

4. R. Brown (1970, 844).
5. F. Hauck, *TDNT* 4:644–647.

governor is triply emphasized by the Greek words listed. We should not be too surprised that "they" get the attention of this fearsome leader without any description of a message being sent in to him, as he has already cooperated with their conspiracy by sending the cohort of arresting troops. The Johannine Passion insists on establishing the shared responsibility of Judeans and Romans for the judgment against Jesus. By coming outside, Pilate is placed in the same position Peter was before encountering the portress and others by the fire (18:16).

The governor's name is given without any further identification, with the apparent expectation that readers are all too familiar with this infamous colonial despot. He is not even noted as being the governor! The idea that Judean leaders would willingly turn over a Jew to this despicable tyrant is a cruel insult to those who wait on the outside. This contrast can be understood more clearly with the help of some background from Josephus about the relationship between Pilate and Judea. Just before Josephus's brief narration of the presence of Jesus in Jerusalem, he tells the story of Pilate's tenure as "procurator of Judea." One of the rare occasions when Pilate's brutal policy of repression was successfully resisted involved his attempt to impose the imperial symbols on the people of Judea:

> Pilate . . . removed the army from Caesarea to Jerusalem . . . in order to abolish the Jewish laws. So he introduced Caesar's effigies [i.e., the Roman eagle], which were upon the ensigns, and brought them into the city. . . . Pilate was the first who brought those images to Jerusalem, and set them up there; which was done without the knowledge of the people, because it was done in the nighttime; but as soon as they knew it, they came in multitudes . . . and interceded with Pilate many days, that he could remove the images; and when he would not grant their requests, because it would tend to the injury of Caesar, . . . he ordered his soldiers to have their weapons privately, while he came and sat upon his judgment seat, which seat was so prepared in the open place of the city, that it concealed the army that lay ready to oppress them: and when the Jews petitioned him again, he gave a signal to the soldiers to encompass them round, and threatened that their punishment should be no less than immediate death. . . . But they threw themselves upon the ground, and laid their necks bare, and said they would take their death very willingly, rather than the wisdom of their laws should be transgressed; upon which Pilate was deeply affected with their firm resolution to keep their laws inviolable, and presently commanded the images to be carried back from Jerusalem to Caesarea.[6]

Despite Pilate's retreat in the face of this massive nonviolent civil disobedience, he revealed his true colors soon thereafter, when another protest arose in Jerusalem after Pilate diverted water to Jerusalem by using Temple funds

---

6. Josephus *Ant.* 18.54–59.

to pay for the scheme. This time, Josephus tells us, "since the people were unarmed, . . . there were a great number of them slain."[7] That this is the person with whom the Judean authorities have conspired to "save the nation" is an incredibly sad commentary on how far, in the eyes of the fourth gospel, they have turned away from the God who sent Jesus into the world to save it.

Having come outside to meet his co-conspirators, Pilate speaks first: "What accusation [*katēgorian*] are you bringing against this person?" Given what we (and those to whom he is speaking) have seen about his involvement in Jesus' arrest, Pilate's words are mocking and sarcastic. He *already knows* what the problem is, or he wouldn't have sent his entire body of troops out to the garden. His words also involve a not so subtle judgment on their intentions. The term *katēgorian* was used previously in 5:45, when Jesus told the Judeans that Moses, not he, "would accuse" (*katēgorēsō*) them to the Father. As was noted there, the one who is the "accuser" in the Hebrew scriptures is *Satan* (Job 1:6; Zech 3:1). Whether this judgment belongs to Pilate or the author of the fourth gospel we cannot say, although it is unlikely to expect that the Roman procurator would be familiar with Jewish theology. In either case, the question suggests that in bringing Jesus to Pilate, the authorities are playing the role of Satan.

Whether this barb is caught by Pilate's addressees or not, they certainly understand the mockery of his question generally and respond in verse 30 in kind: "If this one was not doing wrong [*kakon*], we wouldn't likely have handed him over [*paredōkamen*] to you!" Of course, when Jesus challenged Annas's officer to "bear witness about the wrong [*kakou*]," there was no response, for there is no evidence of Jesus' wrongdoing. Unlike the synoptics, which specifically present the Judean accusation of blasphemy, the fourth gospel avoids the theological justification and sticks with the broader political issue of Jesus' challenge to the status quo that makes his removal necessary. In admitting that they have "handed him over," the accusers put themselves directly in line with Judas, who has each time been labeled as "the betrayer" (*paradidous*; e.g., 18:2, 5).

Pilate, seemingly enjoying the role of taunter, jabs back at them in verse 31: "Take him yourself and judge him according to your Law." He knows they need him to execute their scheme; this much has already been agreed to. His statement is pure verbal torment, as a cat plays with a mouse. As Paul Duke points out, "The truth is, since chapter 5 'the Jews' have been trying furiously to judge Jesus by their own law, with embarrassing results."[8]

But the response of the "Judeans" — identified this way for the first time in the Passion narrative — provides one of the sharpest ironies in the fourth gospel: "It is not lawful [*ouk exestin*] for us to kill [*apokteinai*] anyone." J. Ramsey Michaels tells us that the terms *exestin* and *ouk exestin* are "used in the Gospels predominately to refer to what is either permitted or forbidden to Jews by the law of Moses."[9] Thus, the question is not whether *Roman* law allows colonies

---

7. Ibid. 18.62.
8. Duke (1985, 128).
9. Michaels (1990, 475).

the option of capital punishment, but of the *Torah's* attitude. The word for "kill" shines further light on the question. Rather than using the more common *thanatoun,* the Greek word for death used in the Septuagint for legal killing as "put to death," the choice of *apokteinai* puts the emphasis on killing as in *murder.*[10] It is the word that the fourth gospel has repeatedly used to describe their intent to kill Jesus (e.g., 5:18; 7:1). And as we have seen, there has been no legal basis for the Judeans' condemnation of him. Thus, their statement comes down to an affirmation of the ancient principle, "Thou shalt not kill," which they are trying their hardest to violate, with Pilate's assistance.

The narrator intrudes here to linger on this irony by adding another level to its depth: "This was so that the word [*logos*] of Jesus might be fulfilled [*plerōthē*] which he said, signifying [*sēmainōn*] what kind of death [*thanatō*] he was about to die [*apothnēskein*]." The statement is almost an exact repetition of 12:33, when the narrator noted that Jesus' own statement about being "lifted up out of the earth" signified what kind of death he was about to die. Putting them together, we are to see that Jesus will be "lifted up" in crucifixion — that is, the Roman method of execution — because the Judeans were too hypocritical to kill him themselves as they wanted to do.

### c. *"You Are the King of the Judeans?": 18:33–38a*

Having forced the Judeans to announce their murderous intent, Pilate "enters" (*eiselthen*) the praetorium to face Jesus for the first time. What can Pilate's intentions be in "calling" for Jesus in verse 33? Does he expect fun and games with Jesus just as he did with the Judeans? An imperial power display to show off for the puny colonial troublemaker? Or is he really interested in finding out something about the one who is seen as such a threat to the Judean authorities? Just what have the high priests and Pharisees told him about Jesus?

It is a highly dramatic moment: Pilate the governor versus Jesus the messiah; the power of Rome versus the power of God. On this private stage away from the bloodthirsty accusers, the self-important governor faces the envoy of the Holy One. Pilate's opening line overflows with meaning: "You are the king of the Judeans?" It is one of the rare lines found in the exact same wording in all four canonical gospels (Mk 15:2; Mt 27:11; Lk 23:3), indicating the breadth of the traditional memory that the Roman governor asked this question. But in the particular flow of the Johannine Passion account, it finds its own nuance of meaning.

Pilate's disbelief is transparent: this *nobody* is the one they are so concerned about, the one for whom I dispatched an entire cohort? In addition to expressing his being underwhelmed at the presence of Jesus, the title by which he states his doubts drips with sarcastic mockery of Judean national aspirations. We recall that Nathanael proclaimed Jesus as king of *Israel* (1:49), as did the Jerusalem crowd on Palm Sunday (12:13). The expected messiah is to be the leader of

---

10. Ibid., 478.

God's holy people, Israel, but the Judean authorities are concerned about a *national* ruler. From Pilate's perspective, the "king of the Judeans" is probably Herod, who ruled in grand style under the thumb of Rome.[11] His question casts doubt not only on Jesus' royal status but on the sanity of the Judean authorities whose ire has been so aroused by this apparently harmless person.

Jesus' response in verse 34, though, is sharp, certainly not what the governor would expect from a prisoner confronted with the might of Rome: "Are you saying this on your own, or have others spoken to you about me?" Touché! Jesus penetrates the official facade and gets to the heart of the matter, exposing Pilate's conspiracy with the authorities. His question turns the tables around, embarrassing the governor and putting him on the defensive. It is immediately clear to Pilate that Jesus is a more formidable opponent than he might have expected.

Pilate tries to regain his advantage in verse 35 by creating distance between himself, on the one hand, and what he perceives to be the common identity of Jesus and his accusers, on the other: "I am not a Judean, am I [*mēti egō Ioudaios eimi*]? Your nation and the chief priests have handed you over to me." Pilate, of course, considers his question purely rhetorical. He is a *Roman,* after all, not a mere Judean. But in the symbolics of the fourth gospel, the question bears a closer look. Earlier, we heard Jesus called a Samaritan, a charge he did not refute (8:48–49). Similarly, we found people in Galilee called "Judeans" once it was clear that they did not believe in Jesus (6:41, 51). All along, geographic identity has been a matter not of birthplace or citizenship but of mythic allegiance and way of behaving. To be a "Judean" has meant to align oneself with the prevailing *mythos* of Temple and Torah, to base one's value system on supporting the status quo supposedly grounded in God but in reality built on murder and lies. Most fundamentally, it has meant rejecting Jesus as the one sent from God and his commandment to love. Pilate, the "pagan" ruler, knows nothing about any of this, of course. But to readers, the answer to Pilate's question is probably *yes.* To the extent that Pilate is in league with the accusers who are seeking to kill Jesus, he, too, is a "Judean."

His words attempt to focus, though, on Jesus' relationship with what Pilate perceives to be his "nation." Those who insist on translating *Ioudaioi* as "Jews" fail to consider the significance of this point. Pilate correctly understands that those who have "handed over" Jesus are not people of a particular religious perspective but people whose self-identity is as a *nation.* The answer to Jesus' own question in verse 34 is that the accusers have told Pilate substantially what Caiaphas told the Sanhedrin in 11:50, that Jesus' death is "for the benefit" of the "nation" because he has "made himself" a king.

And the answer to the mystery of "they" is also revealed, as Pilate informs readers (Jesus already knew, of course) that Jesus has been betrayed by the "chief priests." The Pharisees are no longer part of the situation, having been "outranked" by the temple authorities, who, ironically enough, no longer existed

---

11. Cf. Josephus *Ant.* 16.311, referring to Herod the Great as "king of the Jews."

by the time the gospel was written. Those whose religious power is intricately linked with cooperation with the political powers are the accusers of Jesus.

Pilate finishes his retort in verse 35 by inviting Jesus' own "confession": "What did you do?" Jesus' response, rather than answering this question, deals with Pilate's first question, the surprising reality of Jesus' kingship. It is one of the most terribly misinterpreted passages in the fourth gospel:

> My kingdom [*basileia*] is not of this world [*ek tou kosmou*]. If my kingdom were of this world, my officers would be fighting [*ēgōnizonto*] so that I would not be handed over to the Judeans. But now, my kingdom is not from here [*enteuthen*].

How many theologians, preachers, and ordinary Christians have forgone the necessary effort to transform the "world" into the *basileia* because of this passage! From our reading of the entire text and particularly of the Johannine term, *ek tou kosmou,* it should be very clear that Jesus is most certainly *not* claiming that his kingdom is "in heaven." Rather, his kingdom is grounded in a reality totally foreign to the "world," the home of police and soldiers, murderous secret conspiracies and repression of dissent. As David Rensberger expresses it clearly:

> It is not a question of whether Jesus' kingship exists in this world but of how it exists; not a certification that the interests of Jesus' kingdom are "otherworldly" and so do not impinge on this world's affairs, but a declaration that his kingship has its source outside this world and so is established by methods other than those of this world.[12]

Jesus' statement is thus a rejection not only of the world "outside" of his kingdom but of those would-be disciples who seek to establish the messianic kingdom by force. By the time of the fourth gospel, the failure of the Jewish revolutionary groups to secure a military victory over Rome was a reminder not only of the relative weakness of Palestine in the face of the empire but also of the impossibility of achieving God's reign through armed struggle.

I write this with trepidation, for it is easy for a comfortable white male in the United States to speak of rejecting violence, and harder for Salvadorans and others who have mourned the slaughter of tens of thousands of sisters and brothers by "the world." But the Johannine community for whom this text was God's word lived in a situation much more like El Salvador than like North America. They, too, knew the immeasurable pain of persecution and martyrdom. And the voice of Jesus that they raised up as a witness to the entire church is one that categorically rejects the notion of armed struggle, even for the sake of saving Jesus himself from the hands of the Judeans or the Romans.

To North American Christians raised on the *realpolitik* of so-called just-war theory or the ideology of "defending freedom," Jesus' words to the impe-

---

12. Rensberger (1988, 97).

rial procurator may make little sense. Rensberger again speaks clearly to this difficulty:

> The politics of John['s gospel] may seen scarcely recognizable as politics to us. They may seem impractical or irresponsible in their stubborn devotion of all loyalty, political as well as spiritual, to Jesus who had been "raised up" as King of the Jews. But...for the Johannine Christians... they were *real* politics and represented a *real* political option.[13]

To understand more clearly how the fourth gospel presents this political option, it may be helpful to consider Jesus' rhetorical means of expressing his response to Pilate. He makes three separate statements, each containing the rare Johannine but very common synoptic term *basileia.* The first and third are statements of "fact," while the center is a counterfactual statement intended to "prove" the other parts of his claim. The first and third are basically equivalent: the world equals "from here." It is the middle statement that makes Jesus' message clear. He presents as the sole example of what defines the world's kingdom the act of *hypēretai* engaging in "fighting." It is not so much an image of violence as of physical *struggle,* as the Greek term *agōnizomai* suggests. The word is not used elsewhere in the fourth gospel but occurs in the New Testament in images of athletic competition (e.g., 1 Cor 9:25; Col 4:12). The particular object of this struggle in Jesus' image is obtaining the king's release from the hands of the enemy. It is precisely what Peter tried to do at Jesus' arrest (18:10)! But Jesus says that in *his* kingdom, this would *not* happen.

Is Jesus suggesting, then, passive acceptance of violence and oppression? Not at all. Rather, the politics of Jesus involves engaging not in a struggle with the powers to release their grip on God but in relentless *witness* to the truth of what is happening and in mutual love that provides an alternative model for all to see and ponder. The Johannine Jesus does not hesitate to name — sometimes with sarcasm or bitter irony — the evil that suffuses the world. But nowhere in the fourth gospel does Jesus *struggle* against the world. *Life as struggle is exactly what leads the world to violence and deceit.* The world perceives existence as a zero-sum game, in which all people and groups grab for whatever they can at the expense of others. For God, though, life is about love, which is the opposite of this endless competitive striving. The Johannine Jesus has repeatedly called his community of disciples into mutuality, self-sacrifice, and deep intimacy. It may well lead to grief, fear, or trouble, but the response is never to intentionally "fight" the way the world does.

What does Jesus' statement say about poor Peter and his thousands of successors who have taken up the sword to "defend" God from God's enemies? Simply put, that they are not part of his kingdom. There is to be no more fighting in God's name! Those who choose this path are revealing their allegiance to some other sovereign than the one who speaks to Pilate in this passage.

---

13. Ibid., 99–100.

What does this message say to an experienced tyrant like Pilate? It is obviously an inconceivable notion, and Pilate's own response shows that he has not even heard it: "Well, so you are a king, then?" For the governor, the only question at issue is whether *someone's* royal prerogative is being challenged. He has twice heard Jesus say "my kingdom," and that sounds a lot like a claim against one king or another.

Jesus' answer contains words that are found in all four gospels' versions of his response to Pilate's question: "You say it [*su legeis*]." The fourth gospel, though, adds the trailer, "... that I am a king." Thus, the words come both from the mouth of Pilate and the mouth of Jesus: on this much they "agree."

But Jesus' response continues in a uniquely Johannine manner in verse 37b: "For this I have been born [*genennēmai*], and for this I have come into the world: so that I should bear witness to the truth. Everyone who is of the truth [*ek tes alētheias*] is hearing my voice." Jesus confronts Pilate with the theme first heard in the prologue (1:13) but which echoes throughout the gospel: the meaning of being born. Jesus carefully distinguishes what might to non-Johannine ears seem to be two different ways of saying the same thing: "being born" and "coming into the world." For God's agent, the first involves spirit-into-flesh, what *is* participating in *becoming*. But the second involves mission: the deliberate engagement with the realm of darkness. It is a clear refutation of the way of the Qumran community or the gnostics, whose paths led directly away from the world. Jesus has had something to accomplish in the world: witnessing to truth.

This is the nature of Jesus' kingship: to present the way things *are* to those wrongly committed to the way things *seem to be*. While a reading of a modern newspaper or a study of history might suggest that what "is" is violence and oppression, Jesus' cross-based kingship claims just the opposite: that all which the world claims as permanent is really just transitory in the face of God's *is-ness*, God's "truth." The Temple, the empire, and their successors all eventually crumble like sandcastles. It is God's invitation to covenant that "remains." It has been, from the beginning, Jesus' work from his Father to convey this truth to the world, not to condemn it, but to save it from itself.

The invitation even comes to the Roman procurator, in Jesus' remark challenging him to be among those who have ears to hear his voice. Give up being "of the world" and become "of the truth!" Pilate's famous rejoinder hangs in the air as one of the greatest unanswered questions in all history: "What is truth?" What is Pilate really asking in this deceptively simple question? He has been listening to Jesus enough to put aside for at least a moment the issue of Jesus' kingship and crime. Can it be a sincere attempt to understand Jesus' message? Or is it a cynical rejection of this confused prisoner's pretensions to royalty? Is it asked with a sneer or a smile? Whatever might be Pilate's intention, the writer's artful construction leaves it totally open, for generations to ponder without resolution.

### d: "I Find No Cause in Him": 18:38b–40

Neither the narrator nor Pilate waits for an answer, as the procurator returns outside in verse 38b: "After saying this, he again went out [*exēlthen*] toward the Judeans, and said to them, 'I find no cause [*aitian*] in him.'" Pilate may be getting bored with Jesus' highblown rhetoric, but he has not tired of taunting the Judeans. He publicly underscores their lack of compassion and murderous intent that will not rest until they achieve their goal. He does so through the formal announcement of a verdict, the finding of "no cause." Either Pilate perceives Jesus as harmless or he is so sure of the Judeans' response that he takes the "risk" of finding him not guilty.

Pilate continues by taking another jab at the Judeans' lack of compassion in verse 39: "But you have a custom [*synētheia*] that I should release one to you on the Passover. Do you want, therefore, that I should release to you the king of the Judeans?" Both Mark and Matthew describe the practice of releasing a prisoner as *Pilate's* custom (Mk 15:6; Mt 27:15), while Luke does not link the proposal to release a prisoner with custom at all. There is no convincing extrabiblical evidence for such a custom by either Romans or Judeans, however, despite the apparently strong early Christian tradition. The term *synētheia* is not used elsewhere in the fourth gospel and only in one other place in the New Testament (1 Cor 11:16), so it is difficult to get a deeper sense of its meaning here. In the flow of the Johannine narrative, it continues to portray Pilate as taunting and the Judeans as unwilling to budge in their determination to force Pilate's hand.

By linking the custom with the *Passover* (Mark and Matthew refer only to a general practice at festivals), the writer adds to the image of Jesus, the Lamb of God, linking him to the *sacrificial* lamb of the Passover feast (Ex 12:21). The Roman governor unwittingly plays into the unfolding fulfillment of scripture, as the Isaian imagery draws into the foreground along with the Passover story: "Like a lamb led to the slaughter or a sheep before the shearers…" (Isa 53:7; cf. 52:4–53:12).

Finally, Pilate for the first time calls Jesus publicly by the name that aroused all the difficult conversation on the "inside": "king of the Judeans." Note that he does not say, "the one you call 'king of the Judeans,'" but offers the title as a statement of fact. Is Pilate convinced of the truth of the title, or is he just mocking the national aspirations of the high priests? Given the just completed conversation, we must assume that his words are ironic. He does believe Jesus is harmless, but the notion that this bound prisoner could be king of the crowd on the outside is ludicrous.

The Judeans' response in verse 40 adds another wrinkle to the calculus: "They cried out [*ekraugasan*] again, therefore, 'Not this one, but Barabbas.'" This Barabbas was a bandit [*lēstēs*]." The Judeans' "cry" is in sharp contrast with the previous cry, that of the Palm Sunday crowd proclaiming Jesus' entry as king of *Israel* (12:13, *ekraugazon*). Now, the Judeans clamoring for Jesus' death cry out for a different king, Barabbas. They seem to be suggesting that the one described by the narrator as a *lēstēs* is "king of the Judeans." The term *lēstēs,* we might recall, was used by Jesus in the good shepherd discourse as a negative moniker for those who enter the sheepfold the wrong way (10:1, 8). It was used more generally to describe the social bandits who terrorized the wealthy in a raw form of Robin Hood-like, quasi-political rebellion.[14] The synoptics do not use this term for Barabbas, describing him instead in terms of the specific acts of insurrection and murder (Mk 15:7; Lk 23:19). Thus, the Judeans' cry seeks the release of a *violent revolutionary,* one identified by Jesus as someone sneaking into the sheepfold. Even the Judean authorities hope for release from Roman captivity, despite their accommodation to it. But their hopes are in the David-like messiah who will lead with a sword and bring about an era of everlasting peace. To link these hopes with Barabbas is a sad reminder of how narrow their vision has become.

Barabbas plays another role in the particular flow of the fourth gospel. His Hebrew name, *bar-abbas,* means "son of the father." It is a particular irony that the Judeans are selecting not only between two kings but between two "sons of the Father." Given Barabbas's practice, it is clear that he and Jesus have the same differences in paternity as between Jesus and the Judeans in chapter 8.

### e. Scourging the King: 19:1–3

Pilate's response to this cry for Barabbas reveals imperial logic: "Then, therefore [*tote oun*], Pilate received [*elaben*] Jesus and scourged [*emastigōsen*] him." Pilate, although in league with the Judean authorities' death plot from the beginning, has listened to Jesus and found him innocent. He has offered to release him to no avail. Now, he chooses a "middle" course: to torture him for a while. The verb for scourging refers to the particular Roman practice of flogging a criminal with a barbed whip, the *mastix,* although "scourging" is also referred to in the Hebrew scriptures (e.g., Ex 5:14, by Pharaoh; Deut 25:2–3, by the Israelite judge), and a milder form was practiced in the synagogue.[15] It served Roman law by "preparing" a person for execution. Pilate begins the inevitable process of glorifying Jesus.

By describing Jesus as "received" by Pilate, the narrator adds an ironic reminder of the purpose of the entire drama of the incarnation. The prologue told us from the start of the authority given to those who "received" (*elabon*) Jesus. Of course, their "receiving" and Pilate's could hardly be more different. But in form, if not in substance, Pilate unconsciously acts out the process whereby people become "children of God."

Charles Giblin suggests that this act by Pilate marks the midpoint of the encounter between Jesus and the procurator, signaled by the words *tote oun* here and in 19:16.[16] This perspective is consistent with the chiastic structure with

---

14. Horsley and Hanson (1985, 63–85).
15. C. Schneider, *TDNT* 4:515–519.
16. Giblin (1984, 222–223).

which we are working,[17] for it comes at the beginning of the central section of the chiasm. Throughout this "inside" scene, there are no words reported from either Jesus or Pilate. Instead, the centerpiece finds Jesus prepared as a mock king, whose "coronation" begins with a scourging.

In verse 2, we see Pilate's soldiers providing two powerful symbols of royalty for their prisoner: a crown (*stephanon*) of thorns and a purple robe. Matthew and Mark both note the crown of thorns and Mark the purple robe, but Matthew refers to a "scarlet" robe (Mk 15:17; Mt 27:29). The crown is a specific mockery of the emperor's laurel wreath headpiece, also called a *stephanon*.[18] The purple suggests wealth generally (cf. Lam 4:5; Dan 5:7–29), but as a robe, specifically the kingly garment (e.g., Judg 8:26). Whether this outfit is part of Pilate's order to further humiliate Jesus and the Judeans or is spontaneous "fun" on the part of the soldiers, we cannot be sure. Apparently, mocking of political prisoners as would-be kings was a common practice in the ancient world.[19] However, Pilate will soon bring Jesus out wearing the crown and robe, suggesting it is, if not his own idea, at least one he finds fitting.

The soldiers continue in verse 3: "And they were coming toward him and saying, 'Hail [*chaire*], the king of the Judeans!' and they were giving him slaps [*rapismata*]." Their movement is another subtle irony on Jesus' mission, which is to "draw all people to myself" (12:32). Here, he has drawn the most distant of peoples, the imperial officers, to acknowledge his kingship, but only in a mocking fashion. Their greeting, although at one level the usual Roman form of "hello," also marks an ironic contrast with Jesus' repeated Last Supper discourse call for "joy" (14:28 [*echarēte*]; 16:20 [*charan*]; 16:22 [*charēsetai*]). Only Mark (14:65) also reports Jesus being slapped by the soldiers, a particularly personal sort of violence. It has the effect here of removing whatever hint of sincerity there might have been in the royal treatment of Jesus by the soldiers. They are professional killers, trained in violence, who toss a little of it around without a second thought.

The slap also recalls the high priest's officer's slap of Jesus (18:22). The Johannine ideology is consistent throughout: Rome and Judea are equal partners in the violence against the king.

### f. "Look! The Human!": 19:4–8

Given the Judeans' explicit rejection of Pilate's offer to release Jesus, one might expect that all that remains after the scourging and mock coronation is

---

17. Cf. the reverse procedure of Senior (1991, 69), who, although noting that the "chaiastic [*sic*] parallels . . . are quite convincing," goes on to say that "they should not be overemphasized" because "the centerpiece of the chaiastic pattern is not, in fact, the dramatic summit of the trial." Senior's method — which finds the "fact" of the center in the "dynamism" supposedly reaching its pinnacle not in Jesus' ironic coronation but in the apostasy of the Judeans — results in a methodologically undisciplined and theologically misdirected emphasis on the sins of the Judeans rather than on the revelation of the true meaning of Jesus' mission to the world.

18. R. Brown (1970, 875).

19. C. Koester (1994, chap. 6).

to take Jesus away for execution. But, mysteriously, Pilate instead follows a different course of action in verse 4: "And Pilate went out [*exēlthen*] outside again and said to them, 'See, I am leading [*agō*] him to you outside, so that you should know that I am finding no cause in him.' " Both the narrator and Pilate underscore the movement to the Judeans who are "outside," an ironic reversal of the Judeans' threat to cast "outside" anyone who confessed Jesus as the messiah (9:22, 34). But the narrator is more subtle still, for Pilate is also outside, a result of his refusal to hear Jesus' "voice" and be led (10:4; 18:37).

The narrator continually scripts this double movement, which is apparently controlled by the worldly powers but is truly under the guidance of Jesus and the Father. Pilate tells the Judeans to see how he has "led" Jesus out, as if to show his own power to determine the outcome of events. But, of course, Jesus moves throughout this drama totally on his own volition. It is he who will "lead" out his sheep (10:16, *agagein*) to a place of safe pasture. In contrast, Pilate leads Jesus directly into the wolves.

For the second time, Pilate intones that he finds no cause. His behavior begins to take on ritualistic aspects. It also suggests a parallel with Peter's threefold denial of his discipleship. After this second disclaimer, we will not be surprised to hear a third before the scene is completed.

In verse 5, the narrator describes the free movement of Jesus: "Jesus, therefore, came out [*exēlthen*] outside, wearing the thorny crown and the purple robe." Despite Pilate's claim of control, Jesus comes out on his own, complete with royal symbols.

Having been joined by Jesus, Pilate in verse 5b announces the king to the people: "Look! The human [*Idou! Ho anthrōpos*]!" What may be from Pilate's perspective a simple call to draw attention to the pathetic, beaten king echoes Hebrew scripture for the attuned listener:

> And you shall take silver and gold, and make crowns, and you shall put them on the head of Joshua [LXX, *Iesou*], the son of Jehozadak the high priest; and you shall say to him, "Thus says the Lord Almighty, Behold the man [LXX, *Idou anēr*], whose name is The Branch, and he shall spring up from his stem and build the house of the Lord. And he shall receive power, and shall sit and rule upon his throne." (Zech 6:11–13)

Given the fourth gospel's inclusive language, it is not surprising to have the writer put in Pilate's mouth the word *anthrōpos* rather than *anēr* to announce the royal presence.

But the response, sadly but predictably, is less than the Palm Sunday crowd's acclamation. The text states: "When, therefore, the chief priests and the officers saw him, they cried [*ekraugasen*], saying, 'Crucify! crucify!' " Pilate's second "no cause" is matched by the Judeans' second cry, this time with no subtlety at all.

It is interesting that the narrator implicates the officers with the chief priests, a detail no other gospel provides (Mt 27:20: chief priests, elders, crowd; Mk

15:11: chief priests, crowd; Lk 23:13: chief priests, rulers, people). Despite their differences, the synoptics each heap some of the blame on the masses, even if they have been stirred up by the leaders. The fourth gospel, however, limits responsibility to the priests and their employees, keeping the people/crowds at an ambiguous distance. It suggests also a much more contained encounter: rather than portraying Pilate in the face of an enraged multitude, he is shown confronting only his co-conspirators and their minions.

With the call for crucifixion, the last card of the Judean authorities is turned up. It is the first mention of this terrible Roman form of execution in the fourth gospel and, coming from the mouths of the Judeans, has a particularly terrible ring to it. It is like African-Americans in the South calling on the white sheriff to lynch one of their black neighbors. It is one of the most bitter indictments of the Judeans in a text born of the unbearable pain of brotherly rejection.

But Pilate is still not done with the hapless Judeans. He mocks them still again in verse 6b: "Receive [*labete*] him yourself and crucify him, for I am finding no cause in him." Despite all their efforts, they just can't seem to get the job of Jesus' execution accomplished! Do his words also carry an undertone of disgust, as these supposed religious figures come across as bloodthirsty monsters? Given Pilate's own predilection for torture and crucifixion, we should not be too quick to attribute to him distaste at the thought of political murder. Perhaps he simply wants them to acknowledge their own responsibility, rather than seeming to throw it all in his lap. If so, he will get it in the next verse. In the meantime, he issues his third and final "no cause," completing the parallelism with Peter's denial.

In verse 7, the Judeans finally admit openly the rationale for their deadly desire: "The Judeans answered him, 'We have law, and according to the Law, he ought [*opheilei*] to die, because he made himself Son of God.'" Contrary to commentators who hear the Judeans citing a particular statute (e.g., Lev 24:16), the Greek text is anarthrous, indicating not "a" or "the" law but the sum of their law (including the Pharisees' oral tradition?) that prescribes the consequences. The "ought" ironically recalls 13:14, where Jesus told his disciples that they "ought" (*opheilete*) to wash one another's feet in preparation for death. The Judeans' "ought" leads to Jesus' "ought," as the consequences of discipleship become more concrete.

Ever since 5:18, we have heard that the Judeans' problem is that Jesus has been "making himself" something that he is not. Despite the repeated insistence by Jesus that all he does and says comes from the Father and that he does nothing at all on his own, the crux of the matter comes down to this: Who "made" Jesus "Son of God"? Their objection is not to a claim that he is the "messiah," for when challenged to "admit" it, he refused to answer (10:24). Nor do they complain in the terms by which Pilate himself has understood the conflict, that is, king of the Judeans. Their response completely eliminates the political import of the titles "messiah" or "king," seemingly reducing the matter to a religious squabble.

Is this internal justification among the Judeans news to Pilate? Have they withheld this from him during their co-planning? How else to explain the re-action that the narrator notes in verse 8: "When, therefore, Pilate heard this word, he became very much afraid." The procurator was fully at home in the world of political infighting and intrigue; the Roman empire was never short of assassination plots, coups, and betrayals. But the talk of God is outside his realm. Despite the likely condescending attitude with which a Roman would look at a colonial religion, something has spooked Pilate. Suddenly, he has been thrown off course.

In particular, the phrase "Son of God" might have invoked for a Roman not the Jewish messianic hopes but the possibility that Jesus was a "divine man," perhaps marked with special powers.[20] His confident control gone, Pilate is driven to speak with Jesus once again.

### g. *"Where Are You From?": 19:9–11*

The back-and-forth continues as Pilate retreats inside: "And he entered [*eisēlthen*] into the praetorium again and said to Jesus, 'Where are you from [*pothen ei su*]?'" The mocking procurator has been replaced by a frightened man, wondering, like many before him, about Jesus' *pothen*. Earlier, the Judeans had presumed to know where Jesus was from, only to be refuted by Jesus (7:27–8). One might have expected Pilate's question to take on the issue of identity, as in "Who are you?" But Pilate, as always, is an unwitting tool. Even his un-usual question goes to the heart of the matter, for the fourth gospel itself has framed Jesus' identity not so much in terms of who but where from. Regardless of titles, Jesus is from God.

After their previous exchange, we might expect Jesus' response to be some-thing different from what the narrator provides in verse 9b: "But Jesus gave him no answer." Why the sudden silence in the face of Pilate's apparently sincere question? It certainly cannot be because he doubts Pilate would understand; all of Jesus' talk about kingship "not of this world" was not likely to penetrate the imperial mind-set, either. Is it perhaps simply to fulfill the Isaian sheep-before-the-shearers scripture quoted above? As always, the Johannine Jesus is in control, and his mode of behavior is not easily penetrable by those of us mired in the "below."

The silence clearly exasperates Pilate, for his next statement pulls the trump card used by cooperation-seeking judges throughout the millennia: "Are you not speaking to me? Don't you know I have the authority to release you, and I have authority to crucify you?" Our modern North American judges are much more subtle than Pilate, usually threatening "contempt of court" or a longer jail sentence for defendants who don't kowtow in respect to their state-granted authority. Pilate's surprisingly honest basis for his demand reduces the inquiry from what might for a moment have become a true conversation among two

---

20. Carson (1991, 600).

human beings to a typical call for a coerced confession. "Don't answer me because you respect me," the governor says. "Answer me because I have a cross waiting in the wings with your name on it."

At this point, we might come to expect Jesus to remain silent. If he refused to answer the legitimate query, why should he answer the bullying one? But again, Jesus surprises both his interrogator and us with his bold reply in verse 11: "You would have no authority over me at all unless it had been given to you from above [*anōthen*]. This is why the one having handed me over to you has the greater sin [*hamartian*]." It is the first time Jesus has used the *anōthen* metaphor since his encounter with the teacher of Israel, Nicodemus, in chapter 3. There, it was a double entendre, playing "from above" and "again" against one another in relation to birth. Now, it can only mean "from above" in connection with "authority." And yet it still bears a double entendre, albeit a different one. For Pilate, "from above" can only mean from *Caesar,* the one from whom his governorship has been granted. Jesus, of course, means from *God*: Pilate is but a tool in the larger drama of the descent and ascent of the messiah. Just as the official teacher was not likely to pick up the intended sense of *anōthen,* neither is the official procurator. Both Nicodemus and Pilate are captives of their offices, having ceded a share of their humanity to the powers that keep a tight grip on worldly control.

So, from Pilate's perspective, the first part of Jesus' statement is no more than a truism. Although he might hear it as an insult in the face of his threat to crucify Jesus, it would not suggest to him that Jesus is part of a bigger "conspiracy." But the second part of the defendant's response introduces an entirely new theme to the dialogue: the question of "sin." For the Jewish or Christian mind-set of the time of the fourth gospel, *hamartia,* a word with a root meaning of "missing the mark," was associated with the moral culpability of acting against God. In the Hellenistic sense in which the Roman governor might hear it, though, it had less of a sense of personal guilt than simply the making of an error or mistake.[21]

Whether Pilate hears it in this way or as a deeper accusation of cosmic misalignment, it is clearly a way of naming betrayal as the "greater sin" than the carrying out of official political duties. We should not allow this to exculpate the procurator, though: it is a matter of *greater* or *lesser* sin, not of sin versus innocence. "Just following orders" or its more North American equivalent, "just obeying the law," has never been an excuse for violence. But the deliberate violation of the hoped-for covenant fidelity that would exist among the children of the one God is a greater sin. The Judean authorities and Judas together share the responsibility for this breach of trust. However, Jesus' statement is singular: "the one who..." In the end, Judas's fault is greater, for in addition to being part of the ancient covenant, he had walked with Jesus in the new covenant. Without his cooperation, the authorities would not have had their turn. The greatest sin comes from the evil *within* the community, not from the powers in "the world."

---

21. G. Stählin and W. Grundmann, *TDNT* 1:296–302.

### h. "We Have No King but Caesar!": 19:12–16a

For the first time in the scene, we hear in verse 11 that the all-powerful Roman governor is losing his nerve: "After this, Pilate was seeking to release him." When Pilate spoke of the option of release in 18:39, it seemed a matter of political mockery. Now, with the narrator's reliable insight into Pilate's motives, we learn that, despite the previous agreement to serve the Judean authorities' interests, the procurator has been badly shaken. The fun has gone out of the game. Jesus has raised the stakes in a way that has confused Pilate and left him unprepared to continue in the supreme confidence with which he began the encounter. He is ready to end the matter without further action and go back to ordinary work.

But the Faustian deal into which all political authorities enter cannot be nullified quite so easily. Once inside the office, certain consequences follow. His personal desire is to release Jesus, but the accusers also hold a trump card, which they now turn face up in verse 12b: "But the Judeans cried [*ekraugasan*], saying, 'If you release this one, you are not a "friend of Caesar," for everyone who makes himself king is speaking against Caesar!'" It is their third "cry": first for Barabbas, then for crucifixion, now for loyalty to Caesar. The first two cries revealed their own interests and allowed Pilate to keep some distance from their bloodthirsty shouting. Now, though, they appeal to Pilate's interest, and there is no escape.

As Giblin has noted, these shouts are heard from the "inside," where Pilate apparently has remained with Jesus. The lines have been blurred, as the Judeans' cry penetrates the procurator's inner sanctum and destroys his equanimity and his control.[22] With the earlier question of release, Pilate forced the Judeans to choose between two kings: Jesus and Barabbas. Now, they turn the tables, putting Pilate to precisely the same test as between Caesar and Jesus.[23] The wages of sin come back to haunt him. The Judeans may be out for blood, but they are not stupid. They know exactly which button to press.

The term "friend of Caesar" was a common one at the time to refer to loyal servants of the emperor.[24] Coins of the Judean client king Herod Agrippa I during the period 37–44 C.E. bore the inscription *philokaisar*, expressing the allegiance of the Judean ruler to the Roman emperor.[25] Thus, "friend" is used the way U.S. senators refer to each other in debate as "friends." It has nothing to do with affection but everything to do with being partners in the same game. In the Johannine context, it bears the additional irony of contrasting with Jesus' affirmation of his disciples as "friends" if they love him and one another (15:14–15). Unwittingly, the shouting Judeans are challenging Pilate to choose not only among kings but among friends and the meaning of friendship itself.

---

22. Giblin (1985, 232).
23. Duke (1985, 134).
24. R. Brown (1970, 879).
25. Ibid.

The concrete issue for immediate decision is precisely the one Jesus offered to the "Pharisees who were with him" in 9:40–10:18. One cannot have it both ways: either continue your loyalty to the status quo or give it up *now* and follow Jesus. It is the challenge Gandhi gave judges before whom he stood and the one many civil resisters continue to offer to courts: either acknowledge your commitment to a system of violence and oppression by enforcing the law or walk away from it altogether. The usual attempt at the "middle ground" of offering pious platitudes about the sincerity of the opposition while supporting the oppression will not cut it from a Johannine point of view.

Which option will Pilate choose? The narrator draws out the suspense in verse 13: "Therefore, having heard these words, Pilate led Jesus outside, and sat down upon the judgment seat [*bēmatos*] in the place called 'Stone Pavement' [*Lithostrōton*], in Hebrew 'Gabbatha.' " It is undeniable that Pilate's ritual action is in response to the Judeans' final cry. He has heard their words. There is much scholarly debate because of the grammatical ambiguity of the Greek as to whether Pilate himself sat on the judgment seat or put Jesus on the seat. However, given Pilate's fear and desire to release Jesus, it seems terribly out of character to suggest that he would be lampooning his own Roman legal system by placing the would-be Judean king in the place of power.[26]

The seat itself was referred to by Josephus in the passage quoted earlier (see p. 395). It was apparently a public location, from which the governor would pronounce his decisions for all to hear. For the first time in the dance between inside and outside, it is clear that the procurator is positioned for an open audience, beyond the Judeans with whom he has conspired at first and who now pin him down.

The detail of the place-name in both Greek and Hebrew is curious. Why interrupt the dramatic moment with this information? As with previous place-names in the fourth gospel, the clue lies in the link between the name and its association with a particular site (cf. Bethzatha, 5:2; Tiberias, 6:1). The evidence about the *Lithostrōton* points to two possible locations: (1) a yard adjacent to Herod's palace[27] or (2) the courtyard of the fortress Antonia, constructed by Herod on the northwest corner of the Temple Mount.[28] In either case, the Stone Pavement is associated with Herod, the Judean "king," who is never mentioned in the fourth gospel. By specifically linking the name with the "Hebrew" (actually, Aramaic) Gabbatha, the narrator ties Pilate's place of judgment with the cooperation of the Judean authorities in their own friendship with Caesar.

Drawing the suspense out even more, the narrator in verse 14 adds the first time-marker since the beginning of the encounter with Pilate in 18:28: "It was the preparation of the Passover, the sixth hour." The scene that began "early" has taken all morning. What began mostly in darkness has had the bright light of midday cast upon it. The foul deeds will not be covered over. It is the second

---

26. R. Brown (1970, 880–881).
27. Josephus *J.W.* 2.14.8.
28. *HBD* 326.

"sixth hour" in the gospel, the previous one taking place at the Samaritan well. Now, another non-Galilean is faced with the searing vulnerability of noon.

But more significantly, it is the sixth hour of Passover preparation day, the moment at which the Jerusalem priests began their slaughter of the lambs. And even this sacred hour was tainted with the legal chicanery of cultic demands. Brown summarizes the evidence showing that the biblical mandate that the lambs be slaughtered at "evening" (Ex 12:6) was manipulated to accommodate the huge number of lambs needed for the throng of pilgrims. "Evening" became any time after "noon," the beginning of the solar decline.[29] Throughout the afternoon, the bloody business would take place. The narrator has interrupted to let readers know that what Pilate is about to do has this activity in the background.

Finally, in verse 14b, Pilate speaks: "And he said to the Judeans, 'See! Your king!' " Just when we might be expecting him to capitulate directly, he shows one more bit of fight. On his first leading out of Jesus, he had announced him with "See! The human!" Now, it is more specific: Pilate has named this battered person as the Judeans' leader. But in the process, he has tried to reestablish his own distance from Jesus. He is *their* king, not his.

The Judeans will have none of this. There is only one way for Pilate to prove his friendship with Caesar. Eventually, the gamesmanship must stop, and action must be taken. In verse 15, they cry one last time: "Take him away [*aron*]! Crucify him!" The first part of their cry echoes a tremendous range of references in the fourth gospel. The verb *airō* that calls for Jesus' being taken away was used to describe the following activities:

1:29: *taking away* the sin of the world

2:16: *taking away* the doves from the Temple

5:8–12: *lifting up* the mat on the sabbath

8:59: *taking up* stones to throw at Jesus

10:18: *taking away* Jesus' life

11:39, 41: *lifting up* the stone blocking Lazarus' tomb

15:2: *taking away* the unfruitful branches

16:22: not *taking away* Jesus' joy from the disciples

17:15: not *taking away* the disciples from the world

Throughout the narrative, *airō* has signified activity that is central to Jesus' ministry. Now, he is the apparent "victim" of *airō*, but, to readers who have been following closely, this *airō* is the culmination of Jesus' mission to the world.

Pilate, rather desperately, tries in verse 15b one last time: "Shall I crucify your king?" The juxtaposition is horrible. Pilate's last hope is that the reality of what they are seeking will finally dawn on them. But it is no use; their minds are made up. Their final response is one of the most bitter ironies in the Bible:

---

29. R. Brown (1970, 883).

"The chief priests answered, 'We have no king but Caesar!' " The priests of the Chosen People, those at that very moment responsible for the cultic actions celebrating God's covenant with Israel, renounce the relationship altogether. No heavier price could be paid for their achieving their goal than this. An ancient Passover Haggadah expresses what they have given up: "From everlasting to everlasting thou art God; beside thee we have no king, redeemer or savior.... We have no king but thee."[30]

For the fourth gospel, the decision to get rid of Jesus necessarily has had this consequence at least since the Tabernacles discussion. Those who oppose Jesus were not children of God or Abraham but children of the devil. They denied it then but now have been forced to admit the sad truth. The primary manifestation of sin throughout the entire period of Israel's monarchy was the preference for worldly kings rather than God.[31] But now, they have gone one terrible step farther. At least during the monarchy, exile, and postexilic period, the Judean leaders awaited a king of *Israel* who would free them from foreign oppression. Now, they have preferred the oppressor-king himself. From the Johannine perspective, the rift is complete. The Chosen People are those who belong to the Johannine community.

There is still one more thing Pilate can do. The narrator presents the conclusion in verse 16: "Then, therefore [*tote oun*], he handed him over [*paredōken*] to them to be crucified." Pilate cooperates in the crucifixion; he is indeed a "friend of Caesar." But he does so by *handing Jesus back to the chief priests*. He has gotten out of their way by allowing them to share in the imperial power. The scene comes to an end with the placement of Jesus back in the hands of "his own," those who have never received him.

---

30. Cited in Duke (1985, 135).

31. Polzin (1989) presents a brilliant analysis of the Deuteronomic history, concluding that its very raison d'être was the clarification of this premise.

# 25

# Carrying the Cross by Himself

## *The Moment of Glory Arrives*

## John 19:17–30

**A. Chiasm:**

    a: 17: Jesus carries cross alone

      b: 18: "they" crucify Jesus

        c: 19–22: *titulus* controversy

      b[1]: 23–24: soldiers crucify Jesus

    a[1]: 25–30: Jesus on cross, with Beloved Disciple and mother below[1]

**B. Location:** Golgotha, the Place of the Skull

**C. Time:** Passover preparation, the sixth hour

**D. Hebrew scripture context:** Ex 25:22; Ps 22:18, 69; Ex 12:20; Isa 53:12

**E. Social factors:** transition from Judeans as "covenant people" to Johannine community

**F. Themes:** Jesus' death fulfills scripture and completes his mission

**G. Key words:** woven *anōthen*; fulfilled; completed

## 1. THE JOHANNINE CRUCIFIXION NARRATIVE: ALL IS GLORY

How different is the fourth gospel's story of Jesus' death from the synoptics! At one level, this should not surprise us: the Johannine narrative has from the

---

1. Ellis (1984, 266–267) notes this division but rushes to characterize the "B" parallels on the basis of the "soldiers" who crucify Jesus. This misses an essential ambiguity of the scene, as described below.

beginning charted its own course through the story of Jesus' life. But now, at the moment of death, all the stops are pulled out, as the gospel sings the glorious song of the enthronement of the king. Before we look at the scene in detail, it might be helpful to note some of the elements found in, say, Mark, that are not part of the Johannine version and vice versa:

### Elements in Mark's crucifixion narrative not found in the fourth gospel

- Simon of Cyrene helping carry the cross
- Jesus being wine-drugged with myrrh
- movement from third, to sixth, to ninth hours
- the naming of those crucified alongside as *lēstēs*
- the blaspheming bystanders
- the mocking chief priests and scribes
- the reproach of the others on the cross
- darkness from the sixth to ninth hours
- Jesus' cry, "My God, My God, why have you forsaken me?"
- the question of Elijah
- the centurion's proclamation
- the "many other women" looking from afar

### Elements in the fourth gospel's crucifixion narrative not found in Mark

- Jesus carrying the cross alone
- the *titulus* in three languages
- the words "the Nazarene" on the *titulus*
- the argument between the chief priests and Pilate over the written words
- the division of Jesus' outer garment into four pieces, one for each soldier
- the seamless inner garment woven *anōthen*
- the fulfillment of scripture in the apportioning of Jesus' clothes
- the Beloved Disciple at the cross
- the words of Jesus to his mother and the Beloved Disciple
- Jesus' knowledge that all things have been completed
- Jesus' words, "I am thirsty"
- Jesus' words, "It is completed"
- the handing over of Jesus' spirit

The result is two completely different pictures of Jesus' last moments on earth. Mark's story portrays a suffering messiah in the image of Isaiah's Suffering Servant, reviled by all onlookers to the end, feeling abandoned by God, but remaining obedient.[2] John's version shows a royal enthronement, with God's agent fulfilling scripture as he is lifted up in glory for the world to behold.

How different these stories are, too, for us, the readers! Mark's story allows us to identify with Jesus' pain and loneliness, the terror of imperial punishment, the ugliness of death at the hands of the powers. John, on the other hand, keeps Jesus "above" all others in the story and, hence, apart from us as well. We may marvel, wonder, or simply be mystified at Jesus' calm journey to death, but we can hardly begin to identify with his experience.

But the purpose of the fourth gospel throughout has not been to portray a Jesus with whom we could identify, as to inculcate or strengthen our belief that he is the one sent by God and draws people to follow. Despite what appears from "below" to be the final victory by the darkness, Jesus' death is filled with light and glory in the fourth gospel. We *must* learn to see such a fate not as leading us to despair but as teaching us how different are the ways of God from the ways of the world.

## 2. THE MOMENT OF TRUTH:
## JESUS IS LIFTED UP IN GLORY

The imperial power has consented to the fervent desires of the Judean authorities. Jesus is to be crucified as they wish, another troublemaker disposed of by Rome. Or is it by Rome? Although crucifixion was an exclusively Roman form of execution, the fourth gospel's narrator leaves open a small gap at the beginning of the scene that shifts the responsibility for the death itself. In verse 16a, as we have seen, Pilate hands Jesus over "to them to be crucified." Then in verse 16b, the narrator continues: "They therefore received [*parelabon*] Jesus." The "they" in the synoptics is specified as the Roman soldiers (e.g., Mk 15:16), but in the fourth gospel, the continuity of the previous discussion suggests that the "they" is the *chief priests* with whom Pilate was speaking in verse 15. It is the function of these men at this very hour on this very day, we recall, to sacrifice the Passover lambs for the people. Johannine irony never rests.

A further irony in this opening description is the use of the verb *paralambanō*, literally, "to receive alongside." It has been used only twice previously in the fourth gospel: in the central prologue verse wherein we were told that "his own would not receive him [*parelabon*]" (1:11) and in the Last Supper discourse when Jesus promised to come again and "receive" (*paralēmpsomai*, 14:3) the disciples to himself. Now, those who were "his own" and did not re-

---

2. Myers (1988, 383–392) notes the more "hidden" enthronement motif in the Markan narrative as well. In the end, it is a matter not of opposing or inconsistent stories but of emphasis and narrative mode.

ceive him in the sense of believing in him have received him to put him to death, an event that will take Jesus to the place that he will prepare for his new "own."

But having placed Jesus in the hands of "them," the narrator magically transports us to a wholly different scene-within-the-scene in verse 17: "And carrying [*bastazōn*] the cross himself, he went out [*exēlthen*] into the so-called 'Skull Place,' which is called in Hebrew, 'Golgotha.'" Whether Jesus is handed over to the Roman soldiers or the Judean priests is, at a deeper level, irrelevant. Jesus has been in charge of his fate all along. The moment has come for the good shepherd to lay down his life.

We might recall that the verb for "carrying," *bastazo,* was last used in reference to the things that Jesus had to say to his disciples but that they could not "bear" now (*bastazein,* 16:12). Also, it described the stones that the Judeans had previously "carried" in their unsuccessful effort to stone Jesus (*ebastasan,* 10:31). Now, these connotations come together in the carrying of the cross. What the disciples could not bear and what the Judeans could not accomplish, Jesus does willingly and without help.

We have known this was coming for many chapters now, so we might be surprised to realize that verse 17 is the first time in the fourth gospel in which we hear the word "cross." Jesus has spoken instead in terms of two metaphors, "laying down life" and being "lifted up," and the narrator has not dared interfere. Now, the metaphor gives way in part to the physical reality of death, to emphasize that Jesus the Human One really did go through this experience. This question was one of the primary battlefields in which the fourth gospel was used by both sides in the battle between the Johannine community and apostolic churches, on the one hand, and gnostic Christianity, on the other. Although many gnostics quoted the gospel for its dualistic imagery of light/dark, heaven/earth, their conception of the evil of creation and its "demiurge" Creator led them to reject the possibility that Jesus actually subjected himself to physical death.[3] This dispute was much more than an intellectual controversy. The primary implication for the gnostics of their belief in the "illusion" of the crucifixion was to ridicule the Christian embrace of martyrdom as an essential aspect of discipleship. Indeed, one of the main reasons for the eventual rapprochement between Johannine and apostolic Christianity in the second century was the powerful call of the fourth gospel for witness to the powers even unto death. For example, Ignatius of Antioch proclaimed on his way to the lions, "Now at last I am beginning to be a disciple."[4] Thus, a careful reading of the text, despite the exalted theology of glorification, forces us to keep one eye on the historical fact of crucifixion, which the canonical tradition is unanimous in claiming Jesus underwent. The simple word "cross" at the start of Jesus' journey to Golgotha prevents us from indulging for long in gnostic fantasies.

For the last time, Jesus "goes out," as the sequence of comings and goings in the Passion narrative culminates. From Pilate's judgment seat at Gabbatha,

---

3. Pagels (1979, 70–101).
4. Ignatius *Rom.* 5, in Holmes (1989, 104).

to the place of execution at Golgotha, the narrator portrays Jesus' movement as an inevitable part of the plan. The two Hebrew "translation notes" link the two sites, as do the similar-sounding Aramaic words that identify the Stone Pavement and the Skull Place.

Although all four gospels name this place either as "Golgotha" or "Skull," no other details are common to all accounts. Little is known from outside the New Testament about the site, and archaeology has not been able to confirm its precise location. Similarly, whether the name derives from a physical resemblance of the topography to a skull or the frequent executions that took place there, we cannot conclusively determine. But regardless of the haziness of the historical window, the very word "skull" immediately reinforces the deadly destiny of those whose cross leads them there. We do know that most crucified prisoners were left to be scavenged by animals. There can be no doubt of what awaits Jesus at the end of the road.

The narrator jumps past the *via dolorosa* and meets Jesus in midcrucifixion in verse 18, a sentence continuing from the previous verse: ". . . where they crucified him, and with him two others, one on either side [*enteuthen kai enteuthen*], but Jesus in the middle." The fourth gospel completely effaces the others crucified with Jesus, unlike the synoptics, which specify them as bandits (Mk 15:27; Mt 27:38) or criminals (Lk 23:33). Only their location relative to him is noted. Even this gets a Johannine twist! The synoptics refer to the others "on the right and on the left," but the fourth gospel uses a figure of speech to note "either side." The particular word, *enteuthen,* previously expressed a desire to depart "from here" (7:3; 14:31) and, later, differentiated Jesus' kingdom as not "from here" (18:36). Jesus has finally arrived "here," with those next to him described in terms that remind us of the places from which he has come along the way.

The placing of Jesus in the middle between two others also echoes the Septuagint:

And I will make myself known to you, and I will speak to you from above [*anōthen*], the mercy seat between the two cherubs, which are upon the ark of witness [*martyriou*], and in all things [*panta*] I will command you about the children of Israel. (Ex 25:22)

The transformation of the place of crosses and skulls into a site of divine proclamation continues in verses 19–20 with the narrator's description of Pilate's final act in Jesus' lifetime: "Pilate wrote a title [*titlon*] and put it [*ethēken*] upon the cross. It was written, 'Jesus the Nazarene, the king of the Judeans.' This title, therefore, many of the Judeans read, because the place where Jesus was crucified was near the city, and it was written in Hebrew, Latin, Greek." Again, the Johannine differences are most revealing. Whereas Luke and Mark call the words an "inscription" (*epigraphē*, Mk 15:26; Lk 23:38) and Matthew calls them a "charge" (*aitian,* Mt. 27:37), the fourth gospel specifies a "title," befitting the enthronement theme. Furthermore, the words are written in the three languages of the Johannine world, tongues for the entire "world" to understand.

Also, only John adds the words "the Nazarene" to the title otherwise common to all four gospels. It is another ironic note on the world's misunderstanding, as Jesus is proclaimed as king from Nazareth, rather than from God. "Jesus the Nazarene" was twice the response of the arresting party to Jesus' question, "Whom are you seeking?" (18:5, 7). Now, the one they sought is also named "king of the Judeans."

The detail that the place of crucifixion was near the city and therefore the *titulus* was read by many Judeans provides both a plot movement and a character note. From the perspective of plot, we should not be surprised when this reading leads to complaint in the next verse. From the perspective of character, it tells us that the Judeans in Jerusalem found it worth their while to "visit" the Skull Place. What macabre sort of spectator sport is this? Is it like rubbernecking at a freeway accident? But no, this requires going out of one's way to watch someone being tortured to death. Was it a regular practice to witness crucifixions, or was this particular event especially worth watching?

The narrator simply notes the fact and then moves on in verse 22 to focus on the implications of Pilate's words to a particular subset of Judeans, the chief priests, who began to say to Pilate, "You should not be writing 'the king of the Judeans,' but, 'This one said, "I am king of the Judeans."'" Of course, the children of the devil are only acting like their father in urging upon Pilate another lie (8:44), for Jesus never said what they want Pilate to write. They have acted from the beginning from a faulty premise: that Jesus "made himself" equal to God or a king (5:18). Now, though, they are ready to have the procurator seal the frame-up with a false charge, one that Pilate three times refused to use.

We can only imagine the disgust with which Pilate holds these petitioners. Despite being partners in crime and political "realists," they have openly embarrassed him with the threat to report that he is not a "friend of Caesar." Now, they have gotten their execution, but they still want one more favor from him. He might well have offered them the Roman equivalent of "Go to hell!" Instead, he speaks in a profoundly prophetic manner in verse 23: "What I have written, I have written." On one level, it is just another way of saying, "Leave me alone! I've done enough for you already!" But at the deeper level with which the gospel is always concerned, Pilate's writing is an act of cosmic truth-telling by the one who disclaimed knowledge of truth. And at the same time, it is an ironic confirmation of Jesus' response to Pilate's inquiry about Jesus' kingship, "You have said it" (18:37).[5]

The writing on the *titulus* by Pilate is a backdoor way of assuring readers that, although the procurator had apparently turned Jesus over to the chief priests, Rome had not totally disclaimed responsibility for the execution. As Craig Koester puts it, "The placard identified Jewish messianism as a capital offense and reminded the populace that threats to Roman rule would not be tolerated."[6] Now, in verse 23, the matter becomes even more clear: "There-

---

5. Duke (1985, 137).
6. C. Koester (1994, chap. 6).

fore, when the soldiers [*stratiōtai*] had crucified Jesus, they took his robe and made four parts, for each soldier a part." The term for soldiers removes any doubt that those described now as the ones who crucified Jesus are indeed Roman troops. The effect of the ambiguous "they" in verse 16 and the naming of the *stratiōtai* in verse 23 is to reinforce the sense of *mutual responsibility* among both Judea and Rome for Jesus' death. The narrator could not possibly be so bold in creative presentation of the narrative as to actually name the chief priests as the offerers of the Passover sacrifice on the cross. But the more subtle method of leaving open the gap in verse 16 works the same result, while leaving an "out" for those who might object to the historically unlikely suggestion that the priests were directly involved. It is enough in the fourth gospel's ideology for them to have been linked *in spirit* with the crucifixion.

Now, though, the focus has moved from the Judean participation and objections to Pilate's writing to the participation of the Roman soldiers. They are first described as dividing Jesus' "outer garments" (*hamatia,* plural) into four parts. *Himatia* refers to the same items of clothing that the narrator noted Jesus "laying down" at the beginning of the footwashing and "receiving" again at the end (13:4, 12), with a small difference: Jesus' own *himatia* have been replaced by the purple robe given to him earlier by the soldiers (19:2). D. A. Carson suggests the plural makes reference here not simply to the robe but to the other clothes that a Palestinian Jew would have worn: a belt, sandals, and a head covering.[7] Whether as symbols of removing his Roman "authorization" for kingship or of his laying down of his life, the *himatia* become curious souvenirs for the professional executioners.

Is there meaning to the detail of *four* soldiers and four corresponding pieces of clothing? Earlier uses of "four" do not seem to shed light (four months until harvest, 4:35; Lazarus four days dead, 11:17, 39). The text itself provides no added clue, so we are left to open speculation. Can it be a symbol of the Roman empire's control of the "four corners" of the world? Whatever our imaginations might do with the symbolics of fourness, it is clear that the soldiers are perfectly willing to split up Jesus' *himatia,* just as they might expect the wild animals to do with his body when they are done crucifying him. This would not be of particular importance were it not for the care with which the narrator contrasts in verse 24 this action with their treatment of Jesus' "inner garment" (*chitōn):*

> But the inner garment was seamless, woven from above [*anōthen*] throughout the whole. They therefore said to one another, "We should not split [*schisōmen*] it, but let us determine by lots [*lachōmen*] whose it shall be." This was so that the scripture might be fulfilled, "They divided my *himatia* to themselves and upon my garments [*himatismon*] they threw lots." And, indeed, the soldiers did these things [*tauta*].

---

7. Carson (1991, 612).

Only the fourth gospel makes any distinction at all between the *himatia* and the *chitōn*; the synoptics each refer only generally to casting lots for the *himatia* (Mt 27:35; Mk 15:24; Lk 19:24). As usual, each aspect of the description serves a uniquely Johannine purpose.

Although a *chitōn* was a common garment worn next to the skin,[8] the particular details of Jesus' *chitōn* are far from common. The narrator provides three specific descriptive elements: it is "seamless," "woven from above," and woven "throughout the whole." In contrast with Jesus' physical body that can be torn into pieces, his inner life — his oneness with the Father that has been "from the beginning" — is not subject to division. The uniquely Johannine note that the *chitōn* is woven *anōthen* ought to alert readers to the idea that the narrator is not simply referring to a piece of cloth but to the indissoluble essence of the Christ. His being, like those who receive the invitation to be reborn, is from above, which involves a wholeness not found among most human beings, a wholeness that cannot be "split." For the fourth gospel, this distinction between the fragile body subject to suffering and death and the eternal spirit is not akin to the gnostic rejection of the body as evil or corrupt but a realistic recognition of the limits of political power. The conspirators are able — with Jesus' cooperation, of course — to tear his outer garments into pieces. But his inner garment is woven of different stuff, which their methods cannot destroy.

From this perspective, what sense can we make of their determining by lots "whose it shall be"? The answer comes from remembering that the unfolding drama is taking place simultaneously on two planes. From the earthly viewpoint of the soldiers, the *chitōn* is an undershirt, woven in one piece or not, and can be handed over just like Jesus' body has been to them. Their observation of its wholeness simply prevents them from making it worthless to all of them and, unconsciously to them, fulfilling scripture at the same time. We certainly cannot infer that their action somehow bestows on them Jesus' *spirit,* as if it could be given by violence. The narrator makes use of both the double entendre implicit in the question of garments and the fulfillment of scripture through their "earthly" treatment of Jesus' clothes.

The scripture fulfilled is an exact quotation of the Septuagint version of Ps 22:18. It is interesting that the narrator is faithful to the Septuagint even when it generates a distinction from the precise wording of the gospel in which the scripture is supposedly fulfilled. For example, the narrator tells us that the soldiers "determined by lot" (*lachomen*), but the psalm speaks of "casting lots" (*ebalon klēron*). Further, the narrator has gone to the trouble of distinguishing the *himatia* from the *chitōn*, whereas the psalm speaks only of *himatia/himatismon*. The soldiers, though, have not throw lots for the *himatia* at all! The tradition of Psalm 22 was seemingly so deeply associated with Jesus' crucifixion (it begins with "My God, my God, why have you forsaken me?" quoted by the synoptics but not by John) that the author felt the need to include a reference to its fulfillment *somewhere* in the scene. Given the deliberate playing

---

8. BAG 882 references various usages.

down of any description of Jesus' suffering in dying or the mocking of the by-standers (the themes with which the psalm is concerned), no other aspect of the psalm would fit the Johannine theological perspective and the limited scope of the crucifixion narrative. Thus, we have an imperfect fulfillment of scripture that at least meets the apparent need to get Psalm 22 into the story of Jesus' death.

The narrator concludes this part of the scene with the curious affirmation that the soldiers "indeed" did "these things" (*tauta*). Just when we might be wondering whether the entire scene has been fabricated from whole cloth, we are given this assurance that the narrative remains linked with historical reality. The word *tauta* also links what the soldiers have done with Jesus' prediction of the manner in which the disciples will be persecuted and killed (16:3). Beginning with the Last Supper discourse and moving through the Passion narrative, *tauta* has developed a powerful pair of opposing referents: the things Jesus says and does that come from God and the things that the world does because it does *not* know God. The diametrically opposite results — the giving and protecting of eternal life versus the taking and destroying of earthly life — remind readers that one's religious commitment is not simply a matter of verbal formulas or cultic obedience but of one's daily practice of life giving or life taking.

Having completed the picture of the actions of the world in response to the ongoing crucifixion, the narrator shifts in verse 25 to the response of Jesus and his remaining followers: "Standing by the cross of Jesus were his mother, his mother's sister, Mary of Clopas, and Mary Magdalene." It is a silent eloquence that allows these women to stand with Jesus publicly in the face of official scorn. The brightness of their witness contrasts strongly with the darkness of Judas's and Peter's standing "with them," as well as with the brutality and profit seeking of the Roman soldiers. The Greek emphasizes this witness in its word order, which puts the fact of "standing by the cross" before the identification of the women.

The presence of Jesus' mother is startling, though: we have not heard from or seen her since the wedding at Cana, with the exception of the indirect reference to her in 6:42. She has remained completely off stage, an unnamed woman, whose ongoing relationship to Jesus has been unknown to us. But suddenly at the foot of the cross, she is there, watching her son being tortured to death by the authorities.

And she is not alone: with her are other women, although the number and identity of her companions are unclear. Are there four women: Jesus' mother, her sister, Mary of Clopas, and Mary Magdalene? Or are there only three, with Mary of Clopas a description of Jesus' aunt? If there are four, they seem to be faithful counterparts to the four Roman men who share Jesus' garments among themselves.

But the narrator is not really interested in any of them except Jesus' mother, at least for now. In verse 26, we find that these women are not alone, either: "Jesus, therefore, having seen the mother and the disciple whom he was loving standing by . . . " The Beloved Disciple is also there! And his presence only underscores the absence of his "partner," Simon Peter. At the moment of truth, those who remain with the master are three or four women and one man, the man most important to the Johannine community after Jesus himself.

The identifying of this handful of followers and of the Beloved Disciple in particular not only makes us think about Peter but might lead us to wonder about the whereabouts of Jesus' other "beloveds": Martha, Mary, and Lazarus. Why have these special people not come to be with Jesus at this moment? Bethany is just a stone's throw from Jerusalem, and they have been together within the week. Has fear of the Judeans overcome them, too? Perhaps they are there but are not important to Jesus' final task. With this narrative gap, we are left to ponder the fate of these three as well as the countless others who have been with the master along the way but for whatever reasons are seemingly absent now.

The narrator tells us that Jesus sees only two of the group who are mentioned, or at least his vision is focused on them. And the woman he has seen is not described as "his" mother but is twice noted more universally as "the" (*tēn*) mother. It is to this one that he speaks from the cross: "Woman, look! Your son!" His address to her is identical here as it was at Cana, the general title "woman." His words seem to suggest that the women and the Beloved Disciple are not aware of each other's presence. Indeed, there is no reason from within the fourth gospel to suppose that Jesus' mother and the Beloved Disciple know each other at all. Similarly, his following words continue this "introduction": "Next he said to the disciple, 'Look! Your mother!' "

Two aspects of Jesus' life come together under his direction. His past and present are called to form a new relationship toward their mutual future. The woman has her role transposed from being *his* mother to being *the* mother to being the mother of *the beloved one*. At the same time, the Beloved Disciple is challenged to develop his own filial relationship with this woman. And the narrator immediately reveals his response: "And from that hour, the disciple received [*elaben*] her into his own [*idia*]." The usual biblical image of the mother comforting the lost or afflicted one is here reversed, as a one-way response is all that is narrated. What the mother's thoughts or feelings were are a gap that is left wide open.

Many suggestions have been made about the symbolic import of this highly stylized interaction. Are the woman and Beloved Disciple representative of male and female unity in the Johannine community? Of Jesus' success in bringing together bonds of blood and faith into a single unity? Is the mother a new Eve, joined with a sinless man in a re-creation of paradise? Or might she symbolize Israel, the mother of Christians? Is it a final challenge to synagogue and church to heal their divisions in the shadow of the cross? Paul S. Minear adds an intriguing variation on this last possibility in suggesting that the mother's antetype is Rachel, and the Beloved Disciple's antetype is Benjamin, the last child of Rachel whom Jesus restores to her at this unique moment (Genesis 43–45).[9]

All of these possibilities have their own attractions, and we cannot claim the validity of one rather than another. The text does not provide any further clues

---

9. Minear (1977, 119–120).

from which to discern a "right" answer but, as usual, allows us to meditate on these multiple meanings that coalesce around the archetypes of mother and son. But from any of these symbolic perspectives, we see that the Johannine Jesus uses the power of the cross to form new relationships, to heal wounds, to generate new communities just when all seems dust and ashes. The challenge to those who stand at the foot of the cross and ponder its meaning is to be open to "receive" into one's "own" whatever or whoever God may give at that moment. It is in sharp contrast to the violent taking of Jesus' garment by the soldiers, another reminder of the differing methods of God and the world in providing what we need.

This nonviolent bringing together of new community is the final "task" for Jesus to perform on this side of death, as the narrator tells us in verse 28: "After this, having known that all things [*panta*] had now been completed [*tetelestai*], Jesus, so that scripture might be completed [*teleiōthē*], said, 'I thirst.' " The postresurrection perspective of Jesus' prayer at the Last Supper now is enacted before readers' eyes, as we are told that Jesus knows that "all things" are completed (17:4, 23). The circle that opened in 18:4 with the impending arrest and Jesus' knowledge of "all things" that would happen has now come around to its closure.

But one act remains: the final "completion" of scripture. It is an unusual way to express the matter in the fourth gospel, in contrast with the more common sense of "fulfilling" scripture.[10] But it expresses the distinction between something *happening* apart from the actor(s)'s awareness of its deeper meaning (12:38; 13:18; 15:25; 17:12; 18:9) and Jesus' intentional *completion* of the biblical text.

The specific text is Psalm 69, a scripture passage already implicitly invoked at least twice (69:4, "They hated me without cause" [Jn 15:25]; 69:9, "Zeal for your house consumed me" [Jn 2:17]). Now, it is verse 21 that is echoed, but not in Jesus' words as much as in the response narrated in verse 29: "A vessel full of vinegar [*oxous*] was lying there; therefore, they brought toward him a sponge full of vinegar on a hyssop reed, and put it to his mouth." The psalm says of the speaker's enemies, "They gave me vinegar to drink." Thus, what appears to be a good deed in offering the dying man a drink is actually the last act of the enemy in Jesus' lifetime. The word for vinegar suggests a cheap wine commonly used by soldiers.[11] The provision of vinegar would temporarily quench thirst and, hence, prolong the agony, hardly a gesture of compassion. Although the "they" in the fourth gospel are not identified at all, we can hardly imagine them to be the faithful remnant gathered at the cross. But that the narrator even leaves this possibility open might cause us to shudder, as we are challenged to consider the ways in which what seem to us to be acts of love might really be service to some other master.

Jesus' final encounter with the world provides two additional contributions

---

10. Luke uses this same construction in 22:37; cf. Lk 18:31; Acts 13:29.
11. Carson (1991, 620).

to the overflowing Johannine treasure chest of irony. First, Jesus' thirst recalls his conversation with the Samaritan woman at the well, where Jesus asked for a drink (4:7). That thirst was caused by Jesus "having labored on the journey" (4:6). But he never was given a drink in that scene! Now, his earthly labors completed, nothing remains but that unquenched thirst.

Second, the vinegar — sometimes translated as "sour wine" — recalls the abundant wine at Cana, the promise of messianic bounty and celebration. But the wine has gone sour, as the Judeans have murdered the messiah rather than receiving him. It is particularly ironic given the new relationship between the mother, last seen at Cana, and the Beloved Disciple. What should be a time for new celebration is instead remembered with vinegar.

Although the vinegar is mentioned by all four gospels, two details are unique to John. The use of hyssop recalls Moses' command to the people to sprinkle the blood of the lamb on their doorposts with hyssop as a sign to God (Ex 12:22). Psalm 51:7 adds, "Purge me with hyssop and I shall be clean." Now, the hyssop is used to link Jesus for the last time with the earth, as his blood drips from the nail marks to purify the people of sin (1:29).

The second detail is narrated in verse 30: "When, therefore, Jesus received [*elaben*] the vinegar, he said, 'It is completed [*tetelestai*].' " To our surprise, perhaps, it is the *receiving* of the vinegar that is the completion. It may have been initiated by an anonymous "they," but it is the in-charge-until-the-last-moment Jesus whose acceptance of the vinegar provides the final completion. As the Beloved Disciple has "received" the mother in order to initiate the era of the new covenant, so Jesus completes the time of the old by having "received" the sour wine.

Given the narrator's double reference to completion in verse 28, it perhaps seems anticlimactic for Jesus' final words from the cross in the fourth gospel to be, "It is completed." The statement has the effect, though, of confirming the authority of the omniscient narrator, whose credibility will soon be challenged as it has never been before.

The words have an incredibly royal majesty, but not nearly so much as the final acts that the narrator tells of in the rest of verse 30: "And bowing his head, he handed over the spirit." The moment of death for the Johannine Jesus is a *kairos* of high liturgical ceremony. What a contrast with the painful suffering messiah portrayed in Mark and Matthew! Its effect is such as to lead many writers to question whether the Johannine Jesus is even human,[12] so perfect is his unity with God even at the end.

The particular wording for death echoes passages both from earlier in the fourth gospel and from Hebrew scripture. The "handing over" completes the cycle begun with Judas's betrayal in the garden (18:2, 5, 30, 36; 19:11, 16). This time, it is not a betrayal at all but the return of something borrowed to its proper place. It also completes the fulfillment of Isaiah's "sheep to the slaughter" passage, which ends with this powerful image:

---

12. E.g., E. Käsemann, refuted sharply by Thompson (1988).

Through this he shall inherit many, and he will divide
 the spoils of the powerful,
because his life [*psychē*] was handed over [*paredōthē*]
 to death.
And he bore the sins of many, and was handed over
 [*paredōthē*] because of their sins.

(LXX, Isa 53:12)

In true Johannine fashion, the narrator changes the implicit citation to the prophet in one important way: rather than handing over his *psychē*, Jesus hands over the *pneuma*, the spirit that can now be poured out on his disciples (7:39).

How does this awe-ful death leave us feeling? It is certainly not written in a way that evokes the wrenching emotions of the Markan crucifixion or the power of the infinite compassion of the Lukan Jesus. We are left at a distance, perhaps at the base of the cross looking on, perhaps at some greater remove. We are not invited into the experience at all but simply called to witness to its occurrence. Jesus expresses no anger, no sorrow, no despairing cry. Instead, he completes his work with the single-mindedness of a Buddhist monk in prayer amidst the world's strife and violence. Can any of us begin to imagine being this centered on our Sender at such a moment? The fourth gospel calls us at the crucifixion not to tear our hearts out but to bow our heads with Jesus. He has honored his Father by accepting the glory that was his from the beginning. Now it is up to those who remain behind to celebrate that glory and share it as good news in a sin-darkened world.

# 26

# Bound in Spices

## *The Removal of Jesus' Body*

## John 19:31–42

**A. Chiasm:**

    a: 31: Preparation: Judeans ask Pilate to break the legs and take away bodies

      b: 32–34: not break the bones; pierce

        c: 35: witness of Beloved Disciple

      b¹: 36–37: bones not broken; pierced

    a¹: 38–42: Joseph/Nicodemus ask Pilate to take away body: Preparation of the Judeans[1]

**B. Location:** Golgotha and a nearby garden

**C. Time:** Passover Preparation day

**D. Hebrew scripture context:** Ex 12:46; Ps 34:20; Zech 12:10

**E. Social factors:** the Johannine community and the secret believers

**F. Themes:** the necessity of taking sides

**G. Key words:** witness, Preparation/sabbath

## 1. BLOOD AND WATER:
## THE FINAL FULFILLMENT OF SCRIPTURE

It is a rude reminder of the ongoing conduct of the world's business when the narrator in verse 31 immediately returns our attention to the concerns of the Judeans: "Therefore, the Judeans, since it was Preparation, so that the bodies

---

1. Ellis (1984, 273–274).

would not remain [*meinē*] upon the cross on the sabbath — for that sabbath was a great day — asked [*erōtēsan*] Pilate that the legs might be broken and taken away [*arthōsin*]." It is a long, complex sentence with which the narrator informs us of both the motivations and the actions of the Judeans. Its multiple clauses may remind us of the narrator's introduction to the Last Supper discourse, when Jesus' knowledge and goal were stated in a single word burst. There, the themes were love of God and movement out of the world. Here, they are obedience to the Law and movement out of sight.

The narrator begins with a socially powerful time signal. Each Friday for the Jews of the first century (and for many observant Jews today) was the day of Preparation, the eve of the sabbath, upon which all work needing to be done before Sunday would be completed to allow for the strict observance of the day of rest. We have seen several sabbaths in the fourth gospel, but this is the first one in which the day of Preparation played such an important role. Passover, on the other hand, was (and still is) a feast day based on the lunar calendar, to be celebrated on the fourteenth day of the month of Nisan. But because the lunar year does not contain an even multiple of seven days, most years would not find the coincidence of the sabbath preparation and the eve of Passover on the same day. That these two central cultic feasts would fall on the same day in the year Jesus was killed allows for the development of a narrative both symbolic and heavily ironic.

We had been prepared for this fact in 19:14, in a reference that conflates the Passover/sabbath notices into a single time-marker. Now, the narrator focuses on the sabbath Preparation, linking it with Passover through the euphemistic, "the great day."

The Judeans' concern is that the bodies not "remain" on the cross at the sacred moment. It is a crude irony that the Judeans who were so insistent upon causing a death and who have so recently proclaimed their sole allegiance to Caesar are now focused on the intricacies of the Law. The narrator adds insult to injury by contrasting Jesus' oft-repeated challenge to "remain" with him or in his love or in some other relationship (*menein* is used twelve times in 15:4–16) with the worry about his dead body "remaining" on the cross.

Another irony is piled on as the Judeans, at the very moment at which they purport to be acting out their commitment to the God of Moses, prove their dependence on Caesar. The narrator tells us that they "ask" *Pilate* to enable their desire, after Jesus has repeatedly invited his disciples to "ask" (*erataō*) *God* for what they wanted, just as Jesus "asked" throughout chapter 17. Their own actions prove once again the correctness of Jesus' evaluation of them in chapter 8.

The specific request to the governor is that "their" legs be broken and lifted away. According to the narrator, the Judeans are no longer concerned with Jesus in particular but more generically with the scandal of dead bodies on the cross on the great day — or perhaps with hiding their true motivation behind the "religious" reason. The practice of breaking the legs of crucifixion victims was intended as an act of mercy, for it would hasten death and reduce the period of torture. The Judeans, of course, are not concerned with mercy but with the Law, another ironic reversal of the mandate of the prophets: "I desire steadfast love [Heb, *chesed*; cf. Jn 1:17], not sacrifice" (Hos 6:6), and "I hate your festivals, ... but let justice flow like a river" (Amos 5:21, 24).

The text rather strangely suggests if taken literally that the *legs* be taken away; it does not mention bodies or any other noun to link with the verb *arthōsin* at the end of the sentence. The effect is to draw attention away from the "bodies" at the beginning of the sentence to the "legs" at the end, which will be the focus of scriptural fulfillment.

Pilate's response is not narrated directly. We might wonder what he would say to these most persistent petitioners after their mutually revealing dialogue prior to and during the crucifixion. Instead of letting us in on that interaction, the narrator skips over it and shows us in verse 32 the response of the procurator's obedient agents: "The soldiers came, therefore, and did break the legs of the first one and then of the other one crucified with him." The soldiers, ironically like Jesus, are also sent on a mission, which they carry out with good Roman efficiency.

Their order of procedure is curious, though, as they seem to bypass Jesus in order to break the legs of the others first. Only after dealing with the ones on either side do they come to Jesus in verse 33: "As they saw that he was already dead, they did not break his legs." Jesus' death did not follow the expected "schedule." It was not a matter of death by torture but of "handing over the spirit," an event totally controlled by Jesus.

But despite the mootness of leg-breaking, the soldiers are not finished with Jesus' now apparently lifeless body. Verse 34 provides the most remarkable of epilogues: "But one of the soldiers jabbed [*enuxen*] his side [*pleuran*] with a spear [*logchē*], and at once blood and water came out [*exēlthen*]." Why stab an already dead body? Simply for target practice? Or to make absolutely sure that the victim was in fact dead? Paul S. Minear states the matter this way:

> [It is the] final blow for the Pharisees and high priests against the King of Israel. With his spear the soldier verified the full success of their conspiracy. Yet it is at this very moment that the amazing flow of blood and water signaled the failure of that conspiracy.[2]

The verse is totally unprecedented, both in vocabulary and theology. The words for "spear" and "jab" are not found elsewhere in the New Testament, nor is the narrative of a final attack by Rome on the dead Jesus. And with a minor exception,[3] neither is the word for "side," *pleuran,* found in the New Testament. However, it does occur in a significant place in the Septuagint:

---

2. Minear (1984, 72).
3. Acts 12:7, where the angel touches Peter on the "side."

> And God...took from Adam one of his ribs [*pleurōn*], and filled up its flesh. And God formed the rib [*pleuran*] which he received [*elaben*] from Adam into a woman. (Gen 2:21–22)

From the side/rib of Jesus comes not a woman but an unprecedented and immediate flow of blood and water. The usual situation in which blood and water flow like this is, of course, the act of birth. We recall Jesus' words, themselves quoting scripture, about the advent of the spirit: "Out of his belly [*koilias*] will flow living water" (7:38). *Koilia*, although a general term for "belly," is used in both the Septuagint (Gen 25:24; Deut 28:4, 11) and rabbinical texts for "womb."[4] Thus, several aspects of the verse come together to present an image of the soldier's stab allowing Jesus to give birth to the spirit, through the physical symbols of blood and water. In turn, the spirit gives life to the people who are formed from Jesus' *pleuran,* that is, the Johannine community represented by the Beloved Disciple at the foot of the cross. It is fitting that the most egalitarian gospel portrays an androgynous king, whose reign from the cross is succeeded by the birth of a new paraclete to guide his newly born people.

This interpretation is confirmed by the later, more explicit text of 1 John:

> Who is the one conquering the world if not the one believing that Jesus is the Son of God? This is the one having come through water and blood, Jesus Christ; not in the water only but in the water and in the blood; and the spirit is the one bearing witness, because the spirit is the truth. Because three are bearing witness: the spirit and the water and the blood, and the three are in one. (1 Jn 5:5–8)

In addition to providing a powerful image of birth, the flow of blood and water, begun by a Roman spear, confirms the greater power of Jesus' "baptism" than the baptism of John, the one who came baptizing only in water (1:31, 33). John's witness was that the spirit was upon Jesus. That spirit, handed back to the Father in Jesus' dying moment, now flows back onto the earth through the impetus of imperial violence. Jesus' mission began with a baptism in water and ends in a baptism in blood. Both result in invitation to those who dare to believe in Jesus to follow along this dual route.

As the blood and water flow out of Jesus, those who believe are to allow Jesus' blood and water to flow back into themselves by "drinking" it (cf. 4:14; 6:53–56; 7:38).[5] That is, the "living water" that Jesus offered to the Samaritan woman and the blood that he insisted his disciples drink are now revealed also to be symbols of the paraclete, the one who will inspire the community after Jesus' death. The paraclete is both comforter ("living water") and challenge ("blood").

Another significant detail is the description of the fluids "coming out" (*exēlthen*) from Jesus. Throughout the Passion narrative, Jesus has been in

---

4. J. Behm, *TDNT* 3:786–787.

5. Senior (1991, 125–127) notes the links between 6:53–6 and 19:34 as to blood but does not draw out the implications for discipleship.

charge of his comings and goings. Now, in his penultimate "coming out," Rome appears to be in control. But, as the narrator will shortly underscore, this entire scene is a fulfillment of scripture. The imperial power is now, just as in the confrontation with Pilate, given from above. Those who reap the glory of human beings are, at a deeper level, enhancing the glory of God.

The description of the blood and water is followed in verse 35 by a most emphatic insistence on the credibility of the narrative and addresses readers directly for the first time: "And the one having seen has borne witness, and his witness is true, and that one has known that he speaks the truth, so that you [plural] may believe." As Raymond Brown points out, the question of who knows that the testimony is true is highly ambiguous. The possibilities are:

1. the narrator knows that the witness is true

2. Jesus knows that the witness is true

3. God knows that the witness is true

4. eyewitness knows that his own witness is true[6]

Regardless of one's solution to this conundrum, the text insists in the strongest possible way that the narrative is based on personal witness. We should not think of this in modern terms of "scientific" evidence but in the gospel's own terms of speaking the deeper truth that is not always apparent to an observer. That is, we should not hear the text calling us to believe in a biologically improbable "miracle" but in the relationship between Jesus' death and the presence of the otherwise invisible spirit that is a part of Jesus as the first woman was a part of the first human. We recall that one of the most difficult challenges to the disciples during the Last Supper discourse was to accept that Jesus' "going away" was necessary for the coming of the paraclete (16:7, cf. 16:17–18). The true witness is that Jesus' statement was itself true: his death *did* lead to the giving of the spirit to the people of the new covenant. For a community struggling to believe that a person subjected to a brutal imperial execution was truly God's agent, this eyewitness account confirms the validity of their commitment. The direct address to readers shows that the entire gospel has been written with an eye to later believers, including the Johannine community members who were not around to experience the central events for themselves.

But just to make sure that the readers' faith is strong, the narrator goes on in verses 36–7 to quote two passages from Hebrew scripture fulfilled by these last events: "Not a bone of his will be broken [*syntribēsetai*]," and, "They will look on the one they have pierced [*exekentēsan*]." Neither these passages nor the actions that fulfill them are part of the synoptic Passion narratives. Why has the narrator of the fourth gospel focused our attention on them at this particular moment?

---

6. R. Brown (1970, 936–937) lists the first option as the "author," but, given the narrative method used in this book, the more precise option is the "narrator."

The first quotation is a conflation of two different texts, expressing two distinct themes.[7] First is the Passover command about how to prepare the lamb: "A bone of it you shall not break [LXX, *syntripsete*]" (Ex 12:46). The second is a prayer for God's protection of the just: "He keeps all their bones; not one of them shall be broken [LXX, *syntribēsetai*]" (Ps 34:20). As we can see, the narrator has tapped into our previous associations between Jesus' crucifixion and the sacrifice of the Passover lamb to suggest the first text but has also used the precise wording of the psalm to lead us to see how Jesus' death fulfills both themes: he is the new paschal sacrifice of whose flesh the people will eat and also the just one whom the Lord has protected.

The second fulfillment quotation is from Zech 12:10, although, interestingly, from the Hebrew rather than the Septuagint version:

And I will pour out a spirit of compassion and supplication on the house of David and the inhabitants of Jerusalem, so that, when they look on the one whom they have pierced, they shall mourn for him, as one mourns for an only child, and weep bitterly over him, as one weeps over a firstborn.

It is an eschatological passage of God's justice against the bad shepherds of Jerusalem. Thus, with these two fulfillment quotations, the narrator has linked Jesus' death both to the purifying sacrifice of the innocent lamb and to God's eventual justice against those who have misled the people for so long. Those who "look on" will be those who have done the piercing, that is, the Roman empire, which will eventually be besieged by Christians witnessing unto death about their faith in the Crucified One. But as the Roman soldiers were tools also of the Judean authorities, we cannot see this fulfillment as directed exclusively against the empire. The Judeans, too, will look on Jesus, as the Johannine community finds its new place apart from the synagogue, and they will wonder just who this one was whom they sent to an apparently ignoble death.

## 2. IN SECRET, FOR FEAR OF THE JUDEANS: THE FINAL CHALLENGE TO COMMIT

But having found Jesus dead on the cross and the breaking of his bones unnecessary, what is to become of Jesus' body? We recall that the Judean request of Pilate was twofold: to break his legs and to take him away. We might well expect the soldiers to carry out the second part of their command in the next verses. But to our surprise, the narrator in verse 38 shifts our attention away from the immediate confrontation between the Roman troops and the dead Jesus to some time later, with different characters brought on stage: "After these things [*tauta*], a request to Pilate was made by Joseph from Arimathea, a disciple of Jesus but in secret [*kekrymmenos*] for fear of the Judeans, to take away

---

7. Ibid., 937.

[*arē*] the body of Jesus." The translation above is an attempt to preserve the Greek word order, which first tells us that someone made a request of Pilate (again!) and then springs on us the identity of this latest petitioner, one Joseph of Arimathea.

Who is this new figure, brought into the story suddenly at this terrible and glorious moment? We are given a highly ambiguous description of him. Unfortunately, we know little about the location of the place with which he is associated, Arimathea. Brown, though, tells us that of the several possibilities, none is in Galilee. Thus, "Joseph would have been one of the Judean disciples of Jesus."[8] Given what we have seen of Judeans in this story, this is not a good starting point!

He is also described as both "a disciple" and one "in secret for fear of the Judeans." Whatever positive feelings we might have from the first element are dashed to pieces by the second. We recall that the phrase "fear of the Judeans" has been used twice before. First, at the beginning of the Tabernacles gathering, the murmuring crowd kept their talk to themselves for fear of the Judeans (7:13). The second occasion was even more ominous: the narrator's rationale for the blind one's parents' refusal to support their healed son, for fear of the Judeans (9:22). Their fear was that they would be thrown out of the synagogue. This particular concern links "fear of the Judeans" with those among the "rulers" who "believed in him but, because of the Pharisees, would not confess, so that they would not be thrown out of the synagogue, for they loved the glory of people more than the glory of God" (12:42–43). Is this Joseph like the parents, an ordinary person afraid to speak up for Jesus or those associated with him, or like the rulers, whose powerful social status is too much to give up for what they know in their hearts to be the truth?

Two clues lead us to associate Joseph with the latter group. First, the very fact that he is able to obtain an audience with the Roman procurator weighs strongly against the idea that he is simply afraid of official authority like the parents. It is only a bold person of some renown who not only would be admitted into the praetorium but also would be given the privilege of having a request heard. Second, the parents were not identified as disciples at all; they were just scared and confused peasants, the usual victims of institutional threats and oppression. In contrast, Joseph not only is afraid but is also a *disciple*. This double image fits perfectly with the description of the rulers who would not confess so as not to give up the "glory of people." Joseph is not identified directly as either a Pharisee or a ruler, and we should not be too quick to fill in details omitted by the narrator. But as a secret disciple, he falls into the broader category of those who want to have their cake and eat it too, the group most reviled by the Johannine community for its unwillingness to testify to what it has seen and known to be true (cf. 9:40–41).

We should be suspicious of this petitioner for another reason: his request is exactly the one made by the Judeans but not carried out by the soldiers! It is

---

8. Ibid., 938.

also described with the same verb by which the Judeans cried their final cry, "Take him away [*aron*]!" (19:15). We are given no reason for his request as we were with the one in verse 31. This ambiguity leaves open a gap that builds suspense through the following scene: Is Joseph just another Judean trying to "take away" the "unclean" body before the great day, or does his discipleship, albeit secret, lead him to ask for the body for some other reason?

While we await the revelation of Joseph's purpose, the narrator tells us that "Pilate permitted it." The straightforward carrying out of this act follows at the end of the verse: "He came [*ēlthen*] therefore, and took away his body." Is this it? Will we find out what he did with the corpse? Before this mystery is resolved, the narrator in verse 39 springs another surprise on us, with even more force than the appearance of Joseph: "Nicodemus also came [*ēlthen*], the one having come [*elthōn*] to him first *at night.*" Old Nicodemus! In case we have forgotten him, the narrator reminds us in chilling detail of his earlier encounter with Jesus. It was at night, the same time at which Judas, the betrayer, went out (13:30). Both Joseph and Nicodemus are described as coming (*ēlthen*), rather than "coming out" (*exēlthen*) as Jesus was described doing three times in the Passion narrative. Each of Jesus' *exēlthen* represented a movement into the world (18:4; 19:5, 17). In contrast, Joseph and Nicodemus do not "come out," because they are *already in the world.* With this introduction, we do not yet know whether the two are operating together or have come independently to Pilate, perhaps for different reasons. But the common description of their *ēlthen* links them in spirit if not in direct purpose.

The narrator's association of Nicodemus's first visit to Jesus with his present appearance is sly by what it omits. Nicodemus appeared a second time in the story, among the Pharisees who pondered at Tabernacles what to do with this one whom their own officers said spoke like no one else (7:46). We recall that those in charge challenged the officers with the taunt, "Not one of the rulers have believed in him, nor anyone from the Pharisees!" It was precisely Nicodemus's failure at that point to confess his own faith — *if* he had any — that condemned him to being "at best" a member of the "Pharisees who were with him" (9:40). Now, he has returned, without our attention being expressly brought back to this moment of hesitancy. Also, the narrator does not tell us whether Nicodemus, like Joseph, is a "disciple." *Is* he a disciple, too, or is he just another Judean ruler carrying out the requirements of the Law?

Our understanding of his purpose and commitment is confused even further by the narrator's description of what he has brought with him: "a roll of myrrh and aloes weighing a hundred pounds." There can be no doubt of the general import of this burden: they are spices for ceremonial burial. And what are we to make of the tremendous quantity? How are we to picture Nicodemus arriving on the scene with this heavy load? Was he carrying it himself, or did he have unnamed helpers? Or was the supply of spices *already at hand,* waiting for this moment? Whether or not they were brought to the scene that moment or prepared ahead, it is clear that Nicodemus has been *planning* for this event. Even a wealthy ruler does not just have a hundred pounds of myrrh and aloes

sitting around at all times! While it would not have taken much preparation —
Jerusalem would have been filled with merchants ready to sell such items, especially at a feast time — nonetheless, the hundred pounds make certain that
Nicodemus knew Jesus was going to be crucified and, as far as we are told,
made no objection. Instead, he accepts Jesus' death as inevitable and comes
only to bury him.

In addition to being a huge and expensive burden, the hundred pounds of
fancy spices suggest an extravagant burial, one, we might say, fit for a king.
Indeed, defenders of Nicodemus over the centuries have praised him lavishly for
his "generous" and "kind" act that supposedly acknowledges in death what he
would not speak up for in life. But given the gospel's insistence on witnessing
to Jesus, we cannot let Nicodemus off the hook quite so easily. We must wait to
see what he does with these royal burial spices before we can evaluate his place
along the Johannine spectrum of faith.

In verse 40, the narrator moves us several steps toward resolving the suspense: "They received [*elabon*] Jesus' body, therefore, and bound [*edēsan*] it
with bandages [*othoniois*] and the spices, according to the Judean burial custom [*ethos*]." There has been a lot of receiving going on in these last moments:
his outer garments by the soldiers (*elabon,* 19:23), the mother by the Beloved
Disciple (*elaben,* 19:27), the vinegar by Jesus (*elaben,* 19:30), and now Jesus'
body by Joseph and Nicodemus, who are now revealed to be acting together.
Each receipt says something about the receiver's commitment: the soldiers' to
gathering worldly booty; Jesus' to the will of his Father and the fulfillment of
scripture; the Beloved Disciple's to the inclusion of women, Israel, and everything else symbolized by "the mother" into the Johannine community. Now, the
two would-be disciples reveal their own loyalty: to the "Judean burial custom."

The first thing they do with the body is to bind it, a negative symbol connected with the treatment of Jesus before he was handed over to Pilate (18:12,
*edēsan*; 18:24, *dedemenon*). Of course, at the earthly level, this binding is not
an act of imprisonment but one of caretaking, as it attempts to preserve the
body against decay by wrapping it tightly in embalming spices. But this is precisely the problem: the entire burial ritual is conducted to comply with "earthly"
thinking, both about physical decay and about enforcing the Judean custom. The
practice is not described as part of the Law but is an element of the *ethos,* the
traditional way of doing things by which a people define themselves. At this
crucial moment, Joseph and Nicodemus identify with the Judean *ethos.*

The myrrh and aloes are together described by the narrator as "spices"
(*arōmatōn*). The connotation apparent from the Greek of strong *aroma* recalls
the previous occasion for sweet-smelling fragrance: the anointing of Jesus' feet
by Mary of Bethany (12:2–8). Several aspects of the two scenes are in contrast. First, Mary's supply of perfumed oil, valued at three hundred denarii by
Judas, is described as weighing a "pound" (*litran,* 12:3), in comparison with
Nicodemus's "a hundred pounds" (*litras ekaton*). These are the only two uses of
"pound" in the fourth gospel, making the linking of these two scenes unavoidable and leading us to wonder about the monetary value of the men's spices.

Second, her act is named by Jesus as "to keep the day of my burial" (12:7). For Joseph and Nicodemus to smother Jesus' body with spices for burial is to *ignore* Mary's act. Either the men were not present at that supper — suggesting that they were not really disciples at all — or their patriarchal attitude does not see Mary's act as sufficient, despite Jesus' praise of it. In either case, it creates a most negative connection between their act and the anointing at Bethany. Finally, Mary's act results in "the house" being filled with the smell, suggesting the permeation of the entire community by the power of her bold act. The men's act, on the other hand, is not described as having any effect at all, except to fulfill the requirements of the Judean *ethos*.

At the same time, the willingness to deal with a dead body on the eve of a sabbath and Passover would have violated the very *ethos* that the two buriers are so concerned to fulfill. According to Num 9:10–12, contact with a corpse would not negate Passover duties but would delay them for a month, a condition apparently enforced at the time of the fourth gospel.[9] This discrepancy underscores the half-in/half-out nature of Nicodemus's and Joseph's discipleship. How hard they try to have it both ways!

There is still another negative feature of this massive wrapping in spices: they are preparing Jesus' body for a *long* stay in the earth. Whereas Mary's anointing acknowledged the imminence and necessity of Jesus' death, it was open to the possibility of resurrection. The hundred pounds and binding bandages, though, are the materials of a permanent burial. And this, in the end, is the narrator's implicit explanation of their failure to be open disciples: their lack of faith in the power of resurrection allows their fear to overcome their belief in the truth of Jesus' being a teacher sent from God (3:2). Without resurrection hope, they ironically are the ones who remain "bound." The inferior promise of worldly status and the glory of humanity is the cheap reward they reap in place of the glory of God and the matchless gift of eternal life.

This all adds up to a very dark picture of Joseph and Nicodemus, although not one for which we cannot have compassion. For these men rest on the all-too-familiar comfortable cushions of Christianity, from which we offer thanks to God without risk of pain. As David Rensberger powerfully expresses the matter:

> Where is Nicodemus to be found today? This especially we would prefer to leave ambiguous.... Nicodemus is to be found, to begin with the most exact analogy, where Christians in power relate to powerless Christians.... It applies to white Christians in relation to blacks in the United States and in South Africa. It applies to affluent members of church hierarchies in relation to peasants and the poor, in Latin America but certainly not only there. It applies to men in relation to women in nearly all societies. It applies to the educated in relation to the ignorant, the well fed in relation to the hungry, the healthy in relation to the sick.... Certainly it applies to any Christian who has not let this identity be known in a

9. Thomas (1991, 180).

place where real danger might result. This includes those who are reluctant to become known as activists in struggles for justice and for peace, since ... for John the one way in which Christians are known is by their love for one another.[10]

Having painted this sad but home-hitting picture of the reluctant disciples, the narrator continues in verses 41–42 to add further to the image: "In the place where he was crucified there was a garden, and in the garden a new tomb, in which no one had yet been buried. Therefore, because of the Judean Preparation, and because the tomb was near, they laid [*ethēkan*] Jesus there." The twice-mentioned garden brings us full circle, as we recall the garden into which Jesus entered with his disciples just prior to his arrest (18:1). But this is a different garden, one near to Golgotha. It is a place of convenience, which the narrator underscores as the reason for their deposit of Jesus in the new tomb in the garden. They have done what the *ethos* requires, but both sabbath and Passover beckon. There is no time to linger, no need for prolonged mourning or prayer. The business is to be gotten over as quickly as possible.

The mention of the "new" tomb prepares the way for the eventual inspection of the tomb by inquiring disciples. For now, it is a mysterious detail, adding only the suggestion that Jesus is not placed in a common grave but in one reserved for someone special. It is a final poignant ambiguity, as Joseph and Nicodemus, despite their concern about keeping the Law and the *ethos,* treat Jesus' body respectfully. They are not murderers or liars; they have not openly participated in the conspiracy to get rid of Jesus. But their final act shows that they are still struggling to keep one foot in both worlds, just as Jesus is removed, apparently for the last time, from this one.

The last verb used provides one last irony. They have "laid down" Jesus' body, just as he said he would freely lay down his life (*tithēmi,* 10:17). Even the ambiguity of their last act is part of the plan, in fulfillment of Jesus' word. Nothing escapes the oversight of God.

Thus, for the Johannine community, the burial of Jesus by secret disciples presents the final contrast between Judeans and Christians. As Herold Weiss puts it, "The Johannine community has come to understand that its whole life is being lived on the sabbath. ... A Christian community that is concerned with the body of a dead person would be a misguided community." Instead, "Jesus' dead body is the concern of half-believing persons on the periphery of Christianity."[11] For Judeans, the tomb has been filled. For Johannine Christians, the tomb will soon be found empty.

---

10. Rensberger (1988, 115).
11. Weiss (1991, 319–320).

# 27

# "For They Did Not Yet Know the Scripture..."

## *Encountering the Empty Tomb for the First Time*

## John 20:1–18

**A. Chiasm:** 20:1–18

    a: 1: Mary Magdalene is coming [*erchetai*] to tomb; saw

        b: 2–9: Mary Magdalene tells two: taken Lord away

            c: 10: disciples go back to own

        b[1]: 11–17: Mary Magdalene tells two: taken Lord away

    a[1]: 18: Mary Magdalene is coming [*erchetai*] to disciples; seen[1]

**B. Location:** in and around the tomb

**C. Time:** early, on the first day of the week, while still dark

**D. Hebrew scripture context:** Song of Songs

**E. Social factors:** gender and leadership in the Johannine community

**F. Themes:** seeing and believing

**G. Key words:** facecloth (*soudarion*)

---

1. Ellis (1984, 280–281).

# 1. THE MULTILAYERED STRUCTURE
# OF THE FIRST RESURRECTION NARRATIVE

As the new day dawns and the darkness begins to recede, we will probably not be surprised to find the author of the fourth gospel continuing to structure the story with the now-familiar chiastic framing, as set out above. However, the text of 20:1–18 contains another important structural feature that has not been used as frequently: the narrative "sandwich" or intercalation.

We may recall that when Jesus was in Samaria, the author told the story of Jesus' encounter with the woman and her compatriots with an interruption consisting of his conversation with the disciples (4:27, 31–38, surrounded by 4:4–26 and 4:28–30, 39–42). The primary effect was to contrast the Samaritans' stubborn attempt to learn how to overcome cultural prejudices with Jesus' own disciples' confusion. The character of the woman developed from being trapped within preexisting ideas about the messiah and worship — as well as about the role of women — to a faith in Jesus that led her to share the news with her people.

The story of Mary Magdalene's encounter with Jesus at the tomb is structured to achieve a similar result. As we will see, she is introduced as bearing a mind-set not much different from that of those who buried Jesus. But as she persists in getting an answer to her original question, she is given the opportunity to receive a gift much greater than that for which she had dared hope. In the end, like the Samaritan woman, she takes the news about Jesus to her companions, inviting them to a new stage in their discipleship.

At the same time, the disciples with Mary end up confused. Just as those with Jesus in Samaria apparently did not understand the parable of the harvest, so the disciples with Mary do not understand the scripture. Both pairs of stories leave readers in suspense, wondering whether the disciples will ever get the message.

It is interesting to note that the author saves this structural technique for conveying a particular aspect of Johannine ideology: the superior *apostleship* of women. The Samaritan woman actively seeks out her people and leads them to faith, just as Mary Magdalene seeks to share the exciting news with the disciples. It is ironic that the Samaritan woman succeeds in leading to Jesus a people who were totally unprepared for a Jewish messiah, while Mary Magdalene "fails" in convincing the redundantly prepared friends of Jesus of the depth of his victory over the forces of darkness. The contrast thus has a double social function. First, it reinforces Johannine egalitarianism, which stood in contrast to some of the more "Petrine" Christian communities and their emerging sense of a male hierarchical leadership. Second, it serves to remind the Johannine community of its roots in relationships with the "other" and of the challenge to remain on guard against the temptation to arrogance that can so easily come to those who think they have a hold of the truth.

## 2. THE FIRST REACTIONS TO THE EMPTY TOMB

### Chiasm: 20:1–10

a: 1–4: Mary, Peter, Beloved Disciple come to tomb

  b: 5: "other disciple" sees cloths and does not enter

    c: 6a: Peter came following and entered

  b¹: 6b–7: Peter sees cloths

a¹: 8–10: disciples go back to own[2]

If resurrection and death were not as cyclically bonded in the general Christian consciousness as day and night, how might we be feeling as the narrative resumes at the beginning of chapter 20? Is it futile to even attempt to imagine how the story might sound to "untrained" ears? Were there *ever* any readers or hearers of the fourth gospel who were not already familiar with the tradition of the resurrection?

Although we obviously cannot answer the last question with certainty, it seems unlikely that anyone who has followed this far into the Johannine story of Jesus would not have come with at least some idea of resurrection. The concise Pauline and Lukan formulas suggest that "crucified and risen" and "raised from the dead" became hendiadys-like phrases not unlike "grace and truth" in the prologue. That is, together, the terms meant something completely different than either might have meant separately before the Christian experience of Easter.

Thus, it appears that all readers of the fourth gospel, ancient and modern, must engage in an exercise of imagination to place themselves in the position of the characters who come to the tomb in chapter 20. Has Jesus' Last Supper discourse sufficiently conveyed the message of Jesus' going and coming again? Has their witness of Lazarus' emergence from the tomb convinced them of the penultimacy of death? Might those who disappeared from the scene after Jesus' arrest dare to show up again in Jerusalem?

These and many other questions might fill our minds and hearts as we consider how the story can continue after Nicodemus and Joseph have so successfully and completely buried Jesus. The narrator begins in verse 1 with a temporal jump from the imminence of the great Passover sabbath to a new time: "It was the first day of the week [*mia tōn sabbatōn*]." The actual occurrence of the central feast is irrelevant to the Johannine community, which marks its birth by the development of a new sacred time, the "first day of the week." The phrase has not been used previously in the fourth gospel and, in the Greek, bears an ironic note: the day of resurrection is defined in terms of the *sabbath* but in a way that replaces the Judean sabbath in the process.

---

2. Ellis (1984, 282) finds a chiasm from 20:2–9, leaving verses 1 and 10 hanging unattached (he also finds a chiasm from verses 11–17). In addition to this *literary* problem, his suggestion also has the *social* problem of missing the contrast between the disciples' departure from the tomb closing one chiasm and Mary Magdalene's continued presence at the tomb beginning the next one.

Of all the familiar characters who might be brought on stage on this first day, the narrator twists our expectations by speaking not of "the disciples" or any particular member of "the twelve" but of a heretofore obscure woman, Mary Magdalene. We have only heard of her since the crucifixion itself, as she was mentioned without further comment among those gathered at the cross (19:25). All we know at this point is that she was faithful and courageous enough to appear publicly in the midst of the terrible hostility of Jesus' condemnation and death.

What else might we be able to discern about her character and why the narrator chose to bring her to the forefront at this central moment? First, her twice-narrated description as literally "the Magdalen," that is, from the city of Magdela, provides some insight. Although several characters have been associated with particular geographic origins (e.g., Jesus with Nazareth [1:45, 18:5, 7, 19:19]; Philip, Andrew, and Peter with Bethsaida [1:44] and Philip again [12:21]; Lazarus, Mary, and Martha with Bethany [11:1]), no one has been linked as tightly with a place as Mary. Magdela itself has been described as "a thriving, rural community" on the sea of Galilee, between Capernaum and Tiberias.[3] Thus, Mary is immediately and strongly associated with *Galilee,* the place from which Jesus' other named disciples have come (with the possible exception of Judas Iscariot, see p. 170). Two possibilities are suggested. Perhaps Mary was just another of the thousands of pilgrims arriving in Jerusalem for the Passover who, somewhere along the way, heard about Jesus and felt drawn to him. On the other hand, the repetition of her origin might also suggest that she has been with Jesus since at least his last trip to Galilee in 7:1–9. In either case, she comes onto the scene as an outsider to the Judean way of thinking. She is one of the rural hicks, the accursed crowd who does not know the Law (7:49).

Another factor, from outside of the text, also comes into consideration. All four gospels, in one way or another, associate Mary Magdalene with the first visit to the tomb (Mt 28:1, Mk 15:47–16:1, and the longer ending in 16:9; Lk 24:1–10, among other women). The tradition of her presence at the tomb was very strong, despite the minor role she plays in the gospels during Jesus' lifetime. Thus, the author of the fourth gospel, despite the powerful freedom that the text exhibits in picking and choosing among traditions and their chronological order, accepted this common element of the resurrection narratives in beginning the story of the encounter with the empty tomb. As usual, though, the tradition has been shaped and expanded in comparison with the other gospels to fit the particular strategy of the fourth gospel.

Her appearance at the tomb begins with a note of ambiguity. She is described as "coming early [*prōi*], while there was still darkness [*skotias*], to the tomb." It provides an interesting half-empty/half-full contrast with the Markan expression, "And very early [*lian prōi*], on the first day of the week, they [the women, including Mary Magdalene] came to the tomb, the sun having risen." Thus, although Mark seems to emphasize the earliness of the hour even more strongly

---

3. *HBD* 594.

than John, that gospel focuses on the new dawn, while the fourth gospel brings our attention to the ongoing darkness.

Of course, *skotia* has played a central symbolic role throughout the gospel, beginning with the prologue and culminating with the summary of Jesus' mission preceding the Last Supper discourse (1:5; 6:17; 8:12; 12:35, 46). Now, it suggests that Mary's presence is a stumbling one. She walks at night, when people risk injury (11:10). However, *prōi* contrasts with *skotia* to imply that the darkness will soon come to an end. How will the darkness surrounding Mary be dissipated? This introductory suspense will build throughout the scene, until its explosively joyful resolution at the end.

Amidst this combination of darkness and approaching light, the narrator tells us that Mary "is looking at the stone, which had been taken away from the tomb." Both Mary's arrival and her observation are told in the present tense, in contrast with the aorist tense of the burial. The story of Jesus' death is from the past, completed once for all time, but his resurrection is an ongoing reality in the lives of his disciples. The narrator's use of this lively form brings us right into the situation, looking over her shoulder, as it were, at the displaced stone.

The stone, we recall, played a central role in the story of the raising of Lazarus (11:38–41), although no stone has been mentioned on Jesus' own tomb. Does Mary know about Lazarus? The word had certainly spread widely around Jerusalem, as crowds from Bethany dispersed into the capital city sharing their amazement (12:17). But even if Mary has heard this story, will she associate the displaced stone with resurrection?

Verse 2 starts on a hopeful note but immediately offers two surprises: "She is running, therefore, and coming to Simon Peter and toward the other disciple, whom Jesus befriended [*ephilei*]." Her running itself remains ambiguous, although filled with undescribed emotion. Is she afraid, excited, or joyous? The narrator maintains the suspense by shifting our attention from her reaction to her goal. Simon Peter, who was last heard from denying Jesus three times, is suddenly brought back into the story and in connection with one who was present at the cross. *Now* we know that Mary Magdalene is no mere Galilean pilgrim but is an active member of the discipleship community, familiar (as we readers are not!) with the whereabouts of Peter. Wherever he is, he has apparently not completely quit the discipleship mission, for he remains in relationship with one of the faithful ones.

If this reintroduction of Simon Peter surprises us, so much more might the way in which the other object of Mary's running is described. Is this the same person previously described at the cross as the Beloved (*ēgapa*) Disciple, the one to whom Jesus entrusted the care of the mother? It is hard to imagine that some new person is being introduced at this point in the story. Instead, we should hear this description as an unexpected and unexplained demotion of the Beloved Disciple. Why the movement from love to friendship, from *agapē* to *philia*? The story will eventually provide a reason, but for now, it piles up surprises and suspense and leaves readers completely unable to anticipate what might happen next.

Mary reaches her goal at the end of verse 2 and says: "They have taken away the Lord from the tomb, and we do not know where they put [*ethēkan*] him." What an incredibly human mixture of faith and doubt are packed into her few words! She speaks of Jesus as "Lord," a title expressing commitment and faith. But at the same time, rather than celebrating a victory over death, she is lamenting a missing body!

Her statement is also packed with social significance. She speaks collectively both of those she assumes are responsible for stealing the body as well as those not knowing what has happened to it. Although her presence was narrated as a lone visit (in contrast to the Markan and Lukan stories), she is, like so many in the fourth gospel, a representative character. However, no clue is given as to who the "we" are to whom she refers. Whether the other women at the cross or simply other believers, the "we" suggests widespread wonder about the mystery of the empty tomb.

Similarly, the "they" is not specified. Does she think it is the Romans who have done the dastardly deed, the Judean leaders, or simply the all-too-common grave robbers looking for booty from the embalmed body?[4] Or is her complaint about the more generalized "they" whom we tend to blame for things that go wrong or that fail to meet our expectations? Whomever the object of her assumption might be, she is ready to blame *someone* for what she perceives as a problem. The lifted stone has not spoken of resurrection to her. Instead, she picks up the word used by the narrator to describe the act of "putting" Jesus in the tomb, this time to refer to some other, unknown resting place. She, like Nicodemus and Joseph, is simply looking to treat a lifeless corpse with respect.

What will Simon Peter and the "befriended" disciple do with this information? What expectations do they have at this stage? That they are reunited at all is a sign of the beginning of Peter's rehabilitation. The gospel could easily have left them apart, Peter as a denier and the Beloved Disciple as a faithful witness at the cross. But the process of healing and reconciliation among them starts here, as does the healing of the tears between the Johannine community and the apostolic churches. For better or worse, the fates of both disciples and their communities are linked.

Without any discussion or hesitation, the two are described in verse 3 as leaping into action: "Therefore, Peter and the other disciple went out [*exēlthen*] and were coming to the tomb." Like the people of Samaria, the recipients of the message go to see for themselves. Their going out signals another stage in their shared journey, as they, like Jesus who "went out" several times during the Passion narrative, leave their space and venture into newness. Where they have been is omitted in lieu of the more important fact of where they are going.

Peter's partner is now described with the wholly neutral term, "other disciple." It is the same term used for Peter's companion at the high priest's door (18:16), renewing the possibility that the one known to the high priest was in fact the Beloved Disciple. But we should not be too quick to jump to this con-

---

4. R. Brown (1970, 999).

clusion, for being described as "other" is hardly the special reference that is "beloved," and need not imply a unique character at all. Whoever the "other" was at the door, this "other" does not leave Peter behind to get caught by the fire in denial. Instead, they go together on this new stage in their journey.

But only for a moment! In verse 4, the narrator begins a highly stylized account of their movement to the tomb: "The two were running together, and the other disciple ran ahead more quickly than Peter, and came to the tomb first." What began as a shared journey turns into a race, every man for himself. Their unity is broken, as curiosity and suspense overcome the command to remain as one, just as Jesus and the Father are one. It provides the first part of the reason for the shift from "beloved" to "befriended." Even this disciple has not yet fully caught on to the challenge of community!

What is this one expecting as he arrives at the tomb? Are his thoughts and feelings any different from Mary Magdalene's? The narrator, who has previously spent much energy on providing dialogue, is now completely focused on action instead. Thus, instead of conveying the Beloved Disciple's words, we are given in verse 5 a detailed picture of what he does: "And, having bent over, he is looking at the cloths [*othonia*] lying there, but did not enter [*eisēlthen*]." The very cloths with which Jesus had been bound by his buriers are now found "lying" in the tomb. Given the financial value of such cloth, the description removes the possibility of grave robbers, who would have been more likely to take the cloths and leave the body.

The sudden shift from the racing disciple to the cautious one who will not enter a tomb is dramatic, as if a wall of fear or sacred awe or some other unnamed emotion has prevented the disciple from following through. But while we consider the reasons for the Beloved Disciple's behavior, the plot moves on in verse 6: "Therefore, Simon Peter is coming, too, following [*akolouthōn*] him, and he entered [*eisēlthen*] the tomb." It is the ancient fable of the tortoise and the hare, with a theological twist. While the other disciple hesitates, Peter rushes forward into the sacred space of the empty tomb. And yet he is described as *following* the other, a term that means more than simply the already known fact of his having lost the race to the tomb. "To follow" is an expression of discipleship and loyalty. Here, it suggests that Peter, the one who denied Jesus, is now following the Beloved Disciple, the one who remained faithful at the cross. He is not, however, following *Jesus*! It is another expression of the lack of expectation of resurrection. With Jesus gone, Peter has not altogether abandoned the way but has apparently shifted his loyalty from the master who is now dead to the one still alive. But when that one pulls up short, Peter continues on his own, even into the unknown territory of the tomb.

His entry allows him to see not only what the Beloved Disciple saw but more: "And he saw the cloths lying there and the facecloth [*soudarion*], which was on his head, lying not with the cloths but having been rolled up apart [*chōris*] in a separate place." What can this mysterious sight mean to Peter? Is its meaning any clearer to us, reading the story through the lens of resurrection faith?

To begin to unravel the mystery of the *soudarion,* we must pay careful attention to each detail of the narrator's description. Peter's first experience is identical to that of his companion: the burial cloths are lying in the tomb. But Peter's perspective from inside the tomb allows him to behold another element of Jesus' burial wrappings, the *soudarion,* traditionally used to wipe perspiration from one's face or as a covering for the face of a corpse (as in 11:44). The word itself is a loanword from Latin and is not used at all in the Septuagint, although Luke also uses it generically as "handkerchief" (Lk 19:20; Acts 19:12).[5] However, it did find its way into later Jewish writings such as the Mishnah and into the later versions of scripture called the Targums. In particular, it is used to describe the veil covering Moses' face after he speaks with God and returns to the people (Ex 34:33–35).[6]

Not only does Peter see the *soudarion* itself, but he finds it distinct from the other cloths in two ways. It is neatly rolled up, *and* it is "apart" in a separate place. It has not simply been thrown off like the other cloths but has been treated carefully and given its own location in the tomb. Its "apartness" recalls the two previous uses of the word *chōris* in the fourth gospel, both of which use the term negatively to speak of what should not or cannot be "apart." First, nothing "came to be" apart from the Word (1:3). Also, apart from the "vine," "you can do nothing" (15:5). Here, the term has almost the exact opposite connotation: *unless* the *soudarion* is apart from both the other cloths and Jesus' body itself, nothing can continue to happen in the story.

These pieces help us put the puzzle of the *soudarion* together. When Lazarus "came out" from the tomb, he remained bound in the *soudarion* and needed help from others to become free. His "resurrection" was temporary; the murderous conspiracy was likely to achieve its goal of killing him. Even if it did not, nothing in the story suggests that the raised Lazarus did not continue to share the fate of all humans to return to the earth. We would certainly have heard about it if he had not! Jesus, in contrast, has left the *soudarion* behind. Because it is in a different place, Peter's attention has been drawn to it, to recall the bound Lazarus and come to understand what it was he was experiencing.

Also, in contrast with Moses, Jesus will not need a *soudarion* in the future. At this point in the narrative, this contrast opens a gap: Will he not need it because, having returned to God, he will no longer be present with his disciples? Or will his presence be a vulnerable one that is not shielded by a facecloth? In either case, the possibility is strong that the term would have suggested to the Johannine community this contrast with Moses and acted as a "sign" of the fulfillment of Jesus' prediction that he was going back to the Father.[7]

The careful rolling up of the *soudarion* adds another facet to our understanding: Jesus' body was not simply swept up in a passive act that would leave the *soudarion* "lying there" like the other cloths. Rather, Jesus *actively participated*

---

5. BAG 759.
6. Schneiders (1983, 96).
7. Ibid.

in his resurrection. If the "lying" of the burial cloths represents the act of the Father in releasing Jesus from death, the rolled up *soudarion* tells us that, having been invited to "take up" his life again, Jesus did so, in fulfillment of his statement in 10:17–18.[8] This Johannine conception of Jesus' cooperation with the Father stands in contrast with the Pauline and Lukan notion of resurrection as something that happened *to* Jesus through the grace of God (e.g., Rom 6:4; Acts 3:15). But it should not surprise faithful readers of the fourth gospel, who have heard repeatedly from the very beginning of the cooperation of the Word with God in bringing life and light to the world.

This is the sense in which the "apartness" of the *soudarion* recalls the essential link *both* between God and Jesus and between Jesus and the disciples. If the fourth gospel goes out of its way to symbolize the unified activity of Jesus and the Father, it is not for the sake of christology but for the sake of *discipleship.* The readers must be convinced of Jesus' active involvement in his resurrection so that they can be encouraged to actively participate in their own journey back to God, even through the dark corridor of death.

The leaving behind of the *soudarion* also contains a social criticism. Although Jesus' burial narrative does not mention the *soudarion,* it is clear that it entered the tomb in the first place as a result of the meticulous obedience to the Judean burial *ethos* by Nicodemus and Joseph. The well-meaning but tragically misguided secret disciples attempted to contain Jesus within the tradition of Judea, leaving him bound in the tomb in accordance with their own understanding of what was right. But Jesus has actively burst through that limitation. The *soudarion* and all it represents have been consciously abandoned. There is no need for a face veil, and there is no further need for loyalty to an *ethos* that keeps people bound up in the darkness of the tomb. Jesus is the light of the world, and his followers are to walk in the light, even beyond the experience of death.

Is any of this understood by Peter? Based on his earlier misunderstandings, we have precious little basis for expecting him to perceive the meaning behind these subtle yet unmistakable signs. But whether he understands or not, the narrator does not say. Instead, he leaves Peter gaping at the *soudarion* in the tomb while the Beloved Disciple takes his own step forward in verse 8: "Then, therefore, the other disciple entered [*eisēlthen*], the one who came [*elthōn*] first to the tomb, and he saw and believed."

The narrator has carefully noted each stage in the Beloved Disciple's journey: in verse 3, he went out (*exēlthen*), then in verse 4, he arrived (*elthōn*) but in verse 5 did not enter (*eisēlthen*). Now, he does enter, as we are reminded of his having arrived first. The tense has changed from present to aorist: the entry into the tomb is an event from the past, the sight of the *soudarion* no longer being available to the experience of later disciples. The two disciples stand side by side in the tomb, sharing a common experience, but only one believes.

But what exactly *does* he believe at this stage in the story? The narrator has

---

8. Byrne (1985, 88).

led us to interpret this as belief in Jesus' resurrection. The empty tomb, the cloths lying there, the rolled up *soudarion*: all evidence points away from Mary Magdalene's assumption that "they" have taken the body somewhere and toward the fulfillment of Jesus' oft-predicted word that he would receive his life again and return to the Father. It is the joyous culmination of the long journey with Jesus and the beginning of the restored discipleship of Jesus' followers.

Or is it? Just when this conclusion seems inescapable, the narrator knocks the wind out of our sails in verses 9–10. For in verse 9, which is part of the same sentence as verse 8, the narrator continues: "For they did not yet know the scripture that it is necessary for him to rise from the dead." They *still* do not understand! If the Beloved Disciple has perceived that the *soudarion* means Jesus has risen, why would the narrator add this "not yet" statement here? Some commentators, struggling to reconcile the apparent contradiction between resurrection faith and the ignorance of scripture, have interpreted verse 9 to suggest that they did not know *until now*. But this interpretation does violence to the text, which does not say "until now" but speaks of "not yet."

Verse 10 knocks the other legs out from the table supporting the inference of resurrection faith: "Therefore, the disciples went off [*apēlthon*] again to themselves." The carefully staged movement out from where they were and into the tomb is now reversed: they go back *again*. There is no implication that they are leaving the tomb and continuing into a new future. Instead, the narrator clearly tells us that they are returning to a situation they have been in before. In addition, the literal translation provided shows the result of their incomprehension: they are going to *themselves* rather than to others. What began hopefully in verses 3–4 with Peter and the Beloved Disciple's journey "together" has ended with them going back separately, or at least not to share the experience with others. Their problems began when the shared journey became a race: competition has overtaken community, and, burdened with the pursuit of self-interest, they remain unable to understand the meaning of the *soudarion* and the empty tomb.

But the Beloved Disciple, at least, has believed *something*. If not an expression of resurrection faith, what is it that he believed? We now are called to remember that their journey began in response to Mary Magdalene's witness about the tomb being empty and that "they" had taken the Lord's body. The two runners went out to find out if the woman's incredible testimony could be true. The Beloved Disciple, seeing the *soudarion*, discerned that human activity had taken place after Jesus' burial. Indeed, Mary Magdalene's account was accurate! This is what the Beloved Disciple (for the moment reduced to the "other disciple") believed: that the woman's witness was true. But before we infer too much, the narrator stops us and makes clear that resurrection faith continues to elude even the most faithful of followers.

How else to explain their emotionless return? Unlike the women in Mark who are overcome with ecstasy and fear at the sight of the empty tomb (Mk 16:8), the Johannine disciples are described as going back with no particular feelings or goal. They are neither fearful nor ecstatic. They, unlike Mary Magdalene, are not distressed enough to gather the others to share the experience. They simply leave the tomb wordlessly. The reader's expectation of the celebration of resurrection is deflated by the still-dark hearts of Jesus' disciples. And yet the Beloved Disciple's belief in Mary Magdalene's word at least keeps open the possibility that this darkness will eventually be dispelled.

## 3. "WOMAN, WHY ARE YOU WEEPING?"

a: 11–12: "Mary" at tomb, weeping over Jesus' absence

  b: 13: woman, why are you weeping? taken away, put him

    c: 14: turned into things behind and did not know it was Jesus

  b$^1$: 15: woman, why are you weeping? taken away, put him

a$^1$: 16–18: "Mary" at tomb, clinging to Jesus' presence

While the retreat of the leading disciples is both a surprise and a disappointment, the narrator does not linger over it. Instead, the narrative continues by providing still another surprise in verse 11: "But Mary still stood outside the tomb, weeping." The other side of the "sandwich" keeps us at the empty tomb. We had last heard from Mary as she conveyed her news to the leaders. We had not been told at all that she had returned with them to the tomb, as the narrative technique of focusing on one interaction at a time kept our attention on the competition between the racers and their dance at the door of death. They have gone back, but she remains, albeit "outside" the tomb. She may not have seen the sign of the *soudarion,* but she has not given up the idea that the tomb is the right place for her to be, even if only to grieve her missing Lord. Her explicit emotions put the apparent apathy of the others even further into shadow. At least she can feel pain!

And yet her weeping is itself ambiguous, recalling the weeping outside the tomb of Lazarus that generated Jesus' own powerful emotions (11:33). She can grieve, but she is like the others in lacking faith in resurrection. Having shared the news with the others in hope that they might at least share her pain and perhaps help solve the mystery of the absent corpse, she instead experiences their leaving her alone in tears at the tomb.

But, not content simply to cry on the outside, she takes her own step forward in verse 11b–12: "Therefore, while she was weeping, she bent over into the tomb, and saw two angels in white sitting, one toward the head and one toward the feet, where the body of Jesus had been lying." What a difference from what the others saw! If the cloths and the *soudarion* are still there, she does not see them at all. Instead, her sight is open to the only extraordinary vision in the fourth gospel to this point: the presence of "two angels in white." Has anything in the narrative prepared her or us for this experience? Just when we might have expected to observe her own reaction to what the Beloved Disciple and Peter saw, we are startled along with her by this incredible sight from above.

Angels had previously been only a figurative presence in the fourth gospel. The first mention was in Jesus' response to Nathanael's proclamation of faith, when he spoke of "angels of God ascending and descending upon the Human One" (1:51). Some of the crowd experiencing the heavenly voice confirming Jesus' eventual glorification interpret it as the voice of an angel (12:29). But now, the heavenly figures are unambiguously present to the eyes of Mary Magdalene. The narration does not give any indication that such a vision is surprising at all, though, despite what was presumably as rare an experience for ordinary people then as it is now.

But although the narrator has told us that the white-clad occupants of the tomb are angels, does Mary recognize them as such? Other than being dressed in white, what clues might there be about their appearance that would suggest to Mary their true identity?

All we are told to help guide us through this surprising twist in the plot is that they were sitting at the place in the tomb where Jesus' head and feet had been. Jesus' head was the site of the *soudarion,* which is now occupied by an angel. His feet were the object of the other Mary's anointing, the preparation for his burial. Both the sacred (anointing oil) and the profane (*soudarion*) objects of death are replaced by radiant signs of eternal life. Men and a woman, Judeans and a disciple, have prepared Jesus for his death in their own way. But the time of death has passed over. The angels' silent presence itself announces the beginning of the new dawn.

But they do not remain as silent symbols. They take the initiative in verse 13 by challenging Mary's grieving stance: "And they are saying to her, 'Woman, why are you weeping?'" Their form of address immediately recalls Jesus' own twice-used title for his own mother (2:4; 19:26). Their question denies the central assumption of her reality, that Jesus' death is final and that his missing body indicates theft or some other earthly misdeed.

Her response, given this experience, is tragicomic: "She is saying to them, 'They have taken my Lord, and I have not known where they put him.'" Her response to the two angels is almost identical to her statement to the disciples, with one important difference. She continues to perceive the problem as the result of "they" who have taken away the body, but she no longer speaks collectively. "*The* Lord" is replaced with "*my* Lord"; "*we* have not known" is replaced with "*I* have not known." She is feeling utterly alone in the midst of an experience meant to show her that she will never be alone again! She sees these tomb occupants simply as possible answers to her stubborn inquiry about the body. Her tears have blinded her, as she apparently has not the slightest sense that those who question her are "from above."

The chiasm reaches its central point in verse 14 with the narrator's amazingly low-key introduction of the object of her desire: "Having said these things, she turned into the things behind [*eis ta opisō*] and saw Jesus standing, and she did not know it is Jesus." From *soudarion* to angels in white to Jesus himself: the fact of resurrection emerges like a photographic print in the darkroom. Suddenly, without the slightest notice, the narrative affirms the greatest theological reality in all human experience, as if it was as expectable an event as the movement from night to day.

Once again, the narrator has most carefully crafted this climactic moment, building the maximum imaginable suspense into the scene. Getting no further response from the tomb, Mary "turns." The narrator's phrase expresses both the ordinary act of turning around and the profound Johannine sense of rejection of faith. We recall that some of Jesus' disciples, upon being confronted with the necessity of publicly known eucharist, "went off into the things behind [*apēlthon eis ta opisō*]" (6:66). Similarly, the arresting party who retreat at the mention of *egō eimi* are described as going *eis ta opisō* (18:6). Now, the struggling Mary Magdalene repeats this negative movement. But just when we are led to think that she is in the same spiritual place as the disciples who left the tomb to go back home, the narrator slides in the "detail" that "she saw Jesus standing." For a split second, our emotions are reversed from despair to joy, only to be put on the edge of our seats with tension as the narrator immediately adds that she did not know it was him. Who among us is not inclined at this point to shout at Mary, "Open your eyes, woman! There he is right in front of you!"? But mysteriously, something that is not described prevents her from identifying this new visitor to the gravesite. Just as the other disciples did not know the scripture, so she does not know the Lord's presence in her midst.

The suspense could hardly be more intense. Certainly Jesus will complete the revelation and allow his grieving follower's pain to be turned into joy, just as he said he would, won't he (16:22)? The question that holds our attention now is no longer *if* but *how*. What will be the means for this supreme release?

Maddeningly, the narrative holds us in tension for another verse, as Jesus now takes his turn asking Mary the identical question as the angels and then adding his own: "Woman, why are you weeping? Whom are you seeking?" The second inquiry is the same one asked twice to the arresting party (18:4, 7). It is the ultimate Johannine question, the one on which the entire gospel turns. What will Mary's response be?

Before she can speak, the narrator adds another tragicomic element to this incredible scene: "Thinking it was the gardener she is saying...." The *gardener*! Come on, Mary! Her misunderstanding, as frustrating as it may be to readers, serves the function of reminding us that this entire scene is taking place in a garden, still another parallel between this scene and that of Jesus' arrest. It also puts us deeply into the ambiguity of biblical gardens, places both of intimacy and betrayal, in Genesis and in John (18:2). Will Mary's encounter in the garden lead to intimacy or be just another betrayal? What can she possibly say to this "gardener"?

If readers are frustrated at her inability to see, so is she becoming frustrated with the inability of any of these people to answer her questions, which she now states as a demand: "Sir [*kyrie*], if you took him [*ebastasas*], tell me where you put him, and I will take him away." Her previous statements to the disciples and the angels had spoken of "them" taking away (*aran*) the body. Now, she practically accuses the gardener of "carrying off" the body, just as Judas carried the money and the Judeans carried stones to use against Jesus. *She* will now "take away" the body and put it somewhere where she can keep track of it.

It is enough! In verse 16, the curtain is raised in the most simple yet profoundly personal way possible: "Jesus said to her, 'Mary!' Having turned around, she said to him in Hebrew, '*Rabbounei!*' which means 'teacher.'" Finally! The presumed gardener reveals himself as the shepherd, by calling one of his sheep by name and leading her out of her pain (10:3). The physical description of the scene painted by the narrator is confusing and suggests that we should not get caught up — like Mary — in the "earthly" sense of things. In verse 14, we were told that she turned from the tomb to the one standing behind. Having spoken with that one, she now turns again and speaks to the same person. Her turning is not so much another spin on her heels but a *metanoia,* a conversion of heart.

And yet her response is another surprise. She has spoken twice of the absent Jesus as "Lord," a term whose double meaning in Greek (*kyrie*) allows it to be used ironically as an address to the one she thinks is the gardener in her demand for the dead body. Now that her eyes are opened, though, she calls Jesus by the intimate yet lesser title, *Rabbounei,* which the narrator tells us is Hebrew (actually, Aramaic) for teacher. Although we have not heard Mary Magdalene address Jesus at all during his lifetime, seven times previously he has been called "Rabbi" by his disciples or by others (1:38, 49; 3:2; 4:31; 6:25; 9:2; 11:8). It expresses her willingness to continue to be taught by the one whose wisdom has brought her to this moment. Why does the narrator interrupt, though, at this peak moment, with the mundane translation note of a word whose basic form we have already heard many times?

By focusing our attention for a brief moment on the fact that Mary Magdalene addresses Jesus with a Hebrew/Aramaic term, the narrator forces us to see that the rejection of the Judean establishment and the highly critical attitude toward the Law and the related *ethos* are *not a rejection of Jewish people.* It is certainly true from a Johannine perspective that the religious and cultural system represented in the story by the world of the "Judeans" has been replaced by the love commandment within the discipleship community given birth to by Jesus. But the translation note reminds us at this time of Jesus' triumph that those who were with him included many Jews. For a Johannine community under intense persecution by a Judean-Roman conspiracy, the temptation to anti-Jewishness would be extremely powerful. But Mary Magdalene's Hebrew title for the risen Jesus, especially after her difficulty in becoming open to the unexpected reality of resurrection, invites the Johannine community itself to remain open to later Jews who could not or would not accept Jesus as the messiah and his way as from God. Mary Magdalene thus becomes a representative character of all those future people who respect and love Jesus for his wisdom, but are unable to acknowledge him as risen Lord without a direct experience.

With this exchange between Jesus and Mary, the time of celebration has finally arrived, when shepherd and sheep are united. Her tears have been turned into dancing, her grieving to unimaginable joy. However we might expect Jesus to react to her excited acknowledgment of his ongoing life in her midst, it is certainly shocking when we are told his words in verse 17: "Jesus is saying to her, 'Do not cling [*haptou*] to me, for I have not yet ascended to the Father.'" Rather than offer some kind word or other sign of celebration, Jesus reacts strongly to an aspect of Mary's response that was not narrated, her "clinging" to him. Contrary to some of the absurd interpretations of this verse that focus on imaginary problems with "risen bodies" being touched, Jesus does *not* prohibit Mary from *touching* him but from *clinging*. Although the Greek word *haptō* has a wide range of meanings,[9] it seems clear from the context that Jesus' concern is not with physical contact itself but with Mary Magdalene's natural but improper attempt to keep him with her. Having searched for him so hard, she does not want to lose track of him again! Her hug of Jesus is both spontaneously unavoidable and fitting. But her desire to keep him present interferes with his completion of his journey back to the Father. As he told those gathered for the Last Supper discourse, unless he returns to the Father, there can be no paraclete to guide them and lead them to the truths that they have as yet been unable to bear (16:7–13).

Support for this interpretation comes from another source: the shared imagery between this scene and the Song of Songs. We find the following familiar-sounding passages in the Septuagint version of chapter 3 of the Song:

By night ... I sought him whom my soul loves: I sought him, but found him not. (verse 1)

The watchmen who go their rounds in the city found me. I said, "Have you seen him whom my soul loves?" It was as a little while [*mikron*] after I parted from them, that I found him whom my soul loves: I held [*hapheka*] him and did not let him go until I brought him into my mother's house, and into the chamber of her that conceived me. (verses 3–4)

It is apparent that the author of the fourth gospel has modeled Mary's search for Jesus' body in part on this passage. The lover's desire in the Song to hold on to the beloved includes taking him to her "mother's house." Can this carry over into the gospel scene to suggest that Mary wants to take Jesus back to the *synagogue,* the place in which she was "conceived" as a Jewish woman? Or, given the handing of "the mother" to the Beloved Disciple at the cross and Mary Magdalene's relationship with the Beloved Disciple, does it suggest taking Jesus back to be present in the *Johannine community*, where Mary was born *anōthen?* Either possibility is consistent with Jesus' strong rejection of her clinging. The community of faith will have to come to its commitment without his physical presence.

His description of this last leg of his journey in terms of "ascending" fulfills the statements of 3:13 and 6:62. The former narrates as an already completed event (from the perspective of the Johannine community) the ascension of the

---

9. BAG 102–103.

Human One. The latter reference took the form of a rhetorical question put to those who found Jesus' word about "munching flesh" to be too hard: Would seeing the Human One ascend allow them to believe that participating in the eucharistic meal was ordained by God? Now, Jesus' ascension will allow the Johannine community to find the paraclete in their midst, precisely in the fellowship and sharing that result both from the meal itself as well as from the persecution that was the consequence of that participation.

In the first part of Jesus' statement to Mary, he speaks generally of "the" Father. But in the second part of verse 17, the image is made much more personal: "Be going to my brothers and say to them, 'I am ascending to my Father and your Father, my God and your God.'" Are the "brothers" to whom Mary is to take this message the same as the "disciples," or does Jesus have another purpose in mind? At one level, we can interpret "brothers" to imply that whoever shares Jesus' experience of God as Father is his brother (or sister), as common children of God (cf. 1:13). But at the deeper level to which the fourth gospel constantly challenges us to go, we must remember that earlier in the narrative, "brothers" and "disciples" were spoken of as distinct groups (2:12). If we accept Peter Ellis's larger chiastic structure that makes this entire scene parallel to the first Cana scene,[10] then we hear Jesus' command to Mary as calling her to bring a message to the *unbelieving* brothers who left Jesus behind at Tabernacles (7:1–9). Given the wider parallel between the wedding imagery of the Cana story and the Song of Song's nuptial imagery, we should not be too quick to assume that Jesus' reference to "brothers" is simply an intimate way of referring to the disciples.

But the parallelism between "my" and "your" Father and God does include a call to deeper intimacy. Why this sudden interest in the faith of the "brothers," who are not again mentioned? They are clearly people who have mocked Jesus' messiahship, seeing his signs as a desire for earthly glory (7:3–9). The narrator expressly told us that they did not believe, and Jesus in turn mocked their comfortable place in the "world" that cannot hate them as it hates Jesus. At the same time, they have *some* intimacy with Jesus and are distinct from the larger enemy, the "Judeans," found throughout the story. We see them with Jesus only in Galilee. Perhaps they represent hometown people who cannot accept that this familiar person is truly one sent from God. From this perspective, they serve as a symbol for the Johannine community of all the friends and relatives who resist accepting the process that has led people to give up the ways of their community of birth in favor of following the way of Jesus and the Johannine community. How many of us share the experience of finding our commitment to radical discipleship more difficult to swallow among our family than among strangers? Jesus' command to bring this message to the "brothers" challenges the Johannine community not to give up on those who may mock or reject our claim to be in touch with God's spirit as we witness publicly on behalf of the way of Jesus.

---

10. Ellis (1984, 288–289) lists a number of intriguing parallels.

After all the emotion of Mary Magdalene's search for Jesus, we are told nothing further of her feelings in response to this command. How disappointed she must be to have to let go all over again! But instead of letting us in on this experience, the narrator takes us in verse 18 directly to her carrying out of the message, just as the woman of Samaria brought her experience of Jesus back to her people: "Mary Magdalene brought the news to the disciples, 'I have seen the Lord!' and these things [*tauta*] he said to her."

Having addressed Jesus directly as *Rabbounei,* she now reverts to calling Jesus "Lord." But she has brought the message not to the brothers but to the disciples! Has she, too, assumed that these were the same people? Or has she simply taken the news to the first people she could find with the idea of sharing it with the brothers (in Galilee) later? Or might the idea of confronting Jesus' brothers be too frightening or intimidating to her? These questions go unanswered. The narrator focuses instead on her classic proclamation, "I have seen the Lord!" Her faithful conveyance of Jesus' message is reduced to a narrative aside in the face of this primal Christian affirmation. For all time, the news of the resurrection is brought to the community by a word of a woman, the first apostle of the risen Christ.

## 28

# Penetrating the Locked Doors

*Finding Jesus in the Midst of the Community*

### John 20:19-31

A. **Chiasm:** 20:19-29

   a: 19-20a: day; doors locked, Jesus came and stood; showed hands/side

      b: 20b: disciples rejoice at seeing the Lord

         c: 21-23: send you, holy spirit, forgive sins

      b$^1$: 24-25: disciples: we have seen the Lord!

   a$^1$: 26-29: days, doors locked, Jesus came and stood; showed hands/side

B. **Location:** behind locked doors

C. **Time:** evening on the first day of the week

D. **Hebrew scripture context:** Gen 2:7

E. **Social factors:** the Johannine community's mission to the world and relationship to those who come later

F. **Themes:** overcoming fear; believing without seeing

G. **Key words:** peace, locked doors

### 1. THE UNITY OF THE REMAINING RESURRECTION ACCOUNTS

**Chiasm: 20:19-21:25**

a: 20:19-23: Jesus commissions disciples

   b: 24-29: Jesus' presence for Thomas: we have seen the Lord/my Lord

      c: 30-31: purpose of gospel

454

b¹: 21:1–14: Jesus' presence for catch of fish: It is the Lord!

a¹: 15–25: Jesus commissions Peter[1]

Mary Magdalene's inaugural experience of the risen Jesus stands alone. Despite her temporary grief-induced tear-blindness, her eventually open eyes remain for all time the first to see what all people yearn to see: evidence of life beyond the bounds of death. Although there is no description of the risen Jesus' physical appearance, Mary's experience cannot truly be compared with that of those who witnessed the raising of Lazarus. Although the fourth gospel certainly intends the Lazarus narrative to prepare both characters and readers for what has now been told, Lazarus' return to life was penultimate, while that of Jesus is a permanent victory over the evil one. Both her experience and her apostleship remain privileged, unassailable, and apart from the experience of all later believers.

The text protects her experience by keeping it chiastically separate from the other resurrection accounts, which are grouped together as a single larger chiasm. When we reach chapter 21, we will look at the numerous other ways in which the final chapter is integrally linked with the rest of the text, contrary to the still dominant scholarly view that treats it as an "appendix" or "epilogue." For now, it is enough to pay attention to the fact that the accounts of Jesus' appearances to "the disciples" are grouped together as a unit apart from the initial narrative.

As we will see, in contrast with the general view that these stories are included for the sake of confirming the fourth gospel's *christology,* each resurrection account confirms an essential element of *discipleship.* The focus of the gospel is, more than ever, on the function of the Johannine community. How is it to continue after Jesus' final completion of his own mission to the world?

## 2. "AS THE FATHER HAS SENT ME, SO I AM SENDING YOU"

**Chiasm: 20:19–23**

a: 19a: fear

  b: 19b–20: gift of peace

    c: 21: as Father has sent me, I am sending you

  b¹: 22: gift of holy spirit

a¹: 23: forgiveness as antidote to fear

With the beginning of the multilayered chiasms starting in verse 19, the narrator moves us from the initial postcrucifixion site of the tomb and garden to the place where the community is gathered. The introductory description is the

---

1. Ellis (1984, 290–291).

saddest possible confirmation of the failure of those who were at the tomb to believe in the resurrection: "Therefore, being evening on that day, the first of the week, and the doors [_thyrōn_] where the disciples were having been locked for fear of the Judeans..." The day that began with darkness awaiting dawn now has reached evening, as the presence of the light fades back into night. The narrator notes it as "that day," a phrase with eschatological overtones.[2] But it is also described again as "the first of the week," maintaining the emphasis on the particular newness of the Easter event.

At this point, the disciples have presumably received the racers' report about the _soudarion_ and have definitely been given Mary Magdalene's proclamation of having seen the Lord. How have they responded to this incredible news? They are hiding behind locked doors! Their insecurity is concretely political and terribly ironic: "fear of the Judeans" has led them into seclusion. The narrator's attribution of this cause for the locked doors puts them, of course, in the same camp as the parents of the healed blind one and secret disciples like Joseph of Arimathea (9:22; 19:38). Furthermore, they are like the sheep without a shepherd, hiding from the thief/plunderer who threatens to "kill and destroy" them (Jn 10:1–10; see chapter 15, above). Rather than trusting in Jesus-the-door (10:7, _thyra_), their doors are locked. It is a wholly negative evaluation, one for which no exceptions are made. Apparently, even the formerly "Beloved" Disciple has been reduced to this sorry state of fear.

The narrator does not expressly tell us of the disciples' disbelief of Mary Magdalene's report, as does the narrator in Luke (24:11). But their fearful hiding out bears the same implication. In contrast to the people of Samaria who responded positively to the wild claim of a woman of disrepute, the disciples apparently totally ignore Mary's message. Given this "failure" of apostleship, the Johannine community should not be surprised later when its attempt to bring the good news to the "world" is met with scorn and persecution.

At least one positive inference can be made from this first part of the scene: the disciples are still _together_. Despite the statement that Peter and the Beloved Disciple went again "to themselves" in verse 10, the quaking community remains united, even in their shared fear. This ambivalent state of affairs, as it turns out, is the paradigm for community from a Johannine perspective. Their remaining together, even in their paralyzed state, is enough to evoke the experience that is their salvation, as described in the second part of verse 19: "Jesus came and stood in their midst, and is saying to them, 'Peace to you.'"

The locked doors are no barrier to the risen Jesus, although the text offers not the slightest hint of a supernatural explanation of Jesus' appearance. Instead, it focuses on his being "in their midst." And is this not how it is for all gatherings of would-be disciples who shake in fear of the authorities but still claim to believe in the Human One? Somehow, despite all of our cowering, all of our attempts to insulate ourselves from the brunt of police-state threats and violence,

---

2. R. Brown (1970, 1019).

Jesus *is* present in the midst of the community, offering the gift of peace. It is not a matter of mysteriously passing through locked doors of a *room,* but of prayerfully opening the locked doors of our *hearts,* that allows the community to perceive the presence of the Risen One.

Jesus' greeting to them is both ordinary and profound. The common Hebrew phrase *shalom alechem* is as everyday as our "good-bye," a contraction of "God be with ye." But just as "good-bye," when considered in its root meaning, is a powerful prayer for the other, so Jesus' greeting offers the disciples exactly what they need in their locked-up situation. The "peace" Jesus gives is not that which the world gives (14:27; 16:33). The two previous occasions on which Jesus spoke of peace, both in the Last Supper discourse, involved the challenge to allow his peace to give courage that dissipates their fear of the world's persecution. Now that moment has come. Jesus' peace is not the superficial calm that consists of either the mere absence of fighting or the repression and denial of conflict. Instead, it is the centeredness that comes from acknowledging fear but simultaneously trusting in God's victory over the world (16:33).

After Jesus has offered this gift to the community for the first time, the narrator adds a perhaps surprising piece of physical confirmation of his identity in verse 20: "And having said this, he also showed them his hands and his side." At one level, Jesus draws attention to the evidence of crucifixion that "proves" that the one speaking is indeed Jesus. But at the deeper level, the particular focus on "hands" and "side" emphasizes Jesus' authority, which will momentarily be transferred to the discipleship community. Twice previously we have heard that God "has given all things into his hands" (3:35; 13:3) and that those given to Jesus by the Father cannot be snatched out of the hand of the Father, with whom Jesus is one (10:28). His showing his hands to the community, then, is to remind them of what God has given them and of the protection that being in his hands offers them against the world's threats. Similarly, as we have seen, the "side" is the place from which blood and water flowed, symbolic of the birth of the community that is initiated by the sword thrust of Rome. The impending violence of both Judeans and Romans, which the community fears, is, paradoxically, the labor through which the community must go in order to be fully born *anōthen.*

Whether the disciples catch these deeper meanings or not, we are not told. The narrator simply offers the thrill of recognition: "Therefore the disciples rejoiced at seeing the Lord." Their experience is now united with that of Mary Magdalene in "seeing the Lord." It is the explicit confirmation of Jesus' prediction that "I shall see you again, and your heart will rejoice, and your joy no one will take away from you" (16:22).

Then, in verse 21, Jesus repeats the conveyance of peace to the community. If the first *shalom alechem* might have been perceived as an ordinary greeting, the repetition makes clear that it is a meaningful gift that is being offered. And with this gift comes a responsibility: "As the Father has sent me, so I am also sending you." The divine authority that Jesus has been given is *totally transferred to the community.* For those who emphasize the high christological aspects of the Johannine Jesus' relationship with God, equal attention must also be given to the unqualified conveyance of this relationship to the community. There are no limitations or distinctions made whatsoever between Jesus' mission and the mission of the Johannine community. What he began, they (and we) are to continue: to witness God's love to the world and shed light on deeds done in darkness so as to convert them into acts of the light.

And in the fulfillment of the promise made in the Last Supper discourse, Jesus now gives the community what it needs to carry out this sacred mission: "And having said this, he blew in [*enephusēsen*] them and is saying to them, 'Receive holy spirit.'" The act of "blowing in" spirit is directly evocative of God's first act of infusion: "And God...breathed in [LXX, *enephusēsen*] his face the breath of life, and the person became a living soul" (Gen 2:7). That Jesus' act is linked with this initial creation of humanity is emphasized by the shared aorist verb tense in a sentence that otherwise speaks in the present of Jesus' speech. The fearful community, hiding in the dust of its shame, is infused with "holy spirit" from the mouth of Jesus.

It is important to note that the text does not suggest that Jesus is giving them an "entity," "the holy spirit," but rather a share in his relationship with God that flows and blows like the wind (cf. 3:8). Certainly the later Christian understanding of what Jesus has given the disciples here as being the same as "the holy spirit" promised earlier (14:26) and spoken of by the other gospels is not "wrong." But we should at least be aware that in the context of the fourth gospel standing alone, Jesus' gift is identical with that given to the first human, the presence of God that allows life to come into being.

Having challenged the community to receive this gift, Jesus offers them a profound word of wisdom in verse 23: "If you forgive [*aphēte*, literally, 'let go of'] someone's sins, they are forgiven; if you retain them, they have been retained." Although often considered as a parallel to Mt 18:18 in the giving of authority, the Johannine logion is really quite different. Whereas Matthew's Jesus speaks of "binding" and "loosing" on earth and in heaven, the Johannine Jesus speaks of a community reality that is essential to their living out of the love commandment. In contrast with the commission in verse 21, verse 23 does not convey authority or transfer responsibility but reminds them of what life together is about. *If* they hold on to the sins of each other — that is, bear grudges or get stuck in focusing on the imperfections of one another — *then* they will indeed remain focused on sin. *But if* they are able to let go — to accept the human condition that they share and its propensity toward fear, denial, and betrayal — *then* they will be able to move together as Jesus has encouraged them to do.

It also involves the willingness to *acknowledge* this sinfulness, in contrast with those whose foul deeds are done in the dark to avoid reproval by the community (3:19–21). It is something that the community is also reminded of in 1 John, in an A-B-A[1] chiastic passage that emphasizes this need for community confession and forgiveness:

A: If we should say, "We have no sin," we are misleading ourselves and the truth is not in us

   B: If we are confessing our sins, he is faithful and just so that he might forgive [*aphē*] our sins and cleanse us from all injustice

A¹: If we should say, "We have not sinned," we are making him a liar and his word [*logos*] is not in us (1 Jn 1:7–9)

For a community that hides behind locked doors, competes for priority, and denies being related to Jesus to deny its sinfulness would truly be the height of hypocrisy. But the point is not to wallow in guilt but to name the community's sins so as to let go of them and to continue together in the joyous presence of holy spirit in the shared mission to the world.

### 3. "BLESSED ARE THOSE NOT HAVING SEEN BUT HAVING BELIEVED!"

**Chiasm: 20:24–29**

a: 24–25a: Thomas; Lord; seen

   b: 25b: hands; finger, in his side; believe

      c: 26: peace to you

   b¹: 27: finger; hands; in my side; believe

a¹: 28–29: Thomas; Lord; seen[3]

With the gifts of peace and holy spirit, the commission to be sent forth, and the admonition to forgiveness, the community is almost fully prepared for its life together. But the text is not yet completed, for several important matters still need to be addressed. Foremost is one central to a Johannine community that lives two generations after this initial experience and the generations of Christians who follow in their footsteps. What about those who have *not* seen the hands and side of the Lord? How are we to share in these gifts and this mission?

For the sake of those who come later — those for whom Jesus has prayed (17:20–26) — the gospel continues with the story of "doubting Thomas." Verse 24 introduces him: "Thomas, one of the twelve, the one called 'Twin,' was not with them when Jesus came." The specific mention of Thomas as "one of the twelve," is, of course, a two-edged sword. The "twelve" are both the "inside" group referred to three times in 6:67–71 and those from whom the betrayer comes. To mention Thomas at this point as part of this group, which is not otherwise distinguished from "the disciples" throughout the entire gospel, is to mock the apostolic church's claims to authority founded on their continuity with

---

3. Ellis (1984, 295).

the twelve (e.g., Mk 3:14, 16; Lk 6:7; 9:1; Acts 6:2). The member of the twelve is noted here only for his *absence* at the central event of the community's birth!

Thomas in particular, we recall, was the one who brashly or sarcastically (we cannot tell which) challenged his mates to go die with Jesus in Judea (11:16) and disclaimed knowing either where Jesus was going or "the way" (14:5). We have not seen or heard from him since, and the narrator brings him back on stage with this negative introduction, to receive the word of the others in verse 25: "Therefore, the other disciples were saying to him, 'We have seen the Lord!' " Their proclamation is identical to Mary Magdalene's to them in verse 18. Should we be surprised when the absent Thomas is no more ready to accept their witness than they were to accept Mary's?

The form of his expression of doubt is both graphic and emphatic: "Unless I should see the nail prints in his hands and thrust [*balō*] my finger in the nail prints and throw my hand into his side, I will never [*ou mē*] believe." His statement is doubly violent: he will base his faith only on his own forceful touching of the places where Jesus has been most forcefully touched. He also expresses distrust of his own vision: seeing alone will not suffice. He must both see *and* touch the nail prints in Jesus' hands.

What has provoked this most demanding stance? Has Thomas previously had reasons to disbelieve the reports of the other disciples in order to justify this lack of faith in their witness? Or does his strong statement express a deep anger and disappointment in Jesus' willingness to let the powers kill him? If we hear Thomas's earlier statement about going "to die with him" not as courageous but as a bitter and grudging acceptance of Jesus' chosen path and its implications for discipleship, then we should not be overly surprised to find him eager to deny the reality of resurrection. A dead and buried Jesus may be a disappointment to Thomas's messianic hopes, but it allows him to deny the implications of Jesus' death for his *own* future. But a gloriously risen Jesus is the most powerful evidence imaginable that Jesus is indeed the one sent from God, whose commandment *is* the word of God that requires obedience. Perhaps Thomas's previous absence also expresses this desire to be rid of the demands of this martyr messiah who challenged his followers to continue his mission and his method. If so, then his double demand is coherent as stating what he considers an impossibility. His fellow disciples may be seeing visions of the Lord, and, perhaps, under their influence, his own imagination might show him such a sight. But the demand for the violent thrust into the wounds presupposes a bodily present Jesus, not just a ghostly spirit. Such a resurrected Jesus, seemingly impossible, would indeed convince Thomas of the ongoing life of their master.

Rather than narrate a gradual movement toward recognition as in the Mary Magdalene account, the narrator instead brings down the curtain on this gathering, only to raise it again in verse 26 "eight days later." The previous resurrection stories had taken place on the "first day of the week," while the disciples' witness to Thomas is not given its own time reference. But now, eight excruciating days are allowed to pass without description, a week in which the jubilant disciples perhaps wondered whether Thomas would be left permanently outside their newly enspirited community.

The description of Jesus' appearance in verse 26 is subtly yet significantly different from his earlier appearance in verse 19. On the first occasion, the Greek gives us first the word about the "doors having been locked for fear of the Judeans," *then* tells us that "Jesus came and stood in their midst." The effect is to lead us to be conscious both of the protected position of the disciples and of their reason for their enclosure *before* we find Jesus able to penetrate both the locks and their fear. But now, the order of information is different, with an altered effect. Literally, the sentence reads, "Is coming Jesus, the doors having been locked, and stood in their midst." Jesus' coming has been changed from an aorist indicative (*ēlthen*) to a present participle (*erchetai*), changing the context from a completed event to an ongoing reality. Second, Jesus' coming, which we might expect at this point, *precedes* the news that the doors are locked *again,* certainly a surprise given the disciples' proclamation affirming the experience of Jesus' presence to them. Finally, the reason for the locking is omitted, perhaps suggesting that the specific political fear of Judean persecution has been replaced by a more generalized fear of moving out from their security to confront the world with the truth Jesus has given them.

Jesus comes to them again, with their imperfect faith, and again offers his *shalom alechem.* But he has come on a more specific mission this time: to lead Thomas to believe. In verse 27, he speaks to this angry disciple directly: "Bring your finger here and see my hands, and bring your hands and thrust into my side; don't become [*ginou*] unbelieving but believing!" Jesus offers Thomas a physical witness, but not exactly the same way Thomas demanded. He oddly tells the disciple to "bring his finger" in order to "see my hands," then tells him to "bring" his hands to "thrust into my side." He does not offer the opportunity to "thrust" into the nail prints, though. Of course, Thomas was not stating a logical blueprint for his faith but an emotional cry that called out for the seemingly impossible. Jesus' invitation varies from the letter of Thomas's demand to show readers that Johannine faith is not a matter of precisely defined behavior just as we have previously seen that it is not a matter of precisely defined doctrine. Its focus is on moving Thomas off the road of unbelief and toward faith. The particular form *ginou* implies an ongoing process toward either increasing unbelief or increasing faith. Jesus' willingness to allow the doubting disciple to "thrust" his hands into the birthing-place of Jesus both respects the depth of Thomas's feelings and urges him to move past them and into participation in the discipleship community.

Thomas's simple response in verse 28 is one of the most joyously emotional moments in the fourth gospel: "In answer, Thomas said, 'My Lord and my God!'" His confession, which should be seen not as a theological but as a relational statement uttered from the depth of the moment of conversion, restores Jesus as the master of Thomas's heart. His anger and disappointment are washed away in the tears of joy that must accompany this profound experience of the Risen One.

For Thomas, his words are pure emotion, but for the Johannine community, they bear a strong social significance. As the Samaritans' confession of Jesus as "the Savior of the world" expressed their belief in him as greater than Caesar, so Thomas's proclamation challenges the supremacy of the emperor. Domitian, the Roman ruler enthroned from 81–96 C.E., is described in literature of the time as *dominus et deus noster,* "our lord and god."[4] Thus, both the formerly "outsider" Samaritans and the "insider" twelve have produced confessions of Jesus that extol him as supreme leader, the one whose kingdom is both *not of* and *greater than any in* the world.

Even this most happy of moments produces in verse 29 a response from Jesus that contains an edge: "Because you have seen me you have believed? Happy are those not having seen and having believed." His question is similar to his doubting inquiries earlier about Nathanael's faith rooted in the fig tree vision (1:50) and the disciples' faith in response to Jesus' supposedly open speech (16:31). Despite Thomas's affirmation that did *not* ultimately require his hand-thrust into the wounds, Jesus' question leads us to wonder whether Thomas really does get it.

But this mystery is submerged under the fourth gospel's second beatitude (cf. 13:17), which is the real focus of the entire story of Thomas. Few are those who had the chance to see the nail prints or to touch Jesus' side, but countless are those invited to believe on the faith of those sent in Jesus' name. It is these — including the members of the Johannine community — whom the Johannine Jesus urges to the path of faith. To all those throughout the ages who demand physical evidence — only relatively recently thought of under the rubric "scientific proof" — Jesus offers a blessing if they, we, can come to faith on the word of others. For in the end, there is no "proof" that cannot be subjected to further doubt, no "seeing" that cannot be interpreted for or against belief. The last beatitude offers "those" who can respond to this challenge Jesus' own blessing, an aspect of the joy that the world cannot take away.

## 4. THE CHIASTIC CENTER OF
## THE COMMUNITY'S STORIES OF RESURRECTION:
## THE REASON FOR THE FOURTH GOSPEL

What many commentators see as the conclusion of the gospel lies at the very center of the resurrection narratives extending from 20:18 to 21:25. Verses 30–31, which flow from the implicit reference to signs in the demand for "miraculous" proof, are the bridge linking the Jerusalem stories in chapter 20 and the Galilee stories in chapter 21. As the narrator summarized the various responses to Jesus during his lifetime not at the end of the gospel but in the middle (12:37–43), so the resurrection stories are summarized in the middle. Both narrative summaries focus on the role of "signs." Earlier, 12:37 began by

---

4. R. Brown (1970, 1047).

noting the "many signs" Jesus did, then used Isaiah to explain why many have not believed. Now, 20:30 notes the "other signs" that Jesus did, then refers to the fact of the fourth gospel itself to explain the value of believing. Both passages function to summarize what has been narrated already and to introduce what is to follow. Earlier, 12:37–43 set up the narrative that showed us the consequences of the "rulers" preferring the glory of people to the glory of God. Now, verses 30–31 set up the narrative that will show us the consequences of the disciples' commitment to Jesus, that is, the movement of the community beyond the locked doors and into its mission.

Verse 30 continues from the previous scene by referring to what the community has seen: "Jesus, indeed, did many other signs in the sight of his disciples, which have not been written in this book." The narrator suggests that the offer to let Thomas touch his risen body was itself a sign: a physical act that invites the conclusion that Jesus is from God, to those with eyes to see. But it also implies the futility of developing an endlessly long narrative of all Jesus' signs, for more sign-stories would not necessarily mean more believers. Finally, the verse implies that the writer has picked and chosen among the traditions about Jesus, a fact obvious to one familiar with the synoptics but perhaps not to the Johannine community.

The writing of the fourth gospel was an exercise in deliberate collecting and editing of the available tradition, the purpose of which is stated in verse 31: "But these things [*tauta*] have been written so that you may believe that Jesus is the messiah [*christos*], the Son of God, and so that believing, you may have life in his name." It is perhaps surprising to find at this late date that, despite the highly ambiguous attitude of both Jesus and the narrator throughout the text toward the titles given to Jesus, the apparent purpose of the entire gospel is to get us to affirm two specific ones! Of course, the key to the verse is not the titles but the consequence of faith: having life in his name.

From the vantage point of verse 31, we can also see that the purpose of noting the nonnarrated "signs Jesus did in the sight of his disciples" is to assure those who are trying to believe without seeing that the *signs themselves were not keys to faith at all.*[5] Rather, it is the *gospel* that invites participation in the Johannine community. And from within the gospel, to believe that Jesus is "the messiah, the Son of God," is not simply to elevate two titles from among many but to affirm that the picture painted in the narrative is indeed of the one sent by God. Together, the titles put at the chiastic center of the resurrection accounts the same idea found at the chiastic center of the prologue: that worldly sources of being — violence, nationalism, and human glorification — are inferior to the life offered by the way of God's covenant. What was true in "the beginning" remains true at the end. But to complete the circular journey of the fourth gospel, we must return once more to Galilee.

---

5. Cf. Minear (1984, 88), who also suggests that verse 30 refers only to the signs in chapter 20, an interesting but unsupported claim.

# 29

# Fishing at Night in Galilee

*Empowering the Christian Communities
into the Common Mission*

## John 21:1–25

A. **Chiasm:** (see below)

B. **Location:** Sea of Tiberias, in Galilee

C. **Time:** at night, moving into morning

D. **Hebrew scripture context:** Ps 109:31

E. **Social factors:** apostolic Christianity's relationship with Johannine community

F. **Themes:** going on mission

G. **Key words:** boat, fish, bread, gird, shepherd, *agapē/philia*

## 1. THE CONTINUITY OF THE GALILEAN
## RESURRECTION STORIES

Certainly if there were no chapter 21 in the fourth gospel, we might feel "satisfied" that the narrative has come to an end. What aspects of the final verses might lead us to feel this way? No doubt, the last two verses appear to be the narrator's summary. And through the notation of other sign-stories that are not told, the text leads us to feel that the storytelling process has come to an end. Many scholars, on the basis of this "sense of an ending,"[1] have vigorously ar-

---

1. Cf. Kermode (1967).

gued that the gospel "originally" ended with 20:31 and that *someone* added chapter 21 later.

However, many factors argue against accepting this conclusion too quickly. To start with, in contrast with many older manuscripts of Mark's gospel that stop at 16:8 and do not include the stories that later manuscripts add as 16:9–20, there is *absolutely no manuscript evidence for John's gospel without chapter 21.* From a historical standpoint, texts of the fourth gospel are remarkably consistent in continuing past the presumed ending.

Of course, source-oriented scholarship gets around this problem the same way it deals with the "four-source theory" of the origin of the Pentateuch: by positing different "layers" of writing and editing that have become embedded or woven into a single text. To the "trained" reader, these "layers" are obvious, the theory goes. Thus, just as scholars have widely accepted for over a century the theory that the Pentateuch is comprised of "Yahwist," "Elohist," "Priestly," and "Deuteronomic" strands,[2] so mainstream Johannine study has accepted the existence of the Johannine "evangelist," "ecclesiastical redactor," and other academic fictions.

Where a narrative perspective breaks with this consensus is not in denying the *possibility* of such "layers" of composition but in denying the *importance* of discerning them. It may well be that the fourth gospel came to be through a complex process that included many stages of oral sharing, written fragments, and rewritten passages. But what we have and what has apparently always been the "fourth gospel" includes chapter 21 as an integral part of the narrative. Thus, the arguments for discontinuity grounded in source-oriented methods are not refuted so much as ignored as perhaps interesting but ultimately irrelevant tributaries from the gospel's current that leads readers along the path of discipleship.

From a more positive standpoint, what narrative links can be found between chapter 21 and the rest of the gospel? Recent literary scholarship, seeing the text with open eyes, has discovered a wide range of connections that make a strong case for the thematic integration of the final chapter into the overall strategy and purpose of the fourth gospel.[3] For example, Jeff Staley writes:

> [The] division between 20 and 21 is very similar to that of 5 and 6: both chapters 5 and 20 open with scenes at the Sea of Galilee; both chapters 6 and 21 contain food miracles — in chapter 6 the food is bread and fish (bread is emphasized), in chapter 21 the food is fish and bread (fish is emphasized); both chapters contain night stories on the lake where Jesus reveals himself to the disciples; and both chapters end with a discussion about leaving.[4]

---

2. But see recent discourse-oriented scholarship challenging this consensus, e.g., Alter (1981), Sternberg (1985), Rosenberg (1986).

3. See, generally, Breck (1991), Minear (1983).

4. Staley (1988, 68 n. 47).

Paul S. Minear, also seeing the parallels between chapters 6 and 21, notes that the word used in both places for "fish," *opsarion,* is not found anywhere else in the New Testament but in these two texts.[5]

There are many other continuities as well between the final passages and what precedes. A list of the important Johannine thematic words used in chapter 21 that we have previously discussed illustrates this point:

| Johannine word in chapter 21 | place(s) found earlier in John |
|---|---|
| 1. reveal (*phaneröo*) (vv. 1, 14) | 1:31; 2:11; 3:21; 7:4; 9:3; 17:6 |
| 2. Sea of Tiberias (v. 1) | 6:1 |
| 3. Thomas, called Twin (v. 2) | 11:16; 20:24 |
| 4. Nathanael (v. 2) | 1:45–49 |
| 5. Cana of Galilee (v. 2) | 2:1, 11; 4:46 |
| 6. draw (*helkysai*) (v. 6) | 6:44; 12:32; 18:10 |
| 7. Beloved Disciple (vv. 7, 20) | 13:23; 19:26 |
| 8. gird (*diazönnymi*) (vv. 7, 18) | 13:4, 5 |
| 9. charcoal fire (*anthrakian*) (v. 9) | 18:18 |
| 10. leaning upon Jesus' breast at supper (v. 20) | 13:25 |
| 11. remain (*menö*) (v. 23) | 32 verses (of 44 gospel verses total) |
| 12. witness (v. 24) | 35 verses (of 50 gospel verses total) |

In addition to these purely verbal connections, as we shall see, there are a number of ways in which Johannine themes left open earlier in the narrative are completed in chapter 21, in a manner consistent with what has gone before. Thus, however chapter 21 became a part of the text originally, it has been composed in a way that makes for even a "better" ending than the final verses of chapter 20.[6]

## 2. DRAWING IN THE MULTITUDE OF FISH

### Chiasm: 21:1–14

a: 1: Jesus revealed to disciples

 b: 2–6: Peter; boat; fish; draw; got into boat

  c: 7: it is the Lord!

---

5. Minear (1983, 96).

6. One recent deconstructionist-oriented literary critic, though, has made an interesting case for seeing the discontinuity between chapters 20 and 21 from within a reader-response perspective. Braun (1990, 60) says: "John 21, the continuation of a previously closed work, thus constitutes the gospel's permission for the reader to question the sufficiency of its claims concerning 'the truth' and to expose the dark underside of its justly celebrated and eloquent appeal to love." Disagreement with Braun is based not on flaws in his argument but simply on the acknowledgment that different starting perspectives will reach different conclusions. Those who seek to find the gospel's "dark underside" can no doubt find it, while those who search the gospel for its light will see different things. Ultimately, neither perspective is "right" or "wrong"; each simply reveals the differing mind-sets of the reader-writers.

> b¹: 8–13: boat; Peter; fish; draw; got out of boat
> a¹: 14: Jesus revealed to disciples[7]

The new scene opens with what has become a "traditional" Johannine connector: "After these things [*meta tauta*]..." (eight of twelve total uses in the gospels are in John). But in contrast with the previous resurrection stories in which the scene unfolded without any hint that Jesus would participate, this one starts by giving away the show: "Jesus revealed himself again to the disciples, upon the Sea of Tiberias, revealing himself like this." By taking part of the suspense away before the story starts, the narrator shifts the focus immediately from *whether* Jesus will appear to *how* he will appear. We are placed halfway between the position of the disciples (who do not know that Jesus will appear) and that of the narrator (who knows both that he will appear *and* how it will happen).

Without any warning or preparation, we have been moved from the deadly intensity of Jerusalem to the pastoral calm of Galilee. In looking back, we may be surprised to realize that, with the exception of the narrator's passing references to interludes elsewhere (10:40–42; 11:54), the narrative has remained in and around the capital city since the feast of Tabernacles in chapter 7. And, in fact, Galilee itself is barely mentioned at all in chapter 21, the spatial indicator instead being the uniquely Johannine "Sea of Tiberias." The special location recalls the scenes that were narrated in chapter 6: the great crowds who followed because they saw the signs, the feeding of the multitudes with bread and fish, the attempt to make Jesus king, Jesus' nighttime appearance on the sea. Each of these images plays an active part in the scene described in chapter 21 but with plot twists that show how Jesus' mission has now been transferred to the Johannine community.

Verse 2 continues by providing the longest discipleship list in the gospel: "Together were Simon Peter; Thomas, the one called 'Twin'; Nathanael, the one from Cana of Galilee; the sons of Zebedee; and two other disciples." It is an odd list: two uniquely Johannine disciples (Thomas and Nathanael) are now "together" with the universally known Simon Peter, the otherwise purely synoptic sons of Zebedee, and two mysteriously unnamed "other disciples." Conspicuous by his absence — at least explicitly — is the Beloved Disciple, as well as the other important Johannine named disciples, the Galileans Andrew and Philip. The women are not mentioned, either, including the Galilean Mary Magdalene. Are these others gathered somewhere else in Galilee? Or have they tarried in Judea for some reason? Or perhaps they have left the group altogether!

The Johannine disciples who are named share a common trait. They have each revealed their doubts about their relationship with Jesus: Peter, by his denial; Thomas, by his demand for physical proof; and Nathanael, by his doubt that "good" could come out of Nazareth. At the same time, each has also offered an explicit confession of faith: Peter, of Jesus as the "Holy One of God" (6:69);

---

7. Ellis (1984, 298–299).

Thomas, "My Lord and my God" (20:28); and Nathanael, "You are the Son of God, the king of Israel" (1:49). Finally, each has had his "confession" followed by a rhetorical question by Jesus that expressed his own doubts about the depth of the disciple's commitment (6:70; 20:29; 1:50). No other characters in the fourth gospel share this similar pattern of relationship with Jesus.[8] By naming these and only these familiar characters, the narrator reminds us that the relationship of faith is a combination of belief and doubt, courage and cowardice. Our expectations may be aroused that the story will also include this theme.

But why the "sons of Zebedee," who otherwise have not been seen in this gospel? Their individual names found in the synoptics, James and John, are not given but have led many commentators since ancient times to suggest that this late connection is a way of signaling that John, son of Zebedee, was the author of the text. If this was the case, the narrator has certainly conveyed the possibility in an oblique manner, for the sons are not again mentioned in the chapter!

We can only speculate about how broadly the particular synoptic traditions about the brothers were known. But to the extent that they represent leaders in the apostolic churches whom even Paul grudgingly and somewhat sarcastically acknowledged as "pillars" (Gal 2:9), they help balance the presence in this scene of Johannine community symbols (Thomas and Nathanael) with apostolic church symbols, linked by Peter and the two unnamed "others."

The introduction of the scene differs from most earlier settings in having so many named characters on the stage simultaneously. But as we will see momentarily, the briefly differentiated individuals quickly merge back into the homogeneous "disciples."

Verse 3 opens the action: "Simon Peter said to them, 'I am going to fish [*alieuein*].'" It is the only time in the fourth gospel that "fish" is used as a verb. Did the Johannine community know of the tradition of Peter the Fisherman, whom Matthew's and Mark's Jesus describes — together with his brother Andrew — as a "fisher of people" (Mt 4:19; Mk 1:17)? What eventually became the symbol for the bishop of Rome began as a much broader image for Christian faith in general and mission in particular. Early Christian art bore both general fish images as well as the more specific "ICHThYS," based on the Greek, *Iesous Christos, Huois tou Theou, Soter*, Jesus Christ, Son of God, Savior.[9] As we have seen, this acrostic pun would be very much at home in the Johannine community. While we can reach no clear conclusion, it is certainly not impossible that the one known widely as a "pillar" would be considered one of the prime fishers. Thus, Peter's opening declaration could be seen as a statement of missionary intention: he is on his way to begin the task of witnessing to the world.

---

8. Martha's pattern in chapter 11 is somewhat like these in including a "confession" ("You are the messiah, the Son of God, the one coming into the world" [11:27] — two out of three parts of which conform exactly to the narrator's stated goal of the gospel) and a "doubt" ("If you had been here..." [11:21]), but the rhetorical question is placed in another part of the story ("Didn't I tell you that if you believe...?" [11:40]).

9. Chadwick (1967, 277–279).

Or is he? At the same time, Peter's statement could easily be read as suggesting that he has not yet understood what it means to follow Jesus. As Raymond Brown points out, the infinitive form of the verb "to fish" might well connote going back to the old way of life, along the familiar Sea of Tiberias where Peter is said to be from.[10] This is the tension that the narrator's giving away of the eventuality of Jesus' appearance replaces: Is Peter about the task of discipleship or has he, like so many others, gone "back into the things behind" (6:66; 18:6; cf. 20:14)?

As this suspenseful issue is set up, the others, speaking as one, respond: "We are coming with you, too." Whether about mission or avocation, the Galilean group is of one mind, with Peter in the lead.

The narrator continues the story at the end of verse 3: "They went out [*exēlthen*] and got into [*enebēsan*] the boat [*ploion*], and in that night, they caught [*epiasan*] nothing." The familiar symbolism of the boat — the second link with chapter 6 — continues the ambiguous nature of Peter's goal, as the boat is equally representative of both the prosaic occupation and the Christian community itself. But when we are told that the fishing trip is at *night,* faithful readers of the fourth gospel should begin to get suspicious. To paraphrase Nathanael, can anything good come at night in John? Indeed, the answer is immediate, as we are informed that they "caught nothing."

The word for "caught," *epiasan,* is an unusual one to describe fishing or hunting.[11] It has been used six times previously in the narrative, always for the attempts to "arrest" Jesus (7:30, 32, 44; 8:20; 10:39; 11:57). Are the night fishers trying to "catch" Jesus on the lake? Or has the meaning of *epiasan* been extended to refer to catching new members for the Johannine community? At this point, we can be sure of one thing: at least the *narrator* has bigger fish to gather in than those hiding in the dark waters of Tiberias!

Verse 4 takes this grim failure and immediately injects a ray of hope: "It was coming to be [*ginomenēs*] morning." The new description links images from the prologue and the first resurrection story. The "coming to be" of the new light recalls both Genesis and the beginning of the fourth gospel: the approach of newness into the chaotic confusion of the dark waters of night. And as Mary Magdalene's visit to the tomb was "early while still dark" (*prōi skotias eti*), so the empty-handed disciples find morning (*prōias*) coming out of the night.

Given this setting, we should not be too surprised as the narrator continues: "Jesus stood on the beach, but, of course, the disciples had not known that it is Jesus." The first contrast with the chapter 6 water appearance is given here. There, Jesus appeared on the sea itself; now he is on the shore. Their previous offer to take him into the boat (6:21) — that is, to bring him into their community — makes no sense here, for his presence on dry land obviates the need to "protect" him by getting him off the sea and into the "safety" of the boat.

But in addition to this distinction in Jesus' location, there is the further fact

---

10. R. Brown (1970, 1069).
11. BAG 657.

that they do not recognize him at all. We cannot simply chalk up this difference to the supposed changes in "risen bodies," for the text gives no evidence
whatsoever for such a supposition. Indeed, when Jesus came to them within the
locked doors, they *did* recognize him! The narrator's "of course" must be based
not on imagined physical difficulties but on the expectable *disbelief* that Jesus
is once again present. Despite the earlier appearances to the disciples in Jerusalem, they are now back in Galilee, fishing at night. The "of course" underscores
the difference between the narrator's perspective — which is implicitly the same
as that of readers — and that of the disciples. They are now to be seen as about
the ordinary task of catching ordinary fish, while the narrator has suggested that
they *should be* about the extraordinary task of catching people.

The unknown one along the beach now speaks to this misguided bunch in
verse 5: "Little children [*paidia*], you do not have anything to eat, do you?"
Jesus addresses the fishing crew in a way not previously used for the disciples
but found in describing the child of the *basilikos* (4:49) and the child of the
woman in labor (16:21). It is found in 1 John as an address to the writer's
audience (1 Jn 2:14, 18), though, suggesting that it is the proper title for the
members of the community after the resurrection. Its basic meaning is distinct
from *teknon* (1:12; 8:39; 11:52) in that *paidion* refers to immaturity of age or
development, while *teknon* largely connotes the sense of progeny.[12] Thus, Jesus
is speaking to the group not in the sense of "children of God" but in the sense
of those recently born and not yet capable of full understanding. But it is an
affectionate, not a critical, title and introduces Jesus to the scene with positive
regard for those in the boat.

His question to them is stated in terms of their own understanding: they are
failing to take care of their own basic needs. They answer simply and directly,
"no." Whoever they might imagine the stranger on the beach to be is not described, but they are willing to share their despair with him, perhaps in the hope
that he can help. And indeed, in verse 6, he does: "He said to them, 'Cast the net
into the right side of the boat, and you will find some.' " The invitation marks
another contrast with chapter 6, as the imagery shifts from boat/night/water to
eat/fish: on the first occasion, Jesus created the meal for them without their help
(6:11). Now, he offers assistance, but the basic job is up to them to perform.

The specification of the "right side" is consistent generally with the positive
biblical evaluation (along with that of most of the ancient world) of right-ness.
God is described numerous times as acting with the "right hand." But the particular image of being on the right of the receiver of God's invitation fits that
of Ps 109:31: "For he stands at the right hand of the needy, to save them from
those who would condemn them to death."

The narrator goes on to describe the disciples' trusting response to the
stranger's command: "Therefore, they cast, and they were not yet strong enough
to draw [*helkysai*] it in, because of the multitude [*plēthous*] of fish [*ichthyōn*]."
The narrator builds suspense by describing first the disciples' lack of strength,

---

12. A. Oepke, *TDNT* 5:636–640.

then following with the reason for the need for such power. Their inability "to draw" recalls the word of Jesus, "When I am lifted up from the earth, I will draw [*helkyso*] all people to myself" (12:32). Jesus — and, ultimately, the Father (6:44) — does the true drawing, but after the resurrection, it will be accomplished through the vehicle of those who have been sent to continue his work. But they are still "little children" and do not yet have the strength to carry out this aspect of their discipleship.

It is a bountiful harvest, just as Jesus had told them it would be, using the farming metaphor (4:35). The term *plēthous*, used to describe the multitude of fish in the net, was used earlier only to refer to the "multitude of sick, blind, lame, and withered ones" waiting at the Bethzatha pool for healing (5:3). *Helkysai* and *plēthous* underscore the metaphorical quality of the scene, a verbal perspective available once again to readers but not to the characters in the story. The suffering masses in need of salvation are waiting just outside the community, available for initiation as soon as the disciples can muster the strength to draw them in.

Amidst this poignant scene of desire among the weak for food, the narrator narrows the focus in verse 7 down to the question of the stranger's identity and those who claim to know it: "Therefore, the disciple whom Jesus loved said to Peter, 'It is the Lord!'" For the first time since the race to the tomb began, the two key disciples are found together. The narrator springs on us the identity of one of the two "other disciples" noted in verse 2 — unless we see the Beloved Disciple as the unnamed John, son of Zebedee. Whether son of Zebedee or simply "other," the Beloved Disciple is the one to recognize the one who has guided them to the full net.

It is a Johannine version of the Lukan story of the road to Emmaus: as the latter characters came to know Jesus in "the breaking of the bread" (Lk 24:35), so the Johannine disciples come to know Jesus in the drawing of the fish. Having already found Jesus present in the community's gatherings (20:19, 26), the time has come to find him also present in the discipleship mission. This is the key element of faith that the disciples still needed to learn to grow out of being little children. Even in the insecurity and darkness of life outside the locked doors, Jesus would continue to be present as they carried out his commandments. It is the first lesson of chapter 21, one without which the gospel would remain incomplete.

Upon hearing the proclamation of the Beloved Disciple, the still impetuous Peter leaps into action: "Simon Peter, therefore, having heard 'It is the Lord!' girded [*diezōsato*] himself with his cloak, for he was naked, and threw [*ebalen*] himself into the sea." It is an incredibly comic and yet poignant scene, as the one who was going to fish now throws himself into the water. It is both suicidal and baptismal, as the fisherman takes the final plunge into the dark sea.

Many commentators have struggled with what on its face seems an absurd aspect of the scene: Why would a "naked" man tie on his cloak before jumping in for a swim? Is it a question of modesty? Does "naked" not really mean without clothes? To avoid getting caught in this trap, we should note that the verb *diazōnnymi,* to gird, was used previously by the narrator in a crucial symbolic setting. In preparing to wash his disciples' feet, Jesus "girded [*diezōsen*] himself" with a towel, a detail the narrator repeated in the next verse (13:4, 5). As we saw, the footwashing episode reflected a symbolic/ritual way to convey the need for the Johannine community to prepare each other to face death by being intimate with one another. Now, the issue of intimacy shifts its symbolic attachment from feet (which Peter resisted allowing Jesus to wash) to nakedness itself (which Peter covers by girding himself). When Jesus had convinced Peter that failure to allow his feet to be washed would mean disinheritance, Peter went overboard by asking to have his hands and head washed as well. Jesus rejected the need for that, as Peter had already been made "clean." But now, after Peter's swordplay in the garden, his denial of Jesus, his walking away from the tomb without understanding, and his return to his old fishing pursuits, he feels the need for cleansing once more. He goes overboard again, succeeding in getting his head, hands, and feet immersed in the water.

The others do not have this trait of impetuosity, and the narrator tells us in verse 8 that "they came in the little boat [*ploiarion*], for they were not far from land, only about three hundred yards, dragging the net of fish [*ichthyōn*]." The description of their craft as a "little boat" recalls the same distinction in chapter 6, where the disciples' boat was first a *ploion* and then a *ploiarion* (6:17–23). Here, the distinction may symbolize the community with and without Peter's presence. That is, the "boat" is the larger church, including the apostolic communities, while the "little boat" is the Johannine community itself, apart from the other communities.

At the level of plot, the difference between Peter's response and that of the group in the boat is substantial. Peter forgets the mission altogether and goes after the one who stands on the shore. The others, though, keep their eyes on the prize and, despite their inability to "draw" the net into the boat, do manage to drag it to dry land. The image is perhaps not unlike Moses dragging the reluctant but in need of salvation ex-slaves through the parted Red Sea, to the safety of dry land (Ex 14:11–33). Having escaped Egypt, they are no longer captives but are not yet God's people either. Similarly, those caught in the net are now "safe" (although not if one is a fish!) but still remain uninitiated into the community.

In verse 9, their closure of their fishing expedition is narrated with fitting symmetry: "Therefore, they got out [*apebēsan*] onto the land." As verse 3 noted that they "got in" (*enebēsan*) the boat, now they get out. Their nighttime fishing adventure has been converted from an experience of nighttime emptiness into morning bounty.

But the narrator springs a surprise after this prosaic introduction: "They saw a charcoal fire [*anthrakian*] and fish [*opsarion*] lying on it, and bread." Although their nets are still full, a meal has already been prepared. The source of heat is an *anthrakian,* precisely the source of heat that Peter stood around warming himself while Jesus faced the high priest's questions (18:18; not used elsewhere in the New Testament). Will Peter come up from the waters to be given another fireside chance? Once again, the "earthly" sense of the disciples' hunger is subverted to the "heavenly" issues upon which the gospel has turned all along.

Also, the narrator has suddenly switched words for "fish," from *ichthys* in verses 6 and 8 to *opsarion* here. As was noted about the ancient symbolic link between Christianity and the *ichthys,* so the use of that word in describing the catch would underline the sense of gathering in new community members. But now *opsarion* focuses on the physical edibility of fish, as its usage did in 6:9, 11. As the "b" part of the chiasm emphasized fish as the fruit of mission, now the "b¹" section emphasizes fish as community meal.

The bread is thrown in at the end of the sentence, almost as an afterthought. But it serves, as Staley has pointed out, to develop the differing emphases in the meals in chapters 6 and 21.[13] In the first meal, bread was the focus, and fish the add-on (only bread is gathered in the baskets). Now, fish is the focus, and bread the add-on.

The already prepared meal comes with an element of mystery. Has Jesus himself set up this fire and food? If so, the narrator does not say so directly. It simply *is,* awaiting the presence of the disciples. In verse 10, the narrator moves on to tell us of Jesus' next command: "Bring some of the fish [*opsarion*] which you just caught." If there is already fish on the fire, why the command to bring more? Is it a matter of joining those brought to the community by the disciples with those already gathered by Jesus? This interpretation would fit the harvest parable's relationship with the Samaritans brought to faith by their direct experience of Jesus. What he has begun will grow by the ongoing work of the community.

Verse 11 returns our attention to the entire chiasm's primary focus on one disciple: "Therefore, Simon Peter went up and drew the net full of great fish [*megalōn ichthyōn*] onto the land, 153 of them. And although there were so many, the net was not split [*eschisthē*]." All the symbols of the narrative come together in this single verse. The net dragged to shore by the others is drawn up by one man. The strength that they seemed to lack together is found present in this single individual. For a Johannine community centered so clearly on leadership grounded in the guidance of the paraclete, it is a remarkable concession to the role of Peter and the apostolic churches he represents. This strength is underscored by the description of the fish as "great," an adjective not provided in the initial mention of the catch.

The mysteriously specific number of fish given remains completely baffling to readers of the fourth gospel. Imaginations have not failed in attempting to give meaning to a number that certainly was not put in by accident, and yet none of the suggestions is persuasive. Whatever meaning 153 had to the Johannine community, its symbolism is simply lost to us, despite the creative attempts to associate it with the number of known species of fish, numerological relationships among various Johannine and other Christian words, and so on. It does,

---

13. Staley (1988, 68 n. 47).

however, seem to suggest a potentially universal Christian community, one that has room and strength for all who may be drawn into its net.

Regardless of the specifics of 153, it is clear that the narrator is conveying the message that an almost unimaginably huge number of fish have been caught, and yet the net did not split. To the first followers of Jesus, the experience of the explosion of faith commitment throughout the Mediterranean to a person crucified and risen must have been awesome and energizing. By the time of the Johannine community two generations after Jesus, discipleship communities had sprung to life in great numbers, despite persecution and repression. And yet as Acts, 1 John, and Paul's letters show, all was not easy harmony among the various communities. There was no wider agreement about what it meant to follow Jesus then than there is now. To assure the Johannine community that the net would not "split" was a powerful promise that in the midst of adversity, argument, and antipathy, Jesus continued to challenge his disciples to remain united in their battle against the world of darkness. And, for the first time in the fourth gospel, there is a hint that this unity will be shored up by the strong leadership of Peter.

With the full net drawn up onto the land, Jesus issues another invitation in verse 12: "Have your breakfast [*aristēsate*]." Although the verb *aristaō* otherwise connotes the eating of the main meal of the day (e.g., Lk 11:37),[14] it is clear that this meal is the morning one. It is thus in contrast with the community's evening meal (*deipnou,* 12:2; 13:3), at which the theme was preparation for death. The time for death has given way to the time for life, darkness to new light.[15] This is the meal that begins the discipleship journey into the world.

The narrator then follows with an odd interjection: "No one of the disciples was daring to seek [*exetasai*] him out by asking, 'Who are you?' having known that it is the Lord." Given the Beloved Disciple's proclamation and Peter's plunge, we would be surprised if they *did* ask "Who are you?" But the narrator's emphasis is on their simultaneous lack of courage *and* knowledge. They do not withhold their question simply because they have no *need* to ask but because they do not *dare* to ask. The term *exetasai* is not found elsewhere in the fourth gospel and is thus distinct from the two words used repeatedly in the Last Supper discourse for "asking," *erōtaō* and *aiteō*. It bears the connotation of interrogation, something these awe-struck disciples are not about to do at this moment.

Despite the invitation to their meal, the disciples remain paralyzed. Thus, in verse 13, Jesus acts once more: "Jesus is coming and is taking the bread and is giving it to them, and the fish [*opsarion*] likewise." The present tense again brings the scene into the life of readers, who are similarly invited to partake of this meal. Surprisingly, the bread returns to the center of the meal. The wording

---

14. BAG 106.

15. It is interesting that the meal in chapter 6 is not specified, although it is clearly daytime, probably to be thought of as afternoon.

is very close to that of 6:11, the previous narration of Jesus' giving of bread and fish to the people. The subordination of the fish to the bread here allows the text to highlight the parallel aspects of the meals over their differences. It is really the same sharing, that which is Jesus' flesh, the eucharist that marks the community's commitment to Jesus and to each other. Those who have been gathered together as the children of God are to continue to gain strength from this banquet, which is paradoxically both a cause of suffering and a comfort in the face of suffering.

The narrator closes the chiasm with an unusual enumeration in verse 14: "This was already the third time Jesus was revealed to the disciples, having been raised from the dead." It recalls the counting of the signs in 4:54, which stopped with the second one in Cana of Galilee. This seaside experience is marked as the third revelation to the disciples. By doing so, it adds another stitch to the unity of 20:18–21:25, keeping the appearance to Mary Magdalene in a privileged category by itself.

## 3. THE SHEPHERD AND THE WITNESS CONTINUE TOGETHER

**Chiasm: 21:15–25**

a: 15–17: Peter's function as shepherd

  b: 18–19: follow me; death

    c: 20: Peter turned and saw Beloved Disciple

  b¹: 21–23: follow me; die

a¹: 24–25: Beloved Disciple's function as witness[16]

Having appeared to break the consistency of Johannine egalitarianism in favor of the strength of Peter, the fourth gospel has one more task remaining: to answer as clearly as possible the question of the relationship between the apostolic churches (Peter) and the Johannine community (Beloved Disciple). Is the church's mission in the end to be carried out by the brute strength that can carry an overflowing net onto land? Has the love commandment finally been replaced by the "practical" ability to make a big haul? In other words, will the emerging hierarchical and patriarchal control of the church subvert the Johannine theology of self-sacrificing love?

To see how the second part of the scene at the sea works, it is best to introduce the initial dialogue between Jesus and Peter schematically, comparing the precise wording of questions and answers.

---

16. Ellis (1984, 303–304).

| narrator | Jesus | Peter |
|---|---|---|
| Therefore, when they had breakfasted, Jesus said to Simon Peter: | Simon, son of John, do you love [*agapas*] me more than these? | |
| He said to him, | | Yes, Lord, you know [*oidas*] I am friendly [*philō*] for you. |
| He said to him, | Feed my lambs [*boske ta arnia mou*]. | |
| He said to him again a second time: | Simon, son of John, do you love [*agapas*] me? | |
| He said to him, | | Yes, Lord, you know [*oidas*] I am friendly [*philō*] for you. |
| He said to him, | Shepherd my sheep [*poimaine ta probatia mou*]. | |
| He said to him a third time: | Simon, son of John, are you friendly [*phileis*] for me? | |
| Peter was grieved [*elypethē*] because he said to him the third time, "Are you friendly [*phileis*] for me?" and he said to him, | | |
| Lord, you know [*oidas*] all things [*panta*]. You know [*ginōskeis*] that I am friendly [*philō*] for you. | | |
| He said to him, | Feed my sheep [*boske ta probatia mou*]. | |

In what sometimes comes out in translation as a meaningless threefold repetition of the same question that understandably leads Peter to be hurt, several things are going on simultaneously if we take a closer look. First, Jesus twice asks Peter in terms of *agapas* and gets answers in terms of *phileō*. Each time, Jesus responds with a different variation on the command that follows. Twice Peter is to feed, once each for lambs and sheep. Once Peter is to shepherd, only used with sheep. The final question is in terms of *phileis,* which Peter answers the same way as his first two responses. Also, Peter twice states his awareness of Jesus' knowledge with *oidas,* but the last time he uses *ginōskeis.* The narrator, meanwhile, plays simple connector of the dialogue, until the very end. Then, the narrator leaps in both to name Peter's feelings and to tell us why Peter feels as he does: because Jesus has allegedly asked three times about Peter's *phileis.* But as we have just seen, the narrator's own telling of the story shows a significant change in the question on the third asking. What is going on? Has our reliable narrator suddenly crossed us up at the very end?

Many readers have avoided the problem by taking the "easy" way out, suggesting that there is no meaningful difference in the *agapē/phileō* and *oida/ginōskō* contrasts, thus confirming the narrator's apparent viewpoint. But this is hardly credible, given how carefully the text has been crafted. Why in this highly stylized interaction would the writer develop a mixed word usage just for the sake of variety? Why, given the centrality of both love and knowledge in the gospel's theology of discipleship, would such a change be made in word usage without there being an important reason?

From our narrative perspective, we find the differences to be part of the lesson that this passage is told to teach. Each speaker has a different perception of what is transpiring and thus finds himself disappointed at the end, but for different reasons. Peter hears the same question repeated three times — which is what the narrator tells us at the end — and is hurt because Jesus has embarrassed him in front of the others by not accepting the answer he got. For Peter — and for many commentators who end up sharing his viewpoint — there is indeed no difference between *agapē* and *phileō.* Friendship, self-sacrificing love, it's all about the same thing, isn't it? Just two different ways of saying the same thing, right, Jesus? The powerful invitation to lay down their lives for one another that is intended as the heart of the Johannine commitment is reduced by Peter to the commitment of an ordinary fraternity! Thus, Peter states his belief in Jesus' knowledge of all things, but there is an element of anger that wants to reduce Jesus from knowledge that is intimacy to knowledge that is intellectual. The *oida/ginōskō* distinction has not functioned in the gospel as sharply as has the *agupē/phileō* contrast, but *in Peter's mind,* it is a stab at the Lord that comes from what the narrator describes as his "suffering."

From Jesus' perspective, on the other hand, the initial question has not been answered clearly and thus requires repetition. Peter answers both "yes" and then changes Jesus' word, indicating that Peter thinks he is answering the question but that Jesus can hear that he is not. Jesus asks a second time to make sure that Peter heard correctly: "Do you *agapas* me?" Having gotten the same response, Jesus then reduces the question to a demand that Peter *can* hear. In other words, finding Peter incapable at this moment of *agapē,* Jesus settles for *phileō.*

At the same time, Jesus makes explicit the demands on this strong leader of the community. He is to feed and to shepherd, to provide nourishment as Jesus has done through word and eucharist, and to exercise the self-sacrificing guidance that marks the good shepherd (10:15). If Peter cannot understand the question in terms of his relationship with Jesus, perhaps he can get it through his relationship with Jesus' sheep. The phrase "feed my sheep" (*boske ta probatia*) recalls the Ezekiel passage underlying the good shepherd discourse in chapter 10 (Ezek 34:15, LXX: *boskēsō ta probata*), indicating that Jesus is challenging Peter to accept the same divinely empowered leadership that Jesus has been exercising during his ministry.

The alternation between lambs and sheep also brings to mind the dual role of the disciples. They are both like Jesus, the Lamb of God, who will be sacrificed for the sake of the people, but are also those who follow, like the sheep Jesus leads. Peter's leadership involves both functions. He is to help those who are led to slaughter and to put his own welfare behind theirs in watching out for them. Clearly, this shepherding does not mean preventing their deaths but rather preventing their being ensnared by false shepherds, those who would lure them either back to the synagogue or to other improper places of "pasture."

This threefold exchange is also, of course, the symmetrical atonement for Peter's threefold denial, as the charcoal-fire setting suggests. Despite Peter's brash offer at the supper to lay down his life for his master, the pressure of real-life circumstances led him instead to deny being a disciple at all. Now, when Jesus asks if he is ready to make the commitment given all that the fisherman has experienced since that first fireside, Peter unconsciously reveals that he still does not really understand the implications of "loving" Jesus. But despite these limitations, Jesus does command him to perform the crucial community leadership functions of feeding and shepherding.

For the Johannine community, it expresses their ambivalence about the apostolic churches. In the end, they accepted the tradition that puts authority in the hands of the Petrine descendants, but not without pointing out that the one on whom those communities based their power did not really grasp the message of discipleship.

But as Jesus had predicted Peter's denial, he follows up this threefold affirmation with another prediction in verse 18, spoken as a poetic parallel:

> Amen, amen I am saying to you:
> when you were younger, you girded yourself and walked
>      where you willed.
> But when you grow old, you will stretch out your hands,
>      and another will gird you
> and take you where you are not willing.

When Peter predicted his sacrificial loyalty, Jesus responded with a double-amen saying refuting his claim (13:38). Now, ironically, when Peter can only acknowledge *phileō* for Jesus, the master responds with another double-amen saying, this time predicting that Peter will in fact lose his life over his commitment to Jesus. But the parallel contains its own grain of ambiguity. When Jesus spoke of his own call to lay down his life, he emphasized his own willingness to participate in that sign of love (10:18). Peter will eventually lose his life over Jesus — but he will do it *unwillingly.* The actual historical circumstances of Peter's martyrdom, other than its probable location in Rome and date of the late 50s, are lost to us. But for the Johannine community, which obviously was familiar with the tradition of Peter's crucifixion (upside-down, according to legend), the bare fact of Roman execution does not express Peter's complete commitment to Johannine discipleship. Jesus' statement subtly reminds us that the issue for the Johannine community was not the *fact* of dying but the *willingness* to lay down one's life.

Jesus' speech in terms of Peter's "girding" provides an ironic contrast with his having girded himself to jump into the sea. Now we can hear that the narrator's choice of words has linked Peter's baptismal death and his eventual martyrdom. The fisherman who has, for better or worse, been in charge of his own destiny throughout the narrative will, in the end, find his fate determined by another. Is this "another" simply the Romans or is it God, whose will Peter will never completely accept? The text leaves this crucial question open, allowing the Johannine community to continue pondering the character of the one whom Jesus has commissioned as their shepherd.

In verse 19, the narrator appears to speak to those in the audience who are not familiar with this tradition about Peter: "He said this to signify by what sort of death he would glorify God." The sentence is virtually identical to the narrator's commentary on Jesus' words about his *own* death (12:33, 18:32). Thus, despite the ambiguous note about Peter's will, the narrator offers the seal of approval to Peter's future, which binds his fate to that of Jesus. His death, like the Lord's, will be for the glory of God, for regardless of his mixed intentions, the world will see it as a sign of his ultimate commitment to the way of Jesus.

After this narrative explanation, Jesus offers one final word to Peter's commission: "And having said this, he said to him, 'Follow me.'" With this simple call to discipleship, we may notice that it is the only time in the fourth gospel that Jesus has actually invited Peter to follow! As we return to the first discipleship call stories, we find that Jesus named Simon "Cephas" but did not invite his following (1:42). The omission is in stark contrast with the next verse's call to Philip, to whom Jesus *does* say, "Follow me." In addition, we remember that when Peter asked at the supper where Jesus was going, the answer was: "Where I am going you are not able to follow me now; but later, you will follow" (13:36). Before Peter could receive this invitation, he needed to experience all that has unfolded in the gospel. The writer, in a beautiful act of creative molding of the tradition, has saved this call of Simon until the last possible moment.

With this apparent completion of the Peter theme, which has occupied the entire chapter, the narrator has but one remaining task. Verse 20 introduces the issue: "Having turned around [*epistrapheis*], Peter looked at the disciple whom Jesus loved following, the one who at the supper leaned against his breast and said, 'Lord, who is the one betraying you?'" Peter's turning matches Mary Magdalene's turning in 20:14, 16. It also contrasts expressly with 12:40, where the narrator's summary of the first half of the gospel quoted Isaiah's sarcastic plaint about the inability of the leaders to open their eyes and their hearts, "lest they should turn around [*straphōsin*] and be healed." With the call to follow, the process of Peter's conversion begins in earnest.

But in the same movement, Peter sees the Beloved Disciple, of whom the narrator reminds us in great detail. The full-bore recall statement offers several sharp contrasts for the readers: the earlier supper with the current breakfast, the Beloved Disciple's intimacy with Jesus and Peter's *phileō,* and the Beloved Disciple's innocent question about the betrayer and Peter's own recent betrayal. Despite the ambivalent description of the Beloved Disciple at the empty tomb, the narrator recalls his high point in the story to emphasize the virtue of the one on whose faith the Johannine community is founded.

Having seen the Beloved Disciple, Peter asks Jesus one final question: "Lord, what about this one?" It is both a simple and a loaded inquiry. With Peter's commissioning, *he* is now the one at the side of the Lord. The Beloved Disciple is visible at an unspecified distance but apparently out of earshot for Peter and Jesus. And despite the narrator's description of this one as the one Jesus loved, it is Peter whose martyrdom has been predicted. Peter's question is a matter both of ordinary curiosity and apostolic jealousy. From a social perspective, it reads: if ultimate ecclesial authority lies with the martyred Peter and his successors, what about the Johannine community? What is Jesus' will for this different band of disciples?

Jesus' response in verse 22 is sharp and to the point: "If it is my will that he is to remain [*menein*] until I come, what is it to you? You follow me!" The implications are several. First, we hear for the first time the suggestion that Jesus' will for Peter and for the Beloved Disciple are different. Peter is to die a glorious death at the will of another, while the Beloved Disciple is to "remain" until Jesus comes again. Remaining with Jesus has been a theme throughout the gospel, from the first discipleship call (1:39), through the mission to Samaria (4:40), to the vine and branches discourse (15:4–10). As Peter is to incarnate the laying down of life, the Beloved Disciple will model remaining in Jesus' love. It is not for Peter to implicitly claim greater authority because Jesus' will for them is different. His job is simply to understand God's will for him and to live it out with faithful love.

And yet both the apostolic churches and the Johannine community shared one major experience: the execution of their members on behalf of Jesus. The emphasis throughout the Last Supper discourse on the challenge to the disciples to love one another as Jesus has loved them would be pointless without their present undergoing of this fate within the community.

Verse 23 reveals the other social issue underlying Peter's question, withheld from our awareness until now: "Therefore, this word went out among the brothers: that this disciple would not die. But Jesus did not say, 'He will not die,' but, 'If it is my will that he is to remain until I come, what is it to you?' " The Beloved Disciple apparently was not martyred, and at least some people based this on the spurious tradition that Jesus had predicted a unique fate for him that escaped death. And it is among the "brothers" that this word has gone out, that group that has earlier exhibited a lack of faith and to whom Jesus sent the message with Mary Magdalene (20:17). It is not among the *disciples* that this word has spread, though. The Johannine community was itself clear on the word of Jesus, which is repeated verbatim by the narrator. But the false rumor was apparently quite strong and required refuting before the narrative could come to a close.

At the same time, the narrator's explanation defends the integrity of the Johannine community's founder. If, according to this story, love is exhibited by laying down one's life for one's friends *and* the Beloved Disciple did not do so, should his witness be trusted at all? Further, for a community encouraging new members to make a commitment to this sort of love relationship, how could they explain the "failure" of their founder to model this behavior? The narrator's precise repetition of Jesus' word emphasizes that remaining in Jesus' love was not a matter of following a law mandating martyrdom but of bonding one's will to that of Jesus and accepting in faith whatever fate might befall one. This was an important assurance also for those in the community who experienced some of their members dying while others "remained." In the apostolic church, there were many who saw martyrdom as the "proof" of one's discipleship. But for the Johannine community, it is love's willingness to die, not death itself, that marked one as a follower of Jesus.

Having resolved these last questions, the narrator has truly come to the close of the story. In a manner fitting both with Johannine ideology and the growing practice of late first-century and early second-century literary works, the authenticity of the gospel is assured in verse 24: "This is the disciple who is witnessing about these things [*tauta*], and the one having written these things [*tauta*], and we have known that his witness is true." The fact that we have been assuming all along is made explicit: the Beloved Disciple is both the source *and* the writer of the fourth gospel. The double summary use of *tauta* underscores the intimate relationship between the things of the Beloved Disciple and the things of Jesus.

And yet the *narrator* is clearly not the Beloved Disciple, for the verse speaks in the plural of those who know *about* the truth of the Beloved Disciple's witness. Thus, the gospel is ultimately the *community's* story, not just that of the Beloved Disciple. What began as a tradition handed down by one who believed by seeing is claimed by a community that believes and seeks the faith commitment of those who have *not* seen. Jesus did ultimately come to take the Beloved Disciple to his Father's house, but not leaving the Johannine community orphans. They continue to witness to the truth that they have been taught by the paraclete who both advocates for them before the world and comforts them in their grieving. And they continue to challenge readers of their story to make the commitment to the one sent by God, and to have life in his name.

The final verse concludes the narrative on its last ironic note, one that challenges all commentators to laugh at their own efforts: "There are also many other things which Jesus did, which, if they were ever written down, I suppose the world itself could not contain the books being written." As chapter 20 ended with the reminder that the author has chosen among many signs that remain unnarrated, so the entire gospel closes with the reminder that Jesus also did more things than could ever be told. And continues to do such things, in the lives of those who have been his followers through the centuries. Our efforts to understand them, which inevitably use more words than the gospel itself, are the ultimate irony, for, as Isaiah has said:

> For my thoughts are not your thoughts,
>     nor are your ways my ways, says the Lord.
> As high as the heavens are above the earth,
>     so high are my ways above your ways,
>     and my thoughts above your thoughts.
> For just as from the heavens,
>     the rain and snow come down
> And do not return there
>     till they have watered the earth,
>     making it fertile and fruitful,
> Giving seed to the one who sows,
>     and bread to the one who eats,
> So shall my word be
>     that goes forth from my mouth
> It shall not return to me void,
>     but shall do my will,
>     achieving the end for which I sent it. (Isa 55:8–11)

# Abbreviations

| | |
|---|---|
| BAG | W. Bauer, W. F. Arndt, and F. W. Gingrich, *A Greek-English Lexicon of the New Testament and Other Early Christian Literature* |
| *Bib* | *Biblica* |
| *BibT* | *The Bible Today* |
| *BTB* | *Biblical Theology Bulletin* |
| *BJRL* | *Bulletin of the John Rylands University Library of Manchester* |
| *CBQ* | *Catholic Biblical Quarterly* |
| *CurTM* | *Currents in Theology and Mission* |
| *DR* | *Downside Review* |
| *ETL* | *Ephemerides theologicae lovanienses* |
| *ExpTim* | *Expository Times* |
| *HBD* | P. J. Achtemeier, et al. (eds.), *Harper's Bible Dictionary* |
| *Int* | *Interpretation* |
| *ITQ* | *Irish Theological Quarterly* |
| *JBL* | *Journal of Biblical Literature* |
| *JSNT* | *Journal for the Study of the New Testament* |
| LXX | Septuagint |
| MT | Masoretic Text |
| *NB* | *New Blackfriars* |
| *Neot* | *Neotestamentica* |
| *NovT* | *Novum Testamentum* |
| *NTS* | *New Testament Studies* |

| | |
|---|---|
| *RB* | *Revue biblique* |
| *RevExp* | *Review and Expositor* |
| SBLDS | SBL Dissertation Series |
| SBLMS | SBL Monograph Series |
| SBLSP | SBL Seminary Papers |
| SNTSMS | Society for New Testament Studies Monograph Series |
| *SpT* | *Spirituality Today* |
| *SR* | *Studies in Religion/Sciences religieuses* |
| *SVTQ* | *St. Vladimir's Theological Quarterly* |
| *TDNT* | G. Kittel and G. Friedrich (eds.), *Theological Dictionary of the New Testament* |
| *TTJ* | *Toronto Theological Journal* |
| *TWOT* | *Theological Wordbook of the Old Testament* |
| *ZNW* | *Zeitschrift für die neutestamentliche Wissenschaft* |

# Bibliography

## METHODOLOGY AND HERMENEUTICS

Botha, J. 1992. "The Ethics of New Testament Interpretation." *Neot* 26, no. 1:169–194.

Caputo, John. 1987. *Radical Hermeneutics.* Bloomington: Indiana Univ. Press.

Jobling, David, ct al., eds. 1991. *The Bible and the Politics of Exegesis.* Cleveland: Pilgrim.

Kuhn, Thomas S. 1970. *The Structure of Scientific Revolutions.* Chicago: Univ. of Chicago Press.

Lochhead, David. 1993. "The Liberation of the Bible." In *The Bible and Liberation,* edited by Norman K. Gottwald and Richard A. Horsley, 128–141. Rev. ed. Maryknoll, N.Y.: Orbis Books.

McFague, Sallie. 1982. *Metaphorical Theology.* Philadelphia: Fortress.

McKnight, Edgar. 1988. *Post-Modern Use of the Bible.* Nashville: Abingdon.

Ricoeur, Paul. 1975. *Biblical Hermeneutics.* Missoula, Mont.: Scholars Press.

―――. 1981. *Hermeneutics and the Human Sciences.* Cambridge: Cambridge Univ. Press.

Schüssler Fiorenza, Elisabeth. 1988. "The Ethics of Biblical Interpretation: Decentering Biblical Scholarship." *JBL* 107:3–17.

Segundo, Juan Luis. 1976. *The Liberation of Theology.* Maryknoll, N.Y.: Orbis Books.

Sternberg, Meir. 1985. *The Poetics of Biblical Narrative.* Bloomington: Indiana Univ. Press.

Tracy, David. 1981. *The Analogical Imagination.* New York: Crossroad.

―――. 1987. *Plurality and Ambiguity.* San Francisco: Harper and Row.

## BIBLICAL REFERENCE WORKS

Achtemeier, Paul J., ed. 1985. *Harper's Bible Dictionary.* San Francisco: Harper and Row.

Bauer, Walter, William F. Arndt, and F. Wilbur Gingrich. 1957, 1979. *A Greek-English Lexicon of the New Testament and Other Early Christian Literature.* Chicago: Univ. of Chicago Press.

Harris, R. Laird, Gleason L. Archer, Jr., and Bruce K. Waltke. 1980. *Theological Wordbook of the Old Testament.* 2 vols. Chicago: Moody.

Kittel, Gerhard, and Gerhard Friedrich, eds. 1964–1974. *Theological Dictionary of the New Testament.* 9 vols. Grand Rapids: Eerdmans.


## SOCIAL CONTEXT OF SCRIPTURE


Berger, Peter, and Thomas Luckmann. 1967. *The Social Construction of Reality.* Garden City, N.Y.: Doubleday.
Brown, Raymond E., and John P. Meier. 1983. *Antioch and Rome.* New York: Paulist.
Chadwick, Henry. 1967. *The Early Church.* New York: Penguin.
Girard, René. 1986. *The Scapegoat.* Baltimore: Johns Hopkins Univ. Press.
Gottwald, Norman K., and Richard A. Horsley, eds. 1993. *The Bible and Liberation.* Rev. ed. Maryknoll, N.Y.: Orbis Books.
Horsley, Richard A. 1989. *Sociology and the Jesus Movement.* New York: Crossroad.
Horsley, Richard A., and John S. Hanson. 1985. *Bandits, Prophets, and Messiahs.* San Francisco: Harper and Row.
Jeremias, Joachim. 1969. *Jerusalem in the Time of Jesus.* Philadelphia: Fortress.
Kee, Howard Clark. 1989. *Knowing the Truth: A Sociological Approach to New Testament Interpretation.* Minneapolis: Fortress.
Malherbe, Abraham J. 1983. *Social Aspects of Early Christianity.* Philadelphia: Fortress.
Malina, Bruce J. 1981. *The New Testament World: Insights from Cultural Anthropology.* Atlanta: John Knox.
Meeks, Wayne A. 1983. *The First Urban Christians.* New Haven: Yale Univ. Press.
Neusner, Jacob. 1984. *Judaism in the Beginning of Christianity.* Philadelphia: Fortress.
Neusner, Jacob, et al., eds. 1987. *Judaisms and Their Messiahs.* Cambridge: Cambridge Univ. Press.


## HEBREW SCRIPTURE AND
## OTHER NON–NEW TESTAMENT TEXTS


Bloom, Harold. 1990. *The Book of J.* New York: Grove Weidenfeld.
Brueggemann, Walter. 1978. *The Prophetic Imagination.* Philadelphia: Fortress.
———. 1981. " 'Vine and Fig Tree': A Case Study in Imagination and Criticism." *CBQ* 43:188–204.
———. 1985. *The Hopeful Imagination.* Philadelphia: Fortress.
———. 1988. *Israel's Praise.* Philadelphia: Fortress.
Charlesworth, James M., ed. 1983. *The Old Testament Pseudepigrapha.* Vol. 1. Garden City, N.Y.: Doubleday.
Collins, John J. 1984. *The Apocalyptic Imagination.* New York: Crossroad.
Fishbane, Michael. 1985. *Biblical Interpretation in Ancient Israel.* Oxford: Clarendon.
Friedman, Richard Elliott. 1987. *Who Wrote the Bible?* New York: Harper and Row.
Gottwald, Norman K. 1985. *The Hebrew Bible: A Socioliterary Introduction.* Philadelphia: Fortress.
Hanson, Paul D. 1986. *The People Called: The Growth of Community in the Bible.* San Francisco: Harper and Row.
Holmes, Michael W., ed. 1989. *The Apostolic Fathers.* 2d ed. Grand Rapids: Baker.

Josephus. 1987. *The Works of Josephus.* Translated by William Whiston. Peabody, Mass.: Hendrickson.

Pagels, Elaine. 1979. *The Gnostic Gospels.* New York: Vintage.

Polzin, Robert. 1980. *Moses and the Deuteronomist.* Bloomington: Indiana Univ. Press.

———. 1989. *Samuel and the Deuteronomist.* San Francisco: Harper and Row.

———. 1993. *David and the Deuteronomist.* Bloomington: Indiana Univ. Press.

Robinson, James M., ed. 1978, 1988. *The Nag Hammadi Library in English.* San Francisco: Harper and Row.

Rosenberg, Joel. 1986. *King and Kin· Political Allegory in the Hebrew Bible.* Bloomington: Indiana Univ. Press.

Vermes, Geza. 1987. *The Dead Sea Scrolls in English.* 3d ed. Sheffield, Eng.: JSOT Press.

Yonge, C. D., trans. 1993. *The Works of Philo.* Peabody, MA: Hendrickson.

## LITERARY STUDIES

Alter, Robert. 1981. *The Art of Biblical Narrative.* New York: Basic Books.

Berlin, Adele. 1983. *The Poetics and Interpretation of Biblical Narrative.* Sheffield, Eng.: Almond Press.

Booth, Wayne. 1961. *The Rhetoric of Fiction.* Chicago: Univ. of Chicago Press.

Brown, Schuyler. 1988. "Reader Response: Demythologizing the Text." *NTS* 34:232–237.

Chatman, Seymour B. 1978. *Story and Discourse.* Ithaca, N.Y.: Cornell Univ. Press.

De Boer, M. C. 1992. "Narrative Criticism, Historical Criticism, and the Gospel of John." *JSNT* 47:35–48.

Detweiler, Robert. 1985. "What Is a Sacred Text?" *Semeia* 31:213–228.

Eagleton, Terry. 1983. *Literary Theory: An Introduction.* Minneapolis: Univ. of Minnesota Press.

Fowler, Robert M. 1985. "Who Is 'the Reader' in Reader Response Criticism?" *Semeia* 31:5–23.

Funk, Robert W. 1988. *The Poetics of Biblical Narrative.* Sonoma, Calif.: Polebridge.

Frye, Northrop. 1982. *The Great Code: The Bible and Literature.* New York: Harcourt Brace Jovanovich.

Genette, Gérard. 1980. *Narrative Discourse: An Essay in Method.* Ithaca, N.Y.: Cornell Univ. Press.

Jameson, Frederick. 1981. *The Political Unconscious: Narrative as a Socially Symbolic Act.* Ithaca, N.Y.: Cornell Univ. Press.

Jobling, David. 1990. "Writing the Wrongs of the World: The Deconstruction of the Biblical Text in the Context of Liberation Theologies." *Semeia* 51:81–118.

Kermode, Frank. 1967. *The Sense of an Ending.* Oxford: Oxford Univ. Press.

———. 1979. *The Genesis of Secrecy.* Cambridge, Mass.: Harvard Univ. Press.

Moore, Stephen D. 1989. *Literary Criticism and the Gospels: The Theoretical Challenge.* New Haven: Yale Univ. Press.

Phillips, Gary A. 1990. "Exegesis as Critical Praxis: Reclaiming History and Text from a Postmodern Perspective." *Semeia* 51:7–42.

Rimmon-Kenan, Shlomith, 1983. *Narrative Fiction: Contemporary Poetics.* London: Methuen.

Robinson, Lillian S. 1985. "Treason Our Text: Feminist Challenges to the Literary Canon." In *Critical Theory since 1965,* edited by Hazard Adams and Leroy Searle, 572–585. Tallahassee: Florida State Univ. Press.

White, Hayden. 1986. "Historical Narrative as Literary Artifact." In *Critical Theory since 1965,* edited by Hazard Adams and Leroy Searle, 395–407. Tallahassee: Florida State Univ. Press.


## NON-JOHANNINE NEW TESTAMENT STUDIES

Crosby, Michael H. 1988. *House of Disciples: Church, Economics, and Justice in Matthew.* Maryknoll, N.Y.: Orbis Books.

Koester, Helmut. 1990. *Ancient Christian Gospels.* Philadelphia: Trinity Press International.

Myers, Ched. 1988. *Binding the Strong Man: A Political Reading of Mark's Story of Jesus.* Maryknoll, N.Y.: Orbis Books.

Schüssler Fiorenza, Elisabeth. 1983. *In Memory of Her: A Feminist Reconstruction of Christian Origins.* New York: Crossroad.

———. 1991. *Revelation: Vision of a Just World.* Philadelphia: Fortress.

Wink, Walter. 1984. *Naming the Powers.* Philadelphia: Fortress.

———. 1987. *Unmasking the Powers.* Philadelphia: Fortress.


## JOHANNINE STUDIES

Ashton, John. 1991. *Understanding the Fourth Gospel.* Oxford: Oxford Univ. Press.

Bammel, C. P. 1991. "The Farewell Discourses in Patristic Exegesis." *Neot* 25, no. 2:193–207.

Bassler, Jouette M. 1981. "The Galileans: A Neglected Factor in Johannine Community Research." *CBQ* 43:243–257.

———. 1989. "Mixed Signals: Nicodemus in the Fourth Gospel." *JBL* 108:635–646.

Beutler, Johannes. 1990a. "Greeks Come to See Jesus (John 12.20f)." *Bib* 71:333–347.

———. 1990b. "Response from a European Perspective." *Semeia* 53:191–202.

Borgen, Peder. 1965. *Bread from Heaven.* Leiden: Brill.

———. 1968. "God's Agent in the Fourth Gospel." In *Religions in Antiquity,* 137–148. Leiden: Brill.

Braun, Willi. 1990. "Resisting John: Ambivalent Redactor and Defensive Reader of the Fourth Gospel." *SR* 19:59–71.

Breck, John. 1992. "John 21: Appendix, Epilogue or Conclusion?" *SVTQ* 36:27–49.

Brown, Raymond E. 1966. *The Gospel according to John.* Vol. 1. New York: Doubleday.

———. 1970. *The Gospel according to John.* Vol. 2. New York: Doubleday.

———. 1979. *The Community of the Beloved Disciple.* New York: Paulist.

Bultmann, Rudolf. 1971. *The Gospel of John: A Commentary.* Eng. trans. G. R. Beasley-Murray, et al. Philadelphia: Westminster.

Byrne, Brendan. 1985. "The Faith of the Beloved Disciple and the Community in John 20." *JSNT* 23:83–97.

Cahill, P. Joseph. 1976. "The Johannine *Logos* as Center." *CBQ* 38:54–72.

Carson, D. A. 1979. "The Function of the Paraclete in John 16:7–11." *JBL* 98:547–566.

————. 1991. *The Gospel according to John.* Grand Rapids: Eerdmans.

Carter, Warren. 1990. "The Prologue and John's Gospel: Function, Symbol, and the Definitive Word." *JSNT* 39:35–58.

Cassidy, Richard J. 1992. *John's Gospel in New Perspective.* Maryknoll, N.Y.: Orbis Books.

Charlesworth, James H. 1990. *John and the Dead Sea Scrolls.* New York: Crossroad.

Collins, Raymond F. 1976. "The Representative Figures of the Fourth Gospel." *DR* 94:26–46, 119–132.

————. 1980. "Cana (Jn. 2:1–12) — the First of His Signs or the Key to His Signs?" *ITQ* 47:79–95.

Cook, Cornelia. 1991. " 'I Gotta Use Words When I Talk to You': A Literary Examination of John." *NB* 72:365–376.

Cosgrove, Charles H. 1989. "The Place Where Jesus Is: Allusions to Baptism and the Eucharist in the Fourth Gospel." *NTS* 35:522–539.

Crossan, John Dominic. 1983. "It Is Written: A Structuralist Analysis of John 6." *Semeia* 26:3–22.

Cullmann, Oscar. 1975. *The Johannine Circle.* Philadelphia: Westminster.

Culpepper, R. Alan. 1981. "The Pivot of John's Prologue." *NTS* 27:1–31.

————. 1983. *Anatomy of the Fourth Gospel.* Philadelphia: Fortress.

————. 1988. "The Genius of John: A Compositional Critical Commentary on the Fourth Gospel." *RevExp* 85:349–351.

————. 1990. "The Johannine *Hypodeigma*: A Reading of John 13." *Semeia* 53:132–152.

————. 1993a. "The Gospel of John as a Document of Faith in a Pluralistic Culture." SBLSP. Alpharetta, Ga.: Scholars Press.

————. 1993b. "John 5:1–18 — a Sample of Narrative Critical Commentary." Unpublished article.

De Jonge, Marinus. 1971. "Nicodemus and Jesus: Some Observations on Misunderstanding and Understanding in the Fourth Gospel." *BJRL* 53:337–359.

————. 1972–73. "Jewish Expectations about the 'Messiah' according to the Fourth Gospel." *NTS* 19:246–270.

————. 1973. "Jesus as Prophet and King in the Fourth Gospel." *ETL* 49:160–177.

Dewey, Kim E. 1980. "*Paroimiai* in the Gospel of John." *Semeia* 17:81–99.

Draper, J. A. 1992. "The Sociological Function of the Spirit/Paraclete in the Farewell Discourses in the Fourth Gospel." *Neot* 26, no. 1:13–29.

Droge, Arthur J. 1990. "The Status of Peter in the Fourth Gospel: A Note on John 18:10–11." *JBL* 109:307–311.

Duke, Paul D. 1985. *Irony in the Fourth Gospel.* Atlanta: John Knox.

Dunn, James D. G. 1970. "The Washing of the Disciples' Feet in John 13:1–20." *ZNW* 61:246–252.

DuRand, J. A. 1991. "Perspectives on Johannine Discipleship according to the Farewell Discourses." *Neot* 25, no. 2:311–325.

Ellis, Peter F. 1984. *The Genius of John: A Composition-Critical Commentary on the Fourth Gospel.* Collegeville, Minn.: Liturgical Press.

Evenson, Ardy. 1989. "Mary of Magdala." *BibT* 27:219–223.

Fuller, Reginald. 1977. "The 'Jews' in the Fourth Gospel." *Dialog* 16:31–37.

Giblin, Charles Homer. 1980. "Suggestion, Negative Response, and Positive Action in St. John's Portrayal of Jesus." *NTS* 26:197–211.

————. 1983. "The Miraculous Crossing of the Sea." *NTS* 29:96–103.

————. 1984. "Confrontations in John 18,1–27." *Bib* 65:210–231.

————. 1985. "John's Narration of the Hearing before Pilate." *Bib* 66:221–239.

Gittins, Anthony J. 1990. "Grains of Wheat: Culture, Agriculture, and Spirituality." *SpT* 42:196–208.

Grassi, Joseph A. 1986. "The Role of Jesus' Mother in John's Gospel: A Reappraisal." *CBQ* 48:67–80.

Haenchen, Ernst. 1984. *Gospel of John.* 2 vols. Philadelphia: Fortress.

Harvey, Alan. 1972. *Jesus on Trial: A Study in the Fourth Gospel.* London: SCM.

Hawkin, David J. 1990. "Johannine Christianity and Ideological Commitment." *ExpTim* 102:74–77.

Henaut, Barry W. 1990. "John 4.43–54 and the Ambivalent Narrator: A Response to Culpepper's *Anatomy of the Fourth Gospel.*" *SR* 19:287–304.

Hendricks, O. Obery, Jr. 1992. "An Ideology of Domination: A Socio-Rhetorical Study of IOUDAIOS in the Fourth Gospel." Unpublished manuscript (Princeton, N.J.).

Herzog, Frederick. 1972. *Liberation Theology: Liberation in Light of the Fourth Gospel.* New York: Seabury.

Karris, Robert J. 1990. *Jesus and the Marginalized in John's Gospel.* Collegeville, Minn.: Liturgical Press.

Kelber, Werner H. 1990. "The Birth of a Beginning: John 1:1–18." *Semeia* 51:121–144.

Kermode, Frank. 1986. "St. John as Poet." *JSNT* 28:3–16.

Koester, Craig. 1989. "Hearing, Seeing, and Believing in the Gospel of John." *Bib* 70:327–348.

————. 1990a. "Messianic Exegesis and the Call of Nathanael (John 1:45–51)." *JSNT* 39:23–34.

————. 1990b. " 'The Savior of the World' (John 4:42)." *JBL* 109, no. 4:665–680.

————. 1994. *Symbolism in the Gospel of John: Meaning, Mystery, and Community.* Minneapolis: Fortress.

Koester, Helmut. 1986. "Gnostic Sayings and Controversy Traditions in John 8:12–59." In *Nag Hammadi, Gnosticism and Early Christianity,* Charles W. Hedrick and Robert Hodgson (eds.), 97–110. Peabody, Mass.: Hendrickson.

Kurz, William S. 1989. "The Beloved Disciple and Implied Readers." *BTB* 19:100–107.

Kysar, Robert. 1978. "Christology and Controversy." *CurTM* 5:348–364.

————. 1991. "Johannine Metaphor — Meaning and Function: A Literary Case Study of John 10:1–8." *Semeia* 53:81–111.

————. 1992. "The Gospel of John and Anti-Jewish Polemic." *Explorations* 6:1–4.

Leon-Dufour, Xavier. 1981. "Towards a Symbolic Reading of the Fourth Gospel." *NTS* 27:439–456.

Lieu, J. M. 1988. "Blindness in the Johannine Tradition." *NTS* 34:83–95.

Lindars, Barnabas. 1992. "Rebuking the Spirit: A New Analysis of the Lazarus Story of John 11." *NTS* 38:89–104.

Lombard, H. A., and W. H. Oliver. 1991. "A Working Supper in Jerusalem: John 13:1–38 Introduces Jesus' Farewell Discourses." *Neot* 25, no. 2:357–378.

Lowe, Malcolm. 1976. "Who Were the IOUDAIOI?" *NovT* 18:101–130.

MacRae, George W. 1978. *Invitation to John.* Garden City, N.Y.: Image Books.

————. 1986. "Gnosticism and the Church of John's Gospel." In *Nag Hammadi, Gnosticism and Early Christianity,* Charles W. Hedrick and Robert Hodgson (eds.) 89–96. Peabody, Mass.: Hendrickson.

Malatesta, Edward. 1971. "The Literary Structure of John 17." *Bib* 52:190–214.

Malina, Bruce. 1985. "The Gospel of John in Sociolinguistic Perspective." *Colloquium* 48. Berkeley, Calif.: Center for Hermeneutics Studies.

Martyn, J. L. 1979. *History and Theology in the Fourth Gospel.* 2d ed. Nashville: Abingdon.

Matsunaga, Kikuo. 1981. "Is John's Gospel Anti-Sacramental?" *NTS* 27:516–524.

Maynard, Arthur H. 1984. "The Role of Peter in the Fourth Gospel." *NTS* 30:531–548.

Meeks, Wayne A. 1966. "Galilee and Judea in the Fourth Gospel." *JBL* 85:159–169.

———. 1972. "The Man From Heaven in Johannine Sectarianism." *JBL* 91:44–73.

———. 1976. "The Divine Agent and His Counterfeit in Philo and the Fourth Gospel." In *Aspects of Religious Propaganda in Judaism and Early Christianity,* edited by Elisabeth Schüssler Fiorenza. Notre Dame, Ind.: Notre Dame Univ. Press, 43–67.

Mercer, Calvin. 1990. "*Apostellein* and *Pempein* in John." *NTS* 36:619–624.

Michaels, J. Ramsey. 1990. "John 18.31 and the 'Trial' of Jesus." *NTS* 36:474–479.

Minear, Paul S. 1977. "The Beloved Disciple in the Gospel of John." *NovT* 19:105–123.

———. 1983. "The Original Function of John 21." *JBL* 102:85–98.

———. 1984. *John: The Martyr's Gospel.* New York: Pilgrim.

Miranda, José. 1977. *Being and the Messiah: The Message of St. John.* Maryknoll, N.Y.: Orbis Books.

Mlakuzhyil, George. 1987. *The Christocentric Literary Structure of the Fourth Gospel.* Rome: Analecta Biblia.

Moloney, Francis J. 1990. "Reading John 2:13–22: The Purification of the Temple." *RB* 97:432–452.

———. 1991. "A Sacramental Reading of John 13:1–38." *CBQ* 53:237–256.

———. 1993. *Belief in the Word: Reading John 1–4.* Minneapolis: Fortress.

Neirynck, Frans. 1990. "John 21." *NTS* 36:321–336.

Neyrey, Jerome H. 1979. "Jacob Traditions and the Interpretation of John 4:10–26." *CBQ* 41:419–437.

———. 1987. "Jesus the Judge: Forensic Process in John 8:21–59." *Bib* 68:509–542.

———. 1988. *An Ideology of Revolt: John's Christology in Social-Science Perspective.* Philadelphia: Fortress.

———. 1989. "'I Said You Are Gods': Psalm 82:6 and John 10." *JBL* 108:647–663.

O'Day, Gail R. 1988. *Revelation in the Fourth Gospel.* Philadelphia: Fortress.

———. 1991. "I Have Overcome the World (John 16:33): Narrative Time in John 13–17." *Semeia* 53:153–166.

Oliver, W. H., and A. G. Van Aarde. 1991. "The Community of Faith as Dwelling-Place of the Father." *Neot* 25, no. 2:379–400.

Osiek, Carolyn. 1989. "The 'Liberation Theology' of the Gospel of John." *BibT* 27:210–218.

Painter, John. 1986. "John 9 and the Interpretation of the Fourth Gospel." *JSNT* 28:31–61.

———. 1989a. "Quest and Rejection Stories in John." *JSNT* 36:17–46.

———. 1989b. "Tradition and Interpretation in John 6." *NTS* 35:421–450.

Pamment, Margaret. 1983a. "The Fourth Gospel's Beloved Disciple." *ExpTim* 94:363–367.

———. 1983b. "The Meaning of *doxa* in the Fourth Gospel." *ZNW* 74:12–16.

Pancaro, Severino. 1975. "The Relationship of the Church to Israel in the Gospel of St. John." *NTS* 21:396–405.

Pazdan, Mary Margaret. 1987. "Nicodemus and the Samaritan Woman: Contrasting Models of Discipleship." *BTB* 17:145–148.

Petersen, Norman R. 1993. *The Gospel of John and the Sociology of Light: Language and Characterization in the Fourth Gospel.* Valley Forge, Pa.: Trinity.

Phillips, Gary A. 1983. " 'This Is a Hard Saying. Who Can Be Listener to It?': Creating a Reader in John 6." *Semeia* 26:23–56.

Pryor, John W. 1990. "Jesus and Israel in the Fourth Gospel — John 1:11." *NovT* 32:201–218.

Quast, Kevin B. 1989. "Reexamining Johannine Community." *TTJ* 5:293–295.

Reinhartz, Adele. 1989. "Jesus as Prophet: Predictive Prolepses in the Fourth Gospel." *JSNT* 36:3–16.

———. 1992. *The Word in the World: The Cosmological Tale in the Fourth Gospel.* SBLMS. Atlanta: Scholars Press.

Rensberger, David. 1988. *Johannine Faith and Liberating Community.* Philadelphia: Westminster.

Schenke, Hans-Martin. 1986. "The Function and Background of the Beloved Disciple in the Gospel of John." In *Nag Hammadi, Gnosticism and Early Christianity,* Charles W. Hedrick and Robert Hodgson (eds.), 111–125. Peabody, Mass.: Hendrickson.

Schnackenburg, Rudolf. 1990. *The Gospel according to John.* New York: Crossroad.

Schneiders, Sandra M. 1983. "The Face Veil: A Johannine Sign (John 20:1–10)." *BTB* 13:94–97.

———. 1987. "Death in the Community of Eternal Life: History, Theology and Spirituality in John 11." *Int* 41:44–56.

Segovia, Fernando F. 1991a. *The Farewell of the Word: The Johannine Call to Abide.* Philadelphia: Fortress.

———. 1991b. "The Final Farewell of Jesus: A Reading of John 20:30–21:25." *Semeia* 53:167–190.

———. 1991c. "The Journey(s) of the Word of God: A Reading of the Plot of the Fourth Gospel." *Semeia* 53:23–54.

———. 1991d. "Towards a New Direction in Johannine Scholarship: The Fourth Gospel from a Literary Perspective." *Semeia* 53:1–22.

Senior, Donald. 1991. *The Passion of Jesus in the Gospel of John.* Collegeville, Minn.: Liturgical Press.

Snyder, Graydon F. 1971. "John 13:16 and the Anti-Petrinism of the Johannine Tradition." *BR* 16:5–15.

Staley, Jeff. 1986. "The Structure of John's Prologue: Its Implications for the Gospel's Narrative Structure." *CBQ* 48:241–264.

———. 1988. *The Print's First Kiss: A Rhetorical Investigation of the Implied Reader in the Fourth Gospel.* SBLDS. Atlanta: Scholars Press.

———. 1991. "Stumbling in the Dark, Reaching for the Light: Reading Character in John 5 and 9." *Semeia* 53:55–80.

Stibbe, Mark W. G. 1991. "The Elusive Christ: A New Reading of the Fourth Gospel." *JSNT* 44:19–38.

———. 1992. *John as Storyteller: Narrative Criticism and the Fourth Gospel.* SNTSMS. Cambridge: Cambridge Univ. Press.

Sylva, Dennis D. 1988. "Nicodemus and His Spices." *NTS* 34:148–151.

Talbert, Charles H. 1970. "Artistry and Theology: An Analysis of the Architecture of Jn 1,19–5,47." *CBQ* 32:341–366.

———. 1976. "The Myth of a Descending-Ascending Redeemer in Mediterranean Antiquity." *NTS* 22:418–439.

————. 1992. *Reading John.* New York: Crossroad.

Taylor, Michael. 1983. *John: The Different Gospel.* New York: Alba House.

Thomas, John Christopher. 1991. "The Fourth Gospel and Rabbinic Judaism." *ZNW* 82:159–182.

Thompson, Marianne Meye. 1988. *The Humanity of Jesus in the Fourth Gospel.* Philadelphia: Fortress.

Tobin, Thomas H. 1990. "The Prologue of John and Hellenistic Jewish Speculation." *CBQ* 52:252–269.

Tolbert, Mary Ann. 1990. "A Response from a Literary Perspective." *Semeia* 53:203–212.

Tolmie, D. F. 1991. "The Function of Focalisation in John 13–17." *Neot* 25, no. 2:273–287.

Van Den Heever, G. A. 1992. "Theological Metaphorics and the Metaphors of John's Gospel." *Neot* 26, no. 1:89–100.

Von Wahlde, Urban C. 1981. "The Witnesses to Jesus in John 5:31–40 and Belief in the Fourth Gospel." *CBQ* 43:385–404.

Weiss, Herold. 1979. "Foot Washing in the Johannine Community." *NovT* 21:298–325.

————. 1991. "The Sabbath in the Fourth Gospel." *JBL* 110, no. 2:311–321.

Wendland, E. R. 1992. "Rhetoric of the Word: An Interactional Discourse Analysis of the Lord's Prayer of John 17 and Its Communicative Implications." *Neot* 26, no. 1:59–88.

Wiarda, Timothy. 1992. "John 21.1–23: Narrative Unity and Its Implications." *JSNT* 46:53–71.

Woll, D. Bruce. 1980. "The Departure of 'The Way': The First Farewell Discourse in the Gospel of John." *JBL* 99:225–239.

Wuellner, Wilhelm. 1991. "Putting Life Back into the Lazarus Story and Its Reading: The Narrative Rhetoric of John 11 as the Narration of Faith." *Semeia* 53:113–132.

Yee, Gale A. 1989. *Jewish Feasts and the Gospel of John.* Wilmington, Del.: Glazier.

## SCRIPTURE AND DISCIPLESHIP

Auerbach, Jerold S. 1990. *Rabbis and Lawyers: The Journey from Torah to Constitution.* Bloomington and Indianapolis: Indiana University Press.

Batstone, David, ed. 1993. *New Visions for the Americas: Religious Engagement and Social Transformation.* Minneapolis: Fortress.

Berrigan, Philip, and Elizabeth McAllister. 1989. *The Time's Discipline.* Baltimore: Fortcamp.

Bonhoeffer, Dietrich. 1959. *The Cost of Discipleship.* New York: Macmillan.

Coleman, William. 1982. *An American Strategic Theology.* New York: Paulist.

*Community-Based Education.* 1990. Special issue of *Harvard Educational Review* 60.

Douglass, James. 1972. *Resistance and Contemplation.* Garden City, N.Y.: Doubleday.

————. 1980. *Lightning East to West.* Portland: Sunburst.

————. 1992. *The Nonviolent Coming of God.* Maryknoll, N.Y.: Orbis Books.

Freire, Paulo. 1973. *Pedagogy of the Oppressed.* New York: Herder and Herder.

Harris, Maria. 1988. *Teaching and Religious Imagination.* San Francisco: Harper and Row.

Holland, Joe, and Peter Henriot. 1983. *Social Analysis: Linking Faith and Justice.* Maryknoll, N.Y.: Orbis Books; Washington, D.C.: Center of Concern.

Hug, James, ed. 1985. *Tracing the Spirit.* New York: Paulist.

Moore, Allen J., ed. 1989. *Religious Education as Social Transformation.* Birmingham, Ala.: Religious Education Press.

Myers, Ched. 1994. *Who Will Roll Away the Stone?* Maryknoll, N.Y.: Orbis Books.

Schillebeeckx, Edward. 1987. *The Church with a Human Face.* New York: Crossroad.

Winter, Gibson. 1981. *Liberating Creation: Foundations of Religious Social Ethics.* New York: Crossroad.

Wylie-Kellermann, Bill. 1991. *Seasons of Faith and Conscience: Kairos, Confessions, Liturgy.* Maryknoll, N.Y.: Orbis Books.

# Scripture Index

**Genesis**

| | |
|---|---|
| ch. 1 | 149 |
| 1:2 | 53 |
| ch. 2-3 | 373 |
| 2:7 | 217, 458 |
| 2:21-22 | 429 |
| 3:7 | 74 |
| 3:8 | 44 |
| 5:24 | 324 |
| 9:20 | 330 |
| 17:11 | 179 |
| 24:10-61 | 114 |
| 25:24 | 429 |
| 27:35-36 | 73 |
| 27:41 | 337 |
| 28:12 | 74 |
| 28:16-18 | 108 |
| 29:1-20 | 114 |
| 31:19 | 107 |
| 31:34 | 107 |
| 35:4 | 107 |
| 37:5-8 | 337 |
| 41:52 | 267 |
| ch. 43-45 | 422 |
| ch. 47-49 | 291 |
| 48:1-20 | 267 |
| 48:22 | 102 |
| 49:10 | 217 |

**Exodus**

| | |
|---|---|
| 2:15b-21 | 114 |
| 3:14 | 64 |
| 3:14-15 | 361 |
| 3:28 | 109 |
| 5:14 | 403 |
| 7:3-4 | 118 |

| | |
|---|---|
| ch. 11 | 142 |
| 12:6 | 411 |
| 12:21 | 402 |
| 12:22 | 424 |
| 12:46 | 431 |
| 14:11-33 | 472 |
| 16:16 | 145 |
| 16:19-20 | 146 |
| ch. 19 | 143 |
| 19:10-11 | 77 |
| 20:20 | 143 |
| 23:11 | 122 |
| 25:22 | 417 |
| 30:19 | 295-296 |
| 30:30 | 296 |
| 31:12-15 | 124 |
| 34:33-35 | 444 |

**Leviticus**

| | |
|---|---|
| 7:26-27 | 164 |
| 11:44 | 366 |
| 15:8 | 217 |
| 16:22 | 67 |
| 19:17 | 92, 337 |
| 20:26 | 366 |
| 23:39-43 | 173-174 |
| 23:40 | 174, 274 |
| 24:16 | 406 |
| 25:5 | 376 |
| 25:11 | 376 |

**Numbers**

| | |
|---|---|
| 6:1-21 | 375 |
| 9:10-12 | 435 |
| 21:9 | 91 |
| 27:16-18 | 233 |

**Deuteronomy** _____

| | |
|---|---|
| 1:33 | *314* |
| 2:14 | *122* |
| 5:10 | *319* |
| 7:9 | *319* |
| 8:2-3 | *143* |
| 8:3 | *157* |
| 8:15 | *185* |
| 11:1 | *319* |
| 13:6 | *177* |
| 16:13 | *173* |
| 18:15-18 | *65* |
| 18:18 | *48, 146* |
| 18:18-19 | *340* |
| 25:2-3 | *403* |
| 27:26 | *188* |
| 28:4 | *429* |
| 28:11 | *429* |
| 29-34 | *291* |
| 30:11-14 | *91* |
| 30:14 | *137* |
| 30:19 | *179, 284* |
| 32:2 | *144* |

**Joshua** _____

| | |
|---|---|
| ch. 22-24 | *291* |

**Judges** _____

| | |
|---|---|
| 3:15-30 | *379* |
| 8:26 | *404* |
| 13:5 | *375* |

**1 Samuel** _____

| | |
|---|---|
| 1:1 | *267* |
| 2:12 | *35* |
| ch. 8 | *57* |
| 8:5-22 | *383* |
| 8:7 | *265* |
| 8:19 | *265* |

**2 Samuel** _____

| | |
|---|---|
| 7:12-14 | *92* |
| 15:23 | *372* |

**1 Kings** _____

| | |
|---|---|
| 2:37 | *372* |
| 4:24 | *326* |
| 4:25 | *74* |
| 4:26 | *326* |

| | |
|---|---|
| 6:29 | *274* |
| 6:32 | *274* |
| 6:35 | *274* |
| 11:26 | *267* |
| 12:26-29 | *43* |
| 15:13 | *372* |
| 18:37 | *263* |

**2 Kings** _____

| | |
|---|---|
| 2:9-15 | *66* |
| 4:42 | *144* |
| 5:10 | *217* |
| ch. 17 | *107* |
| 17:24-41 | *102* |
| 17:30-31 | *107* |
| 21:9 | *177* |
| 23:4-12 | *372* |

**2 Chronicles** _____

| | |
|---|---|
| 21:12 | *65* |

**Ezra** _____

| | |
|---|---|
| 4:1 | *102* |
| 4:2 | *102* |

**Nehemiah** _____

| | |
|---|---|
| 6:11-13 | *239* |
| 8:15 | *274* |

**1 Maccabees** _____

| | |
|---|---|
| 1:59 | *243* |

**2 Maccabees** _____

| | |
|---|---|
| 6:28 | *299* |
| 6:31 | *299* |
| 10:7 | *274* |

**Job** _____

| | |
|---|---|
| 1:6 | *396* |
| 1:11 | *205* |
| 2:5 | *205* |
| 5:25 | *144* |
| 28:12-14 | *181* |
| 28:20-21 | *181* |
| 29:25 | *320* |

**Psalms** _____

| | |
|---|---|
| 11:5 | *338* |
| 22 | *420-421* |
| 22:18 | *420* |

| | |
|---|---|
| 23:4 | *320* |
| 25:7 | *227* |
| 25:18 | *227* |
| 26:5 | *338* |
| 27:2 | *164* |
| 31:6 | *338* |
| 32:2 | *73* |
| 34:20 | *431* |
| 35:19 | *338, 340* |
| 37:2 | *144* |
| 38:19 | *338* |
| 41:9 | *301* |
| 51:7 | *424* |
| 56:9 | *377* |
| 58:7 | *144* |
| 69:4 | *84, 338, 340, 423* |
| 69:8 | *84* |
| 69:9 | *84, 423* |
| 69:21 | *423* |
| 72:16 | *144* |
| 78:15-16 | *185* |
| 80:8 | *330* |
| 80:14 | *330* |
| 81:15 | *338* |
| 82 | *246, 271-272* |
| 86:17 | *320* |
| 89:36 | *283* |
| 89:38 | *283* |
| 89:51 | *283* |
| 100:3 | *233* |
| 105:40-41 | *185* |
| 107 | *147* |
| 109:31 | *470* |
| 113-118 | *174* |
| 118:25-27 | *274-275* |
| 119:29-34 | *315* |
| 132:17 | *135* |
| 139:21 | *338* |
| 146:8 | *242* |

**Proverbs**

| | |
|---|---|
| 1:20-25 | *183* |
| 1:28-33 | *183* |
| 5:15 | *185* |
| 8:22-31 | *53* |

**Song of Songs**

| | |
|---|---|
| 3:1 | *451* |
| 3:3-4 | *451* |

**Wisdom**

| | |
|---|---|
| ch. 6-10 | *53* |
| 6:16 | *228* |
| 10:5 | *364* |
| 10:16 | *92* |

**Sirach**

| | |
|---|---|
| 4:11 | *92* |
| 15:2 | *92* |
| 24:8 | *58* |
| 38:34 | *354* |
| 39:1-4 | *354* |
| 39:11 | *354* |

**Isaiah**

| | |
|---|---|
| 5:1 | *330* |
| 5:2 | *330* |
| 5:7 | *330* |
| ch. 6 | *285* |
| 6:8 | *287* |
| 8:6 | *217* |
| 9:2 | *54* |
| 9:4 | *54* |
| 9:6 | *9* |
| 9:6-7 | *28* |
| 9:14-16 | *274* |
| 10:25 | *311* |
| 10:27 | *311* |
| 11:1 | *375* |
| 26:17-19 | *351* |
| 27:2-5 | *330* |
| 27:12 | *111* |
| 29:16 | *246* |
| 29:18 | *223* |
| 40:3 | *65* |
| 40:9-11 | *275-276* |
| 41:21-23 | *348* |
| ch. 42 | *67* |
| 43:10 | *301* |
| 43:20 | *185* |
| 48:14 | *347* |
| 52:4-53:12 | *402* |
| 52:6 | *362* |
| 52:13 | *283* |
| 52:15 | *279* |
| ch. 53 | *67, 285* |
| 53:1 | *285* |
| 53:7 | *402* |
| 53:12 | *425* |

**Isaiah (continued)** ――――――

| | |
|---|---|
| 54:13-15 | *163* |
| 55:1-3 | *163* |
| 58:11 | *185* |
| 55:8-11 | *482* |
| 62:4-5 | *79* |
| 64:6 | *346* |
| 64:8 | *246* |
| 64:8-11 | *217* |
| 66:7-8 | *350* |
| 66:10 | *350* |

**Jeremiah** ――――――

| | |
|---|---|
| 2:2 | *106* |
| 2:4-5 | *106* |
| 2:8 | *106* |
| 2:11 | *106* |
| 2:13 | *106* |
| 2:21 | *331* |
| 4:22 | *35* |
| 5:6 | *239* |
| 5:10-11 | *333* |
| 5:13 | *333* |
| 12:10 | *331* |
| 23:1-4 | *233* |
| 24:7 | *360* |
| 31:33-34 | *361* |
| 51:33 | *311* |

**Lamentations** ――――――

| | |
|---|---|
| 4:5 | *404* |

**Baruch** ――――――

| | |
|---|---|
| 3:9-4:4 | *53* |
| 3:29 | *90* |

**Ezekiel** ――――――

| | |
|---|---|
| 3:1-3 | *165* |
| 17:5-6 | *331* |
| 24:2-15 | *234* |
| 24:24 | *301* |
| 34:15 | *478* |
| 36:25-26 | *64* |
| 36:25-27 | *88* |
| 39:17 | *164* |
| ch. 41 | *274* |
| 47:1-5 | *174* |
| 47:1-11 | *185* |

**Daniel** ――――――

| | |
|---|---|
| 2:46 | *377* |
| 5:7-29 | *404* |
| 11:31 | *243* |
| 12:1 | *357* |
| 12:2 | *26* |
| 12:2-3 | *131* |

**Hosea** ――――――

| | |
|---|---|
| 2:4 | *204* |
| 2:13 | *204* |
| 6:6 | *428* |

**Amos** ――――――

| | |
|---|---|
| 5:21 | *428* |
| 5:24 | *428* |
| 9:13 | *111* |
| 9:13-14 | *79-80* |

**Micah** ――――――

| | |
|---|---|
| 2:12-13 | *236* |
| ch. 3 | *234* |
| 5:2 | *187* |
| 5:2-6 | *28* |

**Nahum** ――――――

| | |
|---|---|
| 1:1 | *190* |

**Habakkuk** ――――――

| | |
|---|---|
| 3:16 | *357* |

**Zephaniah** ――――――

| | |
|---|---|
| 1:14-15 | *357* |

**Zechariah** ――――――

| | |
|---|---|
| 3:1 | *396* |
| 3:1-2 | *74* |
| 3:6-7 | *74* |
| 3:9-10 | *74* |
| 3:10 | *74* |
| 6:11-13 | *405* |
| 8:12-13 | *331* |
| 9:9-10 | *275* |
| 9:10 | *325* |
| ch. 10 | *234* |
| 11:9 | *164* |
| 12:10 | *431* |
| 14:7 | *174* |

| | |
|---|---|
| 14:8 | *174, 185* |
| 14:17 | *174* |

**Malachi** ———————————
| | |
|---|---|
| 3:1 | *82* |

**Matthew** ———————————
| | |
|---|---|
| 1:19 | *260* |
| 2:7 | *260* |
| 3:4 | *66* |
| 3:11 | *66* |
| 4:11 | *269* |
| 4:19 | *468* |
| 5:18 | *60* |
| 5:20 | *27* |
| 6:9 | *44, 364* |
| 6:13 | *366* |
| 6:44 | *322* |
| 7:16 | *239* |
| 8:17 | *285* |
| 9:30 | *261* |
| 10:2 | *32* |
| 10:3 | *239* |
| 10:21 | *222* |
| 13:19 | *366* |
| 13:38 | *366* |
| 16:6-12 | *27* |
| 16:16 | *259* |
| 16:18 19 | *32* |
| 18:18 | *458* |
| 18:18-19 | *32* |
| 21:1-9 | *274* |
| 24:29-31 | *129* |
| 25:1-8 | *374* |
| 25:44 | *269* |
| 26:6-13 | *269* |
| 26:36 | *372* |
| 26:51 | *378* |
| 26:57-66 | *392* |
| 26:63 | *392* |
| 27:11 | *397* |
| 27:15 | *402* |
| 27:20 | *405* |
| 27:29 | *404* |
| 27:37 | *417* |
| 27:35 | *420* |
| 27:38 | *417* |
| 28:1 | *440* |

**Mark** ———————————
| | |
|---|---|
| 1:6 | *66* |
| 1:8 | *66* |
| 1:17 | *468* |
| 1:20 | *239* |
| 1:44 | *261* |
| 3:4 | *177* |
| 3:14 | *32, 460* |
| 3:16 | *460* |
| 4:1-20 | *354* |
| 4:5-6 | *202* |
| 4:12 | *286* |
| 5:20 | *130* |
| 5:37 | *45* |
| 6:3 | *162* |
| 6:14-29 | *96* |
| 6:50 | *261* |
| 8:29-30 | *259* |
| 9:2 | *45* |
| 9:44-47 | *33* |
| 10:13-15 | *310* |
| 10:18 | *177* |
| 10:35-45 | *32* |
| 11:1-10 | *274* |
| 11:17 | *235* |
| 11:21-22 | *313* |
| 12:40 | *340* |
| 12:41-44 | *197* |
| ch. 13 | *291, 294* |
| 13:1 | *222* |
| 13:2 | *292* |
| 13:7 | *292* |
| 13:8 | *292* |
| 13:11 | *292* |
| 13:13 | *292* |
| 13:22 | *236* |
| 13:23 | *292* |
| 14:3-5 | *261* |
| 14:3-9 | *269* |
| 14:28 | *241* |
| 14:32 | *372* |
| 14:47 | *378* |
| 14:48 | *235* |
| 14:42-46 | *281* |
| 14:55 | *386* |
| 14:63-64 | *386* |
| 14:65 | *404* |
| 15:2 | *397* |

**Mark (continued)** ——————
| | |
|---|---|
| 15:6 | *402* |
| 15:7 | *403* |
| 15:11 | *405-406* |
| 15:16 | *415* |
| 15:17 | *404* |
| 15:24 | *420* |
| 15:26 | *417* |
| 15:27 | *417* |
| 15:47-16:1 | *440* |
| 16:8 | *446, 465* |
| 16:9-20 | *465* |

**Luke** ——————
| | |
|---|---|
| 1:44 | *135* |
| 1:58 | *135* |
| 2:41 | *222* |
| 3:2 | *382* |
| 3:16 | *66* |
| 6:3 | *322* |
| 6:7 | *460* |
| 6:13 | *32* |
| 7:37-50 | *269* |
| 9:1 | *460* |
| 10:16 | *239* |
| 10:38-41 | *256* |
| 10:38-42 | *41* |
| 11:2 | *44, 364* |
| 11:14 | *130* |
| 11:37 | *474* |
| 14:12 | *218* |
| 15:6 | *218* |
| 15:15-19 | *239* |
| 19:20 | *444* |
| 19:24 | *420* |
| 19:28-44 | *274* |
| 21:1-4 | *197* |
| 22:50 | *378* |
| 22:61 | *324* |
| 23:3 | *397* |
| 23:13 | *406* |
| 23:19 | *403* |
| 23:27 | *350* |
| 23:33 | *417* |
| 23:38 | *417* |
| 24:1-10 | *440* |
| 24:11 | *456* |
| 24:26-27 | *28* |
| 24:35 | *164, 471* |
| 24:38 | *261* |

**Acts** ——————
| | |
|---|---|
| 2:24 | *241* |
| 2:42 | *164* |
| 2:46 | *338* |
| 3:11 | *243* |
| 3:15 | *445* |
| 4:6 | *382* |
| 5:12 | *243* |
| 6:2 | *460* |
| ch. 8 | *278* |
| 9:2 | *315* |
| 9:29 | *277* |
| 18:25 | *315* |
| 19:12 | *444* |
| 28:26-27 | *286* |

**Romans** ——————
| | |
|---|---|
| 6:4 | *445* |
| 10:16 | *285* |
| 11:8 | *286* |
| 13:12 | *374* |
| 15:25 | *269* |

**1 Corinthians** ——————
| | |
|---|---|
| 9:25 | *400* |
| 10:16-17 | *164* |
| 11:16 | *402* |
| 11:20 | *269* |
| 12:12-27 | *33* |

**2 Corinthians** ——————
| | |
|---|---|
| 6:7 | *375* |

**Galatians** ——————
| | |
|---|---|
| 2:9 | *45, 468* |

**Philippians** ——————
| | |
|---|---|
| 1:18 | *340* |

**Colossians** ——————
| | |
|---|---|
| 4:12 | *400* |

**1 Timothy** ——————
| | |
|---|---|
| 3:10 | *269* |

**2 Timothy** ————————
  2:14                              *324*

**2 Peter** ————————
  2:22                              *353*

**1 John** ————————
  1:7-9                            *459*
  1:10                            *206*
  2:1                        *206, 323*
  2:5                              *323*
  2:22                            *206*
  2:14                            *470*

  2:18                            *470*
  2:18-19                    *33, 303*
  2:28-3:12                  *56-57*
  3:10                              *92*
  3:10-12                        *206*
  3:15                              *33*
  3:22                            *201*
  4:1-6                              *98*
  4:8                                *36*
  4:14                            *113*
  4:20                            *206*
  5:5-8                            *429*
  5:10                            *206*

# General Index

Abraham, 52, 68, 98, 112, 179, 202-210, 215, 286, 412
Adam, 52
Aenon near Salim, 96
Andrew, 71, 126, 144, 278, 282, 440, 467-468
angels, 74, 447-448
Annas, 371, 381-389, 392, 397
apocalyptic, 31-32, 292, 357
apostle(s), 32-33, 57, 96, 167, 384
apostolic churches: symbolized by Simon Peter, 32-33, 57, 168-170, 304, 313, 386, 438, 442-447, 472-480; in tension with Johannine community, 32-34, 45, 68, 285, 313-314, 330, 338, 438, 459-460, 475-482
Ashton, John, 42
asking/questioning, 103-104, 256, 263, 318-319, 334, 337, 344, 352-353, 355-356, 361, 363, 386-389, 427, 474
Assyria, 102, 107, 111

Babylonian exile, 42, 102, 265
Babylonians, 102
bandit(s). *See* robber(s)
baptism: in Jewish tradition, 64; in John's gospel, 50, 64, 88-89, 95-96, 101, 298, 304, 429
Barabbas, 402-403, 409
*basilikos,* 117-119, 124, 136, 251
Bassler, Jouette, 161
bearing fruit, 279-280, 331-334, 336, 369, 376
Beloved Disciple, 33, 45, 48, 162, 303-305, 311, 313, 371, 379, 383-384, 421-424, 429, 434, 441-447, 451, 456, 467, 471, 474, 475, 480-482

Bethany (across the Jordan), 63-64, 66
Bethany (near Jerusalem), 250-252, 255, 269, 276, 422, 440, 441
Bethlehem, 187, 208
Bethsaida, 72, 277-278, 440
Bethzatha (Bethesda), 121, 410, 471
betrayal, 168, 270, 294, 298, 300-305, 309, 313, 332, 365, 369, 373, 376, 396, 408, 424, 433, 449, 458, 480
Beutler, Johannes, 279
binding and unbinding, 263-264, 380, 434-435, 444-445, 458
blind one (healed), 45, 172, 214-230, 242, 258, 262, 264, 287, 295, 316, 343, 353, 432, 456
blindness, 198, 214-230, 253, 286, 448
boat(s), 148-151, 469-472
born "of blood," 56, 123, 204-206, 338
born again/from above (*anōthen*), 87-88, 98, 126, 130, 141, 164, 165, 186, 201, 216, 217, 228, 254, 310, 408, 420, 451, 457
born of "will of flesh," 57, 123, 194, 204, 287, 338, 360
born of "will of man," 57-58, 114, 117-118, 123, 338
bridegroom, 79-80, 97-98
brothers, the, 81, 175-177, 250, 452-453, 480
Brown, Raymond, 10, 65, 70, 73, 78, 91, 112, 122, 136, 137, 156, 164, 170, 175, 183, 185, 199, 202, 217, 227, 230, 237, 244, 277, 282, 286, 290, 303, 313, 318, 332, 335, 339, 342, 347, 352, 357, 367, 375, 378, 388, 394, 411, 430, 432, 469
Brueggemann, Walter, 326

Bultmann, Rudolf, 10
burial of Jesus, 271, 294, 431-436, 439,
    441

Caesar, 36-37, 58, 394, 395, 408-412,
    418, 427. *See also* Roman empire
Caiaphas, 58, 250, 266-267, 302, 345,
    371, 379, 381-383, 387, 389-390,
    392-394, 398
Cana, 77-78, 80, 97, 103, 106, 108, 114,
    117-119, 126, 146, 175, 182, 216, 251,
    283, 331, 421-422, 424, 452, 467, 475
Capernaum, 117, 148, 151-153, 166, 175,
    177, 440
Carson, D. A., 145, 345-346, 419
characterization in biblical narrative, 24;
    *See* individual characters in John's
    gospel
charcoal fire, 386, 472, 478
chiasm: definition, 38; role in biblical
    narrative, 38-39
chief priests. *See* priests
children of God, 35, 55-58, 59, 92, 97,
    111, 150, 186, 203, 206, 265-266, 295,
    310, 322, 333, 357, 360, 377, 403, 408,
    412, 452, 470, 475
children of the devil, 56, 92, 205-207,
    215, 265, 377, 412, 418. *See also*
    Satan/devil
Collins, John J., 26
completion pronouncements, 111, 423,
    424
creation, 35-36, 148, 153, 458
crowd(s), 125, 142-143, 146, 151-161,
    177, 179-182, 186-189, 274-276, 279,
    282-285, 387, 397, 402, 405-406,
    440-441, 448
Culpepper, R. Alan, 11, 39, 126, 299,
    308-309, 312
Cyrus of Persia, 102.

David (king of Israel), 186-187, 301, 326,
    372, 378, 403
deafness, 201
Dedication (chanukah), feast of, 50,
    172-173, 231-232, 242-243, 250, 299,
    392
devil. *See* Satan

Dionysus, 77
disciples (as a group): call to follow:
    69-72, 280, 312; mission of, 111-112,
    312, 317, 346, 364-369, 458, 471;
    misunderstanding by, 103, 110-111,
    130, 215-216, 302, 305, 312; intimacy/
    unity, 269, 321-323, 336, 364, 367-369,
    400, 452, 472; remembering scripture/
    Jesus' word(s), 84, 85, 276, 323-324,
    338-339, 344, 356; resistance to Jesus,
    167
division (*schisma*), 187, 221, 229, 238,
    242, 420, 473-474
Domitian, Roman emperor, 23, 462
door(s)/gate(s), 233-238, 384, 456-457,
    461, 463
Duke, Paul D., 114, 198, 213, 214, 228,
    356, 393, 396
dwelling(s), 313-315, 323

Eighteen Benedictions, 20, 187
Elijah, 65-66, 68
Elisha, 144
Ellis, Peter, 39, 129, 148, 213, 232, 452
Ephesus, 49
Ephraim, 267, 276
eschatology, 129, 160, 456
eternal life, 91, 105, 132-133, 137, 154,
    169, 209, 360, 369, 421, 435, 448
eucharist, 50, 153-170, 269-270, 301, 305,
    449, 452, 475
exodus, the, 58, 142-170, 172-173, 177,
    249, 394
eyewitness, 371, 430

farewell discourse genre, 290-292
feet, 260-261, 269-270, 434, 447-448,
    472. *See also* footwashing
flesh: contrast with spirit, 88, 167-168,
    194; Jesus', 164-168, 315, 343, 377,
    431
food and hunger, 103, 110-111, 143-146,
    154-155, 159, 470-475
footwashing, 50, 295-300, 311, 314, 332,
    339, 360, 378, 406, 419, 472
friend(s), 251-253, 281, 316, 335-336,
    338-339, 353, 355-356, 409-412, 418

fulfillment of scripture/Jesus' word(s), 47, 50, 54, 108, 185, 301-302, 338, 340, 364, 378, 397, 402, 415, 419-421, 423, 424-425, 428, 430-431, 434, 436
fundamentalism, 2, 92, 318

Galilean(s), 43, 117, 156-160, 170, 187, 190, 198, 242, 250
Galilee, 43, 71-2, 102, 114, 119, 121, 141-142, 155, 161, 172-173, 175-176, 181, 187, 190, 192, 208, 222, 226, 250, 277-278, 375, 385, 398, 423, 440, 452-453, 467, 470, 475
gaps: role of in reading process, 18-19
garden/gardener, 370, 372-373, 376, 378, 380, 390, 396, 424, 436, 449-450, 455
gate(s). *See* door(s)
Giblin, Charles, 377, 385, 403, 409
gird oneself, 295, 471-472, 478-479
Gittins, Anthony, 279-280
glory of God: as cross, 91, 241, 251, 263, 279, 281, 286, 293, 309-310, 348, 355, 359-360, 371, 425, 479; contrast with glory of humanity, 128, 138, 176, 178, 208, 228, 287, 334, 338, 360-361, 363, 367-368, 430, 432, 435, 463
gnosticism, 34-37, 53, 55, 73, 84, 300, 303, 360, 416, 420. *See also* knowledge
Golgotha, 416-417, 436
good shepherd, 238, 258, 263, 276-277, 285, 293, 295, 312, 354, 356, 373, 378, 384, 403, 416, 450
Greeks, 184, 277-280, 353, 360

Hanson, John S., 21, 187
hate, 176, 337-340, 342-343, 347, 365
healing, 117-119, 123-126, 212-230, 262
Hendricks, Jr., O. Obery, 250
holy spirit/spirit of truth, 320-325, 336, 342, 347, 458-459. *See also* paraclete
honor/shame, 78, 103, 110, 114, 118, 131-132, 207-208, 281, 425, 458
Horsley, Richard A., 21, 187
hour, the, 78, 108, 132, 146, 176, 182, 197, 253-254, 258, 279, 281, 287, 293, 313, 326, 331, 343, 344, 350-351, 355-356, 359-360
Human One (or Son of Humanity), 74-75, 85, 90, 91, 129, 132, 154, 165, 167,

201, 228, 244, 275, 279, 283-284, 299, 309, 416, 448, 452

I AM (*egō eimi*), 64, 109, 124, 149, 159-161, 193, 199, 201, 209-210, 219, 229, 235-236, 238, 257, 262, 286-287, 293, 301, 315, 330-333, 354, 360-362, 364, 366, 376-378, 380, 385, 449
intertextuality, 47
irony, 40
Israel: as biblical people, 21, 58, 68, 89, 97, 179, 217, 397-398; as "nation," 31, 58, 106, 265, 383, 398

Jacob (Israel), 73, 102, 104-109, 111, 114, 337
Jeremias, Joachim, 83
Jerusalem, 63, 72, 83, 102, 107, 109, 111, 114, 121-122, 128, 135, 143, 167, 171, 174, 177, 192, 217, 232, 242, 255, 268, 270, 274, 276-277, 372, 392, 395, 418, 422, 434, 440, 467, 470. *See also* Temple, Jerusalem
Jerusalemites, 180-182, 194, 196, 226
Jews: assimilation of, 27; author's experience, 8; in John's gospel, 450; in modern culture, 8; as part of audience, 53, 60. *See* Judeans
Johannine community: commitment to, 89, 165-166, 481; death and, 258-259; as egalitarian, 57, 438, 475; mission to "world," 162-163, 201, 342, 362-369; as multicultural, 49, 278; opposition with gnostics, 34-37, 290, 401, 416; opposition with Judeans, 128, 132, 138, 156, 166, 180, 206, 290, 311; opposition with Pharisees, 27-29, 66, 87-93, 156, 182, 221, 237, 265; rebirth into, 29, 88-89; schism, 33-34; tension with apostolic churches, 32-34, 36-37, 45, 68, 168-170, 285, 313-314, 330, 338, 416, 438, 442-447, 459-460, 475-482; tension with Qumran community, 30-31, 37, 93, 290, 301, 401
John (the Baptist): as leader of his own community, 54, 96, 101, 136, 151, 209-210, 236, 297; as witness to Jesus, 54, 63-69, 97, 109, 112, 135-136, 181, 249, 285, 336, 342, 375

Jordan river, 64, 66, 96, 151, 249

Joseph (as father of Jesus), 73, 162, 181, 376

Joseph of Arimathea, 371, 431-436, 439, 442, 445, 456

Josephus, 27, 42, 107, 142, 235, 241, 379, 382, 388, 395-396, 410

joy, 97, 327, 335, 343, 345, 350-351, 353, 355, 357, 365, 404, 449-450, 457, 461

Judas (not Iscariot), 322-323, 327, 349

Judas Iscariot, 169-170, 270-272, 276, 278, 293-294, 298, 301, 304-305, 308-309, 313, 336, 347, 365, 373, 376-377, 380, 386, 396, 421, 424, 433, 440, 449-450

Judea, 95, 114, 119, 136, 145, 161, 172-173, 175, 187, 201, 203, 208, 250, 252-253, 266-267, 283, 293, 383, 395, 460

Judeans: as believers, 202; as geographic description, 41-42, 103, 107-108, 121, 170; as ideological opponents of Jesus/ Johannine community, 43, 58, 63-64, 79-80, 83-85, 96-97, 111, 124-139, 161-168, 173, 177-180, 182-187, 196, 198-210, 219, 222-224, 233-236, 242-248, 255-256, 260-264, 270, 272, 301, 311, 316, 322, 342, 355, 366, 371, 374, 379, 383, 386-389, 392, 395-412, 416, 418, 422, 424, 426-428, 432, 442, 450, 452, 456, 461

judging and judgment, 92, 128, 131-134, 180, 194, 200, 208-209, 229-230, 246, 286, 293, 334, 346-348, 371, 392, 393, 410

Karris, Robert, 219

Kermode, Frank, 58

Kidron, 370, 372

king: Caesar as, 146, 412; Herod as, 146, 398, 410; God as, 412; Jesus as, 146, 186, 221, 275-276, 301, 316, 397-412, 414-418

knowledge (or lack): of Jesus, 48, 197, 296, 298-299, 315-316, 343, 349, 360, 362-363, 448, 474; of God, 34, 48, 181, 194, 197, 227, 240, 294, 315-316, 343, 360, 362-363, 369, 421; Hebrew

vs. Greek concept, 35, 302-303; as intimacy, 55, 73, 162, 297, 302-303, 477; of paraclete/holy spirit, 321

Koester, Craig, 107, 113, 123, 146, 217, 418

Koester, Helmut, 84

Lamb of God, 63, 67-69, 98, 293, 342, 402, 478

lay down life, 238-241, 294-300, 335-337, 342-343, 356, 373, 378, 416, 419, 436, 477-480

Lazarus, 133, 250-264, 268-272, 274, 276-277, 280-281, 302, 313, 336, 350, 359, 380, 419, 422, 439, 441, 444, 455

Levitical scapegoat, 67

lifting up of Jesus, 91, 201, 216, 241, 283, 322, 397, 416, 471

light: of the world, 193, 216, 374; vs. darkness, 30-31, 53-54, 92, 135, 148-149, 216, 284, 306, 310, 440-441, 456, 458

living water, 104, 123, 165, 185, 217, 254, 314, 325, 429

*logos*, 52-53, 97, 112, 127, 203, 285, 366, 378, 397, 459

Lord (as title for Jesus), 101, 153, 250-251, 253, 256, 259-262, 296, 299, 304, 312, 316, 322, 339, 353, 442, 448, 450, 453, 457, 460-461, 471, 480

love: as divine attribute, 138; as central commandment, 58, 311-312, 319, 322, 335, 337, 398, 458, 480; *agapē* vs. *philea*, 130, 251-252, 293, 355, 441, 476-479

MacRae, George W., 213

Magdala, 440

Malchus, 378-379, 390

Martha of Bethany, 41, 57, 250-264, 268-269, 422, 440

Mary Magdalene, 57, 175, 269, 310, 421, 438, 440-443, 446-453, 455-457, 460, 467, 469, 475, 479, 481

Mary of Bethany, 41, 57, 250-264, 268-272, 278, 294-296, 305, 422, 434, 440 meals, community: inclusion of women, 26; Pharisees, 26; as symbol/sacrament, 144, 156, 165-166, 269, 294, 473-475

Meeks, Wayne A., 17-18, 46, 90, 141, 187, 200, 290, 359

messiah (*christos*): Jewish expectations, 28, 64-65, 74, 92, 181-182, 187, 226, 283-284, 326, 378, 397-398, 450; title for Jesus, 71, 109-110, 146, 180, 186, 194, 223, 244, 259, 316, 326, 339, 397, 406, 463

Michaels, J. Ramsey, 396

Minear, Paul S., 91-92, 128, 259, 291, 326-327, 389, 422, 428, 466

Miranda, José, 57, 59, 78, 111, 129, 130, 133, 199

misunderstanding, 84, 88, 103-104, 110-111, 130, 200, 214-216, 233, 266, 276, 284, 302, 305, 312, 378, 383, 418, 445-446, 449

Moloney, Francis J., 52, 78, 88, 101

monarchy, 43, 57-58, 102, 372, 412

Moses, 48, 53, 60, 68, 72, 80, 90-92, 98, 107-109, 112, 121-122, 128, 136-137, 139, 143-148, 151, 156-157, 160, 162, 166, 178-179, 186, 199-200, 225-226, 236, 291, 295, 314, 319, 339, 361, 376, 396, 424, 427, 444, 472

mother of Jesus, 41, 78-79, 84, 175, 371, 379, 421-424, 434, 451

my Lord and my God, 461-462, 468

narrator(s): in biblical narrative, 14, 24, 48; in fiction, 14; in historical writings, 24; in John, 48

Nathanael, 72-74, 77, 162, 167, 181, 187, 275, 376, 397, 448, 462, 467-469

nationalism, 101-102, 104, 107-108, 114, 123, 463. *See also* born of "will of man"

Nazareth, 73, 114, 162, 175, 181, 187, 208, 375-376, 418, 440, 467

neighbors, 218-220

Nero, 23, 382

Neyrey, Jerome, 108, 128, 193

Nicodemus, 25, 29, 45, 87-93, 96, 98, 104, 107, 109, 111, 114, 117, 126, 130, 141, 142, 162, 164, 165, 167, 180-181, 185, 186, 188-190, 196, 203, 217, 221, 224, 227, 230, 241, 275, 283, 287, 371, 379, 384, 387, 392, 408, 433-436, 439, 442, 445

night, 87, 216, 268, 300, 306, 308, 394, 433, 469

O'Day, Gail, 113

openly, 177, 180, 199, 244-245, 254, 266, 353, 355-356, 387, 392

Pagels, Elaine, 36

Painter, John, 214

Palm Sunday, 274-277, 281-283, 397, 402, 405

paraclete, 28, 33, 89, 276, 319-321, 323-325, 339, 342, 344-351, 354, 356, 385, 429-430, 451-452, 473

Passover, 50, 83, 84, 141-142, 156, 173, 178, 196, 243, 267-268, 276-277, 284, 293, 363, 372, 386, 394, 402, 410-412, 419, 431, 435-436, 439-440

patriarchy in Bible, 3; 44, 57-58

Pazden, Mary Margaret, 189-190

peace, 319, 325-326, 357, 456-459

Pentecost, 173

persecution, 56, 96, 98, 126-127, 195, 207, 227, 250, 258, 266, 332, 336-340, 342-349, 362, 368, 374, 399, 421, 450, 452, 456-457, 461, 474

Peter, Simon: as symbol of apostolic churches, 32-33, 57, 168-170, 304, 313, 386, 438, 442-447, 472-480; characterization, 41, 71, 162, 259, 278, 296-298, 304-305, 312-313, 315, 321, 339, 344, 357, 371, 378-379, 381, 383-391, 395, 400, 405-406, 421-422, 440-447, 456, 467-480

Petersen, Norman, 53, 60, 90, 92

Pharisees: messiah and, 28-29, 187; as opponents of Jesus/Johannine community, 27-29, 66, 80, 98, 101, 185, 196-198, 208, 220-222, 225-228, 233, 264-265, 277, 302, 343, 373-374, 376, 397-398, 428; as post-70 C.E. Judean establishment, 26, 65-66, 68, 124, 182, 265, 272; oral tradition of, 60, 80, 406; as pre-70 C.E. "liberals," 26-27, 155, 234, 367; resurrection and, 26, 241, 257; as secret disciples, 29,

Pharisees (continued):
  as secret disciples, 87-93, 229-240,
    242, 287, 316-317, 339, 376, 410,
    432-436, 445; sending out officers,
    182-183, 188, 373-374, 392
Philip, 72-73, 143-144, 162, 277-278,
  282, 305, 316-317, 321, 353, 376, 440,
  467, 479
Philo of Alexandria, 52, 128, 130,
  295-296
Pilate, Pontius, 23, 43, 58, 85, 258, 353,
  371, 374, 382, 387, 393-412, 427-428,
  430, 432-434
Polycarp, 36-37
Polzin, Robert, 48
poor, the: as excluded from elite history
  and literature, 4-5; John's gospel and,
  5, 49, 270-271, 305; as subjects of
  gospel, 4; as subjects of literature, 4;
priests (of Jerusalem Temple), 63, 124,
  142, 182, 184, 188, 197, 237, 243, 250,
  265-268, 272, 277, 343, 371, 373-374,
  378-379, 381-390, 392, 397-398, 402,
  404-406, 411-412, 415, 418-419, 428
prologue themes and images, 51, 73, 92,
  138, 148-150, 167, 178, 186, 193, 199,
  284, 287, 293, 295, 304, 315, 332, 342,
  356, 359, 401, 403, 415-416, 439, 441
prophet-like-Moses, 48, 65, 146, 190
prophets, the, 44, 52, 60, 72, 112, 163,
  209, 215, 234, 236, 331, 428
proverbs (*paroimiais*), 353-355
purification and purity, 27, 79, 96-98, 101,
  267, 297-298, 314, 394, 424

Qumran community: as "children of
  light," 30, 284; as messianic alternative,
  30-31, 93, 202, 315, 320, 366
Qumran, 22

reading methods: and the academy, 7-8;
  poetics of biblical narrative, 14-19;
  Christian reading of Hebrew scripture,
  9; and community, 4; deconstruction, 8,
  12; discourse-oriented, 10-13, 39, 96,
  465; intimidation by scope of problem,
  2; narratology/narrative criticism,
  11; New Criticism, 12; and radical
  discipleship, 7; relationship to reader,

  3, 4-8; source-oriented, 10-11, 13-14,
  16-17, 47, 96, 290, 328, 465
receiving (hospitality/acceptance), 55, 97,
  135, 138, 145, 149, 190, 278-279, 293,
  295, 298, 302, 304, 314, 348, 362-363,
  403, 406, 415, 419, 422-424, 434
reign of God, 87-88, 109, 169, 357
remain (*menein*), 68-69, 113, 137, 202-
  203, 252, 254, 280, 323, 332, 334-336,
  363, 401, 427, 456, 480-481
Rensberger, David, 88, 166, 189, 216,
  223, 225-226, 336, 399-400, 435-436
repetition, 95, 308, 335, 350
resurrection: as invitation/promise/threat,
  125, 133, 160-161, 165, 176, 254-257,
  315, 351, 365, 435; of Jesus, 295,
  310, 439, 442-449, 453, 460-461, 470;
  and messiah, 65, 77; as strategy under
  Hellenistic oppression, 26, 131
robber(s)/bandit(s) (*lēstēs*), 233-236, 242,
  402-403
Roman empire: as colonial authority, 107,
  113, 368, 371, 373-374, 394, 419,
  442; destruction of Jerusalem Temple,
  20, 265; response to Christians as
  "atheists," 22-23, 343, 431; taxation
  of Palestine, 21. *See also* Caesar,
  Domitian, Nero
ruler of the world, 283, 325, 327, 347

sabbath, 50, 123-127, 129, 178, 179-180,
  220-221, 226, 427, 435-436, 439
Samaria, 101-102, 107, 142, 203, 216,
  252, 256, 283, 438, 480. *See also*
  Samaritan(s)
Samaritan woman, 25, 57, 70-71, 103-
  115, 119, 124, 132, 141, 154, 157, 159,
  162, 203, 209, 229, 348, 379, 389, 424,
  429, 438, 453
Samaritan(s), 101-115, 117, 119, 132,
  159, 201, 202, 207-209, 278, 280, 346,
  392, 398, 442, 456, 462, 473
Sanhedrin, 87, 124, 135, 182-185, 239,
  265-268, 270, 272, 275, 283, 285, 302,
  326, 333, 345, 366, 374, 384, 386-390,
  392, 394, 398
Satan/devil, 139, 205, 280, 283, 293-294,
  301, 304-305, 309, 343, 362, 365-366,

369, 373, 380, 396. *See also* children of the devil

savior of the world, 113-114, 202, 394, 462

Sea of Galilee (of Tiberias), 45, 142, 440, 467, 469. *See also* Tiberias

Septuagint (LXX), 47-48

Shechem, 107

shepherd(s): as office, 34, 233-240, 242, 245-246, 258, 266-267, 270, 384, 431, 478. *See also* good shepherd

signs, 80, 85, 87, 114, 117-119, 126, 141-142, 145-146, 154-155, 177, 182, 201, 221, 249, 265, 276, 283, 285, 444, 452, 462-463, 475, 481

sin(s), 198-199, 201, 203-206, 215-216, 221-225, 227-230, 287, 339-340, 346, 348, 373, 408-409, 424-425, 458-459

Snyder, Graydon, 300

Solomon, 243, 274, 326, 372

son of God: in Hebrew scripture, 247; as title for Jesus, 55, 92, 98, 209, 234, 244, 247, 251, 254, 259, 299, 318, 359, 406-407, 463, 468

son of man. *See* Human One

spirit of (the) truth. *See* holy spirit, paraclete

spirit, 88, 98, 109, 167, 186, 217, 424-425, 429-430

Staley, Jeff, 39, 58, 68, 126, 171, 219, 220-221, 223, 465

Sternberg, Meir, 14-19, 24, 39, 161

Stibbe, Mark, 373, 384

Sychar, 102

synagogue: as Jewish gathering place, 166-167, 177, 295, 387-389, 451; as post-70 C.E. worship site, 29, 235, 272, 330; expulsion of Christians from, 42, 160, 223-224, 287, 333, 343, 405, 432; wordplay on, 112, 332-333, 387

Tabernacles, feast of, 25, 50, 160, 172-177, 179, 184-185, 192-198, 210, 214-217, 219, 226, 243-245, 250, 251, 260, 274, 282, 311, 314, 319, 342, 412, 432, 433, 452, 467

Tacitus, 23, 258

Talmon, S., 30

Temple, Jerusalem: as ideological center of Judea, 42, 64, 83, 102, 114, 117, 125, 136, 172, 177, 181, 210, 314, 368, 387, 392; destruction of in 70 C.E., 20-21, 193, 243, 272, 314, 383; as economic center of Judea, 42-43, 83, 237, 272; ideologically linked with Torah, 42, 44, 97, 121-122, 127, 132, 174, 183-186, 217, 229, 243, 265, 331, 398; in opposition to Torah, 26

thirst, 103-105, 159, 184-186, 283, 423-424

Thomas (the twin), 254, 258, 278, 315, 321, 459-463, 467-48

Tiberias, 142, 145, 151, 154, 410, 440

tomb of Jesus, 436, 438-453, 455-456, 472

Torah (the Law): as basis for holiness, 31, 127, 142, 155, 189, 199, 215, 217, 225, 246, 283, 315, 394, 396-397, 406, 440; given by Moses, 60, 90, 173, 178-179; ideologically linked with Temple, 42, 44, 97, 121-122, 127, 132, 174, 183-186, 217, 229, 243, 265, 331, 398; in opposition to Temple, 26; as "your Law," 27, 47, 54, 195, 340, 396

Transfiguration, 45

truth, 93, 135, 168, 188, 195, 202, 206-207, 219, 229, 238, 315, 324, 345, 348, 366-367, 400-401, 418, 430, 438, 451, 459, 481

twelve, the, 32-33, 168-170, 259, 301, 440, 459-460, 462

vine, 330-333, 362, 376, 444, 480

water jars, 79, 103, 110

Weiss, Herold, 270, 295, 344, 436

Wendland, E. R., 359

wheat, 279-280

where from (*pothen*), 73, 80, 88-89, 104, 143, 181, 194, 226, 331, 407

Wisdom tradition, 53, 58, 90, 91, 108, 181, 186

witness, 54, 63-64, 112, 128, 134-139, 168, 194-195, 226-228, 238, 244, 276, 282, 287, 302, 342, 346, 388-389, 400-401, 421, 425, 430, 446, 452, 460, 468, 481. *See also* John (the baptist) women: as apostles, 438, 453; as disciples, 33, 259-260; as eucharistic ministers, 269; as witnesses, 112, 421, 446

work(s), 130, 136, 154, 176, 179, 204, 216, 242, 244-245, 253, 306, 317, 340, 401

world (*kosmos*), the, 54, 67, 157, 168, 176, 184, 193, 199, 216, 224, 229, 277-278, 280, 283, 293, 299, 321-322, 327-328, 337-339, 342, 345-347, 356-357, 361-369, 376, 385, 387-389, 399-400, 408, 411, 415, 417, 421, 423, 433, 452, 456-458, 461-462, 468

wrath of God, 98, 126, 129, 283

Yee, Gale, 243